Psychology Research Methods

Psychology Research Methods

A Writing Intensive Approach

Elizabeth Brondolo, Ph.D.
Professor
Director, Collaborative Health Integration Research Program (CHIRP)
Dept. of Psychology
St. John's University
Jamaica, NY
United States

Academic Press is an imprint of Elsevier
125 London Wall, London EC2Y 5AS, United Kingdom
525 B Street, Suite 1650, San Diego, CA 92101, United States
50 Hampshire Street, 5th Floor, Cambridge, MA 02139, United States
The Boulevard, Langford Lane, Kidlington, Oxford OX5 1GB, United Kingdom

Library of Congress Cataloging-in-Publication Data
A catalog record for this book is available from the Library of Congress

British Library Cataloguing-in-Publication Data
A catalogue record for this book is available from the British Library

ISBN: 978-0-12-815680-3

For information on all Academic Press publications visit our website at
https://www.elsevier.com/books-and-journals

Publisher: Nikki Levy
Acquisitions Editor: Joslyn Chaiprasert-Paguio
Editorial Project Manager: Tracy I. Tufaga
Production Project Manager: Bharatwaj Varatharajan
Cover Designer: Mark Rogers

Typeset by TNQ Technologies

Dedication

This book is gratefully dedicated to my family: Tom, Emma, Patrick, Lily, Elena, Kyle, and my father-in-law, Anthony.

Contents

Chapter 3
From building blocks to building hypothesis-testing research

Chapter 4
Public health significance: Finding the evidence

Chapter 5
Public health significance: A focus on populations and sampling

Chapter 6
Writing the public health significance section

Part 2
Theory of the problem

Chapter 7
Theory of the problem: Understanding risk factors and mechanisms

Chapter 8
Theory of the problem: Understanding research designs

Part 3
Theory of the solution

Chapter 11
Theory of the solution: Understanding psychological treatments

Chapter 12
Theory of the solution: Understanding research design for treatment outcome studies

Chapter 13
Theory of the solution: Identifying gaps in knowledge

Chapter 14
Writing the theory of the solution

Part 4
Methods

Chapter 15
Methods: Participant selection and ethical considerations

Chapter 16
Methods: Measuring variables

Chapter 17
Methods: Procedures for study implementation and protection of internal validity

Chapter 18
Writing about research methods

Preface

I love the research process. I love to think about theories, test hypotheses, collect data, and conduct analyses. When the research results are complete, I am excited to refine the hypotheses and start the process again.

And I love teaching psychology research methods. For over 25 years, I have been teaching psychology research methods at St. John's University in Jamaica, NY. St. John's serves students from a wide range of cultural, racial, and socioeconomic backgrounds. They come with different life experiences and with a wide range of educational skills. But they share the desire to *learn how to learn.*

Consequently, over the years, I shifted my approach from teaching *content* related to research methods to teaching the *process* of developing psychological research. I wanted students to become independent learners. I hoped the research methods course could enable them to formulate questions about topics that captured their interest and to research the answers to those questions.

To become independent learners, students need to acquire the intellectual and social foundation necessary for the research process. This intellectual foundation includes competencies in close reading, careful analysis of scientific research, and effective oral and written communication. Students must learn to read scientific articles in depth and to organize and evaluate the information in these articles. They must be able to analyze the material they are reading, to determine if there are consistent patterns in the evidence or gaps in knowledge that must be addressed. And students must be able to write about the information they have gained, communicating ideas in a clear and professional manner.

But this intellectual foundation is not enough. The research process also requires a strong social foundation. Most research in behavioral science is now conducted by research teams composed of several scientists and many junior colleagues. Students need to build a social foundation by acquiring the interpersonal skills that strengthen their ability to collaborate with others.

Learning to build collaborative relationships pays off! The quality of my own work has been greatly enhanced through my collaborations with students and other researchers. And the work is much more fun.

As I taught research methods over the years, I struggled to find a textbook that provided instruction in both the content of research methods and instruction in the foundational processes involved in developing and conducting research. These topics are usually covered in separate texts or in separate portions of a research methods book. To (hopefully) merge these two approaches, I wrote an integrative text, joining instruction in psychology research methods with instruction and practice in building foundational research competencies.

The book chapters present short bursts of didactic instruction accompanied by a series of skills-building exercises. Students learn skills in close reading as they work through excerpts from research articles included in every chapter. They learn to analyze information in these articles as they complete chapter activities designed to help them extract and evaluate the content of the articles. They learn the content of research methods—the technical details of research design and measurement—as they *write to learn* about research (Galbraith, 2015).

The book also includes guidance for developing the "soft skills" necessary to conduct research and to build effective research teams. Each chapter includes a section on "Building Human Capital." These short sections recognize and honor values, including persistence and conscientiousness, which are strengthened as students complete the course work. Students support their ability to collaborate as they evaluate the ideas of others and offer meaningful feedback. They learn to think about and respond to the feedback they receive.

As students complete the assignments and recognize the skills they are developing, they learn to trust themselves and their own competencies. In their collaborative work, they develop skills that develop trust in others. This trust—in themselves and in others—helps students commit to the demanding work involved in producing high-quality proposals and papers.

Many of the students in our research methods class go on to join advanced research labs, including our program, the Collaborative Health Integration Research Program (CHIRP). CHIRP is a research training program focused on developing basic and applied research to reduce health disparities. In CHIRP, students apply the skills they learned in the undergraduate research methods course to real-life clinical problems. (The CHIRP program has a little bird in a lab coat as a logo. You will see the CHIRP science bird engaged in research activities throughout the chapters).

As a health disparities researcher, I depend on collaboration with well-trained students and other faculty. The students' often have great insight into our research participants' lived experiences. The students' understanding increases the relevance and applicability of our research on stress and health. Together, we develop a more comprehensive and in-depth understanding of the factors influencing stress and health, improving our ability to conduct research that is informative for practice and policy.

A Clinical Focus: Building on the Science of Behavior Change

To support student engagement with the challenging process of reading original research, I wanted to harness their natural curiosity about behavioral health. Therefore, this book is written with a clinical focus. The chapter activities ask students to investigate the causes of and treatments for behavioral health disorders. Each chapter focuses on a different disorder. This clinical approach to teaching research methods brings the research questions to life for the students and bridges the gap between science and practice. As they complete the chapters, students recognize the critical importance of research for clinical work.

We base our teaching approach on the National Institute of Health Science of Behavior Change (SoBC) program. This goal of the SoBC program is to facilitate the process of intervention development for behavioral health disorders. The SoBC program advocates a close link between basic mechanistic research and intervention development (Nielsen et al, 2018). Mechanistic research can help clinicians and patients understanding how disorders develop and how treatments work. This knowledge can improve treatment outcomes and guide efforts to tailor treatments to different populations.

In our application of the SoBC approach, students begin by researching the public health significance of research on a behavioral health disorder of their choice. They research risk factors that lead to vulnerability for the disorder and identify specific populations to study based on this risk factor. Next, students learn to think about the "*theory of the problem*"—identifying the biopsychosocial mechanisms that contribute to the development and maintenance of the disorder. They focus on researching links between a risk factor they have identified in their reading and specific psychological mechanisms that may trigger or maintain the disorder. Students develop a "*theory of the solution*" by researching treatments that may modify these mechanisms and reduce symptoms. As they research the "theory of the problem" and the "theory of the solution," they learn the methods involved in conducting the basic and applied research that provides the evidence they need.

To provide the students with some background for evaluating possible mechanisms contributing to the development of behavioral health disorder, Chapter 7 introduces students to some of the concepts in the Research Domain Criteria (RDoC) Matrix from the National Institutes of Mental Health. To provide background needed to evaluate potential treatments, Chapter 11 provides basic information about psychotherapies. This information supplements material typically provided in an

Abnormal Psychology class. If students have not yet taken a class in abnormal psychology, we often make chapters from an Abnormal Psychology textbook available to support the students' understanding before they read empirical articles.

Progress in behavioral science and an accelerating demand for mental healthcare has fueled a major increase in the number of master's level mental health professionals and in the number of training programs to prepare these professionals. Often students in master's programs in mental health-related fields do not receive in-depth advanced training in research methods before they begin clinical practice. This heightens the importance of high-quality research training for undergraduates. As a practicing clinician, I have seen that a solid research foundation in behavioral science strengthens diagnostic acumen and clinical practice.

A Writing Intensive Approach: Writing to Learn

In the writing intensive approach we use for teaching research methods, students master concepts and consolidate their learning as they complete the writing assignments. Many research methods courses, including ours, require students to write a research proposal or a research review paper. These written assignments are often the primary "deliverables" for the course. As instructors may vary in the type of written paper they assign, the book provides instructions to develop a research proposal and a research review paper.

The research proposal assignment described in the book involves developing an APA style proposal for a randomized clinical trial to test the effects of a treatment for a behavioral health disorder of the student's choice. The research review paper assignment involves developing a more detailed literature review and evaluation of the state of the science on one aspect of a behavioral health disorder of their choice. For example, research papers could focus on reviewing studies of the prevalence and risk factors for a behavioral health disorder, studies investigating mechanisms that trigger or maintain the disorder, or studies evaluating treatments for the disorder.

For both assignments, students must read empirical articles, evaluate evidence, and identify gaps in knowledge and needed research. The proposal vs. review paper choice involves a trade-off between breadth and depth. The research proposal forces students to read both basic and applied research as they work through the "theory of the problem" and the "theory of the solution" sections. This approach can provide an opportunity to review a broader range of information and skills. However, this approach sacrifices some depth. In the research paper, students can explore a topic in more detail, but they may master fewer areas. We have tended to use the proposal format in the research methods class and the paper format in the advanced classes as students develop conference papers or work on papers for publication.

The chapter activities support the students' work on either assignment. As they complete the writing activities in the chapters, they complete components of their writing assignments. In the collaborative work, they get feedback on the clarity and quality of their writing.

Each section of the book has chapters focused on guiding and supporting the students writing for that section. Chapter 6 provides guidance for writing about epidemiological research. Chapter 10 provides guidance for writing about the basic observational and experimental research the students read to develop their "theory of the problem." Chapter 14 provides guidance for writing about clinical empirical research and meta-analyses which students read as they develop a "theory of the solution." Chapter 18 provides guidance for writing a section on research methods.

A quick note on terminology. We use the term "articles" to refer to published scientific and clinical journal articles. We use the term "papers" to refer to the students' own work.

The Organization of the Book: Integrating Basic Mechanistic Research and Applied Clinical Science

The book is divided into four sections: Public Health Significance, Theory of the Problem, Theory of the Solution, and Methods. These four sections permit students to learn about both basic and applied research approaches. The transitions among the sections underscore the importance of integrating basic mechanistic research into the development of clinical interventions.

The activities included in each chapter help teach and consolidate learning. The literature search activities help students to generate search terms and to identify appropriate scientific articles. The close reading activities provide practice in reading different types of research articles relevant for the topics covered in that section. Excerpts of articles are presented throughout the chapters. The excerpts are annotated with text boxes next to the material and tables below to help students decipher the complex content presented in the articles.

The analysis activities help students to evaluate the methods and findings of articles they are reading and to compare the results across articles. The writing activities help students formulate their ideas and consolidate their knowledge as they prepare portions of their paper or proposal in each section of the book.

Our research methods class has both a lecture and a lab component. In the lecture section, I review the concepts by working through the chapter activities with the class. We apply the activities to the specific article excerpts provided in the chapters. In the lab sections, the lab instructors work through the same activities, but they apply the activities to articles the students are gathering for their proposals or papers.

Public Health Significance. The first section focuses on establishing the public health significance of the behavioral health disorder the student has chosen. This section is called the "Public Health Significance" because students must read original empirical articles providing information on the operational definitions of the disorder they are studying, its prevalence and the consequences of the disorder for health functioning.

To help students understand these articles, students learn basic descriptive research methods, including strategies for characterizing a disorder, measuring signs and symptoms, and developing a sampling strategy to measure the prevalence of a disorder. Students learn about theories and related hypotheses as they identify proposed and actual relationships among the variables described in the epidemiological articles.

The chapter activities help students read epidemiological research on the characteristics, prevalence, and consequences of the disorder. The close reading activities help students deconstruct the complex information in each scientific article, providing instruction on identifying the constructs, variables, and measurement instruments used in the study. Annotated excerpts provide examples of the concepts.

In the writing activities, students learn to formulate detailed operational definitions of the disorder they are studying. They practice a structured approach to summarizing evidence from empirical papers on the prevalence and consequences of the disorder. Students make an argument for the significance of their paper or proposal by integrating information on different aspects of the public health impact of the disorder.

The Theory of the Problem. In the second section of the book, students learn about the methods involved in basic mechanistic research. This section of the course is called "The Theory of the Problem" because students must read original research articles that examine variables potentially causing the disorder by triggering or maintaining symptoms.

To help students read articles on the effects of these risk factors and mechanisms, the chapters provide information about the research methods used in many basic mechanistic studies. In the close reading exercises, students learn to identify the sampling strategies, research designs, and analytic approaches used to test study hypotheses. In analysis exercises, students learn to evaluate the implications of different research methods for the interpretation of the findings, contrasting the interpretations of observational versus experimental designs.

In the writing exercises, students learn to organize research findings about potential causes of the disorder. They practice describing the results of original research studies examining relationships among risk factors, mechanisms, and symptoms of the disorder. Students make arguments for the type of treatment needed based on the evidence about causes of the disorder.

The Theory of the Solution. In the third section of the book, students learn about the methods involved in applied research. This section of the book is called the "Theory of the Solution" because students read original research articles about potential treatments for behavioral health disorders.

To help them read these articles, students learn about the research designs and analytic strategies used in applied research, including treatment outcome studies. In the close reading exercises, students learn about the methods used in randomized controlled trials, as well as strategies needed to control for experimental bias in treatment outcome studies. In the analysis exercises, they learn to recognize gaps in knowledge about treatment outcome, including threats to internal and external validity present in prior research. The writing exercises guide them as they organize and describe the research findings to understand both the effects of the treatment and the research methods used to evaluate these effects. Students learn to make arguments to justify a treatment outcome study based on the existing evidence.

Methods. In the final section of the book, students learn about implementing research studies. They examine the specific methods used to recruit samples, protect human participants, choose measurement instruments, deliver the independent variable, assess the outcome variable, and establish procedures for insuring the internal validity of the study. The close reading exercises help them comprehend the detailed information provided in the methods sections of empirical articles. The analysis and writing exercises help them organize information about research methodology and evaluate the implications of these methods for the interpretation of the findings.

Together, the four sections of the book, Public Health Significance, the Theory of the Problem, the Theory of the Solution, and Methods, provide students with opportunities to read a wide range of original scientific literature. They develop initial skills in understanding and evaluating the science. As they complete the writing exercises, they learn to make systematic and well-documented arguments about their ideas.

Working through these chapters and writing a proposal or paper is hard work. But at each step along the way, students learn to develop the persistence and conscientiousness necessary for good scholarship, and professional success in general. The focus on behavioral health disorders can motivate students to learn, as almost everyone is concerned about someone with a mental health issue. And the collaborative work can help maintain positivity, as students help each other to find articles or give feedback about their writing. We include the "Building Human Capital" section at the end of each chapter to help students recognize all the skills and values they are gaining.

Acknowledgments

Writing this book has been a collaborative effort, involving students, faculty, many research colleagues, and family members. Amanda Kaur, MS, has been instrumental to the development of this book. She began as a masters student in our advanced research methods course and went on to run the CHIRP program and work with me on many writing projects. She has worked on the development and execution of this project from start to finish. Dr. Faith Unger has been the head lab instructor for the undergraduate research methods course and been a very dedicated partner as we have tested and refined our approach over time. Over the years, the graduate student lab instructors have provided invaluable insights and feedback. Naama Sarig, Kaitlyn Edwards, and Natasha Kostek worked on every chapter. The lab instructors tested every section of the book as it was developed. Students in the psychology research methods class and the advanced research methods class provided feedback on every aspect of the book, and we have tried to incorporate all their suggestions and advice. Rebekha Simons has provided invaluable support for the development of the glossary and editing the manuscript.

The Psychology Department Chair, William Chaplin, PhD, and the Dean of the College of Arts and Sciences, Jeffrey Fagen, PhD, gave insightful feedback about the manuscript, commenting on both the technical aspects and the presentation of ideas. Carolyn Vigorito, PhD, my colleague at St. John's and a former research methods teacher gave me very helpful advice and encouragement about the manuscript. I would also like to acknowledge the advice and ideas of Irene Blair, PhD, from the University of Colorado at Boulder and Allison Jaeger, PhD, of St. John's University for their thoughtful comments and ideas. Many of my ideas reflect the experiences I had at study section meetings held by the NIH, specifically the panels Mechanisms of Emotions, Stress and Health and Clinical Trials Review Committee. However, all mistakes in this book are mine and feedback is always welcome.

I would also like to acknowledge the ongoing contributions of my family. My daughter, Elena Brondolo made very insightful and helpful comments on the manuscript. Ryan Brondolo made the beautiful illustrations. My husband, Tom Brondolo, and daughter, Emma Brondolo, and my sons-in-law, Kyle Bucklin and Patrick Karnik provided so much support during the writing period. Our new family member, Lily May Karnik, provided inspiration.

Reference

Galbraith, D. (2015). Conditions for writing to learn. *Journal of Writing Research, 7*(1), 215–226.

Nielsen, L., Riddle, M., King, J. W., Aklin, W. M., Chen, W., Clark, D., & Weber, W. (2018). The NIH Science of Behavior Change Program: Transforming the science through a focus on mechanisms of change. *Behaviour Research and Therapy, 101*, 3–11.

Chapter 1

Introduction

Psychological science has implications for almost every aspect of life. The knowledge gained from psychological research can increase self-understanding, improve schools and workplaces, support relationships and child development, and promote mental and physical health. Understanding psychological research is worthwhile, but it is difficult. In this book, you will gain knowledge about research methods in psychology that will help you understand and benefit from research in psychological science.

A Clinical Focus

To provide a focus for instruction in research methods, we examine research on **behavioral health disorders**, including smoking, substance use, anxiety disorders, and mood disorders, among other disorders. In each chapter, we will use a different disorder to illustrate the research methods topics. For example, Chapter 3 includes research on posttraumatic stress disorder (PTSD); Chapter 4 includes research on smoking.

If you plan on pursuing graduate study in psychology, understanding psychology research methods is a necessary step. If you are studying psychology because you want to become a clinician, studying research methods in the context of behavioral health disorders can also provide a good foundation for clinical training. In this book, you will learn about the methods used in research on risk factors that increase the chance of developing a behavioral health disorder, research on variables that may cause the disorder, and research on treatments that may help the disorder.

As you read and evaluate the research, you develop *critical thinking skills* that provide a foundation for the development of the *clinical skills* you will need to diagnose behavioral health disorders. As you analyze connections between risk factors and behavioral health outcomes, you learn how treatments can be

Psychology Research Methods. https://doi.org/10.1016/B978-0-12-815680-3.00001-3

tailored to the needs of different individuals. Finally, as new treatments become available, you will be better able to read the research about these treatments and evaluate their costs and benefits.

A Writing Intensive Approach

We use a writing intensive approach to help you learn research methods in psychology. With this approach, you will do more than learn concepts and terms associated with psychological research methods. You will put the knowledge into practice as you complete a major writing assignment on a behavioral health disorder.

The chapter activities develop the reading and writing skills you need to understand and use research. Some chapter activities develop the close-reading skills needed to master the ideas and vocabulary presented in scientific research articles. These activities help you understand, organize and consolidate the knowledge you gain.

The writing activities in this book are designed to help you write a *research proposal* to test the effects of a treatment for a behavioral health disorder or a *research paper* reviewing one aspect of the science on a behavioral health disorder in more detail. When you have completed all the writing activities in the chapters, you will have assembled a research proposal or paper.

If you are writing a research *proposal*, you will read articles about the nature and causes of the behavioral health disorder you are studying and articles about possible treatments for this disorder. You will design a study to test the effects of one treatment versus another for individuals who have the behavioral health disorder you have chosen to study. And you will use the research articles you have read to justify the methods you propose in your study.

If you are writing a research *paper*, you can investigate a topic related to a behavioral health disorder in more detail. For example, you could focus your paper on research about the risk factors, causes, or treatments for the disorder. You will learn to analyze the research to summarize gaps in knowledge and propose new research directions.

Learning by Doing

Our philosophy is that you learn best by doing—by investigating a problem and writing a proposal or a paper. As you read research articles, you will learn a wide range of concepts and methods in psychological research. You will learn about the ideas of other researchers and develop ideas of your own.

Researching and formulating the proposal or paper will give you an opportunity to integrate your new knowledge of research methods, the findings of other researchers, and your own ideas. Writing the proposal or paper will enhance your ability to clearly and systematically communicate ideas and information.

Research is hard work, but it is also very rewarding. And very interesting! We hope you will take the time to appreciate the knowledge you are gaining, and the skills you are developing as you work through the exercises.

At the end of each chapter, you will see a final section entitled "Building Human Capital." This section encourages you to think about the skills you are developing as you write your proposal. These skills will make you a more effective and rigorous researcher on your own and a better collaborator as you work with others. The skills you acquire will stay with you long after you have finished reading the book.

The Scientific Method and the Science of Behavior Change

At the most general level, **the scientific method** involves a cycle of proposing ideas, systematically testing the ideas, reevaluating the ideas based on the results of the tests, and then proposing new ideas. Every cycle increases knowledge. And new knowledge can help us understand and solve problems (Fig. 1.1).

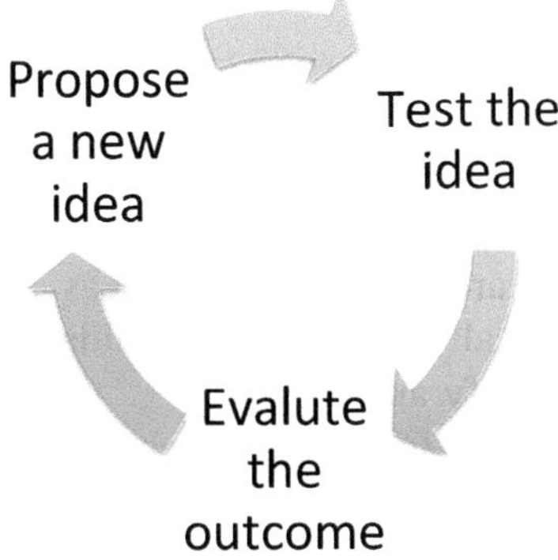

FIGURE 1.1 The scientific method.

The approach to teaching the scientific method presented in this book is consistent with the goals of the National Institute of Health (NIH). In the United States, the NIH is a governmental organization responsible for funding research on health. The NIH approach to evaluating research proposals emphasizes the importance of clearly articulating **the scientific premise** for proposed studies and designing **scientifically rigorous** approaches to testing research hypotheses. For more information about the NIH proposal funding process and a clear explanation of the process of writing these proposals and grant applications see work by William Gerin and colleagues (Gerin, Kinkade, Itinger, & Spruill, 2010).

The conceptual approach used in this book emerges from the NIH's **Science of Behavior Change Program** (Nielsen et al., 2018). The Science of Behavior Change (SoBC) program advocates for the critical role of **basic research** in the development and evaluation of treatments to improve health. The SoBC program highlights the integration of research on how and why individuals develop behavioral health disorders with the process of developing treatments for behavioral health disorders. This process begins with basic research to study risk factors which increase vulnerability and **mechanisms** which can trigger and/or maintain symptoms. These risk factors and mechanisms can provide targets for treatment (see, for example, Czajkowski et al., 2015; Foa & McLean, 2016).

The SoBC program also encourages researchers to understand the **mechanisms of action** for different treatments. The mechanism of action of a treatment is the way the treatments work to improve health. By understanding the mechanisms of action of various treatments, researchers can guide efforts to improve or expand treatment options.

The Culture of Science

The culture of science advocates a rigorous search for knowledge. Scientific researchers challenge ideas and assumptions. They work systematically, and they use validated methods to test hypotheses. They clarify ambiguity.

The reading activities included in each chapter encourage you to read in depth to clarify your understanding. The writing activities encourage you to use clear, thoughtful sentences so your readers can understand exactly what you mean.

The culture of science is also collaborative. The ideas and methods researchers use build on the ideas and methods of others, and their work lays the foundation for future research. Scientists share knowledge and expertise. They check with others to make certain their meaning is clear and all the necessary information is included.

This book offers individual and group activities to encourage both independent thinking and the opportunity to collaborate to test ideas and evaluate each other's work. The ability to collaborate effectively with others is a key requirement for most work. It is especially important in scientific inquiry.

The Products of Scientific Research

Research Articles

Researchers gather new ideas and learn new methods by reading **research articles** of other scientists. After they conduct research studies, they publish their work—their ideas, methods, and findings—in research articles of their own. You will see portions of research articles throughout the book as we present information about research methods. (Research articles are also called research papers, but we use the term research paper to refer to the work you will be producing.)

Original research articles have six sections: an abstract, an introduction section, a methods section, a results section, a discussion section, and a reference section (Fig. 1.2).

- The abstract provides a brief description of the aim of the study, the methods, the results, and the discussion or conclusion. The sections have different purposes, as follows
- The introduction to the article explains the need for the study and justifies the approach
- The methods section explains the actual procedures of the study
- The results section presents the findings or outcomes from the study
- The discussion section provides and interpretation of the findings and their implications
- The reference section includes information about all of the scientific research articles the authors used to make their arguments

Contents lists available at SciVerse ScienceDirect

Journal of Behavior Therapy and Experimental Psychiatry

journal homepage: www.elsevier.com/locate/jbtep

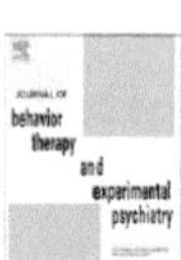

Cognitive-behavioural therapy reduces unwanted thought intrusions in generalized anxiety disorder

Andrea Reinecke[a,*], Jürgen Hoyer[b], Mike Rinck[c], Eni S. Becker[c]

[a] University of Oxford, Department of Psychiatry, Warneford Hospital, OX3 7JX Oxford, UK
[b] Technische Universität Dresden, Germany
[c] Behavioural Science Institute, Radboud University Nijmegen, The Netherlands

ARTICLE INFO

Article history:
Received 3 December 2011
Received in revised form
3 May 2012
Accepted 18 June 2012

Keywords:
Generalized anxiety disorder
Thought suppression
Mental control
Intrusions
Worry
Cognitive-behavioural treatment

ABSTRACT

Background and objectives: Voluntary attempts to suppress certain thoughts can paradoxically increase their intrusive return. Particular impairments in thought suppression are thought to be key mechanisms in the pathogenesis of mental disorders. To assess the role of this processing bias in the maintenance of generalized anxiety disorder (GAD), we investigated whether it is susceptible to cognitive-behavioural treatment (CBT).
Methods: 22 GAD patients and 22 healthy controls (HC) were tested twice within 15 weeks, with patients receiving CBT in between. A subset of patients was additionally tested while waiting for treatment to control for retest effects. Using a mental control paradigm, we measured intrusion frequency during the voluntary suppression of thoughts related to (a) the individual main worry topic, (b) a negative non-worry topic, and (c) a neutral topic. Self-reported worry was measured before and after treatment, and at 6-months follow-up.
Results: Compared to HC, GAD showed specifically more worry-related intrusions. CBT reduced this bias to a healthy level, over and above mere test-retest effects.
Limitations: This study could not clarify whether the demonstrated effect mediates other changes, or how it relates to other cognitive biases in GAD.
Conclusions: The results indicate that thought suppression processes are not only impaired in GAD, but that the impairment is specific to the patients' worries, and that it can be successfully targeted by CBT. This highlights the importance of thought suppression processes in the maintenance of GAD.

1. Introduction

Generalized anxiety disorder (GAD) is characterized by excessive worry regarding a broad range of topics, such as health, financial security and relationships. Patients experience severe difficulty in controlling and stopping worrying thoughts, to a degree that it significantly affects everyday life functioning. The lack of control over worry processes is such a central component of GAD that it has been added as a defining diagnostic criterion to the fourth version of the Diagnostic and Statistical Manual of Mental Disorders (DSM; American Psychological Association, 2000). Following the Metacognitive Model of GAD (Wells, 2005), negative beliefs about worry play an essential role in worry processes spiralling out of control: Concerns that worry thoughts might become uncontrollable, unbearable, or even dangerous, also described as worry about worry, fuel the development of control and avoidance strategies such as reassurance or thought suppression. However, these control attempts prevent experiences that would disconfirm dysfunctional beliefs about worry, thereby reinforcing the relevance and frequency of worry intrusions. This study addresses the impact of cognitive-behaviour therapy (CBT) on such worry intrusions, which we measured using an experimental thought suppression paradigm.

Portions of the introduction section. This section is used to explain the need for the study. The authors will explain the existing knowledge and identify the gaps in knowledge that their study will address.

FIGURE 1.2 Selected components of a research article with highlighted sections of an original research article. *Reproduced from Reinecke et al. (2013).*

2. Materials and methods

Portions of the Materials and Methods section. This section provides information on how the study was done. In psychological research, this section often includes descriptions of the research participants, the testing materials, and the study procedures.

2.1. Participants

Twenty-two patients with a GAD diagnosis and 22 control participants were tested.[1] Patients were recruited from the waiting list of the Dresden University of Technology outpatient clinic for psychotherapy. DSM-IV diagnoses were assessed using the Composite International Diagnostic Interview (CIDI; Wittchen & Pfister, 1997). Six of the patients fulfilled criteria for comorbid major depression and two for a specific phobia. Healthy controls (HC) were recruited via newspaper ads. They were screened for psychiatric diagnoses using the Anxiety Disorders Interview Schedule for *DSM IV* (ADIS; DiNardo, Brown, & Barlow, 1994). To be included in the study, they were required not to clinically or sub-clinically fulfil the criteria of any DSM-IV diagnosis, and not to fulfil any of the criteria for a GAD diagnosis. Educational level, age, and gender were matched between the two groups (*years of education*: GAD $M = 14.3$, $SD = 2.1$, HC $M = 14.3$, $SD = 2.0$, $t(42) = .1$, $p = .943$; *age*: GAD $M = 44.2$, $SD = 13.2$, HC $M = 42.1$, $SD = 14.6$, $t(42) = .5$, $p = .613$; *gender*: GAD 68% female, HC 73% female, $X^2(1) = .1$, $p = .741$).

3. Results

Portions of the Results section. This section provides information about the results of the study. The outcomes of statistical analyses are presented in this section.

3.1. Self-report measures

Before treatment, GAD showed significantly higher depression (IDD) and anxiety (STAIT) scores than HC, both $t(42) > 5.14$, both $p < .001$ (Table 1). Treatment significantly reduced depression (IDD), anxiety (STAIT) and worry (PSWQ, WBSI) scores in GAD patients, all $t(21) > 4.70$, all $p < .001$. Post-treatment worry scores also remained stably reduced over the 6-month follow-up period, PSWQ and WBSI both $t(21) < 1.49$, both $p > .156$. The treatment group GADs (TG) and the waiting group GADs (WG) did not differ from each other on the IDD (TG: $M = 11.6$, $SD = 8.3$; WG: $M = 14.1$, $SD = 5.5$), the STAIT (TG: $M = 51.9$, $SD = 6.0$; WG: $M = 49.5$, $SD = 17.3$), the PSWQ (TG: $M = 58.8$, $SD = 6.7$; WG: $M = 58.6$, $SD = 9.4$), or the WBSI (TG: $M = 49.9$, $SD = 10.0$; WG: $M = 49.8$, $SD = 5.7$), all $t(20) > .75$, all $p < .462$.

FIGURE 1.2 Continued.

Portions of the Discussion section. This section summarizes the purpose of the study and the outcomes. The authors will link the outcomes of the study to existing knowledge. They will provide some interpretation of the findings. They indicate if the findings support their hypothesis or do not, and discuss the implications of the outcomes for science and practice. Finally, the authors present the limitations of their research and suggest directions for future research.

4. Discussion

In this study we investigated whether the previously demonstrated (Becker et al., 1998) increased frequency of worry thought intrusions during a suppression task in GAD patients generalizes to other negative non-worry domains, and whether it improves during CBT. We hypothesized that patients would only differ from controls with respect to the severity of disorder-related worry intrusions, and that this effect would normalize following intervention. The results replicate earlier findings (Becker et al., 1998) by demonstrating that patients with GAD show an increased frequency of worry-related thoughts: While intrusion frequency was not different from healthy controls in the neutral thought condition, GAD patients had significantly more intrusions than controls in the worry thought condition. This effect reflects the uncontrollability of worry which patients with GAD experience (Becker et al., 1998). In addition, our results suggest that thought suppression impairment in GAD is limited to worry thoughts. It does not generalize to other negative non-worry thoughts: GADs and controls had similar intrusion frequencies in the drowning condition.

FIGURE 1.2 Continued.

There are also other types of research articles, such as meta-analyses and systematic reviews. These research articles examine and summarize the findings from many original research articles. A review paper uses a different structure. In this type of paper, the authors present a problem they will review, summarize the findings of existing research, and present conclusions drawn from their review. You will learn to read original research articles and review articles as you work through the chapters.

Writing Research Proposals and Papers

In this book, we provide instructions for developing a scientific writing project, either a research proposal or a review paper. These different kinds of writing exercises have different goals. A research proposal describes a study you would like to conduct. A research paper reviews existing evidence, summarizes themes, and provides guidance for future research. In the next section, we provide an overview of the components of these two kinds of writing projects.

Research Proposals

A research proposal has a very organized structure. Proposals outline the justification for a new study, explain the new knowledge to be gained, and describe the methods to conduct the study. A standard research proposal also includes a discussion of the methods to analyze the data—the information collected from the research participants. As you read articles and work through the chapters, you will learn to read and understand the statistical analyses included in the research articles you read. But it is beyond the scope of this book to provide instruction in writing the statistical analysis plan necessary for a full proposal.

Components of the Proposal

In this book, we focus on research proposals for studies designed to test the effects of a treatment for a behavioral health disorder. The purpose of the proposal is to justify a study to evaluate the treatment and to explain the methods you will use to conduct this evaluation. Each component of the proposal presents part of the justification and methods. As you complete the reading activities for each component of the proposal, you will learn about the research methods described in the articles you read to gather evidence for the proposal. The writing activities will help you learn how to describe your ideas and justify your arguments in a clear and convincing manner (Fig. 1.3).

Introduction. In the first part of the introduction to the proposal, you will establish **the public health significance** of the proposed study. In the remaining parts, you establish the scientific premise of the proposed study. In these sections you explain the **theory of the**

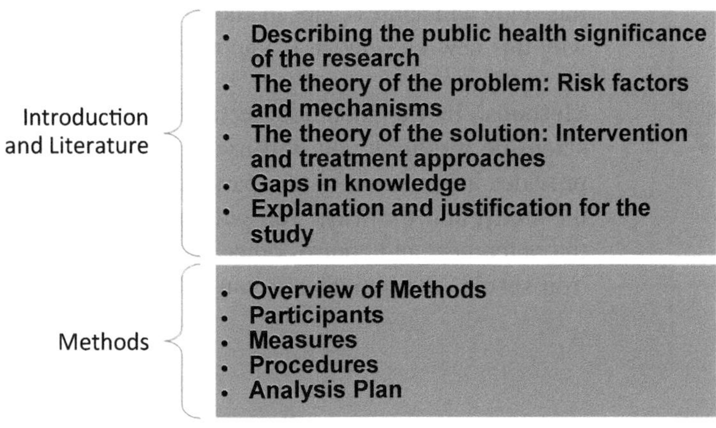

FIGURE 1.3 Components of the research proposal.

problem, identifying some of the causes of the disorder. Next you identify a **theory of the solution**, describing how the treatment you are investigating will address the causes and reduce the symptoms of the disorder. You identify how the proposed study fills **gaps in knowledge** that have not been addressed by prior research. We can look at each part of the introduction in more detail.

PHS

Public health significance. In this section, you explain the nature of the behavioral health disorder you are investigating, and you document the effects the disorder has on public health—the health and well-being of the general population and those at high risk of developing the disorder. Specifically, you describe the disorder you are studying and provide information about the **prevalence** and consequences of the disorder.

TOP

Theory of the problem. In this section, you describe research that explains the causes of the disorder. You can begin to establish causes by identifying who is at risk for the disorder and clarifying the mechanisms which may explain how the symptoms are triggered and maintained.

TOS

Theory of the solution. In this section, you identify an intervention or treatment that may reduce the symptoms of the disorder and justify your choice of treatment to evaluate by reviewing existing research.

GAPS

Gaps in knowledge. In this section, you identify gaps in knowledge or problems with existing research that your study will address. Some of these gaps in knowledge occur because researchers have not fully investigated the treatments. In other cases, the gaps in knowledge occur because there are methodological difficulties with the existing studies. At the end of this section, you write an overview of the study you propose. In this overview, you describe how this study will address gaps in knowledge in the existing studies, and why this new knowledge is important.

METHODS

Methods. In the methods section, you describe the **rigorous scientific methods** you will use to test your ideas. This section provides information on the participants who will be included in the study, and the ways you will deliver the treatment, measure the outcomes, and control other factors that may bias the results. You specify the hypotheses you will be testing.

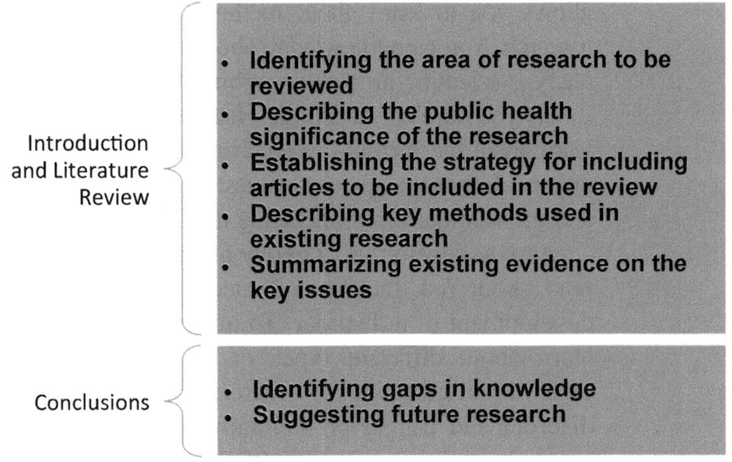

FIGURE 1.4 Components of the research paper.

Components of a Paper Reviewing an Area of Research

There are multiple components to a paper reviewing a specific area of research. If you are writing a review paper, you could review research studies on the public health significance of a disorder, on the causes of a disorder, or on the treatments for the disorder. The purpose of this type of paper is to summarize key themes in the existing research, identify gaps in knowledge, and provide ideas for future research.

As you prepare this paper, you learn how to organize, analyze, and present research findings. As you complete reading activities to prepare your review, you learn different research methods needed to understand the articles you read. The writing activities will help you describe your ideas and present your arguments in a clear and convincing manner.

The components of a research paper of this type can vary, but they often include the sections given in Fig. 1.4.

Basic and Applied Research Methods

As you prepare the proposal and analyze the existing research, you learn methods in basic and applied research. **Basic research** is conducted to understand the characteristics, causes, and effects of a phenomenon, such as a behavioral health disorder. **Applied research** is conducted to solve a "real-world problem," such as finding a treatment for the behavioral health disorder.

Studies of the causes of and treatments for behavioral health disorders are generally too expensive and complex to conduct in an introductory research methods class. But developing a proposal for a basic or applied research study about these causes and treatments allows you to learn about methods from both basic and applied research. You gain knowledge about these methods as you read and analyze scientific articles describing basic and applied research.

As you develop the **Public Health Significance section,** you will learn about the methods researchers use to develop operational definitions of disorders, choose and test research participants for the study, and measure outcomes, including the symptoms of the disorder.

As you develop the **Theory of the Problem section**, you will read about risk factors and mechanisms that contribute to the development of a disorder. To understand this research, you will learn about different types of research designs and methods which are used to identify factors which increase the risk for the disorder and trigger or maintain the symptoms. You will learn more about the statistical methods that are used in these studies.

As you develop the **Theory of the Solution section**, you will read about treatment and intervention approaches. To understand this research, you will learn about the experimental methods used to study treatment outcomes, including the methods involved in conducting randomized controlled trials (RCTs). RCTs are a type of experiment in which different treatments are compared under rigorous experimental conditions to find the most effective option.

As you complete the section on **Gaps in Knowledge**, you will learn to identify sources of bias in research and generate ideas about controlling bias in your own study.

Finally, you will apply this knowledge about concepts in research design and methodology as you develop the methods for your proposal or paper.

Getting Started: Identifying a Disorder to Study

In this book, we choose behavioral health problems for the focus of investigation. Among other disorders, behavioral health problems include *anxiety disorders* (e.g., generalized anxiety disorder, social anxiety disorder, or specific phobias), *mood disorders* (e.g., major depressive disorder or bipolar disorder), and *substance use and related disorders* (e.g., tobacco use disorder or alcohol use disorder).

In this section we include links to videos that provide introductory information about behavioral health problems. We have included links for free videos provided by Kanopy (https://www.kanopystreaming.com/), which includes a collection of media for academic purposes (e.g., documentaries, psychotherapy videos, and more). This content can be accessed via your institution's library or through APA.

We use the categorizations provided in DSM-5 for the behavioral health disorders that are the focus of psychological treatment. We provide a sample of these behavioral health disorders to start the process, but there are many other behavioral health conditions which could be on this list. We can start the process by working on Activity 1.1 in Fig. 1.5.

Activity 1.1: Choosing a Behavioral Health Problem

To start, pick one disorder you want to research further.

- All behavioral health problems deserve attention. It is not necessary to be passionate about treating the behavioral health problem you choose. The best approach is to pick one problem, and then master the skills needed to conduct research on that problem. Once you have learned more about the process, you can modify your choice. Or you can pursue further knowledge about another disorder in another class.
- Review videos and web pages of interest. Which behavioral health problem do you wish to focus on for your proposal?
- ____

FIGURE 1.5 Activity 1.1 identifying a problem that needs a solution.

Creating a Mental Map of the Research Proposal

One goal of this chapter is to introduce a systematic conceptual approach to developing the introduction of the research proposal, including establishing the public health significance and the scientific premise.

We can begin by creating a mental map of ideas and questions that need to be answered about this behavioral health problem. This mental map will help you search for all the information you need to build your proposal. The answers to the questions help develop the **literature review**—a review of the articles about different aspects of the disorder, its causes and its treatment, and a discussion about gaps in knowledge. This literature review establishes the scientific premise of the study and is the largest portion of the introduction to the proposal.

To start building the map, we use our existing knowledge about behavioral health disorders to generate a list of questions that will help us structure our search for a treatment for the disorder. We will supplement our existing knowledge with information from the research literature and other sources. We can start the process by working on Activity 1.2 shown in Fig. 1.6.

Activity 1.2: Creating a Mental Map of the Knowledge Needed to Research the Disorder

Working together, let's start by thinking about one behavioral health problem: anxiety disorders.

What do we need to know about anxiety disorders? What kinds of questions do we need to ask to develop a treatment for anxiety disorder?

Questions

FIGURE 1.6 Activity 1.2 identifying questions we need to ask.

Identifying Question Topics

These different questions can be organized into the different components of the introduction. As you write the proposal, you ask and answer questions concerning these topics. If you are writing a review paper, you may focus on one set of questions (Figs. 1.7 and 1.8). Use the questions in the Activity tables to help you consider different aspects of the research.

FIGURE 1.7 *PHS*, Public health significance; *TOS*, Theory of the Solution; *TOP*, Theory of the Problem.

Questions
Public Health Significance: (Includes questions about the epidemiology of the disorder, such as questions about how many people are affected by the disorder; consequences of having the problem, and risk factors that make people more susceptible to the disorder.) *What is the nature of the problem and how serious a problem is it? How can we define and measure the problem? How many people have this problem? Who is at risk for the problem? What are the risk or vulnerability factors that increase the chances of developing the problem? What happens if the problem is not addressed?*
Theory of the Problem **Risk Factors and Mechanisms:** (Includes questions about the causes of the disorder, including the mechanisms that trigger or maintain the problem.) *What are the causes of this problem? What triggers the initial episode? What maintains the problem – why does it persist?*
Theory of the Solution **Intervention Approaches:** (Includes questions about known treatments for the disorder and questions about the mechanisms of action – the way the interventions work.) *What are different kinds of solutions? How do they work? Are they effective?*
Gaps in Knowledge: (Puts together issues raised in the previous sections. Includes questions about the quality of the evidence concerning known treatments for the disorder. These gaps may include issues related to research methodology, as well as questions about the additional knowledge that needs to be obtained.) *Are better treatments needed? Have the treatments been effectively evaluated? Have there been problems with the validity of the studies or the generalizability of the findings?*

FIGURE 1.8 Questions included in each component of the research proposal.

Activity 1.3: Organizing the Questions into Research Components

In this activity, identify the topics addressed by the questions you or your classmates identified. See which questions go in which category. Sometimes questions may fit into more than one category, depending on how the question is framed. Use Table 1.1 to write in the questions you raised in the section they belong. See if your choices are similar to those in Table 1.2.

TABLE 1.1 Match your questions to the topic

Questions the class asked about the behavioral health problem	Question topics
	Public health significance: Questions about definitions and epidemiology
	Theory of the problem: Questions about etiology
	Theory of the solution: Questions about interventions/treatments
	Gaps in knowledge: Questions about what needs to be known or about necessary corrections to existing methods

TABLE 1.2 Examples of possible questions and their topic

Possible questions	Question topics
What are the symptoms of anxiety disorders? How many people have anxiety disorders? What are the risk factors for the disorders? Who is most likely to be affected by anxiety disorders? How early on can it be detected?	**Public health significance:** Questions about definitions and epidemiology
What causes anxiety disorders? What triggers the first onset of symptoms? What maintains anxiety disorders? Do the triggering or maintaining mechanisms differ depending on the risk factors for the disorder?	**Theory of the problem:** Questions about etiology
What are the treatments? What different components are there to the treatments? How effective are the treatments?	**Theory of the solution:** Questions about interventions/treatments
Are there limitations to the treatments? Do they work better for some types of people or under some circumstances rather than others? Are there problems with the tests of the treatment's effects? Were the methods rigorous? Does more need to be done?	**Gaps in knowledge:** Questions about what needs to be known or about necessary corrections to existing methods

Building Human Capital

In this chapter, we discussed the scientific method and the importance of close and careful reading of scientific articles. We examined the basic structure of a research proposal and a research paper. And we started the search for a behavioral health problem to study. We discussed the different questions that must be asked before investing in a study to test the outcomes of a treatment.

As you worked through these activities, you chose a disorder to study. This decision reflects commitment and a willingness to "just get started." This commitment and engagement will help you stay on track and meet deadlines as you move forward.

You also completed exercises that asked you "What do we need to know about Anxiety Disorders?" To answer this question, you divided the big picture question into smaller, more specific questions. Next you linked these questions together in a logical order. This is the first step to developing a systematic and rigorous approach to thinking about complex problems.

It is hard work to break down the big picture questions and answer each one. But as you do the hard work, you will get better answers to the questions that count!

Terms

Take the time to define each of these terms and consider how to apply them.

Research Terms

Scientific method
Scientific premise
Scientific/Methodological rigor
Basic research
Applied research
Research articles/papers
APA style
Introduction Section
Methods Section
Results Section
Discussion Section
References Section
Statistical analysis plan
Public health significance
Prevalence
Risk Factors
Mechanisms
Intervention
Literature Review
Human Capital

References

Czajkowski, S. M., Powell, L. H., Adler, N., Naar-King, S., Reynolds, K. D., Hunter, C. M., … Peterson, J. C. (2015). From ideas to efficacy: The ORBIT model for developing behavioral treatments for chronic diseases. *Health Psychology, 34*(10), 971.

Foa, E. B., & McLean, C. P. (2016). The efficacy of exposure therapy for anxiety-related disorders and its underlying mechanisms: The case of OCD and PTSD. *Annual Review of Clinical Psychology, 12*, 1–28.

Gerin, W., Kinkade, C. K., Itinger, J. B., & Spruill, T. (2010). *Writing the NIH grant proposal: A step-by-step guide*. Sage.

Nielsen, L., Riddle, M., King, J. W., Aklin, W. M., Chen, W., Clark, D., … Green, P. (2018). The NIH science of behavior Change program: Transforming the science through a focus on mechanisms of change. *Behaviour Research and Therapy, 101*, 3–11.

Reinecke, A., Hoyer, J., Rinck, M., & Becker, E. S. (2013). Cognitive-behavioural therapy reduces unwanted thought intrusions in generalized anxiety disorder. *Journal of Behavior Therapy and Experimental Psychiatry, 44*(1), 1–6.

Part 1

Public health significance

Chapter 2

The building blocks of research: Application to public health significance

In this section of the book, covering Chapters 2–6, we focus on building the public health significance (PHS) section of your research proposal or research paper. We build the proposal by gathering ideas and evidence from scientific articles. To help understand the articles, it will be useful to have knowledge about the overall research process and the methods used to conduct the research that is presented in these articles.

In Chapters 2 and 3, you will learn about the basic building blocks of research that are covered in the research articles, including theories, hypotheses, constructs, variables, and measurement methods. These building blocks work together to move researchers from broad ideas to research projects designed to test specific hypotheses.

As you work through the activities in Chapter 2, you will learn how to develop an operational definition of your disorder, identify variables that can represent your disorder in research studies, and evaluate measurement methods and measurement instruments needed to study the disorder. In Chapter 3, you will learn about the process of generating hypotheses from theories and recognizing the predictor and outcome variables in these hypotheses.

In Chapter 4, you will learn how to find research articles and determine if they are appropriate for your research. You will practice identifying constructs, variables, and measurement methods throughout the articles.

Psychology Research Methods. https://doi.org/10.1016/B978-0-12-815680-3.00002-5

In Chapter 5, you will understand how researchers choose participants to study, determine the prevalence of the behavioral health disorder, and identify the variables which may put people at risk for the disorder.

In Chapter 6, you will learn how to put all the evidence together to write a PHS section.

Building Blocks of Research: Theories, Constructs, Hypotheses, and Variables

Scientists identify a problem they wish to investigate. As they employ the scientific method to conduct their investigation, they rely on the building blocks of science: **theories, hypotheses, constructs, variables, measurement methods**, and **measurement instruments**. On a conceptual level, scientists develop theories about the problem and specify the constructs or ideas that are included in their theory. On an operational or practical level, they identify variables which can be used to represent those constructs in a research study. They choose measurement methods and specific measurement instruments to assess the variable. They develop specific testable hypotheses to examine relations among these variables. In the next section, we will examine each of these building blocks.

Theories

The entire process of psychological science is dedicated to generating and testing theories, and then modifying the theories based on new evidence. **Theories** are proposals about the relations among ideas or constructs. Theories describe relations among constructs, proposing that one idea or construct is related to or causes another (Fig. 2.1).

FIGURE 2.1 The nature of theories.

Constructs

The basic building blocks of theories are constructs. **Constructs** are the ideas that compose the theory. Each disorder can be a construct, each risk factor or mechanism can be a construct, and each treatment can be a construct (Fig. 2.2).

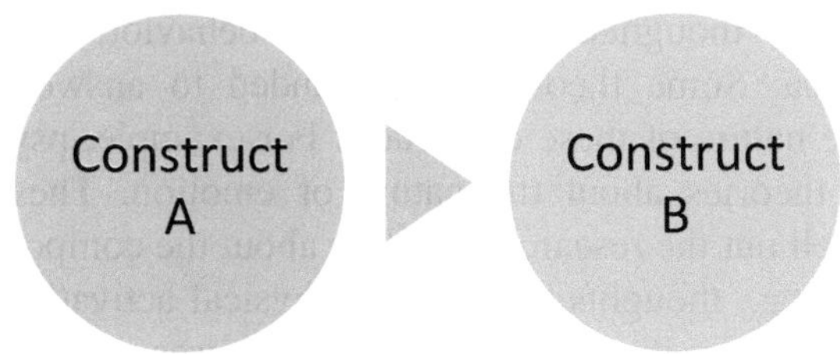

FIGURE 2.2 Theory: Construct A is related to Construct B.

A construct can contain different elements or components. For example, anxiety is a construct. The components of the construct of anxiety can include symptoms such as negative thoughts (e.g., fearful thoughts about the future), feelings (e.g., nervousness), and physical sensations (e.g., tension or restlessness) (Fig. 2.3).

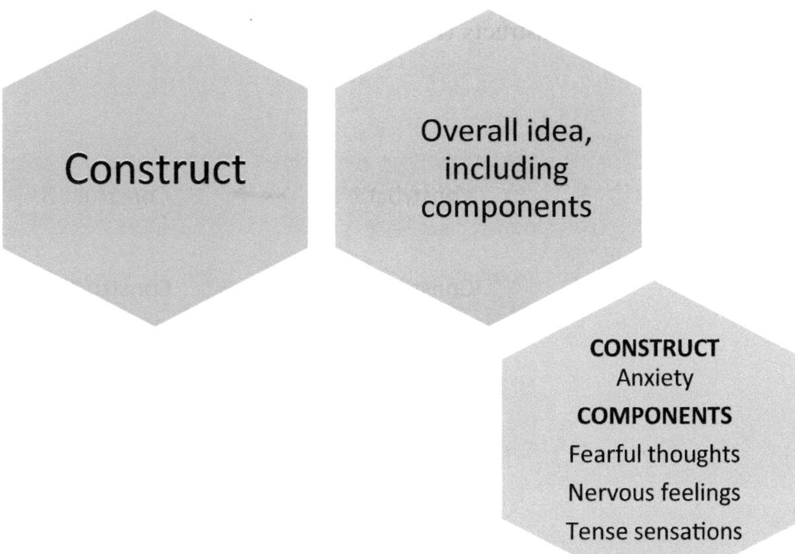

FIGURE 2.3 Anxiety as a construct with multiple components.

Theories and Constructs

A theory is a proposal about relations among constructs—it is a story about the way the constructs work together to produce an outcome. For example, one simple theory proposes that one construct is related to another—Construct A is related to Construct B.

In psychology, we develop theories about constructs including perceptions, thoughts, emotions, and behavior, among other phenomena. Some theories are intended to answer questions about the nature of these constructs. For example, psychologists develop theories about the nature of emotion. These theories might spell out the researchers' ideas about the components of an emotion (e.g., thoughts, sensations, physical activation).

Other theories involve ideas about the causes and consequences of behavioral health disorders. Each of these causes and consequences are also constructs. For example, researchers might develop theories about risk factors that make people vulnerable to the disorder. The researchers might propose that trauma exposure is a risk factor that makes it more likely someone will develop depression. In this example, both the risk factor, trauma exposure, and symptoms of the disorder, depression, are constructs. Psychologists also develop theories about the possible consequences for health and functioning that might occur if someone develops a behavioral health disorder. Functioning and health are also constructs (Fig. 2.4).

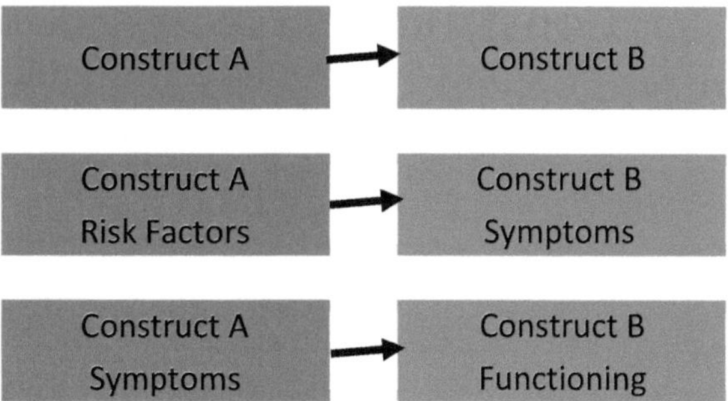

FIGURE 2.4 Theories about causes and consequences.

Variables

Before researchers can investigate a theory, they must figure out how to represent the ideas or constructs in a way they can measure. They must generate variables from the constructs they wish to study. Variables are measurable representations of the underlying constructs (Fig. 2.5).

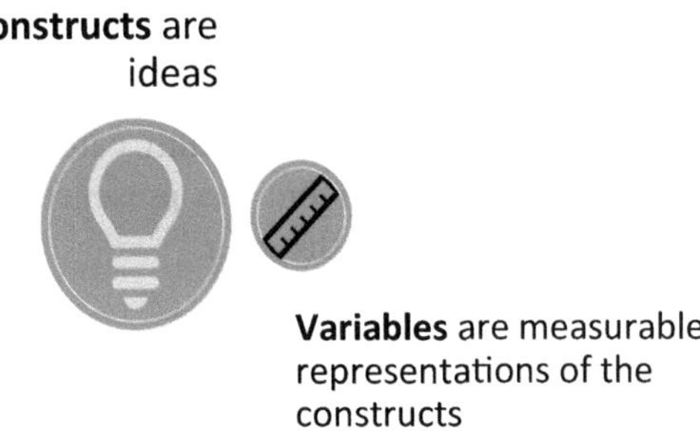

FIGURE 2.5 Constructs and variables.

Variables and Hypotheses

Variables allow theories to generate testable hypotheses (Fig. 2.6).

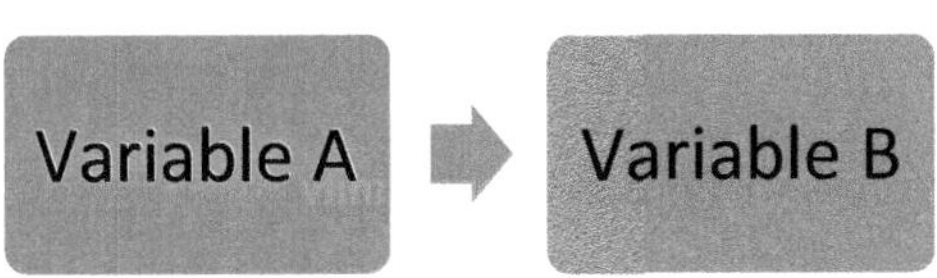

FIGURE 2.6 Hypothesis: Variable A is related to Variable B.

A hypothesis is a prediction generated from the theory. A hypothesis takes the form of a statement about the relations among variables. For example, a theory might suggest that Construct A is related to Construct B. To develop a hypothesis based on that theory, a researcher must specify variables that represent those constructs. The hypothesis might state that Variable A (representing Construct A) is related to Variable B (representing Construct B).

Variables and Constructs

The variables researchers choose to represent the construct reflect the source of the information they collect and the method they use to measure the variable and collect the information they need. The information collected in a research study is called **data**.

Notice that researchers can collect data from many different sources including the research participant, an observer, a health-care provider, or others (see Table 2.1). For example, **research participants** can report on their own symptoms. **Observers**, such as teachers can report on observable evidence or signs of the disorder. Expert observers, including health care providers, can also provide some information about the presence of symptoms known to be associated with the disorder.

TABLE 2.1 Sources of data.
Self
Research staff observers
Experts (e.g., physicians, psychologists)
Educated observers (e.g., teachers, supervisors)
Peers at school or work
Family
Friends
Neighbors/members of the larger community
Other sources of data
Census or other area level data and national or regional databases of resources and stressors

As an example, we can think about the variables that could represent the construct of social anxiety. Anxiety is an internal state—something we feel inside. Researchers cannot directly measure anxiety. But they can use different variables to capture the research participants' social anxiety.

The researcher could ask the research participants—the people being studied—directly about their experiences of social anxiety. This variable could be called *self-reported social anxiety.*

Or the researcher could ask an expert, such as a physician or another healthcare provider, to inquire about the research participant's experiences and to observe the external signs of anxiety shown by the research participant. This variable could be called *healthcare provider—rated social anxiety* (Fig. 2.7).

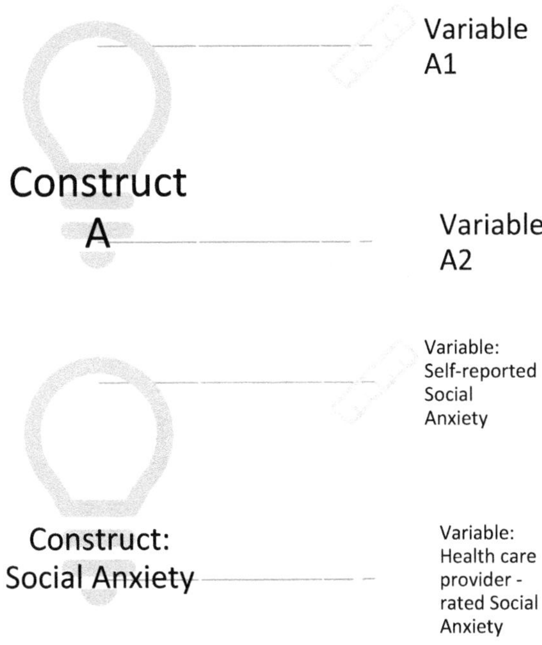

FIGURE 2.7 Deriving variables from a construct.

Both the variables are related to the construct of social anxiety, but they represent different phenomena. Each variable will capture a portion of the overall construct. Different types of information or data can be collected from different sources. In Chapter 16, you will learn how researchers determine how well each variable represents the construct.

Measurement Methods

Data on variables can be collected using several different methods. Some of the **measurement methods** available include surveys, interviews, laboratory tests, diaries, observations, and standardized tests (see Table 2.2).

TABLE 2.2 Measurement methods for collecting data.

Measurement methods (methods for obtaining the data)	Definitions and examples
Survey/questionnaire	Research tools for gathering data—usually in the form of questions or statement inquiring about the opinions or experiences of individuals (e.g., Beck Depression Inventory II, Arousal Predisposition Scale (APS)).
Daily diary	Brief surveys administered one or more times a day over one or more days or weeks either via paper-and-pencil or electronically. Diaries are a form of ecological momentary assessments—assessments which take place in the context of the individual's life.
Interviews	A conversation between the research participant and the researcher. Interviews can be informal or standardized (e.g., Anxiety Disorders Interview schedule).
Observations	A systematic way of "watching what people do". This could involve the researcher observing participants in a laboratory or a naturalistic setting. For example, observing how infants react to a brief separation from their caregiver.
Peer nominations	Asking members of a group to name group members who meet some predetermined criteria. For example, asking a group of students to name the classmates who they consider to be most liked or least liked.
Laboratory tasks	Experiments taking place in a controlled environment to limit the influence of extraneous variables. For instance, participants may be asked to complete a stressful task, such as a math test or a public speaking task. Researchers could collect data on thoughts, feelings, behavioral or physiological responses before, during, or after the task.
Standardized tests	A test that is administered and scored in a consistent manner across individuals (e.g., Scholastic Aptitude Test, Wechsler Intelligence Test, etc.). These data can be compared to **normative data.** These are data collected from large numbers of individuals which allow the researcher to determine how much the participant's score deviate from the average.
Medical or educational charts	Charts are records of information collected in a specific setting (e.g., a school or a medical setting). These charts can include evaluations, observations, and test results. For example, medical charts can include in-depth medical history (e.g., admission and discharge reports: lab and diagnostic tests, consultation notes, etc.).
Physiological measurements	Tests of markers such as heart rate, blood pressure, galvanic skin response, immune function, and cortisol levels among other variables related to the physiological stress response.

For example, both self-reported anxiety and healthcare provider–rated anxiety could be measured with methods including **surveys** or **interviews**. A survey is a document which contains questions about the research topic. The research participant answers these questions and the researcher calculates a score for the survey based on these responses (Fig. 2.8).

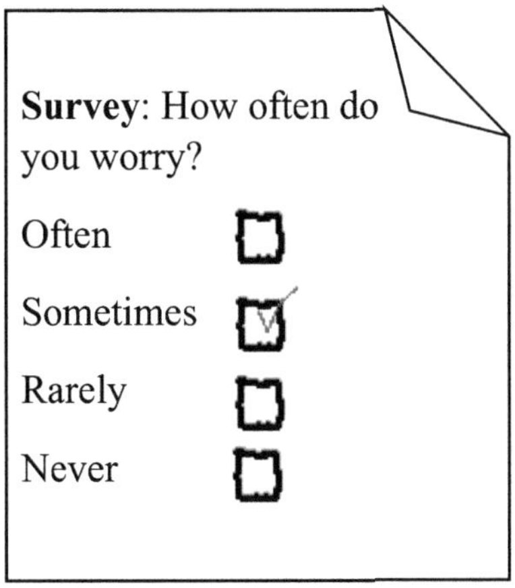

Survey: How often do you worry?

Often ☐

Sometimes ☑

Rarely ☐

Never ☐

FIGURE 2.8 Sample survey item.

An interview is a conversation in which one person asks questions, and the other answers. The responses to the interview are scored to calculate the level of anxiety the participant displays during the interview (Fig. 2.9).

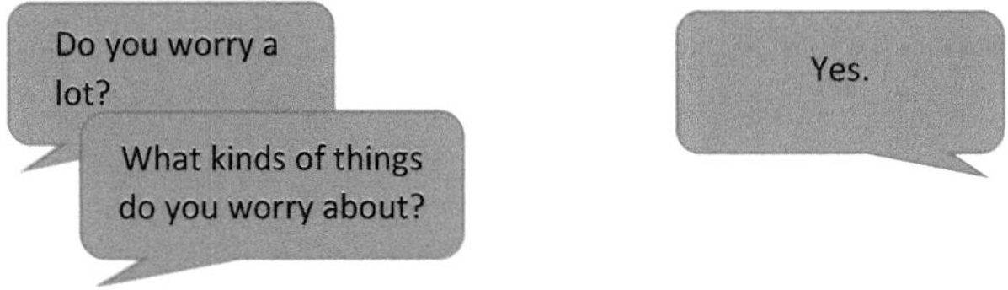

FIGURE 2.9 Sample interview question and answer.

A survey measure of anxiety might contain questions about elements of anxiety (e.g., "How often do you worry?"). The level of self-reported anxiety is reflected in the participants' scores on the survey.

In an interview measure of anxiety, the interviewer might ask the research participant about **symptoms** of anxiety and the interviewer might also notice any observable signs of anxiety. The level of anxiety is reflected in the scores the interviewer assigns based on the participants' responses.

Each method provides different types of data. **Self-report data** can provide information on the person's internal thoughts and feelings in a way that observations cannot capture. The researcher's observations of behavior may provide a good picture of the person's actual behavior in certain situations.

The observations or reports of peers, family, and/or friends can also provide information about the consequences of the disorder—how much the person's problem or symptoms and accompanying behaviors affect their functioning at home, as a friend, as a worker, or in other circumstances. The evaluations from healthcare providers and the results of **standardized tests** can give a picture of how serious the problem is—how much it deviates from normal or expected. The types of information which can be collected from each source are shown in Table 2.3.

Each of these variables is important, but none of the choices captures the complete construct of SAD. Researchers will sometimes include all three variables in the same study. This is called a **multimethod** approach.

Multimethod approaches can provide valuable information. But the research study becomes more complicated and expensive as the number of variables increases. Researchers need to consider whether the source of the data and the type of information gathered will be necessary and sufficient for testing the hypothesis.

TABLE 2.3 Linking sources of data and measurement methods.

What types of information can we obtain?	Who and how can we obtain this information from?
Reports of symptoms, and feelings, thoughts, and actions in the moment	From the participant using daily diaries
Recollections of past feelings, thoughts, and actions	From the participant using surveys or interviews
Observations of the participant's behavior in the moment	Data collected about the participant by a research observer or a professional (e.g., teacher, supervisor) using observational data collection methods
Judgments about the effects of symptoms on functioning	Data collected about the participant from peers, family, friends, or professional observers using surveys or interview methods or peer nominations
Data about the degree to which the person's symptoms deviate from the average	Data obtained from participant using standardized tests, laboratory tasks, or structured interviews which can provide normative data
Examples of data about other factors which may be important to understanding the causes of the disorder	
Data about underlying neurobiological processes contributing to the disorder	Data obtained from the participant using instruments to monitor neurological (e.g., brain function) or physiological (e.g., heart rate) responses at rest and as the participant completes different tasks
Data about other personality factors that may influence the disorder	Data obtained from participant using standardized tests, such as personality inventories, laboratory tasks, or structured interviews
Data about the social or environmental contexts which may influence risk for the disorder or affect the outcome of treatment	Data collected from community surveys, the census, or other government databases on crime, employment, housing, and health (e.g., https://factfinder.census.gov/ or https://www.iustice.gov/)

Measurement Instruments

Once the researcher has identified a source and method, the researcher chooses a specific **measurement instrument** to collect the data.

For example, there are several variables and measurement methods we could use to represent or capture a child's social anxiety symptoms, and each one has at least one measurement instrument available to use to collect the data (Fig. 2.10).

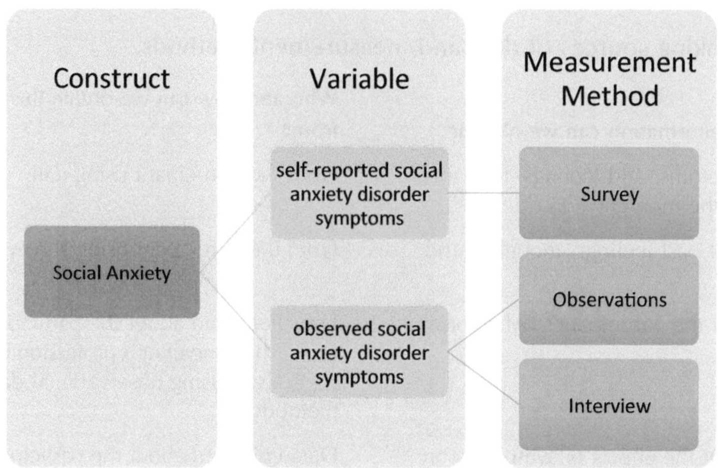

FIGURE 2.10 Documenting the links from the constructs to the measurement method.

If a researcher wished to collect data on the variable "self-reported social anxiety," the researcher could measure this variable by using a survey method to inquire about the child's experiences of anxiety in social situations. One specific survey measurement instrument is the Social Phobia and Anxiety Inventory for Children (Beidel, Turner, & Morris, 1995).

The researcher could collect data on the variable "teacher-reported social anxiety." The child's teachers could provide information about their observations of the child's symptoms of social anxiety. The teachers could be given the specific measurement instrument, the Teacher Report Form (TRF; Achenbach & Rescorla, 2001).

"Parent-reported social anxiety" is another variable. The researcher could ask the participant's parents about the child's social behavior and fears. Parents could be given the specific measurement instrument—the Child Behavior Checklist (Achenbach & Edelbrock, 1991, p. 7).

The specific measurement instrument we choose must be **valid** and **reliable**. A valid measurement instrument yields data that are related to the construct in a demonstrable way. A reliable measurement instrument measures the data in a consistent way.

We will discuss each aspect of the measurement process—from developing an operational definition to choosing a specific measurement instrument—in Chapter 16.

Defining Constructs and Variables

To understand any research article, it is critical to understand the meaning of the constructs the researchers are investigating. Identifying and defining the constructs are the first two steps in close reading of a research article. Many of the important constructs in a study are mentioned in the research abstract. The constructs listed in the abstract of a research article for the PHS section can include the behavioral health disorder, as well as any consequences or risk factors for the disorder, among other constructs. Next, it is critical to identify the variables used to represent the constructs and understand the sources of the data collected on the variables and the measurement method.

Activities 2.1 and 2.2 will help to develop these skills.

Activity 2.1 Recognizing and Defining Constructs

Look at this article by Xu et al. (2012). We provide the abstract and parts of the methods section. This article is investigating gender differences in social anxiety disorder (SAD); (See Fig. 2.11). The authors want to know if men and women differ in how likely they are to develop SAD. They also want to know if men and women with SAD differ in the degree to which they develop alcohol and other substance use disorders.

Journal of Anxiety Disorders 26 (2012) 12–19

Contents lists available at ScienceDirect

Journal of Anxiety Disorders

In the abstract, the authors explain the main ideas of the study. This is a good place to identify the key constructs under investigation.

Gender differences in social anxiety disorder: Results from the national epidemiologic sample on alcohol and related conditions

Yang Xu[a], Franklin Schneier[a], Richard G. Heimberg[b], Katherine Princisvalle[a], Michael R. Liebowitz[a], Shuai Wang[a], Carlos Blanco[a,*]

[a] Department of Psychiatry, New York State Psychiatric Institute, College of Physicians and Surgeons, Columbia University, 1051 Riverside Drive, Unit 69, New York, NY 10032, United States
[b] Adult Anxiety Clinic, Department of Psychology, Temple University, 419 Weiss Hall, 1701 N. 13th Street, Philadelphia, PA 19122-6085, United States

ARTICLE INFO

Article history:
Received 6 April 2011
Received in revised form 10 August 2011
Accepted 10 August 2011

Keywords:
Social anxiety disorder
Social phobia
Human sex differences
Epidemiology

ABSTRACT

This study examined gender differences among persons with lifetime social anxiety disorder (SAD). Data were derived from the National Epidemiologic Survey on Alcohol and Related Conditions ($n = 43{,}093$), a survey of a representative community sample of the United States adult population. Diagnoses of psychiatric disorders were based on the Alcohol Use Disorder and Associated Disabilities Interview Schedule–DSM-IV Version. The lifetime prevalence of SAD was 4.20% for men and 5.67% for women. Among respondents with lifetime SAD, women reported more lifetime social fears and internalizing disorders and were more likely to have received pharmacological treatment for SAD, whereas men were more likely to fear dating, have externalizing disorders, and use alcohol and illicit drugs to relieve symptoms of SAD. Recognizing these differences in clinical symptoms and treatment-seeking of men and women with SAD may be important for optimizing screening strategies and enhancing treatment efficacy for SAD.

© 2011 Published by Elsevier Ltd.

FIGURE 2.11 Excerpts from Xu et al. (2012).

We can make a list of constructs from the article by Xu et al. (2012) on gender differences in SAD. Next, we fill in the definitions of the constructs. Making sure we understand the constructs included in the abstract is a good way to make sure we will understand more about what we read in the article.

We included the methods section of the Xu et al. (2012) article in Fig. 2.12. The information in section 2.2 can help define many of the constructs. Figure 2.13 displays one more excerpt that can help explain what the authors mean when they use the terms "internalizing" and "externalizing disorders".

Continued

Activity 2.1 Recognizing and Defining Constructs—cont'd

2. Method

2.1. Sample

The 2001–2002 National Epidemiologic Sample on Alcohol and Related Conditions (NESARC) is a survey of a representative sample of the United States adult population, conducted by the National Institute on Alcohol Abuse and Alcoholism (Grant, Hasin, Blanco, et al., 2005; Grant, Moore, et al., 2003; Grant, Hasin, Stinson, et al., 2004). The NESARC targeted the civilian population residing in households or group living quarters, 18 years and older. Face-to-face interviews were conducted with 43,093 respondents. The survey response rate was 81%. Blacks, Hispanics, and young adults (age 18–24 years) were over-sampled, with data adjusted for over-sampling, household- and person-level non-response.

The weighted data were then adjusted to represent the U.S. civilian population based on the 2000 Census. All potential NESARC respondents were informed in writing about the nature of the survey, the statistical uses of the survey data, the voluntary aspect of their participation and the Federal laws that rigorously provide for the strict confidentiality of identifiable survey information. Those respondents consenting to participate after receiving this information were interviewed. The research protocol, including informed consent procedures, received full ethical review and approval from the U.S. Census Bureau and the U.S. Office of Management and Budget.

2.2. Measures

2.2.1. Sociodemographic measures

Age, race-ethnicity, nativity, education, marital status, urbanicity, employment status, and insurance type were compared among men and women with lifetime SAD.

2.2.2. DSM-IV diagnostic interview

The diagnostic interview used to generate diagnoses was the NIAAA Alcohol Use Disorder and Associated Disabilities Interview Schedule, DSM-IV Version (AUDADIS-IV; Grant, Dawson, et al., 2003). This structured diagnostic interview designed for lay interviewers was developed to advance measurement of substance use and mental disorders in large-scale surveys.

← In section 2.2.2, the authors describe the interview used to diagnose SAD and to provide information on substance use disorders.

2.2.2.1. Social anxiety disorder. Consistent with DSM-IV (American Psychiatric Association, 1994), diagnosis of SAD required a marked or persistent fear of one or more social or performance situations (here operationalized as at least 1 of 14 social interaction or performance situations, including a residual "other situation" category) in which embarrassment or humiliation may occur. The fear had to be recognized as excessive or unreasonable. Also, exposure to the situation must have almost invariably provoked anxiety (which may

← In section 2.2.2.1, the authors describe how the interviewer establishes a diagnosis of SAD, specifying the criteria that must be met.

Activity 2.1 Recognizing and Defining Constructs—cont'd

have taken the form of a situationally bound or predisposed panic attack), and the feared social situations must have been avoided or else endured with intense anxiety. These latter DSM-IV criteria for SAD helped to further define the feared situation(s) as both excessive and unreasonable. All SAD diagnoses required that the clinical significance criterion of DSM-IV be met (i.e., symptoms of the disorder must have caused clinically significant distress or impairment in social, occupational, or other areas of functioning). The AUDADIS-IV questions used to operationalize the clinical significance criterion were disorder-specific and included: (1) being upset or made uncomfortable by the phobic symptoms and/or avoidance, (2) interference with relationships with other people, (3) interference with occupational or other role responsibilities, (4) restriction of usual activities, and (5) preventing the respondent from engaging in usual activities. Unlike the diagnoses provided by other instruments used in epidemiologic surveys (Alonso et al., 2004; Kessler, Wittchen, et al., 1998; Wittchen, Essau, Zerssen, Krieg, & Zaudig, 1992), AUDADIS-IV diagnoses of SAD excluded persons with SAD symptoms that were substance-induced or due to medical conditions (Grant, Hasin, Stinson, et al., 2004).

In this part of section 2.2.2.2, the authors explain how the interviewer establishes the presence of an alcohol or other substance use disorder.

2.2.2.2. Other psychiatric disorders. As described in detail elsewhere (Grant, Hasin, Stinson, et al., 2005; Grant, Hasin, Stinson, et al., 2004), the AUDADIS-IV also assessed three other DSM-IV anxiety disorders (panic disorder, specific phobia, and GAD) and four mood disorders (major depressive, bipolar I disorder, bipolar II disorder, and dysthymia). All of these disorders followed DSM-IV criteria, required that the clinical significance criteria be met, and ruled out substance-induced episodes or those due to a general medical condition. The AUDADIS-IV questions operationalize DSM-IV criteria for alcohol and drug-specific abuse and dependence for 10 drug classes. Consistent with DSM-IV, a lifetime AUDADIS-IV diagnosis of alcohol abuse required that at least 1 of the 4 criteria for abuse be met prior to interview. The AUDADIS-IV lifetime alcohol dependence diagnosis required that at least 3 of the 7 DSM-IV criteria for dependence be met prior to interview. Drug abuse and dependence and nicotine dependence used the same algorithms (Grant, Hasin, Chou, Stinson, & Dawson, 2004). The AUDADIS-IV assessments of DSM-IV personality disorders have been described in detail previously (Grant et al., 2008; Grant, Hasin, Stinson, et al., 2004). These include avoidant, dependent, obsessive-compulsive, paranoid, schizoid, and antisocial personality disorders. As reported elsewhere, test–retest reliability of the AUDADIS diagnosis of SAD was fair ($\kappa = 0.42–0.46$) (Grant, Hasin, Blanco, et al., 2005; Grant, Moore, et al., 2003), comparable to other interviews used in epidemiological studies (e.g., Ruscio et al., 2008). The reliability ($\kappa > 0.74$) and validity were good to excellent for substance use disorder (Grant, Harford, Dawson, Chou, & Pickering, 1995; Grant, Moore, et al., 2003; Grant, Stinson, et al., 2004; Vrasti, Grant, & Chatterji, 1997).

FIGURE 2.12 The measures section from Xu et al. (2012).

Continued

Activity 2.1 Recognizing and Defining Constructs—cont'd

3.2. Psychiatric comorbidity

Among individuals with lifetime SAD, men were more likely than women to have lifetime alcohol abuse and dependence, drug abuse and dependence, pathological gambling, conduct disorder, and antisocial personality disorder. They were less likely than women to have all mood and anxiety disorders, except bipolar I and bipolar II disorders, for which there were no gender differences (Table 1). Thus, men with SAD were more likely to have comorbid externalizing disorders, whereas women with SAD were more likely to have comorbid internalizing disorders.

FIGURE 2.13 Selected excerpt from Xu et al. (2012).

TABLE 2.4 Selected constructs and their definitions from Xu et al. (2012).

Constructs and definitions from Xu et al. (2012)

Constructs	Definitions	Source of the information for the definition
Lifetime social anxiety disorder (SAD)	SAD is a mental condition that involves disproportionate fears of speaking in certain situations. The episode of anxiety must have lasted more than 6 months and be very distressing. Lifetime social anxiety means the person has had at least one episode of social anxiety lasting 6 months or more over the course of their lifetime.	DSM-5
Internalizing disorders	In this paper, the authors define internalizing disorders as psychiatric disorders including mood disorders such as depression, or other anxiety disorders.	Xu et al. (2012)
Externalizing disorders	In this paper, the authors define externalizing disorders as substance use/abuse disorders, antisocial personality disorder, conduct disorder, or pathological gambling.	Xu et al. (2012)
Alcohol and illicit drug use	The authors use standard criteria to measure alcohol use and abuse. These criteria include: having problems controlling substance use;	ADIS criteria https://www.samhs_a.gov/disorders/substance-use

Activity 2.1 Recognizing and Defining Constructs—cont'd

TABLE 2.4 Selected constructs and their definitions from Xu et al. (2012).—cont'd

Constructs and definitions from Xu et al. (2012)

Constructs	**Definitions**	**Source of the information for the definition**
	wanting to cut down but not being able to; having impairments in social and occupational functioning or health because of substance use and still using; and needing more and more of the substance to have the same feeling.	
There were also other constructs that seemed important but were not directly related to symptoms		
Representative community sample	This refers to the way participants are included in the study. The authors used a strategy to include people in the sample who represented the population and were chosen at random from the individuals available.	Wikipedia
Screening strategies	Strategies used to identify patients with this disorder. The authors are indicating that the information in the paper may influence how men and women could be screened for SAD.	Xu et al. (2012)
Treatment efficacy	The effects of treatment. The authors are indicating that understanding more about gender differences in the consequences of SAD may help make treatments more effective.	Xu et al. (2012)

Activity 2.2 Identifying Constructs, Variables, Measurement Methods, and Measurement Instruments

First, we consider two of the constructs mentioned in the abstract: SAD and substance use disorders. These are the important ideas under investigation. We list these two constructs in the second column of Table 2.4.

Now we can look through the methods section shown in Fig. 2.12 to determine the variables the researchers used to represent SAD and substance use. We also can use the methods section to help us figure out the measurement methods and instruments the researchers used. We filled in Table 2.5 with the information for the construct SAD. Read the excerpts from the Methods section. Fill in the information for the construct substance use disorders. Identify the variable representing substance use disorders, the measurement methods, and the specific measurement instrument used to assess the variable.

TABLE 2.5 Identifying constructs, variables, and measurement instruments.

Author/ date:	Construct	Variable	Measurement method	Measurement instrument
Xu et al. (2012)	Social anxiety disorder (SAD)	Interviewer-rated SAD based on structured interview	Structured diagnostic interview inquiring about symptoms in response to 14 situations	NIAAA Alcohol Use Disorder and Associated disabilities Interview Schedule, DSM-IV version
	Alcohol and other substance use disorders			

The Xu et al. (2012) paper is clear about the constructs, variables, methods, and the measurement instruments. Many articles are not as clear. The authors may simply refer to the variable only by the name of the measurement instrument. In these cases, you may need to look up the name of the measurement instrument to understand the construct, variable, and measurement method which are being used. In other cases, researchers will use multiple measurement instruments for one construct. In this case it is important to understand the variables and measurement methods that are represented by the different measurement instruments. Reading the measures section of the article will help you.

Formal Operational Definitions

Operational definitions are the working definitions researchers use for their constructs. Operational definitions of behavioral health disorders can be obtained from known and "gold standard" sources including:

- Books/Manuals
  - The Diagnostic and Statistical Manual of the American Psychiatric Association (DSM-5)
- Websites created by established and reputable sources
  - Center for Disease Control (CDC)
  - World Health Organization (WHO)
  - American Psychiatric Association (APA)
- Empirical and review articles from peer-reviewed journals, including, for example,
  - Journal of Anxiety Disorders
  - Journal of Clinical Psychology

We can practice by establishing an operational definition of SAD.

The DSM-5 is the "gold standard" for defining behavioral health disorders. The diagnostic criteria of SAD from the DSM-5 include details shown in Table 2.6. The full details of the diagnostic criteria can be seen in the DSM-5 and a broader description of the disorder can be found at the website for the National Institute of Mental Health (www.nimh.gov).

TABLE 2.6 Components of the diagnostic criteria for social anxiety disorder defined by the DSM-5.

Construct:	Components of the construct	Examples of the components
Social anxiety disorder as defined by DSM-5	Symptoms	Fear or anxiety about participating in social situations in which the individual might be observed and potentially judged. Frequent avoidance of feared social situations or the perception that one is enduring the social situation until it is over.
	Clinical impairment	The symptoms, including the fear or avoidance, cause recognizable difficulties in social or professional situations and are distressing to the individual.
	Rule-out conditions	The symptoms are not better explained by another mental condition or are a physiological response to a medication or illicit drug.

The operational definition of a DSM-5 diagnosis of SAD for adults describes both the main idea and the elements of the construct. Here are some sentences which capture the main idea: "The individual with social anxiety disorder experiences significant and disturbing anxiety in social situations in which they may be scrutinized by others. These situations could include public speaking, having a conversation, or meeting unfamiliar people."

This operational definition of the construct of SAD also should recognize that the construct of SAD has multiple elements: symptoms, clinical impairment, and rule-out conditions. The symptoms themselves include multiple components such as *feelings* (i.e., severe anxiety), *thoughts* (i.e., appraisals of situation as more threatening than they are), and *actions* (i.e., avoidance or endurance with distress). The construct of SAD also includes ideas about the *duration* of symptoms (at least 6 months) and the *consequences* of the symptoms (severe distress and impairment).

Activity 2.3 Getting Started on an Operational Definition for the Disorder you are Studying

Develop an operational definition for the construct you are studying. Look up the description of the disorder in the DSM-5. The DSM-5 symptoms for the disorders are available online from reputable sources. There are also descriptive papers which explain the diagnostic criteria and the way they were developed (see, for example, Hasin et al., 2013).

Once you have reviewed the diagnostic criteria for the disorder you are investigating, write out an operational definition in sentences.

____

____

____

____

____

____

Building Human Capital

In this chapter, you learned about basic building blocks of research, including theories, constructs, operational definitions, variables, and measurement methods. You learned about the ways in which researchers can collect data, and evaluate different sources of data and different methods for collecting data. You learned that often there are many measurement instruments that can be used to measure any variable.

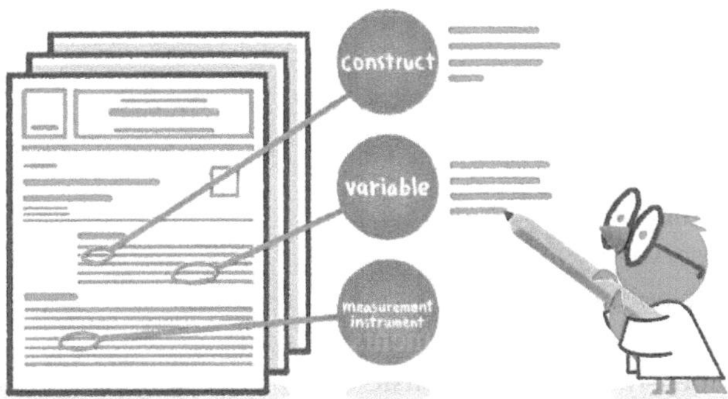

As you completed these exercises, you learned to push yourself to be specific—to move past a general understanding of a construct to develop an operational definition and identify measurable variables.

You had to be patient and conscientious as you defined all the terms and traced the links among constructs, variables, measurement methods, and measurement instruments.

Understanding these constructs and variables can help you think about how the research study might work. You can gain a new kind of creativity as you anticipate what the "story" of the research paper might be—the story of the ways the constructs might work together.

Terms

Take the time to find the definitions and consider how to apply them.

Research Terms

- Theories
- Constructs
- Variables
- Hypotheses
- Measurement methods
- Measurement instruments
- Data
- Descriptive research
- Hypothesis-testing research
- Research participants
- Measurement validity
- Measurement reliability
- Types of measurement methods
  - Daily diaries
  - Expert ratings
  - Interviews
  - Laboratory tasks
  - Medical Charts
  - Observer ratings
  - Peer nominations
  - Physiological measurements
  - Public records (e.g., census data)
  - Standardized testing
  - Surveys

References

Achenbach, T. M., & Edelbrock, C. (1991). *Child behavior checklist*. Burlington (Vt).

Achenbach, T. M., & Rescorla, L. (2001). *ASEBA school-age forms & profiles*. Burlington, VT: Aseba.

Adams, G. C., Balbuena, L., Meng, X., & Asmundson, G. J. (2016). When social anxiety and depression go together: A population study of comorbidity and associated consequences. *Journal of Affective Disorders, 206*, 48–54.

Beidel, D. C., Turner, S. M., & Morris, T. L. (1995). A new inventory to assess childhood social anxiety and phobia: The Social Phobia and Anxiety Inventory for Children. *Psychological Assessment, 7*(1), 73.

Hasin, D. S., O'Brien, C. P., Auriacombe, M., Borges, G., Bucholz, K., Budney, A., … Petry, N. M. (2013). DSM-5 criteria for substance use disorders: Recommendations and rationale. *American Journal of Psychiatry, 170*(8), 834–851.

Xu, Y., Schneier, F., Heimberg, R. G., Princisvalle, K., Liebowitz, M. R., Wang, S., & Blanco, C. (2012). Gender differences in social anxiety disorder: Results from the national epidemiologic sample on alcohol and related conditions. *Journal of Anxiety Disorders, 26*(1), 12–19.

Chapter 3

From building blocks to building hypothesis-testing research

Constructs, theories, variables, and hypotheses are the building blocks of research. In this chapter, we examine different types of research. We consider descriptive and inferential or hypothesis-testing approaches. We explore the differences between experimental and observational research. Understanding these different kinds of research approaches will help you read the articles you need to develop your proposal or paper.

The examples in this chapter are drawn from articles that test hypotheses about the consequences of behavioral health disorders. Many behavioral health problems have consequences for physical and mental health and functioning. These consequences could include additional mental or physical health problems, loss of employment, problems in academic performance, conflict in relationships, or impairments in quality of life, among other outcomes.

If you are writing a proposal, documenting the consequences of the behavioral health disorder is part of the PHS section. This evidence helps you make the argument that your proposed research is significant because the problem you are studying is serious. If you are writing a paper on the public health significance of the disorder, you may wish to review the research on the link between the behavioral health disorder and different consequences for functioning and health. You can review the evidence documenting consequences of a behavioral health disorder and identify gaps in knowledge.

In this chapter, we introduce different types of research approaches. You will learn more about the specific methods used in hypothesis-testing research in Chapters 5 and 12.

Psychology Research Methods. https://doi.org/10.1016/B978-0-12-815680-3.00003-7

Types of Research

Scientists use two different approaches to research: **descriptive research** and inferential or hypothesis-testing research. Descriptive research is research aimed at understanding the characteristics of the construct or phenomenon under investigation. **Hypothesis-testing research** involves testing predictions or hypotheses about how variables relate to each other. The results of hypothesis-testing studies have implications for the theory the researchers are testing.

Descriptive Research

Descriptive research is used to provide information about the construct under investigation. For example, if the construct is a disorder, the results of descriptive research on the disorder might include information about the symptoms associated with the diagnosis and the course or progression of the illness. Other types of descriptive research provide information about the prevalence of the disorder, indicating how many people have the disorder.

Inferential or Hypothesis-Testing Research

In contrast, inferential or hypothesis testing research is aimed at evaluating theories. A theory specifies relations among constructs. Researchers use variables to **translate theories into testable hypotheses**. They identify variables to represent the constructs and generate hypotheses predicting relations among the variables. Hypotheses are formulated as statements about relations among variables.

Variable A is related to Variable B. Variable A causes Variable B.

Researchers conduct studies to determine if these hypotheses are true or false. As researchers develop and test hypotheses, they accumulate **evidence** that will help them determine if their theories are correct.

As you understand how researchers develop and test hypotheses, you will be better able to evaluate the articles on consequences and risk factors you are reading for the PHS section. The evidence from these articles will help you develop your own proposal or paper.

We can consider an example to illustrate the differences between descriptive and hypothesis-testing research. In the article by Xu et al. (2012) on social anxiety disorder (SAD) we examined in the last chapter, the authors used both descriptive research and hypothesis-testing research.

In the abstract the authors write: "*The lifetime prevalence of SAD was 4.20% for men and 5.67% for women.*" This statement provides descriptive information on the prevalence of SAD—the proportion of individuals who have ever had SAD over the course of their lives.

The authors also state: "*Among respondents with SAD, women reported more lifetime social fears and internalizing disorders.*" This statement indicates the authors tested hypotheses about relations between different constructs. They tested hypotheses about the relations among gender, SAD, and a consequence of SAD, **internalizing disorders**.

Developing a PHS section requires that you read both descriptive and hypothesis-testing research. The descriptive research will provide information about the operational definition of the disorder and the prevalence of the disorder. The hypothesis-testing research will provide information on relations between symptoms of the disorder and consequences for health and functioning. Other hypothesis-testing research will identify the risk factors that make people more vulnerable to the disorder. These articles are described in more detail in Chapter 5.

Generating Hypotheses

Theories are stories about relations among constructs. Hypotheses are derived from theory and are statements about relations among variables which represent the constructs. In this chapter, we will examine how those statements are developed and the roles assigned to the variables.

Here is an example. Some researchers propose that one consequence of posttraumatic stress disorder (PTSD) is poor physical health (Pacella, Hruska, & Delahanty, 2013). The theory concerns relations among two constructs: PTSD and physical health (Fig. 3.1).

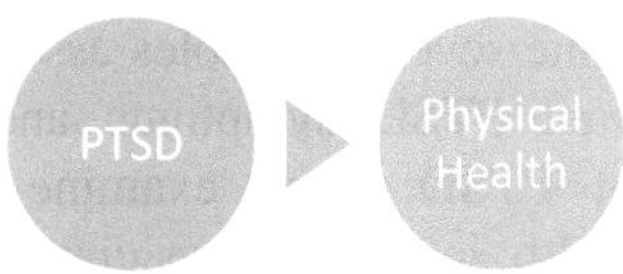

FIGURE 3.1 Theory: PTSD is related to physical health.

To evaluate the underlying theory, researchers must identify variables which can represent the constructs of PTSD and physical health (Fig. 3.2).

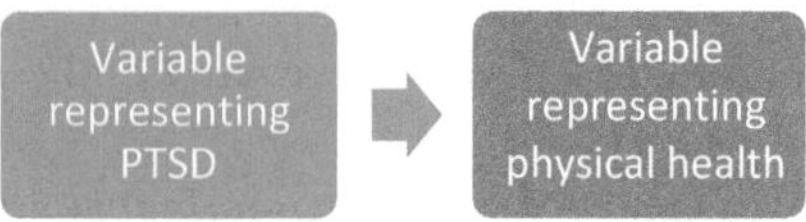

FIGURE 3.2 Hypothesis: Variable A is related to Variable B.

These variables are used to develop hypotheses. Here are some possible hypotheses the researcher could test:

- Healthcare provider's diagnosis of **PTSD** is related to self-reported physical health (Fig. 3.3)

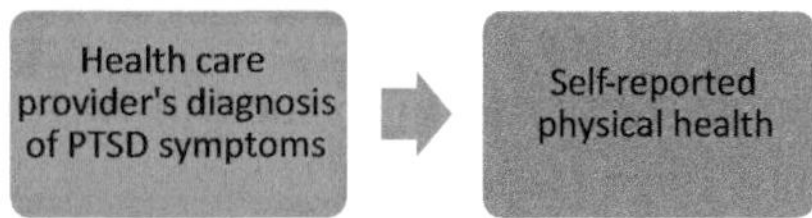

FIGURE 3.3 Hypothesis: Diagnosis of PTSD is related to self-reported health.

Or

- Self-reported **PTSD** symptoms are related to physician's **diagnosis of heart disease** (Fig. 3.4)

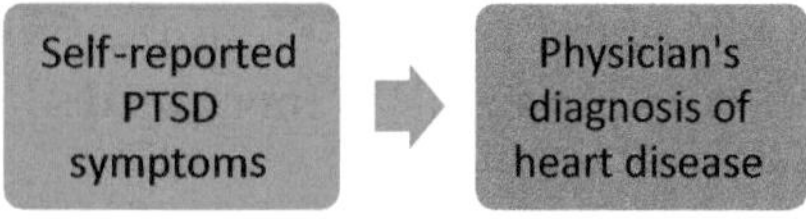

FIGURE 3.4 Hypothesis: PTSD is related to diagnosis of heart disease.

Pacella et al. (2013) conduct a **meta-analysis** to understand how much evidence there is for the theory that PTSD is associated with poor physical health. A meta-analysis is a study that combines the results from many different studies of a given topic (Fig. 3.5).

The authors examine several variables associated with PTSD, including self-reported PTSD symptoms and healthcare provider's diagnosis of PTSD. They examine several variables related to physical health, including physician's diagnosis of heart disease and self-reported physical health (Pacella et al., 2013).

Journal of Anxiety Disorders 27 (2013) 33–46

ELSEVIER

Contents lists available at SciVerse ScienceDirect

Journal of Anxiety Disorders

Review

The physical health consequences of PTSD and PTSD symptoms: A meta-analytic review

Maria L. Pacella, Bryce Hruska, Douglas L. Delahanty*

Department of Psychology, Kent State University, Kent, OH, United States

ARTICLE INFO

Article history:
Received 28 March 2012
Received in revised form 23 August 2012
Accepted 26 August 2012

Keywords:
Medical conditions
Meta-analysis
Pain
Physical health
Posttraumatic stress disorder
Posttraumatic stress disorder symptoms

ABSTRACT

The present meta-analysis systematically examined associations between physical health and post-traumatic stress disorder (PTSD)/PTSD symptoms (PTSS), as well as moderators of this relationship. Literature searches yielded 62 studies examining the impact of PTSD/PTSS on physical health-related quality of life (HR-QOL), general health symptoms, general medical conditions, musculoskeletal pain, cardio-respiratory (CR) symptoms, and gastrointestinal (GI) health. Sample-specific and methodological moderators were also examined. Results revealed significantly greater general health symptoms, general medical conditions, and poorer HR-QOL for PTSD and high PTSS individuals. PTSD/PTSS was also associated with greater frequency and severity of pain, CR, and GI complaints. Results of moderation analyses were mixed. However, consistent relationships emerged regarding PTSD assessment method, such that effect sizes were largest for self-reported PTSD/PTSS and all but one health outcome. Results highlight the need for prospective longitudinal examination of physical health shortly following trauma, and suggest variables to consider in the design of such studies.

© 2012 Elsevier Ltd. All rights reserved.

In the abstract, the authors describe the study. They are investigating the outcomes of 62 studies which tested hypotheses

FIGURE 3.5 Abstract from Pacella et al. (2013).

They find that overall PTSD is related to several different measures of health, but the outcomes depend on the variables which are used to represent PTSD and physical health (Fig. 3.6).

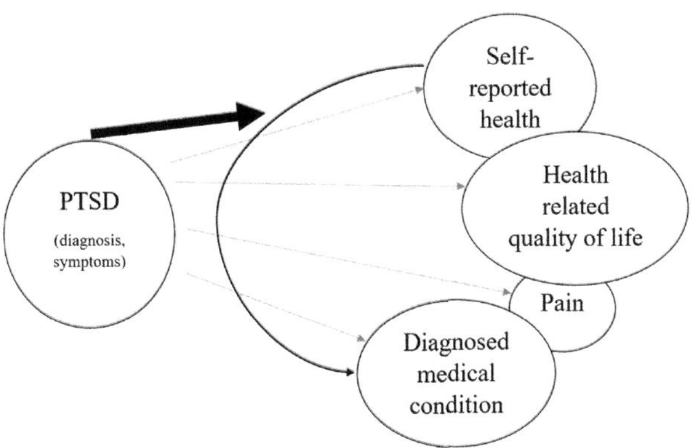

FIGURE 3.6 Mapping PTSD to the associated variables from the Pacella et al. (2013) article.

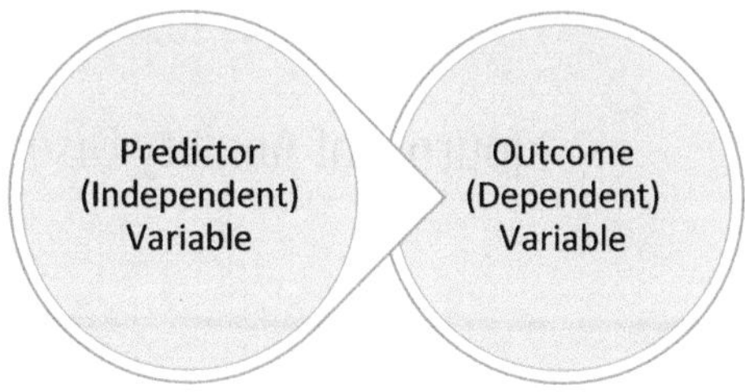

FIGURE 3.7 Predictor and outcome variable.

Assigning Roles to Variables: Considering Predictor and Outcome Variables

Variables have roles in a study. One variable, called the **predictor variable**, is expected to affect another, called the **outcome variable**. For instance, in the example we have been discussing, we could consider "*self-reported PTSD symptoms*" to be the predictor variable and "*physical health*" to be the outcome variable.

In experimental research, the predictor variable is also called the *independent variable* (IV). The outcome variable is called the *dependent variable* (DV). In this formulation, the outcome is dependent on the IV (Fig. 3.7).

A hypothesis states the expected relationship between a predictor or IV and an outcome or DV. The aim of the research study is to test the hypothesis that there is a relationship between the predictor and the outcome.

For example:

- *Hypothesis:* Self-reported PTSD is related to doctor-diagnosed medical illness.
- *Aim:* The aim of the study is to test the relationship of self-reported PTSD to doctor-diagnosed medical illness.

In studies of the consequences of a disorder, it is common for the symptoms of diagnosis of the disorder to serve as the predictor variable and the consequences to serve as the outcome or DV (Fig. 3.8).

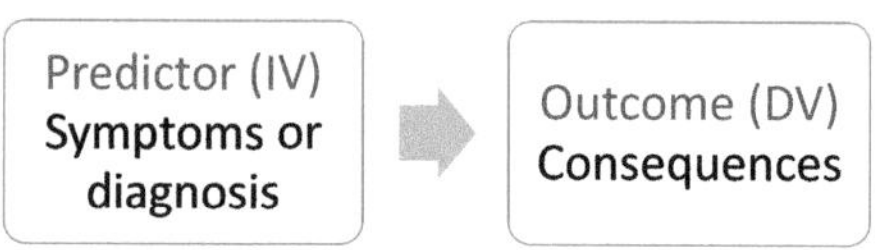

FIGURE 3.8 Symptoms predict the consequences of the disorder.

In contrast, in studies of risk factors, it is common for the risk factor to serve as the predictor (or IV) and the symptoms or diagnoses condition to serve as the outcome (or DV) (Fig. 3.9).

FIGURE 3.9 Risk factor predicts symptoms or diagnosis of a disorder.

Notice that any variable can have a different role depending on the hypothesis being tested and the aim of the study. In a study of consequences, symptoms (or diagnosis) of the disorder serve as the predictor. But in a study of risk factors, symptoms or diagnosis of the disorder serve as the outcome.

Categorical and Continuous Variables: Yes or No vs. More or Less

In the abstract, Pacella et al. (2013) indicate that they examined if the relation of PTSD to physical health depended on whether the predictor was PTSD diagnosis or posttraumatic stress symptoms (PTSSs). The authors conducted these analyses because the variables representing the construct of PTSD can be conceptualized in two ways—as **categorical** variables and as **continuous** variables. Categorical and continuous variables can provide different information.

The different scores on measures of the variable represent different levels of the predictor variable. For variables identified as continuous variables, the scores on a measure of the variable increase in meaningful intervals. The participant's score represents the quantity (or degree, intensity, or amount) of the variable the participant has. For categorical variables, the scores represent the category to which the participant belongs.

Continuous Variables

Here is an example. A scale such as the Posttraumatic Diagnostic Scale (PDS) (Foa, 1995; Foa, Ehlers, Clark, Tolin, & Orsillo, 1999) contains 17 items. Each of the items inquires about symptoms of posttraumatic stress. One question asks if the individual has nightmares, another asks if the individual avoids places that remind him or her of the trauma, and the remaining

"Having upsetting thoughts or images about the traumatic event that came into your head when you didn't want to."			
Not at all or only one time	Once a week or less/once in a while	2 to 4 times a week/half the time	5 or more times a week/almost always
0	1	2	3

FIGURE 3.10 Sample item. *Based on Foa, E. B., Riggs, D. S., Dancu, C. V., & Rothbaum, B. O. (1993). Reliability and validity of a brief instrument for assessing posttraumatic stress disorder.* Journal of Traumatic Stress, 6*(4), 459–473.*

items ask about other symptoms of PTSD. The responses to the items are rated on a Likert-type scale in which the participant chooses from among several answer choices—labeled 0, 1, 2, and 3 (Fig. 3.10).

The average score for each participant can range from 0 to 3, depending on the participant's responses to each item. The researcher can treat the scores on this measure as continuous. Higher scores indicate more symptoms.

When both the predictor and the outcome are continuous, the results of the study can be plotted as shown in Fig. 3.11. This is a plot of a hypothetical relationship between PTSSs and health-related quality of life. (We made up the data.) This plot shows that as PTSSs go up, scores on the measure of health-related quality of life go down.

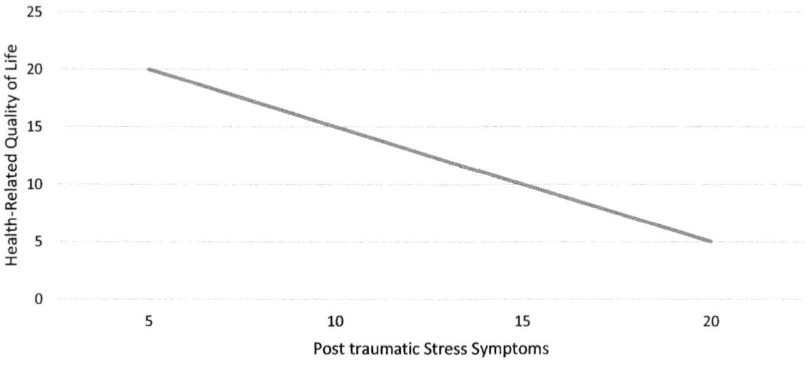

FIGURE 3.11 A hypothetical relationship between posttraumatic stress symptoms and health-related quality of life.

Here are some examples of variables that can be treated as continuous variables. These variables are continuous, because they can increase or decrease in meaningful steps.

- SYMPTOMS can be treated as a continuous variable if the score reflects a count of the number of symptoms or an average of the intensity of symptoms.
- AGE in years is continuous (e.g., 1, 2, 3, 4, 5, etc.).
- EDUCATION can be measured as a continuous variable, if you measure the number of years completed.

Categorical Variables

In contrast, categorical variables are variables in which the scores represent levels of the predictor variable, but the scores do not increase in intervals. Instead, the scores represent mutually exclusive categories. PTSD diagnosis is a categorical variable. An individual either has or does not have a PTSD diagnosis.

Here are some examples of variables which can have scores which reflect categories. We can label each category with a value/number to make statistical analyses simpler.

- DIAGNOSIS: Yes = 1, No = 0
- AREA TYPE: Urban = 2, Suburban = 1, Rural = 0
- HAIR COLOR: Brown = 2, Blonde = 1, Red-headed = 0
- EDUCATION: Completed college = 2, Completed high school only = 1, Completed grade school only = 0

The categories are distinct. One category is not necessarily a higher level than the other even when we use numbers to represent the categories in the dataset. If we label the category Brown Hair = 2, it does not mean that Brown Hair is twice Blonde Hair. They are simply different categories.

The scores on the PDS can also be used to create a categorical variable reflecting probable PTSD diagnosis. To create these categories, the researcher could divide the responses into categories. If the participant's score on the PDS is above a cut-off score, then the person receives a probable PTSD diagnosis. In this case, the participant could be given a score of 1 to indicate the presence of the diagnosis. If the individual does not have a score that reaches the cut-off, the diagnosis score is 0. In this case, there are only two levels of the variable: 1 = probable diagnosis of GAD; 0 = no probable diagnosis of GAD. And the

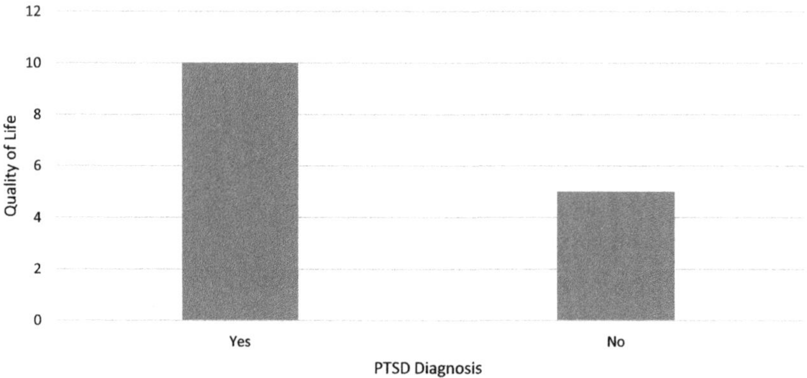

FIGURE 3.12 Hypothetical differences between people with and without PTSD in quality of life.

categories are distinct; an individual can only be assigned a score representing one of the categories.

When variables are categorical, the relationships can be depicted differently. Since the categories are separate, the columns on the histogram are separate, as well (Fig. 3.12).

Hypothesis-Testing Studies: Observational vs. Experimental Research

In some studies, researchers are simply observing variables. They are *measuring* but not *manipulating* the variables. For example, Pacella et al. (2013) include 62 studies in their meta-analysis. In each of these studies, a variable related to PTSD served as a predictor and a variable related to physical health served as an outcome. The researchers conducting these studies measured the variables using different measurement methods and instruments. In some cases, the variables were categorical (i.e., PTSD diagnosis) and in some cases they were continuous. But all the studies involved testing hypotheses about relations between the predictor and outcome variables.

These types of studies are called **observational** or **correlational** studies—studies in which the researchers observe and measure the variables to determine if the predictor is related to the outcome. These studies are not designed to test whether PTSD *causes* poor physical health.

To be able to understand if PTSD is a cause of poor physical health, researchers would need to perform an **experimental** study. In an experimental study, the researcher **manipulates** the independent or predictor variable. The researchers manipulate the independent variable (IV) by assigning participants at random to the different levels of the IV. **Random assignment** means that the condition to which the participant is assigned is determined at random, not by the experimenter or the participant.

If participants have been assigned at random, and if there are differences in the outcomes between those who have been assigned to one level of the IV versus those are assigned to the other, then researchers can assume that the IV is influencing or causing the dependent (outcome) variable. (Provided the researchers control for any other variables that might bias the outcome.)

The studies included in the Pacella et al. (2013) meta-analysis are all observational studies. It is not ethical to randomly assign someone to develop PTSD symptoms to see what happens to their health! In studies of risk factors and consequences, researchers often use observational studies.

In contrast, as you will learn in Chapters 11–14 on the "Theory of the Solution," studies of treatments or interventions often involve true experiments. A **randomized controlled trial (RCT)** is an experiment in which the **causal effects** of a treatment can be evaluated because the IVs are **manipulated,** and participants are assigned **at random** to the different levels of the IV (Fig. 3.13).

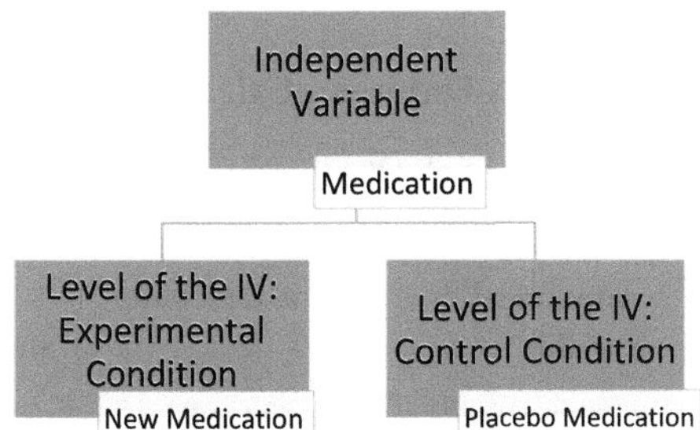

FIGURE 3.13 Randomized control trial.

Activity 3.1: Identifying Predictor and Outcome Variables

We can practice identifying predictor and outcome variables in an original research article on another consequence of PTSD—marital difficulties (Fig. 3.14).

HHS Public Access

Author manuscript

Behav Ther. Author manuscript; available in PMC 2018 March 01.

Published in final edited form as:

Behav Ther. 2017 March ; 48(2): 247–261. doi:10.1016/j.beth.2016.08.014.

Battling on the Home Front: Posttraumatic Stress Disorder and Conflict Behavior among Military Couples

Lynne M. Knobloch-Fedders, Ph.D.,
The Family Institute at Northwestern University

Catherine Caska-Wallace, Ph.D.,
Mental Health Service, VA Puget Sound Health Care System – Seattle Division Department of Psychiatry and Behavioral Sciences, University of Washington

Timothy W. Smith, Ph.D., and
University of Utah

Keith Renshaw, Ph.D.
George Mason University

Abstract

This study evaluated interpersonal behavior differences among male military service members with and without PTSD and their female partners. Couples ($N = 64$) completed a 17-minute videotaped conflict discussion, and their interaction behavior was coded using the circumplex-based Structural Analysis of Social Behavior model (SASB; Benjamin, 1979; 1987; 2000). Within couples, the behavior of partners was very similar. Compared to military couples without PTSD, couples with PTSD displayed more interpersonal hostility and control. Couples with PTSD also exhibited more sulking, blaming, and controlling behavior, and less affirming and connecting behavior, than couples without PTSD. Results advance our understanding of the relational impacts of PTSD on military service members and their partners, and underscore the value of couple-based interventions for PTSD in the context of relationship distress.

Keywords

couples; PTSD; military; interpersonal behavior; Structural Analysis of Social Behavior

Study Overview and Hypotheses

This study was designed to evaluate whether differences in interpersonal conflict behavior distinguish military couples with and without PTSD. Extending work by Miller et al. (2013) and Hanley et al. (2013), we investigated service members (including those on active duty) deployed to Iraq and/or Afghanistan theaters since 2001, focused exclusively on military-specific trauma, and examined PTSD at a diagnostic level of clinical severity. We measured interpersonal behavior broadly, using the circumplex-based Structural Analysis of Social Behavior model (SASB; Benjamin, 1979; 1987; 2000), which has demonstrated utility for detecting the interpersonal correlates of psychopathology in couples (e.g., Knobloch-Fedders, Knobloch, Durbin, Rosen, & Critchfield, 2013). SASB-based behavioral assessments of couple interaction indicate that both hostility and control are associated with relationship dysfunction (Cundiff, Smith, Butner, Critchfield, & Nealey-Moore, 2015; Knobloch-Fedders et al., 2013).

We investigated two primary hypotheses (*Hs*) that evaluated whether the presence of PTSD is associated with differences in couples' conflict behavior. *H1* suggested that military couples with PTSD express more hostility than couples without PTSD (Miller et al., 2013). *H2* predicted that military couples with PTSD exhibit more controlling behavior than couples without PTSD (Taft et al., 2011).

In exploratory follow-up analyses, we also sought to determine whether couples with and without PTSD exhibit interactional differences based on the focus of behavior (e.g., on self or on other). Given the lack of empirical work in this area, no directional predictions were advanced. Instead, we posed two research questions (*RQs*): Do couples with and without PTSD differ in their other-focused (*RQ1*) or self-focused (*RQ2*) behavior?

Behav Ther. Author manuscript; available in PMC 2018 March 01.

FIGURE 3.14 Excerpts from Knobloch-Fedders, Caska-Wallace, Smith and Renshaw (2017).

Let's start by using Table 3.1 to make a list of the constructs included in the abstract and identifying the key terms. Once the list is ready, look up the meaning of any unfamiliar constructs. Then identify the variables used to represent the constructs. Which variables are independent or predictor variables? Which variables are dependent or outcome variables? What is the hypothesis that includes those variables?

TABLE 3.1 Constructs, variables, and hypotheses (Knobloch-Fedders et al. 2017).

Author/Date: Knobloch-Fedders et al. (2017)					
Constructs	**Construct definition**	**Variables**	**Continuous or categorical variable**	**Role (Predictor/ IV or Outcome/ DV)**	**Study hypotheses**
PTSD in couple	Following military service one member of the couple has symptoms including hyperarousal, numbing, reexperiencing, negative cognitions, and mood detachment.	PTSD diagnosis: One member of the couple met criteria or did not	Categorical	Predictor/IV	

Activity 3.1: Identifying Predictor and Outcome Variables—cont'd

TABLE 3.1 Constructs, variables, and hypotheses (Knobloch-Fedders et al. 2017).—cont'd

Author/Date: Knobloch-Fedders et al. (2017)					
Constructs	**Construct definition**	**Variables**	**Continuous or categorical variable**	**Role (Predictor/ IV or Outcome/ DV)**	**Study hypotheses**
Interaction behavior	Interpersonal behaviors exhibited by the members of the couple during conflict interactions in the laboratory.	Observed interpersonal hostility	Continuous	Outcome/DV	Military couples with PTSD will express more hostility than military couples without PTSD.
		Observed interpersonal control	Continuous	Outcome/DV	Military couples with PTSD will exhibit more controlling behavior than military couples without PTSD.

Other key constructs in the abstract include: Circumplex-based structural analysis of social behavior, sulking, blaming, controlling, affirming, and connecting, and relational impacts. However, these are not mentioned directly in the key hypotheses for the study.

We can create a figure displaying the expected relations among the predictor and outcome variables (Fig. 3.15).

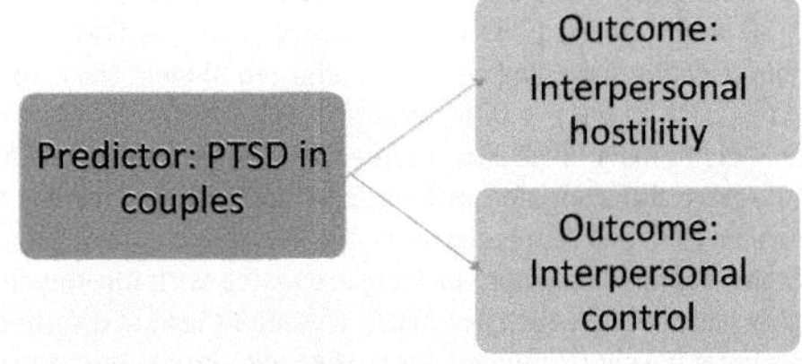

FIGURE 3.15 Relationship among constructs (Knobloch-Fedders et al. 2017).

Continued

Activity 3.1: Identifying Predictor and Outcome Variables—cont'd

Now try it yourself, complete Table 3.2 using an article about another consequence of PTSD, binge eating (Fig. 3.16). The key words to the left of the abstract include constructs that are important to the study.

ELSEVIER

Contents lists available at ScienceDirect

Eating Behaviors

PTSD and depression symptoms are associated with binge eating among US Iraq and Afghanistan veterans

Katherine D. Hoerster [a,b,*], Matthew Jakupcak [a,b], Robert Hanson [c], Miles McFall [a,b], Gayle Reiber [c,d], Katherine S. Hall [e,f], Karin M. Nelson [c,g,h]

[a] *VA Puget Sound Healthcare System, Seattle Division, Mental Health Service, 1660 S. Columbian Way, Seattle, WA 98108, United States*
[b] *University of Washington, Department of Psychiatry and Behavioral Sciences, 1959 NE Pacific Street, Box 356560, Rm BB1644, Seattle, WA 98195, United States*
[c] *VA Puget Sound Healthcare System, Seattle Division, Research and Development Service, 1660 S. Columbian Way, Seattle, WA 98108, United States*
[d] *University of Washington School of Public Health, Departments of Health Services and Epidemiology, 1959 NE Pacific Street, Box 356560, Rm BB1644, Seattle, WA 98195, United States*
[e] *Durham Veterans Affairs Medical Center Geriatric Research, Education, and Clinical Center, 508 Fulton St., Durham, NC 27705, United States*
[f] *Duke University Medical Center, Department of Medicine, 201 Trent Drive, Box 3003 DUMC, Rm 3502 Busse Building, Durham, NC 27710, United States*
[g] *VA Puget Sound Healthcare System, General Internal Medicine Service, 1660 S. Columbian Way, Seattle, WA 98108, United States*
[h] *University of Washington Department of Medicine, 1959 N.E. Pacific St. Seattle, WA 98195, United States*

ARTICLE INFO

Article history:
Received 16 July 2014
Received in revised form 25 November 2014
Accepted 28 January 2015
Available online 4 February 2015

Keywords:
Veterans
Post-traumatic stress disorder
Depression
Obesity
Binge eating

ABSTRACT

Objective: US Iraq and Afghanistan Veterans with post-traumatic stress disorder (PTSD) and depression are at increased risk for obesity. Understanding the contribution of health behaviors to this relationship will enhance efforts to prevent and reduce obesity. Therefore, we examined the association of PTSD and depression symptoms with binge eating, a risk factor for obesity, among Iraq/Afghanistan Veterans.

Method: Iraq/Afghanistan Veterans were assessed at intake to the VA Puget Sound Healthcare System-Seattle post-deployment clinic (May 2004–January 2007). The Patient Health Questionnaire was used to measure depression and binge eating symptoms, and the PTSD Checklist-Military Version assessed PTSD symptoms.

Results: The majority of the sample (N = 332) was male (91.5%) and Caucasian (72.6%), with an average age of 31.1 (SD = 8.5) years; 16.3% met depression screening criteria, 37.8% met PTSD screening criteria, and 8.4% met binge eating screening criteria. In adjusted models, those meeting depression (odds ratio (OR) = 7.53; 95% CI = 2.69, 21.04; $p < .001$) and PTSD (OR = 3.37; 95% CI = 1.34, 8.46; $p = .01$) screening criteria were more likely to meet binge eating screening criteria. Continuous measures of PTSD and depression symptom severity were also associated with meeting binge eating screening criteria ($ps < .05$).

Conclusion: PTSD and depression are common conditions among Iraq/Afghanistan Veterans. In the present study, PTSD and depression symptoms were associated with meeting binge eating screening criteria, identifying a possible pathway by which psychiatric conditions lead to disproportionate burden of overweight and obesity in this Veteran cohort. Tailored dietary behavior interventions may be needed for Iraq/Afghanistan Veterans with co-morbid obesity and psychiatric conditions.

Published by Elsevier Ltd.

FIGURE 3.16 Abstract Hoerster et al. (2015).

Notice that the authors indicate they use both categorical and continuous variables.

Activity 3.1: Identifying Predictor and Outcome Variables—cont'd

TABLE 3.2 Identifying variables and hypotheses.

Author/Date:					
Constructs	**Construct definition**	**Variable**	**Continuous or categorical variables**	**Role (predictor/IV or outcome/DV)**	**Study hypotheses**

Draw a map of the relationships among the constructs. Use shapes and arrows to indicate the constructs and their relationships. You may need to draw more than one map, if the relationships are not clear from the abstract. See if you can figure out which is the predictor and the outcome and label the circles in the model (Fig. 3.17).

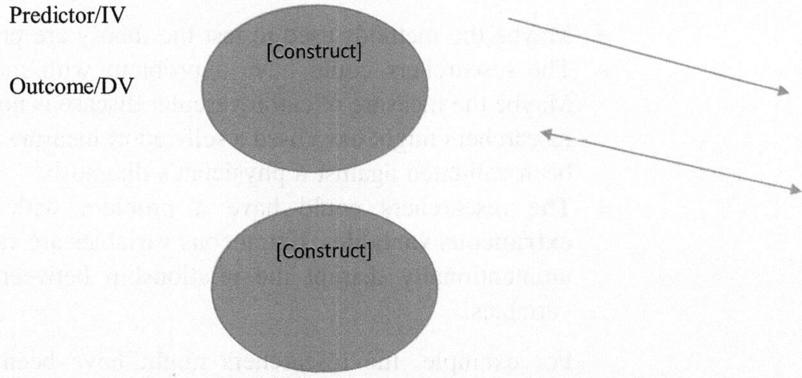

FIGURE 3.17 Mapping the relationship between constructs.

Interpreting the Results of Hypothesis Testing

When researchers develop new studies, they must pay careful attention to the links among the constructs, variables, and measurement methods. This is necessary to insure methodological rigor. When there are strong links—when the construct is well represented by the variable, the measurement method, and the measurement instrument—the internal validity of the study is strengthened. The **internal validity** of the study is the degree to which the study can test the hypothesis it is intended to test. When the researchers have protected the internal validity of the study, we can have more confidence in the interpretation of the findings.

But sometimes, researchers test hypotheses and the outcomes do not confirm the theory.

When researchers get results they do not expect, they need to consider several different possibilities. If the tests do not confirm the hypotheses, then the underlying theory might not be correct and might need to be revised.

- For example, if self-reported PTSD was not related to cardiovascular disease, then the theory about the general relations of PTSD to health might be wrong.
- Or maybe the theory needs to be modified. PTSD might be related to some health outcomes, but not others.

Or…

- Maybe the methods used to test the theory are problematic.
- The researchers could have a problem with measurement: Maybe the measure of cardiovascular disease is not valid. The researchers might have used a self-report measure that has not been validated against a physician's diagnosis.
- The researchers could have a problem with **bias** from **extraneous variables.** Extraneous variables are variables that unintentionally disrupt the relationship between the study variables.

For example, the researchers might have been measuring people too early in the life span, before certain types of cardiovascular disease are apparent. Or the people with PTSD might have been younger than those without PTSD. In this case, age is an extraneous variable unintentionally affecting the outcome.

Problems with measurement or extraneous variables present threats to the internal validity of the study. To prevent these problems, researchers carefully examine the methods of other studies and consider their own methods very carefully. They take the time to consider sources of bias that might affect the outcome. You will learn more about sources of bias and research methods that protect internal validity in Chapter 17.

Building Human Capital

In this chapter you are learning to understand the hypotheses that are generated by theories. You are learning to recognize the variables that make up the hypotheses and understand whether the variables are predictors or outcomes. You have practiced drawing models of the relations among these variables.

These visual models help you to think through your understanding more carefully. When you draw these models, you are checking your understanding of the ideas presented in the articles. These pictures can help you imagine the studies you are reading about in more detail, and help you recognize when you may have left out an important detail. Learning to check your thinking and repair any errors are very important skills for any type of work. You will feel more competent and have more confidence when you know you have taken the time to think things through.

Terms

Take the time to define these terms and apply them.

Research Terms

Evidence
Meta-analyses
Internal validity
Bias
Extraneous variables
Independent or predictor variables
Dependent or outcome variables
Categorical variables
Continuous variables
Manipulated
Observational study
Correlational study
Randomized controlled trial
Experimental condition
Control condition
Random assignment
Placebo

References

Foa, E. B. (1995). *Posttraumatic stress diagnostic scale (PDS)*. Minneapolis: National Computer Systems.

Foa, E. B., Ehlers, A., Clark, D. M., Tolin, D. F., & Orsillo, S. M. (1999). The posttraumatic cognitions inventory (PTCI): Development and validation. *Psychological Assessment, 11*(3), 303.

Hoerster, K. D., Jakupcak, M., Hanson, R., McFall, M., Reiber, G., Hall, K. S., & Nelson, K. M. (2015). PTSD and depression symptoms are associated with binge eating among US Iraq and Afghanistan veterans. *Eating Behaviors, 17*, 115–118.

Knobloch-Fedders, L. M., Caska-Wallace, C., Smith, T. W., & Renshaw, K. (2017). Battling on the home front: Posttraumatic stress disorder and conflict behavior among military couples. *Behavior Therapy, 48*(2), 247–261.

Pacella, M. L., Hruska, B., & Delahanty, D. L. (2013). The physical health consequences of PTSD and PTSD symptoms: A meta-analytic review. *Journal of Anxiety Disorders, 27*(1), 33–46.

Xu, Y., Schneier, F., Heimberg, R. G., Princisvalle, K., Liebowitz, M. R., Wang, S., & Blanco, C (2012). Gender differences in social anxiety disorder: Results from the national epidemiologic sample on alcohol and related conditions. *Journal of anxiety disorders, 26*(1), 12–19.

Chapter 4

Public health significance: Finding the evidence

In this chapter you will learn more about the components of the Public Health Significance (PHS) section of your proposal or paper. You will learn how to identify the kinds of evidence you need and how to search for the scientific articles that can provide each type of evidence. You will start to build your own library of scientific articles.

Public Health Significance

Why do you need a section on the public health significance? When researchers ask the National Institutes of Health or other governmental agencies for money to fund their research, they must document how this research can lead to improvements in the health of the population. Researchers document the public health significance by explaining the nature of the disorder and documenting how common, serious, and/or disabling the problem is. To develop your own PHS section, you will collect and read articles that provide the information you need to make the argument that research on this disorder is important.

If you are writing a proposal for a study concerning a behavioral health disorder, you will include a section on the PHS of addressing your disorder to justify your study. If you are writing a paper reviewing the research on this disorder, you may review and describe studies investigating how common the disorder is and how serious the consequences of the disorder are if it is left untreated. To write this paper, you need to understand how to read articles about the public health significance of the disorder.

Psychology Research Methods. https://doi.org/10.1016/B978-0-12-815680-3.00004-9

Components of the PHS

Researchers develop an argument about the PHS of the study when they answer questions related to these topics:

- **Operational Definition**: What is the nature of the problem—how is it defined and measured? An operational definition of the disorder includes a clear description of the disorder you will be studying.
- **Incidence and Prevalence**: What is the **epidemiology** of this disorder? How common is this problem, how many people are affected?
  - **Incidence** refers to the number of new cases of the disorder in a population over a specific time period (e.g., in a 12-month period).
  - **Prevalence** refers to the number of individuals who have the disorder over a specific time period (e.g., over their lifetime). This includes both existing and new cases of the problem in a population over a given period of time (CDC, 2012).
- **Consequences:** What are the consequences of this problem? Specifically, what are the effects of the problem on mental or physical health or daily occupational, education, or social functioning?
- **Risk factors:** What makes individuals more vulnerable? Risk factors are factors which are associated with differences in the likelihood of developing the disorder.

Communicating the PHS

The PHS is often presented right at the beginning of an article to capture attention by demonstrating the public health impact of the problem. Essentially the authors are saying "This is the problem we are addressing. It is a big and/or serious problem. When this problem is not addressed, there are harmful consequences for the person and the health of the country."

Here is an example of a review article describing the results of interventions to reduce smoking for children and adolescents (Fig. 4.1). Notice that right at the beginning of the article, the authors include information about the prevalence of smoking and information about the consequences of smoking. They also identify risk factors that make young people likely to smoke.

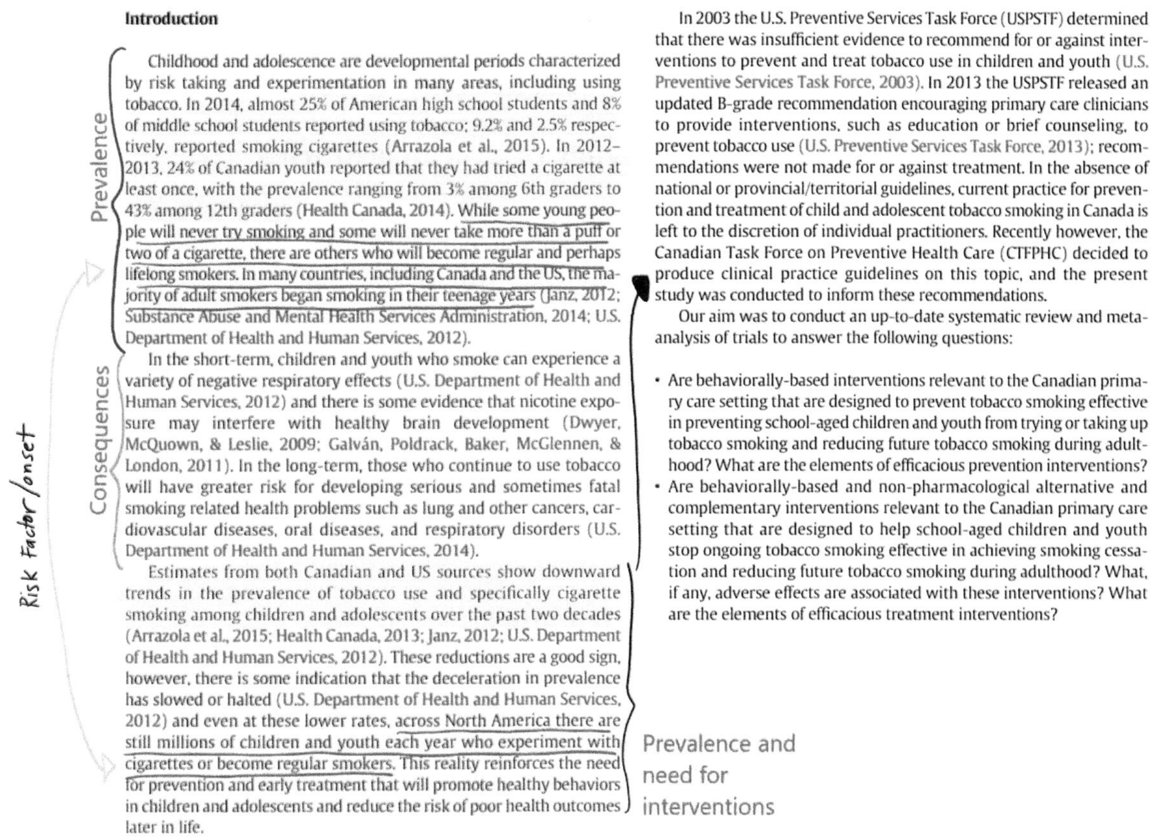

Introduction

Childhood and adolescence are developmental periods characterized by risk taking and experimentation in many areas, including using tobacco. In 2014, almost 25% of American high school students and 8% of middle school students reported using tobacco; 9.2% and 2.5% respectively, reported smoking cigarettes (Arrazola et al., 2015). In 2012–2013, 24% of Canadian youth reported that they had tried a cigarette at least once, with the prevalence ranging from 3% among 6th graders to 43% among 12th graders (Health Canada, 2014). While some young people will never try smoking and some will never take more than a puff or two of a cigarette, there are others who will become regular and perhaps lifelong smokers. In many countries, including Canada and the US, the majority of adult smokers began smoking in their teenage years (Janz, 2012; Substance Abuse and Mental Health Services Administration, 2014; U.S. Department of Health and Human Services, 2012).

In the short-term, children and youth who smoke can experience a variety of negative respiratory effects (U.S. Department of Health and Human Services, 2012) and there is some evidence that nicotine exposure may interfere with healthy brain development (Dwyer, McQuown, & Leslie, 2009; Galván, Poldrack, Baker, McGlennen, & London, 2011). In the long-term, those who continue to use tobacco will have greater risk for developing serious and sometimes fatal smoking related health problems such as lung and other cancers, cardiovascular diseases, oral diseases, and respiratory disorders (U.S. Department of Health and Human Services, 2014).

Estimates from both Canadian and US sources show downward trends in the prevalence of tobacco use and specifically cigarette smoking among children and adolescents over the past two decades (Arrazola et al., 2015; Health Canada, 2013; Janz, 2012; U.S. Department of Health and Human Services, 2012). These reductions are a good sign, however, there is some indication that the deceleration in prevalence has slowed or halted (U.S. Department of Health and Human Services, 2012) and even at these lower rates, across North America there are still millions of children and youth each year who experiment with cigarettes or become regular smokers. This reality reinforces the need for prevention and early treatment that will promote healthy behaviors in children and adolescents and reduce the risk of poor health outcomes later in life.

In 2003 the U.S. Preventive Services Task Force (USPSTF) determined that there was insufficient evidence to recommend for or against interventions to prevent and treat tobacco use in children and youth (U.S. Preventive Services Task Force, 2003). In 2013 the USPSTF released an updated B-grade recommendation encouraging primary care clinicians to provide interventions, such as education or brief counseling, to prevent tobacco use (U.S. Preventive Services Task Force, 2013); recommendations were not made for or against treatment. In the absence of national or provincial/territorial guidelines, current practice for prevention and treatment of child and adolescent tobacco smoking in Canada is left to the discretion of individual practitioners. Recently however, the Canadian Task Force on Preventive Health Care (CTFPHC) decided to produce clinical practice guidelines on this topic, and the present study was conducted to inform these recommendations.

Our aim was to conduct an up-to-date systematic review and meta-analysis of trials to answer the following questions:

- Are behaviorally-based interventions relevant to the Canadian primary care setting that are designed to prevent tobacco smoking effective in preventing school-aged children and youth from trying or taking up tobacco smoking and reducing future tobacco smoking during adulthood? What are the elements of efficacious prevention interventions?
- Are behaviorally-based and non-pharmacological alternative and complementary interventions relevant to the Canadian primary care setting that are designed to help school-aged children and youth stop ongoing tobacco smoking effective in achieving smoking cessation and reducing future tobacco smoking during adulthood? What, if any, adverse effects are associated with these interventions? What are the elements of efficacious treatment interventions?

FIGURE 4.1 Excerpt from Peirson, Ali, Kenny, Raina, and Sherifali (2016).

Scientific Articles

Let's start collecting the scientific articles you need to build the PHS section!

Scientific articles are one of the most important products of science. The business of science is about acquiring knowledge—developing new ideas and accumulating facts. Some of this information is communicated in papers presented at scientific conferences or in discussions in classrooms and meetings. Much of the information is communicated in **peer-reviewed** articles. Peer-reviewed articles are written by scientists and evaluated by other scientists before they are published. The process of peer-review allows other scientists to examine the information and methods presented in the articles.

The products of a culture can provide a lot of information about the values, methods, rules, and language of that culture. As you gather articles to build your proposal or paper, you will learn about the culture of science. You can use these articles to learn about the language and methods of research.

Types of Research Articles

For the PHS section, you will gather information from scientific articles to learn more about the symptoms of the disorder you are studying. These articles will provide information about the prevalence of the disorder, the consequences of the disorder, and the risk factors that increase vulnerability for the disorder.

There are several different types of scientific articles you may need for your proposal or paper, including original research articles, review papers, and clinical papers. These different types of articles are shown throughout this chapter. For the PHS section, you will primarily focus on original research articles and review articles.

Original Research Articles

An original research article describes an **empirical study**. This type of article presents the findings from a research study. The studies presented in original research articles can present **quantitative research** or **qualitative research**.

Articles describing quantitative or qualitative research generally present one study at a time. However, some quantitative articles will describe a short series of related studies. In an article presenting multiple studies, each study addresses a gap in knowledge presented by the previous study.

Quantitative Research Articles. In the last chapter, you reviewed two original research articles: the study on PTSD and marital communication and the study on PTSD and binge eating. The articles presented data from studies in which researchers collected quantitative or numeric data and used statistical methods to test the researchers' hypotheses. The article on PTSD and marital communication was a quantitative research article because the authors measured the outcome—the communication behavior of the couples—quantitatively. They counted the number of times the couples made hostile or controlling remarks. Similarly, the authors of the paper on PTSD and binge eating counted the number of times people with versus without PTSD engaged in binge eating.

Qualitative Research Articles. Qualitative research articles present data from exploratory studies in which researchers use interviews or other methods to understand and describe the nature of a phenomena. Qualitative research approaches can be used to identify the range of concerns or ideas people have about any specific topic; for example, the causes of a behavioral health disorder.

Here is an example of a qualitative research paper on the experiences of smoking among individuals living in disadvantaged (low-income) communities (Fig. 4.2). In this study, the researchers asked participants about all the factors they believed caused people to smoke in their community.

PERGAMON

Health & Place 7 (2001) 333–343

HEALTH & PLACE

www.elsevier.com/locate/healthplace

"It's as if you're locked in": qualitative explanations for area effects on smoking in disadvantaged communities

Martine Stead[a,*], Susan MacAskill[a], Anne-Marie MacKintosh[b], Jane Reece[b], Douglas Eadie[a]

[a] *Centre for Social Marketing, University of Strathclyde, 173 Cathedral Street, Glasgow G4 0RQ, UK*
[b] *Centre for Tobacco Control Research, University of Strathclyde, 173 Cathedral Street, Glasgow G4 0RQ, UK*

Received 14 March 2000; received in revised form 16 March 2001; accepted 1 May 2001

Abstract

Evidence suggests that place of residence may be associated with smoking independently of individual poverty and socio-economic status. Qualitative research undertaken in disadvantaged communities in Glasgow explored possible pathways which might explain this 'area effect'. A poorly resourced and stressful environment, strong community norms, isolation from wider social norms, and limited opportunities for respite and recreation appear to combine not only to foster smoking but also to discourage or undermine cessation. Even the more positive aspects of life, such as support networks and identity, seem to encourage rather than challenge smoking. Policy and intervention responses need to tackle not only individual but also environmental disadvantage.

Keywords: Smoking; Cessation; Deprivation; Area effects; Poverty; Unemployment; Scotland; Qualitative research

FIGURE 4.2 Abstract from Stead, MacAskill, MacKintosh, Reece and Eadie (2001).

Review Articles

A systematic or meta-analytic review article summarizes and evaluates a body of evidence on a topic. These articles are comprehensive—they include every relevant article on the topic of the review. They examine the trends in literature to identify consistent results and identify gaps in knowledge.

A *meta-analysis* is a type of systematic review in which the authors combine quantitative data across studies to see if there are consistent patterns in the findings. The Pacella, Hruska, and Delahanty (2013) paper we reviewed in Chapter 3 is a meta-analysis.

A **conceptual or systematic review** is a type of article which brings together many different types of research to identify themes in the literature and propose new theories or identify gaps in knowledge. The paper by Pierson et al. (2015) introduced at the beginning of this chapter is a systematic review of interventions to reduce smoking among children and adolescents.

The Pierson et al. (2015) paper is a systematic review and meta-analysis of quantitative studies. All the studies reviewed by Pierson and colleagues conducted statistical analyses on quantitative data. The authors combine these data to evaluate trends and patterns.

Researchers can also conduct reviews of qualitative studies. Here is an example of a systematic review of qualitative research on barriers to smoking cessation among pregnant women (Ingall & Cropley, 2010) (Fig. 4.3).

REVIEW

Exploring the barriers of quitting smoking during pregnancy: A systematic review of qualitative studies

Georgina Ingall, Mark Cropley *

Department of Psychology, Faculty of Arts and Human Sciences, University of Surrey, UK

Received 2 March 2009; received in revised form 18 September 2009; accepted 21 September 2009

KEYWORDS
Pregnancy;
Barriers;
Smoking cessation;
Qualitative

Abstract Smoking during pregnancy is widely known to increase health risks to the foetus, and understanding the quitting process during pregnancy is essential in order to realise national government targets. Qualitative studies have been used in order to gain a greater understanding of the quitting process and the objective of this systematic review was to examine and evaluate qualitative studies that have investigated the psychological and social factors around women attempting to quit smoking during pregnancy. Electronic databases and journals were searched with seven articles included in this review. The findings demonstrated that women were aware of the health risks to the foetus associated with smoking; however knowledge of potential health risks was not sufficient to motivate them to quit. Several barriers to quitting were identified which included willpower, role, and meaning of smoking, issues with cessation provision, changes in relationship interactions, understanding of facts, changes in smell and taste and influence of family and friends. A further interesting finding was that cessation service provision by health professionals was viewed negatively by women. It was concluded that there is a shortage of qualitative studies that concentrate on the specific difficulties that pregnant women face when trying to quit smoking.

FIGURE 4.3 Abstract from Ingall and Cropley (2010).

Clinical Articles

Clinical articles, including case studies and theoretical papers, can provide detailed descriptions of a treatment or intervention approach. Some articles will also explain the theory underlying the interventions.

Case studies can provide an example of the way the intervention was implemented with a small number of patients, often with just one patient.

Clinical review or theoretical papers describe the rationale for the intervention and describe how it can be implemented. Here is an example of a theoretical paper which describes the rationale behind interventions to change behavior among medical patients when they are seen in a primary care medical office (Elder, Ayala, & Harris, 1999) (Fig. 4.4).

Theories and Intervention Approaches to Health-Behavior Change in Primary Care

John P. Elder, PhD, MPH, Guadalupe X. Ayala, MA, Stewart Harris, MD, MPH

Content: Providers typically rely on health information and their professional status to convince patients to change. Health-behavior theories and models suggest more effective methods for accomplishing patient compliance and other behavior change related to treatment regimens. Behavior modification stresses the remediation of skill deficits or using positive and negative reinforcement to modify performance. Like behavior modification, the Health Belief Model stresses a reduction of environmental barriers to behavior. Social Learning Theory suggests that perceptions of skills and reinforcement may more directly determine behavior. Self-management models put the above theories into self-change actions. Social support theories prioritize reinforcement delivered through social networks, whereas the Theory of Reasoned Action emphasizes perceptions of social processes. Finally, the Transtheoretical Model speaks of the necessity to match interventions to cognitive-behavioral stages. Strategies derived from each of these theories are suggested herein.

Medical Subject Headings (MeSH): health-behavior change, models, primary care (Am J Prev Med 1999;17(4):275–284) © 1999 American Journal of Preventive Medicine

FIGURE 4.4 Abstract from Elder et al. (1999).

Finding Research Articles to Build Your PHS Section

It's time to search for information about the operational definition of the disorder, the prevalence of the disorder, the consequences of having the disorder, and risk factors for the disorder.

Finding Information on the Operational Definitions

The operational definition of the disorder is the definition you will be using in your proposal or paper. This definition includes all the symptoms associated with the disorder. The operational definition can also include information on how you will conceptualize the disorder—as a diagnosis or as a set of symptoms. An example of the diagnostic criteria used to develop an operational definition is shown in (Fig. 4.5)

Tobacco Use Disorder

Diagnostic Criteria

A. A problematic pattern of tobacco use leading to clinically significant impairment or distress, as manifested by at least two of the following, occurring within a 12-month period:

1. Tobacco is often taken in larger amounts or over a longer period than was intended.
2. There is a persistent desire or unsuccessful efforts to cut down or control tobacco use.
3. A great deal of time is spent in activities necessary to obtain or use tobacco.
4. Craving, or a strong desire or urge to use tobacco.
5. Recurrent tobacco use resulting in a failure to fulfill major role obligations at work, school, or home (e.g., interference with work).
6. Continued tobacco use despite having persistent or recurrent social or interpersonal problems caused or exacerbated by the effects of tobacco (e.g., arguments with others about tobacco use).
7. Important social, occupational, or recreational activities are given up or reduced because of tobacco use.
8. Recurrent tobacco use in situations in which it is physically hazardous (e.g., smoking in bed).
9. Tobacco use is continued despite knowledge of having a persistent or recurrent physical or psychological problem that is likely to have been caused or exacerbated by tobacco.
10. Tolerance, as defined by either of the following:
    a. A need for markedly increased amounts of tobacco to achieve the desired effect.
    b. A markedly diminished effect with continued use of the same amount of tobacco.
11. Withdrawal, as manifested by either of the following:
    a. The characteristic withdrawal syndrome for tobacco (refer to Criteria A and B of the criteria set for tobacco withdrawal).
    b. Tobacco (or a closely related substance, such as nicotine) is taken to relieve or avoid withdrawal symptoms.

FIGURE 4.5 Tobacco use disorder diagnostic criteria from DSM-5.

Information on operational definitions can be gathered from widely available texts in the area that are regarded as the "gold standard." For mental health disorders, the DSM-5 is the gold standard for operational definitions of these disorders. You can also use official websites (e.g., from the NIH) to obtain this information (see Chapter 1 for links).

Finding Information on the Prevalence and Incidence of the Disorder

Information on the prevalence, incidence, and consequences of a disorder can be gathered from original research articles and review articles.

Here is an example of an original research article presenting the results of a large population-based study which investigated the epidemiology of different kinds of smoking among teenagers in the United States (Fig. 4.6). The study provided information about the rates of smoking both e-cigarettes and regular cigarettes

(McCabe, West, Veliz, & Boyd, 2017). This is the type of article that would be very helpful for establishing the public health significance of a study about smoking. Similar articles are available for all mental health and substance use disorders.

HHS Public Access

Author manuscript

J Adolesc Health. Author manuscript; available in PMC 2018 August 01.

Published in final edited form as:

J Adolesc Health. 2017 August ; 61(2): 155–162. doi:10.1016/j.jadohealth.2017.02.004.

E-cigarette use, cigarette smoking, dual use and problem behaviors among U.S. adolescents: Results from a national survey

Sean Esteban McCabe, Ph.D.[a], **Brady West, Ph.D.**[b], **Phil Veliz, Ph.D.**[a], and **Carol J. Boyd, Ph.D.**[a,c,d]

[a]Institute for Research on Women and Gender, University of Michigan, Ann Arbor, MI, 48109

[b]Survey Research Center, Institute for Social Research, University of Michigan, Ann Arbor, MI 48016

[c]School of Nursing, University of Michigan, Ann Arbor, MI 48109

[d]Addiction Research Center, Department of Psychiatry, University of Michigan, Ann Arbor, MI 48109

Abstract

Purpose—There is a need to obtain greater clarity regarding adolescents' e-cigarette use and their use with a wider range of risk behaviors. This study examines the associations among past-month e-cigarette use only, traditional cigarette smoking only, dual use (i.e., concurrent e-cigarette use and cigarette smoking), school-related (i.e., truancy and poor academic performance), and substance-related (i.e., alcohol use, binge drinking, marijuana use, illicit drug use, and nonmedical prescription drug use) risk behaviors.

Methods—Data were collected via self-administered questionnaires from a nationally representative sample of 8,696 high school seniors.

Results—An estimated 9.9% of U.S. high school seniors reported past-month e-cigarette use only, 6.0% reported past-month cigarette smoking only, and 7.3% reported past-month dual use. School-related and substance-related risk behaviors had strong associations with past-month e-cigarette use. Adolescents who only used e-cigarettes had significantly greater odds of all school-related and substance-related risk behaviors relative to non-users. Dual users had significantly greater odds of frequent/daily e-cigarette use as well as all school-related and substance-related risk behaviors relative to those who only used e-cigarettes. Finally, adolescents who engaged in frequent/daily e-cigarette use had significantly greater odds of binge drinking, marijuana use, other illicit drug use and nonmedical prescription drug use, relative to experimental e-cigarette users.

FIGURE 4.6 Abstract from McCabe et al. (2017).

Here is an example of a review paper on the epidemiology of smoking across the world (Fig. 4.7). The authors of this paper have examined the results of many different studies of the prevalence of smoking and organized the findings. They summarize evidence about the consequences of smoking. They highlight knowledge that is consistent across studies and also describe gaps in the literature (Reitsma et al., 2017).

Smoking prevalence and attributable disease burden in 195 countries and territories, 1990–2015: a systematic analysis from the Global Burden of Disease Study 2015

*GBD 2015 Tobacco Collaborators**

Summary

Background The scale-up of tobacco control, especially after the adoption of the Framework Convention for Tobacco Control, is a major public health success story. Nonetheless, smoking remains a leading risk for early death and disability worldwide, and therefore continues to require sustained political commitment. The Global Burden of Diseases, Injuries, and Risk Factors Study (GBD) offers a robust platform through which global, regional, and national progress toward achieving smoking-related targets can be assessed.

Methods We synthesised 2818 data sources with spatiotemporal Gaussian process regression and produced estimates of daily smoking prevalence by sex, age group, and year for 195 countries and territories from 1990 to 2015. We analysed 38 risk-outcome pairs to generate estimates of smoking-attributable mortality and disease burden, as measured by disability-adjusted life-years (DALYs). We then performed a cohort analysis of smoking prevalence by birth-year cohort to better understand temporal age patterns in smoking. We also did a decomposition analysis, in which we parsed out changes in all-cause smoking-attributable DALYs due to changes in population growth, population ageing, smoking prevalence, and risk-deleted DALY rates. Finally, we explored results by level of development using the Socio-demographic Index (SDI).

Findings Worldwide, the age-standardised prevalence of daily smoking was 25·0% (95% uncertainty interval [UI] 24·2–25·7) for men and 5·4% (5·1–5·7) for women, representing 28·4% (25·8–31·1) and 34·4% (29·4–38·6) reductions, respectively, since 1990. A greater percentage of countries and territories achieved significant annualised rates of decline in smoking prevalence from 1990 to 2005 than in between 2005 and 2015; however, only four countries had significant annualised increases in smoking prevalence between 2005 and 2015 (Congo [Brazzaville] and Azerbaijan for men and Kuwait and Timor-Leste for women). In 2015, 11·5% of global deaths (6·4 million [95% UI 5·7–7·0 million]) were attributable to smoking worldwide, of which 52·2% took place in four countries (China, India, the USA, and Russia). Smoking was ranked among the five leading risk factors by DALYs in 109 countries and territories in 2015, rising from 88 geographies in 1990. In terms of birth cohorts, male smoking prevalence followed similar age patterns across levels of SDI, whereas much more heterogeneity was found in age patterns for female smokers by level of development. While smoking prevalence and risk-deleted DALY rates mostly decreased by sex and SDI quintile, population growth, population ageing, or a combination of both, drove rises in overall smoking-attributable DALYs in low-SDI to middle-SDI geographies between 2005 and 2015.

Interpretation The pace of progress in reducing smoking prevalence has been heterogeneous across geographies, development status, and sex, and as highlighted by more recent trends, maintaining past rates of decline should not be taken for granted, especially in women and in low-SDI to middle-SDI countries. Beyond the effect of the tobacco industry and societal mores, a crucial challenge facing tobacco control initiatives is that demographic forces are poised to heighten smoking's global toll, unless progress in preventing initiation and promoting cessation can be substantially accelerated. Greater success in tobacco control is possible but requires effective, comprehensive, and adequately implemented and enforced policies, which might in turn require global and national levels of political commitment beyond what has been achieved during the past 25 years.

In this section the authors provide data on the prevalence of smoking.

FIGURE 4.7 Abstract from Reitsma et al. (2017).

This is a type of article which could be very helpful in describing the public health significance of a study of smoking. Similar review papers on the prevalence of disorders are available for some, but not all, disorders.

Finding Information on the Consequences of the Disorder

Mental health disorders and behavioral health problems, such as smoking, have a wide variety of consequences for health and social and emotional functioning. Searching for the articles which will help you identify the consequences of a disorder often requires knowing a little about the possible consequences, including effects on other aspects of health or functioning. Once you have a little information about possible consequences, the searches can include the term related to the disorder (or behavioral health problem) and terms about possible consequences, such as “mental health,” “physical health,” “role functioning,” “social functioning,” and “quality of life” (Fig. 4.8).

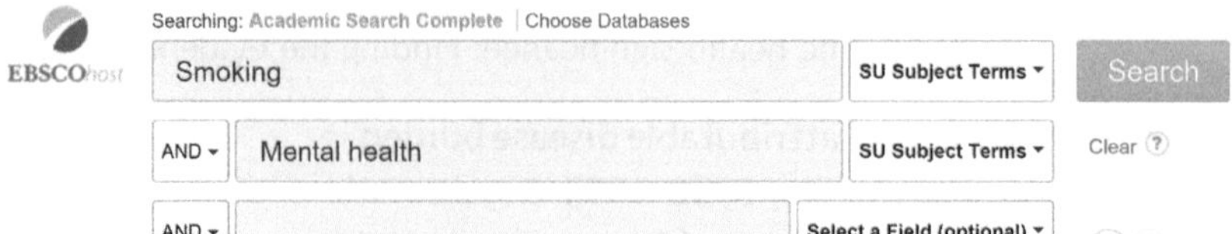

FIGURE 4.8 A sample search for consequences of smoking.

We can look at one example of a paper on the consequences of smoking. Bakhshaie, Zvolensky, and Goodwin (2015) examine mental health outcomes associated with smoking. They find that individuals who smoke are more likely to develop depression (Fig. 4.9).

HHS Public Access

Author manuscript

Compr Psychiatry. Author manuscript; available in PMC 2015 July 01.

Published in final edited form as:

Compr Psychiatry. 2015 July ; 60: 142–148. doi:10.1016/j.comppsych.2014.10.012.

Cigarette smoking and the onset and persistence of depression among adults in the United States: 1994–2005

Jafar Bakhshaie[a], **Michael J. Zvolensky**[a,b], and **Renee D. Goodwin**[c,d,*]

[a]Department of Psychology, University of Houston, 126 Heyne Building, Houston, TX, 77204, United States

[b]Department of Behavioral Sciences, University of Texas MD Anderson Cancer Center, Houston, TX, United States

[c]Department of Psychology, Queens College and The Graduate Center, City University of New York (CUNY), Queens, NY, United States

[d]Department of Epidemiology, Mailman School of Public Health, Columbia University, New York, NY, United States

Abstract

Background—The present study investigated the relationship between daily cigarette smoking and risk of onset and persistence of major depressive disorder (MDD) over a 10-year period among adults in the United States and whether successful smoking cessation reduced the risk for MDD.

Method—Data were drawn from the Midlife Development in the United States Survey (MIDUS; $n = 2101$) Waves I and II. Logistic regressions were used to investigate the relations between smoking and the onset and persistence of MDD, adjusting for demographic characteristics and substance use problems.

Results—Daily smoking in 1994 [OR = 1.9 (1.2–3.2)] and persistent daily smoking (in 1994 and 2005) [OR = 2.2 (1.3–3.7)] were both associated with a significantly increased likelihood of MDD in 2005. Additionally, abstinence, compared to daily smoking, for more than 10 years significantly reduced the risk of MDD in 2005 [OR = 0.5 (0.3–0.87)] and persistent MDD in 1994 and 2005; [OR = 0.5 (0.3–0.87)].

Conclusions—Findings from this study provide new insights into the role of smoking in the onset and persistence of MDD. Namely, among those in mid-adulthood, smoking is associated with greater MDD risk and quitting may help to reduce such risk. These results suggest that there may be merit in targeting smoking to reduce the risk of MDD and the mental health benefits of quitting smoking in the form of reduced risk of MDD could usefully be added to common information listed as reasons to quit.

FIGURE 4.9 Abstract from Bakhshaie et al. (2015).

Finding Information on Risk Factors for the Disorder

A risk factor is a characteristic or situation that makes individuals vulnerable to developing the disorder. Researchers study risk factors when they want to answer these questions: Who is most at risk? What factors make people more vulnerable or susceptible to the problem? Should interventions be targeted at certain groups?

For example, individuals may start smoking for different reasons. Wellman et al. (2016) published a review article on different risk factors for smoking initiation in adolescents. They identified the different factors that are associated with initiation of smoking (i.e., "taking the first puff"). They report that having poor school performance and having peers who smoke are among the risk factors for smoking. Some of these risk factors are related, but not completely overlapping (Fig. 4.10).

Predictors of the Onset of Cigarette Smoking

A Systematic Review of Longitudinal Population-Based Studies in Youth

Robert J. Wellman, PhD,[1] Erika N. Dugas, MSc,[2] Hartley Dutczak, BSc,[2,3] Erin K. O'Loughlin, MA,[2,4] Geetanjali D. Datta, ScD,[2,3] Béatrice Lauzon, MSc,[2,3] Jennifer O'Loughlin, PhD[2,3]

This activity is available for CME credit. See page A4 for information.

Context: The onset of cigarette smoking typically occurs during childhood or early adolescence. Nicotine dependence symptoms can manifest soon after onset, contributing to sustained, long-term smoking. Previous reviews have not clarified the determinants of onset.

Evidence acquisition: In 2015, a systematic review of the literature in PubMed and EMBASE was undertaken to identify peer-reviewed prospective longitudinal studies published between January 1984 and August 2015 that investigated predictors of cigarette smoking onset among youth aged < 18 years who had never smoked.

Evidence synthesis: Ninety-eight conceptually different potential predictors were identified in 53 studies. An increased risk of smoking onset was consistently (i.e., in four or more studies) associated with increased age/grade, lower SES, poor academic performance, sensation seeking or rebelliousness, intention to smoke in the future, receptivity to tobacco promotion efforts, susceptibility to smoking, family members' smoking, having friends who smoke, and exposure to films, whereas higher self-esteem and high parental monitoring/supervision of the child appeared to protect against smoking onset. Methodologic weaknesses were identified in numerous studies, including failure to account for attrition or for clustering in samples, and misidentification of potential confounders, which may have led to biased estimates of associations.

Conclusions: Predictors of smoking onset for which there is robust evidence should be considered in the design of interventions to prevent first puff in order to optimize their effectiveness. Future research should seek to define onset clearly as the transition from never use to first use (e.g., first few puffs).

(Am J Prev Med 2016;51(5):767–778) © 2016 American Journal of Preventive Medicine. Published by Elsevier Inc. All rights reserved.

FIGURE 4.10 Abstract from Wellman et al. (2016). This article organizes and evaluates the evidence for different risk factors for smoking.

To identify risk factors for the disorder under investigation, expand the search for articles by adding in the search term "risk factor" (Fig. 4.11). You can determine if something is a risk factor for the disorder if the article indicates it is related to the disorder. See the highlighted section in (Fig. 4.10).

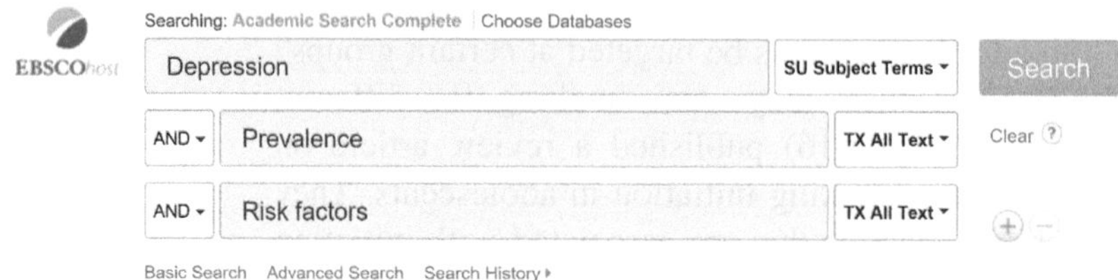

FIGURE 4.11 Sample search for risk factors of a disorder.

As we will see in Part II of the book, studying risk factors can tell us about how disorders develop and provide information about how they could be treated.

For example, the ways in which smoking is initiated and maintained may be different for individuals who have poor school performance (and may have started smoking to reduce stress) versus those who have peers/friends who smoke (and may have started smoking because they were curious about smoking after they saw their peers smoke). If this is the case, the treatment for smoking may need to be adjusted depending on the risk factor. Therefore, it is critical to understand what factors put individuals at risk for the behavioral health disorder.

Assessing the Usefulness of a Particular Paper

How do you know if this paper is helpful to your search for the public health significance of the problem? The **abstract** of the article located at the start of the paper provides a brief summary of the purpose, methods, and findings of the study. You can use this abstract to give you an idea if the article is appropriate for the type of questions you are asking.

Check the abstract and ask yourself these questions. Does the abstract mention the words epidemiology or prevalence? Do the authors provide statistical details (i.e., provide information on the proportion of the population with the problem or the number of new cases)? Does the abstract indicate the authors have identified a specific risk factor related to the disorder? If the article provides this information, then save a copy of the paper by downloading the pdf.

A Practical Tip

Creating a library of articles. You should save these articles in an electronic reference manager such as Mendeley, Zotero, Refworks, etc. These reference managers will allow you to store articles and insert the citations/references in your proposal, and create a bibliography at the touch of a button. Some reference manager programs are free (Mendeley, Zotero), others have to be purchased. Ask your librarian about the reference manager programs available at your school.

If you want to save articles on your own computer, there are many different conventions for saving papers. It can be helpful to have information about the authors, the topic or title, and the year the paper was published. This can help us remember what the article was about and how recent were the findings. We use the authors' names to refer to the paper in the proposal. However, often there are many authors and the paper titles can be very long and may not explicitly mention the information you need from the paper. Very long filenames can be problematic for storage.

It can be more efficient to use the last name of the first author, the year the paper was published, and a few words that describe the study in a way that makes sense to you. The reference managers also allow users to input additional notes. This can be especially useful for jotting down key findings or any other relevant details. This way, as you go through your library, you can figure out what a paper was about or what the key findings were at the click of a button.

For example, here is a full APA style reference for a study on the epidemiology of discrimination in Hispanic individuals. There are many authors of this study and the title is long.

Arellano-Morales, L., Roesch, S. C., Gallo, L. C., Emory, K. T., Molina, K. M., Gonzalez, P., ... Brondolo, E. (2015). Prevalence and correlates of perceived ethnic discrimination in the Hispanic community health study/study of Latinos sociocultural ancillary study. Journal of Latina/o Psychology, 3(3), 160–176.

One possible filename for the pdf of this article could be: Arellano-Morales 2015 prevalence discrimination Hispanic.

This filename would make it easy to search for the pdfs of papers on prevalence. Or if it was important to find papers in your directory on Hispanic populations, it would be easy to find this pdf as well.

Save the pdf of the paper to a directory in your computer that will be easy to find. You could call this directory: Articles about (name of problem). You could create a subdirectory for articles you are using for the public health significance (PHS) section (Fig. 4.12).

Continued

A Practical Tip—cont'd

For example:

C:\articles about smoking\Public Health Significance

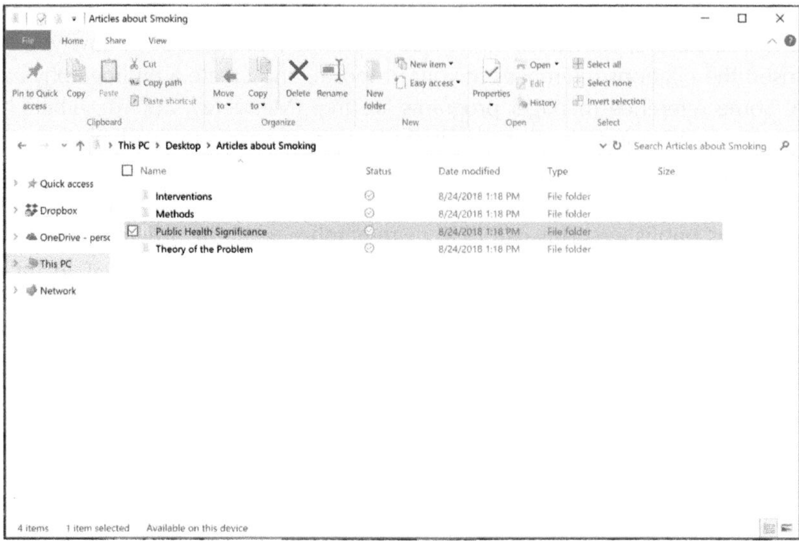

FIGURE 4.12 A sample library.

Activity 4.1: Identifying Articles to Establish the PHS of the Disorder

Now it is your turn to identify articles to establish the PHS of your chosen behavioral health disorder.

Using EBSCO host, ProQuest, or Web of Science search for articles on the epidemiology of the behavioral health problem you want to study. Use search terms such as the prevalence or incidence or epidemiology and the name of the disorder you are studying (e.g., depression). An example of a search is shown in (Fig. 4.13).

FIGURE 4.13 An example of a potential literature search.

Building Human Capital

One of the most important things you will learn as you write this proposal is the importance of being organized. If you are well organized, you will be better able to find the information you need. As you search for articles for each section of the proposal, you will create a library. And as you write the proposal, you will find yourself going back to each of the articles to make sure you understand the information and are reporting it accurately. So keeping things organized and keeping track of where you find each piece of information is critical).

It takes time to be organized. You need to do a little bit of work to store the articles in a way you will remember. And you need to reference the articles when you use information from the articles in your paper or proposal. (We will show you how to do this in later chapters.)

But the time you take upfront to get organized and stay organized will pay off in the long run. And you will have developed good habits you take with you into your future scholarship.

Terms

Take the time to define these terms and apply them.

Research Terms

Epidemiology
Incidence
Prevalence
Peer-reviewed articles
Original research
Empirical articles
Qualitative research
Quantitative research
Systematic reviews
Case studies
Abstract

Clinical Terms

Smoking cessation
Health behavioral change

References

Bakhshaie, J., Zvolensky, M. J., & Goodwin, R. D. (2015). Cigarette smoking and the onset and persistence of depression among adults in the United States: 1994–2005. *Comprehensive Psychiatry, 60*, 142–148.

CDC. (2012). *Principles of epidemiology | lesson 3 - section 2*. Retrieved June 30, 2018, from https://www.cdc.gov/ophss/csels/dsepd/ss1978/lesson3/section2.html.

Elder, J. P., Ayala, G. X., & Harris, S. (1999). Theories and intervention approaches to health- behavior change in primary care. *American Journal of Preventive Medicine, 17*(4), 275–284.

Ingall, G., & Cropley, M. (2010). Exploring the barriers of quitting smoking during pregnancy: A systematic review of qualitative studies. *Women and Birth, 23*(2), 45–52.

McCabe, S. E., West, B. T., Veliz, P., & Boyd, C. J. (2017). E-cigarette use, cigarette smoking, dual use, and problem behaviors among US adolescents: Results from a national survey. *Journal of Adolescent Health, 61*(2), 155–162.

Pacella, M. L., Hruska, B., & Delahanty, D. L. (2013). The physical health consequences of PTSD and PTSD symptoms: A meta-analytic review. *Journal of Anxiety Disorders, 27*(1), 33–46.

Peirson, L., Ali, M. U., Kenny, M., Raina, P., & Sherifali, D. (2016). Interventions for prevention and treatment of tobacco smoking in school-aged children and adolescents: A systematic review and meta-analysis. *Preventive Medicine, 85*, 20–31.

Reitsma, M. B., Fullman, N., Ng, M., Salama, J. S., Abajobir, A., Abate, K. H., … Abyu, G. Y. (2017). Smoking prevalence and attributable disease burden in 195 countries and territories, 1990–2015: A systematic analysis from the global burden of disease study 2015. *The Lancet, 389*(10082), 1885–1906.

Stead, M., MacAskill, S., MacKintosh, A.-M., Reece, J., & Eadie, D. (2001). "It's as if you're locked in": Qualitative explanations for area effects on smoking in disadvantaged communities. *Health & Place, 7*(4), 333–343.

Wellman, R. J., Dugas, E. N., Dutczak, H., O'Loughlin, E. K., Datta, G. D., Lauzon, B., & O'Loughlin, J. (2016). Predictors of the onset of cigarette smoking: A systematic review of longitudinal population-based studies in youth. *American Journal of Preventive Medicine, 51*(5), 767–778.

Further Reading

American Psychiatric Association. (2013). *Diagnostic and statistical manual of mental disorders* (5th ed.). Washington, DC: Author.

Chapter 5

Public health significance: A focus on populations and sampling

In Chapter 4 you found articles which provide information about the public health significance of the disorder. Now it's time to thoroughly read these articles. You will be reading descriptive research articles that present evidence on the prevalence of the disorder, and hypothesis-testing research which examines consequences of the disorder and risk factors for the disorder.

As you read articles on the prevalence of the disorder, you will learn more about how researchers choose the sample of participants for a research study and understand the costs and benefits of different strategies for obtaining a sample of participants.

As you read hypothesis-testing research on risk factors, you will have a clearer idea of the different samples or groups of individuals who may be at risk for the disorder you are studying. If you are writing a proposal for a treatment study for this disorder, this research can help you identify the specific sample you will choose for your proposed study. This will be a sample at high risk for developing the disorder you are investigating. If you are writing a paper reviewing the evidence on the prevalence or consequences of the disorder, these papers can help you identify the types of samples that have been used in prior research. Once you have mastered these concepts, the next chapter—Chapter 6—provides specific information about writing about the prevalence and consequences of the disorder and the risk factors for a disorder.

Psychology Research Methods. https://doi.org/10.1016/B978-0-12-815680-3.00005-0

Understanding Samples and Populations

When researchers want to know how common a disorder is, they look for information about the incidence or prevalence of the disorder. The **incidence** of the disorder refers to the number of new cases which develop in a population over time (e.g., over a year or another period). The **prevalence** of the disorder refers to the proportion of population who has ever had this disorder over time, even if they do not currently have the disorder. **Lifetime prevalence** is the proportion of the population who have ever had the disorder at any time over the course of their lives.

What do researchers mean when they investigate a population? A population includes all the members of a given group. Which group should be studied?

- All people in the United States?
- All people in the world?
- All children?
- All teenagers?

The choice of the larger population group depends on the hypotheses to be tested. For example, imagine a researcher wants to know how many children use substances (i.e., alcohol or recreational drugs). Another way to say this is that they are investigating the prevalence of substance use in a population of children—defined as people under 18 years of age. They cannot measure all children, or all members of any population. Therefore, researchers collect data from a sample (a subset) of this population.

Different Ways to Obtain a Sample

The way the researchers obtain this sample depends on the aim of the study. The researchers can use a form of population-based sampling or a form of convenience sampling (or a combination).

Population-Based Sampling

In **population-based sampling**, researchers are attempting to create a sample that represents the whole population, a sample labeled a **representative sample**. In a population-based or representative sample, the sample reflects the composition of the whole population. These samples are generally created through **random selection,** a process in which individuals from the

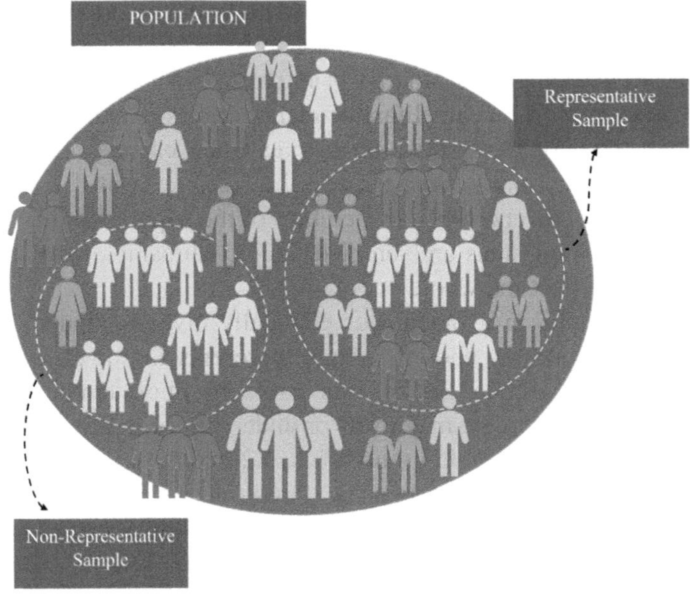

FIGURE 5.1 Depictions of sampling.

population are chosen at random. This means every person in the population of interest (e.g., all adults in the United States or all children in the United States) has an equal chance of being chosen to participate in the study (Fig. 5.1).

Convenience Sampling

As an alternative to population-based sampling, researchers can use **convenience sampling.** Convenience sampling is generally not used in studies of the prevalence of a disorder, but it may be used in studies of consequences and risk factors. In convenience sampling, researchers recruit participants to volunteer for the study. The selection of the participants is not random; it depends on the researchers' recruitment methods and the participants' willingness to volunteer. Many types of basic research on mechanisms and treatment outcome can be done with convenience sampling.

Choosing a Sampling Method

Population-based sampling with random selection is critical for epidemiological studies investigating the prevalence of a disorder in a population. It would be very difficult to obtain an unbiased estimate of the prevalence of the disorder in a population without choosing participants at random from the relevant population.

Random selection can eliminate many sources of bias because each member of the population has an equal chance of being included in the final sample used in the research. But if a population is very diverse or if the members of the population live far apart and not all areas are sampled, the actual sample may not accurately reflect the whole population.

For example, in a racially or ethnically diverse population, researchers hope the chosen sample represents the diversity of the population sample. But in some cases, if simple randomization is used, the sample may over- or underrepresent members of a specific racial or ethnic group (Figs. 5.2 and 5.3).

Therefore, to prevent bias in sampling, researchers have developed alternative strategies to improve the relationship between the population and the randomly selected sample. These strategies include, among others, **stratified random sampling.**

FIGURE 5.2 Population.

FIGURE 5.3 Limitation of sampling.

In stratified sampling, researchers identify groups within the population that should be represented within a sample (e.g., Asian Black, Hispanic, Native American, and White). They identify the proportions of individuals within the sample who should belong to each group depending on their representation within the population. Individuals are selected at random within these groups in the population. Sometimes researchers will overselect members of a group to insure representation of members of the group. If the researchers use a larger sample of members of that group, they are more likely to ensure that they include a group of individuals who represent a range of characteristics within the group.

When researchers want to understand the prevalence of a disorder across the United States, they use a **nationally representative sample**. To obtain a sample that is representative of the United States and includes all the groups you need to study, researchers use different approaches including **multistage random sampling**. In multistage random sampling, researchers randomize inclusion at different levels, such as regions, schools, or addresses.

For example, in the McCabe et al. (2017) study you read about in Chapter 4, the authors wanted to examine the prevalence of smoking among adolescents in the United States. The researchers needed to obtain a nationally representative sample—a sample which included adolescents from across the United States. To create this sample, researchers develop large databases that can be used for studies of prevalence and other issues of public health significance.

In the McCabe et al. (2017) study, the researchers used the Monitoring the Future dataset. This dataset was created using one approach to multistage random sampling. First the researchers chose regions of the country at random, then they chose one or more schools in each area at random, and then they chose one or more classes at random within each school. All students within the classes were asked to participate. Most (more than 79%) of the students in the classes participated. You can read more about how the Monitoring the Future dataset was created at https://www.healthypeople.gov/2020/data-source/monitoring-the-future-study.

Other studies, including the National Study of Drug Use and Health, use a different approach. Researchers first choose census tracts at random, then they choose small areas within the census block at random, then they choose addresses within the smaller areas at random, and then they choose individuals within these addresses. You can read more about how the dataset for this study was created in the 2014 NSDUH Methodological Resource Book (Substance Abuse and Mental Health Services Administration, 2015).

Although creating a sample through the process of **random selection** is challenging, there are important advantages that are essential for a study of prevalence. The use of random selection can eliminate many concerns about bias in the choice of participants. When people are chosen at random, the characteristics of the volunteer do not influence the opportunity to volunteer for the study. Similarly, the researcher's beliefs or expectations also do not influence the opportunity to volunteer for the study.

In convenience sampling, participants may be recruited using many different methods. Participants may be recruited through advertisements, referral from medical specialists or teachers, word of mouth, and other approaches. **Snowball sampling** is a specific form of convenience sampling in which existing research participants recruit other participants who might be appropriate for the study (Fig. 5.4).

Convenience sampling can make recruitment easier and much less expensive. But convenience sampling increases the risk that the characteristics that lead people to volunteer influence the outcome of the study. Therefore, researchers pay

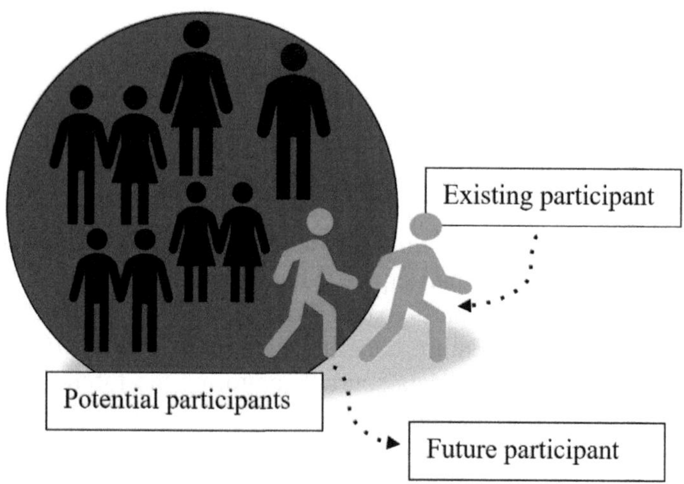

FIGURE 5.4 Snowball sampling.

special attention to the methods they use for recruitment. If they can, they try to identify the ways in which the sample they obtain through convenience sampling differs from a population-based sample. And they often report on the ways in which individuals who agreed to participate or who remained in the study differ from those who did not agree or who did not complete the study.

Activity 5.1: Identifying Sampling Methods

We can identify the sampling methods used in an article which examines one consequence of substance use. Harford, Yi, Chen, and Grant (2018) examine whether substance use increases the risk for exposure to violence (Fig. 5.5). Some studies of consequences use random selection or probability sampling, others do not. As you read about the study, see if the sampling method affects the conclusions you can draw about the association between the behavioral health condition (i.e., substance use) and the consequences (violence) (Table 5.1).

Journal of Affective Disorders 225 (2018) 365–373

Contents lists available at ScienceDirect

Journal of Affective Disorders

journal homepage: www.elsevier.com/locate/jad

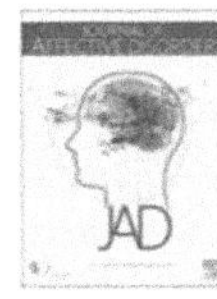

Research paper

Substance use disorders and self- and other-directed violence among adults: Results from the National Survey on Drug Use And Health

Thomas C. Harford[a], Hsiao-ye Yi[a], Chiung M. Chen[a,*], Bridget F. Grant[b]

[a] CSR, Incorporated, 4250 N. Fairfax Drive, Suite 500, Arlington, VA 22203, United States
[b] National Institute on Alcohol Abuse and Alcoholism, National Institutes of Health, 5635 Fishers Lane, Bethesda, MD 20892, United States

A B S T R A C T

Background: Previous studies have identified a violence typology of self- and other-directed violence. This study examines the extent to which substance use disorders (SUDs) as defined by the *Diagnostic and Statistical Manual of Mental Disorders, Fourth Edition (DSM-IV)*, independent of serious psychological distress, major depressive episodes, assault arrest, and criminal justice involvement, are associated with these violence categories.
Method: Data were obtained from the National Survey on Drug Use and Health (NSDUH) pooled across survey years 2008–2015, with a combined sample of 314,881 adult respondents. According to self-report data on suicide attempt (self-directed) and attacking someone with the intent for serious injury (other-directed), violence was categorized in four categories: none, self-directed only, other-directed only, and combined self-/other-directed. Multinomial logistic regression was used to estimate the adjusted odds ratios associated with the risk factors for different forms of violence.
Results: Nicotine dependence and the number of *DSM-IV* SUDs criteria (except the criterion of legal problems) for alcohol, marijuana, and pain reliever use disorders are significantly associated with the self-/other-directed violence categories.
Limitations: Cross-sectional data do not allow assessment of directionality of important factors.
Conclusions: The identification of the combined self- and other-directed violence among adults in the general population extends studies in the adolescent population, and significant correlation between self- and other-directed violence provides additional support for clinical studies that established this association. Findings expand the associated risk factors identified in previous studies for the adult population. Prevention and treatment programs need to address both forms of violence and suicidality.

FIGURE 5.5 Abstract from Harford et al. (2018).

Continued

Activity 5.1: Identifying Sampling Methods—cont'd

TABLE 5.1 Start by making a construct list and filling in definitions of these constructs.

Author date	Constructs	Definitions
Harford et al. (2018)	Substance use disorder	The use/abuse of one or more substances, including alcohol, nicotine, pain relievers, stimulants, and more
	Self-directed violence	For example, suicide attempt
	Other-directed violence	Attacking someone else with the intent to seriously injure or harm
	....	....

Fig. 5.6 The excerpt below explains the sampling and data collection methods.

Study Design:
The study sample is based on the adult sample from the NSDUH, annual surveys of the civilian noninstitutionalized U.S. population ages 12 and older. The NSDUH is sponsored by the Substance Abuse and Mental Health Services Administration and conducted annually under contract with RTI International.

← Here the authors are providing information about the group which organizes and funds the study and the group that collects the data.

The survey collects information on demographics, substance use, and mental health using a combination of computer-assisted face-to-face interviews and audio computer-assisted self-administered interviews.

← Here the authors are providing information about the ways the data are collected. Since the whole sample included over 300, 000 people, the researchers needed to hire many people to collect the data.

Participants are selected by an independent multistage area probability sample design (i.e., census tracts as the first stage followed by census block groups, segments, dwelling units, and individuals) for each of the 50 states and the District of Columbia. Young people are oversampled.

← Here the authors explain the procedures to select participants at random.

FIGURE 5.6 Excerpts from Harford et al. (2018).

Now we can determine how the researchers obtained the sample. See the answers to the following questions in Table 5.2. Did the authors use population-based sampling or convenience sampling? How can you tell?

Activity 5.1: Identifying Sampling Methods—cont'd

TABLE 5.2 Identifying sampling methods.

Author/ Date	Population-based sampling or convenience sampling?	How did you decide which type of sampling was used (what were the keywords that indicated the approach?)	What is the size of the sample?	How were the participants recruited?	Potential limits to generalizability. What groups were included? Were any populations or groups not included?
Harford et al. (2018)	Population based	"National survey on drug use and health"	N = 314, 881	Participants were chosen at random ("independent multistage are probability design"). Participants are then visited by an interviewer and asked to complete an interview (computer/ face-to-face).	Civilian, noninstitutionalized individuals ages 18 and older residing in individual or group quarters. This means studies of high-risk persons—homeless and institutionalized/ incarcerated—are not included. So estimates may be biased toward low end.

Now it is your turn. Identify a study on the prevalence of the behavioral health disorder you are studying and complete Table 5.3.

TABLE 5.3 Identifying the sample in an epidemiological study you are using.

Author/ Date	Population-based sampling or convenience sampling?	How did you decide which type of sampling was used (what were the keywords that indicated the approach?)	What is the size of the sample?	How were the participants recruited?	Potential limits to generalizability. What groups were included? Were any populations or groups not included?
			N =		

Risk Factors: Targeting the Study

Not everyone is at equal risk for every disorder. As we discussed in Chapter 4, risk factors are variables which make it more likely someone will develop a disorder. Identifying variations in risk can help researchers to target their efforts toward a population that needs further research and treatment efforts.

Risk factors can include variables on the personal, family, social group, community/neighborhood, or national level (Braveman, Egerter, & Williams, 2011). On a personal level, risk for many disorders varies depending on demographic and socioeconomic characteristics such as age, gender, race, education, or income, as well as genetic predispositions, behavioral profiles, and personality-related variables. Risk can also be affected by community-level variables such as the characteristics of a neighborhood. For example, on a community or neighborhood level, low levels of neighborhood income, high levels of crowding, high levels of crime, and low levels of social cohesion have all been identified as risk factors for some behavioral health disorders (Alamilla, Scott, & Hughes, 2016). Other risk factors that are associated with health outcomes include local or regional policies and regulations (i.e., concerning childcare or breastfeeding) that may influence health behavior (see Richman & Hatzenbuehler, 2014).

What characteristics could affect risk for the disorder you are investigating?

- Demographic?
- Environmental?
- Social?
- Personal?
- Political?

Understanding the risk factors may provide important information about the etiology or causes of the disorder. Choosing risk factors can provide direction for identifying mechanisms that trigger or maintain the disorder.

For example:

If age is a risk factor, then the mechanisms might involve changes to developmental processes.

If gender is a risk factor, then the mechanisms might involve hormones or gender socialization.

If substance use is a risk factor, then the mechanisms might involve impulse control problems or other consequences of using substances.

How Can You Find Information On Risk Factors?

To find evidence of a risk factor for your disorder, you can use the term "risk factor" combined with the term for your disorder (Fig. 5.7). Or you can use some of the risk factor terms suggested in Table 5.4.

As shown in Table 5.4, constructs which are commonly considered as risk factors for behavioral health symptoms and treatment outcomes include stressors and resources in the family and neighborhood/community (Reardon, 2016; Sampson, Morenoff, & Gannon-Rowley, 2002). As you can see in the table, different measurement methods can be used to gather data on

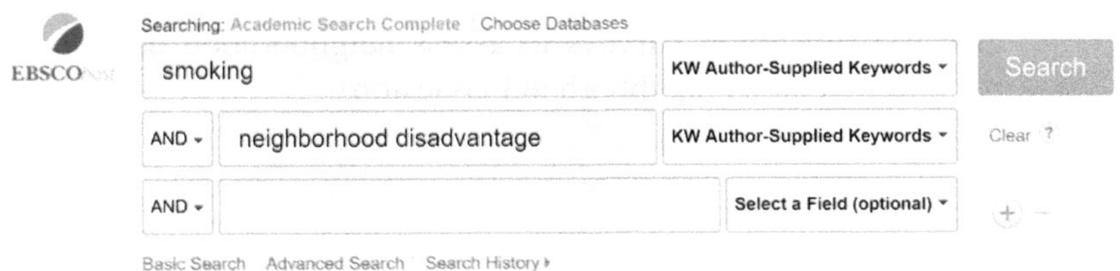

FIGURE 5.7 Sample search.

TABLE 5.4 Examples of risk factor constructs at different levels.

Risk factors considered on an individual level	Example of measurement methods
Family stressors, child maltreatment	Self-reports, child welfare reports
Family resources, attachment	Self-reports, parent reports, observations
Other trauma	Self-reports, police reports
Family history of behavioral health disorders	Self-reports, parents' reports
Personality	Self-reports, personality tests
Age	Self-reports
Gender	Self-reports
Ethnicity or race	Self-reports
Education	Self-reports or educational records
Income or assets	Self-reports, tax returns
Risk factors considered on a community level	
Neighborhood disadvantage	Census data
Neighborhood segregation	Census data
Neighborhood crime and violence	Reports from police reporting services, such as COPSTAT

family and neighborhood stressors and resources. Consequently, there can be many different variables representing the constructs of family stressors and family resources.

For example, the construct of family stressors could include variables such as "Child Maltreatment" or "Domestic Violence" or "Child Neglect." In this case the variables also could be assessed through child reports, records from child welfare agencies, criminal justice organizations, or medical charts, among other measurement instruments.

Neighborhood stressors and resources can be represented by variables derived from the US census, including neighborhood disadvantage or neighborhood crowding. Sometimes researchers also use self-report surveys to assess neighborhood disorder or resources such as neighborhood cohesion).

Using national databases to find information about neighborhood stressors and resources

To find information on community stressors in the social or physical environment, researchers often use information from the census or other national databases (see examples in Fig. 5.8). Here is an example of the type of data on a neighborhood that can be obtained from the census using freely available links (e.g., FFIEC https://geomap.ffiec.gov/FFIECGeocMap/GeocodeMap1.aspx) (Fig. 5.9).

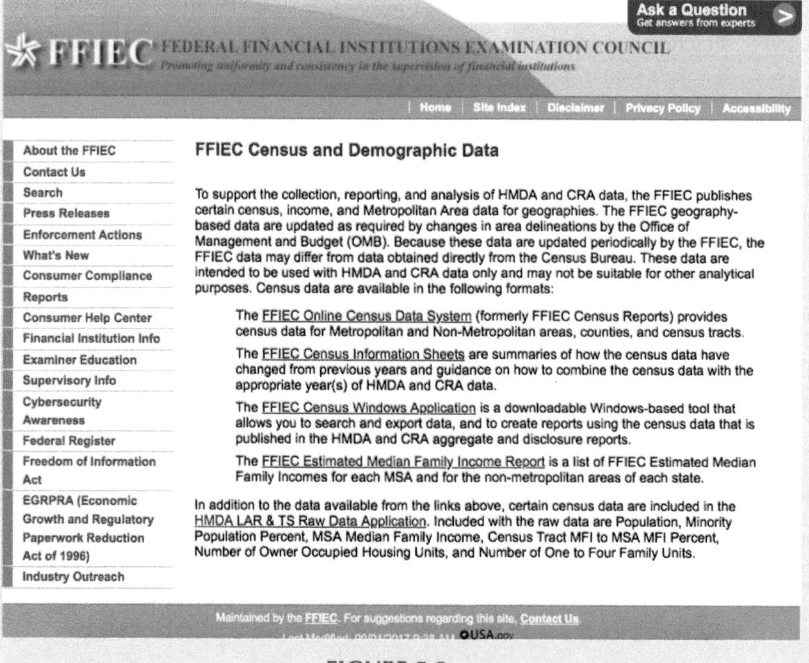

FIGURE 5.8

A Closer Look

Using national databases to find information about neighborhood stressors and resources—cont'd

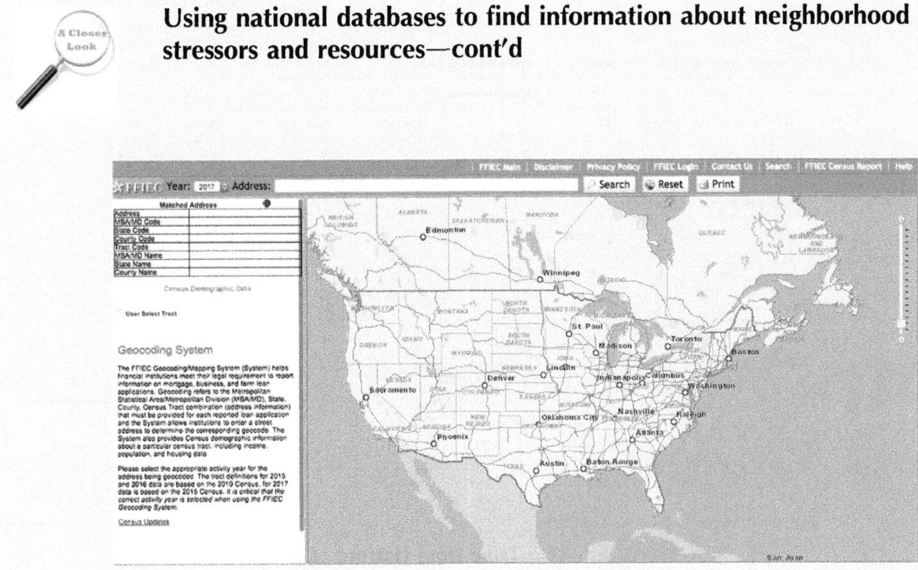

FIGURE 5.9 FFIEC website.

Documenting Risk Factors

To document that a variable is a risk factor, you need quantitative evidence of a relation between the risk factor and the disorder you are studying. There are different ways this quantitative evidence can be provided. The relation between a risk factor and an outcome can be expressed in terms of percentages. For example, a researcher might state that 10% of people with the risk factor have the disorder compared with 5% of people who do not have the risk factor.

Or the relation can be expressed as a relative risk or *odds ratio (OR)* in which the researcher is expressing the likelihood of having the disorder if the person has versus does not have the disorder. Other studies document the relation between the risk factor and outcome by reporting a correlation or regression coefficient estimating the extent of the relation. Or researchers can present differences in symptom scores between those who do versus do not have the risk factor.

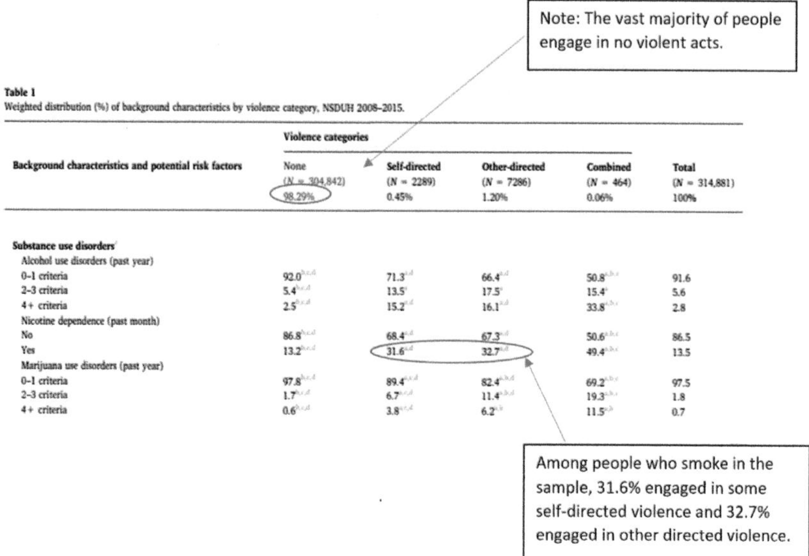

Table 1
Weighted distribution (%) of background characteristics by violence category, NSDUH 2008–2015.

Background characteristics and potential risk factors	Violence categories				
	None (*N* = 304,842) 98.29%	Self-directed (*N* = 2289) 0.45%	Other-directed (*N* = 7286) 1.20%	Combined (*N* = 464) 0.06%	Total (*N* = 314,881) 100%
Substance use disorders[f]					
Alcohol use disorders (past year)					
0–1 criteria	92.0[b,c,d]	71.3[a,d]	66.4[a,d]	50.8[a,b,c]	91.6
2–3 criteria	5.4[b,c,d]	13.5[a]	17.5[a]	15.4[a]	5.6
4+ criteria	2.5[b,c,d]	15.2[a,d]	16.1[a,d]	33.8[a,b,c]	2.8
Nicotine dependence (past month)					
No	86.8[b,c,d]	68.4[a,d]	67.3[a,d]	50.6[a,b,c]	86.5
Yes	13.2[b,c,d]	31.6[a,d]	32.7[a,d]	49.4[a,b,c]	13.5
Marijuana use disorders (past year)					
0–1 criteria	97.8[b,c,d]	89.4[a,c,d]	82.4[a,b,d]	69.2[a,b,c]	97.5
2–3 criteria	1.7[b,c,d]	6.7[a,c,d]	11.4[a,b,d]	19.3[a,b,c]	1.8
4+ criteria	0.6[b,c,d]	3.8[a,c,d]	6.2[a,b]	11.5[a,b]	0.7

FIGURE 5.10 Table from Harford et al. (2018).

Here are the results from the Harford et al. (2018) study examining the relations of substance use to different forms of violence (Fig. 5.10). The authors examine whether meeting criteria for each substance use category is associated with violence. There are low levels of violence overall, but within each category of substance use, the authors examine whether those who meet more criteria for substance use disorders are more likely to engage in some type of violence.

Evaluating the Evidence: Identifying Threats to Validity and Gaps in Knowledge in Epidemiological Studies

Threats to internal validity include any sources of bias which influence the researchers' ability to collect valid data about the prevalence of a disorder or to test hypotheses about the consequences of a disorder or the risk factors for the disorder. **Threats to external validity** include any limitations to the study which affect the ability to generalize the findings to other populations or situations than those used in the original study.

Threats to internal validity can emerge from bias when selecting the sample, choosing the measures, implementing the procedures, and analyzing the data. Threats to internal validity can also emerge from **extraneous variables**. Extraneous variables are variables which are not intentionally included in the study variables and which have unintended effects on the outcomes of a study.

Threats to external validity in a study of prevalence may emerge when the sample is restricted along some dimension (e.g., restricted to noninstitutionalized individuals or to a specific age group).

The threats to validity may not seem clear to you when you first start to read articles. But you will begin to understand these threats as you read more articles. Authors of original research articles include discussions about threats to validity and gaps in knowledge to justify their study. Authors of review articles include discussions about threats to validity seen in the original research and identify gaps in knowledge.

We can briefly consider some of the threats to internal and external validity that may be present in studies of the prevalence and consequences of a disorder, as well as studies of risk factors for the disorder you are studying. We will examine a limited number of threats here. In Chapter 13, we discuss threats to validity to other types of studies, including randomized controlled trials used to evaluate treatment outcome. For more information about the quality and threats to validity of epidemiological studies, see (Carlson & Morrison, 2009; Hassan, 2006; Kim et al., 2013; Zaccai, 2004).

Threats to Internal Validity

Volunteering. One threat to internal validity which faces many studies using both population-based and convenience sampling concerns the nature of **volunteering**. All research participation is voluntary. People who volunteer for research may differ in some important characteristics from those who do not. They may have different levels of extraversion or willingness to take risks, or they may have a greater need for the **compensation given for participation**. These characteristics may influence the outcomes of the study. Therefore, often researchers will try to

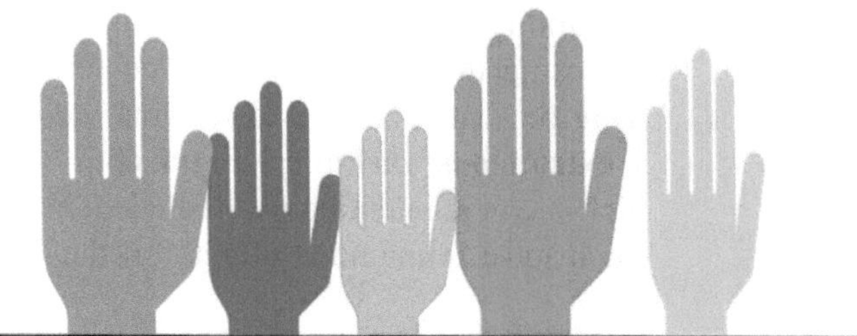

FIGURE 5.11 Volunteer characteristics can affect the internal validity of a study.

investigate the ways in which individuals who volunteer for their study differ from those who do not (Fig. 5.11).

Operational definitions and measurement. A study can experience a threat to internal validity, if the operational definition of the disorder is too narrow or too broad, if the inclusion and exclusion criteria for the study are not clear or correct, or if the measurement of the disorder is not reliable or valid.

In many epidemiological studies, the measurement method chosen may allow the researchers to test many people quickly and inexpensively. But despite advantages in terms of efficiency, the measurement method may present some limitations. The measurement method may not capture the characteristics of the disorder that are most likely to produce consequences. For example, if the assessment includes only self-reported symptoms of a disorder, the data cannot provide information on the signs of the disorder that might be apparent to a healthcare provider. Or if a limited range of symptoms are evaluated, the researchers may fail to capture some crucial components.

If a measurement instrument is not valid for use with individuals from a different culture, the estimates of the prevalence of the diagnosis may not be valid for members of that culture (More on measurement reliability and validity in Chapter 16).

Extraneous variables. In studies of behavioral health disorders, extraneous variables can include any variables that may influence the collection of data on symptoms. For example, fears of stigma may limit the reporting of symptoms of behavioral health disorders, such as bipolar disorder. Feeling disconnected from or untrusting toward the interviewer who is asking about the symptoms may also affect the reports. You will learn about these and other relevant extraneous variables as you read articles about the disorder you are studying.

Threats to External Validity

Strategies for Selecting the Sample. In epidemiological studies, the samples are intended to represent a population. If a sample is supposed to be representative of the population, the study can experience a threat to internal validity if the strategy for selecting the members of the population is biased or ineffective.

The sampling method can also introduce threats to **external validity**. In population-based samples, people from many (although not necessarily all) sociodemographic groups are included. But in convenience sampling, this may not be the case. The researcher may work in an area in which it is difficult to find people from some ethnic or socioeconomic backgrounds (Fig. 5.12). Therefore the findings may not generalize to the types of people who are not included in the research.

There may be other subtle limitations to the generalizability of the results. For example, if researchers intend to test the prevalence of a disorder in a representative sample of all US adults, they need to make sure the sampling method does not introduce bias into the process. If the sampling method relies on being able to directly contact all individuals, the sample may exclude people who are institutionalized for any reason (i.e., they are in prison or a hospital) or if they are overseas in active military service. If these individuals are not included, then the sample does not truly reflect the population of the United States, and the sample is not fully representative.

FIGURE 5.12 Homogenous samples can limit the generalizability of the findings.

Evaluating Studies to Detect Threats to Internal and External Validity

Researchers have developed tools, including short surveys, to help evaluate the quality of the research you are reading. It can be helpful to review these tools to understand the components of research that should be included in articles about prevalence.

For example, Hoy and colleagues developed a survey which includes some of the several questions to help you recognize bias in the sampling and collection of the data and potential bias or difficulties with the measurement of the construct (Hoy et al., 2012). We include several of their ideas in Fig. 5.13.

External Validity
❖ Was the sampling frame a true or close representation of the target population?
❖ Was some form of random selection used to select the sample, OR was a census undertaken?
Internal Validity
❖ Was the study instrument that measured the parameter of interest shown to have validity and reliability?
❖ Was the same mode of data collection used for all subjects?

FIGURE 5.13 Items identified by Hoy et al. (2012) (available on page 937) to recognize sampling bias.

Activity 5.2 Identifying Threats to Validity in Articles

Now you try identifying threats to validity in an original article on the prevalence of your disorder. Consider these questions.

1. What type of sampling was used? What are the limitations to the sample the researchers chose? Were people of all ages, race/ethnicities, or regions included? Were people who are not living in the community included?

____

____

____

____

____

2. How was the disorder measured? What are the limitations to this measurement approach? Does this measurement approach capture many aspects of the disorder?

____

____

____

____

____

Building Human Capital

In this chapter you learned about the prevalence and incidence of disorders and how to find information about prevalence and incidence in research articles. You learned about the strengths and weakness of different types of sampling, and how some types of sampling can introduce bias into a study. You searched for risk factors and you evaluated the statistics on the relationship of the risk factor to the disorder.

You are learning to read closely and carefully. As you complete the table exercises and begin to write your PHS section, you are learning to keep close track of numbers and percentages. You are learning to be systematic in your evaluation of the literature. This type of careful reading will help you in understanding psychology research. Being able to pay attention to the details and understand how to find the relevant information is an important skill for any type of learning.

Terms

Take the time to find the definitions and consider how to apply them.

Research Terms

Incidence
Population
Population-based sampling

Representative sample
Random digit dialing
Convenience sampling
Compensation for participation
External validity
National databases
Census
Dose–response relationship
Odds ratio
Confidence interval
Relative risk ratio

References

Alamilla, S. G., Scott, M. A., & Hughes, D. L. (2016). The relationship of individual-and community-level sociocultural and neighborhood factors to the mental health of ethnic groups in two large us cities. *Journal of Community Psychology, 44*(1), 51–77.

Braveman, P., Egerter, S., & Williams, D. R. (2011). The social determinants of health: Coming of age. *Annual Review of Public Health, 32*, 381–398.

Carlson, M. D., & Morrison, R. S. (2009). Study design, precision, and validity in observational studies. *Journal of Palliative Medicine, 12*(1), 77–82.

Harford, T. C., Yi, H., Chen, C. M., & Grant, B. F. (2018). Substance use disorders and self-and other-directed violence among adults: Results from the National Survey on Drug Use and Health. *Journal of Affective Disorders, 225*, 365–373.

Hassan, E. (2006). Recall bias can be a threat to retrospective and prospective research designs. *The Internet Journal of Epidemiology, 3*(2), 339–412.

Hoy, D., Brooks, P., Woolf, A., Blyth, F., March, L., Bain, C., ... Buchbinder, R. (2012). Assessing risk of bias in prevalence studies: Modification of an existing tool and evidence of interrater agreement. *Journal of Clinical Epidemiology, 65*(9), 934–939.

Kim, S. Y., Park, J. E., Lee, Y. J., Seo, H.-J., Sheen, S.-S., Hahn, S., ... Son, H.-J. (2013). Testing a tool for assessing the risk of bias for nonrandomized studies showed moderate reliability and promising validity. *Journal of Clinical Epidemiology, 66*(4), 408–414.

McCabe, S. E., West, B. T., Veliz, P., & Boyd, C. J. (2017). E-cigarette use, cigarette smoking, dual use, and problem behaviors among US adolescents: Results from a national survey. *Journal of Adolescent Health, 61*(2), 155–162.

Reardon, S. F. (2014). School segregation and racial academic achievement gaps. *RSF: The Russell Sage Foundation Journal of the Social Sciences, 2*(5), 34–57.

Richman, L. S., & Hatzenbuehler, M. L. (2014). A multilevel analysis of stigma and health: Implications for research and policy. *Policy Insights from the Behavioral and Brain Sciences, 1*(1), 213–221.

Sampson, R. J., Morenoff, J. D., & Gannon-Rowley, T. (2002). Assessing "neighborhood effects": Social processes and new directions in research. *Annual Review of Sociology, 28*(1), 443–478.

Substance Abuse and Mental Health Services Administration (SAMHSA). (2015). *National Survey on Drug Use and Health Methodological Resourcebook Section 2: Sample Design Report.*

Zaccai, J. H. (2004). How to assess epidemiological studies. *Postgraduate Medical Journal, 80*(941), 140–147.

Further Reading

Department of Health. (2010). *Methods of sampling from a population* [Text]. Retrieved August 25, 2018, from https://www.healthknowledge.org.uk/public-health-textbook/research-methods/1a-epidemiology/methods-of-sampling-population.

Martínez-Mesa, J., González-Chica, D. A., Duquia, R. P., Bonamigo, R. R., & Bastos, J. L. (2016). Sampling: How to select participants in my research study? *Anais Brasileiros de Dermatologia, 91*(3), 326–330.

Ritchie, J., Lewis, J., Nicholls, C. M., & Ormston, R. (2013). *Qualitative research practice: A guide for social science students and researchers.* Sage.

Chapter 6

Writing the public health significance section

In the last five chapters you have learned about the importance of establishing the public health significance (PHS) of the study, and developed skills in gathering the relevant evidence to build a PHS section. Now you are ready to write the PHS section of your paper or proposal for your chosen behavioral health disorder.

In this chapter we will review the components of the PHS, the purpose of each component, and describe how to write each component. The components you need depend on the type of paper or proposal you are writing. We provide examples for two different types of papers or proposals.

- A proposal to evaluate a treatment for the disorder.
- A paper evaluating the evidence on the PHS of the disorder.

Many other papers or proposals are possible. The examples are used to illustrate the importance of linking the arguments you want to make to the evidence you need. As you think about the purpose of the paper and the list of components, you are challenging yourself to build a logical and well-documented argument.

Documenting the Sources of Evidence

Science is collaborative. Every researcher builds on the ideas and methods of other researchers. And they hope other scientists will build on their ideas and methods.

Science is also rigorous. *Rigor* means that claims are based on evidence. Therefore, in the process of writing about research, researchers are careful to give credit where credit is due. Researchers acknowledge the source of every piece of evidence.

In a proposal or paper written in the style required by the American Psychological Association (APA), the documentation

Psychology Research Methods. https://doi.org/10.1016/B978-0-12-815680-3.00006-2

takes the form of citations after statements about ideas or evidence derived from other researchers' work. For example, when a researcher describes evidence from an article, the researcher cites the source of the evidence. The citation lists the last names of the authors of the articles from which the researcher obtained the evidence and also includes the year of publication.

Here's an example. *The prevalence of subthreshold bipolar disorder was 5.1%* (Judd & Akiskal, 2003).

At the end of the paper or proposal, the full citation will be listed in the bibliography, also called the reference section. For example:

> Judd, L. L., & Akiskal, H. S. (2003). The prevalence and disability of bipolar spectrum disorders in the US population: Re-analysis of the ECA database taking into account subthreshold cases. *Journal of Affective Disorders*, 73(1–2), 123–131.

Fig. 6.1 is an example of a reference section from an APA style paper.

References

Akiskal, H.S., Placidi, G.F., Signoretta, S., Liguori, A., Gervasi, R., Maremmani, I., Mallya, G., Puzantian, V.R., 1998. TEMPS-I: Delineating the most discriminant traits of cyclothymic, depressive, irritable and hyperthymic temperaments in a non-patient population. J. Affect. Disord. 51, 7–19.

Akiskal, H.S., Bourgeois, M.L., Angst, J., Post, R., Moller, H.J., Hirschfeld, R.M.A., 2000. Re-evaluating the prevalence of and diagnostic composition within the broad clinical spectrum of bipolar disorders. J. Affect. Disord. 59 (Suppl. 1), 5s–30s.

Akiskal, H.S., 2002. Classification, diagnosis and boundaries of bipolar disorders. In: Maj, M., Akiskal, H.S., Lopez-Ibor, J.J., Sartorius, N. (Eds.), Bipolar Disorder. Wiley, London, pp. 1–52.

American Psychiatric Association, 1980. Diagnostic Statistical Manual of Mental Disorders, 3rd Edition. American Psychiatric Association, Washington, DC.

American Psychiatric Association, 1994. Diagnostic Statistical Manual of Mental Disorders, 4th Edition. American Psychiatric Association, Washington, DC.

Angst, J., 1998. The emerging epidemiology of hypomania and bipolar II disorder. J. Affect. Disord 50, 143–151.

Angst, J., Preisig, M., 1995. Outcome of a clinical cohort of unipolar, bipolar and schizoaffective patients. Results of a prospective study from 1959 to 1985. Schweiz. Arch. Neurol. Psychiatry 146, 17–23.

Baldessarini, R.J., 2000. A plea for integrity of the bipolar disorder concept. Bipolar Disord. 2, 3–7.

Coryell, W., Turvey, C., Endicott, J., Leon, A.C., Mueller, T., Solomon, D., Keller, M., 1998. Bipolar I affective disorder:

FIGURE 6.1 Sample references section from Judd and Akiskal (2003).

The APA has established rules governing the ways to cite evidence and to prepare a bibliography. These rules can be found in the **APA publication manual** (American Psychological Association, 2010). There are also a number of good websites which explain the rules and provide examples of their applications (Purdue Writing Lab, 2018).

Electronic reference managers, such as Zotero or Mendeley, can be very helpful for preparing the reference section of a paper or proposal. Your school librarian can provide instructions on the use of electronic reference managers. You can also learn how to use them online.

As you read articles, enter the citations for the reference section into a reference manager. This can be done electronically when you search for and find the articles. Electronic reference managers can provide a full reference section at the touch of a button at the end of the paper, once you have entered all the citations into the reference manager (Fig. 6.2).

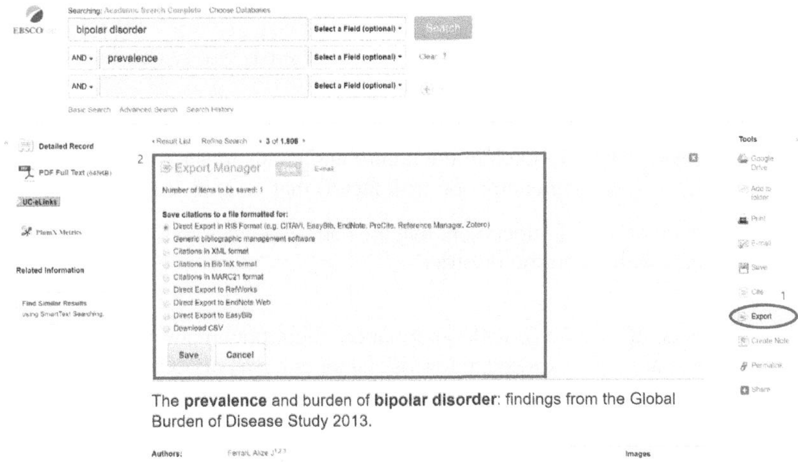

FIGURE 6.2 Exporting references in EBSCO *host*.

It is a good idea to take some time to understand these rules before you start writing. Then you will be prepared to cite your evidence as you write. Staying organized in this way can help you stay on schedule as you complete your paper or proposal.

Components of a PHS Section

The possible components of a PHS section include the information needed to make the arguments about the importance of the study. Table 6.1 lists examples of these components.

TABLE 6.1 Components of a PHS section and their application to different types of papers.

Number	Component	Purpose of the information provided
1.	An operational definition of the disorder	To explain the nature and characteristics of the phenomenon (disorder) you are studying
2.	Evidence of the prevalence of the disorder in the general population	To indicate how common the disorder is
3.	Evidence of the consequences of the disorder	To indicate how serious or disabling the disorder is
4.	Summary of the evidence on the prevalence and consequences of the disorder across multiple studies	To identify consistent and inconsistent themes, to provide information about the prevalence and consequences based on a comprehensive (complete) review of the literature
5.	Threats to internal and external validity in the existing studies	To provide an evaluation of the quality of the available evidence
6.	Gaps in knowledge about the prevalence and consequences of the disorder	To provide a review of the areas of research that are needed
7.	An operational definition of risk factors for the disorder	To explain the nature and characteristics of the phenomenon (risk factor) that you are studying
8.	Evidence of the prevalence of the disorder in individuals with the risk factor	To document that the risk factor increases vulnerability to the disorder
9.	Evidence of the prevalence of the risk factor in the general population	To provide information about how many people are exposed to this risk factor as a way of documenting the likelihood of risk
10.	Summary of the evidence of the relation of the risk factor to the symptoms or diagnosis of the disorder	To identify consistent and inconsistent themes, to provide information about how the risk factor increases the vulnerability to the disorder based on the available literature
11.	Identification of the threats to internal and external validity	To provide an evaluation of the quality of the available evidence
12.	A summary of gaps in knowledge about the relations between the risk factor and the disorder	To provide a review of the areas of research that are needed

Writing a Proposal to Study the Effects of a Treatment

If you are writing a *proposal for a study to evaluate a treatment,* the PHS section is intended to communicate the importance of the problem. In a PHS section, you include *an operational definition*, a statement of the *consequences* of the disorder, and documentation of the *prevalence* of the disorder. The PHS section also includes information about risk factors for the disorder and may also provide some information about the prevalence of the disorder in this high-risk group.

The information on operational definitions, prevalence, and consequences will enable the reader of your proposal to understand the nature and severity of the problem. The information on risk factors helps the reader to understand why you have chosen the sample you have—the individuals who are at risk for the disorder. At a minimum, it would be useful to include information in components 1, 2, and 3 and 7, 8, and 9 listed in Table 6.1 in a PHS section written for this purpose.

Writing a Paper on the Evidence About Prevalence or Risk Factors for the Disorder

Alternatively, if you are writing *a paper reviewing the evidence on the prevalence of a disorder or on the risk factors for the disorder*, you may read many articles about prevalence or risk factors. You can use Table 6.4 to help you organize the findings of the articles you read. In this table you can organize the similarities and differences in the findings across the existing research. For example, you may notice that all the articles provide similar evidence on the prevalence of the disorder or you may notice some articles indicate that the prevalence is higher or lower than expected based on previous studies.

As you read, you can think about the variables that may explain any differences you observe. Then you can evaluate the quality of the data, examining the threats to internal validity and external validity associated with existing research. Finally, you identify remaining gaps in knowledge and make suggestions for future research. For a paper reviewing the evidence on prevalence of the disorder, it would be useful to include information on components 1–6 listed in Table 6.1. For a paper reviewing the evidence on risk factors for the disorder, it would be useful to include information on components 1–3 and 7–12 from Table 6.1.

Assembling the Evidence Needed

Before you start writing, make sure you have all the information you need. It can be very helpful to organize the information into tables. These tables include information about the methods and results of the studies. The information recorded in the tables can provide the detailed guidance for your writing.

Here are some examples of tables used to organize information from articles on the prevalence of bipolar disorder. We completed one example for an original research article on the prevalence of bipolar disorder and another for a review article on the prevalence of bipolar disorder. The tables are accompanied by brief descriptions of the findings and purpose of the articles.

Brief Description of the Article by Judd and Akiskal (2003)

Most studies of the prevalence of bipolar disorder provided information on individuals who met criteria for Bipolar I or Bipolar II disorder, two categories of the disorder. This original research article investigates the prevalence of bipolar disorder using three different categories (Judd & Akiskal, 2003) (Fig. 6.3). In addition to using standard diagnostic criteria for Bipolar I and Bipolar II, they also document the prevalence of subthreshold (sometimes called subsyndromal bipolar disorder). Subthreshold bipolar disorder means the individual has two or more symptoms of bipolar disorder but does not have enough symptoms to meet the criteria for a diagnosis of Bipolar Disorder I or Bipolar Disorder II.

The authors also provide evidence of the consequences of bipolar disorder. The research indicates that any level of bipolar disorder is associated with negative consequences, including more negative health outcomes and poorer occupational functioning, as indicated by the need for disability payments to provide income.

But this article does not provide information on risk factors. It will be necessary to find other articles which provide more information on risk factors for bipolar disorder.

In Table 6.2 we organized the information we gathered from the articles. This made it easy to see what information we had. And it made it easy to see what information we still needed.

ELSEVIER

Journal of Affective Disorders 73 (2003) 123–131

www.elsevier.com/locate/jad

Research report

The prevalence and disability of bipolar spectrum disorders in the US population: re-analysis of the ECA database taking into account subthreshold cases

Lewis L. Judd[a,*], Hagop S. Akiskal[a,b]

[a]*Department of Psychiatry, University of California, San Diego (UCSD), 9500 Gilman Drive, La Jolla, CA 92093-0603, USA*
[b]*Psychiatry Service, San Diego Veterans Health Services, San Diego, CA, USA*

Abstract

Background: Despite emerging international consensus on the high prevalence of the bipolar spectrum in both clinical and community samples, many skeptics contend that narrowly defined bipolar disorder with a lifetime rate of about 1% represents a more accurate estimate of prevalence. This may in part be due to the fact that higher figures proposed for the bipolar spectrum (5–8%) have not been based on national data and have not included all levels of manic symptom severity. In the present secondary analyses of the US National Epidemiological Catchment Area (ECA) database, we provide further clarification on this fundamental public health issue. *Methods:* All respondents in the first wave (first interview) of the ECA household five site sample ($n = 18{,}252$) were classified on the basis of DSM-III criteria into lifetime manic and hypomanic episodes, as well as those with at least two lifetime manic/hypomanic symptoms below the threshold for at least 1 week duration (subsyndromal manic symptoms [SSM] group). Odds ratios were calculated on lifetime service utilization for mental health problems, measures of adverse psychosocial outcome, and suicidal behavior compared to subjects with no mental disorders or manic symptoms. *Results:* As originally reported nearly two decades ago by the primary investigators of the ECA, the lifetime prevalence for manic episode was 0.8%, and for hypomania, 0.5%. What is new here is the inclusion of subthreshold SSM subjects, which accounted for 5.1%, yielding a total of 6.4% lifetime prevalence for the bipolar spectrum. All three (manic, hypomanic and SSM) groups had greater marital disruption. There were significant increases in lifetime health service utilization, need for welfare and disability benefits and suicidal behavior when the SSM, hypomanic and manic subjects were compared to the no mental disorder group. Suicidal behavior was non-significantly highest in the hypomanic (bipolar II) group. Otherwise, hypomanic and manic groups had comparable level of service utilization and social disruption. *Limitations:* Comorbid disorders, which might influence functioning, were not included in the present analyses. *Conclusion:* These secondary analyses of the US National ECA database provide convincing evidence for the high prevalence of a spectrum of bipolarity in the community at 6.4%, and indicate that subthreshold cases are at least five times more prevalent than DSM-based core syndromal diagnoses at about 1%. These SSM subjects, who met the criteria of "caseness" from the point of view of harmful dysfunction, are of great theoretical and public health significance.

Keywords: Epidemiology; ECA; Bipolar I; Bipolar II; Bipolar spectrum; Syndromal symptoms; Hypomania; Mania

FIGURE 6.3 Abstract from Judd and Akiskal (2003).

TABLE 6.2 Information from an original research article on the prevalence of bipolar disorder.

Author/Date: Judd and Akiskal (2003)	
Type of paper: Original or review	**Original**
Population	National sample from NIMH catchment area sample
Sample	18,252 people
Operational definition of the disorder	Individuals were diagnosed with bipolar or subthreshold bipolar disorder based on presence of manic symptoms. To receive a diagnosis of mania, symptoms must be present for 1 week and be accompanied by difficulties, referral, or noticed by friends and relatives. Hypomania, less than 1 week. Subthreshold, two or more symptoms, but do not meet criteria for hypomanic or manic episode.
Measurement strategy	Structured interview
Measurement instrument	Diagnostic interview Schedule
Time frame for reporting	Lifetime
Rates of disorder	0.8% for full manic episodes (Bipolar I diagnosis), 0.5% for hypomanic episode (Bipolar II diagnosis), and 5.1% for subthreshold symptoms.
Definitions of consequences identified	Need for disability or income assistance, suicide, inpatient or outpatient treatment.
Evidence of consequences	All three bipolar groups had higher rates than no bipolar symptom group on all three measures of consequences. For example, 10% of those with mania received disability support versus 7% of those with hypomanic or subthreshold symptoms versus 5% of those with no bipolar symptoms. Among those with manic symptoms 24% committed suicide versus 34% of those with hypomanic symptoms versus 8% of those with subthreshold symptoms versus 2% with no bipolar symptoms.
Definitions of risk factors: Variation by sample characteristics	Risk factors were not specifically investigated.
Evidence of risk factor relation	
Other risk factors?	

Brief Description of Cerimele et al. (2014)

Many people receive treatment from their primary care doctor for common behavioral health problems, such as depression and anxiety. But most articles on the prevalence of behavioral health disorders do not provide information about the number of people who visit primary care clinics who have behavioral health disorders. The review paper by Cerimele et al. (2014) provides good information on the prevalence of bipolar and bipolar spectrum disorders in people who come for primary care (Fig. 6.4).

General Hospital Psychiatry 36 (2014) 19–25

Contents lists available at ScienceDirect

General Hospital Psychiatry

journal homepage: http://www.ghpjournal.com

The prevalence of bipolar disorder in general primary care samples: a systematic review☆,☆☆

Joseph M. Cerimele, M.D. [a,*], Lydia A. Chwastiak, M.D., M.P.H. [a,b], Sherry Dodson, M.L.S. [c], Wayne J. Katon, M.D. [a]

[a] University of Washington School of Medicine Dept. of Psychiatry and Behavioral Sciences, Seattle WA
[b] Harborview Medical Center, Seattle WA
[c] University of Washington School of Medicine Health Sciences Library

ARTICLE INFO

Article history:
Received 23 July 2013
Revised 17 September 2013
Accepted 18 September 2013

Keywords:
Bipolar disorder
Primary care

ABSTRACT

Objective: To obtain an estimate of the prevalence of bipolar disorder in primary care.
Methods: We used the Preferred Reporting Items for Systematic Reviews and Meta-Analyses method to conduct a systematic review in January 2013. We searched seven databases with a comprehensive list of search terms. Included articles had a sample size of 200 patients or more and assessed bipolar disorder using a structured clinical interview or bipolar screening questionnaire in random adult primary care patients. Risk of bias in each study was also assessed.
Results: We found 5595 unique records in our search. Fifteen studies met our inclusion criteria. The percentage of patients with bipolar disorder found on structured psychiatric interviews in 10 of 12 studies ranged from 0.5% to 4.3%, and a positive screen for bipolar disorder using a bipolar disorder questionnaire was found in 7.6% to 9.8% of patients.
Conclusion: In 10 of 12 studies using a structured psychiatric interview, approximately 0.5% to 4.3% of primary care patients were found to have bipolar disorder, with as many as 9.3% having bipolar spectrum illness in some settings. Prevalence estimates from studies using screening measures that have been found to have low positive predictive value were generally higher than those found using structured interviews.

FIGURE 6.4 Abstract from Cerimele, Chwastiak, Dodson, and Katon (2014).

But the article does not provide information on the prevalence of bipolar disorder in people who do not come to primary care. The authors provide no evidence of the specific types of consequences associated with the diagnosis and no information on risk factors. Additional papers will need to be included to be able to report on consequences and risk factors in the PHS section. The findings from the article table displayed in Table 6.3.

TABLE 6.3 Information from a review article on the prevalence of bipolar disorder.

	Cermiele et al. (2014)
Type of paper: Original or review	**Systematic review**
Population	Patients in primary care settings
Sample	
Operational definition of the disorder	Using standard diagnostic criteria for bipolar disorder and bipolar spectrum disorder (subthreshold symptoms) although specifics not mentioned
Measurement strategy	Two methods: 12 studies used structured interviews, 3 studies used mood disorder screening questionnaires
Measurement instrument	Interview tools included, among others, the MINI, the PRIME-MD interview. These are interviews based on the DSM-5 criteria for bipolar disorder. Survey tools included the MDQ (Mood Disorders Questionnaire)
Time frame for reporting	Some studies used 12-month prevalence, others used lifetime prevalence
Rates of disorder	Rates of bipolar disorder or bipolar spectrum disorder ranged from 0.5% to 11.4% in studies that used interviews. Most had prevalence rates up to 4.3%. Survey studies report prevalence of 7%–10%
Definitions of consequences identified	Limited information on consequences. However, part of the diagnosis was based on evidence of impairment associated with the symptoms
Evidence of consequences	No specific evidence included
Definitions of risk factors (variations by sample characteristics)	No information included
Evidence of risk factor relations	No information included
Other risk factors?	

Activity 6.1: Tabling the Information from Sudies on the Prevalence of the Disorder

Now it is your turn.

Identify one or more articles on the prevalence of the disorder you are studying. Complete Table 6.4 to determine if the articles you have obtained contain the evidence you need. In addition to indicating if the article provides the information, provide a brief description of the findings from the article. As you write down the information from the papers, you will have an opportunity to check your thinking.

TABLE 6.4 Assembling the evidence for the PHS section.

	Author/Date:	Author/Date:	Author/Date:
Type of paper: Review or original article			
Population			
Sample			
Operational definition			
Measurement strategy			
Measurement instrument			
Time frame for reporting			
Rates of disorder			
Definitions of consequences identified			
Evidence of consequences			
Definitions of risk factors: (Variations by sample characteristics)			
Evidence of risk factor relations			
Other risk factors?			

It may be helpful to show your thinking, a completed table, and the article itself to a colleague to make sure you are interpreting the material correctly. In your proposal or paper, you do not use the actual words from the article. Instead, you synthesize and report the findings in your own words.

Writing About the Prevalence of the Disorder

To write the PHS section, it may be necessary to read several articles to get all the information you need. You can write short reviews of each of these additional articles to help you keep the information clear. If you use more than one article, you may also need to write a summary of the findings across studies.

Reviewing One Original Research Article on the Prevalence of a Disorder

Here is a sample description of a "made-up" study. (We use "XX" to indicate that we are making up the numbers for the example.) You can use this type of writing template to help you organize the findings. Notice we include information about the authors and date of the study, the research design, the sample and sampling method, the definitions of the disorder, the measurement method and instrument, and the results of the study.

> *Author (2018) conducted a cross-sectional epidemiological study to document the prevalence of depression among young adults. They selected at random a total of XX adults aged XX to XX years of age from New York State using random digit dialing. They defined depression using the symptoms identified in the DSM-V including depressed mood, loss of appetite, impaired sleep and concentration. They examined depression by administering a self-report instrument, the Beck Depression Inventory—II (BDI-II). The authors report that XX% of the sample had mild to moderate symptoms of depression, defined as scores above 10 on the BDI-II.*

Combining Information Across Studies

If you read several articles, the information from each of these articles can be combined to complete the PHS section. You can write sentences which explain and possibly compare the findings from two or more studies. Here is an example of an approach to writing about multiple studies. We are comparing the ways authors from two studies defined and measured the disorders, and we compare the different findings on prevalence.

A study by Authors (year) examined the prevalence of disorder Y, defined as __________________ and measured with _______. In this study the (lifetime) prevalence was XX%. Another review of studies of the prevalence of disorder Y, defined the disorder as __________. The papers reviewed in this article measured the disorder using (name of measurement method) and (name of another measurement method, if more than one was used). This study indicated that the prevalence of disorder Y ranged from YY % to ZZ%.

If the results are different, you can describe these differences. You may wish to explain the differences by examining the methods carefully. For example, the researchers may have used different methods for measuring the disorder or each study may have included samples with different characteristics (e.g., different ages or levels of education).

Activity 6.2: Writing about the Prevalence of the Disorder

The paragraph or paragraph describing concerning the prevalence of the disorder should contain the information listed in Table 6.1 components 1–4 at a minimum.

Write to your paragraphs about the prevalence of the disorder you are studying:

____

____

____

____

____

____

____

____

____

____

____

Writing a paragraph on the prevalence of the disorder.

Writing About the Consequences of the Disorder

Studies of the prevalence of a disorder often provide information about the extent to which the disorder affects the population. The authors provide information about the consequences of a disorder for health, functioning, and quality of life. Information about the impact and severity of the disorder is included to justify the need for the study.

When documenting the consequences of the disorder, researchers provide the types of information presented in Table 6.5.

TABLE 6.5 Information needed when writing about the consequences of the disorder.

The type of consequences that were assessed.
Possible consequences could include:
- Additional impairments in mental or physical health
- Limitations to educational achievement or vocational functioning
- Difficulties in relationships with family, friends, coworkers
- Difficulties in caring for oneself, such as problems managing money or daily routines

The method for measuring the consequences.
Possible methods could include:
- Self-report
- Medical records
- School records
- Employment data
- Family interview
- Other sources

Information about the significance and extent of the association between the disorder and the consequences.

Articles on the consequences of a disorder include information about the relationship between the disorder and the consequences. This information takes the form of comparisons between those who do or do not have the disorder. In some cases, the researchers could report on the proportions of individuals with versus without the disorder who have the consequence (i.e., health difficulties). They might say "*About 10% of people with Disorder XX are unemployed in comparison to 5% of those without the disorder.*"

In other cases, they may report on the odds ratio for having the consequence in one group versus the other. For example, researchers could make statement such as *"Those with Disorder X were more than 1.5 times more likely to develop another mental disorder."* Or they may report group differences in average levels of the consequences. For example, they could write, *"Those with Disorder X had significantly lower levels of relationship satisfaction than those without the disorder."*

The information on the consequences could be summarized in this way.

> *Studies evaluated the effects of Disorder X on physical health, by examining medical records of those with and without Disorder X. They found that those with Disorder X were more likely to be diagnosed with heart disease and diabetes than those without the disorder {Citations}. Additional research indicated that Disorder was also associated with impairments in occupational functioning. Those with the disorder reported that they were less likely to be employed than those without {Citations}.*

The information on the consequences of the disorder also provides evidence about the practical significance of the study. When you write the PHS, you are documenting the consequences for those individuals who have the disorder. But you are also highlighting how many people (or what proportion of the population) are affected by the disorder and its consequences. This information highlights the importance of addressing this problem for public health—for the health of the population. This knowledge is essential for public health officials and healthcare providers who must make decisions about how much and what kind of healthcare to provide.

Activity 6.3: Writing about the Consequences

Clearly explain the consequences of the disorder you are studying in a paragraph. Identify the type of consequences and explain how it is measured. Indicate the outcomes of the study. Make sure to provide correct APA in-text citations.

____

____

____

____

____

____

____

____

____

Writing About the Risk Factors for the Disorder

Researchers also document the risk factors for the disorder—the variables which are associated with a greater likelihood of developing the disorder. In the PHS section, you identify and describe risk factors and document their relationship with the disorder. In the next section of the proposal—the Theory of the Problem—you will review the implications of these risk factors, examining how they are linked to potential causes of the disorder.

There are often multiple risk factors for any condition. Risk factors can include sociodemographic variables (e.g., age, race, gender, and education); biological risk factors (e.g., genetics); social risk factors (e.g., bullying or harsh parenting); personal risk factors (e.g., temperament, personality); and environmental risk factors (e.g., pollution, crowding, trauma exposure). Understanding these different risk factors can help readers understand how and why individuals are more vulnerable to developing a disorder.

The section on risk factors should include the information in Table 6.6.

As we discussed in Chapter 5, researchers document the relations between the risk factor and the disorder by providing statistical information. This information takes the form of comparisons of the prevalence of the disorder in those who do versus do not have the risk factor. The way in which you communicate the information about the risk factor for disorder depends on whether the researchers are using categorical or continuous variables to represent the risk factor or the disorder.

TABLE 6.6 Information that should be included when writing about the risk factors for the disorder.

The type of risk factors that were assessed in the studies reviewed: • Sociodemographic • Biological • Social • Environmental • Personal
The method for measuring the risk factors: • Self-report • Medical records • School records • Employment data • Family interview • Other sources
Identification of a particular risk factor that will be studied in more detail. (For example, if trauma history is a risk factor, then indicate that all participants will have experienced a traumatic event.)
Information about the significance and extent of the association between the risk factor and the disorder.

If researchers report on the proportions of individuals who have the risk factor who also have the disorder, you can summarize their findings by stating *"In this study, 15% of the individuals with the risk factor developed Disorder X in comparison to 10% of the individuals without the risk factor."* In other cases, researcher may report on the odds of having the disorder in those who have the risk factor versus those who do not. You can summarize these findings using statements such as *"Those with Risk Factor A were more than 1.5 times more likely to develop Disorder X than those who did not have the risk factor"*.

Or researchers may report group differences in average levels of the consequences. You can summarize these findings by writing *"Those with Risk Factor A had significantly higher levels of symptoms of Disorder X than those without the risk factor."*

Special Note: Notice that the types of comparisons made in studies of the consequences of the disorder are similar to the types of comparisons which are made in studies of risk factors for the disorder. The difference is that in studies of consequences, the disorder is usually the predictor. In studies of risk factors, the disorder is the outcome. Each type of study you read gives you preparation for understanding the next set of studies. Practice helps!

Activity 6.4: Writing about the Risk Factors

Find several articles presenting information on risk factors for the disorder you are studying. Clearly explain the risk factors for the disorder. Summarize the findings using the clear description of the statistical outcomes. Make sure to provide correct APA in-text citations.

Writing About Threats to Validity and Gaps in Knowledge

When you are making the public health argument for a treatment outcome study, the arguments you are making primarily concern demonstrating the extent and severity of the disorder you are investigating.

On the other hand, if you are writing a paper reviewing the evidence on the prevalence and consequences of a disorder or the risk factors for the disorder, you need to evaluate the quality of the science and identify gaps in knowledge. The quality of the science is affected by threats to validity in the studies. Threats to internal and external validity limit the conclusions you can draw about the articles.

There are many different approaches to writing about threats to validity. One approach is to identify threats associated with each study you examined. Another approach involves summarizing all the available evidence, clearly stating the threats to validity, explaining why this threat is important, and then providing evidence of those threats from specific studies. Citations are needed for every claim.

For example, if the threat to validity involves limitations to the diagnostic criteria, you could write:

One limitation to the existing research is that most researchers limit their investigation to individuals who meet the full criteria for Disorder X. They do not provide any information on the number of individuals with subsyndromal symptoms (i.e., two or more symptoms without meeting the full diagnostic criteria) {Citations}.

Why is this limitation important to note?

Individuals with subthreshold diagnoses may still have impairments in health and functioning. A strict diagnosis may limit the ability of public health authorities to plan for the treatment needs of the population. If they plan to provide treatment only for those who meet the full diagnostic criteria, they may fail to have enough treatment available for all those who are affected by Disorder X, even if they do not meet criteria {Citations}.

What is the evidence?

For example, studies by (authors, date) regarded individuals as meeting the diagnosis for Disorder X if they met DSM-5 criteria for the disorder. If they had some, but not all required symptoms, they were not regarded as having Disorder X {Citations}.

As you summarize the findings and the threats to validity, you will begin to recognize the gaps in knowledge. These gaps in knowledge may reflect information that is necessary but has not yet been studied. For example, researchers may have studied the prevalence in some groups, but not others. Other gaps in knowledge may occur because the existing research has methodological limitations that prevent researchers from drawing clear conclusions. For example, researchers may have used measurement methods that don't capture some aspects of the disorder.

Putting it all Together

The goal of the PHS section of a treatment outcome proposal is to communicate the importance of the problem. The information included must give the reader a sense of the nature of the disorder, the proportion of people who are affected by the disorder, the seriousness of the outcomes if left untreated, and the risk factors for the disorder. This section leads into the theory of the problem. The risk factor section begins the discussion of the mechanisms that may drive the development of the disorder.

Activity 6.5: Peer Review and Collaboration

Put all the components of your PHS section together. Make sure all the citations are correct in APA style. Now share your PHS section with a peer/classmate. Ask your classmate to review each component to make sure it is present, clear, and contains the necessary citations. Use the rubric in Table 6.7. Review your classmate's PHS section and provide the same type of feedback.

TABLE 6.7 Rubric for evaluating the PHS section.

Component	Information included?	Information presented clearly?	Citation included?	Correct APA format?
Operational definition				
Prevalence in general population				
Consequences of disorder				
Risk factor definition				
Risk factor prevalence, if necessary or appropriate				
Prevalence of disorder in population with risk factor				
Gaps in knowledge				

As you prepare your evaluation of your classmate's work, you can use two types of evaluation processes. First, generate a global evaluation of the quality of the work. Next, to check your thinking, and to make sure you are not letting one or two pieces of information color the whole picture, use a rubric or guide to help you review components of your classmate's response. The rubric allows you to systematically evaluate whether the PHS section included all necessary components in the proper format. Using the rubric also allows you to learn about the way you make global judgments and how those judgments are related to the specific components of the task.

Try it out. Begin the evaluation of a classmate's draft of the PHS section. Generate an estimate of the quality of the draft. Check your thinking by reviewing all the components. Does he or she have each piece? Is each piece properly documented and referenced?

Provide constructive feedback. First point out what your classmate has done well in that section. If the person is missing information, can you figure out why that happened? Did the classmate simply forget or did the classmate not understand the need for that information? See if you can generate questions which will help you determine why your classmate made the mistakes he or she did.

Building Human Capital

Two of the most important skills you can learn are giving and getting feedback. It can be uncomfortable to receive both positive and negative feedback. The person receiving feedback may wonder why the feedback was given. The person giving feedback may worry about the way the other person will react to the feedback. But despite the discomfort, it is critical to develop the skills needed to give and get feedback.

Giving feedback involves being sensitive to the other person's awareness of their own strengths and weaknesses. This requires thinking about their capacity to tolerate the negative emotions that can sometimes accompany potentially critical feedback, and their ability to benefit from the information. Think about what you know about this person and how they handle distress. You can also ask them about how comfortable they feel getting feedback.

Benefitting from feedback yourself requires that you trust the person giving the feedback. You benefit the most when you have some self-awareness and the motivation and skills needed to improve.

If you are receiving feedback, you may worry about why the feedback was given. If you do not trust the person providing the feedback, you may not trust the information provided. To build trust over time, it can be helpful to provide a clear explanation for the feedback and to ask for explanations when you receive feedback.

One of the best ways to improve the feedback process is to be positive first, pointing out all the strengths of the work. It can also be important to restate the importance and value of the work. For example, it can be useful to ask the person receiving feedback why the assignment is meaningful to him or her, and what they expect to get out of completing the assignment well.

As you give specific feedback, it is important to be clear about what you think should be improved and why. The rubrics provided can guide this process. The feedback should be informative. You should provide guidance, not harsh judgment.

Take your time giving feedback, do not rush. And ask the other person if the feedback was helpful.

When you receive feedback, think about what you have learned. If the feedback was helpful, say so. The more you give and get feedback, the better your work will be. You will be learning from a wide range of people and beginning to develop your own judgment about what is necessary for high-quality work.

Terms

Take the time to define each of these terms and consider how to apply them.

Research Methods Terms

American Psychological Association (APA)
American Psychological Association Publication Manual
Citations
Reference section
Electronic reference manager
Random selection
Stratified random sampling
Cluster sampling
Multistage sampling

References

American Psychological Association. (2010). *Publication manual* (6th ed.). Washington, DC: American Psychological Association.

Cerimele, J. M., Chwastiak, L. A., Dodson, S., & Katon, W. J. (2014). The prevalence of bipolar disorder in general primary care samples: A systematic review. *General Hospital Psychiatry, 36*(1), 19–25.

Judd, L. L., & Akiskal, H. S. (2003). The prevalence and disability of bipolar spectrum disorders in the US population: Re-analysis of the ECA database taking into account subthreshold cases. *Journal of Affective Disorders, 73*(1–2), 123–131.

Purdue Writing Lab. (2018). *Reference list: Basic rules//purdue writing Lab.* Retrieved August 25, 2018, from https://owl.purdue.edu/owl/research_and_citation/apa_style/apa_formatting_and_style_g uide/reference_list_basic_rules.html.

Part 2

Theory of the problem

Chapter 7

Theory of the problem: Understanding risk factors and mechanisms

In the next section of the book, covering Chapters 7–10, we examine hypothesis-testing research in more detail. We focus on the underlying models and methods used to develop research on the **etiology** or potential causes of behavioral health disorders. The causes of behavioral health disorders can include potential risk factors for the disorder, as well as variables that may trigger or maintain the symptoms of the disorders.

As you read articles on the causes for the behavioral health disorder you are investigating, you will develop a "theory of the problem." In this theory, you are specifying the relations among risk factors for the behavioral health disorder and the mechanisms that may explain the link between the risk factor and the symptoms (Fig. 7.1).

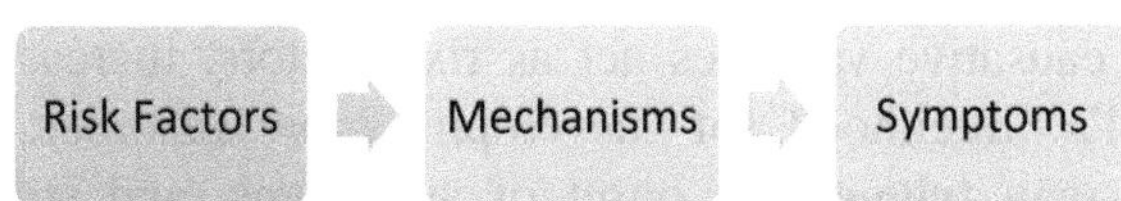

FIGURE 7.1 A model of a theory of the problem.

Examining studies which investigate risk factors and mechanisms provides an opportunity to learn more about basic research methodology. In Chapters 7–10, we discuss the process of building and testing models of the theory of the problem.

In Chapter 7, you will learn more about building **theoretical models** and generating testable hypotheses to examine the causes of behavioral health disorders.

In Chapter 8, you will learn about the different research designs that can be used to test these hypotheses.

Psychology Research Methods. https://doi.org/10.1016/B978-0-12-815680-3.00007-4

In Chapter 9, you will learn how to understand some of the statistical results used to present the outcomes of research studies.

In Chapter 10, you will learn how to explain your theory of the problem and how to write about research on risk factors and mechanisms which provide evidence in support of your ideas.

If you are writing a proposal for a treatment outcome study, the "theory of the problem" sets the stage for the "theory of the solution"—the rationale for the treatment you propose to evaluate. Information about the risk factors and mechanisms contributing to the development of the disorder is critical for justifying the choice of treatment for the disorder. These treatments will address the risk factors or mechanisms to reduce the symptoms of the disorder.

If you are writing a paper reviewing the evidence on different causes for a behavioral health problem, you review and evaluate a wider range of risk factors and mechanisms that may contribute to the development and maintenance of the behavioral health disorder. You may discuss threats to validity in the existing research. As you summarize the literature and identify gaps in knowledge, you will identify areas in need of further research.

Understanding Etiology

Etiology refers to the cause or causes of a disorder. In the case of behavioral health disorders, there can be causes at different stages along the way to the development of the disorder. The causes can occur on biological, psychological, and social levels.

Some causative variables act as risk factors, increasing the individual's likelihood of developing the disorder. Other variables may **trigger** the onset of symptoms, and still other variables may **maintain** the symptoms once they have occurred, and consequently, prevent recovery. Triggering and maintaining variables can be considered the **mechanisms** through which symptoms of the disorder develop and persist.

It is not always easy to distinguish between a risk factor and a mechanism. In this book we distinguish between risk factor variables and mechanism variables by considering the place of the variable in the causal chain. A risk factor variable is a variable further away from the symptoms, a variable which increases the chance that an individual will develop the disorder. In contrast, a mechanism variable is a variable which serves as part of the "fundamental processes involved in or responsible for" developing the symptoms (Merriam Webster, 2018).

Based on this formulation, family history of anxiety disorder is a risk factor. Family history increases the chances that one will develop a disorder. But many other variables may also increase the risk and intervene to promote or to prevent the family history of anxiety disorder from producing anxiety symptoms.

In contrast, a variable such as negative thoughts is considered a mechanism. The negative thoughts are closely tied in time to the onset of the anxiety symptoms, and these negative thoughts are a part of the fundamental processes involved in the onset and maintenance of anxiety symptoms.

Here's an example. Anxiety disorders are among the most common disorders affecting children (Albano, Chorpita, & Barlow, 2003). Childhood anxiety disorders can include separation anxiety disorder, panic disorder, or generalized anxiety disorder, among other disorders. Symptoms can include persistent worries or fears, feelings of anxiety, difficulty remaining calm, and somatic symptoms, such as rapid heart rate or sweating. For children, anxiety disorders can be accompanied by worries about going to school or being separated from parents (Albano et al., 2003). Often children are likely to have symptoms from more than one anxiety disorder at a time (Ginsburg et al., 2014).

There are many potential causes for childhood anxiety disorder, and these various causes can play different roles in the development and maintenance of the disorder at different stages of development. Variables which serve as risk factors increase vulnerability or susceptibility to the disorder. Variables which serve as mechanisms may act more directly to increase or sustain symptoms.

Risk factors for developing anxiety disorder in childhood include, among others, a family history of anxiety disorders or trauma exposure. Risk factors can also include individual characteristics or **traits** that render the person more susceptible to having strong and sustained negative psychological, biological reactions to an anxiety-producing situation (Heim & Nemeroff, 2001; Messer & Beidel, 1994; Rosenbaum et al., 1993).

We can consider one of the risk factors—family history of anxiety disorders—to understand how to think about the pathways linking the risk factors to the disorder. We are asking: How does family history of anxiety disorder lead to childhood anxiety disorder? What are the mechanisms?

Both biological/genetic and psychological pathways may be involved. On a psychological level, researchers have hypothesized that anxious parents may display anxious thoughts and feelings, and children may internalize their parents thoughts and feelings. Parents may also engage in the kinds of parenting behaviors which maintain anxious feelings in children.

For example, researchers have hypothesized that anxious parents might overemphasize the degree to which the world can be threatening, uncontrollable, and dangerous. In turn, children may absorb these descriptions and accompanying displays of emotions, leading to the development of *cognitive vulnerabilities* for anxiety disorder. These cognitive vulnerabilities could include errors in thinking related to catastrophizing or overestimating threats. On a behavioral level, parents who are controlling or overprotective may prevent children from engaging in behaviors which will allow them to challenge their anxious beliefs and develop skills which help them overcome fears (Pereira, Barros, Mendonça, & Muris, 2014).

Healthcare providers can intervene to address the symptoms by targeting the risk factors and the mechanism. They can develop treatment approaches to reduce exposure to risk factors, such as childhood maltreatment, that increase vulnerability. And they can help the individual to modify cognitive vulnerabilities by addressing specific thoughts and behaviors that may trigger episodes of anxiety or maintain anxiety symptoms. In some cases, they may work with parents, helping them to break the cycle of anxious communications with their children (Fig. 7.2).

Developing a Model of the Pathways Among Risk Factors, Mechanisms, and Symptoms

It is often essential to understand the pathways linking the risk factors, mechanisms, and the disorder because treatment for a disorder often addresses the causes of the disorder, including mechanisms triggering or maintaining symptoms. But the etiology or causes of the disorder may not be the same for all individuals. The etiology may depend on the specific risk factors for the disorder. In other words, the mechanisms that cause the disorder may differ depending on the variables that make an individual susceptible to the disorder. Therefore, it can be important to understand the links between risk factors and

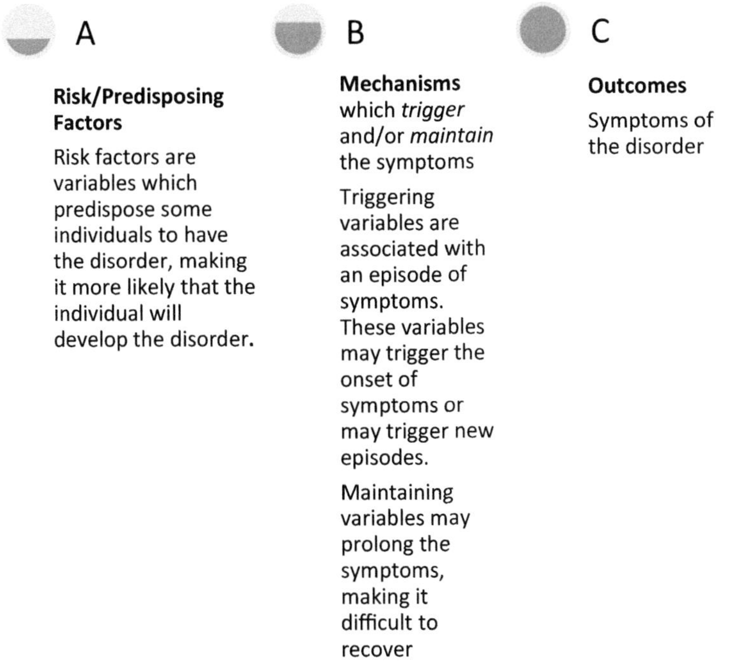

FIGURE 7.2 The A-B-C pathway.

mechanisms to understand how symptoms develop in different circumstances.

As you document relationships among risk factors, mechanisms, and symptoms of the disorder, you build a theory of the problem. We call the relation among the risk factors, mechanisms, and symptoms the A-B-C pathway (Fig. 7.2). Table 7.1 illustrates the types of relationships that must be examined to understand the etiology of the disorder. The table can be used to generate an outline of the kinds of arguments needed to build the theory of the problem.

The theory describes the relations among the A, B, and C constructs. Each aspect of the theory generates testable hypotheses. The hypotheses concern relations among the variables the researcher has chosen to represent the constructs.

To evaluate the theory, the researcher examines the existing evidence supporting each hypothesized link. This includes evidence of a link between the risk factor and the symptoms (the A-C path); evidence of a link between the risk factor and the mechanism (the A-B path); and evidence of the link of the mechanism to the symptoms of the disorder (the B-C path).

TABLE 7.1 Spelling out the A-B-C pathway: The relations among risk factors, mechanisms, and outcomes.

Theories	Constructs	Possible independent variables	Possible dependent variables	Possible hypotheses derived from the theory
Construct A is related to Construct C.	A B	Variable derived from Construct A	Variable derived from Construct B	There is an association between Variable A and Variable C.
Construct A causes Construct B, which causes Construct C.	C	Variable derived from Construct B	Variable derived from Construct C	There is an association between Variable A and Variable B. There is an association between Variable B and Variable C.

The researcher evaluates the existing research to determine if the theory concerning the A-B-C path is supported by the existing evidence.

To develop an A-B-C (risk factors—mechanism—symptoms) model for the disorder you are investigating, you will search for and read research articles that evaluate the A-C, A-B, and B-C pathways, and the full A-B-C pathway, if available. Empirical evidence (i.e., data from a research study) for all three links may not be found in a single paper. Instead, you may need to identify studies testing portions of the A-B-C model. And once the evidence is assembled, gaps in knowledge about this theory may become clear.

Here's an example. Suppose we are writing a proposal to test a new treatment for children's anxiety disorders. In researching the public health significance section, we find some evidence that anxiety disorder in the parents increases their child's risk for anxiety symptoms (Pereira et al., 2014). In this case, the parents' anxiety disorder is the A variable (i.e., the risk factor variable) and children's anxiety symptoms serve as the C variable (i.e., the outcome) (Fig. 7.3).

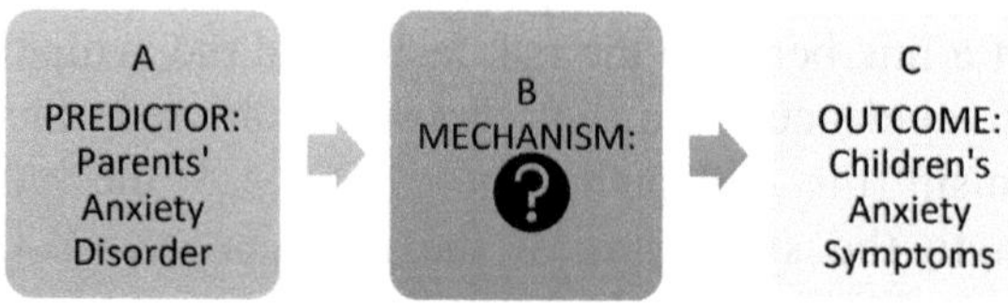

FIGURE 7.3 Parental anxiety disorder is associated with children's anxiety symptoms.

What are the mechanisms that link family history of anxiety disorder to children's anxiety symptoms?

The literature suggests that *cognitive biases* may be a potential mechanism that links parents' anxiety to children's anxiety. Cognitive biases include the tendency to interpret ambiguous situations as threatening and to catastrophize about possible dangers. *Catastrophizing* means anticipating and believing that the worst possible outcome will occur. In turn, these cognitive biases may trigger anxious feelings and maintain those feelings, preventing recovery.

Cognitive biases are one possible mechanism (or B) variable. If there is evidence that parents' anxiety increases children's cognitive biases, that evidence would support an A-B (Risk factor–Mechanism) pathway. If there is evidence of a link between cognitive biases and children's anxiety symptoms, this evidence supports the B-C pathway (Fig. 7.4).

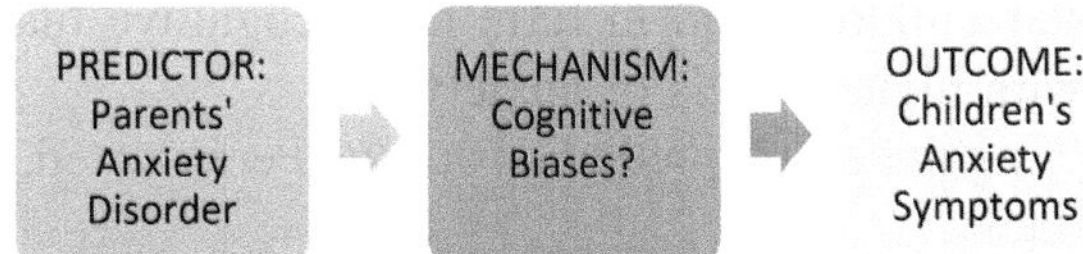

FIGURE 7.4 Cognitive biases may link parental anxiety disorder to children's anxiety symptoms.

Pereira et al. (2014) provide research on this issue.

They tested the relations among parental anxiety, cognitive biases, and children's anxiety symptoms in a study of 12- to 18-year-old children. They examined both mother's and father's trait anxiety, the child's cognitive biases, and the child's anxiety symptoms.

All measures were obtained with self-reports, except the child's anxiety symptoms. The score for the child's anxiety symptoms was a composite of the child's self-reports and the mother's observations.

In this study, the A variable is parental anxiety, the B variable is cognitive bias, and the C variable is children's anxiety (Fig. 7.5).

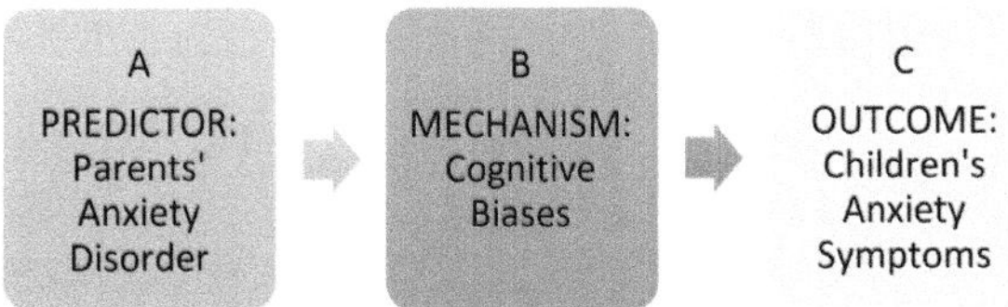

FIGURE 7.5 A-B-C pathway (Parental anxiety–Cognitive biases–Child's anxiety symptoms).

The evidence from the study suggests partial support for the model. Specifically, the authors find some support for the A-C pathway—the risk factor to symptoms pathway. Mother's anxiety was positively associated with the child's anxiety. This is called a positive relation because the direction of the association is positive: As the mother's reports of anxiety increase so do the scores on the measures of children's anxiety.

Pereira et al. (2014) also find some support for the A-B pathway, the risk factor to the mechanism pathway. Mother's anxiety was positively associated with her children's cognitive biases, including catastrophizing and threat interpretation.

Finally, the authors find some support for the B-C pathway, the mechanisms to symptoms pathway. Children's cognitive biases, specifically catastrophizing and threat interpretation biases, were associated with the children's anxiety symptoms.

Pereira et al. (2014) proposed a theory of the problem—a theory that suggests that parental anxiety increases cognitive biases in their children; and in turn, these cognitive biases are associated with higher levels of anxiety.

Table 7.2 organizes the predictions of the Pereira et al. (2014) article in a table.

TABLE 7.2 The A-B-C pathway based on the findings from Pereira et al. (2014).

Theories	Constructs	Possible independent variables	Possible dependent variables	Hypotheses derived from the theory
Parents who are anxious are more likely to have children who are anxious.	Mother's anxiety symptoms	Mother's self-reported anxiety symptoms	Children's self-reported catastrophizing	There is a positive relation between mother's anxiety and child's anxiety (A-C).
	Father's anxiety symptoms	Father's self-reported anxiety symptoms	Children's self-reported threat interpretation bias	There is a positive relation between father's anxiety and child's anxiety (A-C).

TABLE 7.2 The A-B-C pathway based on the findings from Pereira et al. (2014).—cont'd

Theories	Constructs	Possible independent variables	Possible dependent variables	Hypotheses derived from the theory
Parents who are anxious shape cognitive biases in their children, and these cognitive biases lead to symptoms of anxiety in children.	Children's cognitive biases	Children's self-reported catastrophizing	A composite measure of children's anxiety that combines children's self-reports and mother's observations	There is a positive relation between mother's anxiety and child's cognitive biases (A-B).
	Children's anxiety symptoms	Children's self-reported threat interpretation bias		There is a positive relation between father's anxiety and child's cognitive biases (A-B). There is positive relation between child's cognitive biases and child's anxiety symptoms (B-C).

Mediator and Moderator Variables

The picture of the A-B-C relationships or the risk factor—mechanism—symptoms relationship model depicts the mechanism as mediating the relationship between the risk factor and the symptoms.

Mediator Variables

A **mediator variable** is a variable that explains the relationship between two variables. In the case of the Pereira et al. (2014), cognitive biases are proposed as mediator variables, mediating or explaining the relationship between parents' anxiety and their children's anxiety (Fig. 7.6).

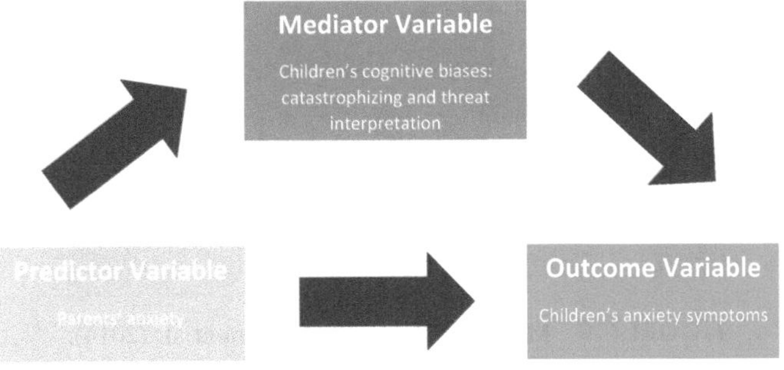

FIGURE 7.6 Mediation.

Moderator Variables

In contrast, moderator variables affect the relations between the predictor and outcome variables. If a variable moderates a relationship between the predictor and the outcome, it could be the case that the relationship is positive for one level of the moderator, and negative for the other level. Or the relationship could be very strong for one level of the moderator variables and weak or nonexistent for the other level (Fig. 7.7).

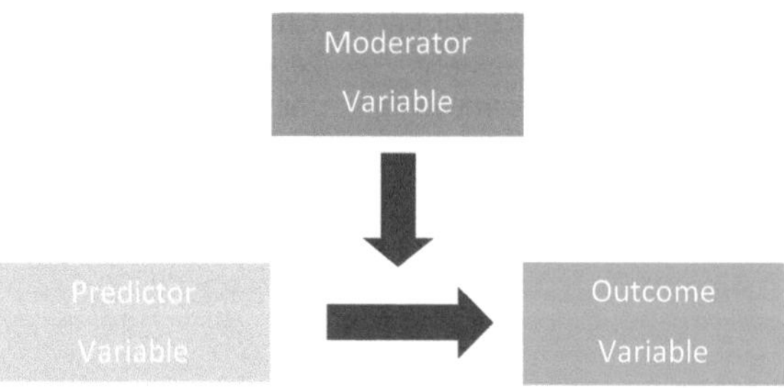

FIGURE 7.7 Moderation.

For example, Pereira et al. (2014) point out that mothers and fathers often have different roles and responsibilities in the family. The authors hypothesized that the parent's role in the family might affect the role of parental anxiety in explaining children's anxiety. They are proposing that the parent's role moderates the relationship between parental anxiety and children's anxiety.

The authors of the Pereira et al. (2014) article did not specifically test moderation. Testing moderation requires specific types of analyses. However, the authors propose and test the effects of parents' anxiety on children's anxiety separately for mothers and fathers. They find a significant relation between mothers' anxiety and children's anxiety, but no relation between fathers' anxiety and children's anxiety (Fig. 7.8).

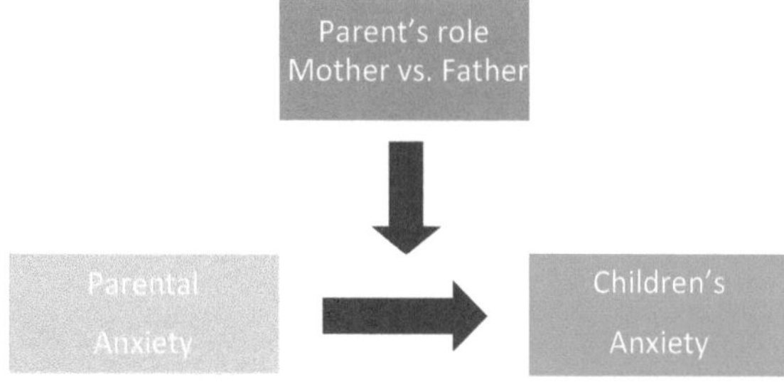

FIGURE 7.8 Moderation based on Pereira et al. (2014).

Researching the Evidence for the "Theory of the Problem"

To generate a theory of the problem, you need to read and evaluate basic research on the risk factors for the disorder and the mechanisms that trigger or maintain the symptoms of the disorder you are studying. Just as you did for the PHS section, you need to read peer-reviewed empirical and review articles. Peer-reviewed articles are articles which have been reviewed by other scientists to determine the quality and accuracy of the research.

But how do you start finding out which mechanisms might contribute to the disorder you are studying? There are so many mechanisms on a biological, psychological, and social level that may trigger or maintain behavioral health disorders.

Descriptions of Potential Mechanisms

Many potential mechanisms can be found in the Research Domain Criteria (RDoC). The RDoC is a template developed by the National Institute of Mental Health to help organize research on the mechanisms that might cause or contribute to mental disorders (National Institute of Mental Health, 2018). This is only one strategy for organizing the research, but it can be a useful approach.

The possible mechanisms are organized into different domains including **cognitive processes, social processes, negative valence, positive valence, and activation** and **arousal**. For each domain, the template identifies constructs and variables on multiple levels, including the levels of genes, molecules, cells, neural circuits, physiological behavior, and self-reports. These different constructs and accompanying variables may play different roles in contributing to or causing a behavioral health disorder. You can see the constructs included in the template at https://www.nimh.nih.gov/research-priorities/rdoc/constructs/rdoc-matrix.shtml.

To simplify the presentation of these ideas, we focus on mechanisms described in the RDoC, but limit our discussion to those mechanisms that can be assessed using constructs associated with behavior and self-report of internal experiences. These mechanisms can be assessed using measurement methods that involve observations, psychological testing, or self-reports. In the following section, we briefly review basic information about some of the mechanisms that might be involved in many psychological disorders. This information is intended to provide basic examples of the kinds of psychological mechanisms that could be involved in behavioral health disorders. Your research will help you identify these and other mechanisms that may play a role in the etiology of the disorder you are studying.

Problems in cognitive processes. Many people with anxiety disorders and mood disorders have difficulty with **cognitive control** (Hofmann, Schmeichel, & Baddeley, 2012; Joormann & Gotlib, 2010). Cognitive control processes include those associated with **executive function (EF)** and **working memory (WM)**. When people have difficulties with EF or WM, they may not be able to shift their attention either toward or away from the feared or disturbing situation as needed. They may not able to shift their attention away from their own internal state to help reduce their distress. They may have more difficulty with the planning and organization needed to develop more effective coping strategies. They may show an **attentional bias**, attending more closely to threatening information (Fig. 7.9).

FIGURE 7.9 Problems with cognitive control processes are linked to many behavioral health disorders.

Therefore, many researchers have investigated the role of different facets of cognitive control (e.g., attentional bias, the capacity to shift perspective, etc.). They examine whether cognitive control–related variables trigger and/or maintain anxiety and mood (Everaert, Bronstein, Cannon, & Joormann, 2018).

Problems in negative valence. The development of different types of behavioral health problems often involves problems in the regulation of **negative emotions and mood** (Sellbom, Ben-Porath, & Bagby, 2008). These problems can include difficulties with **mood reactivity** or emotionality under stress (Gross, 2001). Specifically, individuals who have very intense internal physical and emotional reactions to threats may be more likely to develop some kinds of anxiety disorders and posttraumatic stress disorder (Bar-Haim, Lamy, Pergamin, Bakermans-Kranenburg, & Van Ijzendoorn, 2007; Britton, Lissek, Grillon, Norcross, & Pine, 2011) (Fig. 7.10).

FIGURE 7.10 Problems with negative mood and related thoughts are linked to many behavioral health disorder.

Behavioral health problems can also be triggered and maintained by different negative beliefs or **cognitions** about the self, the world at large, and/or the future (Beck, 2005). Negative beliefs have been associated with depressive symptoms (Young, Klosko, & Weishaar, 2003); posttraumatic stress disorder (Foa, Ehlers, Clark, Tolin, & Orsillo, 1999); and anxiety symptoms (Pereira et al., 2014; Stöber, 2000).

Negative emotions or fear of negative emotions can trigger behavioral responses, including **avoidance**, which can contribute to behavioral health disorders (Dymond & Roche, 2009; Hayes, Wilson, Gifford, Follette, & Strosahl, 1996). Avoidance of anxiety-producing situations prevents recovery and can maintain symptoms (Clark, 1999; Foa & Kozak, 1986; Newman & Llera, 2011). When avoidance leads to a failure to engage in positive activities or self-affirming activities, individuals may become depressed (Borkovec, Alcaine, & Behar, 2004; Newman, Szkodny, Llera, & Przeworski, 2011).

Problems in positive valence. Problems in the regulation of positive mood and pleasure responses can also contribute to behavioral health problems. Some individuals may feel the pleasure associated with certain substances or foods or other activities more intensely than other people do and have a strong drive to have those pleasurable experiences (Beaver et al., 2006). Differences in responsiveness to rewards can have implications for the development of different behavioral health problems as individuals may have a tendency to value immediately available rewards more than those in the future (Bickel et al, 2019). Specifically, differences in **reward sensitivity** has been associated with increased risk for obesity and substance use (Beaver et al., 2006; Kim-Spoon et al., 2016) (Fig. 7.11).

FIGURE 7.11 Problems in the regulation of positive mood or pleasure are also implicated in some behavioral health disorders.

Problems in social processes. Problems in social relationships can also contribute to the development of behavioral health disorders. Difficulties expressing emotion or understanding emotional expression in others can undermine the development of the social skills needed for successful interactions. Problems in social processes may also include difficulties with **mental representations** of the self and others, also called schemas. Both negative schemas about others and impairments in social functioning have been consistently associated with depression (Calvete, 2014; Hammen, 2018).

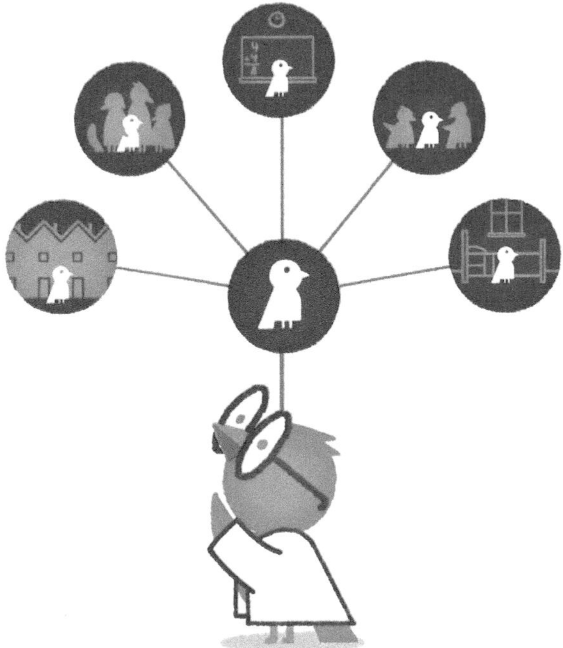

Problems in arousal regulatory systems. Problems in arousal regulatory systems can also contribute to and can also be a symptom of many behavioral health disorders. Problems in arousal regulation can include difficulties regulating energy throughout the day, making it difficult to engage in routine tasks. These problems can also include difficulties in getting to sleep, staying asleep, or maintaining a consistent bedtime and waking routine. Other difficulties can include problems in **circadian rhythms**, the rhythms that set your internal clock and wakefulness, sleep, and energy. Difficulties with arousal and regulatory systems have been associated with mood disorders, especially bipolar disorder (Takaesu, 2018) (Fig. 7.12).

FIGURE 7.12 Problems in arousal and activation have been linked to many behavior health problems.

Creating a cascade of difficulty. All the mechanisms we discussed above can contribute to these problems. These mechanisms can operate in series or in tandem, multiplying the negative outcomes. For example, problems in shifting attention away from a feared situation or negative emotions can leave people unable to reduce the intensity of anxiety they feel (Joormann & Vanderlind, 2014). Although one mechanism can influence another, in rigorous studies, we are careful to separate out each mechanism and clearly identify the variables we are studying.

To understand these psychological mechanisms in more detail, it can be useful to read clinically oriented articles. These papers describe a case or a theory, but they usually do not involve specific tests of hypotheses or include much quantitative data (e.g., Fresco, Mennin, Heimberg, & Ritter, 2013; Hawke & Provencher, 2011; Newman & Llera, 2011). The case illustrations can help you form a mental picture of the way the mechanisms operate.

Establishing a B-C Pathway

Start by gathering evidence about the B-C (mechanism to symptoms) path. This evidence may be found in articles that explicitly test the B-C path. The evidence may also be found in articles that assess the A-C (risk factors to symptoms) path, but also include measures of the B variable (mechanisms). Treatment outcome papers may also include information on the mechanism. In these cases, the researchers may be investigating whether the treatment affects the mediator/mechanism as well as the outcome.

You will need patience and persistence to find the evidence you need to build the A-B-C pathway. Use Google Scholar or a similar search engine. You can also use your library website and services such as EBSCO or Proquest and the specific databases of PsychInfo, PsycArticles, or Medline. It may also be helpful to use Interlibrary Loan Services from your school library if you are having trouble accessing a specific article.

To find evidence on the B-C path, begin by using search terms that include the name of the disorder you are researching and one of the mechanisms. For example, in the first search bar, list the name of the disorder (e.g., a specific phobia, GAD, SAD, depression, smoking) and in the second search bar, list one of the psychological mechanisms listed in Table 7.3 (or use other mechanisms listed in the RDoC). In Table 7.3 we provide examples of mechanisms from different dimensions. Many more mechanisms are possible. Look for the most recent literature—confine the searches to the last five years. Then repeat with a new mechanism (Fig. 7.13).

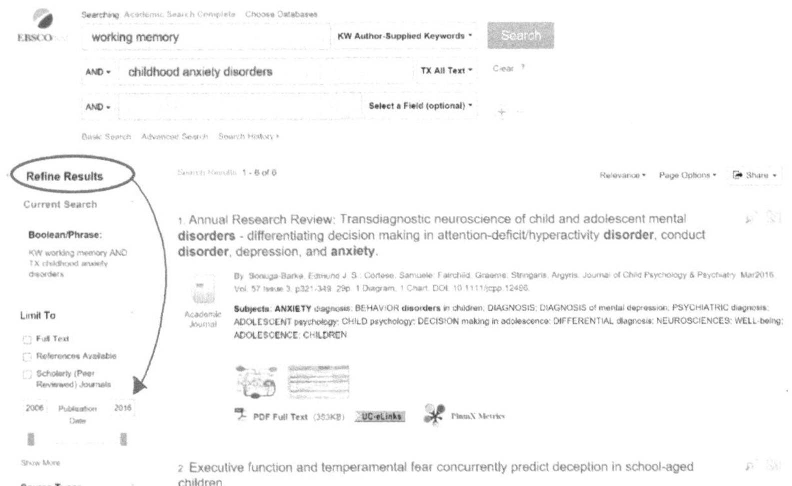

FIGURE 7.13 Sample search of literature for the B-C path.

TABLE 7.3 Finding and tabling evidence for the B-C pathway.

Potential mechanisms	Disorder	Reference
COGNITIVE CONTROL		
Working memory		
Executive function		
Attentional biases		
NEGATIVE VALENCE		
Negative moods		
Negative cognitions		
Maladaptive schemas		
POSITIVE VALENCE		
Reward sensitivity		
Reward Satiation		
Delay discounting		
SOCIAL PROCESSES		
Social isolation		
Attachment and affiliation		
Interpersonal conflict		
AROUSAL		
Circadian rhythm difficulties		
Sleep difficulties		
Regulation of physiological reactivity		

Activity 7.1: Psychological Mechanisms—Finding Evidence for the B-C Pathway

If there are papers which link each of the different mechanisms to the disorder, write down the reference (Author/Date) as shown in Table 7.4. If the article seems appropriate for your topic, download the pdf and save it to the directory you are using to store articles for your proposal.

TABLE 7.4 Mechanisms linked to SAD.

Potential Mechanisms	Disorder: Social Anxiety	Disorder: Social Anxiety
working memory	Judah, Grant, Lechner and Mills (2013)	Moriya (2018)

Not all disorders will be associated with all mechanisms. Practice by pairing the disorder you are studying with at least five different mechanisms to get a more general understanding of the types of mechanisms which may be involved in the disorder. You may be able to add terms to the table if you find different names for these and other constructs. Use Table 7.3 to identify mechanisms for the disorder you are studying.

Understanding the Articles on the Mechanisms to Disorder B-C Pathway

Now it is time to start the close reading of the articles on the B-C path. It is useful to start with articles linking the B (mechanism) to the C (symptoms of the disorder) because we want to make sure there is evidence that the mechanism is related to the disorder. Then we can determine if it is worth examining the A-B articles, the articles that link the risk factor to the mechanism (Fig. 7.14).

The process of obtaining and understanding articles about the B-C pathway can be a little perplexing. When we conceptualize the B-C pathway, we think of the mechanism as the predictor or independent variable (IV) and the disorder or symptoms of the disorder as the outcome or dependent variable (DV). The picture we draw of the model puts the mechanism in the position of the predictor and symptoms of the disorder are in the position of the outcome.

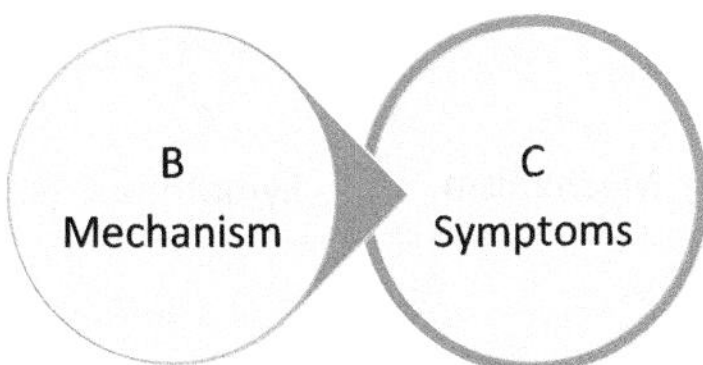

FIGURE 7.14 B to C pathway.

But sometimes you can obtain valuable information about the B-C pathway, even when researchers formulate the problem differently and test the hypothesis in a different way. In these cases, researchers may use the disorder as the predictor and the mechanism as an outcome. They test the hypothesis that symptoms of the disorder predict the level of the mechanism.

Here is an example. Articles about children's anxiety disorders, including separation anxiety, indicate that **attentional biases** are potential mechanisms contributing to the symptoms (Pergamin-Hight, Naim, Bakermans-Kranenburg, van IJzendoorn, & Bar-Haim, 2015). Children are regarded as displaying an attentional bias toward threatening information if they pay greater attention to stimuli that are threatening versus neutral or pleasant. One way to measure attentional biases to threat includes measuring reaction times to threatening stimuli versus less threatening stimuli.

If you are looking for evidence that attentional bias is the mechanism and children's anxiety is the outcome, you might look for an article in which there are sentences with this type of structure: *"Attentional bias to threat was associated with anxiety in children"* or *"Attentional bias to threat predicted fear children's anxiety."* In an article with sentences like these, the mechanism is conceptualized as the predictor and the symptoms are conceptualized as the outcome.

But sometimes researchers might conceptualize the problem differently. Instead of asking if the mechanism predicts the symptoms or the condition, they ask if the condition is associated with the mechanism (Fig. 7.15). They might conduct a study which asks: Are symptoms of Disorder X associated with measures of Mechanism Y?

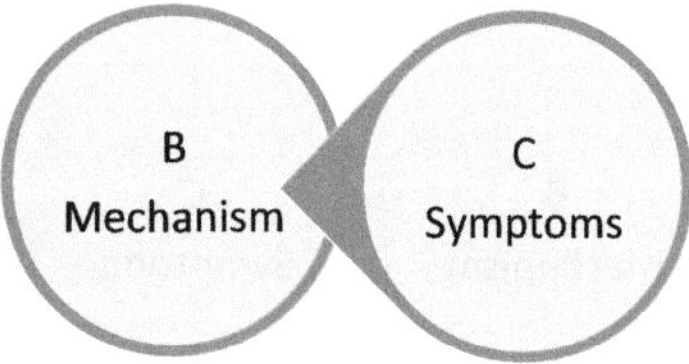

FIGURE 7.15 Is the condition associated with the mechanism?

In this case, the investigators may use continuous measures of both the symptoms and the mechanism. The predictor might be symptoms of the disorder and the outcome is the mechanism.

An article with these types of findings is still examining the B-C pathway. These articles might have sentences with this type of structure: *"Anxiety symptoms were* ***correlated*** *with scores on a measure of attentional bias."* If this is a cross-sectional, correlational study, evidence for the C-B pathway is also evidence for the B-C pathway (Fig. 7.16).

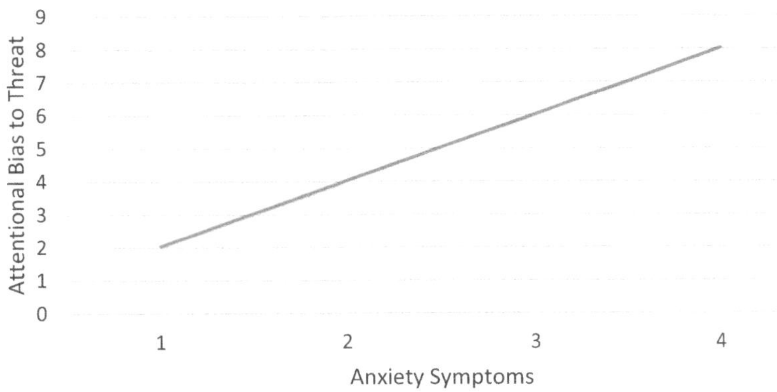

FIGURE 7.16 Correlation.

Sometimes researchers use a similar approach but formulate the question a little differently. They might ask: Do people *with* Disorder X differ from people *without* Disorder X on Mechanism Y? In this case the predictor in the study is a categorical variable. The variable could be "Disorder." The variable has two levels (With the disorder vs. Without the disorder). For example, if we ask the question "Do children with (vs. without) Anxiety Disorder have higher levels of attentional bias?", then the predictor is "Disorder." The predictor has two levels: With Anxiety Disorder and Without Anxiety Disorder. The outcome is Attentional Bias (Fig. 7.17).

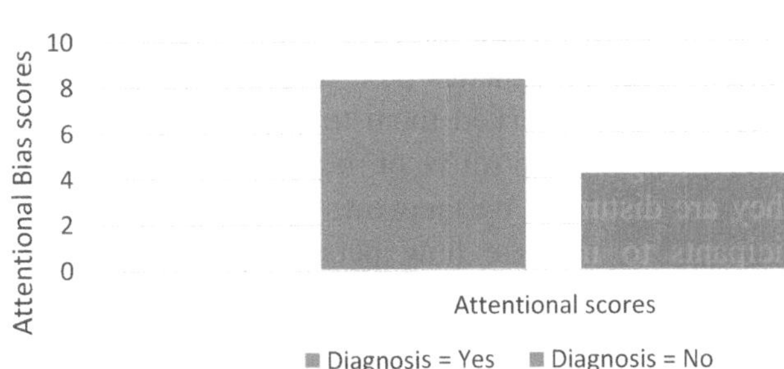

FIGURE 7.17 Notice in this figure, the data are divided by the predictor groups: With versus Without the diagnosis.

In studies in which the authors are using the diagnosis as the predictor, you may see sentences with a structure like this: "*There are differences between those with the disorder and those without the disorder on the mechanism.*" An example related to anxiety disorders might include a sentence like: "*There are differences between children with anxiety disorder and those without anxiety disorder in attentional bias.*"

Authors may also use the terms "healthy controls" or "unaffected individuals" to refer to people without the disorder. Therefore, the sentences may be stated like this: *"There were differences between those with anxiety disorder and healthy controls in attentional bias."*

An article reporting these types of comparisons is likely to be a good article providing evidence for the B-C pathway where C refers to the symptoms and B refers to the mechanism. Even though the disorder is considered the predictor in this study, the data still provide evidence of a link between the mechanism and the symptoms of the disorder.

Table 7.5 may help you think about the differences between the types of studies that can be used to document the B-C path. Imagine we want to build an A-B-C model in which *appraisals* are the B variables and *OCD symptoms* are the C variables. To determine if the articles provide support for the B-C pathway, first we identity the predictor and outcome variables. Next, we determine what type of hypothesis that authors are testing. Table 7.5 lists information from the excerpts from both studies.

We can examine the abstract and text from each paper to understand how to fill in the table (Fig. 7.18).

In the article by Corcoran and Woody (2008), the authors test the hypothesis that appraisals of thoughts (i.e., how people think and feel about their own thoughts) are a mechanism associated with symptoms of OCD. They hypothesize that the more people view intrusive thoughts as disturbing and personally salient, the more likely they are to have OCD symptoms. The authors make this hypothesis clear in the abstract and in the introduction when they state that cognitive theories predict that appraisals of thoughts will lead to OCD symptoms (See highlighted sentences from the introduction given in Fig. 7.19).

To test this hypothesis, the researchers asked participants to read a series of vignettes (i.e., stories) about thoughts they might have. Then they asked them to report how much they appraise these thoughts as positive or negative (i.e., to indicate how much they are disturbed by their own thoughts). They also asked participants to indicate how personally relevant they find these thoughts. They found that negative appraisals are associated with OCD symptoms. The authors frame the hypothesis so that the predictor is the mechanism (appraisals) and the outcome is symptoms of OCD. This approach lines up with a B-C pathway. Notice how this information is listed in Table 5.

As shown in Table 7.5, mechanism the article is discussing is *appraisals.* The outcome was *OCD symptoms.* The authors do not divide people into those with versus without OCD symptoms.

ELSEVIER

Available online at www.sciencedirect.com

Behaviour Research and Therapy 46 (2008) 71–83

BEHAVIOUR RESEARCH AND THERAPY

www.elsevier.com/locate/brat

Appraisals of obsessional thoughts in normal samples☆

Kathleen M. Corcoran*[,1], Sheila R. Woody

Department of Psychology, University of British Columbia

Received 17 May 2007; received in revised form 5 October 2007; accepted 16 October 2007

Abstract

Cognitive theories of obsessive–compulsive disorder (OCD) posit that appraisals about the significance of thoughts are critical in the development and persistence of obsessions. Rachman [(1997). A cognitive theory of obsessions. *Behaviour Research and Therapy*, *35*, 793–802.] proposes that appraisals of unwanted thoughts distinguish clinical obsessions from normal intrusive thoughts; thoughts appraised as important and personally significant are expected to be upsetting and recur. Appraisals are also expected to be related to symptoms of OCD. To explore the features of normal appraisals of obsession-like thoughts, nonclinical participants in two studies rated the personal significance of intrusive thoughts portrayed in vignettes containing prototypical themes associated with primary obsessions: aggressive, sexual, and blasphemous thoughts. Unwanted intrusive thoughts that were described as occurring more frequently were appraised as more personally significant, but participants appraised these socially unacceptable thoughts similarly whether they imagined having personally experienced them or a friend confiding about having experienced them. Appraisals in both studies were related to subclinical OC symptoms and OC beliefs.

Keywords: Obsessive–compulsive disorder; Cognitive theory; Appraisals; Metacognition; Intrusive thoughts

FIGURE 7.18 Abstract from Corcoran and Woody (2008).

Appraisals of obsessional thoughts in normal samples

Obsessive–compulsive disorder (OCD) is characterized by frequent and disturbing obsessions and ritualistic compulsions. The obsessions, which consist of unwanted, intrusive thoughts, images, or impulses, are highly distressing and tend to provoke active resistance in the form of thought suppression and neutralization. While obsessions per se are a unique characteristic of OCD, most people do experience unwanted intrusive thoughts on occasion (Rachman & de Silva, 1978; Salkovskis & Harrison, 1984). Cognitive theories of OCD posit that dysfunctional appraisals about the significance of intrusive thoughts are critical in transforming "normal" unwanted intrusive thoughts into clinical obsessions (Rachman, 1997, 1998; Salkovskis, 1985; Salkovskis, Forrester, & Richards, 1998).

FIGURE 7.19 Selected excerpt from Corcoran and Woody (2008).

Instead, they examine the relations between appraisals and OCD symptoms. They are testing the hypothesis that appraisals are predicted OCD symptoms.

Brief Description of an Article by Libby et al. (2004)

Now we can examine a second study. We describe the study here, Instead of including the article text.

Libby et al. (2004) also examine appraisals and their relation to OCD in a sample of young people ages 11−18 years. They test the hypothesis that people with OCD will differ from those with another anxiety disorder or from healthy controls in their appraisals. The authors specifically evaluate appraisals related to inflated responsibility (i.e., inaccurately appraising oneself as highly responsible for outcomes), thought−action fusion (i.e., appraisals related to the links between what one feels and what one does), and perfectionism (i.e., appraisals related to the need to be perfect). Participants are evaluated to determine their diagnosis and asked to complete questionnaires to assess their appraisals.

In the first analysis in this study, the authors are framing "Diagnosis" as the predictor and "Appraisals" as the outcome. (Here they are testing a C-B path.) In the second analysis, they test the hypothesis that the intensity of appraisals, particularly appraisals related to inflated responsibility, is positively correlated with the severity of OCD symptoms. (Now they frame the analyses as a B-C path.) In both analyses they find evidence for the relations of appraisals to OCD symptoms.

The findings from this study are placed on two lines in the table. This is necessary because two different hypotheses were tested, and two types of analyses were used. In both cases the authors are measuring appraisals and OCD symptoms, but they assign different roles to the variables in each analysis.

In the first analysis, OCD diagnosis is the predictor and different types of appraisals are the outcomes. The levels of OCD diagnosis in the first analysis include having OCD, having another anxiety disorder but not OCD, and having no anxiety disorder (i.e., healthy controls). In this analysis, the authors are testing the hypothesis that having an OCD diagnosis is associated with higher levels of these appraisals.

In the second analysis, appraisal scores are the predictor and OCD symptoms are the outcome. They are testing whether higher levels of these appraisals are associated with higher levels of OCD symptoms.

Researching the A-B (Risk Factor to Mechanism) Pathway

You documented the A-C (risk factor to the symptoms) pathway in the PHS section. Now we need to explain and document the A-B (risk factor to mechanism) pathway.

TABLE 7.5 **Identifying hypotheses.**

Author/date	**The student's B variable**	**The student's C variable**	**Predictor variable in the article**	**Outcome variable in the article**	**Is the author testing the hypothesis that *"People with Disorder X differ from people without Disorder X on Mechanism Y?"* If so, write the hypothesis using the variables included in the study**	**Is the author testing the hypothesis: *"Scores on the measure of the mechanism are associated with scores on a measure of symptoms of the disorder?"* If so, write the hypothesis using the variables included in the study**
Corcoran and Woody (2008)	Appraisals	OCD symptoms	Appraisals	Self-reported symptoms of OCD	No	Yes. The authors hypothesize: Appraisals of thoughts are positively associated with symptoms of OCD.
Libby, Reynolds, Derisley, and Clark (2004) Analysis #1	Appraisals	OCD symptoms	OCD diagnosis (three levels: OCD, another anxiety diagnosis, or healthy control)	Self-reported appraisals of inflated responsibility, thought–action fusion, perfectionism	Yes. The authors hypothesize: People with OCD will have more elevated scores on these appraisals than those with another	No

Continued

TABLE 7.5 Identifying hypotheses.—cont'd

Author/date	The student's B variable	The student's C variable	Predictor variable in the article	Outcome variable in the article	Is the author testing the hypothesis that *"People with Disorder X differ from people without Disorder X on Mechanism Y?"* If so, write the hypothesis using the variables included in the study	Is the author testing the hypothesis: *"Scores on the measure of the mechanism are associated with scores on a measure of symptoms of the disorder?"* If so, write the hypothesis using the variables included in the study
					anxiety disorder or healthy controls, following threatening stimuli.	
Libby et al. (2004) Analysis #2	Appraisals	OCD symptoms	Level of appraisals of inflated responsibility.	Self-reported OCD symptoms	No	Yes, the authors hypothesize: Higher levels of inflated responsibility will be associated with higher levels of OCD symptoms.

Why do we examine the A-B pathway and look at the role of risk factors? The psychological mechanisms predisposing people to the condition or triggering or maintaining the condition may not be the same for everyone. Therefore, in this book we use an approach to understanding treatment development that involves examining the role of risk factors. This permits us to start the process by considering the full context in which the condition develops.

For example, there are many different risk factors which have been associated with anxiety disorders, including trauma, family history of anxiety disorder, and low socioeconomic status. These common risk factors for anxiety disorder may trigger or maintain anxiety disorders through different mechanisms. Some mechanisms may overlap, others may be distinct. For example:

- Trauma can increase negative schemas, stress reactivity, and avoidance (Blascovich, 2013; Brondolo, Eftekharzadeh, Clifton, Schwartz, & Delahanty, 2017.
- Family history of anxiety disorder may be associated with psychological mechanisms including: attentional bias, increased stress reactivity, increased harm avoidance, learned cognitive biases, and avoidance behaviors (Nikolić, de Vente, Colonnesi, & Bögels, 2016; Suveg, Zeman, Flannery-Schroeder, & Cassano, 2005).
- Low socioeconomic status may be associated with negative cognitions and schemas, heightened stress reactivity, and limited coping (Chen, Langer, Raphaelson, & Matthews, 2004; Ewart, Elder, & Smyth, 2014; Hackman, Gallop, Evans, & Farah, 2015; Haushofer & Fehr, 2013).

Context, Mechanisms, and Interventions

The **antecedents** of the mechanisms—the factors that shape the development of these mechanisms—may influence what healthcare providers say and do in the intervention. For example, the

Activity 7.2A: Identifying and Tabling Important Constructs and Variables

Now it is your turn.

Read the abstract and methods section from Summers, Fitch, and Cougle (2014) (Fig. 7.20).

1. First make a construct list and make sure you can define all the constructs and identify the variables. Sometimes authors will not list the name of the variable. They will simply use the name of the measurement tool (the survey or other measure) or task they have chosen to measure the variable that is derived from the construct. You can figure out the variable the researcher is using by reading the description of the measurement instrument in the methods section. This will help you determine if the measurement instrument assesses a self-reported variable or another type of variable. In this article, some of the outcomes include responses to the laboratory tasks. Use Table 7.6 to identify and define constructs and variables.

ELSEVIER

Available online at www.sciencedirect.com

ScienceDirect

Behavior Therapy 45 (2014) 678–689

Behavior Therapy

www.elsevier.com/locate/bt

Visual, Tactile, and Auditory "Not Just Right" Experiences: Associations With Obsessive-Compulsive Symptoms and Perfectionism

Berta J. Summers
Kristin E. Fitch
Jesse R. Cougle
Florida State University

"Not just right" experiences (NJREs), or uncomfortable sensations associated with the immediate environment not feeling "right," are thought to contribute to obsessive-compulsive disorder (OCD) symptomatology. The literature suggests that NJREs are experienced across sensory modalities; however, existing in vivo measures have been restricted to visual inductions (e.g., viewing and/or rearranging a cluttered table). The present study used a large undergraduate sample ($N = 284$) to examine 4 in vivo tasks designed to elicit and assess NJREs across separate sensory modalities (i.e., visual, tactile, and auditory). Task ratings (discomfort evoked, and urge to counteract task-specific stimuli) were uniquely associated with self-report measures of NJREs, OC symptoms (ordering/arranging, checking, and washing), and certain maladaptive domains of perfectionism (doubts about actions, and organization). Findings have implications for experimental research and clinical work targeting NJREs specific to particular senses.

FIGURE 7.20 Abstract and selected sections from Summer et al. (2014).

Activity 7.2A: Identifying and Tabling Important Constructs and Variables—cont'd

This section provides background on the nature of OCD.

Obsessive-compulsive disorder (OCD) is characterized by persistent, unwanted thoughts (obsessions) and/or repetitive behaviors (compulsions) performed to curb associated anxiety or other uncomfortable sensations (American Psychiatric Association, 2013). Research efforts examining the driving forces underlying OC symptomatology have revealed two distinct motivational domains for compulsions: harm avoidance and incompleteness (Summerfeldt, 2004). Compulsions motivated by harm avoidance are intended to reduce anticipatory anxiety associated with a feared consequence or safety concern (Salkovskis, 1991). Compulsions motivated by incompleteness are intended to prevent or quiet uncomfortable sensations associated with the immediate environment feeling "not just right." Pierre Janet first described the construct of incompleteness as "an inner sense of imperfection" when an action or perception was "incompletely achieved" (Janet, 1903, as cited in Pitman, 1987b, p. 266; Rasmussen & Eisen, 1992). These sensations are commonly referred to within the literature as "not just right" experiences (NJREs; Coles, Frost, Heimberg, & Rhéaume, 2003), deficits in the "feeling of knowing" (Rapoport, 1991), and "sensory phenomena" (Miguel et al., 2000). To minimize confusion that may result from differing labels across studies, we will refer to these phenomena as NJREs throughout this paper, both when discussing previous research as well as the current study. Research indicates that NJREs can be experienced across separate sensory modalities (e.g., looking, feeling, sounding "right"; Rosário et al., 2009; Summerfeldt, 2004). NJREs may reflect dysfunction of the sensory-affective system in which sensory and emotional experiences are not effectively used to guide behavior (Summerfeldt, 2004).

This section explains how "not just right" experiences are associated with OCD.

NJREs are strongly related to certain OC symptom clusters, including ordering and arranging, checking, washing, and obsessing (see Taylor et al., 2014, for a meta-analysis). With regard to ordering and arranging symptoms, studies examining both student (Coles et al., 2003; Pietrefesa & Coles, 2009) and clinical samples (Ecker & Gönner, 2008) have demonstrated a unique relationship between NJREs and ordering behavior and the need for symmetry. Compulsions involving symmetry, ordering, and arranging appear to occur more frequently and are rated as more severe when preceded by NJREs (Ferrão et al., 2012).

This section explains how the authors develop the laboratory tasks to evoke "not just right" experiences.

Some researchers have used in vivo tasks to elicit NJREs in a laboratory setting (Coles et al., 2005; Cougle et al., 2011; Fitch & Cougle, 2013). For example, Coles and colleagues (2005) asked participants to view messy or unbalanced stimuli (e.g., an unorganized bookshelf, a dirty area rug, a desk with one drawer ajar) and rate discomfort, urge to change some part of the room, and fear of something bad happening. The results indicated that these tasks were effective in eliciting discomfort (incompleteness/NJREs) and did not evoke feelings of fear or threat (harm avoidance), demonstrating task specificity in eliciting NJREs. Pietrefesa and Coles (2009) designed behavioral tasks to elicit NJREs (e.g., hanging pictures), and found that dispositional incompleteness was related to task-specific feelings of discomfort and a desire to perform tasks perfectly. Cougle and colleagues (2011) assessed discomfort while viewing a cluttered table, which was correlated with NJRE intensity. In vivo measures designed to elicit NJREs have primarily been confined to visual inductions (e.g., cluttered table, crooked pictures). Thus, it is necessary to develop methods of assessing multiple forms of NJREs to capture the full scope of the construct.

FIGURE 7.20 Cont'd.

Continued

Activity 7.2A: Identifying and Tabling Important Constructs and Variables—cont'd

TABLE 7.6 Construct list, definitions, variables, and measures.

Author/Date:			
Constructs	Operational definitions	Variables	Measurement instrument

Activity 7.2B: Identifying Independent and Dependent Variables

Now determine which construct is the IV/predictor and which is the DV/outcome. Use Table 7.7. to identify the the predictor and outcome variables and the key hypotheses.

TABLE 7.7 Predictor and outcome variables, hypotheses, and B-C path.

Author/Date:				
Constructs	Independent Variable	Dependent Variable	Hypothesis	B-C path? Or another path?

Activity 7.2C: Modeling the Relationship

Create a picture of the model as it is described in the article (Fig. 7.21).

Now try this with the rest of the articles that you have identified for the section of the paper on risk factors and mechanisms for the disorder you are studying.

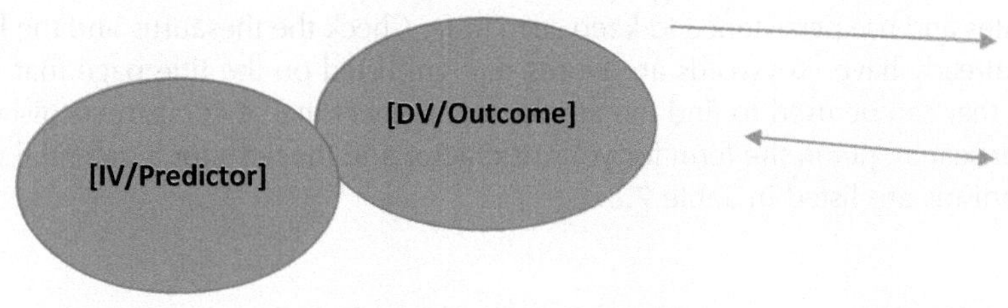

FIGURE 7.21 A model.

instructions and explanations a healthcare provider might give in interventions to reduce stress reactivity are likely to be different for individuals who have high stress reactivity because of trauma versus those who may have inherited a genetic predisposition to high stress activity (Fig. 7.22).

Topics to think about

Think about attentional bias to threat. How could attentional bias to threat develop…

- In people who have a family history of anxiety disorder?
- In people who live in very disadvantaged areas?
- In people who have suffered a traumatic event?

A topic for discussion: Why would it be important to consider the risk factor to mechanism pathway? How could the context in which symptoms develop affect the way we design an intervention?

FIGURE 7.22 Topics to think about.

Activity 7.3: Finding Papers Investigating the A-B Path

Let's practice searching for articles!

Just like Activity 7.1, this activity involves searching for articles. In this case, we are searching for articles which pair the risk factor with the mechanism.

These papers may be more challenging to find. Give yourself enough time to search. Work with your classmates and use persistence to keep searching. Check the thesaurus and the **keywords** in articles you already have. Keywords are words that are listed on the title page that indicate the search terms that can be used to find the article. They reflect the key constructs discussed in the paper. In your search, put in the term for your risk factor and the term for a potential mechanism. These mechanisms are listed in Table 7.8.

TABLE 7.8 Finding papers and investigating the A-B path.

Potential mechanisms	Risk Factor	Reference
COGNITIVE CONTROL		
Working memory		
Executive function		
Attentional biases		
NEGATIVE VALENCE		
Negative moods		
Negative cognitions		
Maladaptive schemas		
POSITIVE VALENCE		
Reward sensitivity		
Reward satiation		
Delay discounting		
SOCIAL PROCESSES		
Social isolation		
Attachment and affiliation		
Interpersonal conflict		
AROUSAL		
Circadian rhythm difficulties		
Sleep difficulties		
Regulation of physiological reactivity		

Activity 7.3: Finding Papers Investigating the A-B Path—cont'd

Fig. 7.23 is an example of an article on an A-B path.

NEW RESEARCH 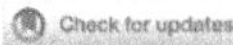

Biases in Interpretation as a Vulnerability Factor for Children of Parents With an Anxiety Disorder

Rianne E. van Niekerk, PhD, Anke M. Klein, PhD, Esther Allart-van Dam, PhD, Mike Rinck, PhD, Pierre M. Souren, MSc, Dr-Ing, Giel J.M. Hutschemaekers, PhD, Eni S. Becker, PhD

Drs. Van Niekerk and Klein contributed equally to this research.

Objective: Children of parents with an anxiety disorder have a higher risk of developing an anxiety disorder than children of parents without an anxiety disorder. Parental anxiety is not regarded as a causal risk factor itself, but is likely to be mediated via other mechanisms, for example via cognitive factors. We investigated whether children of parents with an anxiety disorder would show an interpretation bias corresponding to the diagnosis of their parent. We also explored whether children's interpretation biases were explained by parental anxiety and/or children's levels of anxiety.

Method: In total, 44 children of parents with a panic disorder (PD), 27 children of parents with a social anxiety disorder (SAD), 7 children of parents with SAD/PD, and 84 children of parents without an anxiety disorder (controls) participated in this study. Parents and children filled out the Screen for Child Anxiety Related Disorders (SCARED) questionnaire, and children performed two ambiguous scenario tasks: one with and one without video priming.

Results: Children of parents with PD displayed significantly more negative interpretations of panic scenarios and social scenarios than controls. Negative interpretations of panic scenarios were explained by parental PD diagnosis and children's anxiety levels. These effects were not found for children of parents with SAD. Priming did not affect interpretation.

Conclusion: Our results showed that children of parents with PD have a higher chance of interpreting ambiguous situations more negatively than children of parents without anxiety disorders. More research is needed to study whether this negative bias predicts later development of anxiety disorders in children.

Key words: anxiety, risk factors, affective disorders, developmental psychopathology, interpretation bias

J Am Acad Child Adolesc Psychiatry 2018;57(7):462–470. 

FIGURE 7.23 Abstract from van Niekerk et al. (2018).

Identify the constructs and variables being tested. Determine which is the predictor and which is the outcome (Table 7.9).

TABLE 7.9 Tabling information from an A-B article.

Author/Date	Construct: Risk factor	Construct: Mechanism (mediator)	Construct: Symptoms or Diagnosis, if measured	Variable: Predictor	Variable: Outcome (Mechanism)	Variable: Outcome (Symptom/ Diagnosis)
Niekerk et al, (2018)	Parental anxiety disorder	Negative interpretation bias	Children's anxiety symptoms	Parents' anxiety disorder with 4 levels: parents with panic disorder, parents with social anxiety disorder, parents with both disorder, parents with no anxiety disorders	Children's performance on an ambiguous scenario task in which they are asked to interpret the meaning of a situation	Parents' and children's reports of children's anxiety symptoms (on the SCARED measure)

Continued

Activity 7.3: Finding Papers Investigating the A-B Path—cont'd

What are the findings related to the A-B path? Do the findings support a link between a risk factor and the mechanism? The abstract provides enough information to draw some conclusions, but it is necessary to read the full article to understand the details.

Here is one way to summarize the findings of the van Niekerk article: The findings support a link between parents' panic disorder and children's negative interpretation bias. But they do not support a link between parents' social anxiety disorder and children's interpretation bias. Specifically, children of parents with panic disorder showed more negative interpretation bias than children of parents without anxiety disorder. Children of parents with social anxiety disorder did not differ from children of parents with no anxiety disorder in their negative interpretation bias.

Does this article provide information on the B-C path as well? Yes, the abstract suggests that negative interpretation bias is linked to children's anxiety symptoms, but it is not possible to understand these findings without reading the full article.

Now try to table the information on an article for the A-B (risk factor—mechanisms) pathway that you are reading for your paper or proposal. Use Table 7.10.

TABLE 7.10 Tabling constructs, variables, and results.

Author/ Date	Construct: Risk factor	Construct: Mechanism (mediator)	Construct: Symptoms or diagnosis, if measured	Variable: Predictor	Variable: Outcome (mechanism)	Variable: Outcome (symptom/ Diagnosis)	Does the article provide evidence supporting the A-B pathway? If so, explain the findings.

Building Human Capital

In this chapter you learned a lot of new information. You learned about building a risk factors (A)-mechanism (B)-symptoms (C) model. You learned to understand each part of the A-B-C model. These models reflect the basic research that explains how a disorder develops and who is at risk. This information is critical for understanding how to develop a treatment that is focused on addressing at least some of the causes of a disorder and is targeted at a group of people at risk.

You searched for and found articles. Searching for the articles takes a great deal of discipline and creativity. You need to keep putting in search terms to find the articles you need. You need to read many different articles to find out if you are on the right track. Improving persistence and creativity is very valuable. These are two characteristics you will need for almost any job you might want to do.

As you read the research, you might have noticed that the culture of science is largely an open culture. Knowledge sharing is necessary and encouraged. Researchers build on each other's work. Together they build a body of knowledge.

Take a moment to appreciate the larger culture of science you are joining. Think about the other researchers whose work informs you (and maybe inspires you). Think about others you know now, or might work with in the future, who might benefit from the knowledge you share. Think about the ways in which other people's work supports your own, and your work will support others.

Terms

Take the time to define each of these terms and consider how to apply them.

Research Methods Terms

Etiology
Trigger
Maintain
Mechanisms
Theoretical Model
Mediator
Moderator
Correlated
Keywords
Context

References

Albano, A. M., Chorpita, B. F., & Barlow, D. H. (2003). Childhood anxiety disorders. *Child Psychopathology, 2*, 279–329.

Bar-Haim, Y., Lamy, D., Pergamin, L., Bakermans-Kranenburg, M. J., & Van Ijzendoorn, M. H. (2007). Threat-related attentional bias in anxious and non-anxious individuals: A meta-analytic study. *Psychological Bulletin, 133*(1), 1.

Beaver, J. D., Lawrence, A. D., van Ditzhuijzen, J., Davis, M. H., Woods, A., & Calder, A. J. (2006). Individual differences in reward drive predict neural responses to images of food. *Journal of Neuroscience, 26*(19), 5160–5166.

Beck, A. T. (2005). The current state of cognitive therapy: A 40-year retrospective. *Archives of General Psychiatry, 62*(9), 953–959.

Bickel, W. K., Athamneh, L. N., Basso, J. C., Mellis, A. M., DeHart, W. B., Craft, W. H., & Pope, D. (2019). Excessive discounting of delayed reinforcers as a trans-disease process: Update on the state of the science. *Current Opinion in Psychology, 30*, 59–64.

Blascovich, J. (2013). 25 challenge and threat. In *Handbook of approach and avoidance motivation* (p. 431).

Borkovec, T. D., Alcaine, O., & Behar, E. (2004). Avoidance theory of worry and generalized anxiety disorder. In *Generalized anxiety disorder: Advances in research and practice*.

Britton, J. C., Lissek, S., Grillon, C., Norcross, M. A., & Pine, D. S. (2011). Development of anxiety: The role of threat appraisal and fear learning. *Depression and Anxiety, 28*(1), 5–17.

Brondolo, E., Eftekharzadeh, P., Clifton, C., Schwartz, J. E., & Delahanty, D. (2017). Work-related trauma, alienation, and posttraumatic and depressive symptoms in medical examiner employees. *Psychol Trauma*.

Calvete, E. (2014). Emotional abuse as a predictor of early maladaptive schemas in adolescents: Contributions to the development of depressive and social anxiety symptoms. *Child Abuse & Neglect, 38*(4), 735–746.

Chen, E., Langer, D. A., Raphaelson, Y. E., & Matthews, K. A. (2004). Socioeconomic status and health in adolescents: The role of stress interpretations. *Child Development, 75*(4), 1039–1052.

Chen, E., & Matthews, K. A. (2001). Cognitive appraisal biases: An approach to understanding the relation between socioeconomic status and cardiovascular reactivity in children. *Annals of Behavioral Medicine, 23*(2), 101–111.

Clark, D. M. (1999). Anxiety disorders: Why they persist and how to treat them. *Behaviour Research and Therapy, 37*(1), S5.

Corcoran, K. M., & Woody, S. R. (2008). Appraisals of obsessional thoughts in normal samples. *Behaviour Research and Therapy, 46*(1), 71–83.

Dymond, S., & Roche, B. (2009). A contemporary behavior analysis of anxiety and avoidance. *The Behavior Analyst, 32*(1), 7–27.

Everaert, J., Bronstein, M. V., Cannon, T. D., & Joormann, J. (2018). Looking through tinted glasses: Depression and social anxiety are related to both interpretation biases and inflexible negative interpretations. *Clinical Psychological Science, 6*(4), 517–528. 2167702617747968.

Ewart, C. K., Elder, G. J., & Smyth, J. M. (2014). How neighborhood disorder increases blood pressure in youth: Agonistic striving and subordination. *Journal of Behavioral Medicine, 37*(1), 113–126.

Foa, E. B., Ehlers, A., Clark, D. M., Tolin, D. F., & Orsillo, S. M. (1999). The posttraumatic cognitions inventory (PTCI): Development and validation. *Psychological Assessment, 11*(3), 303.

Foa, E. B., & Kozak, M. J. (1986). Emotional processing of fear: Exposure to corrective information. *Psychological Bulletin, 99*(1), 20.

Fresco, D. M., Mennin, D. S., Heimberg, R. G., & Ritter, M. (2013). Emotion regulation therapy for generalized anxiety disorder. *Cognitive and Behavioral Practice, 20*(3), 282–300.

Ginsburg, G. S., Becker, E. M., Keeton, C. P., Sakolsky, D., Piacentini, J., Albano, A. M., … Caporino, N. (2014). Naturalistic follow-up of youths treated for pediatric anxiety disorders. *JAMA Psychiatry, 71*(3), 310–318.

Gross, J. J. (2001). Emotion regulation in adulthood: Timing is everything. *Current Directions in Psychological Science, 10*(6), 214–219.

Hackman, D. A., Gallop, R., Evans, G. W., & Farah, M. J. (2015). Socioeconomic status and executive function: Developmental trajectories and mediation. *Developmental Science, 18*(5), 686–702.

Hammen, C. (2018). Risk factors for depression: An autobiographical review. *Annual review of clinical psychology, 14*, 1–28.

Haushofer, J., & Fehr, E. (2014). On the psychology of poverty. *Science, 344*(6186), 862–867.

Hawke, L. D., & Provencher, M. D. (2011). Schema theory and schema therapy in mood and anxiety disorders: A review. *Journal of Cognitive Psychotherapy, 25*(4), 257–276.

Hayes, S. C., Wilson, K. G., Gifford, E. V., Follette, V. M., & Strosahl, K. (1996). Experiential avoidance and behavioral disorders: A functional dimensional approach to diagnosis and treatment. *Journal of Consulting and Clinical Psychology, 64*(6), 1152.

Heim, C., & Nemeroff, C. B. (2001). The role of childhood trauma in the neurobiology of mood and anxiety disorders: Preclinical and clinical studies. *Biological Psychiatry, 49*(12), 1023−1039.

Hofmann, W., Schmeichel, B. J., & Baddeley, A. D. (2012). Executive functions and self-regulation. *Trends in Cognitive Sciences, 16*(3), 174−180.

Joormann, J., & Gotlib, I. H. (2010). Emotion regulation in depression: Relation to cognitive inhibition. *Cognition and Emotion, 24*(2), 281−298.

Joormann, J., & Vanderlind, W. M. (2014). Emotion regulation in depression: The role of biased cognition and reduced cognitive control. *Clinical Psychological Science, 2*(4), 402−421.

Judah, M. R., Grant, D. M., Lechner, W. V., & Mills, A. C. (2013). Working memory load moderates late attentional bias in social anxiety. *Cognition and Emotion, 27*(3), 502−511.

Kim-Spoon, J., Deater-Deckard, K., Holmes, C., Lee, J., Chiu, P., & King-Casas, B. (2016). Behavioral and neural inhibitory control moderates the effects of reward sensitivity on adolescent substance use. *Neuropsychologia, 91*, 318−326.

Libby, S., Reynolds, S., Derisley, J., & Clark, S. (2004). Cognitive appraisals in young people with obsessive-compulsive disorder. *Journal of Child Psychology and Psychiatry, 45*(6), 1076−1084.

Merriam Webster. (September 10, 2018). *Definition of mechanism* [Dictionary]. Retrieved September 15, 2018, from https://www.merriam-webster.com/dictionary/mechanism.

Messer, S. C., & Beidel, D. C. (1994). Psychosocial correlates of childhood anxiety disorders. *Journal of the American Academy of Child and Adolescent Psychiatry, 33*(7), 975−983.

Moriya, J. (2018). Attentional networks and visuospatial working memory capacity in social anxiety. *Cognition and Emotion, 32*(1), 158−166.

National Institute of Mental Health. (2018). *Transforming the understanding and treatment of mental illness*. Retrieved September 1, 2018, from https://www.nimh.nih.gov/research-priorities/rdoc/constructs/rdoc-matrix.shtml.

Newman, M. G., & Llera, S. J. (2011). A novel theory of experiential avoidance in generalized anxiety disorder: A review and synthesis of research supporting a contrast avoidance model of worry. *Clinical Psychology Review, 31*(3), 371−382.

Newman, M. G., Szkodny, L. E., Llera, S. J., & Przeworski, A. (2011). A review of technology-assisted self-help and minimal contact therapies for anxiety and depression: Is human contact necessary for therapeutic efficacy? *Clinical Psychology Review, 31*(1), 89−103.

van Niekerk, R. E., Klein, A. M., Allart-van Dam, E., Rinck, M., Souren, P. M., Hutschemaekers, G. J., & Becker, E. S. (2018). Biases in interpretation as a vulnerability factor for children of parents with an anxiety disorder. *Journal of the American Academy of Child & Adolescent Psychiatry, 57*(7), 462–470.

Nikolić, M., de Vente, W., Colonnesi, C., & Bögels, S. M. (2016). Autonomic arousal in children of parents with and without social anxiety disorder: A high-risk study. *Journal of Child Psychology and Psychiatry, 57*(9), 1047–1055.

Pereira, A. I., Barros, L., Mendonça, D., & Muris, P. (2014). The relationships among parental anxiety, parenting, and children's anxiety: The mediating effects of children's cognitive vulnerabilities. *Journal of Child and Family Studies, 23*(2), 399–409.

Pergamin-Hight, L., Naim, R., Bakermans-Kranenburg, M. J., van IJzendoorn, M. H., & Bar-Haim, Y. (2015). Content specificity of attention bias to threat in anxiety disorders: A meta-analysis. *Clinical Psychology Review, 35*, 10–18.

Rosenbaum, J. F., Biederman, J., Bolduc-Murphy, E. A., Faraone, S. V., Chaloff, J., Hirshfeld, D. R., & Kagan, J. (1993). Behavioral inhibition in childhood: A risk factor for anxiety disorders. *Harvard Review of Psychiatry, 1*(1), 2–16.

Sellbom, M., Ben-Porath, Y. S., & Bagby, R. M. (2008). On the hierarchical structure of mood and anxiety disorders: Confirmatory evidence and elaboration of a model of temperament markers. *Journal of Abnormal Psychology, 117*(3), 576.

Stein, M. B., Chartier, M. J., Lizak, M. V., & Jang, K. L. (2001). Familial aggregation of anxiety-related quantitative traits in generalized social phobia: Clues to understanding "disorder" heritability? *American Journal of Medical Genetics, 105*(1), 79–83.

Stöber, J. (2000). Prospective cognitions in anxiety and depression: Replication and methodological extension. *Cognition and Emotion, 14*(5), 725–729.

Summers, B. J., Fitch, K. E., & Cougle, J. R. (2014). Visual, tactile, and auditory "not just right" experiences: Associations with obsessive-compulsive symptoms and perfectionism. *Behavior Therapy, 45*(5), 678–689.

Suveg, C., Zeman, J., Flannery-Schroeder, E., & Cassano, M. (2005). Emotion socialization in families of children with an anxiety disorder. *Journal of Abnormal Child Psychology, 33*(2), 145–155.

Takaesu, Y. (2018). Circadian rhythm in bipolar disorder: a review of the literature. *Psychiatry and clinical neurosciences, 72*(9), 673–682.

Twenge, J. M., & Campbell, W. K. (2002). Self-esteem and socioeconomic status: A meta-analytic review. *Personality and Social Psychology Review, 6*(1), 59–71.

Young, J. E., Klosko, J. S., & Weishaar, M. E. (2003). *Schema therapy: A practitioner's guide*. Guilford Press.

Chapter 8

Theory of the problem: Understanding research designs

In the previous chapter, we examined the types of theories and hypotheses that are generated by research on risk factors and mechanisms. Researchers may begin the process of testing their theories with descriptive research conducted to analyze the nature of the problem. Then they may move to inferential research to permit them to test the hypotheses generated by the theories.

In this chapter, we think about how researchers can test their hypotheses. To collect data, researchers can use both **qualitative** and **quantitative** approaches. To test hypotheses, researchers can use a wide variety **research designs.**

Research designs are the strategies that researchers use to test hypotheses about the relations among variables. Different types of designs can test different types of hypotheses and answer different types of research questions. **Correlational** or **observational** studies can tell us if two or more variables are related, but these methods cannot determine if one variable is the cause of another. **Experimental designs** can permit us to determine if one variable is the cause of another. **Cross-sectional designs** investigate relationships among variables at one point in time. **Longitudinal** or **prospective designs** permit evaluation of changes over time. As you understand these research designs, you will be better able to read the articles you are gathering to develop your theory of the problem.

Descriptive Research: What is the Nature of the Problem?

As we discussed in Chapter 2, descriptive research provides information about the nature of the problem. In research on risk

Psychology Research Methods. https://doi.org/10.1016/B978-0-12-815680-3.00008-6

factors and mechanisms, the problem under investigation is the behavioral health disorder. This type of research can give insight into the way the disorder is experienced, the way people conceptualize or think about the problem, and how many people have it, among other information.

There are different approaches to descriptive research. At the most general level, we can distinguish between quantitative and qualitative approaches to research.

Qualitative Research

As we discussed in Chapter 4, qualitative research can be used to help understand the disorder in more detail. The data generated by qualitative research helps to provide a richer understanding of the context in which the problem occurs. Qualitative research can provide detailed information that can be useful for generating new hypotheses, developing quantitative tools, or designing interventions.

For example, in some types of qualitative research, researchers collect participants' descriptions of their experiences with their behavioral health disorder, including their ideas about the causes and consequences of the disorder. They may use interviews and ask open-ended questions. Researchers can use this information to develop a better way to measure the disorder, or they can use this information to generate new hypotheses about the causes for the disorder. Then, in the next phase of research, researchers can use quantitative methods to test specific hypotheses.

Computer programs can be used to help researchers evaluate the key themes and the messages people communicate about their experiences. These programs and other methods for analyzing the participants' comments provide quantitative outcomes, but they are still methods for generating, not testing hypotheses (Taylor, Bogdan, & DeVault, 2015).

Here is an example of a qualitative study which provides insight into the experiences of women who have depression and anxiety shortly after birth (Highet, Stevenson, Purtell, & Coo, 2014). The researchers interviewed women to identify circumstances in which the women experienced worry and anxiety about themselves and their babies. These experiences could be used to develop survey items about anxiety in these new mothers. These survey items could be used in *quantitative* studies which investigate the causes and consequences of anxiety disorder symptoms in pregnant women and new mothers. From a practical

Women and Birth 27 (2014) 179–184

Contents lists available at ScienceDirect

Women and Birth

journal homepage: www.elsevier.com/locate/wombi

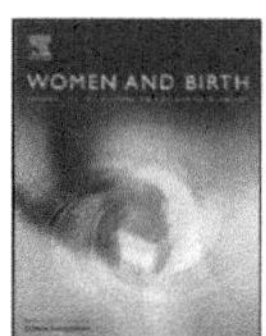

Qualitative insights into women's personal experiences of perinatal depression and anxiety

Nicole Highet[a,*], Amanda L. Stevenson[b], Carol Purtell[a], Soledad Coo[c]

[a] *Centre of Perinatal Excellence, COPE, Melbourne, Australia*
[b] *Centre for Excellence in Child and Family Welfare, Melbourne, Australia*
[c] *Melbourne School of Psychological Sciences, The University of Melbourne, Australia*

ARTICLE INFO

Article history:
Received 1 August 2013
Received in revised form 1 May 2014
Accepted 10 May 2014

Keywords:
Perinatal
Postnatal depression
Anxiety
Symptoms
Personal experiences

ABSTRACT

Background and aim: Symptoms of perinatal depression and anxiety are usually described and understood from a nosological perspective. This research sought to gain insight into women's lived experience of postnatal depression and anxiety, the factors that contribute to these symptoms and the context in which they develop.

Method: Face to face and telephone interviews were conducted with 28 women from metropolitan and rural areas across Australia, who had experienced postnatal depression and/or anxiety within the last five years. Analysis was conducted from a grounded theory perspective.

Findings: Particular symptoms of anxiety and depression develop in the context of the numerous changes inherent to the transition to motherhood and contribute to a common experience of frustration and loss. Symptoms were also associated with feelings of dissatisfaction with the pregnancy and motherhood experience.

Conclusions: The findings provide useful insights into women's experiences of mental health symptoms during the perinatal period, how these symptoms present and the factors involved in their development and maintenance. The need to consider women's perspectives to develop resources and health promotions strategies, as well as within the context of relationships with health professionals is highlighted. The study emphasizes the need for greater, more accurate information surrounding perinatal depression and the need to increase the profile and awareness of anxiety disorders.

FIGURE 8.1 Abstract from Highet et al. 2014.

perspective, these findings can help guide clinicians who wish to understand more about the women's experiences (Fig. 8.1).

Quantitative Approach

Quantitative approaches to descriptive research can also be used to provide information about the nature of a disorder. For example, much of the epidemiological research we reviewed in the PHS section provides quantitative or numerical estimates of the number of people with a disorder. This research may also provide numerical estimates of the number of people who have each

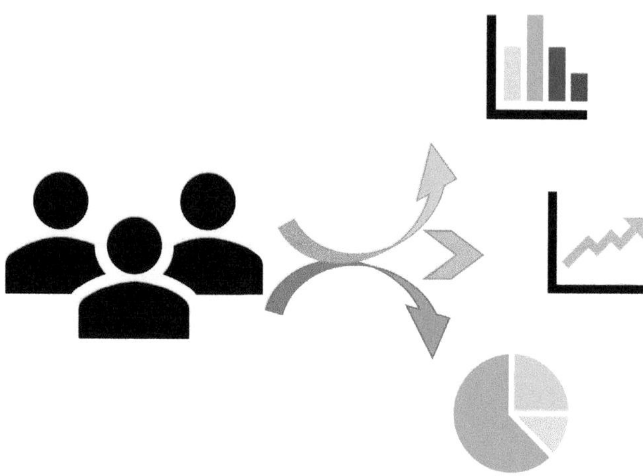

FIGURE 8.2 Moving from ideas to quantitative approaches.

symptom. Research on the overall prevalence or incidence of a disorder is not testing a specific hypothesis. Instead, this type of research is providing numerical or quantitative information about the extent to which the disorder affects the population (Fig. 8.2).

Inferential or Hypothesis-testing in Basic Research Studies Approaches: Are There Relationships Between Two or More Variables?

How do we determine if there are relationships between two or more variables? For example, how do we test the hypothesis that a risk factor is related to a mechanism or to symptoms of a disorder? Both observational and experimental research designs can be used.

Observational Designs

One way to test hypotheses about the relations among variables is to use a correlational or observational design. In these designs, the researcher *assesses* predictor and outcome variables, but does not *manipulate* the predictor variables to determine the effect on the outcome variable. Consequently, correlational designs cannot test causation.

Correlational designs are often used when studying risk factors. This is necessary because many risk factor variables represent constructs that the researcher cannot manipulate. For example, age is commonly investigated as a risk factor for behavioral health disorders. The researcher cannot change the age of the participant. Instead, the researcher must measure the variables as they occur.

Hypothesis 1: **Trauma exposure** is associated with **social anxiety disorder symptoms.**

We can look at an example to understand how risk factors can be studied in a correlational/observational study. A researcher might want to test the hypothesis that trauma exposure is a risk factor for social anxiety disorder (SAD).

The researcher cannot manipulate trauma exposure because the researcher cannot assign some people to experience trauma and others to avoid trauma. Instead, the researcher must measure both trauma and SAD symptoms in all participants. The researcher must use a **correlational design.**

Once the researcher has measured trauma exposure and SAD symptoms, how does the researcher determine if there is an association between trauma and SAD symptoms? The researcher uses **statistical analyses.** Statistical analyses require quantitative data. These analyses estimate the strength and direction of the relations among the variables.

Specifically, the statistical analyses compare the SAD symptoms of people who report they have versus have not been exposed to a traumatic event. The researchers examine the results of the analyses to determine whether the levels of symptoms are higher in the individuals who have been exposed to trauma than those who have not (Fig. 8.3).

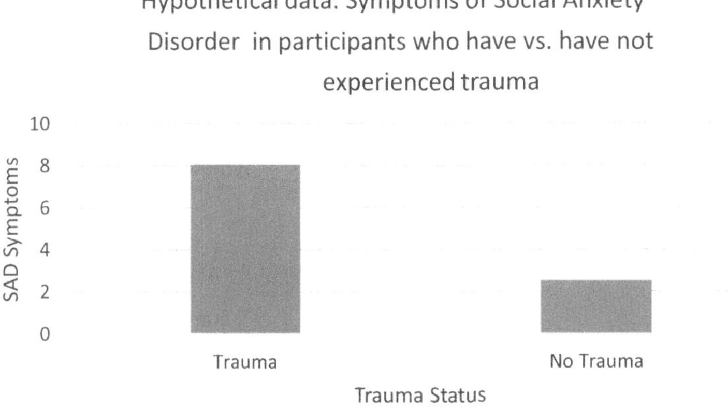

FIGURE 8.3 Depicting hypothetical (made-up) data.

Statistical analyses are also used to determine the statistical significance of the effects, an estimate of the degree to which the relations might have occurred by chance. If the analyses are statistically significant, the hypothesis that trauma is a risk factor for SAD symptoms is supported.

How does the researcher interpret the results of the study?. Just because two variables (A and B) are related, the researcher cannot conclude that one variable (A) causes the other (B). Variable B might cause Variable A. Or it could be that something else (maybe Variable C) causes both Variables A and B.

In our example study, Variable B could cause Variable A. SAD symptoms might cause trauma. One possibility is that people with SAD symptoms are so distracted by anxiety symptoms; they end up at greater risk for accidents or assault.

Or it could be the case that there is a third variable (Variable C) that explains both Variable A and Variable B. For example, high rates of neighborhood violent crime increase the risk for both trauma and anxiety symptoms (Stockdale et al., 2007). Neighborhood violent crime could be a third variable accounting for the relationship between trauma and SAD symptoms. The higher levels of SAD symptoms seen in individuals exposed to trauma may be a function of neighborhood crime levels, not necessarily a function of trauma exposure (Fig. 8.4).

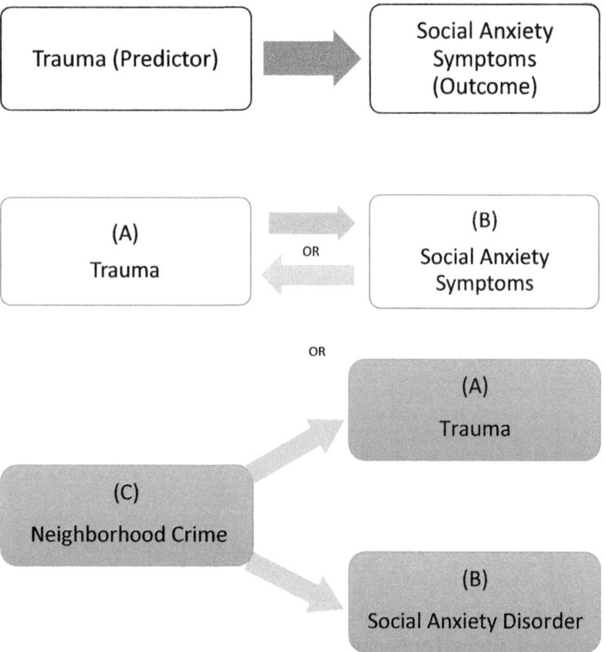

FIGURE 8.4 Modeling relations among variables.

Experimental Designs

Experimental studies permit researchers to test whether one variable is the cause of another. In an experimental study the predictor variable is called the **independent variable (IV)**, and the outcome is called the **dependent variable (DV)**. In an experimental study the IV is **manipulated**. A variable is "manipulated" when the researcher **assigns participants at random** to each level of the IV.

Random assignment means that the choice of assignment to the level of the IV is not influenced by the researcher or the participant. If participants can choose which level of the IV they receive, their attitudes, and not the IV, may affect the outcome. With random assignment, the researcher can examine the effects of the IV on the DV without concerns about bias which might arise if the participant or researcher chooses the assignment.

Experimental studies are generally necessary to evaluate the effects of a treatment. They can also be used to evaluate the role of a mechanism. These studies can help determine if a mechanism causes the symptoms.

Observational Versus Experimental Designs

Observational and experimental studies test different types of hypotheses. In general, observational studies test hypotheses about the relations of a predictor to an outcome. Experimental studies test hypotheses about whether manipulating an IV produces a change in a DV. We can understand this more clearly by looking at some examples.

Here are different types of research designs that can be used to test the hypothesis that intolerance of uncertainty (IU) contributes to anxiety symptoms. IU is a construct which refers to a personal characteristic involving negative beliefs about uncertainty. People who have high levels of IU may believe uncertain situations are dangerous and intolerable. People with IU often experience negative feelings and/or react in avoidant or compulsive ways when situations are uncertain. Researchers have theorized that IU maintains symptoms of depression and anxiety (Buhr & Dugas, 2009, p. 216).

IU has been associated with several different anxiety disorders. The research described in the article by Carleton et al. (2012) uses an observational/correlational design to test the hypothesis that IU is associated with generalized anxiety disorder (GAD). To test this hypothesis, the researchers examined the IU scores in those with GAD as a primary or secondary diagnosis versus healthy controls. They also looked at the extent to which IU was uniquely related to GAD by examining IU in those with depressive symptoms (Fig. 8.5).

Journal of Anxiety Disorders 26 (2012) 468–479

Contents lists available at SciVerse ScienceDirect

Journal of Anxiety Disorders

ELSEVIER

Anxiety Disorders

Increasingly certain about uncertainty: Intolerance of uncertainty across anxiety and depression

R. Nicholas Carleton[a,*], Myriah K. Mulvogue[a], Michel A. Thibodeau[a], Randi E. McCabe[b], Martin M. Antony[c], Gordon J.G. Asmundson[a]

[a] Department of Psychology, University of Regina, Regina, SK, Canada
[b] Department of Psychiatry and Behavioural Neurosciences, McMaster University and Anxiety Treatment and Research Centre, St. Joseph's Healthcare Hamilton, ON, Canada
[c] Department of Psychology, Ryerson University, Canada

ARTICLE INFO

Article history:
Received 17 September 2011
Received in revised form 23 January 2012
Accepted 27 January 2012

Keywords:
Intolerance of uncertainty
IUS-12
Anxiety disorders
Depression
Diagnostic differentiation
Normative
Psychometric properties

ABSTRACT

Intolerance of uncertainty (IU) – a dispositional characteristic resulting from negative beliefs about uncertainty and its implications – may be an important construct in anxiety disorders and depression. Despite the potential importance of IU, clinical data on the construct remains relatively scant and focused on generalized anxiety disorder and obsessive-compulsive disorder. The present study systematically investigated IU, as measured by the Intolerance of Uncertainty Scale-12 (IUS-12), across groups diagnosed with anxiety disorders (i.e., social anxiety disorder, panic disorder, generalized anxiety disorder, obsessive-compulsive disorder) or depression (clinical sample: $n = 376$; 61% women), as well as undergraduate ($n = 428$; 76% women) and community samples ($n = 571$; 67% women). Analysis of variance revealed only one statistically significant difference in IUS-12 scores across diagnostic groups in the clinical sample; specifically, people with social anxiety disorder reported higher scores ($p < .01$; $\eta^2 = .03$) than people with panic disorder. People diagnosed with an anxiety disorder or depression reported significantly and substantially higher IUS-12 scores relative to community and undergraduate samples. Furthermore, IUS-12 score distributions were similar across diagnostic groups as demonstrated by Kernel density estimations, with the exception of panic disorder, which may have a relatively flat distribution of IU. Response patterns were invariant across diagnostic groups as demonstrated by multi-group confirmatory factor analyses, but varied between clinical and nonclinical samples. Overall, the findings suggest IU may serve as an important transdiagnostic feature across anxiety disorders and depression. In addition, robust support was found for the proposed 2-factor model of the IUS-12. Comprehensive findings, implications, and future research directions are discussed.

Operational definition of Intolerance of Uncertainty (IU).

Identification of the predictor variable (diagnoses of anxiety disorder) and a list of the levels of the predictor variable (e.g., GAD, PD, etc.).

Results of comparisons among the different levels of the predictor variable.

FIGURE 8.5 Abstract from Carleton et al. 2012.

Their research uses a correlational or observational design. Carleton et al. (2012) measured variables (i.e., IU, diagnoses). They conducted statistical tests to evaluate the strength of the relations among these variables. They test hypotheses about relationships between IU and diagnoses, but they cannot determine if IU causes a diagnosis of an anxiety disorder (Fig. 8.6).

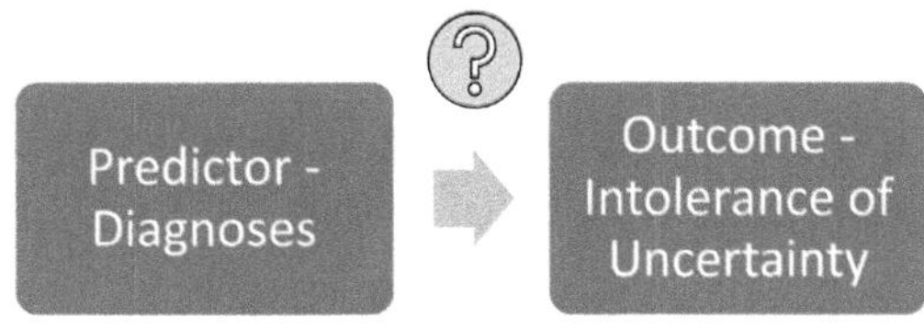

FIGURE 8.6 Hypothesis being tested in Carleton et al. 2012.

In contrast, here is an example of a study which uses an experimental design to test hypotheses about the relations of uncertainty to anxiety. In this study, Ladouceur, Gosselin, & Dugas (2000) manipulate uncertainty and investigate whether the increase in uncertainty is associated with an increase in anxiety symptoms. The authors manipulate uncertainty by assigning participants at random to one of two gambling tasks (Fig. 8.7).

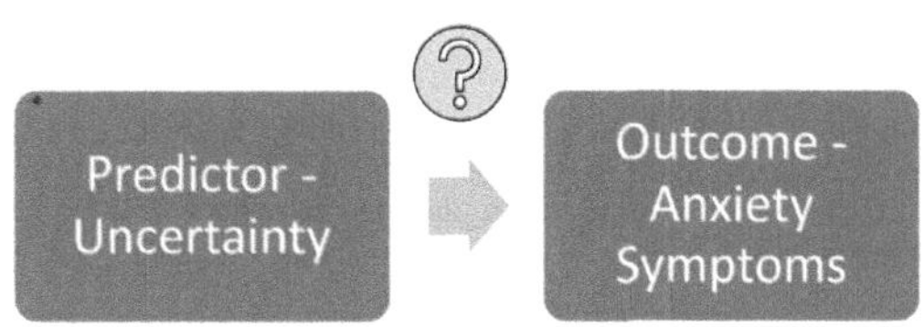

FIGURE 8.7 Hypothesis being tested in Ladouceur et al. 2000.

In the "increasing uncertainty" condition, the participants are given instructions which make them more uncertain about the outcome of the gamble; in the "decreasing uncertainty" condition, the participants are given instructions which decrease their concerns about the outcome. The authors measure whether the individuals in the "increasing condition" worry more than those in the "decreasing uncertainty condition." Because they assign individuals at random to the conditions, and hold other variables the same across conditions, the authors can claim that increasing uncertainty causes increased worry (Fig. 8.8).

We can enter the information on the two studies into a table to help us organize the information about the research design (Table 8.1).

PERGAMON

Behaviour Research and Therapy 38 (2000) 933–941

BEHAVIOUR RESEARCH AND THERAPY

www.elsevier.com/locate/brat

Shorter communication

Experimental manipulation of intolerance of uncertainty: a study of a theoretical model of worry

Robert Ladouceur[a,*], Patrick Gosselin[a], Michel J. Dugas[b]

[a]*Ecole de Psychologie, Université Laval, Ste-Foy, Que., Canada G1K 7P4*

[b]*Department of Psychology, Concordia University, 1455 de Maisonneuve West, Montreal, Que., Canada H3G 1M8*

Received 28 June 1999; received in revised form 28 June 1999

Abstract

Intolerance of uncertainty has been identified as an important variable related to worry and Generalized Anxiety Disorder (GAD) [Dugas, M. J., Gagnon, F., Ladouceur, R., & Freeston, M. H. (1998). Generalized anxiety disorder: a preliminary test of a conceptual model. *Behaviour Research and Therapy, 36*, 215–226; Ladouceur, R., Dugas, M. J., Freeston, M. H., Rhéaume, J., Blais, F., Boisvert, J.-M., Gagnon, F., & Thibodeau, N. (1999). Specificity of Generalized Anxiety Disorder symptoms and processes. *Behavior Therapy, 30*, 197–207]. The goal of the present study was to clarify the relationship between this cognitive process and worry by experimentally manipulating intolerance of uncertainty. A gambling procedure was used to increase intolerance of uncertainty in one group (N = 21) and to decrease intolerance of uncertainty in another group (N = 21). The results indicate that participants whose level of intolerance of uncertainty was increased showed a higher level of worry, compared to participants whose level of intolerance of uncertainty was decreased. These results provide some initial clarifications as to the causal nature of the link between intolerance of uncertainty and worry. These results are coherent with our theoretical model of worry and GAD (Dugas et al., 1998), which stipulates that intolerance of uncertainty plays a key role in the acquisition and maintenance of excessive worry.

In this study, a computerized roulette game was developed in order to increase and decreased intolerance of uncertainty. While taking into consideration the current definition of intolerance of uncertainty, we developed a task whereby the uncertainty of the situation was acceptable for one group, and unacceptable for a second group, without changing either the objective probability of winning (probability of occurrence) or the consequences associated with the situation. The main hypothesis of this study was that, following manipulation of intolerance of uncertainty, participants in the increased intolerance group would report a higher level of worry compared to participants in the decreased intolerance group.

← A description of the ways the independent variable will be administered.

2.4. Increase in level of intolerance

The participants in this group received, several times throughout the experiment, information which led subjects to evaluate their chances of winning (probability) as being unacceptable (e.g. "We already did a study of this type last year, and it's a shame, people had better chances of winning then. People bet on colors, and therefore had one in two chances of winning. Too bad we brought this back to a one in three chance. In fact, I am beginning to notice, by watching people play, that there is a large difference between one chance in three and one chance in two, that is 33 versus 50%. The chances of winning are much worse!").

← A description of the levels of the independent variable.

2.5. Decrease in level of intolerance

The participants in this group received instructions to the effect that the probability of winning, given one chance in three, is high (e.g. "We have already done this with one chance in 36, and people never won, now there is no problem with that, since we have one chance in three to win"). The experimenter also told the participants that it was only a game; if they didn't win, someone else would end up winning so that the Foundation would eventually gets its money.

FIGURE 8.8 Abstract and excerpt from Ladouceur et al. 2000.

TABLE 8.1 Tabling studies using an observational/correlational design and an experimental design.

Author/ Date	What is the predictor or independent variable?	What is the outcome or dependent variable?	Is the design: Experimental? Correlational?	What sentences told you the type of design that was used?	What did the authors do to assess the effects of the predictor/ independent variable?
Carleton et al. (2012)	Diagnostic conditions	IU	Correlational	"The present study systematically investigated IU, as measured by the Intolerance of Uncertainty scale, across groups diagnosed with anxiety disorders, or depression, as well as undergraduate and community samples."	The authors measured both diagnosis and IU in all participants.
Ladouceur et al. (2000)	IU	Worry	Experimental	"The goal of the present study was to clarify the relationship between this cognitive process and worry by experimentally manipulating intolerance of uncertainty."	The authors used an experimental task that involved gambling to manipulate uncertainty. They randomly assigned participants to the condition that increased uncertainty or to the condition that decreased uncertainty. They measured IU after this manipulation.

Understanding the Implications of Different Types of Research Designs

The conclusions we can draw about the study depend on the type of research designs that are used to test relations among risk factors, mechanisms, and symptoms. We can understand these issues more clearly if we examine in more detail the Carleton et al. (2012) study, an observational study, and the Ladouceur et al. (2000) study, an experimental study.

Strengths and Limitations of the Observational Approach

In the Carleton et al. (2012) study, the predictor variable is "patient category." The levels of the predictor variable refer to different kinds of groups, including groups of patients and groups of people who are not patients (i.e., undergraduates and community-dwelling individuals). The outcome variable is IU measured with a survey assessing IU beliefs (see Fig. 8.9).

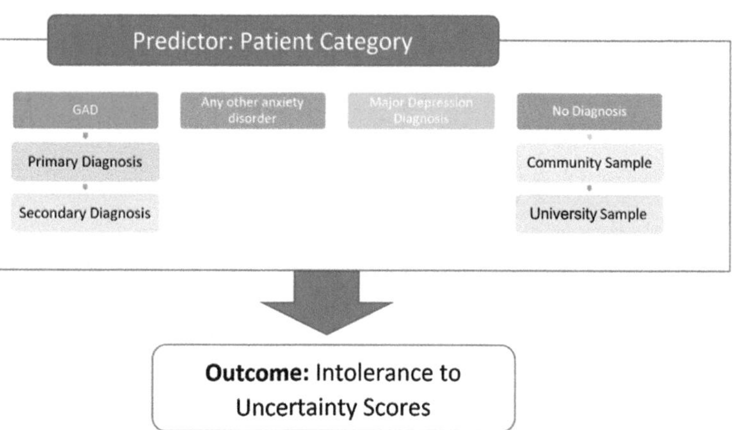

FIGURE 8.9 Depicting the predictor and outcome variables in the Carleton et al., 2012 study.

In this study, the researchers cannot manipulate the IV because they cannot assign people at random to have an anxiety disorder or depression or to have no disorder. Instead, they assess the participants to determine their diagnoses. The researchers used a formal diagnostic interview as their measurement method to assess the participants' diagnoses. The researchers measure self-reported IU in each of the participants by asking the participants to complete a survey measuring IU.

In the statistical analyses, they compare the scores on the IU scale for the different diagnostic groups. (In the next chapter, we will discuss about the statistical analyses they use to test the hypotheses.) The authors find that people with any disorder have higher scores on the IU measure than people without disorders. They find that IU is present across different disorders.

This article provides evidence that IU is related to anxiety symptoms and depression symptoms. Consequently, the findings from this article can provide evidence for the B (mechanism) to C (symptoms) pathway. This is the case, even though the analyses are set up to test a disorder–mechanism pathway.

In addition, the study examines the relations of anxiety diagnosis to IU in a "real-world" sample. Most of the participants were actual patients or individuals living in the community. This enhances the generalizability or external validity of the findings. The results are likely to be relevant for thinking about other patients or community-dwelling adults.

However, the study does not provide other information. The findings cannot tell us if IU causes the symptoms of the disorders. Although researchers observe that IU is related to different types of anxiety symptoms, but they did not manipulate IU. Therefore, they cannot tell if IU predicts or causes these symptoms.

Strengths and Limitations of the Experimental Approach

To determine if IU causes symptoms, researchers need to manipulate IU and then measure symptoms. They need to determine if increasing IU causes an increase in symptoms. The Ladouceur et al. (2000) study we discussed earlier provides an example of an experimental study of IU (see Fig. 8.7 for abstract).

The Ladouceur et al. (2000) study was conducted in the controlled environment of a laboratory, and the participants were college students, not patients. The IV was uncertainty. The DV/outcome was worry. Worry is a principal symptom of GAD and many other anxiety disorders.

This is an experimental study because the researchers were able to manipulate uncertainty. They assigned participants at random either to a condition that increased uncertainty or to a condition that decreased uncertainty. Both conditions involve a gambling task (i.e., roulette played on a computer). The participants were told they were playing to win money for a foundation to help children. Participants assigned to the "Increasing Uncertainty" condition were told that they were unlikely to win because the odds were so poor. Participants assigned to the "Decreasing Uncertainty" condition were told that they were likely to win. They were also told not to worry. The researchers told them someone will win, and the foundation will eventually get the money.

Ladouceur and colleagues insured that participants in both conditions completed the exact same tasks. Both sets of participants played roulette in the laboratory. The only difference between the conditions was the set of instructions provided to the participants: one set of instructions increased uncertainty and the other set decreased uncertainty. These instructions are the "active ingredient" of the study. By keeping everything else the same, except the "active ingredient," the researchers can isolate the effects of the "active ingredient."

The authors use several procedures to improve the internal validity of the study. They assign participants at random to one of the two carefully controlled conditions. They keep the conditions the same except for the instructions about uncertainty. These procedures enable the authors to test the hypothesis that uncertainty *causes* worry (Fig. 8.10).

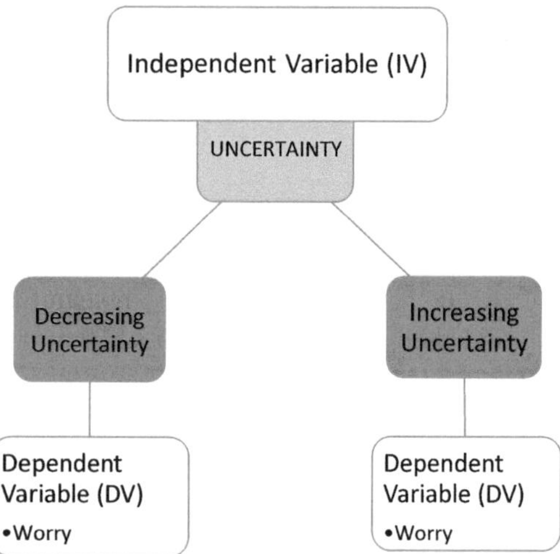

FIGURE 8.10 Depicting independent and dependent variables in the Ladouceur et al., 2000.

The researchers find that the experimental manipulation worked—the participants assigned to the "Increasing Uncertainty" condition felt more uncertain than those assigned to the "Decreasing Uncertainty" condition. Most important, there was an effect of the IV on the DV. The participants in the "Increasing Uncertainty" condition reported more worry than those in the "Decreasing Uncertainty" condition. The authors have experimental evidence that increases in uncertainty causes increases in worry. These data also provide evidence for the B-C path.

However, there are limitations to the external validity or generalizability of the study. The researchers do not know if worry measured in a nonclinical sample is the same experience with the same consequences as worry in a patient sample. And they do not

Activity 8.1: Working on Your Own Articles: Correlational or Experimental Study Designs

Apply the methods of analyzing the research designs of articles to two "theory of the problem" articles you are reading. We modified the table columns to include information about the results of the study. Once you are done, take a look at Chapter 10 to see how to write up the results of your analysis of the articles (Table 8.2).

TABLE 8.2 **Evaluating research designs in two articles of your Choice.**

Author/ Date	What is the predictor or independent variable?	What is the outcome or dependent variable?	Is the design: Experimental or Correlational/ Observational?	What did the authors do to assess the effects of the predictor/independent variables?	What was the outcome of the study: What was the relation between the predictor/IV and the outcome/DV?

Different Types of Experimental Manipulations

In Chapter 7, we discussed different types of mechanisms that might trigger or maintain behavioral health symptoms. These mechanisms included positive and negative valence, cognitive processes, social processes, reward sensitivity, and other mechanisms. Many of these mechanisms can be tested experimentally. In the following sections of the chapter, we review some of the manipulations that can be employed to experimentally test the role of the mechanism in causing the disorder. Here are some examples of methods that can be used to experimentally manipulate the key domains involved in behavioral health disorders. (For a more detailed review of experimental manipulations in psychology, see Abdi, Edelman, Dowling, & Valentin, 2009; Kirk, 2009.)

In experimental manipulations, the researcher isolates the hypothesized "active ingredient" by setting up conditions in which everything is identical except this active ingredient. The active ingredient—the thing that is different between the groups—varies depending on the research hypothesis.

The type of experimental manipulation used in a research study depends on the hypothesis to be tested. For example, LaDouceur et al. (2000) wanted to test hypotheses about uncertainty. They manipulated uncertainty by giving all participants the same type of laboratory task, but systematically varying the instructions that increased or decreased uncertainty.

As another example, researchers might have a hypothesis that color affects mood. They might hypothesize that people will feel better when they work in a room painted yellow than one painted the standard white. To test this hypothesis, the researchers would vary the paint color but keep everything else the same. They could make sure the participants were also doing the same type of work in the yellow and white rooms. To test the hypothesis that paint color affects mood, they could assign the participants at random to the two conditions, such that half the participants worked in a standard white room and half worked in a yellow room (Fig. 8.11).

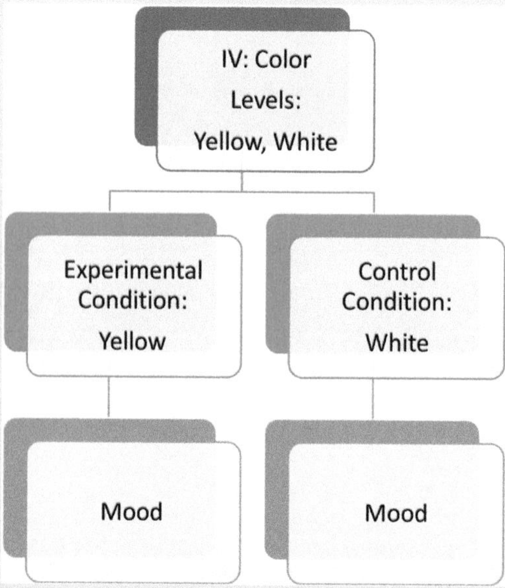

FIGURE 8.11 Depicting the relation between the independent and dependent variables in an experimental manipulation of mood.

Different Types of Experimental Manipulations—cont'd

Experimental Manipulations of Negative and Positive Valence

If researchers want to understand the causal effects of variations in mood on any type of functioning, they might manipulate the participants' mood. To manipulate mood, researchers can use mood induction strategies. Researchers can use many different techniques to induce or elicit changes in mood. For example, to induce a change in sadness, researchers might ask participants to watch a sad movie, listen to sad music, or to read a sad essay. Similarly, to create a positive mood, researchers might ask participants to watch a funny or happy movie, read a happy story, etc. To create a neutral mood, researchers might ask participants to read a boring text, or to watch an informative movie about gardening, or to create lists of instructions for assembling a set of shelves (Westermann, Spies, Stahl, & Hesse, 1996).

If the researchers want to test hypotheses about the effects of mood on an outcome, they could use experimental methods. They could consider the sad mood induction as the experimental condition and neutral mood induction as the control condition. To test the effects of sad mood, the researchers would assign participants at random to either a sad or neutral mood induction. After participants complete the mood induction, researchers could administer a task or test to assess the effects of mood on the outcome of interest. Outcomes could include test performance, changes in eating, other forms of impulse control, or cognition, among other variables.

Fig. 8.12 is an abstract of a meta-analysis of studies which examined the effects of mood induction on eating in eating and weight disorders samples and in samples of healthy controls.

Neuroscience and Biobehavioral Reviews 57 (2015) 299–309

Contents lists available at ScienceDirect

Neuroscience and Biobehavioral Reviews

journal homepage: www.elsevier.com/locate/neubiorev

ELSEVIER

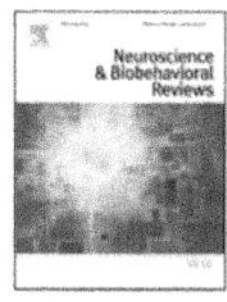

Review

The effects of negative and positive mood induction on eating behaviour: A meta-analysis of laboratory studies in the healthy population and eating and weight disorders

Valentina Cardi*[1], Jenni Leppanen[1], Janet Treasure

Section of Eating Disorders, Psychological Medicine, King's College London, Institute of Psychiatry, London, United Kingdom

ARTICLE INFO

Article history:
Received 15 May 2015
Received in revised form 3 August 2015
Accepted 18 August 2015
Available online 20 August 2015

Keywords:
Eating disorders
Eating
Mood
Test meal
Obesity
Restrained eaters

ABSTRACT

Objective: The aim of this study was to conduct a meta-analysis to quantify the effect of induced negative and positive mood on meal consumption in healthy participants and patients with eating and weight disorders.

Method: The search term "MOOD" was combined with the following keywords: "TEST MEAL" or "LABORATORY FEEDING" or "LABORATORY MEAL" or "TASTE TEST" or "TASTE TASK" to identify the relevant studies.

Results: Thirty-three studies were selected, including 2491 participants. Two meta-analyses compared negative mood or positive mood with neutral mood. Induced negative mood was significantly associated with greater food intake, especially in restrained eaters and binge eaters. Positive mood was also associated with greater caloric intake across groups.

Conclusion: These findings support the causal relationship between negative mood and greater food intake, especially in restrained eaters and binge eaters. Preliminary evidence indicates that strategies to improve positive mood might be of benefit for people with anorexia nervosa and bulimia nervosa, although the size of the effect across a single meal is small.

FIGURE 8.12 Abstract from Cardi, Leppanen, & Treasure, 2015.

Continued

Different Types of Experimental Manipulations—cont'd

Experimental Manipulations of Cognitive Processes

Sometimes researchers want to test hypotheses about the role of cognitive processes in behavioral health disorders. For example, they might want to test hypotheses about the role of **rumination** or **distraction** in sustaining negative mood or triggering depressive symptoms. In this case, they might provide all participants with a stressful task. Next, they might assign participants at random to engage in a rumination task or a distraction task. In a rumination task, participants are asked to think repeatedly about their task performance and how they felt; in a distraction task, participants are given something distracting to do to take their minds off the stressful task. After these tasks, the researchers would measure the outcome. One possible outcome might be depressive symptoms. Researchers could use statistical analyses to determine if the participants in the rumination task had higher depression scores than those assigned to the distraction task (Fig. 8.13).

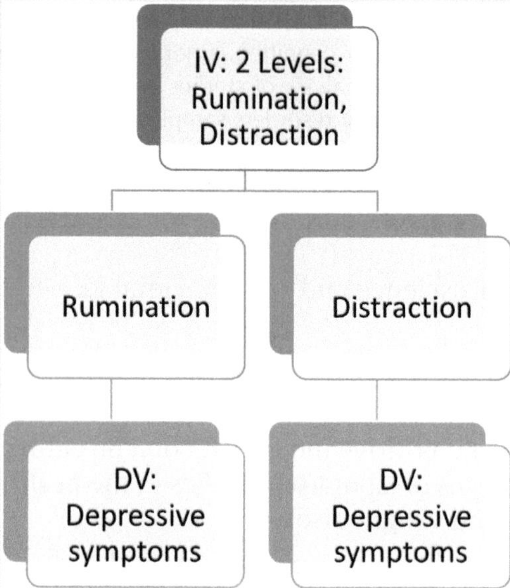

FIGURE 8.13 Depicting the relation between the independent and dependent variables in an experimental test of the effects of rumination.

Researchers can also test hypotheses about factors which might interfere with cognitive performance. For example, researchers hypothesized that making people aware of their membership in a racial minority group which has been stereotyped as less academically competent than the racial majority group would reduce the academic performance of members of the minority group. This is called the **stereotype threat** effect. To test the hypothesis that stereotype threat will reduce academic performance, researchers assigned participants at random to one of two conditions. In the stereotype threat condition, participants were asked to complete information about their race prior to completing an academically challenging test. In the no-stereotype threat

A Closer Look

Different Types of Experimental Manipulations—cont'd

condition, participants completed the same academically challenging test, but were not asked to complete information about their race before the test. Outcomes could include test performance or feelings about test performance (Lewis & Sekaquaptewa, 2016). Researchers can use statistical analyses to determine if participants assigned to the stereotype threat condition (i.e., were asked about race prior to completing the test) had lower scores on the test than participants who did not experience stereotype threats (Fig. 8.14).

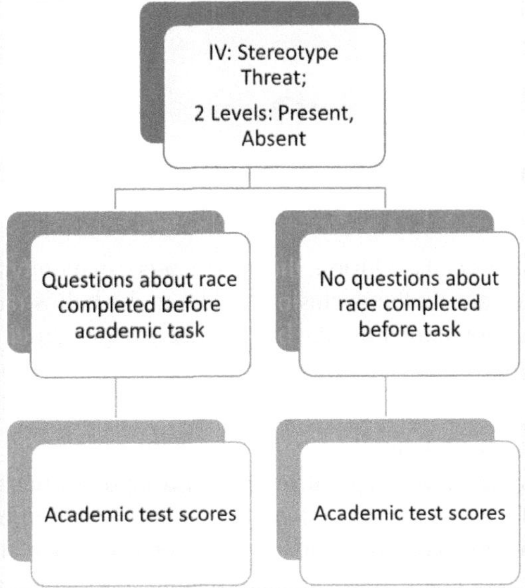

FIGURE 8.14 Depicting the relation between the independent and dependent variables in an experimental manipulation to test the effects of stereotype threat.

Experimental Manipulations of Social Processes

There are many experimental manipulations that can be used to understand disruptions to social processes. In each of these manipulations, the experimenter modifies the social interactions the research participant experiences in the laboratory. Some manipulations include changing the way the **experimenter** or an **experimental confederate** interacts with the research participant. An experimental confederate works with the experimenter to manipulate the independent variable. For example, the researcher might create conditions that vary in the degree to which the experimenter or the experimental confederate treats the participants in a warm or hostile way. Sometimes researchers use computer avatars to act as experimental confederates. For example, a commonly used procedure to evaluate the effects of social exclusion is a computer game called Cyberball. In Cyberball, participants play a game of catch on a computer with avatars of the players depicted on the screen. The Cyberball game can be used to assess the effects of social exclusion on a number of different outcomes, including depressive symptoms, cognitive function, and impulsive behavior (Hartgerink, Van Beest, Wicherts, & Williams, 2015).

Continued

Different Types of Experimental Manipulations—cont'd

The avatars of the players in the Cyberball game (i.e., the research participant and the other players who are actually controlled by the experimenter) toss the ball back and forth to each other (Fig. 8.15).

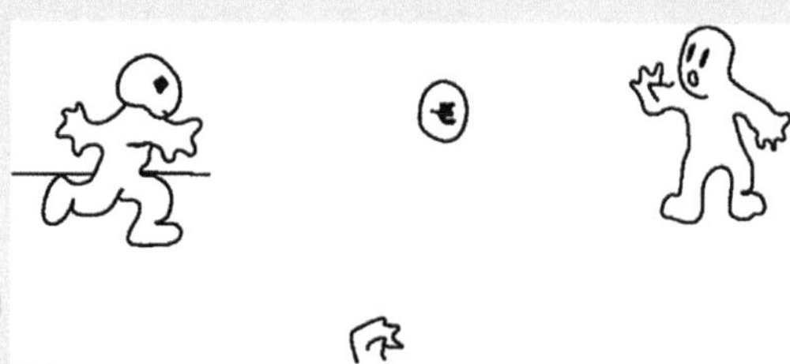

FIGURE 8.15 Depiction of the Cyberball game play. (Hartgerink, Van Beest, Wicherts, & Williams, 2015).

To examine the effects of social exclusion, the researchers can modify the number of times the ball is tossed to the participant. In the exclusion condition the ball is rarely or never thrown to the participant; in the inclusion condition, the ball is tossed to the participant about a third of the time as would be expected in a game with three players. Participants can be assigned at random to either the inclusion or the exclusion condition to experimentally test the effects of exclusion.

Experimental Manipulations of Arousal

Researchers manipulate arousal and arousal regulation using both behavioral and psychopharmacological methods. They can test the effects of medications used to increase or decrease sleep or alertness. Researchers can use different types of experimental conditions to test the effects of sleep deprivation or changes to circadian rhythms on many outcomes.

For example, researchers can manipulate the independent variable by altering the time of day participants are asked to wake up, delaying the onset of sleep, and of sleep duration/or depriving individuals of sleep, among other methods. By isolating components of sleep (e.g., time to bed, interruptions during the night, length of sleep, time at awakening, etc.) during experimental studies, researchers can test hypotheses about the effects of arousal regulation on functioning and health. (See de Bruin, van Run, Staaks, & Meijer, 2017 for review.) They can compare outcomes between participants who sleep normally versus those whose sleep schedule is altered (Fig. 8.16).

Different Types of Experimental Manipulations—cont'd

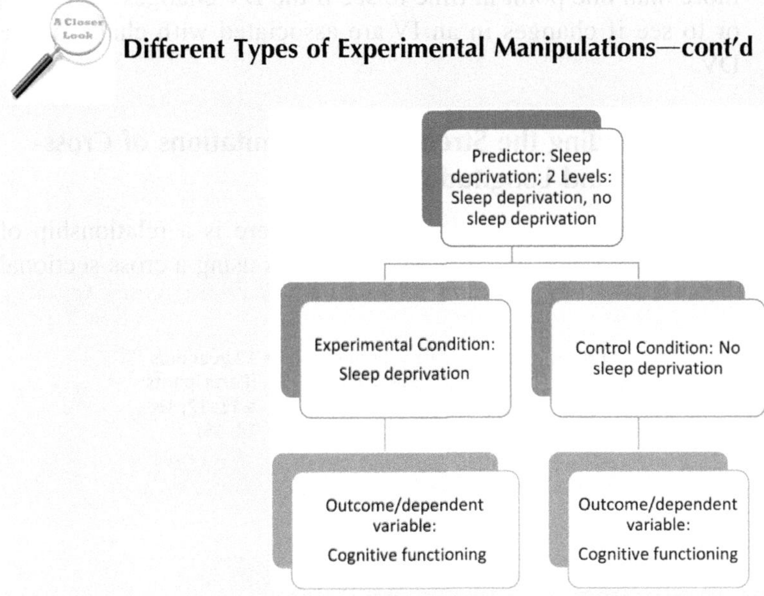

FIGURE 8.16 Depicting the relation of independent and dependent variables in an experimental study to test the effects of sleep deprivation on cognitive functioning.

know if the laboratory manipulation evokes the same kind of worry as the worry experienced by patients during their daily lives.

Cross-Sectional Versus Longitudinal Designs

Some research designs can answer questions that ask about the relationships among variables at one moment in time. Other designs can answer questions that require examining variables over time. The design we chose depends on the questions we need to answer.

Cross-sectional studies examine variables at one moment in time. In cross-sectional studies researchers measure the predictor/IV and outcome/DV at (roughly) the same time. Statistical analyses examine the degree to which they are related, but the analyses cannot determine if one variable triggers the onset of another.

Longitudinal studies allow researchers to test hypotheses about changes over time. Investigators measure participants at more than one point in time to see if the DV changes over time, or to see if changes in an IV are associated with changes in a DV.

Understanding the Strengths and Limitations of Cross-Sectional and Longitudinal Designs

Suppose researchers hypothesize that there is a relationship of age to IU. They could test this hypothesis using a cross-sectional

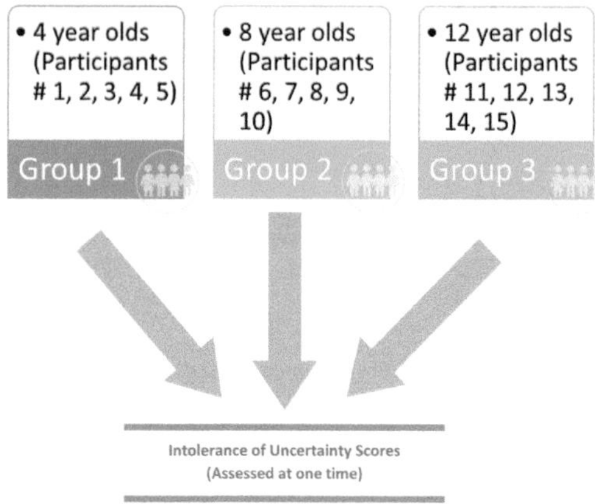

FIGURE 8.17 A cross-sectional design.

design. They could use an observational/correlational study to test the hypothesis that older children have more IU than younger children. They could test different groups of children who are at different ages (e.g., 4, 8, and 12 years) (Fig. 8.17).

In this case:

Predictor = age with three levels (4, 8, and 12 years)
Outcome = intolerance of uncertainty

The researchers might find there is a significant relationship of the predictor to the outcome—a difference among children at different age levels in IU. The results might indicate that older children show higher scores than younger children.

But they would not be able to claim that children develop more IU as they get older. They simply did not test that hypothesis. They tested the hypothesis that older children have more IU than younger children.

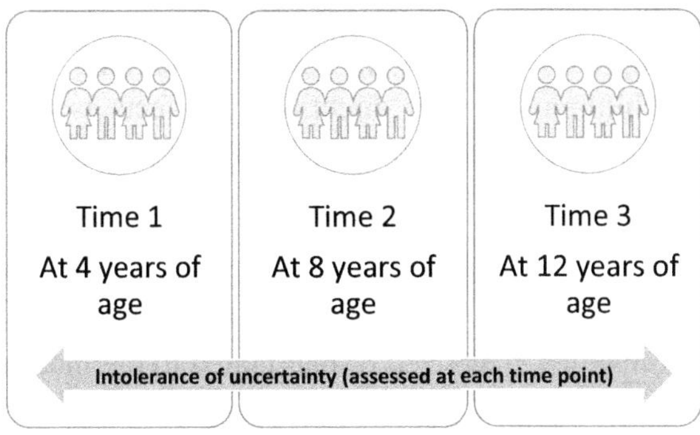

FIGURE 8.18 A longitudinal design.

To test the hypothesis that children get more anxious as they get older, researchers need a longitudinal study. The researchers would need to study one group of children, starting when they were young and retesting as they got older. In this case they are still using observational methods. The predictor is age, and the outcome is anxiety. But in this design the same group of children is tested repeatedly. Now the investigators can examine whether increasing age is associated with increasing anxiety (Fig. 8.18).

There are strengths and limitations to both approaches. (For a review of these issues, see Caruana, Roman, Hernández-Sánchez, & Solli, 2015.)

Cross-sectional studies are easier and generally less expensive. But the researchers cannot control for cohort effects. For example, participants at one level of the predictor might have experienced different circumstances than participants at another level. These circumstances might influence the outcome.

For example, the 12-year-old children in the cross-sectional study might have lived through a period of economic or political uncertainty that the 4-year-old and 8-year-old children did not. This experience, and not their age, might account for their anxiety scores. In this case economic or political uncertainty serves as an extraneous variable which influences the outcome of the study in a way the researcher does not want.

Longitudinal studies are costlier, but they can give greater insight into changes over time. And they can answer questions about the direction of the relations, clarifying which variable predicts changes in the other. In studies examining changes in anxiety as children age, the direction of effects is clear. Age might increase anxiety, but anxiety cannot make children older.

But there are also problems with longitudinal studies. Longitudinal studies are sensitive to **attrition** (dropping out). Participants who drop out may affect the outcome. Second, repeated measurement of variables may affect the outcome. Participants may get sensitized or habituated to the measurement instrument and the measurement process.

Testing Mediation and Moderation

Researchers can use cross-sectional and longitudinal approaches to test hypotheses about mediating and moderating variables.

Testing Mediation

As we discussed in Chapter 7, a mediator is a variable that explains the relationship between the predictor/IV and the outcome/DV. In the A-B-C model, the B variable can be considered a mediator variable. The B variable explains the link between the risk factor (the A variable) and the symptoms (the C variable). Longitudinal research can help researchers test mediation more effectively.

For example, suppose we hypothesize that stress leads to anxiety symptoms through stress-related changes to negative cognitions. If *stress-related negative cognitions* are a mediator, then we would expect to see that *stress* (the A variable) increases *negative cognitions* (the B variable), and we would expect to see that *negative cognitions* increase *anxiety symptoms* (the C variable) (Fig. 8.19).

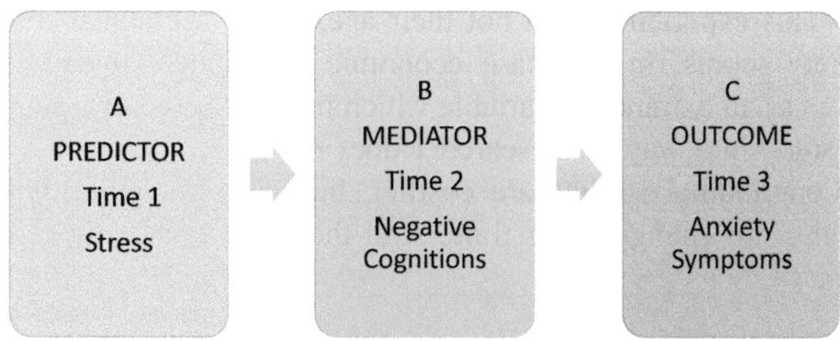

FIGURE 8.19 Model of the A-B-C pathway.

Notice that in this example we are talking about the way variables operate over time; stress increases negative cognitions; negative cognitions increase anxiety symptoms. Longitudinal designs increase the validity of tests of mediation. In a longitudinal analysis we can more clearly see that one variable (the A variable) is associated with changes to the B variable, and in turn, changes in the B variable are associated with changes in the C variable.

Testing Moderation

A moderator is a variable which affects the relationship between the IV and DV, making it weaker or stronger. In studies of risk factors and mechanisms, moderation analyses can help researchers identify whether the mechanisms that lead to symptoms are the same for different risk factors.

Age is a variable that is commonly tested as a moderator. In studies using age as a moderator, researchers are asking if the relations of the predictor to the outcome are the same for younger and older people. For example, the effects of IU on GAD symptoms might be different for children versus adults. Researchers could test the hypothesis that age moderates the relation of IU to GAD symptoms (Fig. 8.20).

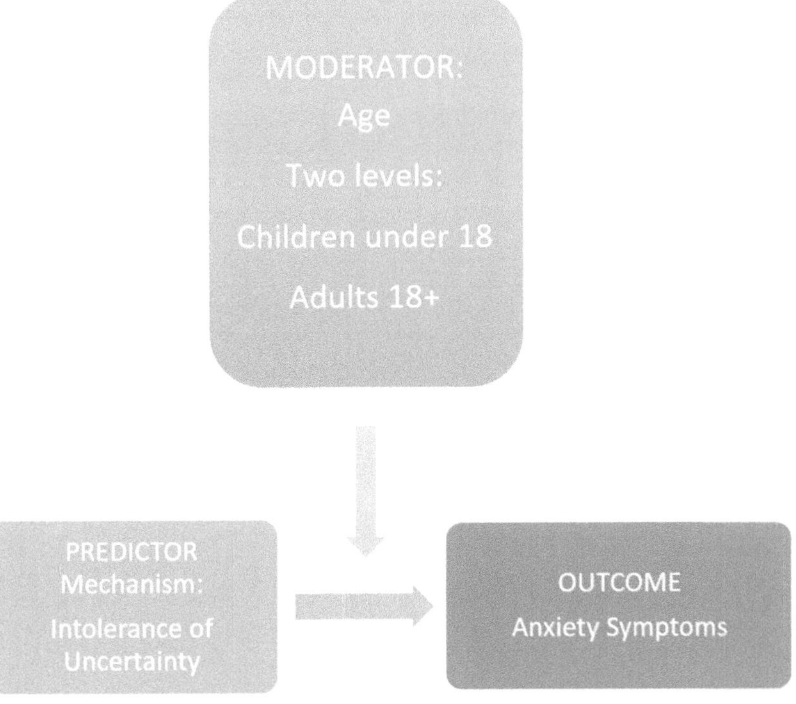

FIGURE 8.20 Depicting moderation of the B-C pathway.

Activity 8.2: Applying Our Knowledge of Design to Analyze Research Articles

We can examine an article using a longitudinal research design to make sure we understand how the design works. We are using an article by Calvete and colleagues (Calvete, 2014).

In this article, Calvete uses a longitudinal design to examine changes over time in the effects of childhood maltreatment on the development of cognitive vulnerabilities and depression. The author tests an A-C model by examining whether two kinds of childhood maltreatment (abuse from parents and abuse from peers) affect the development of depression and social anxiety. The author also tests A-B-C pathway by asking whether the effects of childhood maltreatment on outcomes (i.e., depression or social anxiety) are mediated by cognitive vulnerabilities in the form of maladaptive schemas. Then the author tests whether the A-B-C pathway is moderated by the adolescents' temperament. Variables representing the A, B, and C constructs are measured three times, making this a longitudinal study.

This study is very complex. We use two tables to help organize the information. One table lists and defines the constructs and related variables. The second table presents the research design and the findings. In Chapter 10 you will learn how to write summaries based on your tables.

In these articles we are introducing new constructs, including emotional abuse, maladaptive schemas, and temperament. Take the time to make a construct list to help you understand what these constructs mean (Fig. 8.21).

Activity 8.2: Applying Our Knowledge of Design to Analyze Research Articles—cont'd

Child Abuse & Neglect 38 (2014) 735–746

Contents lists available at ScienceDirect

Child Abuse & Neglect

Emotional abuse as a predictor of early maladaptive schemas in adolescents: Contributions to the development of depressive and social anxiety symptoms☆

CrossMark

E. Calvete*

University of Deusto, Spain

A R T I C L E I N F O

Article history:
Received 19 June 2013
Received in revised form 14 October 2013
Accepted 16 October 2013
Available online 16 November 2013

Keywords:
Parental emotional abuse
Bullying victimization
Temperament
Early maladaptive schemas
Depression
Social anxiety
Adolescents

A B S T R A C T

The schema therapy model posits that maltreatment generates early maladaptive schemas (EMSs) that lead to the development of emotional disorders throughout the life span. The model also stipulates that temperament moderates the influence of maltreatment on EMSs. This study examines (a) whether emotional abuse perpetrated by parents and peers, both alone and interactively with temperament, predicts the worsening of EMSs; and (b) whether EMSs in turn predict an increase in depressive and social anxiety symptoms in adolescents. A total of 1,052 adolescents (M_{age} = 13.43; SD = 1.29) were assessed at three time points, each of which was separated by 6 months. The subjects completed measures of emotional abuse by parents and peers, neuroticism, extraversion, EMSs, depressive symptoms, and social anxiety. The findings indicate that emotional bullying victimization and neuroticism predict a worsening of all schema domains over time. Contrary to expectations, there was no significant interaction between temperament dimensions and emotional abuse. The results confirmed the mediational hypothesis that changes in EMSs mediated the predictive association between bullying victimization and emotional symptoms. This study provides partial support for the schema therapy model by demonstrating the role of emotional abuse and temperament in the genesis of EMSs.

Continued

Activity 8.2: Applying Our Knowledge of Design to Analyze Research Articles—cont'd

Introduction

Childhood maltreatment is a strong predictor of psychological disorders, such as depression and anxiety, during adolescence and throughout the life span (e.g., Alloy, Abramson, Smith, Gibb, & Neeren, 2006; Cicchetti & Valentino, 2006; Hankin, 2005; Harkness, Bruce, & Lumley, 2006; Kim & Cicchetti, 2010; Simon et al., 2009). Specifically, emotional abuse seems to be particularly relevant for the development of depression (Gibb, Butler, & Beck, 2003; Gibb, Chelminski, & Zimmerman, 2007) and social anxiety (Bruce, Heimberg, Blanco, Schneier, & Liebowitz, 2012; Simon et al., 2009). In addition to maltreatment perpetrated by parents, abuse perpetrated by peers has also been identified as a risk factor for the development of depression and social anxiety (e.g., Cole et al., 2013; Reijntjes, Kamphuis, Prinzie, & Telch, 2010).

Cognitive theories posit that the impact of childhood maltreatment on subsequent psychopathology may be mediated by cognitive vulnerabilities, which include negative inference styles and dysfunctional schemas (Gibb, Abramson, & Alloy, 2004; Hankin, 2005). As support for this assumption, diverse models hold that maltreatment experiences contribute to the development of cognitive vulnerabilities (Ingram, 2003). The influence of maltreatment on cognitive vulnerabilities would be particularly strong when early experiences interact with specific temperament dimensions, an aspect that has received scant attention so far. The present study expands these ideas to the concept of early maladaptive schemas (EMSs), a central construct of schema therapy (Young, Klosko, & Weishaar, 2003), and explores the role of emotional abuse, both alone and in interaction with temperament, in the development of EMSs and depression and social anxiety symptoms in adolescents.

↑ This section provides background information. The authors identify childhood maltreatment, and in particular emotional abuse, as an important risk factor for childhood depression. They explain that cognitive vulnerabilities, including maladaptive schemas, may explain the relationship between emotional abuse and depression.

Later in the introduction (sections not shown), the authors hypothesize that the effects may be moderated by temperament. They expect that the effects of emotional abuse on the development of maladaptive schemas and depression. They suggest that temperaments characterized by high negative emotion and low positive emotion may make the effects of emotional abuse worse.

Overview of the present study

The review of the available research indicates that no study has yet examined the conjoint influence of maltreatment experiences and temperament in the worsening of EMSs, as hypothesized by the schema therapy model. The present study aims to examine whether temperament and emotional abuse perpetrated by parents and peers, alone and interactively, contribute to the change of EMSs in adolescents.

← The rationale for the study.

The assessment of the mediational hypothesis proposed in this study requires taking measurements in at least in three waves to examine whether experiences of emotional abuse and temperament at Time 1 (T1) predict the worsening of EMSs at Time 2 (T2) and whether EMSs, in turn, predict an increase in depressive and social anxiety symptoms at Time 3 (T3). Specifically, this study included measures of two temperament dimensions (neuroticism and extraversion), two types of maltreatment experiences (emotional abuse by parents and peers), three schema domains (disconnection/rejection, impaired autonomy, and other-directedness), and depressive and social anxiety symptoms.

← The overview of the methods.

Activity 8.2: Applying Our Knowledge of Design to Analyze Research Articles—cont'd

Method

Participants

The initial sample included 1,281 adolescents aged 13–17 years (593 girls and 688 boys) who were high school students from 51 classrooms at eight educational centers in Bizkaia, Spain. The assessments occurred at three time points, each of which was separated by 6 months: at the beginning of the school year (T1), 6 months later (T2), and 1 year later (T3). Two-hundred twenty-nine adolescents did not complete the measurements at one of the time points; their lack of participation was caused almost entirely by sickness or absence. The attrition rate also included participants who did not respond to some of the questionnaires and were therefore eliminated from the study. Consequently, the final sample consisted of 1,052 adolescents (499 girls and 553 boys) who completed the measures during all three waves of the study (participation rate: 82.12%). The final sample had a mean age of 13.61 years (SD = 1.41) at the beginning of the study. A series of t tests was conducted to examine differences in all study variables at T1 among the 1,052 adolescents who completed the three waves and those who failed to complete the study. None of these analyses were significant.

← This section explains the three times that data will be collected. This section also explains who participated and which variables were collected at each time point.

Regarding the first objective, the results indicate that victimization by peers and neuroticism are independent predictors of the change in the three schema domains assessed in this study. That is, both the experiences of emotional abuse by peers and neuroticism predict a worsening of schemas in the domains of disconnection/rejection, impaired autonomy and performance, and other-directedness. These results are consistent with those obtained in previous cross-sectional studies that showed associations between neuroticism and numerous EMSs (e.g., Muris, 2006; Sava, 2009; Thimm, 2010b) and with previous evidence of predictive associations between temperament and other cognitive vulnerabilities (Mezulis et al., 2006).

Findings indicate that the emotional abuse perpetrated by peers, not the emotional abuse perpetrated by parents, predicts the worsening of the schemas. The predictive association between bullying victimization and schemas is of great importance because it suggests that peer victimization experienced in adolescence is crucial to the development of dysfunctional schemas. In particular, as a consequence of being bullied, adolescents may develop schemas involving thoughts and feelings of being rejected and abused by others (disconnection/rejection), feelings of being defective to some extent (disconnection/rejection), a sense of vulnerability and failure (impaired autonomy), and the need to satisfy the desires of others in an attempt to gain acceptance (other-directedness) and eventually to avoid bullying.

← In this section, the author explains the findings of the study.

FIGURE 8.21 Selected sections from Calvete, 2014—An observational longitudinal design.

Continued

Activity 8.2: Applying Our Knowledge of Design to Analyze Research Articles—cont'd

As a reminder, begin by making a construct list with definitions to make sure you understand what the study is about. We completed the portions of the table for the first two constructs. Complete the rest of the table (Table 8.3).

TABLE 8.3 Making a construct list.

Author/ date	Constructs	Operational definition	Variables	Measurement methods
Calvete, 2014	Emotional abuse		Self-reported emotional abuse from parents Emotional bullying from peers	Self-report surveys: Psychological Abuse Scale of the Conflict Tactics Scale—Parent-to-Child version
	Early maladaptive schemas	Schemas (linked networks of thoughts, feelings, attitudes) which reflect negative ideas Schemas include: Disconnection/ rejection, Impaired autonomy, Other-directedness	Self-reported cognitions associated with the schemas	Self-report surveys: Young schema questionnaire
	Temperament	Characteristic ways of relating, perceiving, thinking	Self-reported personality traits of neuroticism and negative affectivity Self-reported traits of positive affectivity	Self-report survey: NEO personality inventory
	Depressive symptoms			
	Social anxiety			

Activity 8.2: Applying Our Knowledge of Design to Analyze Research Articles—cont'd

Next let's think about the research design and the findings. Here we use a more detailed table to help us organize more of the findings (Table 8.4).

TABLE 8.4 Research design and findings for Calvete (2014).

Author/date	Predictor: Definition	Outcome: Definition	If this is a study testing mediation, what are the A, B, C variables?	If this is a study testing moderation, what is the moderator?	Design: Observational or experimental? If experimental, how was Predictor manipulated?	Cross-sectional or longitudinal? If longitudinal, how many observation periods were there?
Calvete, 2014	Peer bullying and Parental abuse	Early maladaptive schemas (EMS) Symptoms of depression and anxiety	A = Peer or parent maltreatment B = Mediator (early maladaptive schemas) C = Symptoms of depression and anxiety	Temperament: negative and positive affectivity	Observational study	Longitudinal study– variables were measured 3 times, every 6 months Time 1. Abuse and bullying, EMS, temperament, depression and anxiety Time 2. EMS, and depression and anxiety Time 3. Depression and anxiety

Now try the same activity with an article of your choice that you are using for your proposal (Tables 8.5 and 8.6).

TABLE 8.5 Construct list.

Author/date	Constructs	Operational Definition	Variables	Measurement methods

Continued

Activity 8.2: Applying Our Knowledge of Design to Analyze Research Articles—cont'd

TABLE 8.6 Research design and findings.

Author/ date	Predictor: definition	Outcome: definition and measurement method	If this is a study testing mediation, what are the A, B, C variables?	If this is a study testing moderation, what is the moderator?	Design: Observational or experimental? If experimental, how was IV manipulated?	Cross-sectional or longitudinal? If longitudinal, how many observation periods were there?

Building Human Capital

In this chapter, you learned about different types of research designs that can be used to test your theory of the problem—the relations among risk factors, mechanisms, and the disorder. You learned about the differences between correlational/observational versus experimental studies and the differences between longitudinal and cross-sectional studies. You learned about how these designs can help test mediation and moderation.

This was a very long chapter. But, as you worked your way through the material, you developed many skills. You practiced good organizational skills to keep the articles organized and to keep your notes on the articles in order. And you strengthened your conscientiousness and attention to detail as you read the articles and make sure you were getting the facts.

Throughout the process, you worked to overcome boredom and frustration as you read and reread articles to understand all the terms. You improve your patience and persistence as you develop construct lists and learn to carefully read the papers.

There is a lot of information in all the articles you are reading. Much of the information is very interesting and seems important. But it can be overwhelming or confusing to identify the parts you need to build your proposal or paper.

If you commit to using the tables, you will be better able to pull out the information you need. The task of filling out the tables can help you guide your reading and help you identify the information you need. It can be tedious to complete these tables, but you may find you are much more organized and on top of the material when you do. You are gaining the kind of disciplined thinking that is necessary for a good analysis of information.

The tables help you see the different methods more clearly and learn to think critically about the information. The tables help you answer yourself important questions about the quality of the research, including:

How did the authors represent the construct—what variable did they choose?

What were the strengths and weaknesses of using this variable to represent the construct?

Do the measurement methods capture what the authors were trying to investigate?

What research design did the authors use? Are there threats to internal or external validity from the approach used?

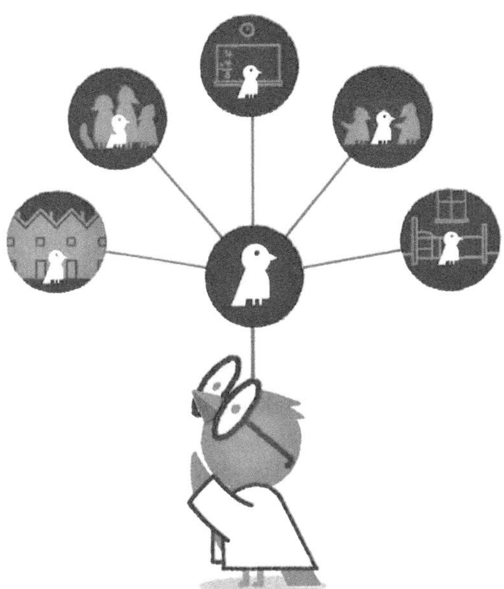

It is hard work! But being able to push yourself—taking breaks as needed—is an important skill for every aspect of your life. Once you know you can push yourself to think systematically and work your way through the difficult material, no one can take that knowledge away! And you will learn a lot about behavioral science in the meantime.

Terms

Take the time to define each of these terms and consider how to apply them.

Research Terms

Research design
Correlation/observational study
Experimental design
Cross-sectional design
Longitudinal design
Prospective design
Statistical analyses
Statistical significance
Manipulation (of a variable)
Random assignment
Mood induction
Experimenter
Experimental confederate

References

Abdi, H., Edelman, B., Dowling, W. J., & Valentin, D. (2009). *Experimental design and analysis for psychology*. Oxford University Press.

de Bruin, E. J., van Run, C., Staaks, J., & Meijer, A. M. (2017). Effects of sleep manipulation on cognitive functioning of adolescents: A systematic review. *Sleep Medicine Reviews, 32*, 45–57.

Buhr, K., & Dugas, M. J. (2009). The role of fear of anxiety and intolerance of uncertainty in worry: An experimental manipulation. *Behaviour Research and Therapy, 47*(3), 215–223.

Calvete, E. (2014). Emotional abuse as a predictor of early maladaptive schemas in adolescents: Contributions to the development of depressive and social anxiety symptoms. *Child Abuse & Neglect, 38*(4), 735–746.

Cardi, V., Leppanen, J., & Treasure, J. (2015). The effects of negative and positive mood induction on eating behaviour: A meta-analysis of laboratory studies in the healthy population and eating and weight disorders. *Neuroscience & Biobehavioral Reviews, 57*, 299–309.

Carleton, R. N., Mulvogue, M. K., Thibodeau, M. A., McCabe, R. E., Antony, M. M., & Asmundson, G. J. (2012). Increasingly certain about uncertainty: Intolerance of uncertainty across anxiety and depression. *Journal of Anxiety Disorders, 26*(3), 468–479.

Caruana, E. J., Roman, M., Hernández-Sánchez, J., & Solli, P. (2015). Longitudinal studies. *Journal of Thoracic Disease, 7*(11), E537.

Hartgerink, C. H., Van Beest, I., Wicherts, J. M., & Williams, K. D. (2015). The ordinal effects of ostracism: A meta-analysis of 120 Cyberball studies. *PloS One, 10*(5), e0127002.

Highet, N., Stevenson, A. L., Purtell, C., & Coo, S. (2014). Qualitative insights into women's personal experiences of perinatal depression and anxiety. *Women and Birth, 27*(3), 179–184.

Kirk, R. E. (2009). *Experimental design. Sage handbook of quantitative methods in psychology* (pp. 23–45).

Ladouceur, R., Gosselin, P., & Dugas, M. J. (2000). Experimental manipulation of intolerance of uncertainty: A study of a theoretical model of worry. *Behaviour Research and Therapy, 38*(9), 933–941.

Lewis, N. A., Jr., & Sekaquaptewa, D. (2016). Beyond test performance: A broader view of stereotype threat. *Current Opinion in Psychology, 11*, 40–43.

Stockdale, S. E., Wells, K. B., Tang, L., Belin, T. R., Zhang, L., & Sherbourne, C. D. (2007). The importance of social context: Neighborhood stressors, stress-buffering mechanisms, and alcohol, drug, and mental health disorders. *Social Science & Medicine, 65*(9), 1867–1881.

Taylor, S. J., Bogdan, R., & DeVault, M. (2015). *Introduction to qualitative research methods: A guidebook and resource*. John Wiley & Sons.

Westermann, R., Spies, K., Stahl, G., & Hesse, F. W. (1996). Relative effectiveness and validity of mood induction procedures: A meta-analysis. *European Journal of Social Psychology, 26*(4), 557–580.

Chapter 9

Theory of the problem: Understanding research results

In the previous chapters, you have learned about research designs used in studies to test hypotheses. As those studies are conducted, data are collected, and statistical analyses are performed on those data. These analyses are used to determine if the data support the hypotheses.

In research articles, the results of statistical analyses on the data collected in the study are presented in the results section. In this chapter, we learn to read and understand the results section of articles on behavioral health disorders. This chapter focuses on studies used to establish the public health significance and investigate risk factors and mechanisms. Chapter 13 describes analyses commonly used in treatment outcome papers.

Psychology Research Methods. https://doi.org/10.1016/B978-0-12-815680-3.00009-8

Quantifying Constructs

To conduct hypothesis-testing research, researchers must **quantify** their ideas. Quantifying ideas requires representing these ideas or constructs with measurable variables.

These variables must be assessed with a measurement instrument that yields quantifiable data. Quantifiable data are data that can be expressed as numbers. For example, researchers can collect **numeric data** on the number of symptoms a participant has, the number of cigarettes the participant smokes each day, or the length of time between mood episodes, among many other types of data. Because each of these variables can be expressed as a number, researchers can use quantitative methods to test many different hypotheses about these variables.

To test hypotheses, researchers perform **statistical analyses** on quantifiable data. The information presented in this chapter assumes you have basic statistical knowledge, generally gained through an introductory statistics course. Knowledge of the definitions of the following terms will be necessary: percentage, mean, median, mode, standard deviation, normal curve, *P* value, and statistical significance. A beginning understanding of standard statistical methods used in behavioral science is helpful. These methods include ANOVA, correlational analyses, regression, and chi-square.

A helpful review of basic statistical principles can be found at:

https://onlinecourses.science.psu.edu/statprogram/review_of_basic_statistics
http://geog.uoregon.edu/bartlein/courses/geog495/lec11.html
http://www.biostathandbook.com/chigof.html
http://www.statsoft.com/Textbook/Multiple-Regression

A refresher on the standards for writing about statistics can be found at https://owl.english.purdue.edu/owl/resource/672/1/

Also

https://web2.uconn.edu/writingcenter/pdf/Reporting_Statistics.pdf

The APA guidelines for reporting statistics results can be found in the APA Manual:

American Psychological Association. (2010). *Publication manual of the American Psychological Association* (sixth ed.). Washington, DC: Author.

The guidelines for reporting analyses in the results can be found in:

Appelbaum, M., Cooper, H., Kline, R. B., Mayo-Wilson, E., Nezu, A. M., & Rao, S. M. (2018). Journal article reporting standards for quantitative research in psychology: The APA Publications and Communications Board task force report. *American Psychologist*, *73*(1), 3–25.

Levitt, H. M., Bamberg, M., Creswell, J. W., Frost, D. M., Josselson, R., & Suárez- Orozco, C. (2018). Journal article reporting standards for qualitative primary, qualitative meta-analytic, and mixed methods research in psychology: The APA Publications and Communications Board task force report. *American Psychologist*, *73*(1), 26–46

Variability: An Essential Concept

Statistical analyses are used to identify and evaluate reliable patterns in the data. One pattern might involve differences between the levels of the predictor/independent variable (IV). For example, researchers may hypothesize that participants at Level 1 of the predictor have higher scores than those at Level 2. Detecting these patterns is one goal of the analyses. The significance of the findings, and their implication for the hypothesis you are testing also depends on understanding the variability among the scores.

The outcome of statistical analyses depends on both the differences in scores associated with the different levels of the predictor/IV and the variability in scores among the participants. Here is a silly example, but one that is easy to understand. Imagine a researcher wants to test the hypothesis that a predictor variable is associated with responses to an outcome variable. In this case the predictor variable is "Type of Food." The variable "Type of Food" has two levels: Pizza and Brussels sprouts. The outcome variable is self-reported liking of the food. Twenty participants are assigned at random to the two levels of the predictor variable. Ten participants receive pizza and 10 receive Brussels sprouts. All participants are asked to complete a survey indicating how much they liked the food they were assigned.

The researcher is testing whether the difference in the scores assigned to pizza and Brussels sprouts across participants is greater than the variability in response to the foods within the groups of participants.

We generated some made-up data for this study. The means which are displayed in Fig. 9.1 demonstrate that there are big differences in scores assigned to pizza and Brussels sprouts. But there is also variability in scores within each of the groups (Fig. 9.2). Look at the raw data in Table 9.1 and the standard deviations in Table 9.2. Not everyone likes pizza, although most people like it a lot. Not everyone dislikes Brussels sprouts, one person likes them a lot. (I do, too!) But, although there is a lot of variability in responses, some consistent patterns emerge. The statistical analyses the researchers use consider both the differences between the levels of the predictor variable (i.e., the differences between pizza and Brussels sprouts) and the variability in the scores among participants.

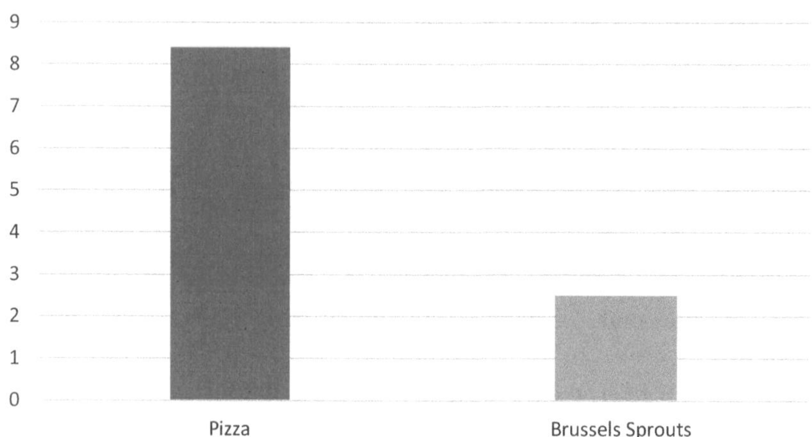

FIGURE 9.1 Mean "Liking" scores for pizza versus brussels sprouts.

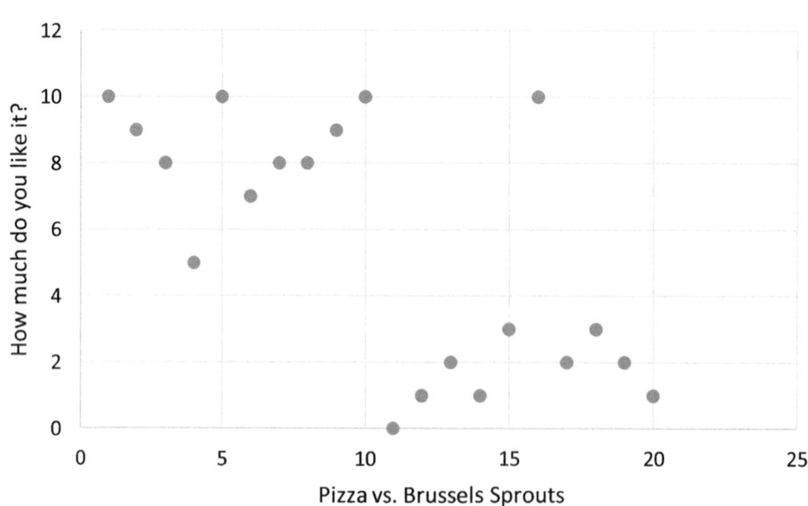

FIGURE 9.2 Variability for "Liking": Pizza versus brussels sprouts.

TABLE 9.1 Raw scores on a measure of liking for pizza versus brussels sprouts.

Obs	Food type (p = pizza, b = brussels sprouts)	Liking (from 1 to 10, with 10 as highest score)
1	p	10
2	p	9
3	p	8
4	p	5
5	p	10
6	p	7
7	p	8
8	p	8
9	p	9
10	p	10
11	b	0
12	b	1
13	b	2
14	b	1
15	b	3
16	b	10
17	b	2
18	b	3
19	b	2
20	b	1

TABLE 9.2 Mean scores on a measure of "Liking" for pizza versus Brussels sprouts.

		Liking	
Level of Food type	N	Mean	Std dev
Brussels sprouts	10	2.50	2.79
pizza	10	8.40	1.57

To test the relations between Food Type and liking, we could use an analysis of variance (ANOVA). The results of the analysis suggest that the differences between the two levels of the predictor variable Food Type (pizza and Brussels sprouts) is greater than the variability among the participants' scores. If the analysis yielded statistically significant results, we could claim that participants in the study liked pizza more than Brussels sprouts. Later in this chapter you will see examples of the results of an ANOVA and learn how to interpret the findings.

The Research Hypothesis and the Null Hypothesis

In scientific studies, researchers are testing hypotheses about relationships among variables.

- In risk factor studies, researchers are testing hypotheses that a particular risk factor is related to the symptoms or diagnosis of a disorder.
- In studies of mechanisms that contribute to the development or maintenance of a disorder, researchers are testing hypotheses about the relations of the mechanism variable to symptoms of the disorder.

The researchers' hypothesis is called the *research or alternative hypothesis*. This hypothesis is referred to as H_1. In general, the research hypothesis in risk factor and mechanism studies states that there *is* a relationship among variables. For example, the general version of one research hypothesis could be stated as follows:

H_1: There is a relationship of the risk factor to symptoms of the disorder.
Or
H_1: There is a relationship of the mechanism to symptoms of the disorder.

The research hypothesis (H_1) is contrasted to the *null hypothesis* (H_0). In most studies of risk factors and mechanisms, the null hypothesis states that there is no relationship between the variables. More accurately, the null hypothesis is stating that the evidence is not strong enough to demonstrate a relationship.

To determine whether there is support for the research hypothesis, researchers use statistical analyses. The analyses provide important information: an estimate of the direction of the relations among variables, an estimate of the strength of the association among the variables, and an estimate of the statistical significance of the relationship.

The direction of a relation between variables can be positive or negative. Variables have a positive relation if the outcome increases as the predictor increases; they have a negative relation if the outcome decreases as the predictor increases (Fig. 9.3). For example, the relation between income and health is positive—as income goes up, people report better health (Marmot, 2002). The relation between income and smoking is negative—as income goes up, the likelihood of smoking goes down (Singh, Williams, Siahpush, & Mulhollen, 2011).

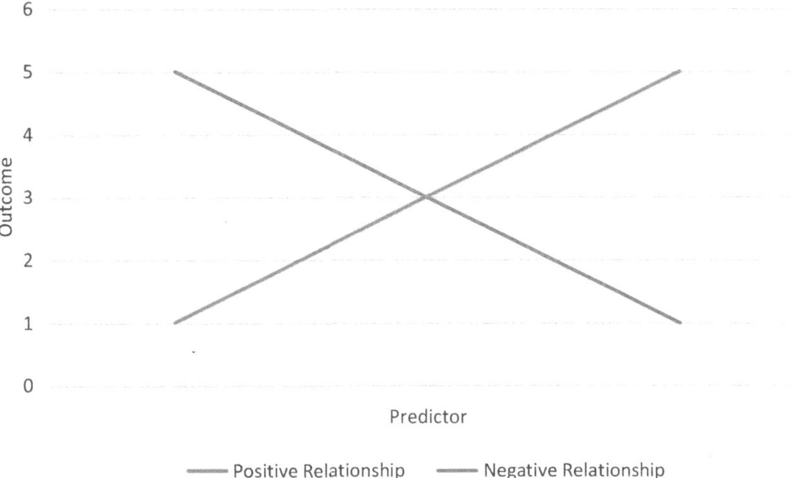

FIGURE 9.3 Positive and negative relationship.

There are various methods for generating the statistical outcomes that provide information about the direction and magnitude of the relations among variables see before (Table 9.3). You may be familiar with some of these statistics including *regression coefficients, correlation coefficients*, and *t-tests,* among other types of statistical information. Later in this chapter we will discuss this statistical information in more detail.

TABLE 9.3 Types of analyses and their associated symbols.

Symbol	Type of analysis
r	Correlation
t	t-test
F	ANOVA
R^2	Regression
χ^2	Chi-square
Wilks' lambda (λ)	MANOVA
Φ	Effect size

Once researchers have estimates of the direction and size of the relations between variables, they need to understand whether the estimates of the relationship and the measure of variability among the scores provide support for their hypothesis and are enough to reject the null hypothesis. The researchers are asking: Is the strength of the relationship large enough and consistent enough to reject the null hypothesis?

Researchers make the decision about whether to accept or reject a hypothesis based on probability theory. As a community, researchers establish standards for the level of error they wish to accept. They specify how often they will accept an error in which they reject the null hypothesis when there really is no relation among the variables. Researchers sometimes frame this idea as the likelihood of obtaining a **false positive**. A false positive occurs when there is no real relation between two variables—the null hypothesis is true. But by chance, the data will indicate that the null hypothesis is false.

To standardize the approach to the possibility of obtaining a false positives, researchers set a standard, called an **alpha level**, which allows them to decide how much error (false positives) they are willing to accept. Researchers do not want false-positive results, but they also don't want false-negative results. Researchers can also make false-negative errors when they set the standard too high and they accept the null hypothesis when it is, in fact, false.

In psychology the alpha level is set at .05. This means that researchers have collectively accepted using an alpha level of .05, and they are willing to accept the possibility that 5% of the time (5/100), errors will be made, and the null hypothesis is true, even it is rejected. When a ***p* value,** the significance level of the statistical test, is less than **.05,** this indicates the test exceeds the standard set by the community of psychology researchers.

To test the hypothesis about relations between food type and liking, we used an Analysis of Variance or ANOVA on our made-up data. The analysis found that the difference between food types was significant and larger than the variability among the scores. The analysis yielded an **F value** of 33.72. This is the ratio of the adjusted values for the differences between the two conditions (Pizza vs. Brussels sprouts) and the variability among the scores. This F value is very large. The output of the statistical analysis shows a p value $p < .0001$, and therefore, it is unlikely that the difference between pizza and Brussels sprouts occurred by chance. A p value of .0001 means the likelihood of incorrectly rejecting the null hypothesis is less than 1 in 10,000.

There is a movement toward another approach to statistical testing. This approach does not frame analyses as permitting the rejection or acceptance of the null hypothesis. Instead, researchers are encouraged to present estimates that provide better insight into the magnitude and consistency of the effects of a given study. Instead of presenting p values, researchers are encouraged to present confidence intervals and to display variability in the data. For further information about recommended approaches to statistical analyses, see (Applebaum et al., 2018).

Here is an example of this approach from a published research article. In the results section of the study, you can see both the general trends or patterns in the data and the variability in scores. The abstract is presented in Fig. 9.4 so you can have an idea of the aims of the study.

Behaviour Research and Therapy 77 (2016) 86–95

Contents lists available at ScienceDirect

Behaviour Research and Therapy

journal homepage: www.elsevier.com/locate/brat

Internet-delivered acceptance-based behaviour therapy for generalized anxiety disorder: A randomized controlled trial

Mats Dahlin [a], Gerhard Andersson [b, c, *], Kristoffer Magnusson [c], Tomas Johansson [e], Johan Sjögren [e], Andreas Håkansson [e], Magnus Pettersson [e], Åsa Kadowaki [f], Pim Cuijpers [g, h], Per Carlbring [d]

[a] Psykologpartners, Private Practice, Linköping, Sweden
[b] Department of Behavioural Sciences and Learning, Linköping University, Linköping, Sweden
[c] Department of Clinical Neuroscience, Karolinska Institute, Stockholm, Sweden
[d] Department of Psychology, Stockholm University, Stockholm, Sweden
[e] Department of Psychology, Umeå University, Umeå, Sweden
[f] Region Östergötland, Linköping, Sweden
[g] Department of Clinical Psychology, VU University Amsterdam, The Netherlands
[h] EMGO Institute for Health and Care Research, The Netherlands

A R T I C L E I N F O

Article history:
Received 1 February 2015
Received in revised form
8 December 2015
Accepted 15 December 2015
Available online 21 December 2015

Keywords:
Internet-based behaviour therapy
Generalized anxiety disorder
Randomized controlled trial
Acceptance
Mindfulness

A B S T R A C T

Generalized anxiety disorder (GAD) is a disabling condition which can be treated with cognitive behaviour therapy (CBT). The present study tested the effects of therapist-guided internet-delivered acceptance-based behaviour therapy on symptoms of GAD and quality of life. An audio CD with acceptance and mindfulness exercises and a separate workbook were also included in the treatment. Participants diagnosed with GAD ($N = 103$) were randomly allocated to immediate therapist-guided internet-delivered acceptance-based behaviour therapy or to a waiting-list control condition. A six month follow-up was also included. Results using hierarchical linear modelling showed moderate to large effects on symptoms of GAD (Cohen's $d = 0.70$ to 0.98), moderate effects on depressive symptoms (Cohen's $d = 0.51$ to 0.56), and no effect on quality of life. Follow-up data showed maintained effects. While there was a 20% dropout rate, sensitivity analyses showed that dropouts did not differ in their degree of change during treatment. To conclude, our study suggests that internet-delivered acceptance-based behaviour therapy can be effective in reducing the symptoms of GAD.

FIGURE 9.4 Abstract from Dahlin et al. (2016).

Dahlin et al. (2016) are comparing changes in generalized anxiety disorder (GAD) symptoms (measured with the GAD-7) over time for participants in an Internet treatment condition versus a wait-list control condition. In Fig. 9.5, we display the way Dahlin et al. (2016) show the results of the statistical model in a table, and the actual responses from individual participants in an accompanying figure. They display the average responses using triangles for the treatment condition and circles for the wait-list control. They label the dashed lines the "model" to explain this is the line generated by the analyses. The table and figure provide a clear visual representation of changes over time in responses to the treatment and control conditions. Their figure illustrates that the participants in the treatment condition showed an earlier and steeper decline in GAD symptoms than did participants in the wait-list control condition.

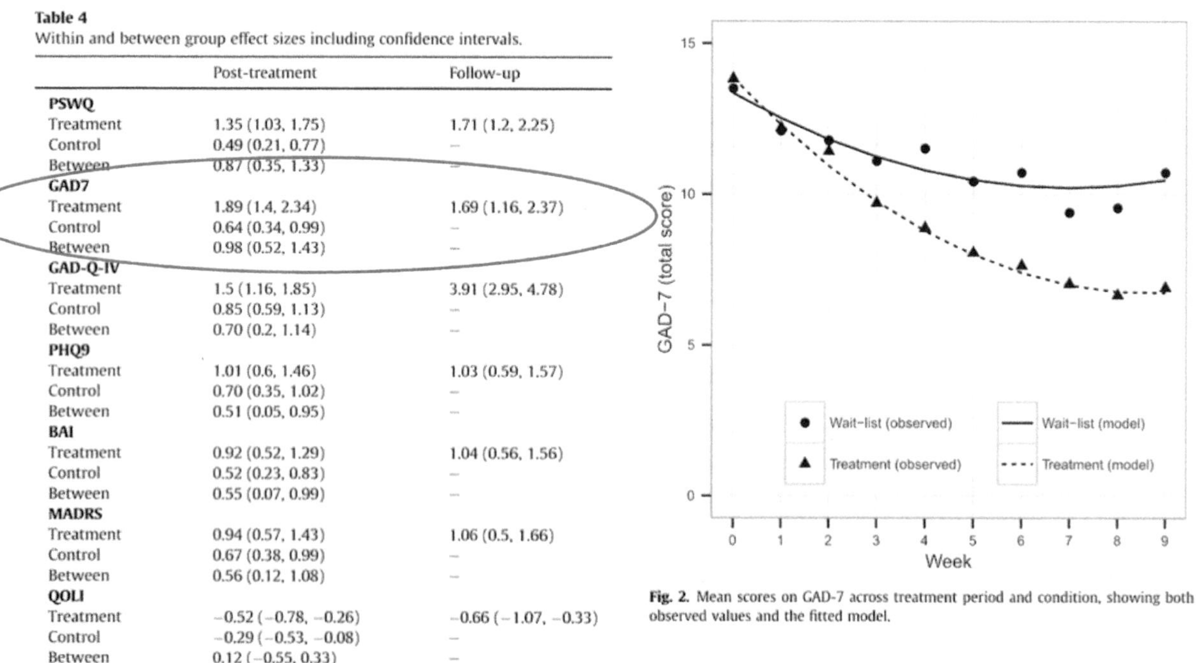

Table 4
Within and between group effect sizes including confidence intervals.

	Post-treatment	Follow-up
PSWQ		
Treatment	1.35 (1.03, 1.75)	1.71 (1.2, 2.25)
Control	0.49 (0.21, 0.77)	–
Between	0.87 (0.35, 1.33)	–
GAD7		
Treatment	1.89 (1.4, 2.34)	1.69 (1.16, 2.37)
Control	0.64 (0.34, 0.99)	–
Between	0.98 (0.52, 1.43)	–
GAD-Q-IV		
Treatment	1.5 (1.16, 1.85)	3.91 (2.95, 4.78)
Control	0.85 (0.59, 1.13)	–
Between	0.70 (0.2, 1.14)	–
PHQ9		
Treatment	1.01 (0.6, 1.46)	1.03 (0.59, 1.57)
Control	0.70 (0.35, 1.02)	–
Between	0.51 (0.05, 0.95)	–
BAI		
Treatment	0.92 (0.52, 1.29)	1.04 (0.56, 1.56)
Control	0.52 (0.23, 0.83)	–
Between	0.55 (0.07, 0.99)	–
MADRS		
Treatment	0.94 (0.57, 1.43)	1.06 (0.5, 1.66)
Control	0.67 (0.38, 0.99)	–
Between	0.56 (0.12, 1.08)	–
QOLI		
Treatment	−0.52 (−0.78, −0.26)	−0.66 (−1.07, −0.33)
Control	−0.29 (−0.53, −0.08)	–
Between	0.12 (−0.55, 0.33)	–

Fig. 2. Mean scores on GAD-7 across treatment period and condition, showing both observed values and the fitted model.

FIGURE 9.5 Figures from Dahlin et al. (2016).

Notice that in the table, they report confidence intervals in parentheses following the estimate. These confidence intervals provide information about the upper and lower boundaries of the estimate. In this example, if the confidence interval does not cross 0 (i.e., both numbers are above 0 or both are below), then the findings are significant.

Understanding the Presentation of the Statistical Analyses

As the goal of this chapter is to help you read scientific articles, it is important to discuss the way the results of statistical analyses are presented in these articles. We include information about interpreting these findings. This information will supplement the understanding you have developed from the courses you have taken in statistical methods.

The sections of the article describing the statistical methods, analyses, and outcomes can seem complicated. But these sections usually follow a pattern. The plan for the statistical analyses is often presented in the *Methods Section* of the articles, whereas the results of the statistical analyses are presented in the *Results Section* of scientific articles.

The results section often presents a series of preliminary analyses followed by inferential analyses. Both the sections on preliminary and hypothesis-testing or inferential analyses contain a series of components. If you understand how the plan and the results are presented in research articles, you can focus your attention on the important pieces of information contained in these sections.

An Analytic Plan or Strategy

The analytic plan for the statistical analyses usually describes methods that will be used for both the preliminary data analyses and the hypothesis-testing or inferential data analyses. It can be helpful to read this section because the authors explain what will be presented in the results section, and they usually provide a concise explanation of the primary hypotheses they plan to test. This information can help you focus your attention as your read the rest of the results section (Fig. 9.6).

2. Methods

2.3. Analytic strategy

First we used independent *t*-tests and chi-square statistics to compare demographic and psychosocial characteristics of participants that were available at FU2 to those who dropped from the study. Next we analyzed the cross-sectional associations between OC cognitions and OC, depressive and anxiety symptoms at baseline using a series of regression analyses. The total III score was separately analyzed as the predictor of OCD symptom severity and subtypes as well as of comorbid anxiety and depressive symptoms. A total of 16 models were analyzed. First, unadjusted regression analyses were conducted to describe the associations between OC cognitions and symptom severity, subtypes and comorbid anxiety and depressive symptoms. In order to measure the unique associations between cognitions and symptoms, and due to possible overlap between various symptoms, we conducted additional adjusted analyses as following: 1) a model testing the association between OCD cognitions and symptom severity, adjusted for the effects of depressive and anxiety symptoms; 2) a model testing the association between OCD cognitions and symptom subtypes, adjusted for the effects of depressive and anxiety symptoms; 3) a model testing the association between OC cognitions and anxiety symptoms, adjusted for OCD severity and subtypes; 4) a model testing the association between OC cognitions and depressive symptoms, adjusted for OCD severity and subtypes. Due to multiple comparisons, we applied the Bonferroni correction with p level of significance at $p < .003$ (.05:16). All analyses were conducted in SPSS (IBM, 21.0).

← In this section, the authors are describing their strategy for handling preliminary analyses. These analyses compare those who did vs. did not drop out of the study. They also examine relations among all the key variables at baseline.

← In this section, the authors are describing the specific hypotheses they want to test. They are specifically interested in the relations between OCD-related cognitions and different kinds of symptoms (OC symptoms. Each of the models controls for different variables.

FIGURE 9.6 Analytic strategy. *From Tibi et al. (2018).*

A Section Explaining Preliminary Analyses

Researchers often conduct preliminary analyses that are necessary to decide how to proceed with the statistical analyses necessary for hypothesis testing. These preliminary analyses are usually presented in the Results section of the article. Preliminary analyses have two goals: (a) to determine if the data are appropriate for the analyses the researcher wants to conduct, and (b) to identify any variables that may influence the analyses in ways that should be avoided to protect the internal validity of the study.

Preliminary analyses to determine if the data meet assumptions of the analyses. One set of preliminary analyses provide information on the degree to which the data collected for the study meet the **assumptions of the analyses** the researchers want to undertake. This is critical because not all kinds of data are appropriate for every kind of statistical test. Each statistical test makes assumptions about the kind of data that are being used. For example, regression analyses generally require that the data are normally distributed. Other analytic strategies do not require the data to meet the assumption of a normal distribution, but they make other assumptions. For a more detailed discussion of these issues see Tabachnick and Fidell (2007). In the preliminary analysis section, researchers provide information on whether the data collected meet the assumptions of the statistical tests they plan to use.

Here's an example. Regression analyses assume **normally distributed data**. Normally distributed data look like the **bell curve** depicted in Fig. 9.7. The responses are distributed around the mean.

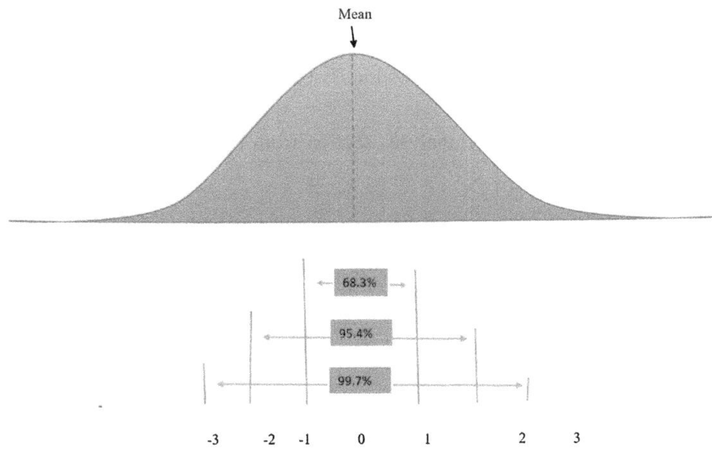

FIGURE 9.7 Normal distribution.

But sometimes data are not distributed this way. Too many participants may have had very high scores (or very low scores). Consequently, the data may be **skewed** (Fig. 9.8).

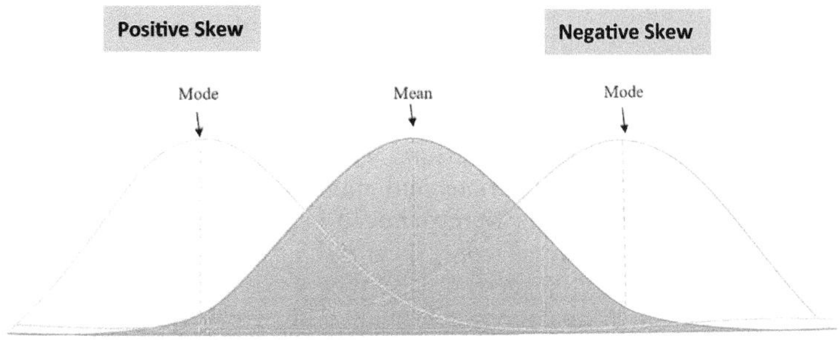

FIGURE 9.8 Skewness.

If the data are not normally distributed, some methods of statistical analyses cannot be used. Therefore, researchers will sometimes **transform** the data to make the distributions more normal.

Here are two examples of preliminary analysis sections. In the first, the data meet assumptions and no further work is needed before the analyses can proceed (Fig. 9.9).

2. Results

2.1. Preliminary data analyses

Prior to carrying out the main statistical analyses, the data were screened to determine whether statistical assumptions were met and to ascertain whether the data were appropriate for further analyses (see Tabachnick & Fidell, 1996, for a review of data screening procedures). The assumption of normality, linearity, homogeneity of variance, as well as multicollinearity and singularity were met for all measures.

FIGURE 9.9 Preliminary analyses section from Buhr and Dugas (2009).

In the second, the data do not meet assumptions. The authors transform the data and make other adjustments, so the analyses can proceed (Fig. 9.10).

Results

DATA SCREENING

Prior to data analyses, distributions, skewness, and kurtosis were examined for scale total scores (ACQ, BSQ, BDI-II, EPQ-N, PSWQ, SIAS, SPS, PI, IUS-PA, IUS-IA). Scores were generally normally distributed with most items demonstrating acceptable levels of skewness and kurtosis (< |1.00|). One exception to this was the PI total score, with a skew of 1.33 and kurtosis of 1.57. A square-root transformation reduced these values to .51 and –.25, respectively. All subsequent analyses were conducted with this transformed variable (PIsqrt). Total scores were then screened for univariate and multivariate outliers. Eight participants were removed because they had standardized total scores greater than 3 on at least one variable, suggesting that they were univariate outliers. Mahalanobis Distance with a chi-square cutoff of 29.59 (10 variables, $p = .001$) indicated one multivariate outlier, which was removed. Thus, the final total was 319 participants, who were used for all subsequent analyses.

FIGURE 9.10 Data screening from McEvoy and Mahoney (2012).

The preliminary analysis section can also be used to describe how the authors combined or organized the variables, handle missing variables, or test if the data fit a pre-specified model (Fig. 9.11).

3. Results

3.1. Preliminary analyses

Participants (n = 91) were excluded if more than 5% of their data were missing, they completed the survey more than once (only the earliest response was analysed), and/or they failed to meet eligibility criteria (under 18 years), thereby resulting in a final sample size of 506 participants. Missing values analysis, using Little's MCAR test, indicated that data was missing completely at random, χ^2 (4) = 5.33, p = 0.255. Accordingly, missing data were replaced using the expectation maximisation method (Muthén & Muthén, 1998–2015; Tabachnick & Fidell, 2013). Data screening indicated no problematic distributional properties as evidenced by acceptable levels of skewness (i.e., <2) and kurtosis (i.e., <7) values, and inspection of histograms (Curran, West, & Finch, 1996; Tabachnick & Fidell, 2013). There were no multivariate outliers (i.e., using a p <0.001 criterion for Mahalanobis D^2) and multicollinearty was not an issue. Descriptive statistics and correlations for all study variables are reported in Table 1. Inspection of the bivariate correlations indicated moderate to large significant associations between trait IU, all disorder-specific IU subscales, cognitive vulnerabilities, and disorder symptoms. Cronbach's alphas for all measures were high (Table 1).

← In this section, the authors describe how they handling missing data.

3.3. Structural model

An examination of the fit statistics revealed that the structural model provided an acceptable fit to the data, χ^2 (2278) = 4809.70, p <0.001, CFI = 0.92, TLI = 0.92, SRMR = 0.06, and RMSEA = 0.05 (90% CI [0.045–0.049]). The standardised parameter estimates for the structural pathways are displayed in Fig. 1.

← In this section, the authors test the assumptions specified by the analyses they wish to use. The data meet all the assumptions, so they can proceed with the analyses.

FIGURE 9.11 Excerpt from Shihata, McEvoy, and Mullan (2017).

Preliminary analyses assessing potential control variables. The second set of preliminary analyses examines potential covariate or control variables. Because research participants often vary in sociodemographic characteristics (e.g., age, gender, race, income, education, etc.), researchers must have a strategy to determine if any of these sociodemographic variables are influencing the analyses. If these sociodemographic variables are related to the predictor or outcome variables, they can present a threat to the internal validity of the study and make it difficult to interpret the findings. A preliminary analyses section which examines the relations of sociodemographic variables to the predictor/IV and outcome/dependent variable is sometimes titled "Demographic differences in key variables" or even "Descriptive statistics and sex comparisons."

To evaluate the effects of potential sociodemographic covariates, researchers conduct analyses that examine if there are any associations between these sociodemographic variables and the predictor or outcome variables in the study. Before she conducts tests on her primary hypotheses, she examines the relations of gender to her predictor and outcome variables. If she finds gender differences in either IU or GAD, she may control for gender in her subsequent analyses (Fig. 9.12).

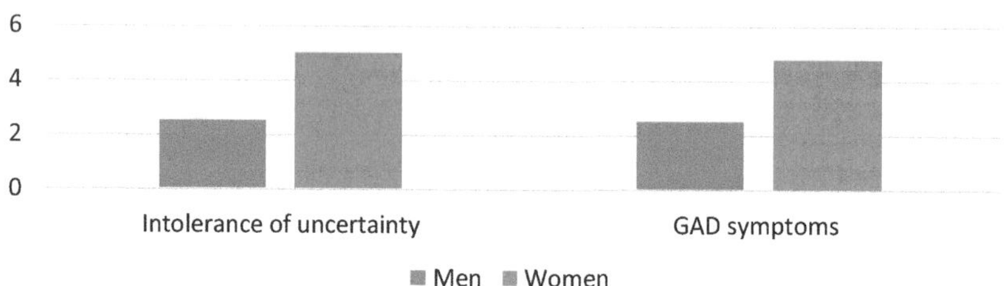

FIGURE 9.12 Gender differences in intolerance to uncertainty and GAD.

When researchers include control variables, they are adjusting the statistical analyses to consider the contributions of these variables. With control variables included in the analyses, sometimes the effect of the predictor/IV is clearer. In other cases, the effects of the predictor/IV may no longer be significant if the effects were partly or fully explained by the control variable. In our hypothetical example, when the researcher uses gender as a control variable, she can determine if the effects of IU on GAD remain significant independent of the effects of gender (Fig. 9.13).

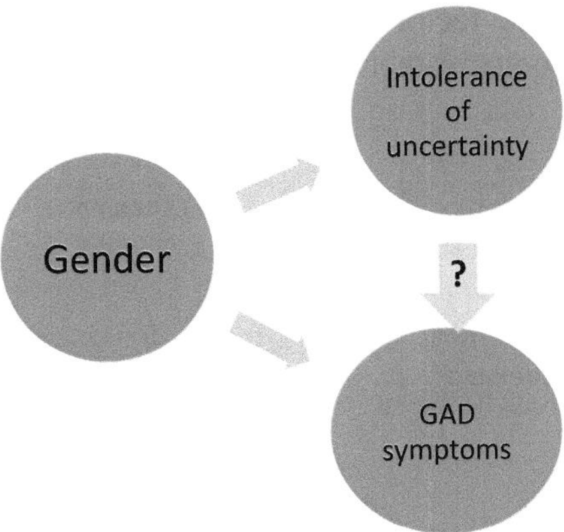

FIGURE 9.13 The role of gender in intolerance of uncertainty and GAD symptoms.

Hypothesis-Testing Analyses

After reporting on the preliminary analyses, researchers report on the hypothesis-testing analyses. This is the section of the results in which *inferential* approaches are used. Inferential approaches are used to test the specific hypotheses the researchers have proposed, the ones essential to the theory. The researchers choose statistical tests depending on the hypotheses they wish to test and the type of data they have collected.

Testing different hypotheses. Researchers might simply hypothesize that there are relations between a predictor and outcome variable. For example, researchers may propose that a risk factor variable is associated with symptoms of the disorder. Researchers can also test hypotheses related to mediation or to moderation. For example, researchers may propose that variables are linked along a pathway. They may test the hypothesis that one or more "mechanism" variables serve as mediators between the risk factor and outcome, two other variables.

Or they might propose that one variable moderates the relations among other variables. For example, they might hypothesize that age moderates the relation between a risk factor and an outcome. The risk factor might have a stronger effect on the outcome for younger rather than older participants (Fig. 9.14).

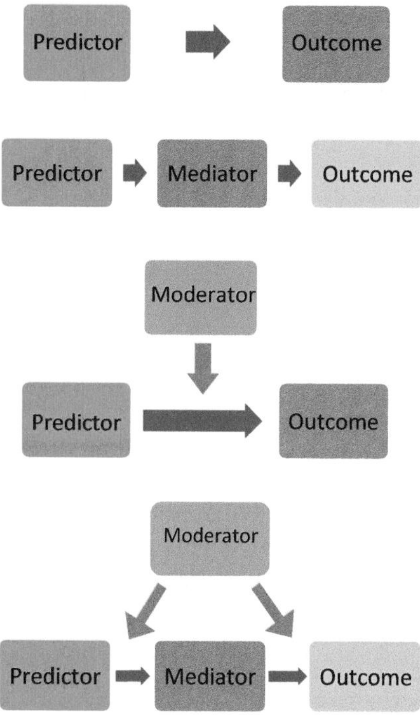

FIGURE 9.14 Different models of relationships among predictor, outcome, mediator, and moderator variables.

The type of analysis chosen to test these hypotheses depends on the nature of the variables. For example, some analytic approaches are best for testing relationships between two or more continuous variables (e.g., regression analyses). Other approaches are appropriate when the predictor is categorical and the outcome(s) are continuous (e.g., analysis of variance, ANOVA or MANOVA). Still other analytic approaches are used when both predictor and outcome are categorical (e.g., chi-square analyses).

The type of approach depends on the number of predictors and outcomes. For example, correlational analyses are appropriate for examining the relations between a single predictor variable and a single outcome variable. Correlational analyses are often used when both predictor and outcome are continuous variables. In contrast, multiple regression analyses are used when there are multiple predictors and one outcome.

Different analyses are used when variables are measured more than once. For example, in longitudinal studies, there are repeated measurements. To analyze the data, the analytic approach might include repeated measures ANOVA or regression, or time series analyses.

The type of analysis also depends on the complexity of the research questions. When researchers are testing a model in which one variable predicts another, a regression model is adequate. But when the researchers propose a model that suggests that one or more variables mediate the relation between the predictor and outcome, then a more complex analysis is needed. These hypotheses can be tested with approaches such as structural equation modeling or process mediational analyses which are derived from regression analyses.

Uncorrected analyses. Often researchers will present simple analyses first. They might present information on relationships among key variables examined one pair at a time, and without correcting for control variables (covariates). Often these analyses can provide data that are valuable for the A-B-C pathways, even when testing one of these pathways is not the primary goal of the study reported in the article.

For example, in the Calvete (2014) article we examined in Chapter 8, the author tested the hypothesis that maladaptive schemas mediated the relation of childhood maltreatment to depressive symptoms. Before the author tests the mediational hypothesis, she examines the uncorrected relations between each of the variables.

The data are presented as shown in the table in Fig. 9.15, with the specific correlation coefficients (the r values) for each analysis presented in the cells of the table.

Table 1
Descriptive statistics and correlations between variables.

	1	2	3	4	5	6	7	8	9	10	11	12	13	14	15	16
1. Parental emotional abuse	1															
2. Emotional abuse by peers	.17**	1														
3. Neuroticism	.21**	.27**	1													
4. Extraversion	−.06	.07*	−.06	1												
5. T1 Disconnection/rejection	.32**	.42**	.52**	.12**	1											
6. T1 Impaired autonomy	.29**	.31**	.39**	.03	.70**	1										
7. T1 Other-directedness	.27**	.37**	.48**	−.01	.80**	.64**	1									
8. T2 Disconnection/rejection	.28**	.37**	.46**	−.10**	.68**	.51**	.60**	1								
9. T2 Impaired autonomy	.27**	.30**	.38**	−.04	.54**	.66**	.48**	.73**	1							
10. T2 Other-directedness	.24**	.33**	.43**	−.04	.59**	.45**	.67**	.82**	.65**	1						
11. T1 Depression	.31**	.32**	.48**	−.05	.63**	.53**	.55**	.48**	.44**	.45**	1					
12. T2 Depression	.27**	.28**	.43**	−.10**	.51**	.43**	.44**	.65**	.56**	.56**	.58**	1				
13. T3 Depression	.25**	.25**	.43**	−.15**	.47**	.40**	.38**	.53**	.47**	.46**	.53**	.67**	1			
14. T1 Social anxiety	.17**	.36**	.49**	−.16**	.67**	.49**	.70**	.56**	.43**	.56**	.47**	.39**	.37**	1		
15. T2 Social anxiety	.18**	.33**	.40**	−.16**	.52**	.38**	.54**	.71**	.55**	.73**	.35**	.49**	.45**	.61**	1	
16. T3 Social anxiety	.17**	.29**	.37**	−.16**	.47**	.36**	.47**	.55**	.44**	.57**	.35**	.45**	.55**	.55**	.66**	1
Mean	9.05	7.82	24.43	20.73	2.32	2.48	2.88	2.21	2.32	2.74	17.64	16.24	25.86	41.53	40.56	39.85
Standard deviation	3.29	2.66	7.74	6.07	0.82	0.94	0.93	0.84	0.94	0.97	9.04	9.62	9.44	12.73	13.36	13.55
Range	6–24	6–24	11–55	10–50	1–6	1–6	1–6	1–6	1–6	1–6	0–60	0–60	0–60	18–90	18–90	18–90

* $p < .05$.
** $p < .001$.

E. Calvete / Child Abuse & Neglect 38 (2014) 735–746

FIGURE 9.15 Table of correlations from Calvete (2014).

These numbers provide an estimate of the magnitude of shared variance between the members of the pair. For example, in the table, the correlation coefficient expressing the relation between peer emotional abuse at Time 1 and depressive symptoms at Time 1 is 0.32. You can also see two small asterisks (**) next to the number. In the Notes section of the table, the authors explain that this asterisk means the p value is $< .001$, and the findings are statistically significant.

Final set of inferential analyses. Now researchers apply all the knowledge they have gained from their preceding analyses to the final hypothesis-testing analyses. In these analyses, researchers generally include all relevant control variables. They combine the predictor and outcome variables in ways which permit them to evaluate their primary hypotheses. Before we examine the section containing the inferential analyses in more detail, we can complete an activity to help us recognize the components of the results section.

Activity 9.1: Identifying the Components of a Results Section

Pick a paper of your own and identify all the sections in the results section. What section title or sentences do the authors use that allow you use Table 9.4 to tell what the purpose of the section is? Remember that not all papers present the components of a results section in the same way.

TABLE 9.4 Identifying components for the results section.

Author/Date	Was this section present?	What section title or sentences gives you the information?
Analytic plan		
Preliminary analyses – meeting assumptions of analyses.		
Preliminary analyses-examining covariates		
Uncorrected analyses		
Hypothesis testing analyses with covariates included		

Understanding the Inferential Analyses

When you prepare to read a results section, it helps to keep the information you need in mind. Think about the A-B-C model you are examining. Look for evidence related to that model. This can help you stay focused as you try to determine if the article provides relevant information. Once you find the information you need, you can read further to find out if the evidence supports your hypotheses or does not.

For example, suppose you are writing about mechanisms that are involved in GAD. You might wonder if IU is a mechanism triggering or maintaining GAD. If there is evidence linking GAD and IU, these data would support using IU as a mechanism.

In the abstract of the Carleton et al. (2012) article we examined in Chapter 8, the authors describe analyses which examine if different types of GAD diagnoses differ in IU. This suggests that the article could provide information relevant to our hypothesis about a relationship between IU and GAD symptoms—information that is relevant to the possible B to C pathway.

As is the case with many empirical articles, the Carleton et al. (2012) article is complex.

In the primary analyses of the Carleton et al. study (2012), the predictor can be labeled *Diagnosis Group*. The variable "Diagnosis Group" has many levels. To define the levels, the authors have combined assessments of diagnosis and the recruitment strategy (i.e., University vs. community). Therefore, the levels of the predictor variable correspond to the composition of the groups rather than the diagnosis itself.

Some levels correspond to groups of participants with different primary or secondary diagnoses of GAD. Two other levels reflect two additional groups they expect will have no diagnosis, one group was recruited from the community and one from the University. In Fig. 9.16, you can see how the authors describe all the levels of the predictor variable. They refer to each level as a group.

The first ANOVA (replicating Ladouceur et al., 1999) collapsed diagnostic groups creating groups with a principal diagnosis of GAD ($n = 63$; i.e., with or without an additional diagnosis of another anxiety disorder), an additional diagnosis of GAD ($n = 49$; i.e., another principal diagnosis, but with a concurrent additional diagnosis of GAD), a principal diagnosis of any other anxiety disorder ($n = 225$; i.e., no principal or additional diagnosis of GAD), a principal diagnosis of MDD ($n = 21$), the undergraduate sample ($n = 428$), and the community sample ($n = 571$).

FIGURE 9.16 Excerpt from Carleton et al. (2012).

In the authors' primary analyses, the predictor "Diagnosis Group" has six levels:

1. A principal diagnosis of GAD
2. A secondary diagnosis of GAD (with a primary diagnosis of social anxiety disorder (SAD), panic disorder (PDA), or obsessive compulsive disorder (OCD)
3. A primary diagnosis of another anxiety disorder (PDA, OCD, or SAD) but *no* GAD diagnosis
4. A primary MDD diagnosis with or without an additional GAD diagnosis

5. No known diagnosis (University sample)
6. No known diagnosis (Community sample)

The authors examine three outcomes: the full IU score, and two dimensions of IU called Inhibitory IU and Prospective IU.

Information about the primary hypothesis is in the hypothesis-testing or inferential analyses sections. Sometimes this section is labeled with a brief title explaining the content of the section. In the Carleton et al. (2012) article, this section is titled *"Distribution estimations and ANOVA results."* In this section, the authors describe the results of the analyses of variance (ANOVAs) they conduct to test the main hypotheses of the study (Fig. 9.17).

The first ANOVA (replicating Ladouceur et al., 1999) collapsed diagnostic groups creating groups with a principal diagnosis of GAD ($n = 63$; i.e., with or without an additional diagnosis of another anxiety disorder), an additional diagnosis of GAD ($n = 49$; i.e., another principal diagnosis, but with a concurrent additional diagnosis of GAD), a principal diagnosis of any other anxiety disorder ($n = 225$; i.e., no principal or additional diagnosis of GAD), a principal diagnosis of MDD ($n = 21$), the undergraduate sample ($n = 428$), and the community sample ($n = 571$). Statistically significant differences were identified for the total score, $F(5, 134.32) = 70.14$, $p < .001$, $eta^2 = .20$, the prospective IU subscale, $F(5, 134.61) = 46.05$, $p < .001$, $eta^2 = .14$, and the inhibitory IU subscale, $F(5, 134.32) = 83.02$, $p < .001$, $eta^2 = .23$. Tukey post hoc comparisons were conducted to assess for individual differences between group means. The results of the Tukey post hoc comparisons were generally comparable for the total and subscale scores. There were no statistically significant differences between participants with a principal diagnosis of GAD, an additional diagnosis of GAD, a principal diagnosis of any other anxiety disorder, or a principal diagnosis of MDD (i.e., all $ps > .10$). In contrast, all of the aforementioned clinical groupings reported statistically significantly higher scores than both the undergraduate and community samples (i.e., all $ps < .01$). There were no statistically significant differences between the undergraduate and community samples. Given that no differences were found from this first ANOVA, only the second ANOVA results are presented in detail; however, the results of the first ANOVA are available from the authors upon request.

← An explanation of all the levels of the predictor variable.

← Statistical sentences explaining the main outcomes of the study.

← Post-hoc analyses.

FIGURE 9.17 Excerpt from Carleton et al. (2012).

In this ANOVA the authors are testing the hypothesis that individuals with either a primary or secondary GAD diagnosis or a diagnosis of depression will have higher IU scores than those without a GAD diagnosis or those who are from a nonclinical sample (and presumably do not have any diagnosis). They compare the six levels of the predictor on the outcomes.

They provide a figure showing the distribution of scores on the IU measures (the outcome) for the different samples of participants they have. The distribution of scores is shown in Fig. 9.18. Higher scores on the IU measure are on the right side of the graph. The levels of the predictor with any clinical diagnosis have peaks which are to the right of those for the University and community sample on the graph.

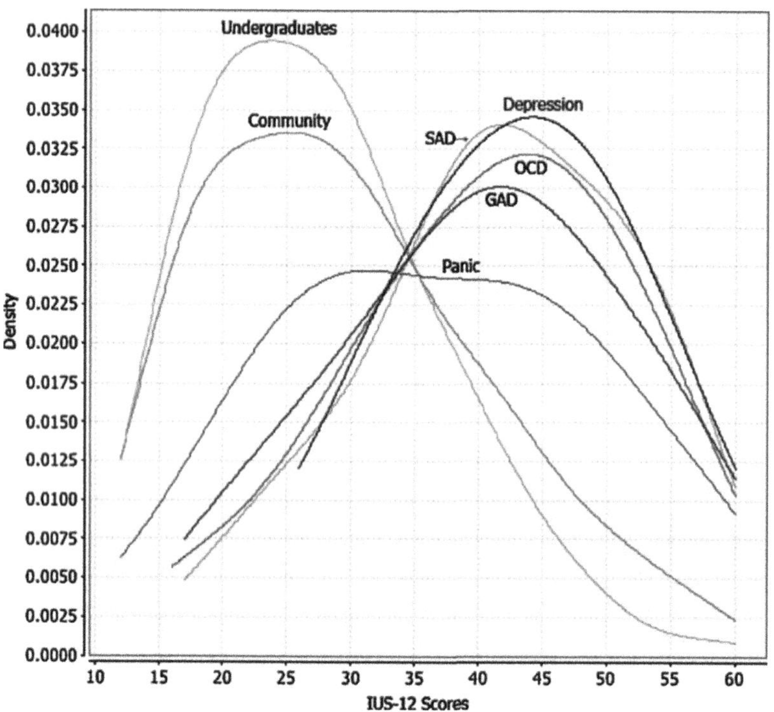

Fig. 1. Kernel density estimation of IUS-12 scores across groups, with density reflecting frequency of cases along IUS-12 scores.

FIGURE 9.18 Figure from Carleton et al. (2012) showing the distribution of scores for different groups.

Statistical sentences. As you can see in Fig. 9.17, the authors present the results of the analyses using word sentences and statistical sentences. The statistical sentences (e.g., $F(5, 134.32) = 70.14$, $P < .001$, $eta^2 = 0.20$) provide important information about the tests used and the methods of analyses. The statistical sentences in the Carleton et al. (2012) article support the authors' statements in words. The statistical sentences indicate that the estimates of the relationships of the predictor (Diagnosis Group) to the outcomes (IU and subscales) are significant.

We will examine each part of the statistical sentence in more detail. But, we provide a very simplified version of these ideas. We use this information to help insure you understand the analyses you are reading. For a detailed understanding of the ideas and procedures involved, see Tabachnick and Fidell (2007).

The first statistical sentence is $F(5, 134.32) = 70.14$, $P < .001$, $eta^2 = 0.20$.

The letter that begins the statistical sentence provides us with information about the type of analysis that was performed. In the analysis plan the authors indicated they would use an analysis of variance (ANOVA). The "F" in the statistical sentences confirms that they did use an ANOVA, since "F" indicates an ANOVA of some kind (Fig. 9.19).

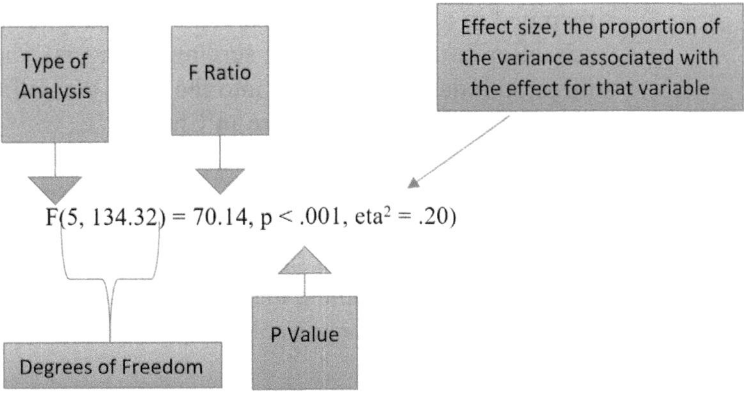

FIGURE 9.19 Reporting results for an F-test.

The F statistic. The F statistic is a ratio of the explained variance to the unexplained variance. In the simplest form:

$$F = \frac{\text{Explained variance}}{\text{Unexplained variance}}$$

As we have discussed, variance refers to the spread of the scores. The explained variance is the variation among the scores that is expected or explained. If the researchers have hypothesized that the predictor variable will be associated with a difference in scores, then they have explained those differences. For example, in the Carleton paper, the authors hypothesize that the predictor, Diagnosis Group, will explain differences in scores on the IU measure.

The **unexplained variance** results from error in the model. This error reflects all the variations among scores from all the participants that are not explained by the predictor. These variations might reflect individual differences among the participants (i.e., the predictor variable might operate differently in different people).

The unexplained variance might also reflect **measurement error**. Measurement error can occur when researchers use unreliable measures or have problems with the testing. Unexplained variance can also occur if the researchers use procedures that are not well controlled and allow different sources of bias to influence the outcome. For example, if the community sample was recruited in a setting which served only young people (e.g., at a school or community center serving teenagers), the researchers might introduce an age bias into the data. We will discuss these different sources of bias more in Chapter 16.

Degrees of freedom. In the statistical sentence $F(5, 134.32) = 70.14$, $p < .001$), the **degrees of freedom** are 5 and 134.32. The degrees of freedom provide information necessary to generate the statistics in the model. In an ANOVA analysis, the degrees of freedom adjust the outcomes to reflect the number of levels of the predictor variable and the number of **observations** included.

In the Carleton et al. (2012) paper the authors must make significant adjustments to the degrees of freedom. They describe using a Welch correction because the sample sizes for each of the levels of the predictor are varied. Some groups are large, and some are very small. These differences violate assumptions of ANOVA. Consequently, they must correct the degrees of freedom to adjust the analyses.

***p* values.** The p value in the sentence is $p < .0001$. In psychological science, the alpha level is set to 0.05, to make sure that it is difficult to reject the null hypothesis. Therefore, researchers regard statistical analyses with a p value $< .05$ as statistically significant, meaning the value exceeds the threshold of set by the alpha value.

Eta^2. The eta is a measure of the amount of variance associated with the predictor variable. In this case, the eta^2 is 0.20. This means that "Diagnosis Group" predicts about 20% of the variance in IU scores.

Post hoc analyses. It is important to know that there is a significant effect of the predictor on the outcome. But we also need to know the direction of the effect. We need to understand which level of the predictor had the higher score.

In the article by Carleton et al. (2012), the statistical analyses we described earlier indicate that there is a significant effect of Diagnosis Group on IU. But that is not enough information to help us understand the results of the study. We need to know which diagnosis groups are significantly different from each other.

We can look at the means for each group to get an idea of the direction of the differences. But to determine if these differences are statistically significant, we need to conduct post hoc statistical tests. *These post hoc analyses are performed only if the overall effect is significant.* In the post hoc analyses, the researchers compare each level of the predictor to every other level on average IU scores. They include special statistical controls necessary because the authors may be comparing many different levels.

In the Carleton et al. (2012) article, the results of the post hoc analyses reveal that there were no differences in average levels of IU among the first four levels of the predictor (primary diagnosis of GAD, secondary diagnosis of GAD, no diagnosis of GAD, or primary diagnosis of MDD). Participants on these four levels of the predictor had scores on the IU scales that were not different from each other. On the other hand, scores for these groups' participants differed from participants on the two levels which had no diagnosis.

One more note about word and statistical sentences. The word sentences the authors use to present the statistical results do not always have the same format. Sometimes authors will write a sentence such as *"There is a main effect of the predictor on the outcome"* or *"One level of the predictor had a higher score on the outcome than the other*."

For example, imagine a study in which there is one predictor (GAD diagnosis, with two levels: GAD vs. no GAD) and one outcome, negative cognitions. Each of these sentences communicates the same idea about the results:

> "There is a main effect of GAD diagnosis on negative cognitions." And the sentences
> "Those with GAD had IU scores which differed from those without GAD."
> "There were statistically significant differences in IU between groups with and without GAD."

Knowing the type of words used to communicate the results and understanding the possible sentence structures used can help you recognize the findings in the results section.

Activity 9.2: Reading Statistical Sentences

Imagine a study in which the predictor/independent variable is Diagnosis and the outcome/dependent variable is Symptoms. The predictor/independent variable has two levels: Disorder A and Disorder B. There are 50 participants in the sample, half of whom have Disorder A. The researchers hypothesize that the participants who have Disorder A will have higher scores on a measure of negative cognitions than the participants who have Disorder B. The results of the analysis can be expressed using this statistical sentence ($F(1,48) = 5.25$, $p < .01$). What does the statistical sentence tell us? Explain each element of the statistical sentence in detail. What additional information would we need to know to which group (Disorder A or Disorder B) had higher scores?

____

____

____

____

____

Activity 9.3: Questions to Answer about the Theory of the Problem Articles

For each theory of the problem article you use, answer these questions:

1. What is the aim of the study?

   ____

2. What type of article is this: risk factor to outcome, risk factor to mechanism, mechanism to outcome? Or risk factor to mechanism to outcome?

   ____

3. Are there multiple hypotheses being tested? If so, what are the hypotheses?

   ____

   a. For each hypothesis, what is the IV/predictor and DV/outcome?

      ____

   b. For each hypothesis, is the IV a risk factor or a mechanism?

      ____

   c. For each hypothesis, is the DV a mechanism or outcome?

      ____

4. What types of statistical analyses are used in the study?

   ____

5. What are the word and statistical sentences used to describe the results of the main hypotheses?

   ____

6. What evidence does the study provide?

   ____

7. How does the evidence from this article support the arguments you are making for your paper?

   ____

Building Human Capital

Thinking About Numbers: A Focus on Yourself and Others

Some people feel very nervous when they must understand numbers or statistics. They get worried they will miss something, not understand the rules, or find it too complicated to understand. When they get nervous, they may avoid thinking about the numbers.

Did you feel that way?

What did you do to push yourself to look carefully at the statistics? How did you make yourself concentrate and check the details and your understanding of the material? Ask a classmate about his/her experiences working with the numbers. What strategies did your classmate use to stay focused on understanding the material? As you understand the statistical sentences in the articles you are reading, how do you feel? Are you gaining some knowledge and confidence?

Terms

Take the time to define each of these terms and consider how to apply them.

Statistical Terms

Quantify
Numeric data
Statistical analyses
Variability
F ratio
False positive/Type I error
False negative/Type II error
Alpha level
P value
Assumptions of the analyses
Normally distributed data/bell curve
Skew
Transform (data)
Factor analyses
Degrees of freedom
Observations
Sum of squares
Mean squares
Post hoc analyses

References

Appelbaum, M., Cooper, H., Kline, R. B., Mayo-Wilson, E., Nezu, A. M., & Rao, S. M. (2018). Journal article reporting standards for quantitative research in psychology: The APA Publications and Communications Board task force report. *American Psychologist, 73*(1), 3–25.

Buhr, K., & Dugas, M. J. (2009). The role of fear of anxiety and intolerance of uncertainty in worry: An experimental manipulation. *Behaviour Research and Therapy, 47*(3), 215–223.

Calvete, E. (2014). Emotional abuse as a predictor of early maladaptive schemas in adolescents: Contributions to the development of depressive and social anxiety symptoms. *Child Abuse and Neglect, 38*(4), 735–746.

Carleton, R. N., Mulvogue, M. K., Thibodeau, M. A., McCabe, R. E., Antony, M. M., & Asmundson, G. J. G. (2012). Increasingly certain about uncertainty: Intolerance of uncertainty across anxiety and depression. *Journal of Anxiety Disorders, 12*, 468–479.

Dahlin, M., Andersson, G., Magnusson, K., Johansson, T., Sjögren, J., Håkansson, A., … Carlbring, P. (2016). Internet-delivered acceptance-based behaviour therapy for generalized anxiety disorder: A randomized controlled trial. *Behaviour Research and Therapy, 77*, 86–95.

Marmot, M. (2002). The influence of income on health: Views of an epidemiologist. *Health Affairs, 21*(2), 31–46.

McEvoy, P. M., & Mahoney, A. E. (2012). To be sure, to be sure: Intolerance of uncertainty mediates symptoms of various anxiety disorders and depression. *Behavior Therapy, 43*(3), 533–545.

Shihata, S., McEvoy, P. M., & Mullan, B. A. (2017). Pathways from uncertainty to anxiety: An evaluation of a hierarchical model of trait and disorder-specific intolerance of uncertainty on anxiety disorder symptoms. *Journal of Anxiety Disorders, 45*, 72–79.

Singh, G. K., Williams, S. D., Siahpush, M., & Mulhollen, A. (2011). Socioeconomic, rural-urban, and racial inequalities in US cancer mortality: Part I—all cancers and lung cancer and Part II—colorectal, prostate, breast, and cervical cancers. *Journal of Cancer Epidemiology, 2011*.

Tabachnick, B. G., & Fidell, L. S. (2007). *Using multivariate statistics*. Allyn & Bacon/Pearson Education.

Tibi, L., van Oppen, P., van Balkom, A. J., Eikelenboom, M., Hendriks, G.-J., & Anholt, G. E. (2018). The relationship between cognitions and symptoms in obsessive-compulsive disorder. *Journal of Affective Disorders, 225*, 495–502.

Chapter 10

Writing the Theory of the Problem

In the last three chapters you have learned about building a model of the causes of the disorder, and you have gathered evidence about the pathways among risk factors, mechanisms, and symptoms of the disorder. Now you will learn about writing the Theory of the Problem, explaining your risk factors and mechanisms. You will learn more about organizing complex scientific information and developing strategies for writing the different components of the Theory of the Problem.

The Theory of the Problem—the explanation of the risk factors and mechanisms—is another portion of the **literature review**, the review of the evidence you have obtained from scientific articles. The components you include in this section depend on the purpose of your paper or proposal. In this chapter we focus primarily on building the Theory of the Problem section for a proposal for a study to evaluate treatment outcomes. We also provide guidance for papers evaluating the state-of-the-science on causes for the disorder. Many other types of papers and proposals are possible.

In a research proposal for a treatment outcome study, the Theory of the Problem section explains information about the potential causes of the disorder. The literature reviewed provides more detail on the risk factors you have identified, describes the nature of potential mechanisms that may trigger or maintain the symptoms, and explains the potential relationships among risk factors, mechanisms, and the symptoms. The goal is to identify targets for treatment.

As you write the paper or proposal, you will continue to refine skills in linking the arguments you want to make to the evidence you need. In this section of the paper, the arguments you are making need to be explained in a straightforward manner. You will need to carefully evaluate the evidence you have gathered and clearly explain the findings to the reader.

Psychology Research Methods. https://doi.org/10.1016/B978-0-12-815680-3.00010-4

Components of the Theory of the Problem Section

The possible components of a Theory of the Problem section include the information needed to make the arguments required for the paper or proposal. Table 10.1 lists examples of these components. The chapter includes examples of different ways to use the information you have gathered about risk factors and mechanisms depending on the type of paper or proposal you are writing. When you write about the evidence needed for each component, the statements you write should be accompanied by the correct bibliographic citations, written in APA style.

TABLE 10.1 Components of the Theory of the Problem Section and their application to different types of papers.

Component	Purpose of the information
1. Summary of evidence on the risk factor and symptoms (A-C pathway). The risk factor(s) is identified in the PHS, but the evidence supporting the link between the risk factor and the symptoms of the disorder is reviewed in more detail in this section.	To provide a clear review of the state-of-the-science on the relations of the risk factor to the symptoms of the disorder.
2. Operational definitions of the potential mechanisms.	To explain the characteristics and function of the mechanism variables.
3. A presentation of the evidence of the links between the risk factors and the mechanism (A-B pathway) across several studies.	To document the ways this risk factor may contribute to the symptoms by affecting the mechanism.
4. A presentation of the evidence of links between the mechanism and the symptoms of the disorder (B-C pathway) across several studies.	To document the relations of the mechanism to the symptoms of the disorder.
5. Threats to internal and external validity seen in existing studies of the A-B (risk factor to mechanisms) pathway.	To provide an evaluation of the quality of the existing literature.
6. Gaps in knowledge presented by the existing literature on the A-B pathway.	To provide a review of areas of new knowledge which are needed.
7. Threats to internal and external validity seen in existing studies of the B-C pathway.	To provide an evaluation of the quality of existing knowledge.
8. Gaps in knowledge presented by the existing literature on the B-C pathway.	To provide a review of areas of new knowledge which are needed.
9. A summary of the implications of the evidence for treatment.	To provide direction for the development of treatment approaches.
10. A summary of the implications of the existing evidence and gaps in knowledge for future research.	To provide direction for the development of future studies on the risk factors and mechanisms which contribute to the development and maintenance of a disorder.

Writing a Proposal for a Study to Evaluate a Treatment for the Disorder

In a proposal for a study to evaluate a treatment for a disorder, the Theory of the Problem section enables the reader to understand the types of risk factors or mechanisms identified as contributing to the disorder. This section explains the A-B-C (risk factor–mechanism–symptoms) pathways that form the "Theory of the Problem." This section is necessary to prepare the reader to understand the treatment you will propose in your "Theory of the Solution" section. The treatment will address the mechanisms and symptoms of the disorder.

At a minimum, it would be useful to include information in components 1, 2, 3, 4, and 9 highlighted in Table 10.1.

Writing a Paper Reviewing the Evidence Concerning Causes of the Disorder

If you are writing a paper reviewing the evidence on the causes of a disorder, you may read many articles about the risk factors and mechanisms. These articles permit a more comprehensive examination of the evidence. Your review of the research may focus more on the A-B (risk factors to mechanisms) path or it may focus more on the B-C (mechanisms to symptoms) path.

In an approach to a paper reviewing evidence for the A-B or B-C pathway, you summarize the findings across these articles, and identify variables that are documented risk factors and/or mechanisms. You examine the similarities and differences in the findings across the existing research. Some evidence may support the hypothesis that a variable is a risk factor for the development of a disorder, and other evidence may not support the hypothesis. You can summarize the existing evidence, highlighting risk factors or mechanisms for which the data are consistent and those for which the data are less consistent or mixed.

Next, you examine possible explanations for mixed findings—thinking about the variables or study methods that may explain differences in the results. In the process, you may identify threats to internal validity and external validity associated with existing research. This analysis and your reading will help you identify gaps in knowledge. You use these gaps to guide the development of a section describing topic areas in need of further research. Chapter 8 provides a general discussion of the threats to validity and Chapter 16 provides details about possible methodological problems that may be present in basic research.

If you are focusing on the A-B path, you would include sections 1, 2, 3, 5, 6, 9, and 10 at a minimum. If you are focusing more on the B-C path, you would include sections 1, 2, 4, 7, 8, 9, and 10 at a minimum.

Assembling the Evidence Needed

In the PHS section, you defined the risk factor and presented initial evidence on the A-C pathways (i.e., the links between the risk factor and symptoms pathway). In the Theory of the Problem section, you expand on this review and the remaining pathways. Specifically, you explain the link between the risk factor and symptoms by providing evidence on the link between the risk factor and the mechanism (A-B path) and the mechanism to the symptoms of the disorder (B-C path).

The evidence you present may come from articles which provide systematic or meta-analytic reviews, if they are available. The evidence will also come from specific original empirical research articles that present data on the pathways you need to document.

For an undergraduate research methods class, a teacher may require students to read a small portion of available articles on each topic. Each of the articles gives the student some information about the topic and experience in reading and reporting on scientific articles. The focus is on understanding how to read the articles and use the evidence.

In contrast, when graduate students are preparing a thesis, or a researcher is preparing a proposal to request funding for research, they are expected to conduct comprehensive reviews of all the literature in the specific area. This will allow them to understand the state-of-the-science—the full range of knowledge about the topic. This comprehensive review will allow them to identify gaps in knowledge that should be addressed in the new research.

Putting all the Evidence into Tables

To help organize the information, it is useful to make tables summarizing the evidence for each section. These tables build on the work already done in the activities included in the previous chapters. It is important to note that there is no single correct way to organize these tables. The format we present below is a suggestion. But some form of tabling can help you keep the information organized and guide your analysis of the research.

The tables we use here include a wide range of information about the methods used to test the hypotheses. You need this information to write a description of the study. The tables also include information about the hypotheses tested and the results. This allows you to organize evidence across studies, as you compare the tables for each of the studies.

You can use the information in the tables to help you write brief descriptions of the studies. These written descriptions of the studies can provide a portion of the literature review for your paper or proposal. These descriptions include the following information:

- the aim of the study, specifying the hypotheses the authors wanted to test
- a description of the methods used to test the hypotheses, including information about the sample, research design, and measurement of the key variables
- a summary of the results, indicating if the data provide support for the hypothesis or do not

We can practice completing a table and translating the data into a written description of the study. Let's consider an A-B-C pathway in which childhood trauma is the risk factor, attachment style is the mechanism, and PTSD symptoms are the outcome (Fig. 10.1). This A-B-C pathway is based on research suggesting that childhood trauma affects attachment style (i.e., the way individuals are able to develop relationships). Problems in attachment style may lead to increased risk for PTSD.

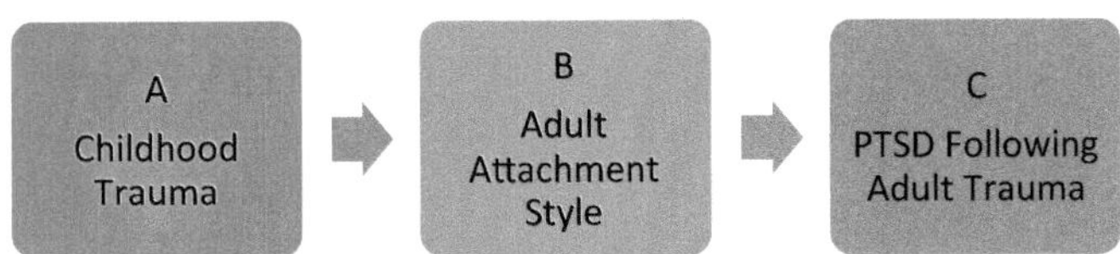

FIGURE 10.1 Example of an A-B-C pathway.

The A-B Studies: Tabling the Evidence for the Relationship of the Risk Factor to the Mechanism

A paper by Rholes et al. (2016) examines the relations between childhood trauma and attachment styles (Fig. 10.2). Table 10.2 summarizes the findings from this original research article on the A-B path, the path between the risk factors and the mechanism. These tables include some aspects of the methods, including sampling, measurement, and research design that are specific to studies of the risk factor to mechanism. An example of a completed table is presented to help you see how to organize the findings and provide a model. Then, a sample description of the study is provided (Fig. 10.2).

TABLE 10.2 Results of studies evaluating the risk factor to mechanism pathway (A-B pathway).

Author/ Date	Sample description, n, sociodemographic information	Sampling: Convenience sample or population-based sample	Research design (experimental, observational, cross-sectional, longitudinal)	Predictor: Risk factor definition	Predictor: Risk factor measurement or manipulation	Outcome: Mechanism definitions	Outcome: measurement	Findings: Provide word and statistical sentences	Limitations
Rholes, Paetzgold, & Kohn, 2016)	510 adults 58% women 78% White 9% Black Mean age = 34	Convenience sampling drawn from Amazon Mechanical Turk	Correlational, cross-sectional	Self-reported Childhood trauma	Child Trauma Questionnaire with 25 items measuring childhood emotional abuse, physical maltreatment, sexual maltreatment, emotional neglect, physical neglect	Disorganized, anxious, and avoidant attachment styles. Disorganized attachment is a style characterized by confusion and anger and anxiety in close relationships. Anxious attachment is a fearful attachment, concerned about rejection. Avoidant attachment is an emotionally distant style, the person can detach completely.	Adult Disorganized Attachment Scale. Self-report scale with nine items assessing the degree to which individuals view romance and interactions with partners as scary and traumatic. Anxious and avoidant attachment were measured with the Experiences in Close Relationships Scale.	Childhood trauma was positively associated with all three attachment types. Correlations: disorganization $r = 0.33$, avoidant $r = 0.28$, anxious 0.27	All self-report measures, only cross-sectional so reports of trauma are retrospective and may be affected by current relationship experiences.

Personality and Individual Differences 90 (2016) 61–65

Contents lists available at ScienceDirect

Personality and Individual Differences

journal homepage: www.elsevier.com/locate/paid

Disorganized attachment mediates the link from early trauma to externalizing behavior in adult relationships

W. Steven Rholes [a,*], Ramona L. Paetzold [b], Jamie L. Kohn [c]

[a] Department of Psychology, Texas A & M University, College Station, TX 77843-4235, USA
[b] Department of Management, Texas A & M University, College Station, TX 77843-4221, USA
[c] Kenan-Flagler Business School, University of North Carolina at Chapel Hill, Chapel Hill, NC 27599, USA

ARTICLE INFO

Article history:
Received 28 August 2015
Received in revised form 20 October 2015
Accepted 22 October 2015
Available online 30 October 2015

Keywords:
Disorganization
Attachment style
Externalizing behaviors
Violence
Aggression

ABSTRACT

This study investigates the mediating effects of attachment disorganization in adulthood, along with the organized attachment styles of anxiety and avoidance, to determine whether the connections between early childhood traumatic experiences and externalizing behaviors in adult romantic relationships can be explained by an attachment model that directly assesses a dimensional measure of adult disorganization. In our study, we used 510 adults who were U.S. citizens, all of whom completed online scales that provided retrospective information about childhood trauma, attachment working model information, and current experiences regarding relationship patterns. Our results indicated that adult disorganization mediated the effects between childhood and adult experiences. We also contrasted fearful avoidance with disorganization as mediators, demonstrating that they appear to be different constructs (as is sometimes contested in the literature) and can provide conflicting information about childhood to adult linkages. Our findings suggest that disorganization in adulthood mediates important relationships between early trauma and later adult externalizing outcomes, similar to outcomes seen for disorganization in childhood and adolescence. We therefore extend the existing literature, demonstrating that results from developmental psychology are relevant to social psychologists who study attachment theory in romantic relationships.

↑ The abstract provides a description of the authors' aims. In this paper, the authors test the hypothesis that childhood maltreatment is associated with adult attachment styles. They assess three different types of attachment styles: anxious, avoidant and disorganized. maltreatment to attachment styles.

Notice that this study might be useful to help document the A-B pathway for our example study.

→

The figure displays the authors' A-B-C model

A: childhood maltreatment

B: attachment styles

C: angry, aggressive relationships

The authors are interested in predicting aggressive behavior. We can still use the information in the article for the A-B pathway, even though we are interested in predicting PTSD.

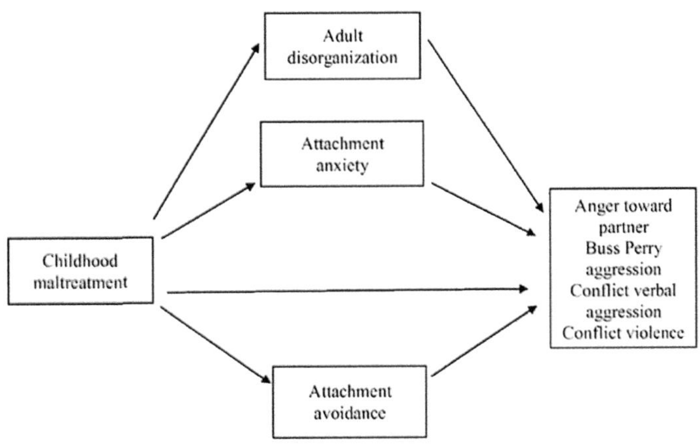

Fig. 1. Mediating model for hypothesis 1.

FIGURE 10.2 Abstract and selected excerpts from Rholes, Paetzold, & Kohn, 2016.

2. Method

→ This part of the methods section tells us who is in the study.

2.1. Participants and procedure

Participants included 510 adults who were U.S. citizens (58% women) and registered for and recruited via Amazon's Mechanical Turk (AMT; www.MTurk.com). Each participant who completed the survey, which was about their romantic relationships, personality, emotions, behaviors, and life events, received $1. Most participants were white (79%), with 9% identifying themselves as African American, 5% as Asian American, and 3% as Hispanic. On average, participants were 34.1 years old ($SD = 11.3$), with ages ranging from 21 to 80 years old. Half of participants (51%) had a college degree, and 47% reported having a full-time job. Most participants (78%) reported being in a current dating or marital relationship.

2.2. Measures

→ This part of the methods section describes all the measures that the authors used.

As you read the measures, you can determine that this is a correlational, cross sectional study in which all measures were given at the same time.

2.2.1. Disorganization

Disorganized attachment was measured using the Adult Disorganized. Attachment scale (ADA) (Paetzold et al., 2015). The ADA consists of 9 items, each rated on a 7-point scale, from 1 (*strongly disagree*) to 7 (*strongly agree*). Sample items include "I find romantic partners to be rather scary," "It is normal to have traumatic experiences with the people you feel close to," "Strangers are not as scary as romantic partners," and "Compared to most people, I feel generally confused about romantic relationships." Cronbach's alpha for the current sample was .91.

2.2.2. Attachment orientations

The Experiences in Close Relationships Scale (ECR; Brennan, Clark, & Shaver, 1998) was used to assess attachment orientation. The 36-item scale contains two subscales measuring anxious attachment style ($\alpha = .95$) and avoidant attachment style ($\alpha = .95$). Participants rated how well each item describes their feelings in close relationships. Each item was rated on a 7-point scale, from 1 (*strongly disagree*) to 7 (*strongly agree*). Eighteen items assessed anxiety and 18 items assessed avoidance, with higher dimensional scores indicating either greater anxious or avoidant attachment. We also collected data on the Fearful Avoidance Scale dimension of the Relationship Questionnaire (RQ; Bartholomew & Horowitz, 1991), with instructions telling participants to focus on close relationships.

2.2.3. Childhood maltreatment experiences

Childhood experiences of maltreatment and neglect were measured retrospectively using the Child Trauma Questionnaire (Bernstein et al., 1994). The 25-item scale ($\alpha = .95$) asked participants to rate how often they experienced five components of childhood trauma: emotional maltreatment, physical maltreatment, sexual maltreatment, emotional neglect, and physical neglect. Items were rated on a 5-point scale, from 1 (*never true*) to 5 (*very often true*). Scores were summed across the subscales and had a possible range of 25 to 125, with higher scores indicating greater frequency and variety of childhood trauma.

FIGURE 10.2 Cont'd

Table 1
Means, Standard Deviations, and Correlations of Study Variables.

Measures	*M*	*SD*	1	2	3	4	5	6	7	8	9	10
1. Disorganized attachment	2.31	1.24	-									
2. Avoidant attachment	2.91	1.30	.66	-								
3. Anxious attachment	3.19	1.39	.52	.38	-							
4. Fearful avoidance	11.15	4.67	.46	.57	.44	-						
5. Partner abuse	42.34	19.58	.56	.37	.31	.25	-					
6. Childhood maltreatment	43.12	19.83	.33	.28	.27	.25	.45	-				
7. Anger toward partner	2.97	1.10	.56	.41	.44	.35	.41	.23	-			
8. BP total aggression	10.65	4.13	.58	.41	.52	.37	.50	.35	.65	-		
9. Conflict verbal aggression	6.58	5.66	.39	.27	.39	.29	.44	.27	.52	.65	-	
10. Conflict violence	1.54	3.89	.40	.29	.19	.07	.54	.38	.33	.45	.48	-

Note. All correlations are significant at the .001 level, except for that between conflict violence and fearful avoidance, which is not significant.

↑ This is a table of correlations among all the A-B-C variables. There are significant correlations of childhood maltreatment to anxious (r = .27, p<.001), avoidant (r = .21, p < .001) and disorganized (r = .33, p < .001) attachments styles.

FIGURE 10.2 Cont'd

Study description. *In this study,* Rholes et al. (2016) *examined the relations among childhood trauma, adult attachment styles, and aggressive behavior in romantic relationships. In their model, childhood trauma is a risk factor and adult attachment styles are the potential mechanisms explaining the link between childhood trauma and aggressive behavior. The authors study these relations in a sample largely composed of White adults with a mean age of 34. The authors measure both recollections of childhood trauma and adult attachment style using self-report surveys. The authors find that childhood trauma is positively associated with all three types of insecure attachment styles in adults: disorganized attachment, anxious attachment, and avoidant attachment. This article provides evidence in support of the relation of the risk factor, childhood maltreatment, to the mechanism, attachment styles.*

Activity 10.1: Tabling the Methods and Results of an A-B, Risk Factor to Mechanism Article

Create a table for the A-B studies you are using for your paper (Table 10.3). Once you have completed the table, write a brief description of each study. Describe the aim, methods, and results, and explain the implications for your paper. See if you can identify similarities and differences across the studies.

TABLE 10.3 Original empirical research articles: A-B articles.

Author/Date	Sample descriptions, sociodemographic information	Sampling: Convenience sample or population-based sample	Research design (experimental, observational, cross-sectional, longitudinal)	Predictor: Risk factor definition	Predictor: Risk factor measurement or manipulation	Outcome: Mechanism definitions	Outcome: measurement	Findings: Provide word and statistical sentences	Limitations

Brief Study Description:

____

____

____

____

____

The B-C Studies: Tabling the Evidence on the Relations of the Mechanism to the Symptoms

Assembling the evidence for the B-C pathway requires a similar approach. As was the case for the observational studies you examined in the A-B pathway, the instruments used to measure the mechanism may vary from study to study. That is, some studies may use variables that rely on self-reports, other variables may rely on expert, parent, or teacher reports. Outcomes can also be defined differently. The outcomes could include one or more symptoms of the disorder or the outcome could be the presence of the diagnosis.

Both cross-sectional and longitudinal or prospective designs may be used. However, the studies used to examine the relationship of the mechanism to the disorder (i.e., B-C pathway studies) can use different methods than those used in the risk factor to disorder studies (A-C pathway studies). Studies examining the relationship of the mechanism to the disorder may use experimental methods in addition to correlational or observational methods. Therefore, when experimental designs are used, the independent variable (IV)—the mechanism—may be manipulated instead of simply measured.

Let's look at an example of an original research study examining a B-C path in which the mechanism (B variable) is attachment style and the outcome (C variable) is the symptoms of a disorder, PTSD following adult trauma (Fig. 10.3).

Journal of Affective Disorders 155 (2014) 295–298

Contents lists available at ScienceDirect

Journal of Affective Disorders

journal homepage: www.elsevier.com/locate/jad

Brief report

The role of adult attachment style, birth intervention and support in posttraumatic stress after childbirth: A prospective study

Susan Ayers[a,*], Donna Jessop[b], Alison Pike[b], Ylva Parfitt[b], Elizabeth Ford[c]

[a] School of Health Sciences, City University London, London, UK
[b] School of Psychology, University of Sussex, Brighton, East Sussex, UK
[c] Brighton and Sussex Medical School, Brighton, East Sussex, UK

ARTICLE INFO

Article history:
Received 31 May 2013
Received in revised form
18 October 2013
Accepted 19 October 2013
Available online 30 October 2013

Keywords:
Posttraumatic stress
Attachment
Birth
Labour
Support
Postpartum

ABSTRACT

Background: There is converging evidence that between 1% and 3% of women develop posttraumatic stress disorder (PTSD) after childbirth. Various vulnerability and risk factors have been identified, including mode of birth and support during birth. However, little research has looked at the role of adult attachment style in how women respond to events during birth. This study prospectively examined the interaction between attachment style, mode of birth, and support in determining PTSD symptoms after birth.
Method: A longitudinal study of women ($n=57$) from the last trimester of pregnancy to three months postpartum. Women completed questionnaire measures of attachment style in pregnancy and measures of PTSD, support during birth, and mode of birth at three months postpartum.
Results: Avoidant attachment style, operative birth (assisted vaginal or caesarean section) and poor support during birth were all significantly correlated with postnatal PTSD symptoms. Regression analyses showed that avoidant attachment style moderated the relationship between operative birth and PTSD symptoms, where women with avoidant attachment style who had operative deliveries were most at risk of PTSD symptoms.
Limitations: The study was limited to white European, cohabiting, primiparous women. Future research is needed to see if these findings are replicated in larger samples and different sociodemographic groups.
Conclusions: This study suggests avoidant attachment style may be a vulnerability factor for postpartum PTSD, particularly for women who have operative births. If replicated, clinical implications include the potential to screen for attachment style during pregnancy and tailor care during birth accordingly.

2.1. Measures

Adult attachment style was measured using the Adult Attachment Questionnaire (Simpson et al., 1996) which has subscales of avoidant attachment (i.e. negative views of others, tendency to avoid/withdraw from intimacy in relationships; $\alpha=.83$) and ambivalent–anxious attachment (i.e. negative self-views regarding relationships, excessive preoccupation with abandonment, loss and partners' levels of commitment; $\alpha=.79$). Complications/intervention during birth was measured using type of birth i.e. women who had operative births (assisted vaginal deliveries or caesarean sections, $n=34$) compared to those who had spontaneous vaginal deliveries ($n=23$). Birth support was measured using the support subscale of the Support and Control in Birth questionnaire (Ford et al., 2009; $\alpha=.90$). PTSD was measured using the PTSD Diagnostic Scale (Foa et al., 1997) in relation to childbirth. The re-experiencing, avoidance, and hyper-arousal symptoms subscales follow DSM-IV symptom criteria and were combined to provide a total PTSD symptom score ($\alpha=.89$).

3. Results

PTSD was significantly correlated with avoidant attachment style ($r=.35$, $p=.008$), mode of birth ($r=.41$, $p=.002$) and birth support ($r=-.27$, $p=.04$) but not ambivalent–anxious attachment ($r=.23$, $p=.09$). Ambivalent–anxious attachment style was therefore not entered into subsequent regression analyses. Hierarchical multiple regression analysis was used to explore (i) whether attachment, birth type and birth support influenced mothers' PTSD scores and (ii) whether attachment moderated any impact of birth type or birth support on PTSD (see Table 1).

At step 1, avoidant attachment accounted for 12.30% of the variance in PTSD scores ($F(1, 54)=7.58$, $p=.008$); a more avoidant attachment style was associated with more PTSD symptoms.

FIGURE 10.3 Abstract from Ayers, Jessop, Pike, Parfitt, & Ford, 2014.

Ayers et al. (2014) conducted a longitudinal study to examine the relations of adult attachment style to PTSD symptoms in women who are in their third trimester of pregnancy. They measured attachment style before pregnancy and PTSD symptoms 3 months after delivery. Attachment style before pregnancy is the B variable and PTSD symptoms 3 months after delivery are the C variable. If the authors find a relation of attachment style to PTSD symptoms, this article could be used to support the B-C pathway.

The Ayers et al. (2014) article discusses other variables as well, including the mode of delivery (e.g., forceps assisted delivery) and the availability of support during delivery. But these variables are not relevant to the B-C pathway. The authors do not mention childhood trauma, which is the risk factor (A variable) in our A-B-C pathway. Therefore, the only information we put in the table from the Ayers et al. (2014) article is information related to the B-C pathway (Table 10.4).

TABLE 10.4 Methods and results from Ayers et al. 2014.

Author/ Date	Sample description, n, sociodemographic information	Sampling: Convenience sample or population-based sample	Research design (experimental, observational, cross-sectional, longitudinal)	Predictor: Risk factor definition	Predictor: Risk factor measurement or manipulation	Outcome: Mechanism definitions	Outcome: measurement	Findings: Provide word and statistical sentences	Limitations
Ayers et al., 2014	57 women who were pregnant and delivering their first baby. Majority were White middle class, college educated.	Convenience sampling	Correlational, longitudinal	Attachment styles. Attachment styles are ways of relating to others and anticipating interactions with others. Anxious attachment reflects anxious concerns about rejection and a desire for reassurance. Avoidant attachment involves an ability to detach and disengage.	Adult Attachment Questionnaire	PTSD symptoms 3 months after birth	Self-reported survey—PDS inquiring about symptoms of hyperarousal, avoidance and reexperiencing about childbirth trauma	Avoidant attachment style, but not ambivalent anxious attachment style, was positively correlated with PTSD symptoms.	All data are collected through self-reports. Hard to know if the findings would be the same with a group that differed in race or socioeconomic status.

Brief description. *In this study,* Ayers et al. (2014) *used a longitudinal design to examine the relations between attachment styles and PTSD after women give birth to their first child. They examine the women's attachment styles during their last trimester of pregnancy and PTSD symptoms 3 months after giving birth. The authors used self-report surveys to measure two attachment styles, avoidant attachment and ambivalent, anxious attachment using. A self-report survey of PTSD symptoms was used to assess PTSD. The authors found that an avoidant attachment style, but not an anxious attachment style, predicts the development of PTSD following childbirth. These results provide support for the hypothesis that specific types of attachment styles predict the development of PTSD following a potentially traumatic event.*

Activity 10.2: Tabling the Methods and Results of a B-C, Mechanism to Outcome Original Article

Table the results of the articles you are reading for the B-C path (Table 10.5). Then write a short summary of the article, explaining the aims, methods, results, and implications.

TABLE 10.5 **Original empirical research articles: B To C articles.**

Author/Date	Sample descriptions, sociodemographic information	Sampling: Convenience sample or population-based sample	Research design (experimental, observational, cross-sectional, longitudinal)	Predictor: Risk factor definition	Predictor: Risk factor measurement or manipulation	Outcome: Mechanism definitions	Outcome: measurement	Findings: Provide word and statistical sentences	Limitations

Brief Study Description:

____

____

____

____

____

Tabling Meta-Analyses

The tables for the A-B or B-C sections may include information gathered from meta-analyses and systematic reviews as well as from original research articles. Tables organizing the findings from meta-analyses require slightly different formatting, as you can see in this section on assembling information from meta-analyses on studies examining the B-C pathways (Fig. 10.4; Table 10.6).

Journal of Anxiety Disorders 35 (2015) 103–117

Contents lists available at ScienceDirect

Journal of Anxiety Disorders

The relationship between adult attachment style and post-traumatic stress symptoms: A meta-analysis

Sarah Woodhouse[a], Susan Ayers[b,*], Andy P. Field[a]

[a] School of Psychology, University of Sussex, United Kingdom
[b] School of Health Sciences, City University London, United Kingdom

ARTICLE INFO

Article history:
Received 20 August 2014
Received in revised form 14 July 2015
Accepted 15 July 2015
Available online 8 August 2015

Keywords:
Attachment
Posttraumatic stress
Trauma
Social bonds
Social cognition
Meta-analysis

ABSTRACT

There is increasing evidence that adult attachment plays a role in the development and perseverance of symptoms of posttraumatic stress disorder (PTSD). This meta-analysis aims to synthesise this evidence and investigate the relationship between adult attachment styles and PTSD symptoms. A random-effects model was used to analyse 46 studies (N=9268) across a wide range of traumas. Results revealed a medium association between secure attachment and lower PTSD symptoms ($\hat{\rho} = -.27$), and a medium association, in the opposite direction, between insecure attachment and higher PTSD symptoms ($\hat{\rho} = .26$). Attachment categories comprised of high levels of anxiety most strongly related to PTSD symptoms, with fearful attachment displaying the largest association ($\hat{\rho} = .44$). Dismissing attachment was not significantly associated with PTSD symptoms. The relationship between insecure attachment and PTSD was moderated by type of PTSD measure (interview or questionnaire) and specific attachment category (e.g. secure, fearful). Results have theoretical and clinical significance.

FIGURE 10.4 Abstract from Woodhouse, Ayers, & Field, 2015.

TABLE 10.6 Summarizing the results of meta-analyses or systematic reviews to evaluate the mechanism to the disorder (B-C pathway).

Author/ Date	Systematic review or Meta-analysis	Number of studies and participants included	Primary focus of meta-analysis	Mechanism, definitions	Mechanism measurement	Outcomes studied	Research designs of articles included in analyses	Control variables	Findings	Limitations
Woodhouse, Ayers, & Fields, 2015	Meta-analysis	46 studies, 9268 participants	Relations of adult attachment style to PTSD symptoms following trauma Multiple forms of trauma	Adult attachment style—defined as self-reported mental representation of others in close relationships and reports of behavior and feelings in these relationships	A variety of self-reported attachment style questionnaires. Broad categories—secure and insecure attachment, also subcategories of anxious, avoidant, fearful, dismissing, preoccupied	Self-reported PTSD symptoms or interview for PTSD symptoms	Correlational, cross-sectional	Studied many potential covariates, including sociodemographic. No effects for age, gender, trauma type, marital status, type of sample.	Insecure attachment was positively associated with PTSD symptoms; whereas secure attachment was negatively associated with PTSD symptoms. Fearful attachment is type of insecure attachment most closely associated with PTSD.	All self-report. Cross-sectional only. Effects stronger with self-report PTSD symptoms, suggesting common method variance is an explanation. People endorse fear-related PTSD symptoms and fearful attachment.

Brief description. Woodhouse, Ayers, and Fields (2015) *conducted a series of meta-analyses to understand the relationship of adult attachment styles to PTSD symptoms in 46 studies of individuals exposed as adults to a variety of traumatic events. The studies were all cross-sectional and correlational. All studies used self-reported attachment style. Most, but not all, studies used self-reported PTSD symptoms. The authors examined different ways to categorize attachment styles. They found an insecure attachment style was positively associated with PTSD symptoms or diagnosis, whereas a secure attachment style was negatively associated with PTSD symptoms. Fearful attachment styles were the type of attachment style most closely associated with PTSD symptoms. The data were consistent across trauma types, gender, and marital status. However, the effects were stronger when the PTSD symptoms were assessed with self-report measures than with interviews.*

Activity 10.3: Tabling the Methods and Results of an B-C, Mechanism to Outcome Meta-analysis

Use Table 10.7 meta-analysis of studies of either the A-B path or the B-C path, if there is one available for your topic. Complete the table and write a brief summary of the findings, describing the aim of the article, the number and type of studies included (i.e., observational or experimental), the overall results, and the implications for your paper. If you are tabling the results of a meta-analysis on an A-B pathway, replace the column for "Outcomes studied" with "Risk factors studied".

TABLE 10.7 Meta-analyses: A-B or B-C articles.

Author/Date	Systematic review or Meta-analysis	Number of studies and participants included	Primary focus of meta-analysis	Mechanism, definitions	Mechanism measurement	Outcomes studied	Research designs of articles included in analyses	Control variables	Findings	Limitations

Continued

Activity 10.3: Tabling the Methods and Results of an B-C, Mechanism to Outcome Meta-analysis—cont'd

Brief Study Description:

____

____

____

____

____

Evaluating the Evidence: Examining Threats to Internal and External Validity

How good is the evidence for each pathway? As you read the articles on each of these paths, you may wonder about the quality of the evidence you are reading. You may notice that the studies have threats to internal and external validity. If you are writing a proposal for a study to test treatment outcomes, you may search for risk factors and mechanisms that have high-quality evidence supporting their effects. (You will learn to evaluate evidence about treatments in Chapter 13 and learn to write about these evaluations in Chapter 14.)

If you are writing a paper on the causes of the disorder, you review the evidence on the A-B or B-C pathway in more detail. As you write, you identify the strengths of these different studies and the threats to validity they face. This review will guide your suggestions for areas in need of further research.

Let's examine some of the threats to internal and external validity that can be seen in risk factor and mechanism studies. We review these issues in general. The specific threats depend on the details of the research area.

Threats to Internal Validity

As we have discussed in Chapter 6, threats to validity include any threats to the ability to test the hypothesis the researcher wishes to test. In general, these threats can come from limitations or bias in the sample, measurement methods, and analyses. Let's examine some threats from each of these categories.

Sources of bias in the sample. Many of the studies included in the A-B path or B-C path do not select their samples at random and do not use population-based samples. Instead, the researchers rely on some form of convenience sampling. Convenience sampling is faster and less expensive than population-based sampling. But researchers must be sure that the sample itself does not introduce bias.

One source of potential bias can come from the **inclusion** and **exclusion criteria** used for the study. Inclusion criteria are the characteristics an individual must have to be included as a participant in the study. Exclusion criteria are characteristics that would render an individual ineligible to participate in the study.

For example, in the studies on the role of childhood trauma to attachment and PTSD symptoms, researchers include individuals with any type of childhood trauma. However, other research suggests that different types and intensities of trauma exposure have different effects on attachment (Erozkan, 2016; Liotti, 1999). Therefore, the failure to find a relation between child trauma and PTSD could be a function of the types of trauma experienced by the participants.

Some inclusion or exclusion criteria can introduce a "third variable" or "extraneous variable" problem. A third variable or extraneous variable problem occurs when another variable is linked with the original predictor variables and affects the outcome. For example, many types of trauma, including violent assaults, domestic violence, and childhood maltreatment, are more likely to occur to individuals who have low socioeconomic status (i.e., low levels of education and income) (Kohl, Jonson-Reid, & Drake, 2009; Lee, Coe, & Ryff, 2017). Therefore, when researchers are measuring trauma exposure, they may also be measuring socioeconomic status as well. Researchers may need to control for socioeconomic status to distinguish between the effects of trauma and the effects of socioeconomic status.

Sources of bias in the measurement. The type of measurement method can also introduce a source of bias. When the instruments used to measure both the predictor and the outcome share similar characteristics, the responses to those measurement methods may reflect the participants' reactions to the type of instrument. This problem is called **common method variance**.

For example, in the meta-analysis on the association of attachment to PTSD, the authors report the findings are stronger when self-report measures of PTSD are used. The attachment measures are also self-report.

Studies which use both self-report measures of attachment and self-report measures of PTSD symptoms may have results which are inflated by common methods—both measurement methods involve self-report. For example, the close relationship of fearful attachment style to PTSD may partly reflect the fact that the questions on both self-report surveys use similar language—both ask about anxiety and fear.

Sources of bias in the methods and study design. Another potential threat to internal validity concerns the nature of the research design. If the study uses cross-sectional, correlational methods, it can be difficult to determine both the direction and causal nature of the relations between the predictor and outcome variables. For example, the authors of the studies we have examined hypothesize that attachment style predicts PTSD symptoms, but it could be that PTSD symptoms influence attachment style (Solomon, Dekel, & Mikulincer, 2008). Longitudinal studies are needed to understand the direction of effects. Without experimental studies, the researchers cannot determine if attachment style causes PTSD symptoms or if attachment styles are simply associated with those symptoms.

Finally, all studies need good procedures to control for extraneous variables that may influence the outcome of the study. These variables can be introduced by accident at any phase of the study. A careful review of the existing studies and some pilot testing can guide the researcher as he or she tries to reduce these threats to validity.

Threats to External Validity

As we have discussed in Chapter 6, threats to external validity include any threats to the ability to generalize the findings of the study to different populations, measurement methods, or testing settings, among other variables.

Threats to generalizability from the sample. All samples have limits. In some cases, the individuals included in the sample have specific characteristics which are important to the research. This limits the ability to generalize the findings of the study to other members of the population who do not have those characteristics. In the Ayers et al. (2014) study, the sample was limited to pregnant women, most of whom were White and all of whom were getting ready to deliver their first child. This means the data on the role of attachment style to PTSD may not be generalizable to people who are not pregnant, who are not White, or who have already given birth to other children.

Threats to generalizability from the measurement approach. Results obtained from one type of measurement method may not be replicated or generalize to another type of measurement method. We have some evidence this is the case in studies of attachment and PTSD. For example, the relation of fearful attachment style to PTSD symptoms was much stronger when the PTSD symptoms were measured using self-report instruments versus interviews (Woodhouse et al., 2015).

Threats to generalizability from the research methods or design. Research studies occur in specific circumstances. Findings which emerge clearly in laboratory studies with good **experimental control** may not emerge in field studies conducted in "real-world" settings. These "real-world" settings may introduce a host of extraneous variables which may obscure the relation between the predictor and outcome. For example, if researchers measured attachment styles and PTSD symptoms in the laboratory, they don't know if the findings of the study will generalize to observations of attachment in the home during the participants' daily activities. Additional research is needed to make the link between data obtained in the laboratory and real-world outcomes.

We can see examples of some of these threats to internal and external validity by reading a little more from the Woodhouse et al. (2015) meta-analysis on the studies of attachment styles as a predictor of PTSD symptoms. In the section on Limitations, the authors identify some gaps in knowledge (Figs. 10.5).

4.1. Limitations

Despite the rigour with which this meta-analysis was conducted, the results should be interpreted in the context of the following limitations. Firstly, moderator analysis was conducted only on the relationship between insecure attachment and PTSD symptoms. The analysis was structured to provide critical information whilst avoiding repetition. However, this is at the detriment of some finer detail on lower level insecure attachment categories. Furthermore, confirmation of the mechanisms underlying the relationship between attachment and PTSD symptoms could not be established by this meta-analysis for two reasons. First, although emotion-regulation (Benoit et al., 2010), self-worth (Lim et al., 2012), self-esteem and representations of others (Ortigo et al., 2013), social support (Muller & Lemieux, 2000) and coping strategies have all been found to have mediating or moderating effects on the relationship, there were too few studies investigating these moderators to pool in the current analysis. Second, causality cannot be determined by pooling data that quantifies *associations* between attachment and PTSD symptoms. Although attachment theory is based on the assumption that that attachment style affects the development of PTSD because an individual's attachment style is determined at a young age, and should be relatively stable over time (Bowlby, 1982), the opposite causal hypothesis is theoretically plausible. In other words, the traumatic event, and even the symptoms themselves, may change attachment style (Weinfield et al., 2000; Zhang & Labouvie-Vief, 2004). Indeed, adult attachment styles have been found to be labile in some studies (Baldwin & Fehr, 1995; Davila et al., 1997; Guðmundsdóttir et al., 2006). Until a greater number of longitudinal studies have been published the causal underpinnings of the relationship between attachment style and PTSD remains open.

← This section highlights a threat to validity that occurs because there are not enough studies available to draw certain conclusions about the data. These conclusions involve testing hypotheses about the role of other factors, including emotion regulation, self-esteem and other variables in the relations of attachment to PTSD.

← This section highlights a threat to validity that occurs because most of the studies are cross-sectional. This makes it difficult to determine if attachment predicts PTSD or if PTSD (or the trauma that produces PTSD) affects attachment.

Another potential limitation was the focus on *adult* attachment, which excludes valuable insights from research investigating the relationship in child populations. The adult inclusion criteria enabled us to provide a more focused analysis, however, by failing to include the child literature we are unable to comment on possible generalisations and similarities/differences between the two populations. This may have considerable theoretical and clinical benefit so should be examined in future.

← This section highlights a limitation to the external validity of the study. The authors point out that they examine only the effects of adult attachment on PTSD. They do not have information on the way attachment affects symptoms in children.

Finally, the poor reporting of effect sizes in papers included in the analyses led to incomplete data. For example, some papers might report the effect size for anxious attachment and PTSD symptoms but not for avoidant attachment and PTSD symptoms. Unless studies routinely report effect sizes for all attachment categories, any meta-analysis will be based on only a subset of the relevant data.

FIGURE 10.5 Excerpt from Woodhouse et al., 2015.

Writing Brief Summaries: General Templates

Here are some templates for writing about the results of original research articles using a correlational design.

The aim of the study by (Author(s)) was to test the hypothesis that the mechanism (name of mechanism) was related to the outcome (symptoms or diagnosis of disorder). The mechanism was conceptualized and measured … (add details). The outcome was conceptualized and measured with … (add details). The author(s) tested the hypothesis in a sample containing … (describe in detail). A (correlational, cross-sectional, or longitudinal design) was used. The authors found … (summarize the results).

If the study was an experiment and the mechanism was manipulated, the template is slightly different because the summary must describe the experimental design and the manipulation of the independent variable. There are many different types of manipulations that can be used to assess the effects of the independent variable (IV) when the IV is a mechanism. For example, if the mechanism was mood, then participants might be assigned at random to different types of mood inductions, such as happiness inductions or sadness inductions (Ferrer, Grenen, & Taber, 2015). If the mechanism was uncertainty, participants might be assigned at random to a condition which makes people feel uncertain or a condition which makes people feel certain, as was done in the article by LaDoceur (2000). In this case the template incorporates information on the design as well.

The aim of the study by (Author(s)) was to test the hypothesis that the mechanism (name of mechanism) was related to the outcome (symptoms or diagnosis of disorder). The researchers operationalized the mechanism by (describe how the test of the mechanism was implemented (e.g., the instructions or task provided to the participants). The researchers assigned participants at random to the levels of the IV (explain experimental and control conditions). The outcome was conceptualized and measured with … (add details). The author(s) tested the hypothesis in a sample containing … (describe in detail). The authors found that (explain findings by identifying differences between the experimental and control conditions in the outcomes).

Here is a template for writing about the results of meta-analyses:

The evidence of the links between the mechanism (identify the mechanism) and the outcome (symptoms or diagnosis of disorder XXX) was reviewed by authors XXX in a (systematic review or meta-analysis). They examined cross-sectional (or longitudinal), correlational (or experimental) studies which examined the relationship of the mechanism to the disorder. The mechanism was defined as ______, and studies used measurement methods including (list types of measurement methods). The outcome was defined as (add details), and studies used measurement methods including (add details). The authors found (most, some, a few, none) of the studies supported this link, indicating a (consistent, mixed, or nonexistent) relationship of the risk factor to the outcome. Moderators of these effects included (list and explain or state that no moderators were tested). The authors indicated the quality of the evidence was (poor, moderate, good). Limitations to the existing data included (list).

Summarizing the Evidence

Now that you have tabled and described the articles included in your paper or proposal, you can consider the evidence overall. Do the studies support the A-B-C pathway overall? Is there evidence for each component: A-C, A-B, B-C?

Start by reviewing the evidence you provide in the tables. Consider all the results. Are all the findings supportive of the hypothesis? Are there differences among the findings?

You may also obtain this information by reading meta-analyses and systematic reviews. For example, in the meta-analysis by Woodhouse et al. (2015) the authors find that not all the studies support the hypothesis that attachment styles lead to PTSD following trauma. The data are more consistent for some types of attachment styles than for others.

The way you summarize and evaluate the research depends on the purpose of the proposal or paper. If you are building an A-B-C argument to justify a focus for treatment, your summaries will be more succinct. You will provide evidence for each pathway and summarize the relations among the pathways at the end.

If you are writing a paper reviewing the evidence on one of the pathways, you will review more papers and provide a more detailed summary of the evidence. After this section, you will include an evaluation of the evidence, highlighting threats to internal and external validity and identifying gaps in knowledge.

You can start the summary section by indicating which studies examined the pathway. For example, you could write...

> *Examples of studies examining the link between the (name of risk factor) and the (name of mechanism) can be found in (Author #1, Year) and (Author #2, Year) (etc.).*

If the evidence is consistent—meaning the evidence is all in agreement—you can write a summary sentence like this:

The data indicate that childhood trauma is associated with adult attachment styles, with childhood trauma positively associated with an insecure attachment style (Hocking, Simons, & Surette, 2016; Rholes et al., 2016). Specifically, childhood trauma is associated with an anxious attachment style, although there is also evidence linking childhood trauma with other insecure attachment styles (Rholes et al., 2016).

A template for a summary sentence when the data are consistent is as follows:

The data indicate that the (risk factor or mechanism) is associated with the outcome (either mechanism or symptoms) in each of these studies.

If the evidence is not consistent, researchers may write:

Many studies, but not all studies, show the expected relationship between the predictor (describe) and the outcome (describe).

Researchers will include the references for the studies that do show the expected relationship and the references for the studies that do not. The sentence will look like this:

Many studies (references for positive studies), but not all studies (references for negative studies), show the expected relationship between the predictor (describe) and the outcome (describe).

If this conclusion comes from a systematic review or a meta-analysis, you can write:

Evidence from a meta-analysis (or a systematic review) indicates that some but not all studies show the expected relation between the predictor (describe) and the outcome (describe) (reference from the meta-analysis).

Writing Clearly about the Evidence

The goal in these summary sentences is to communicate ideas in a clear and unambiguous way. As you write, keep in mind some general principles. Make sure your writing is clear and the meaning is not ambiguous. Shorter sentences are generally easier to understand than longer sentences. Quotes are generally not used. It is better to put the ideas into your own words.

The reader should be easily able to understand what the predictor/IV and outcome/dependent variable (DV) and methods of each study are. The reader should also be able to understand the findings and understand the consistency or inconsistency across studies. The clarity of these sentences depends on the clear labeling of the predictor/IV and outcome/DV variables.

The sentences also make clear the nature of the relation between predictor and outcomes. If the predictor and outcome are continuous variables, the direction of the relations is mentioned (i.e., positive or negative). If the predictor is categorical, the findings for all levels of the predictor are mentioned (e.g., those with a history of childhood trauma had higher scores on a measure of insecure attachment than did those without a history of childhood trauma). The sentences also indicate the consistency of the findings, indicating whether all, most, or only some of the research provides evidence in support of the hypothesized relation.

All sentences with evidence should include citations. All the in-text citations and bibliographic citations should adhere to the APA format.

Writing About Threats to Validity and Gaps in Knowledge

As we discuss in Chapter 6 in the section on writing about threats to validity, there are many possible strategies that can be used when describing these threats to validity and gaps in knowledge. However, in general, if you are writing a paper reviewing the state-of-the-science, there are five pieces of information which should be included.

1. An operational definition of the specific threat to validity. This includes a clear explanation of the specific type of threat, such as a biased sample or limited measurement, among other threats.
2. The importance of the threat. This includes a discussion of the ways in which this threat undermines the ability to test the hypothesis or generalize the findings.
3. The evidence supporting the existence of the threat. This includes examples (with citations) from the specific studies in which the threat was identified.

4. Gaps in knowledge created by these threats to validity. Threats to validity limit the ability to interpret findings from existing studies. This is a summary of the new information needed given the threats to validity in existing studies.
5. Future research. This includes a discussion of the types of studies which need to be conducted or the changes to the methods which would need to address the gaps in knowledge.

Putting it all Together: Writing a Summary Paragraph

As you summarize the evidence for the Risk Factors and Mechanisms section and explain your "Theory of the Problem," you need to include information about all the pathways.

If you are writing a proposal, your summary paragraph includes a statement about the PHS section, and statements about the evidence for and against the A-B and B-C pathways.

The summary paragraph also includes an explanation of the implications for the development of an intervention. The goal is to provide direction for the treatment outcome study to be proposed. The discussion of the evidence explaining the risk factor and its link to the mechanism identifies the group of individuals who will be targeted for the intervention. The group will include individuals with the risk factor. The B-C pathways identify the mechanisms that may be targeted by the treatment.

The general framework for a proposal summary paragraph is presented below.

> *The findings indicate that A is a risk factor for C (add references). Treatment will be targeted to individuals who have risk factor A. Risk factor A is linked to a mechanism B, which (triggers/maintains) condition C (add references). Mechanism B is an important target for treatment. Treating B may reduce the symptoms of C.*

If you are writing a summary paragraph for a paper on the causes of the disorder, your summary paragraph will include information on the evidence, as well as information on potential gaps in the literature, implications of the findings, and recommendations for future research.

The general framework for a review paper summary paragraph is presented below. (If you wrote about a B-C paper, just substitute the mechanism for the risk factor and the symptoms for the mechanism.)

The findings indicate that A is a risk factor for C (add references). Researchers hypothesized that A is linked to C through mechanism B (add references). A has been defined as _____ (add references). B has been defined as _____ (add references). Researchers have examined the evidence linking A-B using explain the different types of designs used; e.g., experimental and/or correlational, cross-sectional and/or longitudinal. Provide the references for the articles using these different types of designs (e.g., cross-sectional designs (references), longitudinal designs (references)). The findings indicate that (most, some, none) of the studies support the relation of the A-B pathway (add references). The findings are stronger in studies using (describe sample or measure or design which produces the clearest results) (add references).

As you learn more about the research area, you will also add additional summary sentences of this type.

Remaining gaps in the literature include (describe) ______. Future research is needed to investigate ___________.

Building Human Capital

Persistence and Attention to Detail

Examining the evidence and summarizing the findings take a great deal of effort, persistence, and conscientiousness. You will need to go back several times to make sure you have read the studies correctly and are describing the methods and results accurately. Take your time. Check your work.

If you have trouble pushing yourself to do the hard work, think about what kinds of support you need to keep you focused and willing to go back and check your work. Do you need to work with someone else? Does talking over your ideas help? Does breaking up the work into smaller chunks help you? Would a gym break help you keep up your energy? Or would calling a friend for a short chat in between reading the articles keep you motivated?

Think about what you gain as you make the tables and write the summaries. Does working hard make you trust yourself more? Do you feel proud of your effort and your outcomes? Are you willing to take more risks because you know you have the discipline and persistence to follow through? Take the time to tell someone important to you about the efforts you are making and the skills you have learned.

Terms

Take the time to define each of these terms and consider how to apply them.

Research Terms

Literature Review
Inclusion Criteria
Exclusion Criteria
Common Method Variance
Experimental Control

References

Ayers, S., Jessop, D., Pike, A., Parfitt, Y., & Ford, E. (2014). The role of adult attachment style, birth intervention and support in posttraumatic stress after childbirth: A prospective study. *Journal of Affective Disorders, 155*, 295–298.

Erozkan, A. (2016). The link between types of attachment and childhood trauma. *Universal Journal of Educational Research, 4*(5), 1071–1079.

Hocking, E. C., Simons, R. M., & Surette, R. J. (2016). Attachment style as a mediator between childhood maltreatment and the experience of betrayal trauma as an adult. *Child Abuse & Neglect, 52*, 94–101.

Kohl, P. L., Jonson-Reid, M., & Drake, B. (2009). Time to leave substantiation behind: Findings from a national probability study. *Child Maltreatment, 14*(1), 17–26.

Lee, C., Coe, C. L., & Ryff, C. D. (2017). Social disadvantage, severe child abuse, and biological profiles in adulthood. *Journal of Health and Social Behavior, 58*(3), 371–386.

Liotti, G. (1999). Understanding the dissociative processes: The contribution of attachment theory. *Psychoanalytic Inquiry, 19*(5), 757–783.

Rholes, W. S., Paetzold, R. L., & Kohn, J. L. (2016). Disorganized attachment mediates the link from early trauma to externalizing behavior in adult relationships. *Personality and Individual Differences, 90*, 61–65.

Solomon, Z., Dekel, R., & Mikulincer, M. (2008). Complex trauma of war captivity: A prospective study of attachment and post-traumatic stress disorder. *Psychological Medicine, 38*(10), 1427–1434.

Woodhouse, S., Ayers, S., & Field, A. P. (2015). The relationship between adult attachment style and post-traumatic stress symptoms: A meta-analysis. *Journal of Anxiety Disorders, 35*, 103–117.

Part 3

Theory of the solution

Chapter 11

Theory of the solution: Understanding psychological treatments

In the next section of the book, covering Chapters 11–14, we examine **applied research**, specifically applied treatment outcome research. In the Theory of the Problem (TOP) section of this book, you examined many methods used in **basic** research. Now, as you develop a Theory of the Solution (TOS), you will learn more about methods used in applied research. And you will build your capacity to make clear arguments about the steps in the research process.

As you read articles to help you identify treatments for the behavioral health disorder you are investigating, you will develop a TOS. The TOS is a theory about how a treatment can reduce the symptoms of a behavioral health disorder. The treatment may operate by affecting the variables that trigger or maintain the symptoms of the behavioral health disorder.

In this book, we focus on developing links between the TOP and the TOS. The mechanisms which contribute to the problem guide your search for treatments for the disorder. This is an approach recommended by researchers working on the science of behavior change (Czajkowski et al., 2015; Nielsen et al., 2018). This approach can make the search for treatment more efficient and potentially more effective (Fig. 11.1).

Psychology Research Methods. https://doi.org/10.1016/B978-0-12-815680-3.00011-6

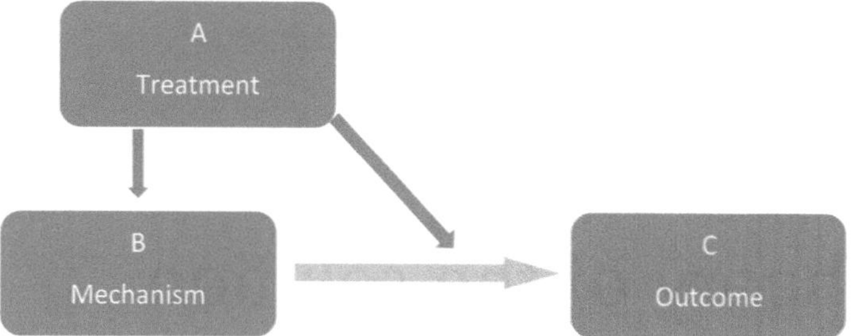

FIGURE 11.1 A model of the theory of the solution.

In Chapter 11, you will learn about different treatments and the delivery of these treatments. You will examine and evaluate the evidence available on the effects of these treatments.

In Chapter 12, you will learn about the research designs used to test hypotheses about the effects of treatment. You will learn about open label and randomized clinical trials, and the statistical methods used to evaluate them.

In Chapter 13, you will examine the gaps in knowledge concerning the treatments you have chosen and identify ways to address threats to internal and external validity.

In Chapter 14, you will learn how to write about treatment outcome research and present a TOS.

If you are writing a proposal for a treatment evaluation study, the TOS section provides a description of the treatment you choose, a rationale for your choice, a discussion about the gaps in knowledge about this treatment, and the way the methods you propose can address those gaps.

If you are writing a paper evaluating different treatments for a behavioral health problem, you can review and evaluate different treatment approaches and discuss threats to validity in the existing research. As you summarize the literature and identify gaps in knowledge, you will identify areas in need of further research.

A Little Background Information About Psychological Treatments

To identify an effective treatment, you follow the same strategies you used to identify risk factors and mechanisms. You search the scientific literature for articles about possible treatments. Then you examine the evidence on the effects of the treatment.

Although comprehensive treatments for many behavioral health problems include biological and pharmacological treatments, in this book we focus on psychological treatments or therapies. In general, students in psychology have taken courses which provide the background to understand these psychological treatments. There are many psychological treatments for behavioral health problems. A short list of some of the available treatments includes: cognitive behavioral therapy (CBT), acceptance and commitment therapy, dialectical behavior therapy, and brief psychodynamic psychotherapy. You may have learned about these treatments if you have taken a course in abnormal psychology.

To get started reading the scientific articles to build a TOS, you need to understand a little more about the psychological treatments themselves. This information can help you think about the treatment approaches that may be useful for individuals with the disorder you are investigating. To write your proposal or paper, you will need to read more about different treatments, and you may benefit from watching videos of the implementation of these therapies.

Wikipedia (https://en.wikipedia.org/wiki/List_of_psychotherapies) and websites associated with NIH or NAMI can give you a general overview of the treatment approaches, but you will need to verify your understanding with peer-reviewed literature.

You can also learn more about these treatments using resources listed in (Fig. 11.2).

Videos Access through your institution's library

- Kanopy streaming video (https://www.kanopy.com/)
- psycTHERAPY streaming video (https://www.apa.org/pubs/databases/streaming-video/index.aspx)

Books Available via multiple platforms

- What works for whom? By Anthony Roth and Peter Fonagy
- A guide to treatments that work By Peter E. Nathan and Jack M. Gorman

Others Available online

- NIMH
- American Psychiatric Association

FIGURE 11.2 Resources for learning about psychological treatments.

Psychotherapies: The Big Picture and Some Details

The Big Picture

Psychological treatments are designed to reduce symptoms and improve functioning. Treatments may target different mechanisms to achieve the goal of symptom reduction and improved functioning. At the most general level, all psychotherapies are composed of treatments to change:

- *The way people think:* Treatments focused on thoughts can include efforts to change the content of the thoughts, as well as the process of thinking, attending, or shifting perspective. Treatments focused on the way people think (i.e., cognitive treatments) often focus on how people think about their own feelings and behavior.
- *The way people feel:* Treatments focused on emotions aim to reduce inappropriate negative feelings, increase appropriate positive feelings, and improve the regulation of emotion.
- *The way people act:* Treatments focused on behavior aim to improve the degree to which people can do more of what they want to do and less of what they do not want to do. The goal is to improve the link between the person's intentions and the person' actions.

Most treatments include components that affect thoughts, feelings, and actions, but they may differ in the emphasis they place on the importance of addressing thoughts, feelings, or actions. There are also other important variations in the type and nature of treatments. Treatments or therapies differ in the specific treatment components they use to achieve changes in thoughts, feelings, and actions. The therapy sessions may involve training to build skills and knowledge, or the therapy sessions may be less structured and provide participants an opportunity to explore thoughts and feelings. Some therapies combine both approaches. Treatments can be delivered in different modalities (e.g., individual, group, or family treatment).

The treatments can be delivered in different formats (e.g., face-to-face or on the web). The therapies can be delivered by a wide range of different individuals, from licensed psychologists to peers. And they can be delivered in a wide variety of settings, from a hospital to the patient's home.

In the next section we will provide some basic background information on:

- Treatment packages
- Treatment components
- Treatment modalities
- Treatment delivery formats
- Treatment settings
- Therapist qualifications

Treatment Packages and Components

Many psychological treatments have more than one component (Kazdin, 2008). For example, CBT has multiple components, depending on how you define it. These components can include relaxation therapy, cognitive restructuring, and exposure components, among others. When you specify an approach, such as CBT or Mindfulness or Brief Psychodynamic Psychotherapy, you need to be clear about which components you are including and why.

Some treatment components are more commonly used with anxiety disorders (e.g., exposure therapy) (Abramowitz, Deacon, & Whiteside, 2011). Others are more commonly used for depression (e.g., behavioral activation) (Martell, Dimidjian, & Herman-Dunn, 2013). Treatment components can be combined. A list of some treatment components is included in Table 11.1, but many other treatment components have been developed. References to articles describing the listed components are also included.

TABLE 11.1 Treatment components and references.

Components	References
Acceptance	Hayes, S. C., Strosahl, K. D., & Wilson, K. G. (2011). *Acceptance and commitment therapy*. New York, NY: Guilford Press.
Attention training	Knowles, M. M., Foden, P., El?Deredy, W., & Wells, A. (2016). A systematic review of efficacy of the attention training technique in clinical and nonclinical samples. *Journal of Clinical Psychology, 72*(10), 999–1025.
Behavioral activation	Hopko, D. R., Lejuez, C. W., Ruggiero, K. J., & Eifert, G. H. (2003). Contemporary behavioral activation treatments for depression: Procedures, principles, and progress. *Clinical Psychology Review, 23*(5), 699–717.

Continued

TABLE 11.1 Treatment components and references.—cont'd

Components	References
Cognitive restructuring	Deacon, B. J., Fawzy, T. I., Lickel, J. J., & Wolitzky-Taylor, K. B. (2011). Cognitive defusion versus cognitive restructuring in the treatment of negative self-referential thoughts: An investigation of process and outcome. *Journal of Cognitive Psychotherapy, 25*(3), 218. Heimberg, R. G. (2002). Cognitive-behavioral therapy for social anxiety disorder: Current status and future directions. *Biological Psychiatry, 51*(1), 101–108.
Decision-making treatments	Duncan, E., Best, C., & Hagen, S. (2008). Shared decision making treatments for people with mental health conditions. *Cochrane Database of Systematic Reviews, 1.*
Exposure therapy	Foa, E. B. (2011). Prolonged exposure therapy: Past, present, and future. *Depression and Anxiety, 28*(12), 1043–1047.
Eye movement desensitization therapy (EMDR)	Oren, E., & Solomon, R. (2012). EMDR therapy: An overview of its development and mechanisms of action. *Revue Européenne De Psychologie Appliquée/European Review of Applied Psychology, 62*(4), 197–203.
Habit reversal	Heinicke, M. R., Stiede, J. T., Miltenberger, R. G., & Woods, D. W. (2020). Reducing risky behavior with habit reversal: A review of behavioral strategies to reduce habitual hand-to-head behavior. *Journal of applied behavior analysis, 53*(3), 1225–1236.
Mindfulness mediation	Baer, R. A. (Ed.). (2015). *Mindfulness-based treatment approaches: Clinician's guide to evidence base and applications.* Elsevier.
Motivational interviewing	Miller, W. R., & Rose, G. S. (2009). Toward a theory of motivational interviewing. *American Psychologist, 64*(6), 527.
Problem-solving, goal selection	D'Zurilla, T. J., & Nezu, A. M. (2010). Problem-solving therapy. *Handbook of Cognitive-Behavioral Therapies, 3,* 197–225.
Psychoeducation	Sin, J., Jordan, C., Barley, E., Henderson, C., & Norman, I. (2015). Psychoeducation for siblings of individuals with severe mental illness. *Cochrane database of systematic reviews (publication no. 10.1002/14651858).(Art. no.: CD010540. Pub. 2).*
Relaxation training	Francesco, P., Mauro, M. G., Gianluca, C., & Enrico, M. (2010). The efficacy of relaxation training in treating anxiety. *International Journal of Behavioral Consultation and Therapy, 5*(3–4), 264–269. https://doi.org/10.1037/h0100887
Schema therapy	Hawke, L. D., & Provencher, M. D. (2011). Schema theory and schema therapy in mood and anxiety disorders: A review. *Journal of Cognitive Psychotherapy, 25*(4), 257.
Self-monitoring	Cohen, J. S., Edmunds, J. M., Brodman, D. M., Benjamin, C. L., & Kendall, P. C. (2013). Using self-monitoring: Implementation of collaborative empiricism in cognitive-behavioral therapy. *Cognitive and Behavioral Practice, 20*(4), 419–428.
Social skills training	Willis, D., Siceloff, E. R., Morse, M., Neger, E., & Flory, K. (2019). Stand-alone social skills training for youth with ADHD: A systematic review. *Clinical Child and Family Psychology Review, 22*(3), 348–366.

Each of these treatment components addresses a different aspect of behavioral health disorders. For example, attention training can help individuals suffering from anxiety to move their attention away from feared stimuli to allow them to reduce the intensity of distress (Fergus, Wheless, & Wright, 2014).

Cognitive restructuring and schema therapy can help individuals identify and challenge underlying negative cognitions and schemas (Beck, Emery, & Greenberg, 2005; Young, Klosko, & Weishaar, 2003).

Exposure-based approaches can help individuals habituate to the sensations of anxiety and to the feared stimuli. Response prevention exercises can help stop individuals from engaging in compulsive behavior and avoiding negative emotions or avoiding the feared stimuli (Wheaton et al., 2016).

Behavioral activation can provide individuals with greater skills and experience in engaging in positive goals. Behavioral activation exercises can also help individuals reduce avoidance (Jacobson, Martell, & Dimidjian, 2001).

Both psychoeducation and acceptance-based treatments encourage individuals to accept the nature of their condition and focus on improving the quality of their life (Hayes, Stosahl, & Wilson, 2011).

Treatment Modalities

The therapeutic relationship is thought to be an important part of delivering the treatment (Lambert & Barley, 2001). In many cases, having the relationship with the therapist helps people to make the changes needed. However, other relationships, including among peers, group therapy members, or among family members may also support change (Horvath, Del Re, Fluckieger, & Symonds, 2011).

The treatment modality refers to the members of the treatment process, including who provides the treatment and who receives the treatment the treatment. Examples of different modalities include:

- *Individual therapy:* Usually, individual therapy consists of sessions with one trained therapist for a period from 30 to 60 minutes, although some prolonged exposure therapy sessions may last for up to 2 hours. The treatment involves both building the relationship and engaging in the specific treatment components to help individuals build skills and/or explore their thoughts and feelings (Roth & Fonagy, 2006).

- *Group therapy:* There are many different types of group therapy, but groups for specific disorders can have as few as 2 or as many as 30 or more individuals, although many psychotherapy groups have about 6 participants. Some groups focus on building skills, others allow individuals to explore their feelings (Haen & Aronson, 2016). There is usually one experienced leader, and there may also be a coleader. Some self-help groups, including narcotics anonymous (NA) and alcoholics anonymous (AA), are led by the members themselves and do not require trained leaders.
- *Family therapy:* Sometimes all members of a family may participate and work directly with a therapist trained in family therapy. Other times only one family member and the identified patient may meet with the therapist. Specific treatment components help individuals change family relationships to improve support and decrease interpersonal stress, as well as to build skills, and/or explore thoughts and feelings (Gurman & Kniskern, 2014).

Treatment Delivery Formats

Therapies can be delivered in many different formats, including the following:

- Face-to-face sessions.
- On the web.
- As part of an app.
- Via virtual reality technology.

Each of these formats has advantages and disadvantages in terms of effectiveness and cost. Face-to-face formats may facilitate the development of a therapeutic relationship (Martin, Garske, & Davis, 2000). Web-based treatments can reduce cost and provide more privacy for some types of therapy (Khanna & Kendall, 2015). App-based treatments can provide support in real time as individuals face challenges or they can provide prompts to help people remember to avoid temptation or practice positive health habits (Donker et al., 2013). Virtual reality approaches may make it easier for individuals to practice coping skills in response to the situations that are highly distressing (Powers & Emmelkamp, 2008).

Types of Therapists

Different types of therapists can provide treatments. Treatment can be delivered by trained therapists or peer therapists or parents. There is a growing body of literature that suggests that carefully trained peer therapists can be of great help (Cabassa et al., 2017).

Treatment Settings

Treatment can be delivered in different types of settings, ranging from a consulting office in an academic medical center to the individual's home or workplace or on the street. For individuals who have phobias or anxiety that occurs in specific places (e.g., at home, in stores or on planes or in the park), therapists may make home visits or conduct therapy in the location which evokes distress for the patient (Kazdin & Blase, 2011).

Ancillary or Common Factors Across Treatments

Treatments have components that researchers hypothesize are the "active ingredients." These active ingredients differ depending on the therapy, but they are the ingredients the researchers hypothesize are the components that make the treatment effective in reducing symptoms and improving functioning (McAleavey & Castonguay, 2014). For example, in acceptance and commitment therapy, researchers hypothesize that acceptance and mindfulness approaches are among the unique active components (Hayes-Skelton, Roemer, & Orsillo, 2013). In exposure-based therapies, the researchers hypothesize that it is being exposed to the feared stimuli and one's own emotional responses to the stimuli that are the components that reduce anxiety (Foa & McLean, 2016).

However, in addition to the hypothesized active component of the therapy, all treatments have some common factors. These factors often include variables that are associated with the way therapy is delivered (McAleavey & Castonguay, 2014). For example, some common factors include the relationship with the therapist, time spent attending to the problem, and expectations of improvement.

Table 11.2 lists some ancillary or common factors that are shared across many, but not all, therapies. For example, most psychotherapies involve a relationship with a therapist, but some web-based therapies or bibliotherapy may not.

One of the challenges in treatment outcome research is determining which of these common factors are active ingredients and which are not. One common factor, the relationship with the therapist, may be an important part of helping the individual reduce symptoms and improve functioning. Other common factors, such as time spent in a therapy office, may not be as essential to improvement. Therapy delivered in other settings or over the computer might be effective as well.

Table 11.2 displays different types of common factors and how they may differ across treatment modalities (i.e., individual vs. family therapy) and across delivery systems (i.e., face to face vs. the web).

TABLE 11.2 Examples of common factors.

	Individual face-to-face CBT	Family CBT	Web-based CBT
Therapeutic alliance	X	X	–
Relationship with trained and committed therapist	X	X	–
Attention devoted to the problem/issues	X	X	X
Time spent focusing on problem	X	X	X
Time spent in a therapy office	X	X	–
Expectations of improvement	X	X	X
Credible (believable) treatment	X	X	X
Support and guidance	X	X	?
Therapeutic questioning and discussion.	X	X	–
Therapist feedback about the patients' symptoms and functioning	X	X	Sometimes, the treatment is facilitated by clinicians.

Activity 11.1: Understanding Different Treatment Approaches

Watch two or three short videos of different approaches or read clinical articles and complete Table 11.3.

TABLE 11.3

Video name	What was the condition being treated?	What was the name of the therapy?	What techniques did the therapist use which were part of the "active ingredient"	What common factors did you notice? Specifically, what other activities or circumstances occurred to support the process of therapy?

Continued

Activity 11.1: Understanding Different Treatment Approaches—cont'd

We can also read clinical or review articles to understand more about treatments. Gu and colleagues (2015) describe mindfulness-based cognitive therapy and provide a good discussion of these therapies and explains how they work. The discussion of the treatment and the mechanism of action are included in Table 11.4.

TABLE 11.4 Understanding the treatment.

Author/ Date	What is the type of therapy	What is the theory of the treatment? What do the authors say about why they think this treatment will work?	Describe the treatment itself. What are the components of the treatment? What does the therapist do? What does the patient do?	How is the treatment supposed to work? What mechanism is it supposed to address?	Does this treatment seem like a reasonable approach for your participants, given their condition and risk factor?
Gu, Strauss, Bond, & Cavanagh, 2015	Mindfulness Cognitive Behavior therapy and Mindfulness stress reduction	These therapies are hypothesized to work by teaching people skills in present moment awareness. They help the person be aware of their thoughts and feelings and to view these thoughts and feelings with acceptance and self-compassion.	The therapist teaches the skills, the patient practices. The components include exercises which promote self-awareness, emotion regulation, relaxation, and exposure to one's own feelings and thoughts.	The treatment is supposed to reduce stress reactivity, interrupt rumination, improve self-monitoring, teach principles of self-compassion, improve attentional flexibility and other kinds of cognitive flexibility, and improve values clarification.	This could be a good treatment for GAD since it seems like it could help people become aware of their worrying and maybe accept that things are sometimes uncertain.

A Closer Look

Primary, Secondary, or Tertiary Prevention

As you have been thinking about risk factors, mechanisms, and symptoms, you may have been wondering—Why don't we just prevent these problems? Why don't we reduce the risk factor, so we can prevent the problem? Why are we treating the mechanisms and the symptoms? Isn't that too late in the game?

Primary prevention—or risk factor reduction—makes sense when there are **modifiable risk factors**. Modifiable risk factors are risk factors we can change. Public health primary prevention treatments are often used to address risk factors (Dixon & Evan, 2014).

For example, if trauma is a risk factor, there are many public health approaches to reduce trauma exposure (Foa, Keane, Friedman, & Cohen, 2008; Rose et al., 2002). We can try to prevent trauma from motor vehicle accidents or crimes. And we can offer parenting programs to reduce the trauma that comes from child abuse and neglect (Sanders, Kirby, Tellegen, & Day, 2014). The programs to prevent risk factors are called primary prevention programs.

But not all risk factors are modifiable. And sometimes trauma or other events cannot be prevented. We need to have treatments to address the consequences of risk factors that were not modified or cannot be modified. These are called secondary prevention treatments. Treatments are called tertiary prevention treatments if they are addressing the disabling consequences of a condition (Joseph, Williams, Ownby, Saltzgaber, & Johnson, 2006).

In this book, we focus on secondary prevention treatments, but the methods could also be used to study primary or tertiary prevention treatments as well.

Finding the Evidence

We can look at the evidence for different treatments. Start by searching for articles to help you determine which treatments have been used for the disorders and mechanisms you have been studying.

Next, assemble a library of articles about the treatment. This library will be helpful as you design your study. Your library may include clinical articles, systematic reviews and meta-analyses, and original research. Clinical articles will help you understand the nature of the disorder and the therapies; review articles will help you understand the state of the evidence and the gaps in knowledge; and original research will give you further information and ideas about how treatment outcome studies operate.

Activity 11.2: Searching for Treatments for the Disorder

Use Google Scholar or an equivalent search engine to search for treatments used for the disorder you are studying. Use Table 11.5 which lists treatment components to guide your search, but be aware that there are many other possible treatment components we have not listed. Use the terms for the treatments or treatment components and the terms for the disorder in the search bars in Fig. 11.3. When providing an example in Table 11.5, we used OCD as a sample disorder.

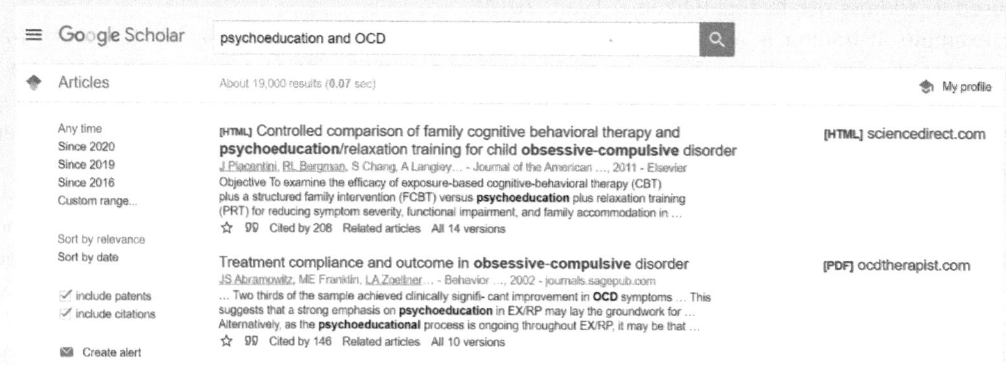

FIGURE 11.3 A sample search using a treatment and a disorder term together.

When articles come up in the search, read the abstracts to see if the articles link your disorder to the treatment component.

Now complete the same activity substituting your mechanism for the disorder as one search term and a treatment or treatment component as another search term. Determine if the therapy component or component has been used to address the mechanism. See Fig 11.4.

In searches for articles which examine the relation between the treatment and the mechanism, you do not have to include the term for your disorder. You are looking to see if the treatment has been used for the mechanism, even if the treatment was used for another disorder. This will still be useful evidence for you.

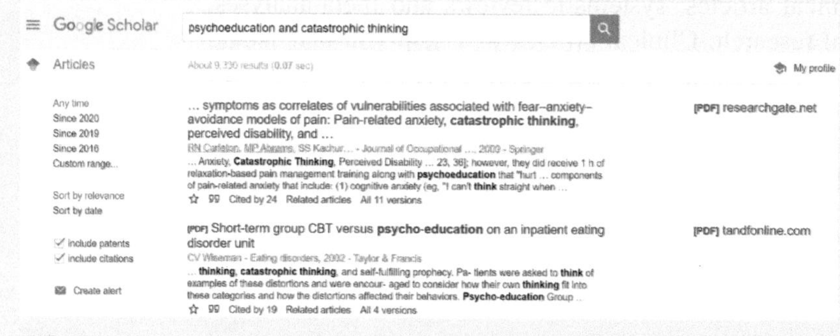

FIGURE 11.4 A sample search using a treatment and a mechanism term together.

Activity 11.2: Searching for Treatments for the Disorder—cont'd

Searches for treatments for the disorder and treatments that address the mechanism may yield similar articles. Once you read the papers, you may find the treatment has been targeted to both the mechanism and the symptoms of the disorder. That will be helpful, even if the search reveals that the researchers have not studied individuals with the disorder you are studying.

Once you have completed Table 11.5 for both the disorder and the mechanism, you will have a better sense of the types of treatments that have been used to treat your disorder and address the mechanism. Now you can assemble articles to see what the evidence says about the types of treatment that are most effective.

Fig. 11.5 is an example of one original research article that came up in a search for psychoeducation and OCD. We demonstrate how to complete the table using the reference for this article.

Controlled Comparison of Family Cognitive Behavioral Therapy and Psychoeducation/ Relaxation Training for Child Obsessive-Compulsive Disorder

John Piacentini, Ph.D., R. Lindsey Bergman, Ph.D., Susanna Chang, Ph.D., Audra Langley, Ph.D., Tara Peris, Ph.D., Jeffrey J. Wood, Ph.D., James McCracken, M.D.

Objective: To examine the efficacy of exposure-based cognitive-behavioral therapy (CBT) plus a structured family intervention (FCBT) versus psychoeducation plus relaxation training (PRT) for reducing symptom severity, functional impairment, and family accommodation in youths with obsessive-compulsive disorder (OCD). **Method:** A total of 71 youngsters 8 to 17 years of age (mean 12.2 years; range, 8–17 years, 37% male, 78% Caucasian) with primary OCD were randomized (70:30) to 12 sessions over 14 weeks of FCBT or PRT. Blind raters assessed outcomes with responders followed for 6 months to assess treatment durability. **Results:** FCBT led to significantly higher response rates than PRT in ITT (57.1% vs 27.3%) and completer analyses (68.3% vs. 35.3%). Using HLM, FCBT was associated with significantly greater change in OCD severity and child-reported functional impairment than PRT and marginally greater change in parent-reported accommodation of symptoms. These findings were confirmed in some, but not all, secondary analyses. Clinical remission rates were 42.5% for FCBT versus 17.6% for PRT. Reduction in family accommodation temporally preceded improvement in OCD for both groups and child functional status for FCBT only. Treatment gains were maintained at 6 months. **Conclusions:** FCBT is effective for reducing OCD severity and impairment. Importantly, treatment also reduced parent-reported involvement in symptoms with reduced accommodation preceding reduced symptom severity and functional impairment. **Clinical Trials Registry Information**—Behavior Therapy for Children and Adolescents with Obsessive-Compulsive Disorder (OCD); http://www.clinicaltrials.gov; NCT00000386. J. Am. Acad. Child Adolesc. Psychiatry, 2011;50(11):1149–1161. **Key words:** obsessive-compulsive disorder, cognitive behavioral therapy, functional impairment, family accommodation

FIGURE 11.5 Abstract from Piacentini et al. (2011).

Continued

Activity 11.2: Searching for Treatments for the Disorder—cont'd

TABLE 11.5 Table for documenting interventions, symptoms, and mechanisms.

	Symptoms	Mechanisms
Psychoeducation	Piacentini et al (2011)	
Relaxation training		
Mindfulness mediation		
EMDR		
Attention training		
Cognitive restructuring		
Schema therapy		
Exposure therapy		
Social skills training		
Behavioral activation		
Habit reversal		
Self-monitoring		
Decision making treatments		
Motivational interviewing		
Other components		
Other components		
Other components		
Other components		
Other components		

Finding Different Types of Articles

There are several different kinds of articles that are useful for a TOS section: Systematic or meta-analytic reviews, clinical articles, and original research articles. Each of these articles has an important role to play in developing your paper or proposal. *But only meta-analyses and original empirical research papers can provide evidence in support of or against the use of a treatment.* Be sure you understand what type of article you are reading as you collect your evidence.

Systematic or meta-analytic reviews of treatment outcomes. It is helpful to start your search for information about a treatment by reading review papers. Just as you found when you read reviews and meta-analyses about the public health significance of the disorder or the associated risk factors and mechanisms, review articles on treatments provide a systematic overview of the findings about treatments for a disorder. This information can provide an idea about the best kind of treatments for the disorder. The authors try to be comprehensive—they include every relevant paper on the treatment for the condition. They examine the trends in literature. They present data indicating which treatments have the most scientific support. Search for review including the term "systematic review" or meta-analysis" in the search (Fig. 11.8).

In a meta-analysis, the authors typically show a list of all the studies reviewed, with a description of the treatments that were tested. These meta-analyses can give you a good idea about:

1. The overall evidence in favor of a treatment.
2. Moderating factors that influence treatment outcome.
3. The gaps in knowledge—the types of evidence that are missing.

Here is an example of a meta-analysis article which provides data on the overall effectiveness of treatment for anxiety disorders (Fig. 11.6). Springer et al. (2018) find that across studies only about 50% of adults with anxiety disorders improve sufficiently that they can be considered to have recovered and no longer have an anxiety disorder after treatment. The results vary across conditions, with treatment showing better outcomes for GAD than SAD, for example. But the findings overall suggest better methods are needed.

ELSEVIER

Contents lists available at ScienceDirect

Clinical Psychology Review

journal homepage: www.elsevier.com/locate/clinpsychrev

Review

Remission in CBT for adult anxiety disorders: A meta-analysis

Kristen S. Springer[a], Hannah C. Levy[a], David F. Tolin[a,b,*]

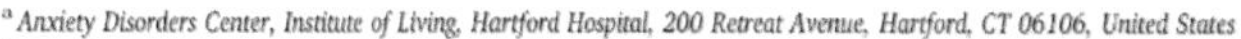
[a] Anxiety Disorders Center, Institute of Living, Hartford Hospital, 200 Retreat Avenue, Hartford, CT 06106, United States
[b] Department of Psychiatry, Yale University School of Medicine, 300 George St. New Haven, CT 06511, United States

HIGHLIGHTS

- There is no universally accepted definition of remission in anxiety disorders.
- We conducted a meta-analysis of remission in cognitive-behavior therapy (CBT).
- The overall remission rate for the intent-to-treat samples was 48% at post-treatment and 54% at follow up while the remission rate for completer samples was 53% at post-treatment and 56% at follow up.
- Remission rates differed by definition, diagnosis, and various patient factors.
- Although CBT is effective for anxiety, there is significant room for improvement.

ARTICLE INFO

Keywords:
Anxiety
CBT
Remission
Meta-analysis
PTSD
OCD

ABSTRACT

Currently there is no universally accepted definition of remission in anxiety disorders. This may be causing significantly different estimates of treatment efficacy across anxiety disorders. The aim of this paper was to determine not only the overall remission rate in cognitive-behavioral therapy (CBT) for anxiety disorders, but also to examine whether the different definitions of remission lead to significantly different remission rates. From the initial 228 abstracts reviewed by the authors, 100 articles were retained. The overall mean remission rate was 51.0%. Remission rates were highest when remission was defined as good end state functioning or no longer meeting criteria for the primary diagnosis. Studies of posttraumatic stress disorder had the highest remission rates, while those of obsessive-compulsive disorder and social anxiety disorder had the lowest remission rates. Rates of remission differed by certain demographic (e.g., older age) and clinical (e.g., medication use) characteristics. Although CBT is an empirically supported treatment for anxiety disorders, it is clear that there is room for improvement, as many patients do not achieve remission status.

FIGURE 11.6 An example of a meta-analytic paper from Springer, Levy, and Tolin (2018).

Other meta-analyses, including the example by Cuijpers et al. (2014), provide insight into potential moderators of treatment outcome (Fig. 11.7). As we have discussed, moderators are variables which affect the relationship between the predictor/independent variable (IV) and the outcome/dependent variable (DV). In treatment outcome studies, moderator variables may allow researchers to understand the situations or characteristics that affect treatment outcome. These moderators could include variables such as the characteristics of the patient, the type of outcome, the type of therapy setting, or treatment provider, among other variables.

Clinical Psychology Review 34 (2014) 130–140

Contents lists available at ScienceDirect

Clinical Psychology Review

Psychological treatment of generalized anxiety disorder: A meta-analysis

CrossMark

Pim Cuijpers [a,b,c,*], Marit Sijbrandij [a,b], Sander Koole [a,b], Marcus Huibers [a,b], Matthias Berking [c,d], Gerhard Andersson [e,f]

[a] Department of Clinical Psychology, VU University Amsterdam, The Netherlands
[b] EMGO Institute for Health and Care Research, The Netherlands
[c] Leuphana University, Innovation Incubator, Division Health Trainings Online, Lueneburg, Germany
[d] Philipps-University Marburg, Germany
[e] Department of Behavioural Sciences and Learning, Linköping University, Sweden
[f] Department of Clinical Neuroscience, Psychiatry Section, Karolinska Institutet, Stockholm, Sweden

HIGHLIGHTS

- Cognitive behavior therapy (CBT) is effective in the treatment of GAD.
- CBT also has considerable effects on depression in GAD.
- There are not enough studies examining the long-term effects.
- There are not enough studies comparing CBT with care-as-usual or placebo.

ARTICLE INFO

Article history:
Received 20 April 2013
Received in revised form 11 October 2013
Accepted 2 January 2014
Available online 10 January 2014

Keywords:
Generalized anxiety disorder
Cognitive behavior therapy
Psychotherapy
Meta-analysis
Randomized trial
Comparative outcome studies

ABSTRACT

Recent years have seen a near-doubling of the number of studies examining the effects of psychotherapies for generalized anxiety disorder (GAD) in adults. The present article integrates this new evidence with the older literature through a quantitative meta-analysis. A total of 41 studies (with 2132 patients meeting diagnostic criteria for GAD) were identified through systematic searches in bibliographical databases, and were included in the meta-analysis. Most studies examined the effects of cognitive behavior therapy (CBT). The majority of studies used waiting lists as control condition. The pooled effect of the 38 comparisons (from 28 studies) of psychotherapy versus a control group was large ($g = 0.84$; 95% CI: 0.71–0.97) with low to moderate heterogeneity. The effects based on self-report measures were somewhat lower than those based on clinician-rated instruments. The effects on depression were also large ($g = 0.71$; 95% CI: 0.59–0.82). There were some indications for publication bias. The number of studies comparing CBT with other psychotherapies (e.g., applied relaxation) or pharmacotherapy was too small to draw conclusions about comparative effectiveness or the long-term effects. There were some indications that CBT was also effective at follow-up and that CBT was more effective than applied relaxation in the longer term.

FIGURE 11.7 An example of a meta-analytic paper from Cuijpers et al. (2014).

Some meta-analyses point out other moderators of outcomes. In the meta-analysis by Cuijpers et al. (2014), the authors combine the results of 41 studies including over 2000 patients to understand the state-of-the-art on psychological treatments for GAD. Cuijpers et al. (2014) point out an important moderator of outcomes, the source of data. Doctors' reports of patient improvement are more likely to reveal positive outcomes than are patients' reports of their own improvement.

The Cochrane Library (https://www.cochrane.org/about-us) contains the highest quality systematic reviews of areas in health and healthcare. The reviews published in the Cochrane collection provide guidance for establishing best practices in many areas of medicine and psychology.

To find systematic or meta-analytic reviews, add the terms meta-analysis or systematic review to the search terms. These terms should already include a type of treatment and your disorder (Fig. 11.8).

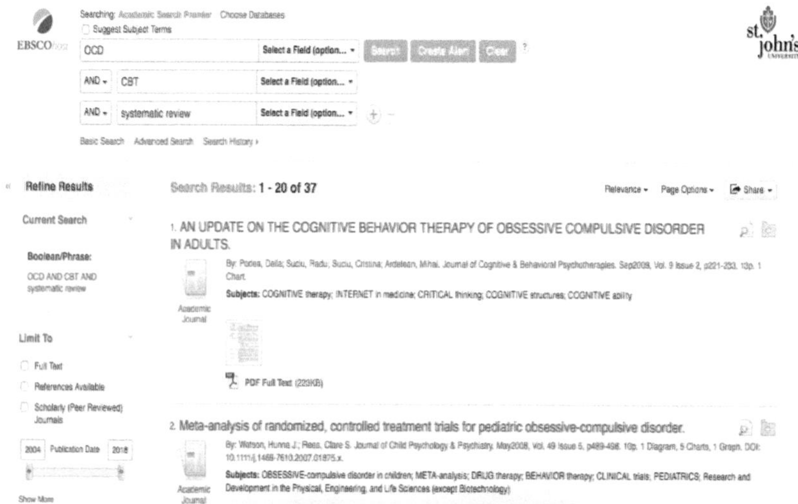

FIGURE 11.8 An example of search terms.

Clinical or theoretical articles. Once you have gained enough information from systematic reviews to choose a therapy for your disorder, it is time to learn more about the treatment. Clinical articles contain this information.

Clinical or theoretical articles generally include a description about a behavioral health problem and a treatment to address the problem. The articles usually provide a theoretical rationale for the therapy and can help the reader understand why the therapy might affect symptoms of the disorder. The articles sometimes identify mechanisms which have been identified as contributing to improvement. These articles may include a case study describing the implementation and response to treatment.

Clinical articles can describe both the disorder and the treatment for the disorder in a clear and straightforward manner. These articles may cite a broad range of literature, but they are not intended to give a comprehensive picture of the field. Instead, they are intended to present a new theory and to describe a clinical situation. They describe the therapy, but do not provide evidence from a rigorous study to document the treatment's effects.

For example, this paper by Fresco and colleagues provides a detailed discussion of emotion regulation therapy for GAD and includes a case study (Fig. 11.9). This paper can help clarify the rationale for emotion regulation therapy and provide insight into the way the therapy should work. The paper does not present quantitative data on the outcomes of the therapy.

Available online at www.sciencedirect.com

Cognitive and Behavioral Practice 20 (2013) 282-300

Cognitive and Behavioral Practice

www.elsevier.com/locate/cabp

Contains Video [1]

Emotion Regulation Therapy for Generalized Anxiety Disorder

David M. Fresco, *Kent State University*
Douglas S. Mennin, *Hunter College*
Richard G. Heimberg, *Temple University*
Michael Ritter, *G.V. (Sonny) Montgomery VA Medical Center*

Despite the success of cognitive behavioral therapies (CBT) for emotional disorders, a sizable subgroup of patients with complex clinical presentations, such as patients with generalized anxiety disorder, fails to evidence adequate treatment response. Emotion Regulation Therapy (ERT) integrates facets of traditional and contemporary CBTs, mindfulness, and emotion-focused interventions within a framework that reflects basic and translational findings in affect science. Specifically, ERT is a mechanism-targeted intervention focusing on patterns of motivational dysfunction while cultivating emotion regulation skills. Open and randomized controlled psychotherapy trials have demonstrated considerable preliminary evidence for the utility of this approach as well as for the underlying proposed mechanisms. This article provides an illustration of ERT through the case of "William." In particular, this article includes a case-conceptualization of William from an ERT perspective while describing the flow and progression of the ERT treatment approach.

FIGURE 11.9 Abstract from Fresco, Mennin, Heimberg, and Ritter (2013).

Original empirical studies. As you have learned when reading articles for the PHS and Risk Factors and Mechanisms sections of the paper, original research papers describe the results of a specific research study. For an original research paper to use in your *TOS section*, you need papers that compare an experimental treatment to a control treatment. To find relevant empirical papers that describe appropriate studies for the TOS, look for these words in the title or abstract ("comparison," "randomized controlled trial (RCT)," "versus" (one treatment vs. another). In addition to using search engines, you can find references for these articles in the reference section of review articles. Knowledge about these treatments will help you to justify your choices of treatment and your control treatment.

Here are some examples of articles which describe randomized clinical trials comparing an experimental treatment to a control condition/treatment. The title of the articles provide ideas about the search terms, such as randomized clinical trial, that will be useful as you search for evidence.

Arch, J. J., Eifert, G. H., Davies, C., Vilardaga, J. C. P., Rose, R. D., & Craske, M. G. (2012). Randomized clinical trial of cognitive behavioral therapy (CBT) versus acceptance and commitment therapy (ACT) for mixed anxiety disorders. *Journal of Consulting and Clinical Psychology*, *80*(5), 750.

Hedman, E., Andersson, E., Ljótsson, B., Andersson, G., Rück, C., & Lindefors, N. (2011). Cost-effectiveness of Internet-based cognitive behavior therapy versus cognitive behavioral group therapy for social anxiety disorder: Results from a randomized controlled trial. *Behaviour Research and Therapy*, *49*(11), 729–736.

Safer, D. L., & Jo, B. (2010). Outcome from a randomized controlled trial of group therapy for binge eating disorder: comparing dialectical behavior therapy adapted for binge eating to an active comparison group therapy. *Behavior Therapy*, *41*(1), 106–120.

Activity 11.3: Using Meta-Analyses to Choose a Treatment

Search for an article presenting a meta-analysis that evaluates treatment outcomes for your disorder. In a search engine such as Google or the databases in your school library, use the search term for your disorder, and add the terms "meta-analysis" and "treatment outcome" to find the meta-analyses you need. As you read, try to get the gist of the article. At this point, you don't need to understand all the details of the meta-analyses.

Notice that the meta-analysis may help you answer these questions:

- What are the treatment components that have been tested?
- Do the data support the treatment you are considering?
- Do the authors suggest a better alternative?

Begin by reading the excerpts from the meta-analysis article by Firth et al. (2017) shown in Fig. 11.10. Use Table 11.6 to help you sort out the evidence. See if the meta-analysis indicates that the treatment affects the mechanism you are studying in addition to the symptoms of the disorder).

Journal of Affective Disorders 218 (2017) 15–22

Contents lists available at ScienceDirect

Journal of Affective Disorders

journal homepage: www.elsevier.com/locate/jad

Review article

Can smartphone mental health interventions reduce symptoms of anxiety? A meta-analysis of randomized controlled trials

Joseph Firth[a,*,1], John Torous[b,c,1], Jennifer Nicholas[d,e], Rebekah Carney[a], Simon Rosenbaum[d,e], Jerome Sarris[f,g,h]

[a] Division of Psychology and Mental Health, Faculty of Biology, Medicine and Health, University of Manchester, UK
[b] Department of Psychiatry, Beth Israel Deaconess Medical Canter, Harvard Medical School, Boston, MA, United States
[c] Harvard Medical School, Boston, MA, United States
[d] Black Dog Institute, UNSW Australia, Australia
[e] School of Psychiatry, Faculty of Medicine, UNSW Australia, Australia
[f] Department of Psychiatry, University of Melbourne, The Melbourne Clinic, Melbourne, Australia
[g] Centre for Human Psychopharmacology, Swinburne University of Technology, Hawthorn, Australia
[h] NICM, School of Science and Health, University of Western Sydney, Australia

ARTICLE INFO

Keywords:
e-health
mhealth
Apps
Panic disorder
Anxiety disorders
Obsessive-compulsive disorder

ABSTRACT

Background: Various psychological interventions are effective for reducing symptoms of anxiety when used alone, or as an adjunct to anti-anxiety medications. Recent studies have further indicated that smartphone-supported psychological interventions may also reduce anxiety, although the role of mobile devices in the treatment and management of anxiety disorders has yet to be established.

Methods: We conducted a systematic review and meta-analysis of all randomized clinical trials (RCTs) reporting the effects of psychological interventions delivered via smartphone on symptoms of anxiety (sub-clinical or diagnosed anxiety disorders). A systematic search of major electronic databases conducted in November 2016 identified 9 eligible RCTs, with 1837 participants. Random-effects meta-analyses were used to calculate the standardized mean difference (as Hedges' g) between smartphone interventions and control conditions.

Results: Significantly greater reductions in total anxiety scores were observed from smartphone interventions than control conditions ($g = 0.325$, 95% C.I. = 0.17–0.48, $p < 0.01$), with no evidence of publication bias. Effect sizes from smartphone interventions were significantly greater when compared to waitlist/inactive controls ($g = 0.45$, 95% C.I. = 0.30–0.61, $p < 0.01$) than active control conditions ($g = 0.19$, 95% C.I. = 0.07–0.31, $p = 0.003$).

Limitations: The extent to which smartphone interventions can match (or exceed) the efficacy of recognised treatments for anxiety has yet to established.

Conclusions: This meta-analysis shows that psychological interventions delivered via smartphone devices can reduce anxiety. Future research should aim to develop pragmatic methods for implementing smartphone-based support for people with anxiety, while also comparing the efficacy of these interventions to standard face-to-face psychological care.

FIGURE 11.10 Abstract from Firth et al. (2017).

Continued

Activity 11.3: Using Meta-Analyses to Choose a Treatment—cont'd

We have completed the table for the first article. Fill out the rest with a meta-analysis on treatments for the disorder you are studying.

TABLE 11.6

Documenting Findings from Meta-Analytic Papers								
Author/Date of meta-analysis	**Disorder being treated**	**Types of treatments examined**	**Number of studies examining the treatment**	**Type of control groups used in studies of these treatments**	**Findings supporting and not supporting the treatment. How many or how strong are the positive findings? How many or how strong are the negative findings?**	**Factors that may explain differences in outcomes, if known.**	**Mechanism? Is there evidence that the treatment affects the mechanism you are studying?**	**Limits to existing knowledge (e.g., outcomes tested, groups tested, treatment delivery differences)**
Firth et al (2017)	Symptoms of anxiety disorders, multiple diagnoses, subthreshold and diagnosed anxiety disorder	Smart phone interventions, using cognitive and behavioral interventions	9 studies, 1837 participants	Some studies in analysis used wait-list control, some used active controls, including control conditions which controlled for attention, user engagement	Moderate to strong effects when comparing smartphone intervention to wait list control, less strong, small positive effect for comparisons to active controls	Type of control condition. Length of intervention	No information	Many different kinds of anxious people. Not many active control groups. Inadequate trials with long term outcomes.

Building Human Capital

As you read about treatments, you may find that you don't always understand how the treatment works. You may need to look for videos or clinical papers to understand more about what really happens in the therapy. Or you may talk to clinicians to ask how the therapy is used in real life.

As you write the TOS, you may find that you are developing your curiosity and your ability to search for new and important

information. You are learning to identify the kinds of questions you need to ask, and the strategies you need to answer them.

And as you read more, you may wonder if the treatment you are reading about is the best approach. You may begin to develop your own ideas about approaches that might also work. If you have had your own therapy, you may think about what helped you. See if you can imagine in your own mind how the therapy operates.

Working through the step-by-step details of how you think the therapy might work gives you mental skills in breaking down ideas. The ability to break down complex ideas into distinct parts is a very valuable skill. You are learning to use your own experience and your own thoughtful imagination to guide your own reasoning and questioning.

Terms

Take the time to define each of these terms and consider how to apply them:

Treatment packages
Treatment components
Treatment modalities
Treatment delivery formats
Treatment settings
Therapist qualifications

References

Abramowitz, J. S., Deacon, B. J., & Whiteside, S. P. (2011). *Exposure therapy for anxiety: Principles and practice*. Guilford Press.

Baer, R. A. (Ed.). (2015). *Mindfulness-based treatment approaches: Clinician's guide to evidence base and applications*. Elsevier.

Beck, A. T., Emery, G., & Greenberg, R. L. (2005). *Anxiety disorders and phobias: A cognitive perspective*. Basic Books.

Cabassa, L. J., Camacho, D., Vélez-Grau, C. M., & Stefancic, A. (2017). Peer-based health interventions for people with serious mental illness: a systematic literature review. *Journal of Psychiatric Research, 84*, 80–89.

Cohen, J. S., Edmunds, J. M., Brodman, D. M., Benjamin, C. L., & Kendall, P. C. (2013). Using self-monitoring: Implementation of collaborative empiricism in cognitive-behavioral therapy. *Cognitive and Behavioral Practice, 20*(4), 419–428.

Cuijpers, P., Sijbrandij, M., Koole, S., Huibers, M., Berking, M., & Andersson, G. (2014). Psychological treatment of generalized anxiety disorder: A meta-analysis. *Clinical Psychology Review, 34*(2), 130–140.

Czajkowski, S. M., Powell, L. H., Adler, N., Naar-King, S., Reynolds, K. D., Hunter, C. M., ... Peterson, J. C. (2015). From ideas to efficacy: The ORBIT model for developing behavioral treatments for chronic diseases. *Health Psychology, 34*(10), 971.

Deacon, B. J., Fawzy, T. I., Lickel, J. J., & Wolitzky-Taylor, K. B. (2011). Cognitive defusion versus cognitive restructuring in the treatment of negative self-referential thoughts: An investigation of process and outcome. *Journal of Cognitive Psychotherapy, 25*(3), 218.

Dixon, D. L., & Evan, M. S. (2014). Primary prevention of cardiovascular. *Circulation, 129*(2), S49–S73.

Donker, T., Petrie, K., Proudfoot, J., Clarke, J., Birch, M. R., & Christensen, H. (2013). Smartphones for smarter delivery of mental health programs: A systematic review. *Journal of Medical Internet Research, 15*(11).

Dryden, W. (2007). *Dryden's handbook of individual therapy*. Sage.

Duncan, E., Best, C., & Hagen, S. (2008). Shared decision making treatments for people with mental health conditions. *Cochrane Database of Systematic Reviews, 1*.

D'Zurilla, T. J., & Nezu, A. M. (2010). Problem-solving therapy. *Handbook of Cognitive-Behavioral Therapies, 3*, 197–225.

Fergus, T. A., Wheless, N. E., & Wright, L. C. (2014). The attention training technique, self- focused attention, and anxiety: A laboratory-based component study. *Behaviour Research and Therapy, 61*, 150–155.

Firth, J., Torous, J., Nicholas, J., Carney, R., Rosenbaum, S., & Sarris, J. (2017). Can smartphone mental health interventions reduce symptoms of anxiety? A meta-analysis of randomized controlled trials. *Journal of Affective Disorders, 218*, 15–22.

Foa, E. B., Keane, T. M., Friedman, M. J., & Cohen, J. A. (Eds.). (2008). *Effective treatments for PTSD: Practice guidelines from the International Society for Traumatic Stress Studies*. Guilford Press.

Foa, E. B., & McLean, C. P. (2016). The efficacy of exposure therapy for anxiety-related disorders and its underlying mechanisms: The case of OCD and PTSD. *Annual Review of Clinical Psychology, 12*, 1–28.

Francesco, P., Mauro, M. G., Gianluca, C., & Enrico, M. (2010). The efficacy of relaxation training in treating anxiety. *International Journal of Behavioral Consultation and Therapy, 5*(3–4), 264–269. https://doi.org/10.1037/h0100887

Fresco, D. M., Mennin, D. S., Heimberg, R. G., & Ritter, M. (2013). Emotion regulation therapy for generalized anxiety disorder. *Cognitive and Behavioral Practice, 20*(3), 282–300.

Gu, J., Strauss, C., Bond, R., & Cavanagh, K. (2015). How do mindfulness-based cognitive therapy and mindfulness-based stress reduction improve mental health and wellbeing? A systematic review and meta-analysis of mediation studies. *Clinical Psychology Review, 37*, 1–12.

Gurman, A. S., & Kniskern, D. P. (2014). *Handbook of family therapy*. Routledge.

Haen, C., & Aronson, S. (2016). *Handbook of child and adolescent group therapy: A practitioner's reference*. Taylor & Francis.

Hawke, L. D., & Provencher, M. D. (2011). Schema theory and schema therapy in mood and anxiety disorders: A review. *Journal of Cognitive Psychotherapy, 25*(4), 257.

Hayes, S. C., Strosahl, K. D., & Wilson, K. G. (2011). *Acceptance and commitment therapy: The process and practice of mindful change*. Guilford Press.

Hayes-Skelton, S. A., Roemer, L., & Orsillo, S. M. (2013). A randomized clinical trial comparing an acceptance-based behavior therapy to applied relaxation for generalized anxiety disorder. *Journal of Consulting and Clinical Psychology, 81*(5), 761.

Heimberg, R. G. (2002). Cognitive-behavioral therapy for social anxiety disorder: Current status and future directions. *Biological Psychiatry, 51*(1), 101–108.

Heinicke, M. R., Stiede, J. T., Miltenberger, R. G., & Woods, D. W. (2020). Reducing risky behavior with habit reversal: A review of behavioral strategies to reduce habitual hand-to-head behavior. *Journal of Applied Behavior Analysis, 53*(3), 1225–1236.

Horvath, A. O., Del Re, A. C., Flückiger, C., & Symonds, D. (2011). Alliance in individual psychotherapy. *Psychotherapy, 48*(1), 9.

Jacobson, N. S., Martell, C. R., & Dimidjian, S. (2001). Behavioral activation treatment for depression: Returning to contextual roots. *Clinical Psychology: Science and Practice, 8*(3), 255–270.

Joseph, C. L., Williams, L. K., Ownby, D. R., Saltzgaber, J., & Johnson, C. C. (2006). Applying epidemiologic concepts of primary, secondary, and tertiary prevention to the elimination of racial disparities in asthma. *Journal of Allergy and Clinical Immunology, 117*(2), 233–240.

Kazdin, A. E. (2008). Evidence-based treatment and practice: New opportunities to bridge clinical research and practice, enhance the knowledge base, and improve patient care. *American Psychologist, 63*(3), 146.

Kazdin, A. E., & Blase, S. L. (2011). Rebooting psychotherapy research and practice to reduce the burden of mental illness. *Perspectives on Psychological Science, 6*(1), 21–37.

Khanna, M. S., & Kendall, P. C. (2015). Bringing technology to training: Web-based therapist training to promote the development of competent cognitive-behavioral therapists. *Cognitive and Behavioral Practice, 22*(3), 291–301.

Knowles, M. M., Foden, P., El-Deredy, W., & Wells, A. (2016). A systematic review of efficacy of the attention training technique in clinical and nonclinical samples. *Journal of Clinical Psychology, 72*(10), 999–1025.

Lambert, M. J., & Barley, D. E. (2001). Research summary on the therapeutic relationship and psychotherapy outcome. *Psychotherapy: Theory, Research, Practice, Training, 38*(4), 357.

Martell, C. R., Dimidjian, S., & Herman-Dunn, R. (2013). *Behavioral activation for depression: A clinician's guide*. Guilford Press.

Martin, D. J., Garske, J. P., & Davis, M. K. (2000). Relation of the therapeutic alliance with outcome and other variables: A meta-analytic review. *Journal of Consulting and Clinical Psychology, 68*(3), 438.

McAleavey, A. A., & Castonguay, L. G. (2014). Insight as a common and specific impact of psychotherapy: Therapist-reported exploratory, directive, and common factor interventions. *Psychotherapy, 51*(2), 283.

Miller, W. R., & Rose, G. S. (2009). Toward a theory of motivational interviewing. *American Psychologist, 64*(6), 527.

Nielsen, L., Riddle, M., King, J. W., Aklin, W. M., Chen, W., Clark, D., … Green, P. (2018). The NIH science of behavior change program: Transforming the science through a focus on mechanisms of change. *Behaviour Research and Therapy, 101*, 3–11.

Oren, E., & Solomon, R. (2012). EMDR therapy: An overview of its development and mechanisms of action. *Revue Européenne De Psychologie Appliquée/European Review of Applied Psychology, 62*(4), 197–203.

Piacentini, J., Bergman, R. L., Chang, S., Langley, A., Peris, T., Wood, J. J., & McCracken, J. (2011). Controlled comparison of family cognitive behavioral therapy and psychoeducation/relaxation training for child obsessive-compulsive disorder. *Journal of the American Academy of Child & Adolescent Psychiatry, 50*(11), 1149–1161.

Powers, M. B., & Emmelkamp, P. M. (2008). Virtual reality exposure therapy for anxiety disorders: A meta-analysis. *Journal of Anxiety Disorders, 22*(3), 561–569.

Rose, S. C., Bisson, J., Churchill, R., & Wessely, S. (2009). Psychological debriefing for preventing post traumatic stress disorder (PTSD). *Cochrane Database of Systematic Reviews, 2*.

Roth, A., & Fonagy, P. (2006). What works for whom? A critical review of psychotherapy research. Guilford Press.

Sanders, M. R., Kirby, J. N., Tellegen, C. L., & Day, J. J. (2014). The triple P-positive parenting program: A systematic review and meta-analysis of a multi-level system of parenting support. *Clinical Psychology Review, 34*(4), 337–357.

Sin, J., Jordan, C., Barley, E., Henderson, C., & Norman, I. (2015). Psychoeducation for siblings of individuals with severe mental illness. *Cochrane Database of Systematic Reviews* (Publication no. 10.1002/14651858) (Art. no.: CD010540. Pub. 2).

Solomon, P. (2004). Peer support/peer provided services underlying processes, benefits, and critical ingredients. *Psychiatric Rehabilitation Journal, 27*(4), 392.

Springer, K. S., Levy, H. C., & Tolin, D. F. (2018). Remission in CBT for adult anxiety disorders: A meta-analysis. *Clinical Psychology Review, 61*, 1–8.

Wheaton, M. G., Galfalvy, H., Steinman, S. A., Wall, M. M., Foa, E. B., & Simpson, H. B. (2016). Patient adherence and treatment outcome with exposure and response prevention for OCD: Which components of adherence matter and who becomes well? *Behaviour Research and Therapy, 85*, 6–12.

Willis, D., Siceloff, E. R., Morse, M., Neger, E., & Flory, K. (2019). Stand-alone social skills training for youth with ADHD: A systematic review. *Clinical Child and Family Psychology Review, 22*(3), 348–366.

Young, J. E., Klosko, J. S., & Weishaar, M. E. (2003). *Schema therapy: A practitioner's guide*. Guilford Press.

Chapter 12

Theory of the solution: Understanding research design for treatment outcome studies

Does the treatment you chose work? What are the effects of the treatment? Is it better than other treatments in reducing symptoms of the disorder?

To answer these questions, you need to understand more about how researchers test hypotheses about treatment effects. In this chapter, you will learn about the research designs that are used to test treatment outcomes and understand the components of these designs. You will also be introduced to some of the statistical analyses used in treatment outcome studies.

Research Designs

Uncontrolled Trials

Let's start with the simplest case. Before researchers undertake the effort and expense of a randomized clinical trial, they need some basic information about the feasibility, acceptability, and effects of the treatment. They want to make sure they understand materials, methods, and participants they will need to formally test their hypotheses about the effects of treatment in more rigorous studies. And they want to identify any problems (e.g., side effects) participants experience when they try this treatment.

Therefore, researchers may start out with an uncontrolled trial of the effects of the treatment. In an uncontrolled trial of a

Psychology Research Methods. https://doi.org/10.1016/B978-0-12-815680-3.00012-8

treatment, all participants receive the same treatment. There is no contrasting or control treatment. The researchers use an uncontrolled trial to answer the question: "Does this treatment produce a change in symptoms over time?"

In this type of study, **Time** is the predictor variable. The primary outcome or dependent variable (DV) is likely to be symptoms of the disorder. The researcher hypothesizes that the treatment will produce changes in symptoms over time.

To test this hypothesis, the researcher measures the symptoms several times. One or more measurements occur before the treatment begins and the other measurements are made after the treatment. Sometimes, researchers will also measure changes in outcomes as the treatment proceeds, adding additional assessment periods during the treatment period (Table 12.1).

TABLE 12.1 Possible times for measuring outcome in a demonstration project.

Timing	Before treatment	During treatment	Immediately after treatment	Follow-up
Measure of symptoms	X	X	X	X

We can look at an example (Fig. 12.1).

Journal of Affective Disorders 173 (2015) 216–220

Contents lists available at ScienceDirect

Journal of Affective Disorders

journal homepage: www.elsevier.com/locate/jad

Preliminary communication

Effectiveness and acceptability of accelerated repetitive transcranial magnetic stimulation (rTMS) for treatment-resistant major depressive disorder: An open label trial

Alexander McGirr[a], Frederique Van den Eynde[c], Santiago Tovar-Perdomo[c], Marcelo P.A. Fleck[b,c], Marcelo T. Berlim[b,c,*]

[a] Department of Psychiatry, University of British Columbia, Vancouver, British Columbia, Canada
[b] Depressive Disorders Program, Douglas Mental Health University Institute and McGill University, Montréal, Québec, Canada
[c] Neuromodulation Research Clinic, Douglas Mental Health University Institute, Montréal, Québec, Canada

ARTICLE INFO

Article history:
Received 4 October 2014
Received in revised form
15 October 2014
Accepted 28 October 2014
Available online 11 November 2014

Keywords:
Major depressive disorder
Treatment resistant depression
RTMS
High-frequency rTMS
Accelerated rTMS
Open-label trial

ABSTRACT

Background: Major depressive disorder (MDD) is a significant cause of worldwide disability and treatment resistance is common. High-frequency repetitive transcranial magnetic stimulation (HF-rTMS) has emerged as a treatment for MDD, and while efficacious, the daily commitment for typical 4–6 weeks of treatment poses a significant challenge. We aimed to determine the effectiveness and acceptability of an accelerated rTMS protocol for MDD.
Methods: In this naturalistic trial, 27 patients with moderate to severe chronic and treatment-resistant MDD were treated with twice-daily HF-rTMS (10 Hz) applied over the left dorsolateral prefrontal cortex for 2 consecutive weeks (60,000 pulses). The primary outcomes were rates of clinical remission and response (16-item Quick Inventory of Depressive Symptomatology post-treatment score ≤ 6, and $\geq 50\%$ reduction, respectively). Secondary outcomes were self-reported anxious symptoms, depressive symptoms and quality of life, and dropout rates as a proxy for acceptability.
Results: Ten (37.0%) patients met criteria for clinical remission and 15 (55.6%) were classified as responders, with comparable outcomes for both moderate and severe MDD. Clinician-rated improvements in depressive symptoms were paralleled in self-reported depressive and anxious symptoms, as well as quality of life. No patient discontinued treatment.
Limitations: This study is limited by short treatment duration that might be lengthened with corresponding improvements in effectiveness, limited duration of follow-up, small sample size, and an open-label design requiring randomized controlled replication.
Conclusion: An accelerated protocol involving twice-daily sessions of HF-rTMS over the left DLPFC for 2 weeks was effective in treatment-resistant MDD, and had excellent acceptability. Additional research is required to optimize accelerated rTMS treatment protocols and determine efficacy using sham-controlled trials.

FIGURE 12.1 Abstract from McGirr, Van den Eynde, Tovar-Perdomo, Fleck, & Berlim, 2015.

In this study, the researchers administer a new form of therapy, called accelerated, repetitive transcranial magnetic stimulation (rTMS). They examine the changes in clinician-rated depressive symptoms from before the treatment started to the end of the 2-week treatment period. The authors call this uncontrolled trial an open trial because all participants receive the treatment, and all are aware of the treatment they are receiving (i.e., they all know they are receiving rTMS).

Time is the predictor. Treatment cannot be a predictor variable because everyone receives the same treatment (rTMS). Since all participants received the treatment, it is not possible to compare the results of this treatment to any other treatment or even to a no-treatment condition. Consequently, we cannot know if the participants would have improved over time even without treatment. We also cannot know if this treatment is better than no treatment or other treatments.

Randomized Controlled Trials

Given the limits of uncontrolled trials, researchers developed other research designs to test hypotheses about the effects of treatment. The most common and "gold standard" approach to testing treatment effects is the randomized controlled trial (RCT).

In an RCT to evaluate the effects of treatment, the independent variable (IV) can be called TREATMENT. To start, investigators consider two levels of TREATMENT. At least one of these treatments is an **experimental treatment** (sometimes called the experimental condition) which contains one or more active ingredients. These are the active ingredients which the researcher believes will produce benefits. Another level of the IV TREATMENT is a **control or comparison treatment/condition.** The choices of experimental and control treatments are shaped by the hypotheses you propose to test.

(In more advanced studies, researchers may include multiple experimental or control conditions, as we will discuss in Chapter 13.)

Since RCTs use an experimental design, participants are **assigned at random** to the different levels of the IV (i.e., experimental vs. control).

The researcher examines differences between the participants in the experimental treatment and those in the control treatment by assessing changes to their symptoms from before the treatment to after the treatment. The statistical analyses will examine whether the participants in the experimental treatment improved more over time than the participants in the control treatment (Table 12.2; Fig. 12.2).

TABLE 12.2 Assessments by levels of IV and time.

Time period	Pretest (before treatment)	Posttest (after treatment)
Treatment groups		
Experimental	Symptom scores	Symptom scores
Control	Symptom scores	Symptom scores

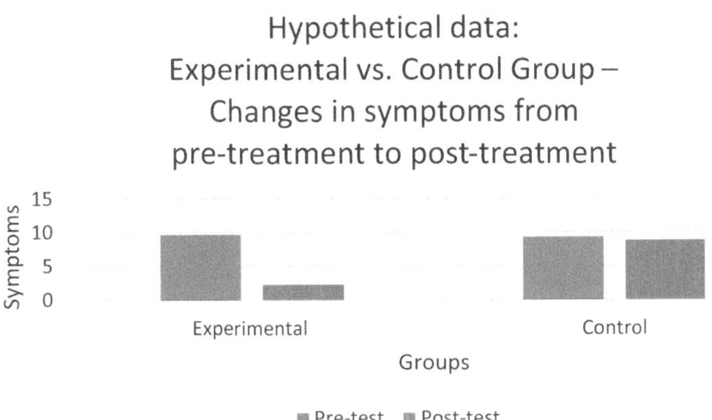

FIGURE 12.2 Depicting changes over time for the experimental and control group using hypothetical data.

Sometimes, researchers add one or more additional measurement periods at points after the treatment has ended. These follow-up evaluations are used to test the hypothesis that the effects of treatment persist over time.

Experimental and Control Treatments

The Experimental Treatment

The decision about which experimental and control conditions should be included in the study depends on the hypotheses to be tested (Fig. 12.3).

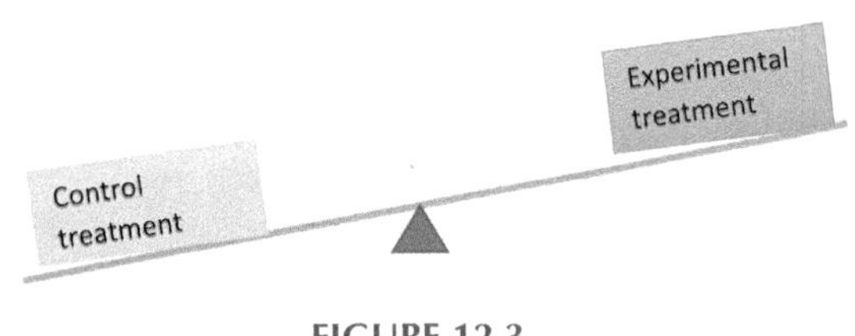

FIGURE 12.3

In the initial phases of research, researchers are asking the question: Does this treatment package work? Is it better than no treatment at all?

As researchers find evidence in support of the treatment, they may want to test hypotheses about different components of the treatment to find out which component is the active component responsible for any benefits of treatment. Later they may want to test hypotheses about new or more cost-effective ways to deliver the treatment.

Therefore, depending on the hypothesis the researcher wants to test, experimental treatments can contain:

- A new active ingredient (or a better combination of active ingredients)
- A more effective approach for delivering the active ingredient
- A more efficient (e.g., cost-effective) method to deliver the active ingredients

The Control Treatment

In an RCT, the researcher is comparing the experimental treatment to a control treatment. This control treatment is used to permit the researcher to pinpoint what is producing the outcome. The type of control or comparison treatment/condition depends on the hypothesis the researcher wishes to test.

Here are some possible control treatments:

- A no-treatment control
- A placebo control—controlling for everything but the active ingredient
- A positive control—comparing two or more active treatments

Let's look at some examples to see how the hypothesis to be tested determines the choice of experimental and control treatments/conditions.

Does the Experimental Treatment Reduce Symptoms?

In the early days of developing a treatment, the researcher may be interested in understanding the benefits and side effects of a new approach. In these cases, researchers may include a no-treatment control. The participants in the no-treatment control are tested just as the participants in experimental treatment are. But they do not receive treatment.

An RCT including a no-treatment control is an improvement over an uncontrolled trial when it comes to testing the feasibility, acceptability, and efficacy of the treatment. With a no-treatment control researchers are now able to determine if any changes seen in the experimental treatment are not simply a function of the passage of time. Since no treatment is involved, researchers sometimes call this the *control condition,* instead of the control treatment (Fig. 12.4).

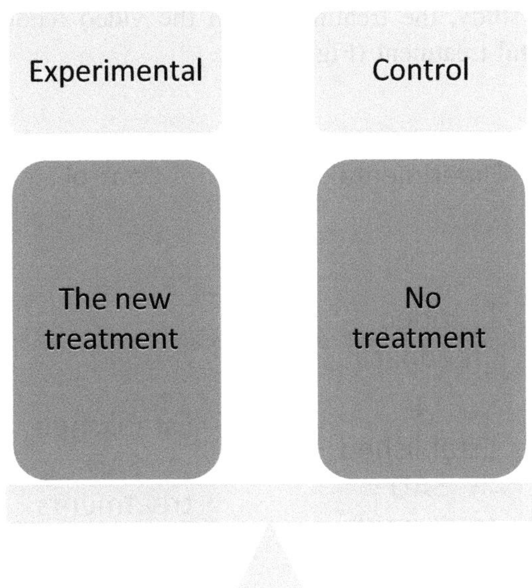

FIGURE 12.4

Does a new method of treatment improve the outcome? In this case, researchers are asking if a new treatment approach improves on the outcomes delivered by existing and successful approaches. Here is a specific example.

Parr and Cartwright-Hatton (2009) have noted that it is very difficult to treat social anxiety disorder (SAD). Previous basic research on SAD indicated that one mechanism that may trigger and maintain SAD involves distorted self-perceptions. Individuals jump to conclusions that their self-presentations are very shameful or negative.

This theory led Parr and Cartwright-Hatton (2009) to generate a new kind of treatment. The researchers hypothesized that videotaping the patients with SAD and showing them the videos would provide them with realistic feedback. They hypothesized that this accurate and realistic feedback might change their self-perceptions.

The researchers designed SAD-specific video exercises to help patients with SAD change their self-perceptions. The researchers tested the hypothesis that an SAD-specific treatment with video feedback will produce better outcomes than an SAD-specific treatment without the video component.

In this study, the treatment with the video feedback is the experimental treatment (Fig. 12.5).

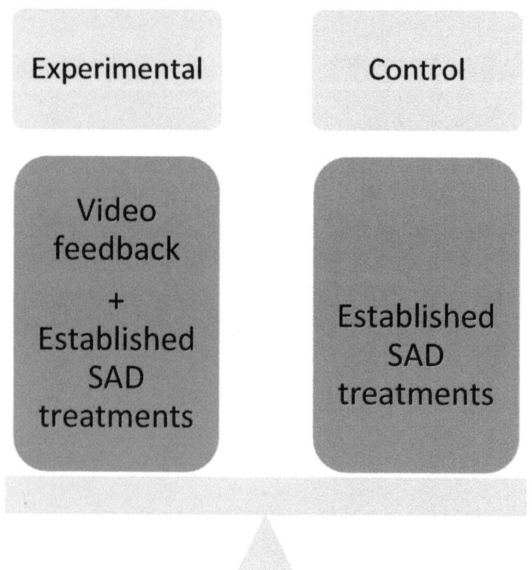

FIGURE 12.5 (Parr & Cartwright-Hatton, 2009; Warnock et al., 2017).

Is there a better way to deliver the treatment? Researchers might want to consider a new approach for delivering an existing treatment. For example, Barrett, Healy-Farrell, and March (2004) wondered if the outcome of cognitive behavioral therapy (CBT) for OCD in children would be better if the CBT was delivered in a family context. They developed the family approach and tested the hypothesis that family CBT (FCBT) is more effective than individual child-focused CBT delivered by a therapist. The FCBT is the experimental treatment (Fig. 12.6).

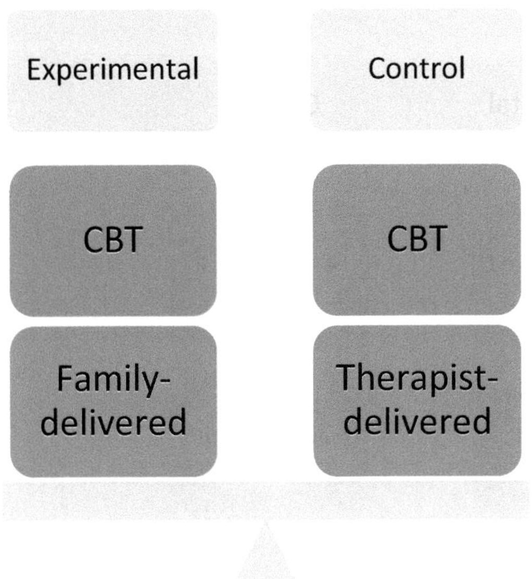

FIGURE 12.6 Comparisons made in Barrett et al., 2004

Will this treatment work outside the medical center in "more real life" circumstances? Once a treatment is established and shown to be effective, researchers may want to understand how to deliver the treatment to the widest number of people, at the lowest costs, without diminishing the benefits of treatment.

Specifically, they want to determine if a lower cost approach to treatment will be as effective as the original version. More cost-effective approaches could include a new delivery system (e.g., using a web-based approach instead of face-to-face therapy) or a new treatment modality (e.g., group therapy) that will permit the researchers to treat more people with fewer resources. In this case the hypothesis the researcher is testing is that these new (potentially less costly) versions of the intervention will produce results that are no different from the old version.

For example, in the Barrett et al. (2004) paper about FCBT treatments for OCD, the authors also compared the effects of family treatment delivered to one family at a time to the effects of a group treatment in which multiple families are treated together. The group approach is the experimental treatment (Fig. 12.7).

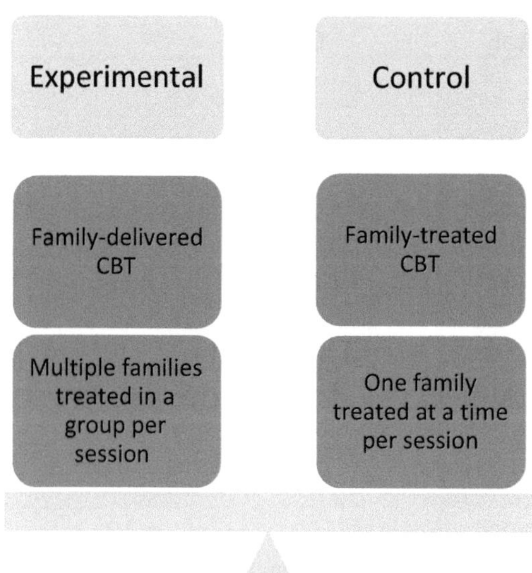

FIGURE 12.7 Comparisons made in Barrett et al., 2004

Efficacy and Effectiveness

Sometimes researchers are examining whether a treatment works under controlled conditions. They may test a new treatment in very controlled conditions at an academic medical center clinic using highly selected patients who have only the condition they are investigating and no other conditions. In this case, the researcher is testing the **efficacy** of her new approach. A treatment is efficacious (i.e., has efficacy) if the treatment produces a good outcome under controlled conditions (Glasgow, Lichtenstein, & Marcus, 2003).

Once the researcher has established efficacy, it's time to test the **effectiveness** of a treatment. A treatment is effective if the treatment works under real-world conditions. These real-world conditions might involve including patients who have other comorbid conditions or using

Efficacy and Effectiveness—cont'd

newly trained therapists, or delivering the therapy in less than ideal settings, such as a busy medical practice. Sometimes, treatments that work well in a very selected sample do not work (or do not work *as well*) in people who have other conditions. Or the treatments do not work as well in the more complicated and busy conditions in a regular medical or psychology practice.

Testing the effects of treatment under "real-world" conditions is one kind of **translational research**. In translational research, the researcher is moving the findings from "bench to bedside." They are taking findings obtained in the controlled conditions of a laboratory (or an academic medical center) and testing them in more real-world conditions to see how they apply in the "real world." The "real world" for treating behavioral health disorders might include settings such as the local doctor's office or a mental health clinic or school or a workplace (Woolf, 2008).

Superiority and Noninferiority Trials

There are different objectives to RCTs—different types of hypotheses that researchers can test. In **superiority trials**, the researchers want to demonstrate that their new approach is better than the control approach. The first three types of studies described in this chapter are superiority studies. Investigators test the hypotheses that the new program is better than no treatment; that the SAD-specific treatment plus video is better than SAD-specific treatment alone; or that family-delivered CBT is better than individual CBT.

Noninferiority trials compare treatments to make sure the newer, more efficient or less costly treatment is as effective as the original version. In noninferiority trials, the treatment delivered by the new system (e.g., web-based CBT) can be considered the experimental treatment. The old system (face-to-face) is the control. The hypothesis that is being tested is that the experimental treatment is not inferior to—not worse than—the old treatment (Fig. 12.8).

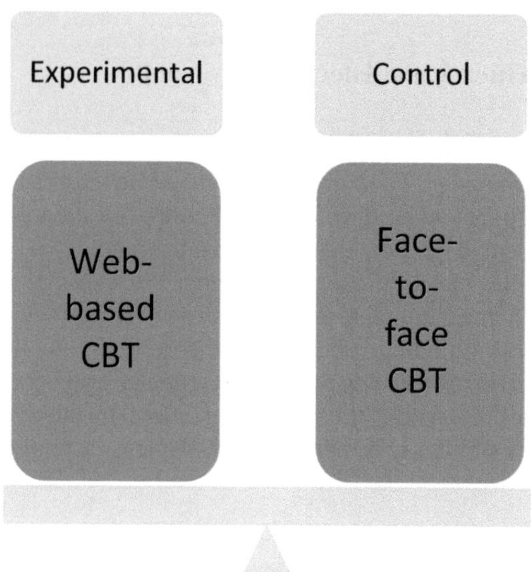

FIGURE 12.8 Comparisons made in Andrews, Cujipers, Craske, McEvoy, & Titov, 2010.

There are also **equivalence trials** in which researchers are testing to see if two active treatments, such as CBT and ACT, produce equivalent effects. When two treatments have equivalent effects, this means the outcomes do not substantially differ across the treatments.

Having equivalent treatments can be helpful in practice. Two treatments that, on average, produce similar outcomes can provide more treatment choices. People can choose the kind of treatment that they prefer and know they are getting a treatment that has evidence supporting its use.

If you are writing a research proposal to test the effects of a treatment, you might choose to test the superiority of a new treatment, or you can test whether a new approach to delivering the treatment is acceptable (i.e., not inferior to the standard method).

If you are writing a research paper on different kinds of treatments for a disorder, you may wish to review different treatment approaches and different delivery systems, reviewing the costs and benefits of each approach.

Understanding Original Empirical Article on Treatment Outcomes

In Chapter 7, you examined how to read the results section of Theory of the Problem articles. In this chapter you will examine the results section of treatment outcome studies—studies you need for the theory of the solution. As you examine the results, you will learn more about how these studies are designed. This knowledge will be helpful as you design your own proposals or write your research paper.

Understanding the Analytical Plan and Statistical Methods

To understand the effects of the treatment, researchers can use many different types of analyses. The approach to the analyses depends on the hypothesis to be tested and the research design that is used.

Uncontrolled or open-label trials. Let's start with the simplest case. Before researchers undertake the effort and expense of a randomized clinical trial, they may try an uncontrolled trial of the effects of the treatment. All participants receive the treatment. The researcher is interested in determining if there are changes in outcomes over time. ***Time*** is the predictor. The primary outcome or DV is likely to be symptoms of the disorder (Table 12.3).

TABLE 12.3 Possible times for measuring outcomes in a demonstration project.

Timing	Before treatment	During treatment	Immediately after treatment	Follow-up
Measure of symptoms	X	X	X	X

The statistical analyses measure changes in symptoms over time. The researcher can use methods related to analysis of variance to compare the symptom scores before treatment to those after the treatment. Alternatively, if they have multiple measurements, the researchers can use methods related to regression to examine the trends in the changes in symptoms over time.

Let's look at an example of the results of an uncontrolled open-label trial on rTMS by McGirr et al. (2015) we discussed earlier (Fig. 12.9).

Journal of Affective Disorders 173 (2015) 216–220

ELSEVIER

Contents lists available at ScienceDirect

Journal of Affective Disorders

journal homepage: www.elsevier.com/locate/jad

Preliminary communication

Effectiveness and acceptability of accelerated repetitive transcranial magnetic stimulation (rTMS) for treatment-resistant major depressive disorder: An open label trial

Alexander McGirr [a], Frederique Van den Eynde [c], Santiago Tovar-Perdomo [c], Marcelo P.A. Fleck [b,c], Marcelo T. Berlim [b,c,*]

2.4. Statistical analyses

Statistical analyses were performed with IBM SPSS v19. Continuous variables were compared using Student's *t*-test, and dichotomous comparisons were performed using χ^2 comparisons. Change in clinical variables as a function of rTMS was performed using repeated measures ANOVA. Statistical significance was set at $\alpha \leq .05$.

A. McGirr et al. / Journal of Affective Disorders 173 (2015) 216–220

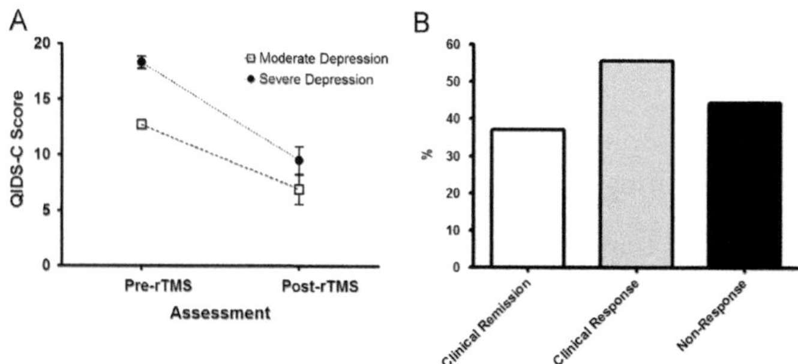

Fig. 1. Clinical response and remission.

Repeated measures ANOVA revealed similar degrees of self-reported depressive symptom improvement according to the QIDS-SR-16 (Mauchly's $W=1.00$; $F(1, 26)=53.19$, $p<.001$). This was mirrored in improvement in self-reported anxious symptomatology (BAI score of 52.00 ± 25.49 pre-rTMS vs 44.00 ± 17.06 post-rTMS; Mauchly's $W=1.00$; $F(1,26)=24.40$, $p<.001$) and perceived improvement in quality of life (WHOQOL-BREF score of 66.99 ± 11.91 pre-rTMS vs 77.81 ± 13.33 post-rTMS; $F(1,26)=29.16$, $p<.001$).

FIGURE 12.9 Selected excerpts from McGirr et al. 2015.

McGirr et al. (2015) examined the changes in clinician-rated depressive symptoms from before the treatment started to the end of the 2-week training period. The researchers used a repeated measures ANOVA to test the hypothesis that there would be reductions in depressive symptoms from pretreatment to posttreatment. In this repeated measures ANOVA, the predictor variable "Time" has two levels: Pretreatment and posttreatment.

The results of the repeated measures ANOVA indicated a significant effect of Time on depressive symptoms. The statistical sentence showing this effect is: ($F(1,26) = 53.19$, $p < 0.001$). But the information in this statistical sentence cannot tell us about the direction of the effects—whether the symptoms go up or down over time.

By looking at Fig 12.9, we can see the direction of the effects. The findings indicate that there is a significant decrease in symptoms over time, even in a small sample. The authors also report the number of participants (10 out of 27) who showed substantial improvement. These data are encouraging, but in an open-label trial we cannot determine if it is the treatment that produced this effect or simply the passage of time or participants' expectations about the outcomes, among other possibilities.

Randomized controlled trials. We need RCTs to conduct experimental tests of hypotheses about the effects of treatment. In an RCT researchers are testing the effects of the IV treatment. Treatment has at least two levels: experimental and control. In complex studies, researchers may include several experimental treatments and/or several controls. The researchers also test the effect of Time—the way symptoms change over time from pretreatment to posttreatment (and even to follow-up).

Parallel and Cross-Over Designs

In many treatment outcome studies, researchers assign participants at random to either the experimental or control conditions. The conditions are implemented in parallel, they occur at the same time. Parallel designs allow researchers to test many participants at once. Since all participants receive only one treatment, researchers do not have to be concerned about exposure to one treatment affecting the outcomes associated with the next treatment, a phenomenon called **carryover effects**. In contrast, another, less common approach to testing treatment outcome involves using a **cross-over** design. In a cross-over design, the participants receive all levels of the IV. They are assigned at random to the order in which the experimental and control conditions are delivered. Specifically, participants are assigned at random to either receive the control condition first or to receive the experimental condition first. This is critical to permit researchers to evaluate order effects and carryover effects. **Order effects** occur when the order in which the participant received the treatments affects the outcome.

Analyses of Parallel Designs

In a parallel design, treatment is a **between-person** IV. A between-person IV is the variable representing the condition to which the participant has been assigned at random. Participants are assigned at random to either the experimental or the control treatment. Scores from participants assigned to the experimental treatment are compared to scores from participants assigned to the control treatment. In Fig. 12.10, participants number 1, 2, 3, 4, and 5 are assigned to the experimental treatment and participants number 6, 7, 8, 9, and 10 are assigned to the control treatment. If there is a significant difference between the scores of those assigned to the experimental treatment vs. those assigned to the control treatment, then there is a significant overall effect of Treatment.

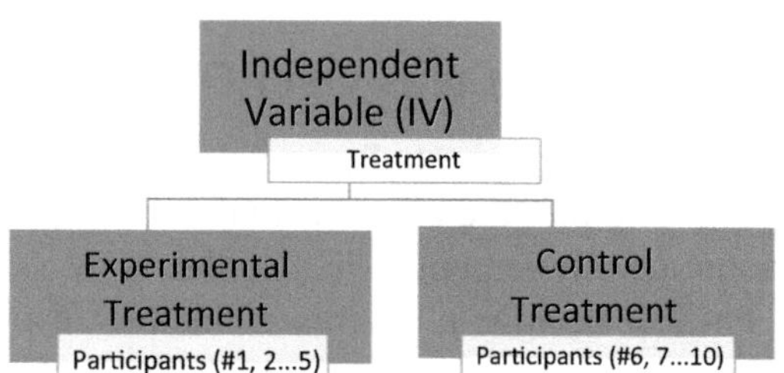

FIGURE 12.10 Comparing participants in the experimental treatment to participants in the control treatment condition.

In contrast, Time is a **within-person** IV. All participants are tested at two or more points in time. At a minimum, scores are obtained at pretreatment, before the treatment begins; and scores are obtained at posttreatment, after the treatment has been completed. Participants' scores at one time are compared with their scores at another. If there is a significant difference in scores between time points, then there is a significant overall effect of Time (Fig. 12.11).

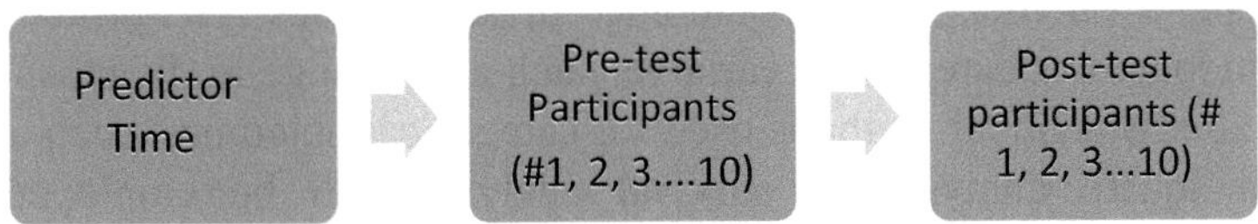

FIGURE 12.11 Comparing the same participants across time.

Researchers are testing the effects of both Treatment and Time, and they are most interested in testing the hypothesis that changes over Time in outcomes are different for the two treatments. They are interested in testing the interaction between Treatment and Time.

The researchers can rephrase this hypothesis by stating that "*The Experimental Treatment is better than the Control Treatment in decreasing the symptoms over time.*"

There are several different statistical methods that can be used to test these general hypotheses. The methods the researchers use depend on:

a) The primary outcome
b) The number of outcomes assessed overall
c) The number of times outcomes are assessed
d) The level of missing data

We introduce several of these approaches to help you understand the results presented in articles describing RCT results. We focus on analytic approaches for parallel RCTs as these are the more common type of RCTs for psychological approaches. For more information on understanding the outcomes of RCTs see Faulkner, Fidler, & Cumming, 2008.

Primary and Secondary Outcomes

In most studies, researchers will measure many outcomes. But to insure the analyses are fair and not biased by multiple statistical tests, they must specify a **primary outcome**.

Researchers choose a primary outcome based on the theory of the solution. The theory of the solution includes the researchers' ideas about what the treatment should be able to change and the clinical relevance of the outcomes. There are many different primary outcomes which could be chosen, including among others, a reduction in symptoms, the remission of symptoms, improvement in functioning, or prevention of hospitalization.

The statistical methods used to evaluate treatment outcome depend on the primary outcome. In some cases, the primary outcome is a categorical variable, such as a change in diagnostic status. Statistical methods used for categorical outcomes, such as chi-square analyses or survival analyses will be employed. In other cases, the primary outcome is a continuous outcome (e.g., reductions in the level of symptoms or improvements in the level of functioning). In this case the statistical approach can include types of analyses of variance or regression methods.

Let's look at examples of categorical and continuous treatment outcomes.

Categorical outcomes. There are several possible categorical outcomes of RCTs. One outcome includes changes in diagnostic status—having or no longer meeting criteria for the diagnosis. The participant has shown a reduction in the intensity or types of symptoms such that they no longer have symptoms that meet the diagnostic criteria. Researchers may use this approach to highlight an outcome that has **clinical significance** as well as statistical significance—a change in symptoms or functioning that is noticeable and valuable to the patient and the healthcare provider.

To test the hypothesis that the experimental treatment will be better than the control treatment in producing a change in diagnostic status, researchers include only participants who meet diagnostic criteria for a disorder at the pretreatment assessment point. After the treatment, at **posttreatment assessment**, the researchers compare the proportion of participants in the experimental and control conditions who still meet the diagnostic criteria for the disorder.

Other primary outcomes include clinically relevant changes in symptoms or social and occupational functioning. Researchers can use established criteria for evidence of clinical improvement. For example, there are surveys which permit experts (usually trained clinicians) to rate the participants' global clinical improvement in symptoms and functioning. Analyses can examine differences in the proportion of participants in the

Experimental and Control Groups who have made clinically significant changes.

We can look at an example in Fig. 12.12.

NEW RESEARCH

Controlled Comparison of Family Cognitive Behavioral Therapy and Psychoeducation/ Relaxation Training for Child Obsessive-Compulsive Disorder

John Piacentini, Ph.D., R. Lindsey Bergman, Ph.D., Susanna Chang, Ph.D., Audra Langley, Ph.D., Tara Peris, Ph.D., Jeffrey J. Wood, Ph.D., James McCracken, M.D.

Objective: To examine the efficacy of exposure-based cognitive-behavioral therapy (CBT) plus a structured family intervention (FCBT) versus psychoeducation plus relaxation training (PRT) for reducing symptom severity, functional impairment, and family accommodation in youths with obsessive-compulsive disorder (OCD). **Method:** A total of 71 youngsters 8 to 17 years of age (mean 12.2 years; range, 8–17 years, 37% male, 78% Caucasian) with primary OCD were randomized (70:30) to 12 sessions over 14 weeks of FCBT or PRT. Blind raters assessed outcomes with responders followed for 6 months to assess treatment durability. **Results:** FCBT led to significantly higher response rates than PRT in ITT (57.1% vs 27.3%) and completer analyses (68.3% vs. 35.3%). Using HLM, FCBT was associated with significantly greater change in OCD severity and child-reported functional impairment than PRT and marginally greater change in parent-reported accommodation of symptoms. These findings were confirmed in some, but not all, secondary analyses. Clinical remission rates were 42.5% for FCBT versus 17.6% for PRT. Reduction in family accommodation temporally preceded improvement in OCD for both groups and child functional status for FCBT only. Treatment gains were maintained at 6 months. **Conclusions:** FCBT is effective for reducing OCD severity and impairment. Importantly, treatment also reduced parent-reported involvement in symptoms with reduced accommodation preceding reduced symptom severity and functional impairment. **Clinical Trials Registry Information**—Behavior Therapy for Children and Adolescents with Obsessive-Compulsive Disorder (OCD); http://www.clinicaltrials.gov; NCT00000386. J. Am. Acad. Child Adolesc. Psychiatry, 2011;50(11):1149–1161. **Key words:** obsessive-compulsive disorder, cognitive behavioral therapy, functional impairment, family accommodation

FIGURE 12.12 Abstract from Piacentini et al. 2011.

Piacentini et al. (2011) test the hypothesis that FCBT will be better than a combination of Psychoeducation and Relaxation Training in improving OCD outcomes in children with OCD. They assign children and their families at random to the experimental treatment (FCBT) or the control treatment

(Psychoeducation and Relaxation Training). The treatment is delivered in 12 sessions over 14 weeks. They assess outcome variables before and after the treatment period (i.e., at baseline and at the end of 14 weeks).

The primary outcome is overall clinical improvement. They measure clinical improvement by having expert raters complete the Clinician Global Impressions of Improvement Scale. Participants are rated on a 1–7 scale with score 1 indicated "very much improved" and a score of 2 indicating "much improved." In contrast, a score of 7 indicated "very much worse." The authors create a categorical variable reflecting improvement level from these scores. If the participant receives a score of 1 or 2, the authors regard the participant as improved. Scores higher than 2 indicate that the participant was not much improved.

The authors examine the proportion of children in each treatment condition who were improved by the end of treatment. They find that 57.1% of the children assigned to the FCBT were improved versus 27.3% of the children in the Psychoeducation and Relaxation Group. They used chi-square analyses and found the differences between groups were significant.

Continuous outcomes. Researchers can use other strategies to evaluate changes in the levels of symptoms or functioning. These strategies allow them to take advantage of the full range of responses. Participants' outcomes are not classified into improved or not-improved categories. Instead, the researchers use the full range of responses and measure changes over time in the levels of symptoms. This is often a preferred approach in behavioral science research (Appelbaum et al., 2018; Levitt et al., 2018).

Let's look at the data to see how these analyses could be conducted. We can imagine the outcome of a study in which 20 people are assigned at random to different treatments, with 10 assigned to the Experimental Treatment and 10 assigned to the Control Treatment. Table 12.4 provides an example of a displaying symptom scores for different levels of the IV at different points in time for a made-up study.

TABLE 12.4 Differences in symptoms over time between the levels of the IV.

	Pretreatment symptoms	Posttreatment symptoms
Experimental condition	8.3	2.7
Control condition	8.2	7.9

Notice that in this example, the estimates of symptom scores for participants in the Experimental and Control treatments are similar at pretreatment but differ at posttreatment assessments. Over time, it appears that changes in scores from pretest to posttest are much greater for the participants in the Experimental Treatment (i.e., changes from 8.1 to 2.8) than those in the Control Treatment (i.e., changes from 8.3 to 8.0).

But are those differences statistically significant? The statistical analyses used to test the significance of these differences depend on the number of outcomes and the number of times the participants are tested and the amount of missing data.

As one approach, researchers can use a Repeated Measures or **Mixed Models ANOVA** to test one outcome over two points in time or a **Repeated Measures MANOVA** if they have multiple measures of related symptoms.

When researchers use these approaches, they test the **interaction of Treatment X Time** to determine if there are differences between the Experimental and Control treatments in changes in symptoms over time.

The interaction effect is an estimate of differences among all four of the cells in the table. (In Table 12.4 the cells represent the different combinations of treatment and time.)

Table 12.5 displays a print-out from a **mixed models analysis of variance** we performed on the data we made up to illustrate this example.

TABLE 12.5 Mixed models analysis of variance from hypothetical data.

Type 3 Tests of Fixed Effects

Effect	Num DF	Den DF	Chi-Square	F Value	Pr > ChiSq	Pr > F
time	1	18	139.24	139.24	<.0001	<.0001
treatment	1	18	60.18	60.18	<.0001	<.0001
treatment*time	1	18	112.36	112.36	<.0001	<.0001

The interaction effect is highlighted in blue. The statistical sentence we could use to express this effect is ($F(1,18) = 112.36$, $p < 0.0001$). The statistical sentence indicates the interaction is significant.

If the estimate for the interaction is significant, researchers conduct additional **post hoc tests** or after-the-fact tests to see which pairs of differences between the cells are significant and account for the overall interaction effect. They are interested in the results of four post hoc tests. The first two tests determine if the two treatments differ in pretreatment scores or in posttreatment scores. Then the next two tests determine if the effects of Time (i.e., the changes from pretreatment to posttreatment) are significant for the Experimental Treatment or the Control Treatment.

The researchers are hoping to see that participants in the Experiment and Control treatments do not differ in symptoms at pretest, but they do differ at posttest. Essentially, the researchers hope the participants in the Experimental and Control treatments start with the same level of symptoms, but the participants in the Experimental Treatment have lower symptoms after treatment.

The researchers also examine the post hoc analyses to determine if pretest to posttest change for the participants in the Experimental Treatment were significantly greater than the pretest to posttest change for the participants in the Control Treatment. This would allow them to conclude that the Experimental Treatment was associated with a reduction in symptoms whereas the Control Treatment was not.

The results of the **post hoc analyses** comparing these different combinations of Treatment and Time are shown in Table 12.6. The results indicate that the differences between the estimates for the pretreatment and posttreatment scores were significant for the Experimental Treatment ($t = -15.84$, $p < .0001$) but not the Control Treatment ($t = -.85$, $p < .4073$).

TABLE 12.6 Results of post-hoc comparisons.

Differences of Least Squares Means

Effect	time	treatment	time	treatment	Estimate	Standard Error	DF	t Value	Pr > |t|
treatment		0		1	2.5500	0.3287	18	7.76	<.0001
time	post		pre		-2.9500	0.2500	18	-11.80	<.0001
treatment*time	post	0	pre	0	-0.3000	0.3536	18	-0.85	0.4073
treatment*time	post	0	post	1	5.2000	0.4130	33.6	12.59	<.0001
treatment*time	post	0	pre	1	-0.4000	0.4130	33.6	-0.97	0.3397
treatment*time	pre	0	post	1	5.5000	0.4130	33.6	13.32	<.0001
treatment*time	pre	0	pre	1	-0.1000	0.4130	33.6	-0.24	0.8101
treatment*time	post	1	pre	1	-5.6000	0.3536	18	-15.84	<.0001

This is the comparison between the pre-test and post-test symptoms scores for the Control Treatment. The effects are non-significant.

This is the comparison between the Experimental and Control condition symptoms scores at Post-test. The effects are significant.

This is the comparison between the Experimental and Control Treatment symptoms scores at pre-test. The effects are non-significant.

This is the comparison between the pre-test and post-test symptoms scores for the Experimental Treatment. The effects are significant.

Fig. 12.13 displays these results in a picture. Notice the line representing the scores for the Experimental Treatment shows a decrease in symptoms from pretreatment to posttreatment. The line representing the scores for the Control Treatment shows essentially no change in symptoms.

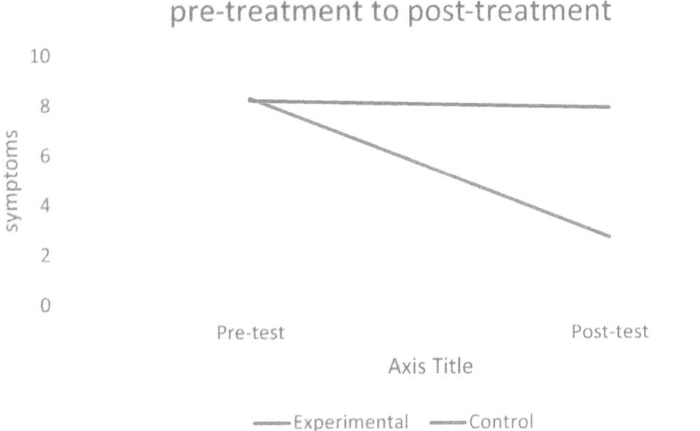

FIGURE 12.13 Changes in symptoms from pre- to posttreatment.

Multiple assessment points. In many clinical trials, participants are tested at more than two points in time. They may be tested at pretest and posttest, but also during the treatment period or at follow-up, after the treatment has ended. If researchers are measuring participants at multiple assessment times and the times of assessment are not completely consistent across the participants, they may use a special form of mixed modeling to examine trends in the changes over time. Hierarchical linear modeling (HLM) is one example of these procedures. HLM allows researchers to see the rate of change over time and compare groups on the differences in the rates of change.

For example, a study by Piacentini et al. (2011) tests the hypothesis that FCBT will be superior to a combined psychoeducation and relaxation training to reduce OCD in children. All participants were assigned at random to either the experimental treatment (FCBT) or the control (Psychoeducation and Relaxation). One outcome included improvement in OCD symptoms.

Piacentini et al. (2011) use HLM to understand rates of change in children's scores on a measure of OCD symptoms, the Children's YBOCS. They find a significant interaction between Treatment Condition X Time. When they examine the data further, they find that the scores show a faster decline in the FCBT group than the PRT (Fig. 12.14).

OCD Severity

The HLM analysis comparing the rate of change in CYBOCS total scores in FCBT and PRT yielded a statistically significant slope by treatment interaction, $t = 2.25$, $p < .05$. The means in Table 3 (and Figure 2) show that the nature of this interaction effect was a faster decline in CYBOCS scores over time in FCBT as compared to PRT. FCBT led to a 46.2% reduction in CYBOCS total score as compared to a 32.0% reduction for PRT.

FIGURE 12.14 Excerpt from Piacentini et al. 2011.

Missing Data: Intent-to-treat Analyses

The statistical tests used and results of the study also depend on the completeness of the data. Researchers can have missing data if participants do not complete all the measurements. They must have a method that allows them to handle these missing data on both a conceptual and technical level.

Missing data presents a special problem for treatment outcome studies because the interpretation of the missing data can be unclear. Data could be missing because the participants drop out of the program. In this case, the missing data could reflect treatment failure. If researchers only include the data from those participants who complete the treatment, they could be biasing the outcome.

Since missing data can reflect the failure of the treatment, researchers often conduct two sets of analyses: **Intent-to-treat** and **completer analyses.** The intent-to-treat analyses include all participants who enrolled in the study; the completer analyses include only those who complete the treatment.

In intent-to-treat analyses, researchers must use a strategy to replace the missing data that do not introduce bias. There are many other methods for handling missing data. For a discussion of these issues, see Bell, Fiero, Horton and Hsu (2014).

In contrast, completer analyses include only those who have completed the treatment and have posttest scores. The analyses are difficult to interpret because those who complete the study may not represent the full sample originally recruited into the study. The smaller sample of completers may not accurately reflect the randomization. More of the completers may have been assigned to the experimental group (or to the control group). Or the completers may differ on other variables (Gupta, 2011).

Let's look at an example from the Piacentini et al. (2011) article.

In intent-to treat analyses, Piacentini et al. (2011) find that 57.1% of the children assigned to the FCBT were improved versus 27.3% of the children in the Psychoeducation and Relaxation Training. In contrast, when only those children who completed the study were included in the analyses, the authors find that 68.3% of the participants assigned to FCBT group improved versus 38.3% of the participants assigned to Psychoeducation and Relaxation Training.

The direction of the effects is similar. In this case, but not in all research, the outcomes from the intent-to-treat and completers analyses are both significant and in the same direction. As you read research on treatment outcome, you can look at the authors' use of intent-to-treat analyses and missing data. This will help you decide how to interpret the results of the study.

Activity 12.1: Understanding the Results of a Treatment Outcome Study

Here is the abstract and the results section of an article describing the results of a randomized controlled trial comparing two types of internet-based treatments: CBT and Interpersonal Psychotherapy (Fig. 12.15).

Continued

Activity 12.1: Understanding the Results of a Treatment Outcome Study—cont'd

Journal of Anxiety Disorders 28 (2014) 410–417

Contents lists available at ScienceDirect

Journal of Anxiety Disorders

Cognitive behavior therapy versus interpersonal psychotherapy for social anxiety disorder delivered via smartphone and computer: A randomized controlled trial

Jesper Dagöö[a], Robert Persson Asplund[a], Helene Andersson Bsenko[b], Sofia Hjerling[c], Anna Holmberg[d], Susanne Westh[d], Louise Öberg[e], Brjánn Ljótsson[f], Per Carlbring[g], Tomas Furmark[c], Gerhard Andersson[a,h,*]

[a] Department of Behavioural Sciences and Learning, Linköping University, Linköping, Sweden
[b] Department of Psychology, Umeå University, Umeå, Sweden
[c] Department of Psychology, Uppsala University, Uppsala, Sweden
[d] Department of Social Sciences, Division of Psychology, Mid Sweden University, Östersund, Sweden
[e] Department of Psychology, Lund University, Lund, Sweden
[f] Department of Clinical Neuroscience, Division of Psychology, Karolinska Institute, Stockholm, Sweden
[g] Department of Psychology, Stockholm University, Stockholm, Sweden
[h] Department of Clinical Neuroscience, Section of Psychiatry, Karolinska Institute, Stockholm, Sweden

ARTICLE INFO

Article history:
Received 30 August 2013
Received in revised form 26 January 2014
Accepted 18 February 2014
Available online 25 March 2014

Keywords:
Cognitive behavior therapy
Interpersonal psychotherapy
Social anxiety disorder
Smartphone
Internet

ABSTRACT

In this study, a previously evaluated guided Internet-based cognitive behavior therapy for social anxiety disorder (SAD) was adapted for mobile phone administration (mCBT). The treatment was compared with a guided self-help treatment based on interpersonal psychotherapy (mIPT). The treatment platform could be accessed through smartphones, tablet computers, and standard computers. A total of 52 participants were diagnosed with SAD and randomized to either mCBT ($n = 27$) or mIPT ($n = 25$). Measures were collected at pre-treatment, during the treatment, post-treatment and 3-month follow-up. On the primary outcome measure, the Liebowitz Social Anxiety Scale – self-rated, both groups showed statistically significant improvements. However, mCBT performed significantly better than mIPT (between group Cohen's $d = 0.64$ in favor of mCBT). A larger proportion of the mCBT group was classified as responders at post-treatment (55.6% versus 8.0% in the mIPT group). We conclude that CBT for SAD can be delivered using modern information technology. IPT delivered as a guided self-help treatment may be less effective in this format.

3.2. *Treatment effects*

3.2.1. *Primary outcome measure (LSAS-SR)*

Results for the primary outcome measure are presented in Table 3. The two groups did not differ significantly on the LSAS-SR at pre-treatment, $M = 60.19$ (SD = 18.95) for mCBT and $M = 65.72$ (SD = 27.15) for the mIPT group: $t(50) = -0.86$, n.s. On the LSAS-SR pre/post, both treatment groups showed significant improvements at the $p < .05$ level; mCBT: $t(24) = 6.18$, $p = .001$; mIPT: $t(21) = 2.75$, $p = .01$. Within-group Cohen's d effect sizes were large for mCBT ($d = 0.99$), and small for mIPT ($d = 0.43$). The between group effect size was moderate ($d = 0.64$). Results for the weekly measurements on the LSAS-SR are presented in Fig. 2 for illustration.

3.2.4. *Clinical significance*

The number of participants meeting the criteria for clinically significant improvement was calculated for the LSAS-SR. In the mCBT group there were 55.6% ($n = 15$) who were classified as responders at post-treatment compared to 8.0% ($n = 2$) in the mIPT group, and this difference was statistically significant $\chi^2(1) = 9.07$, $p = .04$.

414 J. Dagöö et al. / Journal of Anxiety Disorders 28 (2014) 410–417

Table 3
Means, SD's, within and between group effect sizes (Cohen's d), confidence intervals, F-values and significance levels for primary and secondary outcome variables.

Measure	Group	Pre	Post-est. values	Within group ES			Between group ES			F-values (1, 49)
		$n = 52$ M (SD)	$n = 52$ M (SD)	d	CI lo	CI hi	d	CI lo	CI hi	
LSAS-SR	mCBT	60.19 (18.95)	38.93 (23.18)	0.99	0.58	1.39	0.64	0.06	1.22	5.18*
	mIPT	65.72 (27.15)	54.41 (25.19)	0.43	0.09	0.77				
SIAS	mCBT	45.15 (15.81)	34.30 (14.76)	0.71	0.35	1.07	0.72	0.14	1.30	5.83*
	mIPT	50.12 (14.06)	44.54 (13.76)	0.40	0.11	0.70				
SPS	mCBT	32.59 (11.31)	23.42 (12.15)	0.78	0.30	1.27	0.63	0.05	1.22	2.97
	mIPT	37.64 (15.07)	31.30 (12.81)	0.45	0.12	0.77				
BAI	mCBT	17.30 (9.25)	14.79 (10.97)	0.25	−0.31	0.81	0.46	−0.10	1.03	2.09
	mIPT	19.80 (12.12)	20.02 (11.56)	−0.02	−0.41	0.37				
MADRS-S	mCBT	11.70 (5.09)	10.44 (4.77)	0.26	−0.16	0.67	0.88	0.28	1.47	7.25**
	mIPT	14.08 (6.30)	14.62 (4.77)	−0.10	−0.61	0.42				
QOLI	mCBT	1.09 (1.58)	1.41 (1.66)	−0.20	−0.55	0.16	0.37	−0.25	0.99	0.12
	mIPT	0.37 (1.59)	0.82 (1.51)	−0.29	−0.72	0.13				

Abbreviations: mCBT, mobile-based cognitive behavior therapy; mIPT, mobile-based interpersonal therapy; Pre, pre-treatment; Post, post-treatment; LSAS-SR, Liebowitz Social Anxiety Scale – Self Report; SIAS, Social Interaction Scale; SPS, Social Phobia Scale; MADRS-S, Montgomery-Åsberg Depression Rating Scale-Self Report; BAI, Beck Anxiety Inventory; QOLI, Quality of Life Inventory.

* $p < .05$ significance level for effect of group (ANCOVA).

** $p < .01$ significance level for effect of group (ANCOVA).

FIGURE 12.15 Selected excerpts from Dagöö et al., 2014.

Activity 12.1: Understanding the Results of a Treatment Outcome Study—cont'd

In Table 12.7, we include the results from the Dagöö et al. (2014) article. To complete columns 3, 4, and 5 in this table, we needed to consider the type of variables used: continuous or categorical variables. In the Dagöö et al. (2014) study, the primary outcome is continuous. The outcome is measured by taking the difference between the pretreatment and posttreatment scores. Since both the pretreatment and posttreatment scores are continuous variables, the difference score is as well. The authors compare the pretreatment to posttreatment differences for each treatment. In the next step, they examine the effect size of the differences to see if the pre-post changes are larger for the experimental and control conditions.

The next column in the table provides space to indicate if the authors used other ways of measuring the primary outcome. If the authors used a categorical variable, such as the proportion of participants who made a major improvement or who no longer have the diagnosis, you can complete column 6 in the table.

Finally, in the last column of the table, it's useful to include a plain language description of the results. This analysis will help you understand what potential gaps in knowledge might be. One possible gap could occur if there is still a large proportion of participants who do not improve. In the Dagöö et al. (2014) paper, the proportion of participants who improve is much greater for the mCBT group than the miPT group. But a large proportion of participants fail to improve.

Now it's your turn. Use one of the original research articles you are using for your "theory of the solution" to complete the second line of the table.

TABLE 12.7 Tabling the results of a treatment outcome study.

Author/Date	What are the experimental & control treatments?	What is the primary outcome?	What are the methods of analysis that are used?	What are the word and statistical sentences that refer to the main outcomes?	Did the authors report the number of participants with a clinically significant outcome? If so, how was it defined?	A plain language translation of what the findings mean. Is one level of the IV better than the other?
Dagoo et al. (2014)	Internet-based CBT adapted for mobile phones Internet-based self-guided Interpersonal Therapy	Self-reported social anxiety disorder symptoms assessed with a scale (LSAS-SR) that asks about avoidance in 24 social situations	Intent-to-treat analyses. Paired sample t-test to compare pre and post treatment scores for each group. Tests of effect size to compare how large the differences from pre-to post treatment are for the two treatments.	"On the LSAS-LR pre-post both treatment groups showed significant improvements at the $p < .05$ level (MCBT: $t(24) = 6.18$, $p < .007$; mIPT: $t(21) = 2.75$, $p = .01$." Cohen's d was larger for the mCBT group than the mIPT group.	Yes, they report that more people in the mCBT group (55.6%) than the mIPT (8%) achieved a clinically significant recovery according to previously validated criteria.	Yes, both groups improve. The mCBT group improves to a greater degree and more individuals in the mCBT vs. the mIPT group improve.

Building Human Capital

In this chapter you identified different questions researchers ask as they evaluate treatments. Sometimes researchers are testing the hypothesis that one treatment is better than another. Other times they want to demonstrate that a more cost-effective treatment is not inferior to the original version. You learned about the different research designs and statistical analyses used in treatment outcome studies.

As you consider the hypotheses the researchers are testing and examine the results of their studies, you are developing skills in close reading and critical analysis. You are strengthening your ability to work through very difficult material.

You are also developing the ability to evaluate and tolerate complex situations. The results of the studies are not always clear. Some studies may find the treatment is effective, other studies may find it is not. Even in the same study, the treatment may improve one set of symptoms, but not another. Some treatments may work for some people under some conditions. There may be moderators of treatment outcome.

This ability to understand that there may be complex answers to difficult scientific questions is part of becoming a capable and mature thinker. See if you can identify other places in your life where it has been helpful to understand that sometimes the answer is "It depends…".

Terms

Take the time to define each of these terms and consider how to apply them.

Research Terms

Uncontrolled Trial
Randomized Controlled Trial
Pretest (before treatment)
Posttest (after treatment)
Experimental Treatment
Control Treatment
Efficacy
Effectiveness
Superiority Trial
Equivalence Trial
Noninferiority Trial
Between-person effects
Within-person effects
Categorical Outcome
Continuous Outcome
Clinical Significance
Chi-Square Analyses
Post hoc
Intent-to-treat Analyses
Completer Analyses
Mixed models analyses
Analysis of Covariance
Difference scores

References

Andrews, G., Cuijpers, P., Craske, M. G., McEvoy, P., & Titov, N. (2010). Computer therapy for the anxiety and depressive disorders is effective, acceptable and practical health care: A meta-analysis. *PloS One, 5*(10). https://doi.org/10.1371/journal.pone.0013196

Appelbaum, M., Cooper, H., Kline, R. B., Mayo-Wilson, E., Nezu, A. M., & Rao, S. M. (2018). Journal article reporting standards for quantitative research in psychology: The APA Publications and Communications Board task force report. *American Psychologist, 73*(1), 3.

Barrett, P., Healy-Farrell, L., & March, J. S. (2004). Cognitive-behavioral family treatment of childhood obsessive-compulsive disorder: A controlled trial.

Journal of the American Academy of Child & Adolescent Psychiatry, 43(1), 46–62.

Bell, M. L., Fiero, M., Horton, N. J., & Hsu, C. H. (2014). Handling missing data in RCTs: A review of the top medical journals. *BMC Medical Research Methodology, 14*(1), 118.

Dagöö, J., Asplund, R. P., Bsenko, H. A., Hjerling, S., Holmberg, A., Westh, S., … Andersson, G. (2014). Cognitive behavior therapy versus interpersonal psychotherapy for social anxiety disorder delivered via smartphone and computer: A randomized controlled trial. *Journal of Anxiety Disorders, 28*(4), 410–417.

Faulkner, C., Fidler, F., & Cumming, G. (2008). The value of RCT evidence depends on the quality of statistical analysis. *Behaviour Research and Therapy, 46*(2), 270–281.

Glasgow, R. E., Lichtenstein, E., & Marcus, A. C. (2003). Why don't we see more translation of health promotion research to practice? Rethinking the efficacy-to-effectiveness transition. *American Journal of Public Health, 93*(8), 1261–1267.

Gupta, S. K. (2011). Intention-to-treat concept: A review. *Perspectives in Clinical Research, 2*(3), 109.

Levitt, H. M., Bamberg, M., Creswell, J. W., Frost, D. M., Josselson, R., & Suárez Orozco, C. (2018). Journal article reporting standards for qualitative primary, qualitative meta-analytic, and mixed methods research in psychology: The APA Publications and Communications Board task force report. *American Psychologist, 73*(1), 26–46.

McGirr, A., Van den Eynde, F., Tovar-Perdomo, S., Fleck, M. P., & Berlim, M. T. (2015). Effectiveness and acceptability of accelerated repetitive transcranial magnetic stimulation (rTMS) for treatment-resistant major depressive disorder: An open label trial. *Journal of Affective Disorders, 173*, 216–220.

Parr, C. J., & Cartwright-Hatton, S. (2009). Social anxiety in adolescents: The effect of video feedback on anxiety and the self-evaluation of performance. *Clinical Psychology & Psychotherapy, 16*(1), 46–54.

Piacentini, J., Bergman, R. L., Chang, S., Langley, A., Peris, T., Wood, J. J., & McCracken, J. (2011). Controlled comparison of family cognitive behavioral therapy and psychoeducation/relaxation training for child obsessive-compulsive disorder. *Journal of the American Academy of Child & Adolescent Psychiatry, 50*(11), 1149–1161.

Warnock-Parkes, E., Wild, J., Stott, R., Grey, N., Ehlers, A., & Clark, D. M. (2017). Seeing is believing: Using video feedback in cognitive therapy for social anxiety disorder. *Cognitive and Behavioral Practice, 24*(2), 245–255.

Woolf, S. H. (2008). The meaning of translational research and why it matters. *The Journal of the American Medical Association, 299*(2), 211–213.

Further Reading

Ferguson, C. J. (2009). An effect size primer: A guide for clinicians and researchers. *Professional Psychology: Research and Practice, 40*(5), 532.

Flannery-Schroeder, E. C., & Kendall, P. C. (2000). Group and individual cognitive-behavioral treatments for youth with anxiety disorders: A randomized clinical trial. *Cognitive Therapy and Research, 24*(3), 251–278.

Staring, A. B. P., van den Berg, D. P. G., Cath, D. C., Schoorl, M., Engelhard, I. M., & Korrelboom, C. W. (2016). Self-esteem treatment in anxiety: A randomized controlled crossover trial of Eye Movement Desensitization and Reprocessing (EMDR) versus Competitive Memory training (COMET) in patients with anxiety disorders. *Behaviour Research and Therapy, 82*, 11–20.

Suveg, C., Jones, A., Davis, M., Jacob, M. L., Morelen, D., Thomassin, K., & Whitehead, M. (2018). Emotion-focused cognitive-behavioral therapy for youth with anxiety disorders: A randomized trial. *Journal of Abnormal Child Psychology, 46*(3), 569–580.

Chapter 13

Theory of the solution: Identifying gaps in knowledge

To guide the development of new research, scientists examine what is already known and look for gaps in the existing knowledge base. Identifying gaps in knowledge is an essential part of the process of establishing the scientific premise for the study. As these gaps are identified, they provide direction for new research. And as they address these gaps with new research findings, knowledge grows.

In Chapter 6, you learned about threats to validity and gaps in knowledge pertinent to understanding the public health significance of the disorder. In Chapter 10, you learned about threats to validity and gaps in knowledge related to studies of risk factors and mechanisms. In this chapter, you will learn how to identify gaps in knowledge and the threats to validity that are specific to treatment outcome studies.

Information about gaps in knowledge can come from many sources. Researchers can review available meta-analyses and systematic reviews. They can examine limitations to the studies described in original research articles.

There are also many different types of gaps in knowledge. Researchers may find a gap in knowledge about beneficial treatments for a disorder. They may find that many people are not helped by existing treatments. Or researchers may find that many people get a little bit better, but the disorder still has a detrimental effect on health and quality of life. Gaps in knowledge can also occur when new theories leading to new treatments are developed, but the effects of these new treatments have not yet been tested. Gaps in knowledge emerge when there are unaddressed threats to internal and external validity in the existing studies.

Psychology Research Methods. https://doi.org/10.1016/B978-0-12-815680-3.00013-X

If you are writing a research proposal, you use these gaps to justify the study you are proposing. If you are writing a paper reviewing existing treatments, you identify these gaps as areas in need of future research. We will review each type of gap in the following sections.

Identifying Gaps by Understanding the State-of-the-Science

As we have discussed in the earlier chapters, meta-analyses and systematic review articles can provide a big picture view of scientific knowledge about the topic under study. At the end of the review article, researchers will often summarize information about what is known and what is not yet known. The authors will identify gaps in knowledge and identify areas in need of future research. Original research articles also include a **limitations section** in the discussion section of the article. Additional gaps in knowledge can often be found in those sections of the article.

Let's look at an example. The Richards and Richardson (2012) meta-analysis examines the efficacy of computerized therapy for depression. The authors report that there is evidence for the effectiveness of these computerized therapies. However, there are also limitations to the effects of these therapies, and there are significant gaps in knowledge about the conditions under which these treatments are most effective (Figs. 13.1 and 13.2).

We can consider the threats to validity and gaps in knowledge the authors identify in the discussion section. One of the most important issues they raise was related to the problem of drop-outs or attrition. In some cases, more than half the participants dropped out of treatment before the course of treatment was complete.

The researchers also noted a second gap in knowledge. Some programs included additional contact with live therapists; others did not. In general, participants made better progress in programs which provided some contact with therapists than those that did not. However, there is a lack of knowledge about the types and intensity of therapist contact that produce the best outcomes.

The authors also describe many limitations within the existing literature. For example, studies differed in the choice of control groups and the length of time patients were followed once treatment was complete. There were inconsistencies in the ways the treatment programs were presented. Technical problems with the computerized method of treatment delivery may have reduced the quantity and intensity of the treatment that was delivered. Variations in methods made it more difficult to draw conclusions about the effects of the treatments across studies.

Clinical Psychology Review 32 (2012) 329–342

Contents lists available at SciVerse ScienceDirect

Clinical Psychology Review

Computer-based psychological treatments for depression: A systematic review and meta-analysis

Derek Richards [a,*], Thomas Richardson [b]

[a] University of Dublin, Trinity College, Dublin, Ireland
[b] Professional Training Unit, School of Psychology, University of Southampton, Southampton, UK

ARTICLE INFO

Article history:
Received 19 July 2011
Received in revised form 3 February 2012
Accepted 16 February 2012
Available online 28 February 2012

Keywords:
Psychological treatment
CBT
Depression
Meta-analysis, systematic review
Computer-based
Internet-delivered

ABSTRACT

The aim of the paper was to systematically review the literature on computer-based psychological treatments for depression and conduct a meta-analysis of the RCT studies, including examining variables which may effect outcomes. Database and hand searches were made using specific search terms and inclusion criteria. The review included a total of 40 studies (45 published papers), and 19 RCTs (23 published papers) were included in a standard meta-analysis. The review describes the different computer-based treatments for depression, their design, communication types employed: synchronous, asynchronous, and face-to-face (F:F); alongside various types and frequency of support delivered. The evidence supports their effectiveness and highlights participant satisfaction. However, pertinent limitations are noted. Across 19 studies the meta-analysis revealed a moderate post-treatment pooled effect size $d = .56$ (95% confidence interval [CI] $-.71$, $-.41$), $Z = 7.48$, $p < .001$). Supported interventions yielded better outcomes, along with greater retention. The results reported statistically significant clinical improvement and recovery post-treatment. The review and meta-analysis support the efficacy and effectiveness of computer-based psychological treatments for depression, in diverse settings and with different populations. Further research is needed, in particular to investigate the influence of therapist factors in supported treatments, the reasons for dropout, and the maintenance of gains post-treatment.

FIGURE 13.1 Abstract from Richards and Richardson, 2012

4. Discussion

It is only recently that research has attempted to use computer-based interventions for treating depression in specific population groups. One early study by Spek, Nyklicek, et al. (2007), Spek et al. (2008) investigated the efficacy of an online intervention for treating subthreshold depression in over 50's. The subgroup analysis demonstrated a post-treatment effect size of $d = .34$ for studies with specific populations which contrasts a pooled effect size of $d = .60$ for all other RCT studies and comparisons showed the difference to be significant. The results support the overall effectiveness of computer-based interventions for depression, however the potential for specific populations, while encouraging, is unclear at present and future research is needed.

RCT studies are largely heterogeneous regarding samples and treatments. It is therefore important to be tenative about the extent to which the results can generalize to all those with depression. Also research in naturalistic settings does not require nor seek to achieve the same levels of eligibility and exclusion as do many RCTs.

The interventions themselves may be problematic, perhaps there is a lack of functionality, multimedia, interactivity, that might engage any user and support adherence. Proudfoot et al. (2003) reported negative features of the program as a cause of dropout. Meyer et al. (2009) noted that with their program it would be interesting to investigate what added components might enhance the program and increase engagement and adherence.

5. Conclusion

The review and meta-analysis support the efficacy and effectiveness of computer-based psychological treatments for depression, in community, primary, and secondary care, and with diverse populations. As well as reductions in self-reported symptoms, computer-based interventions can also produce clinically significant improvements and recovery in depression. Supported interventions yield better outcomes, along with greater retention. Further research is needed, in particular to investigate the influence of therapist factors in supported treatments, the reasons for dropout, the maintenance of gains post-treatment, the potential for shorter treatments, and treatments with diverse population groups.

Problems in external validity- lack of treatments with diverse populations.

←Threats to internal validity – lack of adherence to strict inclusion criteria and problems with drop-outs

←Threats to internal validity – problems with the dose and delivery of treatment

FIGURE 13.2 Selected excerpts from Richards and Richardson, 2012

Identifying gaps in knowledge helps researchers set priorities for new investigations. For example, given the high drop-out problem in computerized treatment of depression, researchers may want to conduct basic research to identify causes for drop out. This knowledge could be used to develop **adjunctive interventions** (i.e., add-on treatments) that help people persist and complete the course of treatment. In other studies, researchers may want to identify the types of computer problems participants encountered and attempt to develop effective remedies for these technical issues. Overall, meta-analytic reviews can help guide researchers and encourage them to focus their attention on the issues that need to be addressed to improve the quality and consistency of these interventions.

Problems in Internal and External Validity Common to Original Treatment Outcome Studies

Every study has limitations and faces threats to validity. There are threats to internal and external validity that are common to treatment outcome studies. As you read, you will determine if any of these threats are seen in the studies of treatments for the disorder you are studying.

As shown in Table 13.1, there are threats to internal validity from many sources. These can include threats from the delivery of the independent variable, threats from the choice of participants, threats from the measurement methods, and threats from other sources of bias.

There are problems with external validity that are common to many treatment outcome studies. As shown in Table 13.2, these problems concern limits to generalizability across samples, measures, and methods.

Threats to Internal Validity: Mismatch Between the Hypothesis and the Choice of Control Conditions

One of the biggest challenges facing researchers is identifying the correct control group to test the primary hypotheses of the study. The choice of the control condition depends on the theory and the specific hypotheses the researchers want to test. Sometimes ethical, financial, or conceptual concerns restrict researchers' ability to choose the control condition. In these cases, the study may face threats to internal validity and the interpretation of the data is made more difficult.

For example, suppose a researcher has a theory that suggests that a new important therapeutic component is valuable. The

TABLE 13.1 Examples of threats to internal validity.

	Source
Participants	**Inclusion criteria**: Criteria are not well specified and people without disorder are included. **Exclusion criteria**: Criteria are not well specified and people with other comorbid disorders are unintentionally included. **Statistical power**: Not enough participants to permit the effects to emerge because of variability/heterogeneity in response.
Measures	**Measurement quality**: The measures are not reliable or valid. The measures do not fully capture the phenomena. **Measurement timing**: Timing of the testing obscures the results. The testing is meant to capture immediate effects of the treatment, but posttesting occurs before treatment is over and capitalizes on ongoing treatment effect. Or, posttesting occurs too long after treatment is over, and degradation of the effects begins. **Bias in measurement**: The measurement methodology introduces bias. For example, the person evaluating the outcome and/or the participant is not blind to the assignment of the participants.
Methods	**Delivery of the independent variable**: The treatment is not fully specified, and there are problems with the quality or dose of treatment. Specifically, components might have been omitted or other, nonspecified components might have been included. **Comparison conditions**: The control group is different from the experimental group on many components of treatment. The delivery of treatment is not the same across the experimental and control conditions, and this is not intentional. **Sources of bias in the delivery of the independent variable**: Problems with therapist training, fidelity to the treatment, patient or therapist expectations. **Extraneous variables**: Other variables are introduced that influence the outcome. These variables can come from any source, including the testing circumstances or context.
Data analyses	**Match of hypotheses, data, and analyses**: The analyses introduce bias or are not appropriate for the methods, data, or hypotheses.

TABLE 13.2 Examples of threats to external validity

Source	
Participants	**Inclusion criteria**: Participants are limited to a specific diagnosis. **Exclusion criteria**: Participants cannot have additional diagnoses. **Too much homogeneity**: Participants are limited to one sociodemographic group (e.g., single age, gender, race, SES, location, etc.).
Measures	**Type of measures**: Outcome measures are limited to a specific method (e.g., only self-report). **Timing of measures**: Outcome measures are administered only at one moment in time (limits to follow up).
Methods	**Therapist training**: Therapists are limited to those with a particular type of training or qualifications. **Treatment modality**: Treatment is delivered in only one modality (e.g., only to the individual vs. to a group of family). **Treatment delivery system**: Treatment is delivered in only one format (e.g., face-to-face vs. via the web or other system). **Setting characteristics**: Treatment is delivered in only one setting (e.g., academic medical center vs. outpatient clinic or school or workplace or hospital). **Treatment duration**: Treatment effects are seen for a short period of time, shortly after treatment terminates. No assessment of longer-term effects.

theory predicts that adding this new component to the standard treatment will improve the effectiveness of treatment. The researcher hypothesizes that this component will make the NEW THERAPY more effective than other therapies.

What control condition should the researcher choose? If the researcher chooses a Wait-List Control, the researcher cannot test the hypothesis. If the researcher finds the NEW THERAPY is better than a Wait-List Control, the researcher only knows that the NEW THERAPY is better than no treatment (i.e., Wait-List Control). To determine if the NEW THERAPY is better than other active treatments, the control condition needs to include other active treatments known to be effective. A reasonable comparison would be: Experimental Treatment = NEW THERAPY; Control Treatment = OLD THERAPY WITHOUT THE NEW COMPONENT.

How do researchers decide on a control condition or treatment? Let's read through an example of a study by van der Heiden, Muris, and van der Molen (2012) in which researchers consider the importance of theories for the choice of the control condition/treatment (Fig. 13.3).

Behaviour Research and Therapy 50 (2012) 100–109

Contents lists available at SciVerse ScienceDirect

Behaviour Research and Therapy

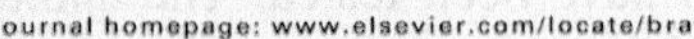

journal homepage: www.elsevier.com/locate/brat

Randomized controlled trial on the effectiveness of metacognitive therapy and intolerance-of-uncertainty therapy for generalized anxiety disorder

Colin van der Heiden[a,*], Peter Muris[b,c], Henk T. van der Molen[b]

[a] Outpatient Treatment Center PsyQ, Max Euwelaan 70, 3062 MA Rotterdam, The Netherlands
[b] Institute of Psychology, Erasmus University Rotterdam, Burgemeester Oudlaan 50, 3062 PA Rotterdam, The Netherlands
[c] Clinical Psychology Science, Faculty of Psychology and Neuroscience, Maastricht University, Universiteitssingel 40, 6200 MD Maastricht, The Netherlands

ARTICLE INFO

Article history:
Received 21 April 2011
Received in revised form
24 November 2011
Accepted 12 December 2011

Keywords:
Generalized anxiety disorder
Metacognitive therapy
Intolerance-of-uncertainty therapy
Randomized controlled trial
Cognitive-behavioral therapy

ABSTRACT

This randomized controlled trial compared the effectiveness of metacognitive therapy (MCT) and intolerance-of-uncertainty therapy (IUT) for generalized anxiety disorder (GAD) in an outpatient context. Patients with GAD ($N = 126$) consecutively referred to an outpatient treatment center for anxiety disorder were randomly allocated to MCT, IUT, or a delayed treatment (DT) condition. Patients were treated individually for up to 14 sessions. Assessments were conducted before treatment (pretreatment), after the last treatment session (posttreatment), and six months after treatment had ended (follow-up). At posttreatment and follow-up assessments, substantial improvements were observed in both treatment conditions across all outcome variables. Both MCT and IUT, but not DT, produced significant reductions in GAD-specific symptoms with large effect sizes (ranging between 0.94 and 2.39) and high proportions of clinically significant change (ranging between 77% and 95%) on various outcome measures, and the vast majority of the patients (i.e., 91% in the MCT group, and 80% in the IUT group) no longer fulfilled the diagnostic criteria for GAD. Results further indicate that MCT produced better results than IUT. This was evident on most outcome measures, and also reflected in effect sizes and degree of clinical response and recovery.

Gap in knowledge - treatments need

Theory of the Problems

Although recent comprehensive meta-analyses have shown cognitive-behavioral therapy (CBT) to be efficacious as compared to wait-list or treatment-as-usual control groups (Hunot, Churchill, & Silva de Lima Teixeira, 2007; Mitte, 2005), the effects produced by this treatment provide a good example of the discrepancy between statistically and clinically significant change. Several studies have shown CBT to lead to statistically significant improvements and large effect sizes in patients with GAD (Covin, Ouimet, Seeds, & Dozois, 2008), but only about 50% of treatment completers achieve high end-state functioning (Hunot et al., 2007) or recovery (Fisher, 2006) following treatment. A possible explanation for these relatively poor results might be that most CBT treatments are not based on a specific theoretical model for GAD (Wells, 1995).

In an attempt to improve the understanding and treatment of GAD the theoretical conceptualization of GAD has undergone considerable scrutiny and refinement in the past 15 years. Contemporary models of this disorder emphasize the avoidance of internal affective experiences, with some of them assuming a special role for aberrant cognitive processes (Behar, Dobrow DiMarco, Hekler, Mohlman, & Staples, 2009). One prominent example is the metacognitive model, which proposes that negative beliefs about worry, resulting in "worry about worry", play a key role in the development and maintenance of GAD (Wells, 1995). An alternative account is the intolerance-of-uncertainty model (Dugas, Gagnon, Ladouceur, & Freeston, 1998), which is based on the idea that patients with GAD become distressed and upset when confronted with uncertain or ambiguous situations, and experience persistent worry in response to such events. Empirical support has emerged for both of these GAD models (for an overview of studies, see Dugas & Robichaud, 2007 and Wells, 2009), and interestingly specific treatment programs have been developed that target to correct the presumed distorted cognitive processes underlying the disorder. So far, a limited number of studies has provided support for the efficacy of these treatment programs (Dugas et al., 2003, 2010; Dugas, Francis, & Bouchard, 2009; Ladouceur et al., 2000; Wells & King, 2006; Wells, Welford, King, Wisely, & Mendel, 2010). However, this evidence is preliminary given the methodological shortcomings of most of these studies, such as the fairly small sample sizes and the lack of active control groups. Nevertheless, the results of a recent review on the clinical significance of psychological treatments for GAD indicate that both of these theory-based cognitive interventions for GAD seem to produce clearly superior recovery rates as compared to more traditional cognitive-behavioral interventions (Fisher, 2006).

Given their promising potential for the treatment of GAD, the present study was conducted to compare the effectiveness of metacognitive therapy (MCT) and intolerance-of-uncertainty therapy (IUT) in a large sample of clinically referred patients with GAD. The study was set-up as a randomized controlled trial so that it became possible to demonstrate the effectiveness of both treatments as compared to a delayed treatment (DT) control condition and to explore whether one type of treatment produced better results than the other.

TOP - experimental avoidance

TOP - intolerance of uncertainty

Summary of existing knowledge

FIGURE 13.3 Abstract and selected excerpts from Van der Heiden, Muris, & Van der Moelen, 2012.

Van der Heiden and colleagues (2012) point out that CBT treatments are effective, but not for everyone. In fact, they claim CBT treatments for GAD are effective for just over half the people who have been tested. The authors hypothesize that the available CBT treatments are not directly addressing the mechanisms that have been identified to trigger or maintain GAD. They wish to test the hypothesis that targeting treatment to the underlying mechanism will improve outcomes.

To address this issue, the authors identify two important mechanisms that may be involved in the development of GAD: *Experiential avoidance* and *intolerance of uncertainty*. There are validated treatments to address these specific mechanisms. *Metacognitive therapy* is intended to help people stop engaging in experiential avoidance and develop the skills they need to achieve their goals. *Intolerance of uncertainty therapy* is intended to address the cognitive biases that drive intolerance of uncertainty. The authors compare metacognitive therapy and intolerance of uncertainty therapy to see if addressing the underlying mechanisms will result in improvements in outcome.

To test their hypotheses, the researchers are comparing two different active treatments: metacognitive therapy and intolerance of uncertainty therapy for GAD. They wish to see if one treatment, metacognitive therapy, is better than intolerance of uncertainty treatment. By contrasting the two active treatments, metacognitive therapy and intolerance of uncertainty therapy, they can determine if treating one mechanism is better than treating another mechanism to achieve reductions in GAD symptoms.

But the authors recognized it is not enough to compare these two treatments to each other. They also compare these two active treatments to a delayed treatment group—a kind of wait-list control. In this way, they can test whether treatment is better than no treatment. This allows the researchers to ensure that any improvements shown after either active therapy are not simply a function of time.

The one hypothesis the authors cannot test using these control groups is whether treatment specifically focused on a mechanism is better than more general CBT treatment for anxiety. They do not compare the two focused treatments to a general CBT protocol. They rely on the evidence from recent meta-analyses which confirm that each of the new treatment approaches is better than general CBT.

Threat to Internal Validity: Problems with Quality and Dose of Treatment

The internal validity of a treatment outcome study requires that the dose and quality of treatment that is delivered is adequate to produce the desired outcome. In trials of medications or other biological therapies, the quality of the treatment is insured by regular inspections of the factories or laboratories that produce the medications or the other instruments that deliver the treatment. The dose of the medication or other treatment can be precisely specified. Extensive pilot testing is conducted to determine the effects of different dosages.

In psychological treatments the issue of specifying the "dose" or insuring the quality of the treatment is more complicated. The quality of the treatment delivery can be affected by the therapists' training, commitment, and fidelity to the treatment protocol (Bellg et al., 2004).

If the therapists' skill level and commitment are not adequate, this may result in a reduced dose or accuracy of the treatment being delivered. If they don't address this issue, any differences between treatment groups in treatment outcome might be a function of differences in the quality and commitment of the therapists, not the quality of the treatment itself (Fig. 13.4). To

Therapist characteristics, recruitment and training

The therapist teams consisted of four (MCT) and five (IUT) staff psychologists of the participating mental health care center. All of them were familiar with the provision of CBT manuals, and all but one were certified cognitive-behavioral therapists. The mean age of the therapists was 33.9 years (range 26–48; MCT: 36.0 years; IUT: 32.2 years), and they had on average 5.6 years of clinical experience (range 0–7; MCT: 5.0 years; IUT: 6.0 years). Prior to the study, therapists' confidence in the treatment they had to deliver was 7.0 on a 10-point scale, with 10 reflecting maximal confidence (range 5–8; MCT: 6.5; IUT: 7.4). The mean number of patients treated by each therapist was 15.3 in the MCT condition (range 8–25), and 12.0 in the IUT condition (range 7–17). *T*-tests revealed no significant differences between the therapists in the two treatment conditions with regard to age [$t(7) < 1$], degree of clinical experience [$t(7) < 1$], degree of confidence in the treatment they had to deliver [$t(7) = 1.49$, $p = .18$], and number of patients treated [$t(7) < 1$].

FIGURE 13.4 Excerpt from van der Heiden et al., 2012.

counter this problem, researchers evaluate the therapists' commitment and determine if the therapist is delivering the treatment as intended. You can see an example of the ways in which researchers handle these problems in the article by van der Heiden et al. (2012).

Another potential threat to the internal validity of a treatment outcome study can occur if the treatment the participants receive is insufficient or incomplete in some way. To address this issue, researchers will often conduct pilot tests to determine the dose of treatment needed (i.e., the number or length of sessions). Participants can also receive incomplete treatment if the therapist does not show fidelity to the treatment protocol. If the therapist does not adhere to the protocol with **fidelity**, they are not consistently or accurately follow the treatment protocol, and it is therefore hard to tell why a treatment does not work. An effective treatment might fail if it was not delivered consistently and accurately. To address this issue, researchers can conduct **fidelity checks,** monitoring treatment sessions to determine if components were delivered correctly.

Here is an example of an approach to checking the fidelity of treatment used by van der Heiden and colleagues (2012) to address threats associated with poor quality implementation (Fig. 13.5).

All therapists were briefly introduced to the treatment program by providing them with the treatment manual, and a 1 h information meeting in separate groups. During the first year of the study, therapists were supervised biweekly by the principal investigator (CvdH) in separate group sessions for MCT and IUT. After the first year, supervision was on average provided once per two months. At these meetings all active cases and therapy notes were reviewed to ensure adherence to protocols and treatment quality. Adherence to the protocol was further evaluated through an assessment of 71 randomly selected recordings of treatment sessions by trained clinical psychology students (at a master level), who rated the therapists' behaviors against session-by-session intervention checklists that closely followed the content of the treatment manuals. This treatment integrity check revealed that the therapists closely followed the treatment manuals (i.e., in only 3% of the sessions they applied interventions that were not described in the manual).

FIGURE 13.5 Excerpt from van der Heiden et al., 2012.

Threats to Internal validity: Problems with Inclusion and Exclusion Criteria

Not all treatments work for all individuals. There are many moderators of treatment effects. For example, a treatment may not work for individuals with comorbid disorders or mild (or severe) forms of the disorder. Without clear specification of the types of patients for whom this treatment is hypothesized to work, it is hard to know if the treatment does not work, or if patients without the condition or patients with other comorbidities were included. To address this problem, researchers often include very detailed inclusion and exclusion criteria.

Here are the inclusion and exclusion criteria used in the study by van der Heiden and colleagues (2012). Notice the authors are very specific about excluding individuals who have disorders other than GAD (Fig. 13.6).

Patients

Patients were recruited between February 2005 and November 2008. Diagnosis was established using the Structured Clinical Interview for DSM-IV axis-I (SCID-I; First, Spitzer, Gibbon, & Williams, 2001), which was administered by a trained clinician. A second clinician re-assessed the diagnosis in a separate intake-interview. Inclusion criteria were as follows: (1) primary DSM-IV-TR diagnosis of GAD, (2) age between 18 and 65 years, (3) fluency in spoken Dutch, (4) willing to accept random allocation to one of the three study conditions, and (5) either free of or stable on psychoactive medication for at least six weeks. Exclusion criteria were kept to a minimum to enhance the clinical representativeness of the sample. Patients were only excluded if they (1) met the DSM-IV-TR criteria for severe major depressive disorder that required immediate treatment, psychotic disorder, or bipolar disorder, (2) suffered from mental impairment or an organic brain disorder, (3) had substance abuse requiring specialist treatment, (4) received a concurrent psychological treatment for any Axis I or II disorder, or (5) were not willing to refrain from making any medication changes during treatment. Thirty-eight of the 165 potentially eligible patients did not meet inclusion criteria, of which 33 refused randomization. One patient met exclusion criteria (meeting criteria for a psychotic disorder), leaving 126 entering the two outpatient treatment programs (MCT = 54, IUT = 52) and the DT condition. For ethical reasons, only 20 patients were allocated to the DT condition.

FIGURE 13.6 Excerpt from van der Heiden et al., 2012.

Threats to Internal Validity: Sources of Bias in Experimentation

One type of bias is called expectation effects, also called Rosenthal effects. Rosenthal effects describe a relationship between expectations and performance. In other words, patient expectations can influence outcomes. For example, researchers have found that higher expectations about performance are associated with better performance (Rosenthal, 1994).

Patients often have information about different types of treatments, which can influence their expectations of benefit. These expectations can affect motivation and optimism about change. In turn, motivation and optimism, and not the components of the treatment, may be responsible for symptom improvement. To identify and address patient expectation effects, researchers often measure patient expectations prior to treatment.

Observation effects (also called Hawthorne effects) are another form of bias. Observation effects occur when participants are aware that they are being observed (McCambridge, Witton, & Elbourne, 2014). These effects may influence change during the treatment period and produce effects. However, when the observation period is over, effects may diminish. This suggests that the process of being observed and monitored, as opposed to the changes associated with the treatment itself, may account for symptom reduction. To address some of the threat associated with observation effects, researchers sometimes measure symptoms at a follow-up period several months after the treatment has been completed.

Threats to Internal validity: Problems with Measurement

Poor reliability and validity in the instruments used to evaluate treatment outcome will undermine the ability to detect effects of treatment. To address this issue, researchers will document the appropriateness and quality of the measurement instruments they employ.

Figure 13.7 provides an example of a description of the **primary outcome measure** from an article by Dagöö et al., 2014 (Fig. 13.7).

2.7. Outcome measures

2.7.1. Primary outcome measure

The LSAS-SR was used as the primary outcome measure. The LSAS-SR measures the degree of avoidance and fear in 24 social situations (13 performance and 11 interaction situations). Fear and avoidance are rated separately for each situation on a scale from 0 (no fear/never avoid) to 3 (severe fear/usually avoid). The clinician-administered version of the LSAS has good psychometric properties (Heimberg et al., 1999). In a comparison of the psychometric properties of the self-report and clinician-administered formats of the LSAS there was little difference between the two versions on any scale or subscale score (Fresco et al., 2001). They were both internally consistent and had essentially identical subscale intercorrelations. The discriminant validity of the two forms of the LSAS was shown to be strong (Fresco et al., 2001).

FIGURE 13.7 Excerpt from Dagöö et al., 2014.

Threats to External Validity: Limits to the Characteristics of Participants

Often a treatment is developed and tested with one group of highly selected patients. These patients may have no comorbid disorders and have adequate resources and limited stressors. However, with this selected sample, the researchers do not know if the results of the treatment will generalize to other populations, including those who have been other disorders.

Another threat to generalizability across patient groups includes concerns about **volunteer bias**. There is substantial evidence that individuals who volunteer to participate in research studies differ from individuals who do not (Lönnqvist, Verkasalo, & Bezmenova, 2007). Some evidence suggests that people who volunteer for psychological research are more conscientious than others. They also have other personality dimensions which may make them better able to respond to psychological treatments. Therefore, it may not be known if the effects of treatment tested in the context of a research study will generalize to individuals who receive the treatment outside the context of research.

Threats to External Validity: Therapist and Setting Characteristics

Tests of the treatment may be conducted with highly trained and supervised therapists. The researchers do not know if the results will be the same if the treatment is delivered with less well-trained or unsupervised therapists, including peer therapists.

The original treatment may have been offered in the controlled conditions of a medical center. The researchers do not know if the treatment will work in less controlled setting like a community clinic or private practice office.

Threats to External Validity: Generalizability of Treatment Modality and Delivery System

The treatment may have originally been offered in an individual modality in a face-to-face encounter. The researchers may not know if the treatment effects will generalize to a group or family modality or to delivery via computerized formats or peer support networks.

Threats to External Validity: Maintenance and Generalization Across Time

The treatment may show benefits when it is evaluated immediately after completion. However, the researchers may not know if the effects will be maintained and generalize across settings and over time.

Activity 13.1: Understanding How Threats to Validity Affect the Ability to Test Hypotheses

Review each of the threats in Table 13.3. Then pick three threats. How would each of the threats affect the conclusions you could draw about the results of a study comparing an Experimental and Control treatment?

TABLE 13.3 Threats to validity.

Source	Threat to internal validity	How does this threat affect the interpretation of the results?
Participants	Inclusion criteria: Not well specified and people without disorder are included.	
	Exclusion criteria: Not well specified and people with other comorbid disorders are included.	
	Too small a sample; insufficient statistical power.	
Measures	The measures are not reliable or valid.	
	The measures do not fully capture the phenomena.	
	The measures introduce bias (e.g., presentation biases).	
	The measurement methodology introduces bias (e.g., halo effects or Hawthorne effects).	
Methods	The therapists are not fully trained.	
	The therapists are not committed.	
	The treatment is not fully specified, and other components could be included.	
	Timing of the testing obscures the results (e.g., testing is too soon after treatment and does not show delayed effects or capitalizes on ongoing effects).	
	The control group is different from the experimental group on many components of treatment.	

Continued

Activity 13.1: Understanding How Threats to Validity Affect the Ability to Test Hypotheses—cont'd

TABLE 13.3 Threats to validity.—cont'd

Source	Threat to internal validity	How does this threat affect the interpretation of the results?
Extraneous variables	The delivery of the treatment is not the same across the two treatments and this is not intentional (e.g., one treatment uses a different room or place than the other).	
	The experimenter knows which participants received which treatment.	
	Participant bias (e.g., one treatment is more widely recognized via social media and changes expectations).	
	The therapists vary in important characteristics which influence the outcome.	
	Other sources of bias.	
Data analyses	The analyses introduce bias or are not appropriate for the methods or hypotheses.	

Activity 13.2 Identifying the Threats to Validity in Original Research Studies

The limitations section of research papers provides information about threats to validity that the researchers have identified. The limitations can generally be found in the discussion section. Some researchers explicitly label the limitations section. Others do not use titles but have clear topic sentences indicating that the paragraph(s) will be discussing limitations.

Let's look at the limitations identified by van der Heiden et al. (2012) (Fig. 13.8).

Study limitations and strengths

The results of this study should be interpreted in the context of various limitations. First of all, as therapists in the trial only received minimal training in the treatment they had to deliver, it could be argued that a more extensive training program would have resulted in better treatment results. However, the positive results of the current study suggest that reasonable outcomes are achievable within the framework of clinical practice without lengthy specialist training. As both treatments use common CBT interventions to address the specific cognitive mechanisms that are supposed to maintain the disorder, therapists may have to modify their practice rather than learn new techniques. This suggestion is supported by the comparison of both the ESs and the degree of clinical significance as documented in the current study with those of other efficacy studies on MCT and IUT (Dugas et al., 2003; Fisher, 2006; Ladouceur et al., 2000; Wells & King, 2006; Wells et al., 2010). Second, it could be argued that IUT performed less well as a result of the reordering of interventions and/or the change in exposure modality as compared to the original manual as described by the developers of IUT (Dugas & Ladouceur, 2000). Related to this, it should be noted that the developers of IUT themselves made an important change in the most recent refinement of their treatment program, by adding a specific component (i.e., uncertainty recognition and behavior exposure) during which patients learn to recognize uncertainty-inducing situations and manifestations of IU, and to expose themselves to such situations and manifestations (Dugas & Robichaud, 2007). As the current study already started in 2005, this component was not included in the IUT-manual. As a result, IU has not been as thoroughly addressed as it is in the most recent version of IUT (Dugas & Robichaud, 2007). However, as the ESs and clinical significance rates as found in the current study were nicely in keeping with, or higher than those of other efficacy were nicely in keeping with, or higher than those of other efficacy studies on IUT for GAD, including a recent study on the effectiveness of the latest version of IUT (Dugas et al., 2003, 2010; Fisher, 2006; Ladouceur et al., 2000; see Table 5), there seems to be no indication that the changes in the IUT-manual or the use of an older version of IUT have negatively influenced its effectiveness.

A third limitation of the current study is that the principal investigator executed the randomization procedure, and trained and supervised the therapists in both treatment conditions. Training and supervision of therapists in distinct conditions by different trainers, preferably the developers of MCT and IUT, would have improved the study. Furthermore, although therapists in the treatment conditions did not differ significantly on several important therapist characteristics, differences in therapist competence cannot be ruled out. Future studies would benefit from using a therapist cross-over design, in which the same group of therapists deliver both treatments in blocks. The reliance on single self-report measures for each symptom and process characteristic can be regarded as a fourth limitation. As we used self-report questionnaires (which are of course susceptible to a social desirable response style) and structured diagnostic interviews, a multitrait–multimethod approach would have been preferable (Kotov, Watson, Robles, & Schmidt, 2007). In addition, clinician ratings such as the Hamilton Anxiety Rating Scale (HAM-A; Hamilton, 1959) could have been included. Fifth, although we included a check on the diagnosis by a second clinician, the administration of two independent diagnostic interviews of course represents the most rigorous way to establish diagnostic reliability. The lack of an evidence-based approach for GAD as a control condition is a sixth limitation, as it limits the understanding of the unique or incremental benefits of MCT and IUT. To tackle this point, future studies should explore the effectiveness of these new cognitive approaches relative to regular CBT or pharmacotherapy. Seventh and finally, rates of discontinuation in the treatment groups were substantial (almost 30% in both conditions), although considerably lower than both the mean rate of dropouts in clinical settings of 47% as found in a meta-analysis of outpatient psychotherapy studies (Wierzbicki & Pekarik, 1993), and the dropout rate of 72% recently found in an outpatient effectiveness study for patients with GAD (Kehle, 2008). But even when dropouts were included in the analyses, results were relatively good in terms of the diagnosis-free (>60% in both conditions) and recovery (MCT > 60%, IUT almost 50%) percentage.

Besides these limitations, the study also has a number of strengths. It was conducted within an outpatient community mental health center, and interventions were applied by therapists who worked within this routine setting. The study included both an active and a passive control condition, and a treatment integrity check was performed. Further, the study was conducted independent of the seminal MCT and IUT teams. And finally, it used a comparatively large, clinically representative sample of GAD patients, that was relatively unselected.

FIGURE 13.8 Selected excerpts from van der Heiden et al. (2012).

Continued

Activity 13.2 Identifying the Threats to Validity in Original Research Studies—cont'd

Remember in the van der Heiden et al. (2012) study, the authors compare two types of treatments (MCT and IUT).

The authors acknowledge several threats to internal validity. Here are three of the points they make: (1) They may not be able to fully test the hypothesis because the therapists received only brief training in the methods and may not have delivered an adequate dose of the treatments. (2) The authors also report some concerns about experimenter bias. The authors of the paper randomized the participants and did all the training of the therapists. (3) They acknowledge that they use limited outcome measures, relying on a single measure of self-reported symptoms (Table 13.4).

Now it is your turn. Examine one original research article. Fill in the second line of the table with the threats to validity identified by the authors.

TABLE 13.4 Identifying threats to validity.

Author/date	Threats to external validity	Explained in plain language	Threats to internal validity	Explained in plain language
van der Heiden et al. (2012)			Possible limitations to the dose and quality of treatment.	They may not be fully able to test the hypothesis because the therapists received a limited amount of training in treatment delivery and may not have delivered an adequate dose of the treatment.
			Possible experimenter bias.	The author of the paper randomized the participants and trained the therapists.
			Limited outcome measures.	They relied on a single measure of self-reported symptoms.

Activity 13.3: Identifying Threats to Validity from Review Articles

Read the discussion section of the review article in Fig. 13.9 and see if you can identify the threats to validity mentioned by the authors. In Table 13.5, include one threat on each line. Try to explain the threat in your own words. Then try to consider how future researchers could address this threat. We provide one example.

Journal of Psychiatric Research 47 (2013) 33–41

Contents lists available at SciVerse ScienceDirect

Journal of Psychiatric Research

journal homepage: www.elsevier.com/locate/psychires

Cognitive-behavioral therapy for obsessive-compulsive disorder: A meta-analysis of treatment outcome and moderators

Bunmi O. Olatunji[a,*], Michelle L. Davis[b], Mark B. Powers[b], Jasper A.J. Smits[b]

[a] Department of Psychology, Vanderbilt University, 301 Wilson Hall, 111 21st Avenue South, Nashville, TN 37203, USA
[b] Department of Psychology, Southern Methodist University, Dallas, TX, USA

ARTICLE INFO

Article history:
Received 25 April 2012
Received in revised form
13 August 2012
Accepted 16 August 2012

Keywords:
Obsessive compulsive disorder
Cognitive-behavioral therapy
Moderation

ABSTRACT

The present investigation employed meta-analysis to examine the efficacy of cognitive-behavioral therapy (CBT) for obsessive–compulsive disorder (OCD) as well as potential moderators that may be associated with outcome. A literature search revealed sixteen randomized-controlled trials (RCTs) with a total sample size of 756 participants that met inclusion criteria. Results indicated that CBT out-performed control conditions on primary outcome measures at post-treatment (Hedges's $g = 1.39$) and at follow-up (Hedges's $g = 0.43$). Subsequent analyses revealed few moderators of CBT efficacy. Neither higher pre-treatment OCD ($p = 0.46$) or depression symptom severity ($p = 0.68$) was significantly associated with a decrease in CBT effect size. Similarly, effect size did not vary as a function of 'type' of CBT, treatment format, treatment integrity assessment, blind assessment, age of onset, duration of symptoms, percentage of females, number of sessions, or percent comorbidity. However, active treatments showed smaller effect sizes when compared to placebo controls than when compared to waitlist controls. Effect sizes were also smaller for adult RCTs than child RCTs. Likewise, older age was associated with smaller effect sizes. However, an association between age and effect size was not observed when examining child and adult samples separately. This review indicates that while CBT is efficacious in the treatment of OCD, more research is needed to identify processes that may predict more favorable treatment responses.

FIGURE 13.9 Abstract and Selected excerpts from the discussion section of Olatunji, Davis, Powers, & Smith, 2013.

Continued

Activity 13.3: Identifying Threats to Validity from Review Articles—cont'd

3. Discussion

The present meta-analytic investigation suggests that CBT is effective in the treatment of OCD and that disorder-specific symptom reduction continue to be observed at follow-up. Although findings were robust against the 'file drawer problem', few data points were available for follow-up assessments. This is an important limitation of the literature on the efficacy of CBT for OCD and more treatment outcome research aimed at delineating the lasting effects of psychological treatments for OCD are needed. Few moderators of outcome were also observed in the present investigation. Regarding the important question posed by Paul (1967) of what treatment, by whom, is most effective for this individual with that specific problem, and under which set of circumstances, it may be the case that CBT is generally effective for most individuals under most circumstances. The finding that higher pre-treatment OCD symptom severity, pretreatment depression symptom severity, and percent comorbidity were not significantly associated with a decrease in effect size highlights the effectiveness of CBT for patients with wide range of symptom complexity. Accordingly CBT should translate well to community clinics where OCD patients with more symptom severity, more depression, and more comorbid conditions are likely to present. The present findings did reveal that CBT is perhaps more effective for children with OCD relative to adults with OCD. However, the prescriptive implication of this finding is less clear. Although CBT should clearly be a first-line treatment for children and adults with OCD, it remains unclear if a distinction between children and adults would predict a different pattern of outcomes between two, or more, treatment modalities. Unfortunately, the majority of RCTs that have been evaluated for the treatment of OCD have focused mainly on the efficacy of CBT. The availability of more RCTs examining the efficacy of non-CBT based OCD treatments will be valuable in identifying prescriptive variables that will facilitate individually tailored OCD treatment.

The exclusive focus on CBT treatments specifically also limits inferences that can be made about psychological treatments for OCD more broadly. The use of only well-controlled RCTs of CBT for OCD is perhaps another limitation of the study as it resulted in the availability of a relatively small number of studies for various comparisons. Although the use of well-controlled RCTs does allow for greater confidence in the present findings, there is a need for more well-controlled RCTs of CBT for OCD that will allow for more substantive examination of moderators of treatment outcome. However, the very nature of RCTs may render them ill-suited for detecting important predictors, especially if stricter eligibility criteria and more rigid delivery of treatment protocols eliminate the very factors that influence how OCD patients respond to treatment. Accordingly, effectiveness trials in community settings may have value in efforts to identify predictors of treatment outcome. The assessment of OCD as a unitary outcome is also a limitation of the present investigation. Prior research suggests that OCD consists of distinct symptom dimensions (Mataix Cols et al., 2005). Mataix-Cols et al. (2002) found that OCD patients with higher scores on the hoarding dimension were more likely to drop out prematurely from a randomized trial of CBT and to improve less than nonhoarding OCD patients. In a meta-analysis, patients with primary obsessive thoughts without rituals tended to improve less with CBT than those who had overt motor rituals (Christensen et al., 1987). Future research is needed to examine the extent to which prognostic and prescriptive moderators of CBT vary across the putative symptom dimensions of OCD.

← In this section, the authors identify a concern with external validity. They report that there are almost no studies with repeated assessments after the treatment was over. This makes it difficult to determine if the effects persist after the end of the treatment.

← The authors are making an argument that the strict inclusion and exclusion criteria used in RCTs may limit the generalizability of the findings. The evidence suggests that having more than one disorder or having a complex set of symptoms may affect whether CBT works. Therefore, researchers do not know if the CBT treatments will work with patients who have more than one disorder or do not meet the exclusion or inclusion criteria for any other reason.

→ The authors are concerned that there have been limited studies comparing CBT to other treatments. That limits the ability to test whether CBT is better than other treatments or simply better than no treatment.

FIGURE 13.9 cont'd.

Activity 13.3: Identifying Threats to Validity from Review Articles—cont'd

TABLE 13.5 Identifying threats to validity from review articles.

Author/ Date	Identify a threat to validity mentioned in the Olatunji et al. article	Describe this threat in your own words	What is one approach researchers could take to address this threat in future studies?
	"The exclusive focus on CBT specifically limits the inferences that can be made about psychological treatments for OCD."	Too few studies used other active treatments as comparisons. Therefore, it is difficult to tell if CBT is the best treatment.	Researchers could compare CBT to another active treatment for OCD.

Building Human Capital

In this chapter, you focused on understanding the research articles well enough to get ideas for new research. You learned to identify gaps in knowledge that occur because of threats to internal and external validity. You learned about specific threats facing treatment outcome studies.

To improve knowledge, scientists must be willing to take the risk to share their ideas and findings and to receive feedback on their work. Effective scientists understand that feedback does not represent a personal threat. Instead, they recognized that constructive or corrective feedback reflects a shared appreciation for the value of scientific knowledge and is essential in the process of improving this knowledge.

The best scientists are those who are willing to learn. And often they are learning from their mistakes and the mistakes of others. That is how they grow, and how the knowledge moves forward.

The willingness to learn is an important quality. We can learn best when we actively listen and are interested in what others have to say. And we learn when we are willing to share ideas and receive feedback.

Think about the ways you have been open and received feedback as you completed the work in this book. How did you improve your competence as a result of getting this feedback from peers or instructors? How did you help yourself appreciate the feedback you receive? How did you improve your ability to give feedback to others?

Terms

Take the time to define each of these terms and consider how to apply them.

Research Terms

Fidelity Check
Rosenthal Effect
Hawthorne Effect
Volunteer Bias
Expectancies
Primary Outcome Measure

References

Bellg, A. J., Borrelli, B., Resnick, B., Hecht, J., Minicucci, D. S., Ory, M., … Czajkowski, S. (2004). Enhancing treatment fidelity in health behavior change studies: Best practices and recommendations from the NIH Behavior Change Consortium. *Health Psychology, 23*(5), 443.

Dagöö, J., Asplund, R. P., Bsenko, H. A., Hjerling, S., Holmberg, A., Westh, S., … Andersson, G. (2014). Cognitive behavior therapy versus interpersonal psychotherapy for social anxiety disorder delivered via smartphone and computer: A randomized controlled trial. *Journal of Anxiety Disorders, 28*(4), 410–417.

van der Heiden, C., Muris, P., & van der Molen, H. T. (2012). Randomized controlled trial on the effectiveness of metacognitive therapy and intolerance-of-uncertainty therapy for generalized anxiety disorder. *Behaviour Research and Therapy, 50*(2), 100–109.

Lönnqvist, J. E., Verkasalo, M., & Bezmenova, I. (2007). Agentic and communal bias in socially desirable responding. *European Journal of Personality: Published for the European Association of Personality Psychology, 21*(6), 853–868.

McCambridge, J., Witton, J., & Elbourne, D. R. (2014). Systematic review of the Hawthorne effect: New concepts are needed to study research participation effects. *Journal of Clinical Epidemiology, 67*(3), 267–277.

Olatunji, B. O., Davis, M. L., Powers, M. B., & Smits, J. A. (2013). Cognitive-behavioral therapy for obsessive-compulsive disorder: A meta-analysis of treatment outcome and moderators. *Journal of Psychiatric Research, 47*(1), 33–41.

Richards, D., & Richardson, T. (2012). Computer-based psychological treatments for depression: A systematic review and meta-analysis. *Clinical Psychology Review, 32*(4), 329–342.

Rosenthal, R. (1994). Interpersonal expectancy effects: A 30-year perspective. *Current Directions in Psychological Science, 3*(6), 176–179.

Chapter 14

Writing the theory of the solution

In the last three chapters, you have learned about treatments for behavioral health disorders and gathered evidence to document the effects of treatments. Now you will learn about writing the "Theory of the Solution" (TOS) to explain the interventions or treatments. The interventions or TOS section is another portion of the **literature review.** Writing the TOS section of the literature review will give you more skills in communicating ideas and supporting evidence.

In this chapter, we provide guidance for writing a proposal for a treatment outcome study and for a paper to review the evidence on different treatments for a behavioral health disorder. If you are writing a proposal for a treatment outcome study, the sections on the TOP (Theory of the Problem) and the TOS establish the **scientific premise** of the study. In the TOS, you continue to establish the scientific premise by identifying a treatment which will be used to address the disorder. You describe the available knowledge on the specified treatment, identify gaps in knowledge, and specify the way the proposed study will provide that information. If you are writing a paper to evaluate available treatments for a specified disorder, you use this section to explain different treatment approaches, evaluate the evidence supporting these different treatments, and identify gaps in knowledge and directions for future research.

Components of a TOS Section

The specific components you include in the TOS section depend on the purpose of your paper or proposal. Table 14.1 lists examples of these components.

Psychology Research Methods. https://doi.org/10.1016/B978-0-12-815680-3.00014-1

TABLE 14.1 Components of the TOS section and their application for different types of proposals or papers.

Component	Purpose of the information
• For a proposal: An operational definition and description of the specific treatment to be evaluated in the proposed study. • For a review paper: Operational definitions and descriptions of the specific treatments to be evaluated in the review paper. • In each case the descriptions provide information on the components of the treatment, as well as information on the modality of treatment and the delivery system.	• To provide a clear description of the treatment so the reader understands exactly what is being studied.
• A description of the theory of the treatment(s), including a discussion of the ways the treatment may work and the mechanisms the treatment may affect.	• To give the reader insight into the ways the treatment may work. This section provides an opportunity to link the choice of treatment to the theory of the problem (i.e., the mechanism hypothesized to contribute to the disorder).
• For the proposal: A review of the empirical evidence concerning the specific treatment to be tested in the proposed study. • For the paper: A review of the empirical evidence concerning the specific treatments to be evaluated in the review paper. • In both cases, the review of the evidence may include an evaluation of outcomes including symptoms of the disorder and the potential mechanisms.	• To provide evidence for the specified treatment or the state-of –the art of treatment for the disorder.
• For the proposal: A review of threats to validity seen in existing studies of the specific treatment to be studied in the proposed study. • For the paper: A review of threats to validity seen in existing studies of treatments for the disorder.	• To provide an evaluation of the quality of the existing literature. To understand the specific limitations to the existing knowledge.
• Gaps in knowledge concerning the treatment for the disorder. These gaps can be a function of limited research on the topic or problems interpreting the existing research because of threats to internal or external validity.	• For a proposal To articulate the scientific premise of the proposed study. • For a review paper: To summarize existing gaps in knowledge to provide an overview of needed research.
• For a proposal: An overview of the methods of the proposed research, including the use of a control group, and an explanation of the ways in which these methods will address existing gaps in knowledge.	• To justify the proposed research methods.

TABLE 14.1 **Components of the TOS section and their application for different types of proposals or papers.—cont'd**

Component	Purpose of the information
• For a paper: Address future directions for research - A summary of the types of research that is needed to address existing gaps in knowledge.	• To provide direction for future research.

Writing a Proposal for a Study to Evaluate a Treatment for the Disorder

The TOS section of the proposal helps to explain why a study evaluating the effects of the treatment is necessary. The TOS section enables the reader to understand the treatment that you are proposing to test and the evidence supporting this treatment. The section also points out gaps in knowledge about the treatment as it applies to the disorder you are studying. These gaps could be related to a lack of evidence for treatment effects, limited treatment effects, inadequate control treatments, or other problems with the methods of the study. At a minimum, it would be useful to include information in components 1, 2, 3, 4, 5, and 6 listed in Table 14.1 in a TOS section written for this purpose.

Writing a Paper Reviewing the Evidence on Existing Treatment(s) for the Disorder

A paper reviewing the evidence on different treatments for the disorder provides an overview of the state-of-the-science, so the reader can determine which treatment approaches are most effective and identify gaps in knowledge which must be addressed in future research.

To prepare a paper reviewing the evidence on different treatments, you may read articles about many different treatments for the disorder. As you read these articles and table their methods and results, you will be able to assemble a more comprehensive examination of the evidence. You can use these tables to help you identify consistencies and inconsistencies in evidence across the articles, identify themes across these papers, and consider variables that may explain differences in outcomes across studies. Summarize the evidence about the effects of the treatment and identify

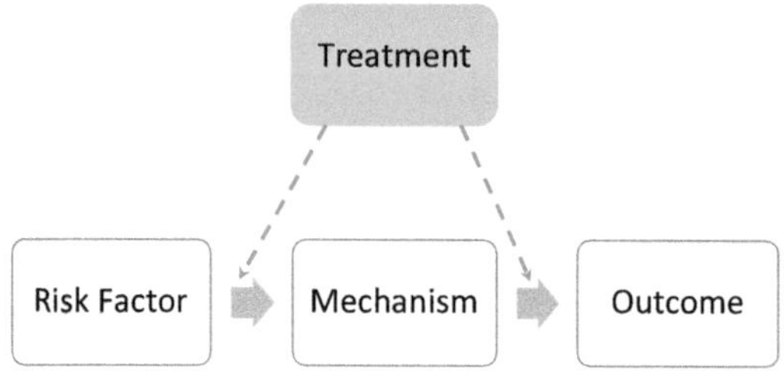

FIGURE 14.1 Treatment may affect the mechanism to interrupt the link of risk factor to the disorder.

threats to internal validity and external validity associated with existing research. Finally, you can enumerate remaining gaps in knowledge and provide ideas for future research. For a paper of this type, you would include Sections 1, 2, 3, 4, 5, and 7 at a minimum.

Starting the Process: Describing the Treatment and Understanding How it Works

Components 1 and 2 of the TOS help the reader understand how the TOP leads to the TOS. For these components, you provide detailed descriptions of the treatment or treatments, so the reader is clear about the nature of the treatments being studied. Next, you explain the **mechanisms of action** of the treatment. The mechanism of action is how the treatment works—the processes that produce the outcomes.

An Operational Definition and Description of the Specified Treatment(s)

Start with components 1 and 2 from Table 14.1. In these components, you describe the treatment in detail. Next, you describe the theory behind the treatment, explaining the mechanism of action. This section provides an opportunity to specify how the treatment affects the mechanisms that trigger or maintain the symptoms of the disorder. In Fig. 14.1 you can see some possible examples for how the treatment may improve outcomes by affecting the link between risk factor and mechanism or between the mechanism and the outcomes.

The description of the treatment should include information about the basic components of the treatment. For example, if you are planning to use a cognitive behavioral therapy (CBT) treatment, include a description of the components of CBT you wish to include (e.g., psychoeducation, cognitive restructuring, relaxation, and exposure and response prevention). It is important to indicate which are the key components, the components hypothesized to produce the benefit. For example, one key component for a condition such as OCD might be exposure and response prevention.

The description of the treatment should also include the modality of treatment (i.e., individual, family, group), the delivery format (i.e., a face-to-face, web, virtual reality, or other format), the setting in which the treatment is delivered, and the qualifications of the therapists, particularly if they are not licensed professionals.

The way you describe the treatment depends on whether you are proposing to test a treatment or if you are reviewing evidence about the effects of the treatment.

- If you are writing a proposal to test the effects of a treatment, you provide a detailed description of the treatment you propose to test.
- If you are writing a paper reviewing different treatments for the disorder you are studying, these descriptions provide details about the different treatments which were used in the articles you describe in your paper. You could describe each of the treatments in one section before you review the evidence about the treatment's effects, or you could describe each treatment before you review the evidence for its effects.

Templates for describing the treatment. These templates can be used to describe the treatment you purpose to test or to describe the treatment employed in studies you are reviewing.

To describe the proposed treatment. *The proposed treatment, (name of treatment), is intended to reduce symptoms of (disorder). The treatment involves (list components). The treatment will be provided in a (describe modality) format using a (describe delivery format). The treatment will be delivered in (describe setting) by (describe therapist qualifications).*

To describe a treatment used in a study you are reviewing for your proposal or paper. *Authors (date) tested the effects of (name of treatment) to reduce symptoms of (disorder). The treatment involved (list components). The treatment was delivered (describe modality) using a (describe delivery format). The treatment was delivered in (describe setting) by (describe therapist qualifications).*

If you need additional information about a treatment, you can obtain further information about the treatment by reading clinical articles or viewing videos about the treatments. In clinical articles, authors describe treatments and often include a case example.

Let's look at a description of treatment presented in an original empirical article (Fig. 14.2).

Controlled Comparison of Family Cognitive Behavioral Therapy and Psychoeducation/ Relaxation Training for Child Obsessive-Compulsive Disorder

John Piacentini, Ph.D., R. Lindsey Bergman, Ph.D., Susanna Chang, Ph.D., Audra Langley, Ph.D., Tara Peris, Ph.D., Jeffrey J. Wood, Ph.D., James McCracken, M.D.

Objective: To examine the efficacy of exposure-based cognitive-behavioral therapy (CBT) plus a structured family intervention (FCBT) versus psychoeducation plus relaxation training (PRT) for reducing symptom severity, functional impairment, and family accommodation in youths with obsessive-compulsive disorder (OCD). **Method:** A total of 71 youngsters 8 to 17 years of age (mean 12.2 years; range, 8–17 years, 37% male, 78% Caucasian) with primary OCD were randomized (70:30) to 12 sessions over 14 weeks of FCBT or PRT. Blind raters assessed outcomes with responders followed for 6 months to assess treatment durability. **Results:** FCBT led to significantly higher response rates than PRT in ITT (57.1% vs 27.3%) and completer analyses (68.3% vs. 35.3%). Using HLM, FCBT was associated with significantly greater change in OCD severity and child-reported functional impairment than PRT and marginally greater change in parent-reported accommodation of symptoms. These findings were confirmed in some, but not all, secondary analyses. Clinical remission rates were 42.5% for FCBT versus 17.6% for PRT. Reduction in family accommodation temporally preceded improvement in OCD for both groups and child functional status for FCBT only. Treatment gains were maintained at 6 months. **Conclusions:** FCBT is effective for reducing OCD severity and impairment. Importantly, treatment also reduced parent-reported involvement in symptoms with reduced accommodation preceding reduced symptom severity and functional impairment. **Clinical Trials Registry Information**—Behavior Therapy for Children and Adolescents with Obsessive-Compulsive Disorder (OCD); http://www.clinicaltrials.gov; NCT00000386. J. Am. Acad. Child Adolesc. Psychiatry, 2011;50(11):1149–1161. **Key words:** obsessive-compulsive disorder, cognitive behavioral therapy, functional impairment, family accommodation

FIGURE 14.2 Abstract and selected excerpt from Piacentini et al. 2011.

Treatment Conditions

Child CBT Plus Family Intervention. The Child CBT Plus Family Intervention (FCBT) protocol consisted of 12 sessions, 90 minutes each, delivered over 14 weeks according to a detailed treatment manual since published.[27,28] The first 10 sessions were delivered weekly with 2-week intervals between the last two sessions to foster generalization and smooth termination from treatment. The initial two sessions involved both the patient and parents and focused on educating the family about OCD, presenting the treatment rationale, creating a symptom hierarchy, and implementing a behavioral reward system for treatment participation. Thereafter, the first hour of each session centered on individual ERP, and the last half hour was devoted to family sessions focusing on psychoeducation designed to correct misattributions about childhood OCD, to reduce feelings of blame and guilt, and to promote increased treatment compliance and awareness. Emphasis was placed on helping parents to disengage from their child's OCD behaviors, promoting developmentally appropriate patterns of family interaction, and addressing relapse prevention and maintenance of therapeutic gains. Although both parents (or primary caregivers) were strongly encouraged to attend all sessions, to enhance sample generalizability this was not an explicit requirement of participation. However, at least one parent attended each FCBT session. To enhance the developmental sensitivity of FCBT, the treatment manual presented techniques in preferred order of administration but provided alternative wordings and examples for different ages. The developmentally appropriate use of language and examples was a key focus of ongoing therapist supervision.

FIGURE 14.2 con'd

← In this section, the authors describe the treatment dose (i.e., the number and length of the sessions, the treatment modalities, and the components of the treatment).

The authors explain both the individual treatment component and the family treatment component.

Fig. 14.3 describes the treatment in the Piacentini article.

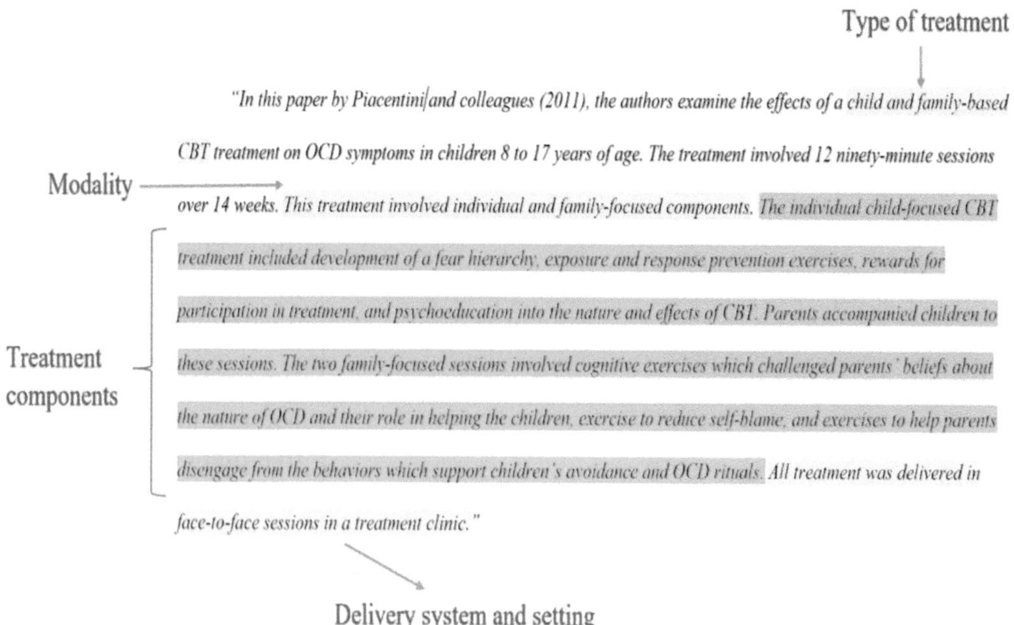

FIGURE 14.3 Annotated treatment description.

Activity 14.1: Identifying and Describing Components of a Treatment

Now it is your turn.

In the next Figure you will see another original research article on a family-based treatment for OCD. Freeman et al. (2008) describe preliminary results of an RCT to test the effects of a family-based CBT treatment for young children with OCD (Fig. 14.4). See if you can answer these questions and then use this information to write a paragraph describing the treatment.

1. Identify the treatment components.

____

____

____

____

____

2. How is the treatment delivered? Describe the modality of treatment, the delivery format, the setting of service delivery, and the qualification of the therapist.

____

____

____

____

____

Activity 14.1: Identifying and Describing Components of a Treatment—cont'd

Early Childhood OCD: Preliminary Findings From a Family-Based Cognitive-Behavioral Approach

JENNIFER B. FREEMAN, PH.D., ABBE M. GARCIA, PH.D., LISA COYNE, PH.D., CHELSEA ALE, B.A., AMY PRZEWORSKI, PH.D., MICHAEL HIMLE, PH.D., SCOTT COMPTON, PH.D., AND HENRIETTA L. LEONARD, M.D.

ABSTRACT

Objective: To examine the relative efficacy of family-based cognitive-behavioral therapy (CBT) versus family-based relaxation treatment (RT) for young children ages 5 to 8 years with obsessive-compulsive disorder (OCD). **Method:** Forty-two young children with primary OCD were randomized to receive 12 sessions of family-based CBT or family-based RT. Assessments were conducted before and after treatment by independent raters blind to treatment assignment. Primary outcomes included scores on the Children's Yale-Brown Obsessive Compulsive Scale and Clinical Global Impressions-Improvement. **Results:** For the intent-to-treat sample, CBT was associated with a moderate treatment effect ($d = 0.53$), although there was not a significant difference between the groups at conventional levels. For the completer sample, CBT had a large effect ($d = 0.85$), and there was a significant group difference favoring CBT. In the intent-to-treat sample, 50% of children in the CBT group achieved remission as compared to 20% in the RT group. In the completer sample, 69% of children in the CBT group achieved a clinical remission compared to 20% in the RT group. **Conclusions:** Results indicate that children with early-onset OCD benefit from a treatment approach tailored to their developmental needs and family context. CBT was effective in reducing OCD symptoms and in helping a large number of children achieve a clinical remission. *J. Am. Acad. Child Adolesc. Psychiatry,* 2008;47(5):593–602. **Key Words:** obsessive-compulsive disorder, cognitive-behavioral therapy, family-based treatment. Clinical trial registration information—Family-Based Treatment of Early Childhood Obsessive-Compulsive Disorder. URL: http://www.clinicaltrials.gov. Unique identifier: NCT00055068.

Exposure with response prevention (EX/RP) is the behavioral treatment of choice for OCD in both adults and children,[7] but previous studies have not adequately addressed the efficacy of EX/RP for children with early childhood–onset OCD. Although children as young as age 7 have been included in previous randomized controlled trials of EX/RP, they were underrepresented in those samples relative to older children and adolescents. For example, in the Pediatric OCD Treatment Study I, 18 of 112 (16%) children were younger than age 9, 11 of 18 (10%) of children younger than age 9 received a CBT-containing condition, and the mean age of the sample was 11.8 years.[8] This is important because young children with OCD may require specific adaptations to the traditional EX/RP treatment regimen.

These adaptations may be required for younger children due to their developmental needs and family context. Developmentally, younger children generally have less sophisticated emotion awareness and expression skills than older children. Such developmental differences are likely to affect the acquisition and application of skills that are integral to EX/RP, such as the development of fear hierarchies. Younger children are also less adept at comprehending abstract concepts such as the treatment rationale for EX/RP. All of these factors may limit a young child's ability and willingness to engage fully in exposure-based treatment.[9]

With regard to family context, younger children rely on parents for guidance and direction more so than do older children. Coupling this developmentally normal level of dependence with the fact that OCD tends to pull family members into rituals, parents may be more likely to inadvertently reinforce or even actively accommodate a young child's rituals.[9–15]

For the above-mentioned reasons, we believe that young children experiencing OCD require a treatment approach uniquely tailored to their developmental needs and family context.

FIGURE 14.4 Abstract and selected excerpts from Freeman et al. 2008.

Continued

Activity 14.1: Identifying and Describing Components of a Treatment—cont'd

Intervention Programs

Both treatment protocols (CBT and RT) consisted of 12 sessions delivered during the course of 14 weeks. The first 10 sessions were delivered weekly, followed by two biweekly sessions. The first two sessions (90 minutes each) were conducted with parents only, and the remaining sessions (60 minutes each) were conducted jointly with parents and children. For more detail about the family-based CBT program, see also Choate-Summers et al.[32]

Family-Based CBT. The overall focus of treatment is to provide both child and parents with a set of tools to help them understand, manage, and reduce OCD symptoms. The primary components of the treatment are as follows.

Psychoeducation. Ensuring that parents clearly understand the treatment program and rationale before children are introduced to treatment lays the groundwork because many young children will not fully understand the treatment rationale. Young children will vary in what they grasp, but can most often understand the concept of being the "boss" of OCD behaviors. To increase parent and child engagement and motivation, psychoeducation is presented as simply as possible via simple, engaging modalities, including the use of visual imagery, metaphors, and developmentally relevant examples.

Parent Tools. Parents are provided with a set of tools used throughout treatment to increase the child's motivation for change and to more effectively manage their child's OCD symptoms. The central parenting tools include differential attention, modeling, and scaffolding.

Child Tools. The goal of the EX/RP component for the child is to have parents and children actively work together to develop a hierarchy and implement EX/RP. This is accomplished by distilling the core concepts of treatment and making it fun (where possible). Home-based practice of EX/RP is facilitated by a reward program introduced early in treatment.

Family-Based RT. The primary components of the treatment were affective education (helping children identify both negative and positive feelings and recognize the connection between stress and anxiety), relaxation training including progressive muscle relaxation and verbally cued guided imagery to attain a relaxation response, and the use of a reward system to encourage relaxation practice between sessions.

Therapist Training and Supervision. All study therapists were clinical psychology interns, postdoctoral fellows, and clinical psychologists with expertise in the application of behavior therapy with anxiety disorders, parent behavior management training, and relaxation and family-based treatment. Doctoral-level clinical psychologists (J.B.F., A.M.G.) provided all of the training and supervision. Training included didactic instruction, familiarization with the treatment manuals, and role-playing of treatment procedures. All of the therapy sessions were videotaped and discussed in weekly group supervision.

Therapist adherence and competence in both treatment conditions were monitored through the use of therapy manuals, ongoing supervision, and regular monitoring and rating of videotaped therapy sessions. Adherence and competence measures developed specifically for this study were rated by study clinicians who were not the provider for that case. Raters were trained until they reached at least 80% agreement. Fifteen percent of taped treatment sessions from each condition were selected to ensure equal representation of age and sex of patient, as well as session number. In the CBT condition, 92% (n = 33) of the sessions were perfectly adherent (all of the required elements present), 5% (n = 2) of the sessions missed one required component, and 3% (n = 1) of the sessions were rated as nonadherent. Notably, this last case was prematurely terminated from the study because another anxiety diagnosis became primary. In the RT condition, no tapes were rated as nonadherent. In both CBT and RT, no tapes were rated as including proscribed treatment elements.

FIGURE 14.4 con'd

Explaining the Mechanism of Action

The mechanisms of action are the processes by which the treatment acts to change symptoms. The researchers who develop or test a treatment describe these mechanisms of action when they are explaining the theories about how the treatment works. The description of the theory can often be found in the clinical articles that explain the practice of the treatment and is often available in the articles presenting a treatment outcome study.

Presenting a theory of the mechanisms of action of a treatment in the TOS is like explaining the mechanisms that trigger or maintain the symptoms of a disorder in the TOP. In this case, you are explaining how the treatment interrupts the mechanisms that trigger or maintain the symptoms.

Here is an example:

> Piacentini et al. (2011) provide a discussion of the mechanisms of action for the family component of the treatment. They make the argument that *parents' accommodation behaviors* serve as a mechanism maintaining the child's OCD symptoms. Parents accommodate their child's OCD when they allow children to engage in rituals and help them avoid feared situations. Parents may accommodate their children because they are concerned the child will experience distress. As you can read in the description of the treatment, Piacentini et al. (2011) make the argument that family-based CBT decreases OCD symptoms, in part, because the treatment interrupts the family accommodation behaviors. We can draw a model of the effects of this treatment (Fig. 14.5).

A template for describing the mechanism of action of the treatment. *Authors (date) describe the theory and practice associated with (name of therapy). The theory proposes that people develop the (name of disorder) because of (description of mechanisms that trigger and maintain symptoms). The (name of treatment) includes specific components such as (names of treatment components). The treatment component or components operate by (describe the mechanism of action—how the therapy affects the mechanisms which trigger or maintain the symptoms).*

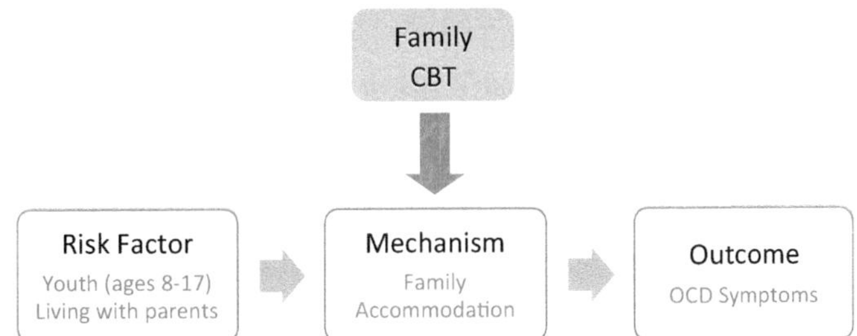

FIGURE 14.5 Visual presentation of treatment model from Piacentini et al. 2011.

Activity 14.2: Describing the Treatment and the Theory Underlying the Treatment

Using one of the articles you have chosen for your TOS section, answer the questions below.

1. Describe the treatment, including the components, delivery system, modalities, and therapists.
2. What are the mechanisms of action described in this article? How do the authors claim the treatment works?

____

____

____

____

____

____

____

____

____

Does the Treatment Work? Summarizing the Evidence

Now it's time to answer the question: Is there evidence that this treatment reduces symptoms and addresses the mechanism? To answer this question, you organize, describe, and evaluate the research on the treatments for the disorder.

The evidence about the treatments may come from articles which provide systematic or meta-analytic reviews, if they are available. Cochrane reviews on treatments for a disorder can be especially helpful in preparing the overview of the evidence. The evidence will also come from specific empirical original research articles that present data on the treatments you are interested in studying.

For an undergraduate research methods class, a teacher may require students to read a small portion of available articles on each topic. Each of the articles gives the student some information about the topic and experience in reading and reporting on scientific articles. The focus is on understanding how to read the articles and use the evidence.

In contrast, when graduate students are preparing a thesis, or a researcher is preparing a proposal to request funding for research, they are expected to conduct comprehensive reviews of all the literature in the specific area. This will allow them to understand the state-of-the-science—the full range of knowledge about the topic. This comprehensive review will allow them to identify gaps in knowledge that should be addressed in the new research.

Assembling the Evidence Needed: Putting the Evidence into Tables

As you have done in previous chapters, you can make tables to help organize the information on treatment outcome. These tables build on the work already done in the exercises for the previous chapters and will help you organize the findings from all the studies you review for each treatment.

The tables we use here include a wide range of information about the methods used to test the hypotheses. You need this information to write a description of the study. The tables also include information about the hypotheses tested and the results. This is the information which will provide evidence about the effects of the treatments.

Not all studies will reveal the same patterns. A summary table organizing findings across studies will help you understand the overall level of support for the different treatments. If the tables are completed correctly, the task of writing a summary of the evidence in support of each treatment will be straightforward.

In addition, the tables can guide other sections of your proposal or paper. If you are writing a proposal, the evidence from these articles will help you choose treatment modalities, delivery formats, and therapist qualifications. If you are writing a paper reviewing these studies, the evidence can help you evaluate the effects of the treatment modalities, delivery formats, and therapist qualifications. The written descriptions of the studies and the summary of the evidence provide a portion of the literature review for your paper or proposal.

Activity 14.3: Organizing the Findings of Original Research Articles on Treatment Outcome

We can practice tabling the methods and findings of an original research article on a treatment. We use the article by Piacentini et al. (2011) to provide an example (Fig. 14.6). The abstract and methods were presented earlier in the chapter. Now we have added more information on the procedures and results.

We have documented the methods and the results in Table 14.2. The table guides the writing of a brief description of the findings.

Now it's your turn. Using Table 14.3, table the findings from the article you chose in the earlier activity. Table the information about the methods and results.

Continued

Activity 14.3: Organizing the Findings of Original Research Articles on Treatment Outcome—cont'd

METHOD

Procedure

Interested families completed a telephone screening to ascertain potential eligibility. Qualifying families were then invited to the Clinic to complete informed consent/assent and a baseline eligibility evaluation. Outreach efforts, including flyers, print ads, and mailings, were specifically targeted toward media outlets and providers serving predominantly minority populations to enhance the representativeness of the study sample. Diagnostic eligibility was determined by the Anxiety Disorders Interview Schedule, Fourth Edition (ADIS-IV),[25] administered along with the Children's Yale–Brown Obsessive Compulsive Scale[26] and a battery of standardized self-report measures assessing functional impairment, family dynamics, and comorbid symptomatology.

After completion of the baseline assessment and final determination of eligibility, participants were randomly assigned to either active (FCBT) or comparison (PRT) treatment. To minimize a potential treatment by therapist confound, therapist assignment was balanced over time so that each therapist treated participants in both treatment conditions. Trained evaluators blinded to treatment condition conducted assessments with families at baseline, at treatment weeks 4 and 8, and post-treatment (week 14). Positive responders to either intervention completed follow-up assessments at 1 and 6 months post-treatment to examine the durability of observed treatment gains.

FIGURE 14.6 Selected excerpts from the methods and results section from Piacentini et al. 2011.

RESULTS

Responder Status

Intent-to-treat analyses with the CGI-I revealed a significantly higher response rate at week 14 for FCBT as compared with PRT (57.1% versus 27.3%; $\chi^2 = 5.40$, $p < .05$). Analysis of treatment completers yielded similar results (68.3% versus 35.3%, $\chi^2 = 5.40$, $p < .05$).

OCD Severity

The HLM analysis comparing the rate of change in CYBOCS total scores in FCBT and PRT yielded a statistically significant slope by treatment interaction (t = 2.25, $p < .05$). The means in Table 3 and Figure 2 show that the nature of this interaction effect was a faster decline in CYBOCS scores over time in FCBT as compared with PRT. FCBT led to a 46.2% reduction in CYBOCS total score as compared with a 32.0% reduction for PRT. In contrast, the ANCOVA comparing post-treatment CYBOCS scores did not reach significance ($F_{1, 69} = 2.67$, $p < .14$). The between-groups ITT ES at post-treatment was 0.40.

To examine clinically significant improvement, week 14 CYBOCS scores for treatment completers were categorized into an ordinal scale: 1 (remitted [<11]), 2 (subclinical [11-15]), 3 (moderate [16-24]), and 4 (severe [>24]) (Table 4). An ordinal regression analysis testing the difference between the treatment groups on these severity categories post-treatment indicated that a higher proportion of children in FCBT fell into the less severe CYBOCS categories than children in PRT ($\chi^2 = 3.81$, $p = .05$). Rates of clinical remission, defined as CYBOCS total score <11,[7] were 42.5% for FCBT versus 17.6% for PRT ($\chi^2 = 3.24$, not significant).

Family Accommodation

HLM analysis of FAS-PR total scores yielded a marginally significant slope by treatment group interaction effect (t = 1.95, $p = .05$). The means for the FCBT group declined from baseline to post-treatment on the FAS-PR, but there was less improvement for the PRT group (post-treatment ITT ES = 0.42) (Table 3).

Family Accommodation as Predictor of Response

Given preliminary prior evidence for the role of family accommodation as a potential predictor of outcome,[19] lagged time-varying covariate analyses were undertaken in HLM to determine whether reductions in FAS scores at a given time point were associated with corresponding reductions in CYBOCS or COIS-R scores at the following time point. Group (within-person) centering was used. FAS-PR scores (at time t, beginning with baseline) were the only predictors at level 1. Level 2 predictors were added after testing the basic level 1 model across groups, in which interactions with treatment group were specified at level 2. CYBOCS or COIS-RC or COIS-RP scores (at time t + 1, beginning with week 4) were the DVs in three separate models. For the CYBOCS level 1 model, there was an association between the slope of the FAS and the CYBOCS total score, such that for each one-point reduction in FAS scores compared with an individual's overall mean score across time points at a particular assessment (e.g., week 4), their CYBOCS score also declined an average of .27 points compared with their overall mean score across time points at the following assessment (e.g., week 8) (t = 2.68, $p < .01$). There was no treatment group by slope interaction effect for the CYBOCS model. However, for the COIS-RC model, a treatment group by slope interaction effect did emerge (t = −2.75, $p < .01$). For the FCBT group, a 1-point reduction in FAS-PR scores (relative to one's own mean across time) at a particular assessment corresponded with a 1.2-point reduction in COIS-RC scores at the following assessment. This effect was reduced by more than 50%, to a 0.48-point corresponding reduction in COIS-RC scores in the PRT group. There was no significant effect found in the COIS-RP model.

Durability of Treatment Response

Of 28 initial FCBT responders, 26 (93%) completed follow-up assessments, with 81% (21/26) maintaining their positive response status (CGI-I <3) at 1 month and 73% (19/26) at 6 months post-treatment. Mean CYBOCS total scores for these 26 subjects were as follows: post-treatment: mean = 9.7 (95% CI = 6.0-12.0); 1-month follow-up: mean = 4.1 (95% CI = 2.8-5.3); 6-month follow-up: mean = 3.2 (95% CI = 1.8-4.5). Of the six PRT responders, five (83%) completed the 1- and 6-month follow-up assessments, although CGI-I data were missing for one subject at 6 months. Overall, 60% (3/5) maintained their positive response at 1 month and 75% (3/4) at 6 months. Mean CYBOCS total scores for these subjects were as follows: post-treatment: mean = 9.8 (95% CI = 5.3-14.3); 1-month follow-up: mean = 4.2 (95% CI = 1.1-7.3); 6-month follow-up: mean = 3.4 (95% CI = −0.6-7.4).

FIGURE 14.6 con'd

Activity 14.3: Organizing the Findings of Original Research Articles on Treatment Outcome —cont'd

TABLE 14.2 Methods and Results from a treatment outcome study.

Author/ Date	DV: Disorder and definition of disorder	Measurement instrument for the DV	Experimental treatment with description	Control treatment with description	Mechanism	Modality and delivery system (Face-to-face, web-based, group, individual, etc.)	Setting and therapist qualifi-cations	Participant characteristics and n	Primary hypothesis	Outcome	Limitations
Piacentini et al. (2011)	Primary diagnosis of OCD from DSM-V from ADIS and YBOCS score greater than 15.	Clinical global improvement from CGI scale, physician ratings of symptoms.	Family plus individual CBT (FCBT), with exposure and focused on reducing avoidance and disrupting the tendency of family members to give into the child's OCD symptoms.	Psychoeducation and relaxation (P&R) included detailed information about OCD and progressive muscle relaxation.	Family accommodation-family tendency to make adjustments to allow child to avoid anxiety-producing threats. Measured with Family Accommodation Scale – revised.	Both face-to face. Experimental delivered in 14, 90-min sessions with. 1 hour devoted to exposure and 30 min devoted to work with the families to address ideas and behaviors associated with managing the child's OCD. Control: 14, 90 min sessions including education about OCD and behavioral contracting for practicing relaxation. Family involvement for first two sessions.		Final sample is 71 children with a primary diagnosis of OCD and no comorbid conditions. 8 to 17 years old. 36.6% were boys.	FCBT > P&R in reducing OCD symptoms.	FCBT was associated with greater improvements in CGI, in the number of children who achieved remission, and also reductions in family accommodations. most in FBCT maintained gains.	Limited information on the role of family accommodation in predicting outcome. Delivered in controlled setting with highly trained therapist.

Activity 14.3: Organizing the Findings of Original Research Articles on Treatment Outcome —cont'd

TABLE 14.3 Table of the methods and results of original research articles.

Author/ Date	DV: Disorder and definition of disorder	Measurement instrument for the DV	Experimental treatment with description	Control treatment with description	Mechanism	Modality and delivery system (face-to-face, web-based, group, individual, etc.)	Setting and therapist qualification	Participant characteristics and n	Primary hypothesis	Outcome	Limitations

Writing Descriptions of the Evidence from Original Research Studies and Meta-Analyses

Descriptions of original research articles and meta-analyses are used to explain the evidence on the effectiveness of the treatment and to identify gaps in knowledge. In this section of this chapter, we focus on reporting the evidence on treatment effects. In the next section, we report on gaps in knowledge.

Describing Original Research Articles

Descriptions of original research articles are helpful to provide the reader with a clear understanding of the methods and the findings of the outcome studies.

The descriptions include the following information:

- ✓ The aim of the study, specifying the hypotheses the authors wanted to test
- ✓ A description of the experimental and control conditions, identifying the differences between these two conditions
- ✓ A description of the methods used to test the hypotheses, including information about the sample, research design, and measurement of the key variables
- ✓ A summary of the results, indicating if the data provide support to the hypothesis that the treatment is effective or not here is an example of paragraphs describing the Piacentini et al. (2011) we tabled in Table 14.2.

The study by Piacentini et al. (2011) tested the hypothesis that family and child CBT was superior to psychoeducation and relaxation training in reducing OCD in children. The sample included only children, and all children lived with their parents. All child participants were assigned at random to either the experimental treatment (Family and Child CBT) or the control (Psychoeducation and Relaxation). The primary outcome variables included clinical ratings of improvement in OCD symptoms, decreases in the levels of OCD symptoms, and remission of OCD diagnosis. Secondary outcomes included measures of family accommodation; a mechanism hypothesized to maintain OCD symptoms.

The results supported the hypotheses about the effects of family-based CBT and the role of family accommodation. At the end of the treatment, children in the Family CBT treatment were more likely than those in the control group to show a clinically significant improvement in OCD symptoms; they had significantly lower levels of OCD symptoms than those in the control group, and they were more likely to have a remission of symptoms. Participants in the Family CBT treatment also showed an improvement in family accommodation. Changes in family accommodation were associated with a decrease in OCD symptoms in both experimental and control conditions.

Templates for a description of a treatment study

Here is an example of a description of a simulated (made-up) treatment outcome article which can provide a template for describing the treatment and the results:

Authors (date) conducted a randomized controlled trial to evaluate the effects of (TREATMENT) to reduce (disorder). Participants included (number of participants) individuals with a diagnosis of (DISORDER) who were recruited from (SOURCE OF RECRUITMENT). Participants were assigned at random to receive either Experimental Treatment or Control Treatment. The Experimental consisted of the following components: X, Y, and Z. Component X is hypothesized the main active ingredient. The authors suggest that Component X acts by (EXPLAIN MECHANISM OF ACTION). The treatments were both delivered by a (DESCRIBE THERAPIST QUALIFICATIONS AND ASSESSMENT OF QUALITY OF TRAINING). The sessions were offered in (MODALITY OF TREATMENT AND DELIVERY SYSTEM).

Participants were tested before and after intervention. The researchers found that participants assigned to the Experimental Treatment versus the Control Treatment had (REPORT OUTCOME OF ANALYSES OF PRIMARY AND SECONDARY OUTCOMES WHICH ARE CONTINUOUS VARIABLES. THIS WILL INCLUDE THE SYMPTOMS AND MECHANISM IF REPORTED) (describe the mechanism) (If information about categorical outcomes is available, report this as well.). About XX% of participants in the Experimental Treatment versus YY% in the Control Treatment demonstrated a clinically significant improvement, defined as (describe clinically significant improvement as defined by authors).

(Note: In many studies the control treatment and the experimental treatment are not matched for all components except the "active ingredient". In these cases, you need to describe the ways in which the treatments overlap and differ.)

Activity 14.4: Describing the Results of an Original Research Article

In Activity 14.1 you wrote a description of a treatment from one of your own articles, and in Activity 14.3 you tabled the results. Now write a description of the results. Use the templates to guide you, and make sure you include all components needed for the description: the aim, the experimental and control treatments, the methods, findings, and conclusions.

____

____

____

____

____

____

____

Journal of Psychiatric Research 47 (2013) 33–41

Contents lists available at SciVerse ScienceDirect

Journal of Psychiatric Research

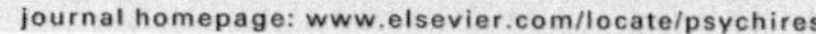

journal homepage: www.elsevier.com/locate/psychires

Cognitive-behavioral therapy for obsessive-compulsive disorder: A meta-analysis of treatment outcome and moderators

Bunmi O. Olatunji [a,*], Michelle L. Davis [b], Mark B. Powers [b], Jasper A.J. Smits [b]

[a] Department of Psychology, Vanderbilt University, 301 Wilson Hall, 111 21st Avenue South, Nashville, TN 37203, USA
[b] Department of Psychology, Southern Methodist University, Dallas, TX, USA

A R T I C L E I N F O

Article history:
Received 25 April 2012
Received in revised form
13 August 2012
Accepted 16 August 2012

Keywords:
Obsessive compulsive disorder
Cognitive-behavioral therapy
Moderation

A B S T R A C T

The present investigation employed meta-analysis to examine the efficacy of cognitive-behavioral therapy (CBT) for obsessive–compulsive disorder (OCD) as well as potential moderators that may be associated with outcome. A literature search revealed sixteen randomized-controlled trials (RCTs) with a total sample size of 756 participants that met inclusion criteria. Results indicated that CBT outperformed control conditions on primary outcome measures at post-treatment (Hedges's $g = 1.39$) and at follow-up (Hedges's $g = 0.43$). Subsequent analyses revealed few moderators of CBT efficacy. Neither higher pre-treatment OCD ($p = 0.46$) or depression symptom severity ($p = 0.68$) was significantly associated with a decrease in CBT effect size. Similarly, effect size did not vary as a function of 'type' of CBT, treatment format, treatment integrity assessment, blind assessment, age of onset, duration of symptoms, percentage of females, number of sessions, or percent comorbidity. However, active treatments showed smaller effect sizes when compared to placebo controls than when compared to waitlist controls. Effect sizes were also smaller for adult RCTs than child RCTs. Likewise, older age was associated with smaller effect sizes. However, an association between age and effect size was not observed when examining child and adult samples separately. This review indicates that while CBT is efficacious in the treatment of OCD, more research is needed to identify processes that may predict more favorable treatment responses.

FIGURE 14.7 Abstract from Olatunji et al., 2013

Describing the Results of Meta-Analyses and Systematic Reviews

Meta-analyses can provide a valuable summary of the evidence for the treatment. Let's look at an example by Olatunji, Davis, Powers, and Smits (2013) (Fig. 14.7). This article describes a meta-analysis of studies of CBT treatments for OCD. The authors conclude that there is good evidence supporting the use of CBT for OCD when CBT is compared with no treatment (wait-list control). The data from this study also provide some evidence that the benefits were not affected by the treatment modality or delivery format. The benefits were also present for children and adults, but the effects were stronger for children.

The results also highlight some gaps in the literature which we will discuss in the next section—Identifying threats to validity and gaps in knowledge.

The data from a meta-analysis can be described by indicating how many studies were reviewed, the size of the meta-analytic overall sample, as well as clinical characteristics of the samples included in the studies. The clinical characteristics include the types of diagnoses or symptoms of the participants. The

Activity 14.5: Writing Brief Descriptions of the Evidence from Meta-Analyses

We can examine the meta-analysis by Olatunji et al. (2013) in more detail. Read the excerpts in Fig. 14.8 of the methods and results of the meta-analysis. Check your understanding against the information included in Table 14.4. Then examine a meta-analysis of treatment outcome studies on the disorder you are studying.

1. Method

1.1. Study selection

Treatments were classified as CBT if they included cognitive techniques (e.g. cognitive restructuring, behavioral experiments, etc.), behavioral techniques (e.g. in-vivo exposure, imaginal exposure, etc.), acceptance/mindfulness techniques (e.g. engaging in valued behaviors despite anxiety), or a combination of these strategies.

1.3. Procedure

Control conditions were classified into two categories: placebo or wait-list. Treatments that were categorized as placebo included: stress management training (SMT), relaxation (R), pill placebo, and anxiety management (AM). Wait-list (WL) was defined as a control condition in which participants did not receive any treatment for OCD symptoms for a specified amount of time. Six of the sixteen studies utilized placebos (5 psychological placebos and 1 pill placebo) as the control condition, 9 of the 16 studies had wait-list as the control condition, and 1 of the 16 studies included both a placebo condition and a wait-list condition.

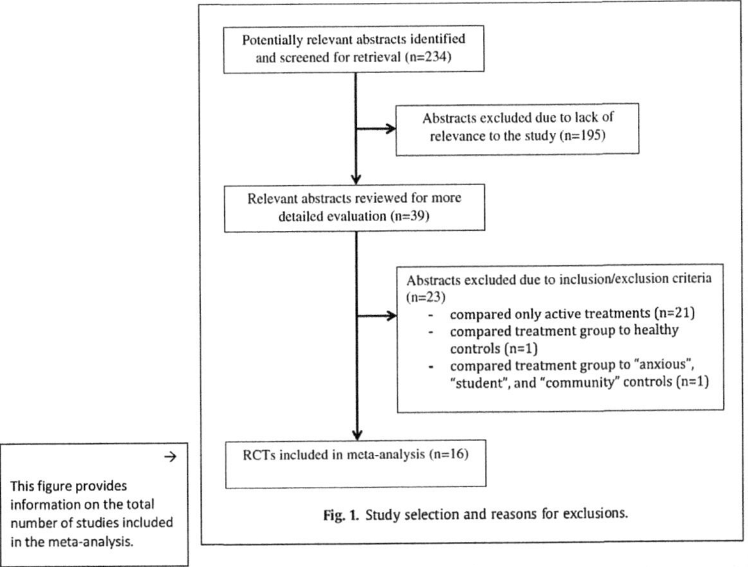

Fig. 1. Study selection and reasons for exclusions.

FIGURE 14.8 Selected excerpts from Olatunji et al. 2013.

Continued

Activity 14.5: Writing Brief Descriptions of the Evidence from Meta-Analyses—cont'd

Table 1
Studies included in the meta-analysis.

Study	Conditions	N	Sample	Mean age	# Of sessions	Primary outcome measure	Secondary outcome measure
Anderson and Rees (2007)	CBT vs. WL	51	Adult	33.7	10	YBOCS	BDI
Barrett et al. (2004)	CBT vs. WL	53	Child	11.8	14	CYBOCS	CDI
Bolton and Perrin (2008)	CBT vs. WL	20	Child	13.2	12	CYBOCS	None
Cordioli et al. (2003)	CBT vs. WL	47	Adult	36.5	12	YBOCS	HAM-D
Fals-Stewart et al. (1993)	CBT vs. Psych PL	93	Adult	30.5	12	YBOCS	BDI
Fineberg et al. (2005)	CBT vs. Psych PL	47	Adult	39.3	12	YBOCS	None
Foa et al. (2005)	CBT vs. Pill PL	41	Adult	34.3	23	YBOCS	HAM-D
Freeston et al. (1997)	CBT vs. WL	29	Adult	35.8	12	YBOCS	BDI
Jones and Menzies (1998)	CBT vs. WL	21	Adult	38.5	10	MOCI	BDI
Lindsay et al. (1997)	CBT vs. Psych PL	18	Adult	32.8	15	YBOCS	BDI
O'Connor et al. (1999)	CBT vs. WL	26	Adult	37.3	5	YBOCS	None
Simpson et al. (2008)	CBT vs. Psych PL	108	Adult	39.2	17	YBOCS	HAM-D
Twohig et al. (2010)	CBT vs. Psych PL	79	Adult	37.0	8	YBOCS	BDI-II
Whittal et al. (2010)	CBT vs. Psych PL vs. WL	73	Adult	31.5	12	YBOCS	BDI
Wilhelm et al. (2009)	CBT vs. WL	29	Adult	33.4	22	YBOCS	BDI
Williams et al. (2010)	CBT vs. WL	21	Child	13.6	10	CYBOCS	CDI

Note. CBT = Cognitive Behavior Therapy, WL = Waitlist, PL = Placebo, CYBOCS = Children's Yale-Brown Obsessive Compulsive Scale, MOCI = Maudsley Obsessional-Compulsive Inventory, YBOCS = Yale-Brown Obsessive Compulsive Scale, BDI = Beck Depression Inventory, BDI-II = Beck Depression Inventory-II, CDI = Children's Depression Inventory, HAM-D = Hamilton Rating Scale for Depression.

←This table describes each of the 16 studies included and provides information on the number of participants in the studies.

2. Results

2.1. Question 1: does CBT outperform the control conditions on primary OCD outcome measures at post-treatment and follow-up?

The post-treatment analysis included 16 studies with 756 participants. Consistent with prediction, Fig. 2 shows that CBT outperformed control conditions on primary outcome (i.e., OCD symptoms) measures at post-treatment showing a large effect size (Hedges's $g = 1.39$ [SE = 0.18, 95% CI: 1.04–1.74, $p = 0.000$]). The follow-up analysis included 3 studies with 111 participants. CBT outperformed control conditions on primary outcome measures at follow-up showing a medium effect size (Hedges's $g = 0.43$ [SE = 0.16, 95% CI: 0.12–0.74, $p = 0.01$]).

2.4. Question 3: is higher pre-treatment severity and depression associated with lower effect sizes?

The analysis for pre-treatment severity included 16 comparisons with 756 participants and revealed that higher pre-treatment severity was not significantly associated with lower effect size ($\beta = 0.05$, $p = 0.46$). The analysis for pretreatment depression included 14 comparisons with 751 participants and showed no significant relation between pre-treatment depression and effect size ($\beta = -0.02$, $p = 0.68$).

2. Results

2.1. Question 1: does CBT outperform the control conditions on primary OCD outcome measures at post-treatment and follow-up?

The post-treatment analysis included 16 studies with 756 participants. Consistent with prediction, Fig. 2 shows that CBT outperformed control conditions on primary outcome (i.e., OCD symptoms) measures at post-treatment showing a large effect size (Hedges's $g = 1.39$ [SE = 0.18, 95% CI: 1.04–1.74, $p = 0.000$]). The follow-up analysis included 3 studies with 111 participants. CBT outperformed control conditions on primary outcome measures at follow-up showing a medium effect size (Hedges's $g = 0.43$ [SE = 0.16, 95% CI: 0.12–0.74, $p = 0.01$]).

2.4. Question 3: is higher pre-treatment severity and depression associated with lower effect sizes?

The analysis for pre-treatment severity included 16 comparisons with 756 participants and revealed that higher pre-treatment severity was not significantly associated with lower effect size ($\beta = 0.05$, $p = 0.46$). The analysis for pretreatment depression included 14 comparisons with 751 participants and showed no significant relation between pre-treatment depression and effect size ($\beta = -0.02$, $p = 0.68$).

2.5. Question 4: does effect size vary as a function of treatment type, control type, mean age, percentage of females, number of sessions, and comorbidity?

The following analyses were completed using fully random effects categorical moderator analyses. First, we examined effect size as a function of two different treatment types: CT (3 studies) and ERP (12 studies). There were no significant differences in the magnitude of effect sizes in these two treatments: CT (Hedges's $g = 1.84$ [SE = 0.46, 95% CI: 0.94–2.74, $p = 0.00$]) and ERP (Hedges's $g = 1.35$ [SE = 0.20, 95% CI: 0.96–1.74, $p = 0.00$]). We also examined effect size as a function of two different control types: placebo (7 comparisons: 1 pill placebo and 6 psychological placebos) and waitlist (12 comparisons). Studies employing waitlist controls (Hedges's $g = 1.67$ [SE = 0.19, 95% CI: 1.31–2.04, $p = 0.00$)] showed larger effect sizes than studies using placebo controls (Hedges's $g = 0.92$ [SE = 0.20, 95% CI: 0.53–1.33, $p = 0.00$]). There were no significant differences after removing the study utilizing a pill placebo from the placebo control comparison ($n = 7$; Hedge's $g = 0.85$ [SE = 0.22, 95% CI: 0.43–1.28, $p = 0.00$)].

There were no significant differences in effect size between group ($n = 9$, Hedges's $g = 1.53$ [SE = 0.24, 95% CI: 1.06–2.00, $p = 0.00$]) and individual formats ($n = 10$, Hedges's $g = 1.24$ [SE = 0.22, 95% CI: 0.82–1.66, $p = 0.00$]). A significant difference in effect size was seen between adult ($n = 13$, Hedges's $g = 1.08$ [SE = 0.12, 95% CI: 0.85–1.32, $p = 0.00$]) and child populations ($n = 3$, Hedges's $g = 2.50$ [SE = 0.28, 95% CI: 1.94–3.05, $p = 0.00$]) with child populations being associated with significantly larger effect sizes. There were no significant differences in effect size between studies including treatment integrity checks ($n = 9$, Hedges's $g = 1.47$ [SE = 0.23, 95% CI: 1.01–1.92, $p = 0.00$]) and studies without treatment integrity checks ($n = 7$, Hedges's $g = 1.21$ [SE = 0.29, 95% CI: 0.65–1.77, $p = 0.00$]) or in studies with blind assessors ($n = 7$, Hedges's $g = 1.43$ [SE = 0.27, 95% CI: 0.90–1.95, $p = 0.00$]) and studies without blind assessors ($n = 9$, Hedges's $g = 1.31$ [SE = 0.25, 95% CI: 0.82–1.80, $p = 0.00$]).

FIGURE 14.8 con'd

Activity 14.5: Writing Brief Descriptions of the Evidence from Meta-Analyses—cont'd

TABLE 14.4 Completing a table for Olatunji et al. (2013) meta-analysis.

Author/ date	Number of studies and participants included	Primary outcome of the meta-analysis	Experimental treatments studied (include information about type and modality of treatment, delivery system, etc.)	Control treatment studied	Possible moderators	Mechanisms	Findings
Olatunji et al. (2013)	16 studies with 756 participants	OCD symptoms, measured with the YBOC or Children's YBOC	CBT (i.e., included exposure-based treatments or acceptance in which individuals participated in a feared activity even if it was disturbing)	Wait-List (WL) control or a psychological placebo condition, such as stress management training, relaxation, pill placebo, or anxiety management training	Age, type of control group, treatment type, illness severity, or comorbidity	Not assessed formally	Large effects of CBT (Hedges $g = 1.39$, $CI = 1.04 - 1.74$, $p < 0.001$). CBT worked better in children than adults, and CBT worked better when compared to WL control than psychological placebo.

Write a brief description of the results of the Olatunji et al. (2013) meta-analysis.

____

____

____

____

____

____

____

Activity 14.6. Recognizing Patterns in the Findings

As you read meta-analyses and original research articles, table the results, see if you can find patterns across the studies, and answer the following questions.

Do some studies support the use of this treatment? If so, which studies provide this support? Include the authors' names and year of publication.

____

____

How effective is the treatment overall? What proportion of participants get better?

____

____

____

____

____

Do some studies find that there are no effects of the treatment on the symptoms? If so, which studies do not find this evidence? Include the authors' names and year of publication.

____

____

____

____

____

Can you identify any variables that might explain the differences in treatment outcome? Do the outcomes differ depending on the disorder being tested? The sample? The treatment delivery system? The setting? The treatment modality? The therapist training?

____

____

____

____

____

description should also include the findings, including a description of the effect sizes, and the overall conclusions.

For example, the findings of a meta-analysis could be summarized using this template: "*In a meta-analytic review, Authors (date) indicate that there is evidence supporting the use of Treatment X to address symptoms of Disorder Y. Specifically, a total of # (supply the number) articles were included in this meta-analysis, permitting evaluation of the responses of #Y individuals.*

The data came from randomized controlled trials (RCTs) in which patients with disorder Y (and other disorders?) were studied. Treatments which were evaluated included A, B, and C. The findings indicate (small, medium, or large) effects of treatment A (or B or C) on symptoms of disorder Y (and other disorders)."

Identifying Threats to Validity and Gaps in Knowledge

Now, it is time to identify threats to internal and external validity and identify gaps in knowledge. We have identified many threats to validity and gaps in knowledge in Chapter 13. You can identify threats to validity on your own as you read research articles. You can also find them in the discussion and limitations sections of many original research articles. Meta-analyses also have sections devoted to identifying threats to validity and gaps in knowledge.

Writing the Gaps in Knowledge Section

Learning to recognize and write about these gaps in knowledge is critical to making effective scientific arguments. If you are writing a proposal for a treatment outcome study, the section summarizing gaps in knowledge serves to justify the study you are proposing. You justify the study by explaining the gaps in knowledge you have identified and how your proposed study will address those gaps.

If you are writing a research paper reviewing the treatments for the disorder you are studying, the section summarizing gaps in knowledge is the section in which you describe future research needs. You will link all relevant gaps in knowledge to ideas for future research.

More information about gaps in knowledge related to methodological problems with research is presented in Chapters 15-18 in which the methods used in research studies are explained in more detail.

Here is the section from the Piacentini et al. (2011) article in which the authors explain the gaps in the literature and the importance of closing those gaps to justify the study they have conducted (Fig. 14.9).

The need for expanded research in this area is driven by several additional concerns. Perhaps most important is the realization of substantial room for improvement in treatment outcomes for pediatric OCD, particularly in light of findings that more than one-half of study participants fail to achieve symptom remission in response to CBT,[7] regardless of treatment condition. One potential target for optimizing the efficacy of existing approaches is the inclusion of intervention techniques to address family factors that may undermine response.[15-17] In particular, accommodation (i.e., participation in rituals and/or modification of routines) is highly common among families of OCD youth[15,17] and may mediate the link between symptom severity and functional impairment.[17] Family accommodation is thought to be a barrier to treatment inasmuch as it reinforces avoidance behaviors and undermines exposure-based exercises.[15]

Unfortunately, research evaluating systematic efforts to address family accommodation and related factors is complicated by the heterogeneous nature of the literature with regard to the intensity and structure of family involvement, especially because some level of parental involvement in treatment is typically specified for OCD youth. Barrett et al.[4] attempted to clarify confusion over what constitutes a "family treatment" by defining individual child + family interventions (FCBT) as those treatments that specify structured weekly intervention sessions focused on changing family dynamics as opposed to primarily individual child treatments that include family members in a less structured or less frequent manner, often as a brief check-in at the end of individual sessions. Using this definition, only two studies, one Type 1 (N = 77)[12] and one Type 2 (N = 40),[18] have critically evaluated FCBT, and only one[18] found post-treatment changes in family dynamics, with families receiving intensive FCBT demonstrating greater reduction in family accommodation compared with those receiving weekly treatment. Moreover, in a partially overlapping sample of children receiving FCBT through one of two separate open-label studies (N = 49), decreases in family accommodation over the course of treatment predicted reduced symptom severity and OCD-related impairment post-treatment.[19] Although these findings require replication under controlled conditions, they suggest that efforts to target relevant family dynamics may lead to improved treatment outcomes.

Finally, only one prior published controlled FCBT trial for childhood OCD has employed a credible psychosocial comparison condition.[20] Although that study included a relaxation training comparison condition similar to that used here, that study was primarily a feasibility trial (N = 42) that was not powered to address efficacy adequately and that differed from the current study in several important ways, including a the use of a parent-focused, play-therapy protocol designed for use with 5- to 8-year-old children. As a result, generalization of findings to youngsters more than 8 years of age, who comprise the largest share of treatment-seeking youth with OCD, is limited. Unfortunately, the absence of rigorous comparative efficacy data for exposure-based CBT versus a credible psychosocial intervention limits conclusions about the efficacy of this treatment and its active ingredients, and impedes its potential classification as a "well-established" or even "probably efficacious" evidence-based intervention according to current guidelines.[4,10]

FIGURE 14.9 Selected excerpts from Piacentini et al. (2011).

Notice how the authors justify their research by making a series of critical points about the public health significance, the mechanism, and the need for methodological rigor.

1. From a public health perspective, the authors point to a need for improved treatment approaches, as many children fail to improve using current methods.
2. From a TOP perspective, the authors hypothesize that addressing a mechanism known to maintain OCD symptoms

will improve outcomes. They document the limited research in this area.

3. From a methodological rigor perspective, they point to threats to internal validity which have limited the interpretation of prior studies. Specifically, they focus on limitations to the control treatments/conditions in existing studies, making it difficult to know which treatments provide the best outcomes. They also identify threats to external validity, pointing out that prior treatment has focused on young children, 5–8 years. They emphasize the need to include older children as well, as they are more likely to seek treatment.

Activity 14.7: Writing a Summary of Gaps in Knowledge

Now it is your turn. Write a summary of two threats to validity identified in the meta-analysis or original research article you are reading for your paper or proposal. See if you can identify and describe future directions for research that would address those gaps.

Wrapping up the TOS: Proposing the Study or Providing Future Directions

If you are writing a proposal, the final paragraphs of the TOS provide an overview of the gaps you wish to address and the methods you will use to address these gaps. In this chapter, you learned about gaps in knowledge related to limitations to the effects of treatment, to the delivery system or modality, or to the choice of control conditions. In Chapters 15–18, you will consider more detailed methodological difficulties that may create gaps in knowledge. You may add gaps or refine your discussion of gaps as you learn more about study methods.

Here are some possible examples based on the treatment effects, treatment delivery methods, or limited control conditions.

The treatment outcome research has focused only on treatment delivered using a (identify a modality or delivery system) format. In this case, you may be addressing this gap by testing a new approach—maybe a web-based or group treatment.

The treatment outcome research has not included _________ individuals (identify characteristics or diagnoses of individuals who are likely to need treatment but have not been studied, such as children or people with comorbid disorders, etc.). In this case, you may be proposing that you will address this gap by treating this group.

The treatment outcome research has not included active control conditions or control conditions which permit identification of the active ingredient in the experimental treatment. In this case, you may be proposing an active control group, particularly one which contains all the elements of the experimental treatment except the active ingredient.

Next, you explicitly state the hypothesis you wish to test and provide a brief overview of the methods. In treatment outcome studies, this generally involves specifying the characteristics of the sample, identifying the experimental and control conditions, and describing the primary outcome.

Here is an example of the summary of the findings and overview of the study from the Piacentini et al. (2011) article (see Fig. 14.10). In this summary, Piacentini et al. (2011) provide a brief overview of the state-of-the-science and gaps in knowledge, list their hypotheses, and describe their methods. They make the connection between gaps in knowledge and their hypotheses and methods.

Notice Piacentini et al. (2011) clearly describe the contrast between the experimental and control conditions. In an experimental study to evaluate treatment outcome—a randomized controlled trial—the contrast between the experimental and control treatment is a very important consideration that affects the internal validity of the study. As we discussed in Chapter 12, the hypothesis that the researchers can test depends on the differences between the experimental and control conditions.

Let's look back at the example in Fig. 14.10. Piacetini et al. (2011) point out that the control condition they chose, Psychoeducation and Relaxation, provides many components which are equivalent to those in the Family- and Child-Based CBT. They

> The goal of the current study was to examine, in randomized controlled fashion, the efficacy of a manualized multi-component treatment that included individual child–focused exposure-based CBT plus a concurrent family intervention designed to facilitate family disengagement from the affected child's OCD symptoms (FCBT) and a comparison individual treatment comprising psychoeducation about OCD and systematic relaxation training. The PRT included several active elements common to quality CBT to enhance its credibility and to provide a more stringent test of FCBT. Despite earlier negative trials,[13,14] more recent studies have found exposure-based CBT to be superior to psychosocial comparison treatment for youth with non-OCD anxiety.[21,22] Based on these studies as well as prior adult OCD research,[23] we hypothesized that FCBT would prove superior to PRT in reducing OCD severity, associated impairment, and family accommodation of OCD symptoms. In addition, and to provide more information regarding the potential mechanisms underlying FCBT, we also examined the temporal relationship between changes in family accommodation and changes in OCD symptom severity and impairment.

FIGURE 14.10 Selected excerpt from Piancentini et al. (2011).

write that this control condition permits them to provide an active comparison treatment which may also improve OCD. If the Family and Child treatment does better, they can claim the introduction of the Family Component and Child CBT is better than other active treatments.

When you describe the control condition, it is important to indicate how the control condition will address a gap in knowledge, and to identify the differences between the experimental and control conditions.

Here is a template for writing about your choices for the experimental and control conditions:

> *Prior studies have used several types of controls (provide a list of active and no-treatment controls). There have been limited tests using XXX type of control conditions. In this study, we propose using a XX control condition. The Experimental and Control conditions are matched for characteristics including (list common*

factors and any other variables that are the same across the two conditions). The Experimental treatment differs from the Control Condition only in XX. Since the treatments will be matched for all components except XX, the study will permit us to test if the experimental component produces a change in outcomes.

If you are writing a paper reviewing the research on treatment outcomes, you use this section to review the primary gaps in the literature and identify future directions for research. The future directions could include the need for different control conditions or different delivery formats, depending on the gaps in knowledge identified. State the gaps in simple and clear sentences. Tie the future directions to the gaps you have identified.

Putting it all Together

The TOS section of your proposal or paper has many different components. Here we list all the sections that should be included. Check to see if you have all components. Ask a colleague or classmate to read through these sections to make sure the ideas and writing are clear (Table 14.5).

TABLE 14.5 Components of the proposal.

Component for proposal	Components for paper reviewing treatments	Does your proposal or paper have this section?
Description of treatment, including all components, delivery format, modality, setting, and therapist qualifications	Description of treatment, including all components, delivery format, modality, setting, and therapist qualifications	
Description of potential mechanism of action	Description of potential mechanism of action	
Evidence about the effects of treatment	Evidence about the effects of treatment	
Threats to internal and external validity in existing research	Threats to internal and external validity in existing research	
Identification of gaps in knowledge	Identification of gaps in knowledge	
Summary of proposed study	Directions for future research	

Building Human Capital

This section on the TOS has been hard work! You learned to find and read treatment outcome studies and meta-analyses of these studies. You learned how to think critically as you identified threats to validity. You learned to make careful scientific arguments as you specified gaps in knowledge that should be addressed and proposed strategies to address them.

Each step of the way you wrote sections of your paper or proposal. You worked to write clear straightforward sentences. You tried to eliminate ambiguity from the research and from your writing. You have learned to take a complex problem and break it into smaller steps, working on each part in turn. You developed some trust in the process. You noticed that if you are conscientious in your work, and take it one step at a time, you can accomplish a lot.

Now that you have finished this section, you can be proud of your perseverance and your new skills in critical thinking and writing).

Terms

Take the time for find the definitions and consider how to apply these terms.

Research Terms

literature review
gaps in knowledge
threats to validity
scientific premise

References

Freeman, J. B., Garcia, A. M., Coyne, L., Ale, C., Przeworski, A., Himle, M., ... Leonard, H. L. (2008). Early childhood OCD: Preliminary findings from a family-based cognitive-behavioral approach. *Journal of the American Academy of Child & Adolescent Psychiatry, 47*(5), 593–602.

Olatunji, B. O., Davis, M. L., Powers, M. B., & Smits, J. A. (2013). Cognitive-behavioral therapy for obsessive-compulsive disorder: A meta-analysis of treatment outcome and moderators. *Journal of Psychiatric Research, 47*(1), 33–41.

Piacentini, J., Bergman, R. L., Chang, S., Langley, A., Peris, T., Wood, J. J., & McCracken, J. (2011). Controlled comparison of family cognitive behavioral therapy and psychoeducation/relaxation training for child obsessive-compulsive disorder. *Journal of the American Academy of Child & Adolescent Psychiatry, 50*(11), 1149–1161.

Part 4

Methods

Chapter 15

Methods: Participant selection and ethical considerations

In the first 14 chapters, you learned how to conceptualize research. Now in the final section of the book, covering Chapters 15–18, you will learn how research is put into practice and the ideas are implemented. These chapters discuss in more detail the research methods used to test hypotheses and evaluate theories.

The methods of a study are written in a *methods section*. The methods section of a proposal or original research paper is like a general instruction manual for the study. The different parts of the methods section describe decisions about the characteristics of participants; measurement methods and instruments; procedures for experimental manipulations, treatments, and assessment; and data management and analyses. As you read the methods section of an article, you will understand how the researchers translated ideas into action.

The activities in these chapters cover strategies for choosing participants, measures, and procedures. Once you have completed these activities, you will be able to communicate the ways in which you intended to translate your hypotheses into action. The methods section describes all the materials and processes necessary to test hypotheses.

To ensure methodological rigor, the choice of methods is influenced by the most up-to-date knowledge about the field. The characteristics of the study participants reflect knowledge gained from studies of the epidemiology of the disorder. The choices of measurement methods are influenced by the measurement strategies used in other basic and applied research studies of the

Psychology Research Methods. https://doi.org/10.1016/B978-0-12-815680-3.00015-3

disorder and by research from studies of the best methods in assessing variables. The methods used to control for extraneous variables are influenced by limitations identified in prior research and basic research on the nature of the problems you are studying.

As you work through the next four chapters, you will learn about the process of designing a research study and writing a methods section.

In Chapter 15, you will learn more about the structure of the methods section and the strategies involved in choosing participants for a research study. This chapter also provides information about ethical considerations in research.

In Chapter 16, you will learn about how to choose and measure all the variables included in the study.

In Chapter 17, you will learn about the procedures used to implement each step of the study. You will learn more about research procedures used to control for experimental bias.

In Chapter 18, you will learn about and practice writing the methods section. As you write the methods section, you include enough detail to enable other scientists to evaluate what you have done, and potentially replicate and extend the study. The methods section you write for your proposal will provide the reader with a clear understanding of the study methods. The information is needed to determine the strengths and weaknesses of the approach for testing the hypotheses.

Components of the Methods Section

The methods section generally has many different components. In this section of the book, we focus primarily on describing the methods of treatment outcome studies focusing on human (vs. animal) participants. We will describe each of the components of the methods section, with very limited attention to the data management and analyses strategies. Information about writing data management and analyses strategies can be found in a work by Gerin, Kapelewski, Itinger, and Spruill (2010). The different sections of the methods are identified in Table 15.1.

TABLE 15.1 Components of a methods section and their purpose.

Components	Purpose
1. Overview: A brief description of the entire study. Usually just a few sentences long.	To provide the reader with a "big picture" understanding the methods. The researcher can include information about the type of participants, the nature of the research design (i.e., experimental, correlational, longitudinal, etc.), and the primary outcome measures.
2. Participants: A description of the participants.	To provide information about the eligibility criteria (i.e., inclusion and exclusion criteria) to help the reader understand the individuals for whom the outcomes and knowledge apply. To help the reader recognize the limits to generalizability (external validity).
3. Measures: A section describing the measurement methods and measurement instruments.	To provide information about the variables the researchers use to represent the constructs in the theory. In a correlational study, this section includes information about the predictor and outcome variables. In an experimental study, this section includes information about primary, secondary, and other dependent variables. Information is provided about the timing and procedures for assessment. This information is necessary for identifying threats to internal validity, including issues with the observation of assessments and the expectations of participants and researchers. This information is also necessary to provide information about the degree to which the study assesses whether outcomes generalize over time, a potential threat to external validity. (In a correlational study, information about the research design is provided here. The discussion of the timing indicates whether a cross-sectional or longitudinal approach is being used.)
4. Independent variables: A description of the experimental manipulations, if applicable. In a treatment outcome study, this section provides information on the experimental and control treatments.	To provide information about the predictor/independent and the designs used to test the relations among these variables. This section will help the reader clarify the hypotheses being tested. Information is also provided about the ways in which researchers will insure the reliability and validity of the experimental manipulation—the delivery of the levels of the independent variable. In an experimental study, information about the research design is often included here. The details about the process of random assignment are included. Specific information about controlling for bias in the assignment of experimental and control conditions is discussed.
6 A section identifying potential sources of bias and strategies for controlling bias.	To provide information about any other potential threats to internal validity and strategies for addressing these threats.
7. A section describing the plans for the data management and data analysis.	To provide information about the statistical methods to be used to manage the data and evaluate the outcomes.

Making Choices About the Methods to Use

Researchers choose methods that allow them to achieve scientific rigor. They are trying to find a way to test their hypothesis and limit threats to internal and external validity. But the approach they choose must be feasible and cost-effective. Table 15.2 includes a list of the methodological issues the researchers must consider.

TABLE 15.2 Issues to consider when choosing research methodology.

Components of research design	Major issues to consider	Dimensions to consider			
Strategies for choosing and recruiting participants	Balancing efficiency of recruitment with the need for a sample representative of the population	Type of sampling: Population-based sampling or convenience sampling	Eligibility criteria (i.e., inclusion and exclusion criteria)	Recruitment strategies (e.g., focused on general population or targeted population)	
Strategies for measuring variables	Insuring reliability and validity of measurement	Source of the data: Self-report Experts (doctors, teachers) Family Peers Researcher Instrumentation	Methods of data collection: Surveys Diaries Interviews Tests Tasks Observation Physiological recording		
Strategies for assessing effects—choosing the right research design	Balancing tight experimental control versus ecological validity	Qualitative versus quantitative approach	Observational/correlational versus Manipulation/experimental approach Or quasi-experimental approach	Cross-sectional versus longitudinal approach	Laboratory studies Observational field studies Workplace/structured settings

TABLE 15.2 Issues to consider when choosing research methodology.—cont'd

Components of research design	Major issues to consider	Dimensions to consider			
Strategies for controlling sources of bias that can influence the outcome	Minimizing bias: Controlling extraneous variables, participant bias, and experimenter bias	Controlling participant bias: Blinding, Careful subject selection, Randomization Reducing demand characteristics-Controlling expectancy and Observer effects	Controlling experimenter bias: Double-blinding, Controlling halo effects	Controlling unintended or extraneous variables in the procedures or setting	Insuring the reliability and validity of measurement tools and the procedures (i.e., treatment fidelity)

Let's look at an example to understand how researchers weigh the costs and benefits of different approaches. In the Smith et al. (2017) study, the authors are searching for low-intensity treatments for depression that are inexpensive and can be widely distributed (Fig. 15.1). Low-intensity treatments are treatments which are low cost and which do not require substantial resources from a treatment provider. These types of treatment are necessary because there are many people who cannot afford or do not want to engage directly with a therapist face-to-face.

Internet Interventions 9 (2017) 25–37

Contents lists available at ScienceDirect

Internet Interventions

journal homepage: www.elsevier.com/locate/invent

Help from home for depression: A randomised controlled trial comparing internet-delivered cognitive behaviour therapy with bibliotherapy for depression

Jessica Smith[a], Jill M. Newby[a,b,*], Nicole Burston[a], Michael J. Murphy[a], Sarah Michael[a], Anna Mackenzie[a], Felicity Kiln[a], Siobhan A. Loughnan[a], Kathleen A. O'Moore[a], Benjamin J. Allard[a], Alishia D. Williams[a,c], Gavin Andrews[a]

[a] Clinical Research Unit for Anxiety and Depression (CRUfAD), University of New South Wales at St Vincent's Hospital, Darlinghurst, NSW, Australia
[b] School of Psychology, University of New South Wales, Australia
[c] Department of Social and Behavioural Sciences, Utrecht University, the Netherlands

ARTICLE INFO

Keywords:
Depression
Internet-delivered cognitive behavioural therapy
Bibliotherapy

ABSTRACT

Major Depressive Disorder (MDD) is a leading cause of the Global Burden of Disease. Cognitive Behavioural Therapy (CBT) is an effective treatment for MDD, but access can be impaired due to numerous barriers. Internet-delivered CBT (iCBT) can be utilised to overcome treatment barriers and is an effective treatment for depression, but has never been compared to bibliotherapy. This Randomised Controlled Trial (RCT) included participants meeting diagnostic criteria for MDD (n = 270) being randomised to either: iCBT (n = 61), a CBT self-help book (bCBT) (n = 77), a meditation self-help book (bMED) (n = 64) or wait-list control (WLC) (n = 68). The primary outcome was the Patient Health Questionnaire 9-item scale (PHQ-9) at 12-weeks (post-treatment). All three active interventions were significantly more effective than WLC in reducing depression at post-treatment, but there were no significant differences between the groups. All three interventions led to large within-group reductions in PHQ-9 scores at post-treatment (g = 0.88–1.69), which were maintained at 3-month follow-up, although there was some evidence of relapse in the bMED group (within-group g [post to follow-up] = 0.09–1.04). Self-help based interventions could be beneficial in treating depression, however vigilance needs to be applied when selecting from the range of materials available. Replication of this study with a larger sample is required.

FIGURE 15.1 Abstract and methods from Smith et al. (2017).

1. Introduction

Depressive Disorders – including Major Depressive Disorder (MDD) – are a global public health concern and a leading cause of disease burden (Ferrari et al., 2013), with burgeoning individual and societal costs (Ustun et al., 2004). Recent NICE (2009) guidelines recommend non-drug interventions such as cognitive behavioural therapy (CBT) as a first line treatment for mild to moderate depression (www.nice.org.uk/CG90), but dissemination of CBT can be limited due to inadequate resources (Shapiro et al., 2003), particularly in certain geographical locations (Cavanagh, 2014). To address these treatment barriers, there has been a recent surge in innovative ways to deliver CBT (Andersson et al., 2012), specifically in the development of more accessible internet and computerised therapies for the treatment of common mental disorders (Marks et al., 2003).

← In this section, the authors explain the PHS and the need for the study. The authors explain the need for low intensity interventions which could be more easily delivered to many people.

The authors then go on to explain internet-based CBT therapies.

Internet-delivered CBT (iCBT) programs are based on face-to-face CBT treatment manuals, and typically deliver psycho-education and the key CBT skills (e.g., cognitive restructuring, behavioural activation) via lessons or modules, supplemented with homework activities and practical exercises to complete between lessons. The concept of 'guided iCBT' typically takes the form of a therapist or coach supporting the patient throughout the course; this is a distinct difference to unguided iCBT which takes place without support - a purely 'self-help' format.

The stages in CBT for depression can be generalised and represented in manuals and 'self-help' books. Bibliotherapy - including self-help books - are commonly used to teach self-help tools and strategies (Den Boer et al., 2004), with their usefulness to treat depression - when compared to controls - largely supported (Gregory et al., 2004). However as numerous self-help books are widely available for depression - whereby a specific self-help program is presented and is typically worked through independently - the evidence-base to support them is relatively small (McKendree-Smith et al., 2003), making their impact difficult to establish.

← The authors explain how bibliotherapy - reading self-help books - may help people manage their depressive symptoms. The authors describe the purpose of the study.

It is not known whether guided iCBT represents an advance in efficacy over the numerous CBT self-help books widely available for treating depression. This question is especially pertinent in an increasingly digital age; however access to the internet is not completely ubiquitous, especially for those on lower incomes (Cline and Haynes, 2001) and those living in rural and remote areas where internet access can be limited. Therefore the first aim of the current study was to compare an evidence-based guided iCBT course (Perini et al., 2009), the 'Sadness' program, versus unguided access to a self-help book based on CBT for depression. Participants in the CBT self-help book group were provided with a leading self-help book free of charge, 'Beating the Blues' (Tanner and Ball, 2012), which they completed without any form of guidance.

FIGURE 15.1 (*Continued.*)

2. Method

2.1. Design

The current study utilised a randomised controlled trial design to compare an iCBT program, a CBT self-help book, a meditation self-help book, to a wait-list control for participants meeting diagnostic criteria for MDD. Participants were assessed at pre-treatment, mid-treatment, post-treatment and at 3 months post-treatment.

← This section provides an overview of the study, explaining the different levels of the independent variable and the randomized controlled trial design.

2.2. Inclusion/exclusion criteria

Inclusion criteria were: (i) aged over 18 years (ii) prepared to provide contact details of their General Practitioner (iii) had access to internet and printer, (iv) resident in Australia, (v) fluent in written and spoken English, (vi) a score between 5 and 23 on the Patient Health Questionnaire 9-item scale (PHQ-9), (vii) met criteria on the Mini International Neuropsychiatric Interview Version 5.0.0 (MINI) (Sheehan et al., 1998) for DSM-IV criteria for MDD on structured telephone diagnostic interview, (vii) if taking medications for anxiety or depression, were on a stable dose for at least 8 weeks at time of intake interview, and (viii) had not commenced face to face CBT within 4 weeks at time of intake interview. Exclusion Criteria included psychosis or bipolar disorder, drug or alcohol dependency, benzodiazepine use, severe depression PHQ-9 total scores > 24, or current suicidality.

← Section 2.2 and parts of section 2.4 describe the participants in the study. In section 2.2, the authors describe the inclusion and exclusion criteria. Then in section 2.4, the authors explain how many people were recruited, how many were eligible for participation, and how many were assigned to the different levels of the independent variable.

Finally, in section 2.9 the authors explain the power analysis they performed to determine how many participants they needed to test their hypotheses.

2.4. Participant flow

Details of the participant flow are displayed in Fig. 1. A total of 1143 applicants applied online for the study between May 2013 and February 2015. Of these, 549 applicants were excluded after completing initial online screening questions and received an email with information about alternative services. Five hundred and ninety four applicants passed the online screening phase and were telephoned for a diagnostic interview. A further 324 individuals were excluded at telephone interview stage, leaving 270 applicants who met inclusion criteria and were randomised.

Eligible participants were randomised based on a random number sequence generated at www.random.org by an independent person not involved in the study. Group allocation numbers were concealed from the interviewer with the use of opaque sealed envelopes, which were opened once the applicant was deemed eligible to participate. Participants provided electronic informed consent before being enrolled in the study. This study was approved by the Human Research Ethics Committee (HREC/13/SVH/29) of St Vincent's Hospital Sydney, Australia. The trial was prospectively registered on ANZCTR (ACTRN12613000502730).

2.3. Procedure

← In section 2.3, the authors explain how participants were recruited. They explain how they tested participants to determine if they met the inclusion and exclusion criteria.

Participants were recruited via the Virtual Clinic (www.virtualclinic.org.au), the research arm of the Clinical Research Unit for Anxiety and Depression, based at St Vincent's Hospital, Sydney and the University of New South Wales. Potential applicants viewed advertisements in the form of leaflets and posters and on social media. Applicants completed online screening questionnaires about demographic information and depressive symptoms as assessed on the PHQ-9 (Kroenke et al., 2001), after reading details about the study. Participants who met online screening criteria then participated in a brief telephone interview. Trained interviewers administered a structured diagnostic interview which consisted of the Mini International Neuropsychiatric Interview Version 5.0.0 (MINI) (Sheehan et al., 1998) MDD and risk assessment modules to confirm whether applicants met for DSM-IV criteria for MDD. Full risk assessment modules (where necessary) were completed by a psychiatry registrar to assess suicidal ideation and determine suitability for the study.

FIGURE 15.1 *(Continued.)*

2.5. Interventions

2.5.1. Sadness program (iCBT)

The Sadness program was delivered through www.virtualclinic.org.au. The program has been evaluated in four previous trials and its efficacy has been established (Perini et al., 2008, 2009, Titov et al., 2010, Watts et al., 2013) (between-groups effect sizes: d = 0.8–1.3, within-group pre-post effect sizes: d = 0.9–1.0). The program consisted of 6 online lessons completed over a 12 week period and participants were instructed to complete one lesson every 1–2 weeks of the program. It follows an illustrated story, with a main character who learns how to manage her depressive symptoms using CBT skills. The program content delivers evidence-based CBT including psycho-education, cognitive restructuring, graded exposure, problem solving, effective communication and relapse prevention, with downloadable weekly homework documents (PDF) containing practical tasks to implement between lessons as well as extra resources and patient 'recovery stories' to read.

← In section 2.5, the authors explain each level of the four levels of independent variable: iCBT, Book 1 (Beat the Blues), Book 2 (Silence Your Mind), and Wait List Control.

2.6. Clinician contact

All participants completing the iCBT course received email and/or phone contact with the technician after the first two lessons to answer any questions about the program and to encourage them with the remainder of the course, then as requested. In cases of increased distress, particularly elevated distress and or suicidal intent was reported, the clinician made contact with the participant. Participants in the bCBT and bMED groups with elevated distress were emailed to inform them that their distress was elevated and where to get appropriate external support. The clinician did make contact with participants in these groups who reported suicidal intent.

← In section 2.6, the authors explain how contact with clinicians is a component of iCBT. Participants in other treatments will be contacted by cliniciansif they are suicidal or otherwise in need of emergency help.

In section 2.5, they explain how therapists contacted participants. This contact is a part of the iCBT program.

↘

2.5.2. Beating the Blues (bCBT) (Tanner and Ball, 2012)

This is a self-help book designed to help people overcome depression and was posted to participants in this group, along with a short (one page) welcome letter from the book authors introducing participants to the concept of cognitive therapy and advising them to tackle the issues presented in the book systematically and one at a time. Participants were asked to work through each of the 12 chapters over 12 weeks and advised to read roughly one chapter per week. The book is self-guiding: the content is based on CBT and organised into various parts, including: Understanding Depression, Our Thinking Habits, Looking After Your Needs and Living with Someone Who is Depressed. The course content is presented in Table 6. Questionnaires and reminders to complete questionnaires were emailed to participants in this group with clinical contact occurring only if a participant reported active suicidal intent. In cases of elevated or increased distress response scores, participants were emailed to advise them where to gain additional support - including telephone counselling numbers, visiting their general practitioner or Emergency Services. No guidance or encouragement was offered.

2.5.3. Silence your mind (bMED) (Manocha, 2013)

This is a self-help book aimed at teaching people to meditate and was posted to participants in this group, along with an instructional DVD, information booklet and a brief (two page) letter from the author introducing participants to the mediation technique described in the book and advising them to practice the technique for at least 10 min per day. Participants were asked to work through each of the 13 chapters over 12 weeks and advised to read roughly one chapter per week. The book is self-guiding: the content is based on a meditative approach called Mental Silence and is organised into various parts, including: What is Meditation, Meditation is Mental Silence, Health, Wellbeing and the non-mind, Helping our Young People, Flow and Optimal Being, and The Brain in Meditation. The course content is presented in Table 7. Questionnaires and reminders to complete questionnaires were emailed to participants in this group with clinical contact only occurring if a participant reported active suicidal intent. In cases of elevated or increased distress response scores, participants were emailed to advise them where to gain additional support - including telephone counselling numbers, visiting their general practitioner or Emergency Services. No guidance or encouragement was offered.

2.5.4. Wait-list control group (WLC)

Participants randomised to the wait-list control (WLC) were able to continue with any course of treatment already specified at intake interview but were withdrawn from the study if they commenced a new treatment during the course of the 12 week waiting period, for example

FIGURE 15.1 (*Continued.*)

In section 2.7, the authors explain all the measurement methods and instruments to assess diagnosis, outcomes, and potentially extraneous variables. The details are included in each of the sections 2.7.1 – 2.7.4.

2.7. Measures

2.7.1. Diagnostic status

The *Mini International Neuropsychiatric Interview Version 5.0.0* (MINI (Sheehan et al., 1998)) MDD and risk assessment modules were administered at intake, and then again at 3 month follow-up for the intervention group participants (assessors were not blinded to the intervention condition).

← In section 2.7.1 they describe themeasurement instruments they use to assess depression to insure the participants meet the inclusion criteria.

In sections 2.7.2 and 2.7.3, the authors explain the instruments they use for the primary outcome and the secondary outcome. ↘

2.7.2. Primary outcome measure

The *Patient Health Questionnaire – 9* (PHQ-9, (Kroenke et al., 2001) is a 9-item self-report scale that was used to assesses DSM-IV criteria for MDD. Participants were asked to rate the frequency of symptoms (including frequency of suicidal ideation with the question "thoughts that you would be better off dead, or of hurting yourself in some way"), over the past two weeks. The scale range is: 0 = not at all, 1 = several days, 2 = more than half of the days and 3 = nearly every day, with total scores ranging from 0 to 27. The PHQ-9 has shown to have excellent reliability and validity (0.86; (Kroenke et al., 2001).

2.7.3. Secondary outcome measures

The *Kessler-10 Psychological Distress Scale* (K10; (Kessler et al., 2002) is a 10-item self-report scale that was used to measure non-specific psychological distress over the past two weeks. Rated on a 5-point scale, higher scores indicate higher distress levels. The K10 has excellent psychometric properties (Furukawa et al., 2003).

The *Generalised Anxiety Disorder 7*- item scale (GAD-7; (Spitzer et al., 2006)) was used to measure generalised anxiety disorder symptoms over the past two weeks on the same 4-point scale as the PHQ-9. Scores range from 0 to 21, and this scale has good reliability and validity (0.83; (Spitzer et al., 2006).

The *NEO-Five Factor Inventory - Neuroticism Subscale* (NEO-FFI, (Costa and McCrae, 1985)) is a 5-point self-report scale which was used to measure the personality dimension of Neuroticism and has good psychometric properties (Cuijpers et al., 2005).

2.7.4. Expectancy of benefit and patient satisfaction

Prior to the start of their respective intervention, participants in iCBT, bCBT and bMED were asked to provide a treatment expectancy rating. Participants were asked to provide a rating ranging from 1 to 9 about how logical the therapy offered to them seemed, and how successful they thought the treatment will be in reducing their symptoms of depression (where 1 = not at all, 5 = somewhat, and 9 = very). To examine treatment satisfaction, participants were asked at post-treatment i) how satisfied they were that the program taught them the skills to manage depression and ii) their confidence in recommending the program to a friend with similar problems (range: 1 = not at all, 5 = somewhat, and 9 = very).

← In section 2.7.4, the authors explain other measures they use to assess extraneous variables that may distort the results of the study. In this study, the authors regard expectations about treatment as one of the potential extraneous variables.

In section 2.8, the authors explain the timing of all the measurements– when they give the tests.

2.8. Outcome measurement

At baseline, participants provided basic demographic details (e.g., age, marital status, gender, employment and educational history), depression history and treatment, and current comorbid physical illnesses (6 questions from the 2007 National Survey of Mental Health and Wellbeing (Teesson et al., 2011).

All four groups completed outcome measures at baseline, mid-point (Lesson 4 for iCBT and week 6 for the book groups and WLC), post-treatment (one week after Lesson 6 for iCBT or at the end of the 12 weeks for the book groups and WLC) and at 3-month follow-up (for iCBT and the book groups only). The iCBT group completed the K10 before commencing every lesson.

FIGURE 15.1 (*Continued*).

The Smith et al. (2017) study specifically examines the effects of low-intensity treatments. They compare three different types of low-intensity treatments: Internet-based cognitive behavioral therapy (iCBT) and two types of bibliotherapy to a wait-list control. Bibliotherapy involves providing books that individuals can read on their own to treat their symptoms. The authors examine the effects of these treatments on symptoms of depression. The researchers hypothesize that each of the low-intensity interventions will be better than the wait-list control approach in reducing depressive symptoms.

As we consider the study hypotheses, you can see how they influence each aspect of the methods from choosing participants to administering the interventions. We can examine the links between the hypotheses and the methods.

Participants. In sections 2.2–2.4 of Fig. 15.2 the authors describe the participants in the study and how they recruited them. As the authors are testing treatments for depression, they must include those who are depressed. But because they are testing the effects of low-intensity treatments, they must make sure the treatment is appropriate for the level of depression. In this case the authors exclude people with severe depression or other severe psychiatric illness because these individuals are likely to need more intensive treatments than are being offered in the current study.

The treatments require reading and some computer expertise. Therefore, they choose participants who can read and speak English, since all the treatments are presented in written English.

Independent variable. In section 2.5 of Fig. 15.1, the authors describe the levels of the IV. The IV is treatment and the researchers include three types of active treatments: iCBT, a self-help book providing instructions for meditation, and a self-help book providing instruction on CBT for depression. They provide information about each active treatment so the reader can understand how the different books or iCBT may produce different outcomes.

Measurement. In section 2.7 of Fig. 15.1, the authors explain the way they measure the outcomes. They provide information about the two different measures of depression they use (i.e., one self-report and one interview measure). The use of these two different measures permits them to understand if the treatment affects both internal perceptions of depressive symptoms and observable signs of depression.

The authors also provide information about the timing of the **assessments.** If they want to test the hypothesis that these interventions provide lasting effects, they need to measure the outcomes at some point after the therapy has finished. They choose to measure outcomes at four points in time: before treatment, midway through treatment, at the end of treatment, and 3 months later.

In the following sections of the chapter, you will learn how to consider each component of the methods for conducting the research.

Choosing Participants

The part describing research participants includes a description of the research participants' characteristics, the methods for obtaining these participants, and the strategies used to protect their rights (Table 15.3). The criteria for including participants in the study must be clearly linked to the study hypotheses. The justification for the choice of participants must reflect the most up-to-date information on the epidemiology and characteristics of the condition and the nature and demands of the intervention.

TABLE 15.3 Information included in the participants component.

Sections of the participants' component	Purpose
The size of the sample, n	To identify the number of participants to be included in proposed study.
Eligibility criteria: Inclusion and exclusion criteria	To clarify the characteristics that the participants must have to be included in the study, and to identify the characteristics which would exclude the participants from the study.
Recruitment procedures	To describe the procedures used to recruit the participants into the study.
Ethical procedures for conducting research	To describe procedures for informing participants about the study, for obtaining consent for participation, and for protecting the participants' rights.

As you work through this chapter and consider the human participants' component for a research proposal, you will answer these questions:

- How many participants are needed and how do you know?
- What are the inclusion and exclusion criteria that guide the choice of participants?
- How do you recruit these participants to volunteer for the study?
- How do you protect the rights of human participants?

If you are writing a proposal to study treatment outcome, the participants' component describes the types of participants you intend to recruit and why. In a paper reviewing studies about a treatment, you examine the component describing the participants in the articles you review. You examine this component to understand the choices the researchers made about participant selection and determine if those choices presented threats to internal or external validity.

The Number of Participants Needed (n)

Choosing the correct number of participants is a complex task, but it is critical for the internal validity of the study. If you do not recruit and test enough participants, you will not be able to test the hypothesis. The test of the hypothesis may fail because you don't have enough participants to show a difference between levels of the independent variable (IV). On the other hand, if you choose too many participants, you are wasting resources. And you may end up with a statistically significant effect, even if the effect is very small and may not have clinical relevance.

The decision about the number of participants to recruit is based on the size of the effect you expect and the variability in responses across participants. In a treatment outcome study, the expected **effect size** reflects both the magnitude of the difference in scores between the levels of the IV (i.e., the experimental and control conditions) and the variability among the scores.

How do you find out the magnitude of the effect you should expect? You can read other articles and look at the size of the differences in the means (or estimates) for the experimental and control group. In many cases researchers conduct a small **pilot study** to get an idea of the size of the difference between the groups. A pilot study is a preliminary study that is designed to provide an initial test of the hypothesis or to determine the feasibility of the approach or the variability in response.

Researchers look at more than the size of the difference in the scores for the experimental and control groups. Researchers also look at the variability in the scores. Not everyone will respond to the experimental and control treatments in the same way. Some people may improve, some may improve a little, and others may get worse. Therefore, an effect size reflects both differences among the levels of the IV and variability among the scores.

Power analyses. In general, to find the number of participants you will need to recruit, it is necessary to conduct a **power analysis**. A power analysis tells you how many participants you need to test to have adequate statistical power to test your hypotheses. Power refers to the likelihood that you will reject the null hypothesis when it is reasonable to do so.

In psychology we accept a power level of 0.80, and an alpha level of 0.05. When researchers establish a sample size designed to give them 80% power (power = 0.80), they are indicating that they are willing to accept a level at which about 80% of the time they will be correct in rejecting the null hypothesis if the p level is below 0.05 (Faul, Erdfelder, Lang, & Buchner, 2007). In Fig. 15.2, notice the description of the power analyses and sample size provided for the Smith et al. (2017) study.

2.9. Power calculations

Prior to commencement of the trial, a power calculation was conducted to set the minimum sample size needed. At 0.8 power (alpha = 0.05), 100 participants per group were needed to have the power to detect a 0.4 effect size difference in efficacy between groups. However, due to unanticipated difficulties with recruitment during the time-period set out for the study, the final sample (N = 270) fell short of the sample size needed (N = 400).

FIGURE 15.2 Example of power analysis calculation from Smith et al. (2017).

For a simple study, you can conduct power analyses yourself using an online power calculator. Check out online tools and power analyses. The following webpage includes examples of online power calculators for various research designs: http://statpages.info/#Power. For more complex designs, researchers often hire a statistical consultant who can guide them in conducting these power analyses.

Eligibility Criteria

The eligibility criteria for a study include both the inclusion and exclusion criteria. The **inclusion criteria** include the characteristics the participants must have to be in the study, and the **exclusion criteria** include the characteristics the participant must *not* have to be in the study. These criteria must be set correctly to avoid threats to internal validity. But the eligibility criteria also create limits to the external validity of the findings.

A study may face a threat to internal validity, if the inclusion criteria are not clear, specific, or consistently applied. The researchers must describe the criteria used to determine if the participants have the condition (or the risk factor) that the treatment is designed to treat. If the criteria are not clear or applied consistently, treatment outcomes may be difficult to interpret. For example, the treatment might fail, but the researcher does not know if the failure to get the expected results occurred because the treatment didn't work *or* because the participants didn't have the disorder the researcher was studying.

The study may also face a threat to internal validity if the researcher does not exclude participants with other conditions that may affect their ability to respond to treatment. If the researcher does not exclude people with other disorders, then it is unclear if the treatment didn't work because it is not an effective treatment *or* if it does not work because the treatment is not intended to work with people who have other disorders.

On the other hand, if all people with other disorders are excluded from the study, there will be limits to the generalizability of the findings—a threat to external validity. The results may indicate that the treatment is effective, but the researcher does not yet know if the treatment can be effective for people with other disorders.

Applying the Eligibility Requirements

As you generate the eligibility criteria (the inclusion and exclusion criteria), you balance the need to protect the internal validity of the study against the desire to generalize the results across different populations and conditions.

For example, if you are studying depression, the inclusion criteria must include having symptoms of depression.

But what should the exclusion criteria be? The epidemiological literature indicates that many people with depression are almost four times more likely than those without depression to also have a substance use disorder, and other research suggests that people with substance use disorders are more likely to be depressed (Grant et al., 2015; Lai, Cleary, Sitharthan, & Hunt, 2015). If you are focusing your treatment on depression, should you exclude people who have a substance use disorder?

If your treatment is targeted specifically at depressive symptoms, then including participants with substance use disorder symptoms may be problematic. The substance use symptoms may not respond to this treatment. Therefore, if the treatment does not appear to work, then it is unclear if the treatment does not work or if the substance use symptoms are limiting the success of the treatment.

On the other hand, there will be significant limits to external validity—the generalizability of the findings to most people with depression. This will occur if many individuals with depression have substance use disorders and you exclude all people with those disorders.

Applying the Eligibility Criteria. To operationalize the inclusion criteria, researchers specify the assessment strategies they will use to determine if the potential participant meets the criteria. For example, if one inclusion criteria is having a diagnosis, the assessment strategies can include tests or interviews that are used to determine if the participant meets diagnosis criteria for the disorder. Activity 15.1 provides some practice in applying the eligibility criteria.

Activity 15.1: Eligibility Criteria

Review the eligibility criteria listed in the methods section of the article presented in Fig. 15.3. See if you can determine what the inclusion and exclusion criteria are. Identify how and when participants were assessed for eligibility in each article. We complete Table 15.4 to answer these questions: Why did the researchers use these methods? What are possible advantages and disadvantages of these methods in terms of efficiency, threats to internal validity, and threats to external validity?

Next complete Table 15.4 with an article you are using for your proposal or paper.

Activity 15.1: Eligibility Criteria—cont'd

Behaviour Research and Therapy 77 (2016) 86–95

Contents lists available at ScienceDirect

Behaviour Research and Therapy

journal homepage: www.elsevier.com/locate/brat

Internet-delivered acceptance-based behaviour therapy for generalized anxiety disorder: A randomized controlled trial

Mats Dahlin [a], Gerhard Andersson [b, c, *], Kristoffer Magnusson [c], Tomas Johansson [e], Johan Sjögren [e], Andreas Håkansson [e], Magnus Pettersson [e], Åsa Kadowaki [f], Pim Cuijpers [g, h], Per Carlbring [d]

[a] Psykologpartners, Private Practice, Linköping, Sweden
[b] Department of Behavioural Sciences and Learning, Linköping University, Linköping, Sweden
[c] Department of Clinical Neuroscience, Karolinska Institute, Stockholm, Sweden
[d] Department of Psychology, Stockholm University, Stockholm, Sweden
[e] Department of Psychology, Umeå University, Umeå, Sweden
[f] Region Östergötland, Linköping, Sweden
[g] Department of Clinical Psychology, VU University Amsterdam, The Netherlands
[h] EMGO Institute for Health and Care Research, The Netherlands

A R T I C L E I N F O

Article history:
Received 1 February 2015
Received in revised form
8 December 2015
Accepted 15 December 2015
Available online 21 December 2015

Keywords:
Internet-based behaviour therapy
Generalized anxiety disorder
Randomized controlled trial
Acceptance
Mindfulness

A B S T R A C T

Generalized anxiety disorder (GAD) is a disabling condition which can be treated with cognitive behaviour therapy (CBT). The present study tested the effects of therapist-guided internet-delivered acceptance-based behaviour therapy on symptoms of GAD and quality of life. An audio CD with acceptance and mindfulness exercises and a separate workbook were also included in the treatment. Participants diagnosed with GAD ($N = 103$) were randomly allocated to immediate therapist-guided internet-delivered acceptance-based behaviour therapy or to a waiting-list control condition. A six month follow-up was also included. Results using hierarchical linear modelling showed moderate to large effects on symptoms of GAD (Cohen's $d = 0.70$ to 0.98), moderate effects on depressive symptoms (Cohen's $d = 0.51$ to 0.56), and no effect on quality of life. Follow-up data showed maintained effects. While there was a 20% dropout rate, sensitivity analyses showed that dropouts did not differ in their degree of change during treatment. To conclude, our study suggests that internet-delivered acceptance-based behaviour therapy can be effective in reducing the symptoms of GAD.

FIGURE 15.3 Abstract and selected excerpts from Dahlin et al. (2016).

Continued

Activity 15.1: Eligibility Criteria—cont'd

2. Material and methods

2.1. Recruitment and inclusion

Participants were recruited via advertisement on the internet and two websites, www.studie.nu and www.kbt.info/oro. As a result of an initial slow recruitment flyers were posted on the campuses of Linköping University and Umeå University and in the central city of Umeå. Participant were requested to go to the website to learn more about the study and register for participation. The web site included a description of the study's purpose and an outline, as well as a presentation of the people involved and a instruction on how to register for the study. After registration the participants were asked to complete a battery of online measures which consisted of Penn State Worry Questionnaire (PSWQ) (Meyer, Miller, Metzger, & Borkovec, 1990), Generalized Anxiety Disorder Questionnaire-IV (GAD-Q-IV) (Newman et al., 2002), Generalized Anxiety Disorder Scale-7 (GAD-7) (Spitzer, Kroenke, Williams, & Lowe, 2006), Beck Anxiety Inventory (BAI) (Beck, Epstein, Brown, & Steer, 1988), Montgomery Åsberg Depression Rating Scale Self-Assessment (MADRS-S) (Svanborg & Åsberg, 2001), Patient Health Questionnaire-9 (PHQ-9) (Kroenke, Spitzer, & Williams, 2001), and Quality of Life Inventory (QOLI) (Frisch, Cornell, Villanueva, & Retzlaff, 1992). Previous studies have demonstrated good psychometric properties of online administration of pencil and paper questionnaires (Andersson, 2014; Carlbring et al., 2007). The screening phase also included questions concerning ongoing or prior treatments and demographic data.

Inclusion criteria were: (a) minimum 18 years old, (b) a Swedish postal address, (c) 45 points or more on the PSWQ, (d) 30 points or less on MADRS-S, (e) meeting the diagnostic criteria for GAD (according to the DSM-IV), (f) no ongoing alcohol or substance abuse, (g) no ongoing psychological treatment, (h) if on medication it should be on a stable dose (at least three months with same dosage) and (i) no active suicidal ideation. Participants meeting at least criteria a-d in the online screening were subsequently contacted for a diagnostic interview over the telephone. The interview was used as a way to ensure that all inclusion criteria were fulfilled through questions regarding eventual uncertainties from the online screening and through a diagnostic interview based on the Structural Clinical Interview for DSM-IV Axis I disorders (SCID-I) (First, Gibbon, Spitzer, & Williams, 1997). Four graduate students, with training in SCID, conducted the interviews under supervision. The purpose of the diagnostic interview was to determine the presence of GAD (criteria e) and the absence of severe depression. It consisted of two parts from SCID-I: the Research Version for Generalized Anxiety Disorder (SCID-I RV, GAD), and the Clinical Version for Depression (SCID-I CV, Depression). The result from the online screening and the interview were discussed in a referral group consisting of the four students, a licensed psychiatrist and two clinical psychologists. In total 215 individuals registered on the study's website and finally 103 participants met the inclusion criteria. We did not exclude persons with a previous history of psychological treatments but required that treatment had to be finished. Included participants were invited to take part in the study and were randomized to either treatment or a control condition. A flowchart showing registration, inclusion, randomization and dropout is presented in Fig. 1. Demographic data on the 103 participants is presented in Table 1.

← Notice that in the description of the inclusion criteria the authors also include the exclusion criteria. They do this by writing that participants must NOT have certain characteristics to be eligible.

FIGURE 15.3 *(Continued)*.

Activity 15.1: Eligibility Criteria—cont'd

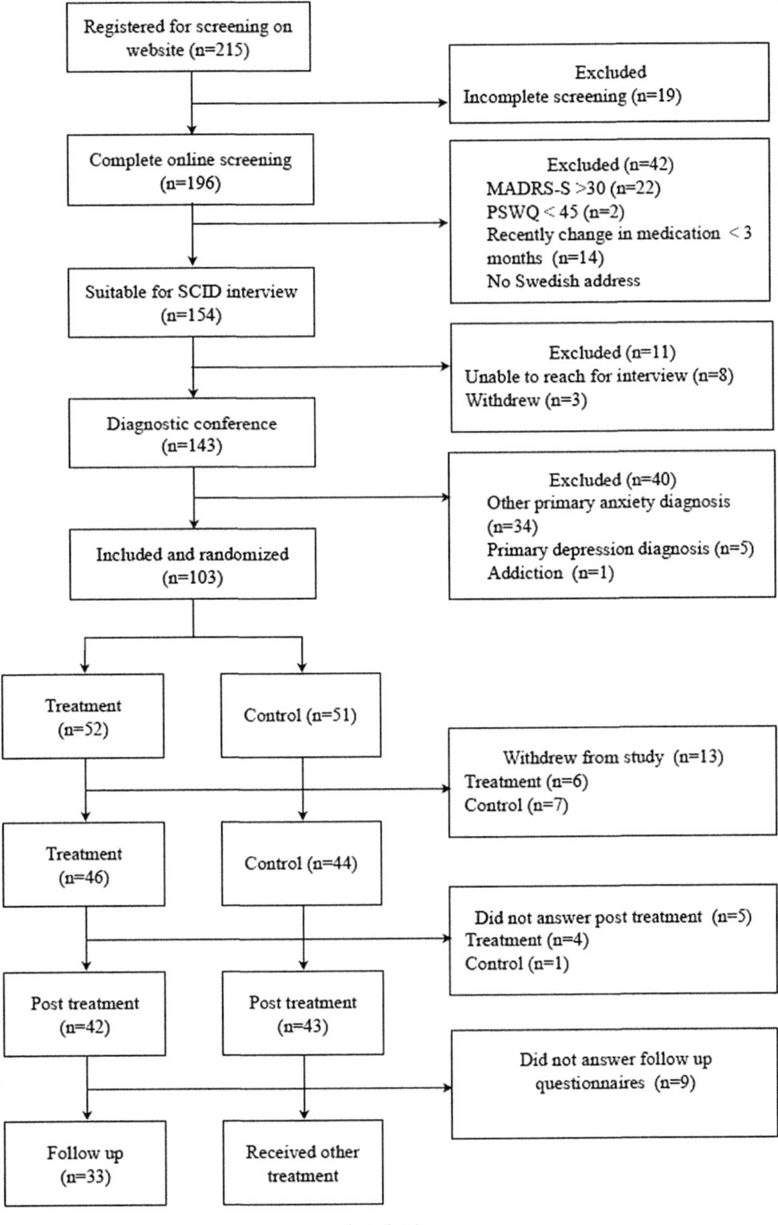

Fig. 1. Flowchart.

FIGURE 15.3 *(Continued).*

Continued

Activity 15.1: Eligibility Criteria—cont'd

TABLE 15.4 Eligibility criteria.

Author/ date	Eligibility/ inclusion criteria	Methods of assessment	Exclusion criteria	Why were people with these conditions excluded from the study?	Benefits and costs of inclusion and exclusion criteria
Dahlin et al. (2016)	- At least 18 years of age - Swedish postal address (indicating full time resident in Sweden) - Meet criteria for GAD according to DSM-VI - Have sufficient symptoms to warrant treatment (i.e., scores of 45 or above on Penn State Worry Questionnaire (PSWQ))	Initial eligibility is evaluated through online surveys inquiring about worry, anxiety, and other symptoms. If patients met initial inclusion criteria, then a follow-up structured diagnostic interview was performed.	- No active suicidal ideation - No current alcohol or substance use disorder - No current psychotherapy - Medication regimen is likely to be changed during the study	**Safety concerns:** Internet therapy may not be adequate for very distressed patients. **Comorbidity concerns:** The treatment is specific to GAD, so if participants have other difficulties, including substance use disorders, these other symptoms may obscure benefits of treatment. **Concerns about internal validity:** If patients are in other treatments it may not be clear which treatment is producing the outcome.	**Benefits**: The sample includes people with GAD including those who are less likely to have substance use comorbidities. People who can complete the initial online surveys used to establish eligibility are also likely to be able to handle the technical demands of Internet therapy. **Limitations**: It is unclear if people with other comorbidities are excluded. Many people with GAD also abuse substances, so there may be limits to the generalizability of the findings. The authors will not know if this treatment could

Activity 15.1: Eligibility Criteria—cont'd

TABLE 15.4 Eligibility criteria.—cont'd

Author/ date	Eligibility/ inclusion criteria	Methods of assessment	Exclusion criteria	Why were people with these conditions excluded from the study?	Benefits and costs of inclusion and exclusion criteria
				Concern about internal validity: If medications are changed during the study, it may not be clear if it is the medication change or the experimental treatment that is producing the effect.	work with many people affected by GAD who also have substance use problems.

Recruitment Strategies

Recruitment strategies are the strategies used to attract and engage participants into the research study. For population-based sampling, in which every member of a population has an equal chance of being recruited, researchers choose individuals at random from the general population. Once individuals are identified as potential participants (e.g., their numbers have been chosen), research assistants call and try to recruit them into the study. Some will agree, others will not.

For convenience sampling, the procedures are different (Etikan, Musa, & Alkassim, 2016). Researchers can use many strategies to "get the word out"." They can recruit from the general population by advertising in social or print media or on radio or TV. They can post flyers in areas in which potential participants might see them. They can recruit from services for individuals with the target disorder (e.g., doctor's office or programs for people with those conditions). They can ask healthcare providers or existing participants to refer others to the study.

There are costs and benefits associated with each of these approaches, and there are implications for the external and internal validity of the study. We can consider the costs and benefits of each recruitment strategy by evaluating its efficiency and effectiveness in obtaining participants who meet the eligibility criteria. We can also examine the effects of the recruitment approach on the characteristics of the participants likely to be recruited using this method (see Table 15.5).

TABLE 15.5 Examples of strengths and limitations of different approaches to recruitment.

Recruitment strategy	Strengths	Limitations
From mental health clinics and doctor's offices	**Efficiency and effectiveness**: The sample is generally prescreened. Many people with the condition may be available.	The sample may be limited to people with more severe or disturbing symptoms.
	Participant characteristics: Participants are likely to be motivated for treatment. Participants are familiar with treatment process.	The researcher won't know if the new treatment will work with individuals who are less motivated or less capable of obtaining services on their own. The researcher won't know if the treatment will work with individuals who are less familiar with the processes of psychological therapy.
Recruiting from the general population through media advertisements	**Efficiency and effectiveness:** The method can reach many people at once.	Many people may not have the disorder. The researcher will have to carefully screen participants for eligibility.
	Participant characteristics: Participants may vary in the intensity of the symptoms of the disorder. Participants may come from more diverse backgrounds.	Some of the diversity in characteristics may present limitations to the internal validity of the study, depending on the hypothesis. Researchers will need to determine if participants have comorbid disorders or other conditions or circumstances that may undermine the response to treatment.

In a treatment outcome study, recruiting participants through their mental healthcare providers may be an effective and efficient method. This approach will provide participants who are already identified as having a disorder, and therefore, are likely to pass the eligibility requirements for a study of that disorder. This recruitment strategy is likely to be efficient as researchers will not have to screen many people to find the few participants who have the disorder.

This strategy may also affect some important participant characteristics, including motivation for and experience with psychological treatment. Participants who have already experienced treatment may be individuals who are motivated to get help.

On the other hand, participants recruited from healthcare providers' offices may have other characteristics that could be problematic and limit the interpretability of the findings. First, if they are already receiving treatment, many participants may not want more treatment. Participants who are recruited from the offices of their mental healthcare providers already have some experience with treatment. Therefore, the researcher will not know if the new treatment works with individuals who have never had any therapy experience. Participants who are recruited from mental healthcare providers may also have more education or income than others, and this may limit the researchers' ability to determine if the treatment works with those who have fewer resources.

Activity 15.2: Identifying Recruitment Strategies

We can take another look at the Dahlin et al. (2016) paper.

Describe the recruitment strategies used in the Dahlin et al. (2016) article.

____
____
____
____
____

Now look at the limitations section of the article (Fig. 15.4).

Continued

Activity 15.2: Identifying Recruitment Strategies—cont'd

There are at least three important limitations to the study. First, as with many ICBT studies we used a self-recruited sample and the level of education was very high (e.g., many had a university education). Moreover, even if GAD is common among women there were few men in the trial. Second, we used a waiting-list control group and while we did collect weekly ratings from all participants an active control group with a credible control treatment would have answered the question of the relative merits of internet-delivered acceptance-oriented behaviour therapy. A non-inferiority study against our previous ICBT program would have required a much larger sample. Third, we used mainly self-report outcomes and comorbidity was only partly assessed (depression). In light of recent transdiagnostic forms of ICBT (Titov et al., 2014) it would have been informative to see how much these comorbid conditions would be influenced by a specific treatment for GAD.

FIGURE 15.4 Limitations of Dahlin et al. (2016) study.

Do the authors identify limitations to their ability to interpret the data as a function of the types of recruitment strategies they used? If yes, explain.

____

____

____

____

____

Now try this with an article you are using for your research. What recruitment strategies did the authors use? How do these recruitment strategies place limitations on the interpretation of the findings?

____

____

____

____

____

Ethical Conduct of Research

When people choose to participate in research, it is a great gift to the researchers. The researchers have an obligation to treat that gift with respect. A code of conduct for the ethical treatment of research participants has been developed. This conduct emerged from moral concerns and respect for those who participate in the research process.

This code of conduct and the principles of human participants research are described in the Belmont Report. Here is the link to Belmont report (https://www.hhs.gov/ohrp/regulations-and-policy/belmont-report/index.html).

This code of conduct was also developed as a function of significant maltreatment of research participants and an international consensus that this maltreatment is unacceptable.

For more information, see:

Brandt, A. M. (1978). Racism and research: The case of the Tuskegee Syphilis Study. *Hastings Center Report, 8*(6), 21–29.

Jones, J. H. (1993). Bad Blood: Tuskegee Syphilis Experiment. Simon & Schuster (Eds.). The Free Press, New York, NY.

Office of Human Research Protections (https://www.hhs.gov/ohrp/regulations-and policy/regulations/45-cfr-46/index.html)

NIH Office of Extramural Research: Protecting Human Research Participants (Certificate Course) https://phrp.nihtraining.com/users/login.php

Principles of Ethical Conduct. The overall ethical approach emphasizes the rights of the individual to make informed and free choices about participation in research. Ethical treatment of research participants centers around three **principles of ethical conduct**: respect for persons, beneficence, and justice. There are also principles that apply specifically to the treatment of animals in research.

Beneficence and Justice

Research can have both costs and benefits. The principles of ethical conduct require researchers to consider important questions when evaluating their own research.

- Are the benefits and costs of the study distributed fairly?
- Are the costs/risks minimal compared to the benefits for the individual and society?

When recruiting human participants into research, it is important to take care to make sure their rights are respected. If the study is a high-risk study, the costs must be distributed fairly across all types of people. High-risk research cannot be limited to individuals who are vulnerable, including those who are poor or otherwise marginalized. Similarly, high potential benefit studies cannot be limited to those with more advantages.

Respect for Persons

When individuals participate in research, they are choosing to give their time and to share their ideas, feelings, actions, or physiological responses with the researchers. This is a precious contribution. And the individuals making this contribution must be treated with respect and care.

All research participation must be voluntary, and individuals must have the right to withdraw. They must be informed about the purpose, procedures, risks, and benefits of the study. Their participation in the research and responses to study materials, including responses to the tests or interviews or surveys, must be kept confidential. When it is appropriate, participants are compensated for their time and effort. But the level of compensation must not be so high that participants will take on excessive risks to receive the reward.

Institutional Review Boards. In the past, researchers did not always protect the safety and rights of their research participants, particularly when they belonged to marginalized communities. A history of some of the most egregious examples of rights violations can be found in https://www.cdc.gov/tuskegee/timeline.htm.

To ensure this protection, institutions, including schools and hospitals, have established **Institutional Review Boards** (IRBs). These boards are composed of community members and a wide variety of experts. The members of the IRBs evaluate research to determine the benefits of the research and to identify potential costs or risks to the participant. They determine if the protections against risk are adequate, and if the strategies used to inform individuals about the study (including its risks and benefits) are appropriate and effective. All studies conducted at a university or college must be reviewed by an IRB.

Informed Consent. Researchers must develop an **informed consent form** which explains the study, the procedures, the risks, and the benefits for participants. The informed consent must be written in clear language at the participants' reading level, to make sure that the participants understand what participation requires. It can be helpful to review the consent directly with the participants by reading it out loud together or highlighting each point. The procedure for reviewing the consent with the participants must include time for the participants to ask questions. The study cannot be truly voluntary if participants are not making an informed choice.

Notice that the consent form provides information about the purpose of the study and the risks and benefits of participation.

The consent form also communicates important information about the participants' rights, including the right to withdraw at any time.

Participants are entitled to confidentiality. The consent also emphasizes the ways in which the **confidentiality** of the participants' data will be protected. This means the researchers must tell the participants who will have access to their data, and they must protect the data from being released to or observed by others. The consent form provides contact information of the investigator and the chair of the IRB, so the participants will know who to contact with questions or concerns.

Fig. 15.5 is a sample of a consent form we used in one of our studies:

ST. JOHN'S
UNIVERSITY

Informed Consent for the study entitled: Stress, working memory and health study

You are being asked to take part in a research study. The aim of this study is to understand the ways stress affects mood, and health behavior. Stress may be related to the way you feel and the decisions you make to support your health.

This study will take about 15 minutes of your time. You will be given surveys which ask about your background (i.e., age, education, and other factors); your experiences of different kinds of stressors, including discrimination, your mood and health habits, including use of cigarettes and alcohol, among other behaviors.

We do not provide you with specific feedback about your responses to the questionnaires. Instead, we will provide all people who participate with information about mental health resources. If you notice you are indicating health concerns and wish for assistance in making an appointment with a health provider, we can offer you assistance at the time.

There are no physical risks to participation. You may become uncomfortable as we ask about life stressors and symptoms. If you become distressed, you can ask to speak to the Principal Investigator, Dr. Elizabeth Brondolo. She is a licensed clinical psychologist.

The cost to you for participating in this study is the time you spend participating. To compensate you for the time you spend participating, you will receive breakfast as well as $10. You may also feel good about helping to investigate the effects of stress on health.

It is your choice to participate in the study. You may withdraw from the study at any time. Your decision to participate or not to participate will not affect your education, employment or treatment in any way. You may skip any questions you do not wish to answer.

All information collected in this study will be treated confidentially. You will be assigned a study number, and this number and not your name will be attached to all information. All information gathered in this study will be kept in a password protected computer file at St. John's University. In line with Food and Drug Administration (FDA) and National Institutes of Health (NIH) guidelines, research records will be kept for 7 years upon completion of the study. After these 7 years, staff members at St. John's University will shred and dispose of these records.

The results of this study may be published using information from all the participants in the study as a group. Your name will not be published and no one will be able to identify you from any published information.

If you have questions about this study, you can directly contact Dr. Elizabeth Brondolo, the principal investigator of the study, at [phone number] or at [email]. If you have general questions about participating in research, you may call [name], Chair of the Institutional Review Board of St. John's University at [phone number].

FIGURE 15.5 Example of an informed consent.

CONSENT TO PARTICIPATE IN THE
STRESS, WORKING MEMORY AND HEALTH STUDY

I have read the above information about the Stress, Working Memory, and Health Study. I have asked all the questions that I have, and these questions have been answered. I give my consent to participate in a research project investigating stress, work memory, and health practices. I have been given a copy of this form for my own records and I have been told that I may ask additional questions as they arise at any time.

I understand that there are no significant physical risks associated with my participation.

I understand that I may withdraw my consent to participate in this project at any time and signing this form does not take away my legal rights.

____
Participants' name (print)

____
Participant's signature/date

____
Research assistant signature and date

FIGURE 15.5 (*Continued*).

The Use of Deception

Sometimes researchers must use deception in their research. In these cases, if the participants have knowledge of the purpose or procedures of the study, the study results will not be interpretable. For example, studies of the "bystander effect" investigate whether people will help others if they observe them experiencing a harmful or dangerous situation. The researchers cannot generally tell the participants that the researchers are studying whether people will act in an empathic way toward a bystander. This knowledge would likely change the participants' behavior. And it would be impossible to tell if the participants acted the way they did because they had empathy or because they knew they were being observed.

Therefore, researchers will provide a cover story to explain the study.

When researchers use deception, they must justify the need for deception. The IRB will carefully examine that the benefits of deception outweigh the risks. Researchers must document that the study could not be done without deception. This is critical, since it is not possible to give full informed consent if you do not know what the purpose of the study is. Therefore, at the end of the study, the investigators debrief the participants and provide information about the true nature of the study. And they discuss the participants' reactions to the deception.

Building Human Capital

When you conduct research, you and your participants are in it together. To the extent possible, they need to understand why this research is important. They need to know what risks they are undertaking and what benefits they may gain.

It would be a good idea to take part in a research study yourself. Many schools have programs where students can participate in faculty or graduate student research. Ask about opportunities to participate.

If you feel reluctant to participate in research at all, think about why? Are you worried about confidentiality or about possible harm to you? About finding something out about yourself that you don't want to know?

What would make you feel more comfortable or more willing to participate? Does the informed consent form for the study address your questions? Have you noticed how researchers try to address those concerns?

As you examine these issues, think about what you would do if you were the researcher. How do you want to treat the participants in a study you are conducting?

Terms

Take the time to define each of these terms and consider how to apply them.

Research Terms

Assessment
Effect Size
Pilot Study
Power Analysis
Alpha Level
Power
Eligibility Criteria
Recruitment Strategies
Ethical Conduct of Research
Belmont Report
Principles of Ethical Conduct of Research
Institutional Review Board
Confidentiality
Informed Consent

References

Dahlin, M., Andersson, G., Magnusson, K., Johansson, T., Sjögren, J., Håkansson, A., … Carlbring, P. (2016). Internet-delivered acceptance-based behaviour therapy for generalized anxiety disorder: A randomized controlled trial. *Behaviour Research and Therapy, 77*, 86–95.

Etikan, I., Musa, S. A., & Alkassim, R. S. (2016). Comparison of convenience sampling and purposive sampling. *American Journal of Theoretical and Applied Statistics, 5*(1), 1–4.

Faul, F., Erdfelder, E., Lang, A. G., & Buchner, A. (2007). G* power 3: A flexible statistical power analysis program for the social, behavioral, and biomedical sciences. *Behavior Research Methods, 39*(2), 175–191.

Gerin, W., Kapelewski, C., Itinger, J. B., & Spruill, T. (2010). *Writing the NIH grant proposal: A step-by-step guide*. Sage Publications.

Grant, B. F., Goldstein, R. B., Saha, T. D., Chou, S. P., Jung, J., Zhang, H., … Hasin, D. S. (2015). Epidemiology of DSM-5 alcohol use disorder: Results from the national epidemiologic survey on alcohol and related conditions III. *JAMA Psychiatry, 72*(8), 757–766.

Lai, H. M. X., Cleary, M., Sitharthan, T., & Hunt, G. E. (2015). Prevalence of comorbid substance use, anxiety and mood disorders in epidemiological surveys, 1990–2014: A systematic review and meta-analysis. *Drug and Alcohol Dependence, 154*, 1–13.

Smith, J., Newby, J. M., Burston, N., Murphy, M. J., Michael, S., Mackenzie, A., … Williams, A. D. (2017). Help from home for depression: A randomised controlled trial comparing internet-delivered cognitive behaviour therapy with bibliotherapy for depression. *Internet Interventions, 9*, 25–37.

Chapter 16

Methods: Measuring variables

In this chapter we discuss the methods for measuring the study variables. The strategies used to measure variables are described in the section entitled "*Measures*" in the Methods Section of an article. In the Measures portion of the Methods section, researchers justify and describe their choices of the **measurement methods** and **measurement instruments**. These sections are critical to establishing the scientific rigor of the study.

As we discussed in Chapter 2, choosing the measurement method requires choosing the source of data and the method used to collect the data (i.e., surveys, instrument, etc.). Choosing a measurement instrument requires identifying a specific instrument which is both reliable and valid. If the measurement method is appropriate to test the hypothesis and the measurement instruments are reliable and valid, the internal validity of the study will be strengthened.

If you are writing a research proposal for a treatment outcome study, you will include a description of the measures you plan to use to measure the variables in the study. If you are writing a paper evaluating existing research, you review the measurement methods of other studies. You describe the approach used in the articles you review and consider issues in internal and external validity raised by the measurement approach the authors employed.

Components of the Measures Part of the Methods Section

In general, a **measures section** describes the instruments used to measure the variables in the study and sometimes also includes information about the timing of measurement. The descriptions of

Psychology Research Methods. https://doi.org/10.1016/B978-0-12-815680-3.00016-5

the measurement instruments generally identify the variable the instrument is measuring, explain the measurement method, provide a description of the type of scores the instrument provides, and also offer some information about the psychometric properties of the instrument, including information on the reliability and validity of the measurement instrument. See Table 16.1.

TABLE 16.1 The measures components.

Information	Purpose
Operational definition of the variable, including the source of the data and the measurement method.	To clarify the specific variable that will be assessed.
Name and description of each measurement instrument.	To identify the specific measurement instrument to permit the reader to obtain information about the way the variable was assessed. This permits the reader to understand how the measurement method is linked to the hypothesis.
Information on reliability and validity of each measurement instrument.	To provide detailed information about the quality of the measurement instrument.

The measurement methods depend on the hypotheses to be tested. For example, some hypotheses include variables which involve internal experiences, some include variables that involve observable behavior, and others include variables that involve responses to laboratory tasks or standardized tests. Data on variables which involve internal experiences (e.g., thoughts or feelings) may be collected from the participant himself or herself, using self-report measurement instruments. In contrast, data on variables which focus on observable behavior (e.g., social behavior or health behavior) require the researcher to collect the data through observational methods. These observations may come from the researcher or from those who know the participant well, such as coworkers, bosses, teachers, or family members.

The choice of a specific measurement instrument depends on the **reliability** and **validity** of the instrument. **Measurement reliability** refers to the degree to which the measurement instrument elicits consistent scores. Depending on the study, it may be important to have:

- consistency in scores across different questions in a survey;
- consistency in scores across different raters who are observing behaviors; or
- consistency in scores across different measurement periods.

Measurement validity refers to the degree to which the measurement instrument assesses the construct it is intended to measure. Different types of measurement validity capture the degree to which scores on the measurement instrument:

- reflect the full range of characteristics associated with the construct;
- are associated with other measures of the construct; or
- are correlated with scores on measures of other variables in ways that are consistent with existing theories about the construct.

Let's look at an example of a measures section in a research article. The article by Dear et al. (2015) describes a randomized controlled trial to test different approaches to treating generalized anxiety disorder (GAD). Notice how the authors identify every measure they include and identify the role (e.g., primary outcome, secondary outcome) of each measures. They provide details on the reliability and validity of each instrument (Fig. 16.1).

2.2.1. Primary measure

Generalized anxiety disorder 7-Item scale (GAD-7; Spitzer et al., 2006).

The GAD-7 is a 7-item measure of the symptoms and severity of general anxiety, which is based on the DSM-IV diagnostic criteria for GAD (Löwe et al., 2008). The GAD-7 has good internal consistency and good convergent and divergent validity with other anxiety and disability scales (Kroenke et al., 2010a; Dear et al., 2011). Scores range from 0 to 21 and Cronbach's α in the current study was .87.

2.2.2. Secondary measures

Patient health questionnaire-9 Item scale (PHQ-9; Kroenke et al., 2001a)

The PHQ-9 is a 9-item measure of symptoms of depression based on the DSM-IV diagnostic criteria for major depressive disorder (Kroenke et al., 2001b). The PHQ-9 has good internal consistency (Titov et al., 2011) and is sensitive to change (Kroenke et al., 2010b). Scores range from 0 to 27 and Cronbach's α in this study was .84.

Mini-social phobia inventory (MINI-SPIN; Connor et al., 2001).

The 3-item MINI-SPIN is a measure of social anxiety symptoms based on DSM-IV criteria for social anxiety disorder (Connor et al., 2001; Weeks et al., 2007). The MINI-SPIN has good internal consistency and adequate convergent validity with other standardized measures of social anxiety (Weeks et al., 2007; Osório et al., 2010). Scores range from 0 to 12 and Cronbach's α in this study was .88.

Panic disorder severity scale—self report (PDSS-SR; Houck et al., 2002).

The PDSS-SR is a 7-item measure of panic disorder symptoms. Psychometric evaluations suggest that it has high internal consistency, good test-retest reliability and is sensitive to treatment-related change (Houck et al., 2002). Scores range from 0 to 28 and Cronbach's α in the current study was .92.

← This section presents the primary outcome measure. GAD symptoms are the primary outcome because the study is designed to test the hypothesis that the interventions will reduce GAD symptoms.

The authors describe the measurement instrument, the GAD-7. They explain the development of the measure and how it is linked to DSM-IV diagnostic criteria.

The authors provide a description of the way the responses are scored. The authors also provide information about the internal consistency of the measure when they report the Cronbach's alpha = .87.

FIGURE 16.1 Measures section from Dear et al. (2015).

2.2.3. Tertiary measures

Kessler 10-item scale (K-10; Kessler et al., 2002).

The K-10 is a ten-item measure of general psychological distress with total scores ≥22 associated with a diagnosis of anxiety and depressive disorders (Andrews & Slade, 2001). Scores range from 0 to 50 and Cronbach's α in the current study was .87.

Sheehan disability scale (SDS; Sheehan, 1983).

The SDS is a 3-item measure of disability with high internal consistency (Leon et al., 1997). Scores range from 0 to 30 and Cronbach's α in the present study was .85.

NEO-five factor inventory—neuroticism subscale (NEO-FFI-N; Costa & McCrae, 1985).

The neuroticism subscale of the NEO is a 12-item measure of a general tendency to experience negative emotional states and sensitivity to stress (Clark et al., 1994; Griffith et al., 2010), which is considered a higher-order risk factor for anxiety and depression (Cuijpers et al., 2005; Spinhoven et al., 2009). Scores range from 0 to 48 and Cronbach's α in the current study was .77.

2.2.4. Other measures

Mini international neuropsychiatric interview version 5.0.0 (MINI; Lecrubier et al., 1997).

The MINI is a brief diagnostic interview developed to determine the presence of current Axis-I disorders using DSM-IV diagnostic criteria. It has excellent inter-rater reliability and adequate concurrent validity with the composite international diagnostic interview (World Health Organization, 1990).

FIGURE 16.1 *(Continued.)*

Hypotheses and Measurement Methods

The choices of measurement methods depend on the researchers' conceptualization of the predictor and outcome variables and the hypothesis to be tested. At the start of the study, the researcher asks:

1. What measurement method should be used to collect the data on the predictor and outcome variables?

2. What or who should be the source of the data?

3. What measurement instrument should be used?

The answers to these questions about the source and type of data depend on the capacity of the source of the data to provide reliable reports; the ability of the measurement instruments to provide reliable and valid data; and the resources available to conduct the study.

We can look at an example.

Suppose researchers want to determine if a risk factor, such as trauma exposure, is linked to having a behavioral health disorder, such as GAD. First, the researchers must clarify their choice of constructs. Are they hypothesizing that trauma leads to a GAD diagnosis? Or do they think trauma increases GAD symptoms, even if the symptoms do not meet diagnostic criteria?

Second, the researcher must determine which variable or variables will represent that construct. Several variables can represent the construct "diagnosis," including self-reported diagnosis, healthcare provider diagnosis, and structured interview diagnosis.

The data on the variable can be collected using different measurement methods, including self-report surveys, structured interviews, medical charts, and expert observations. The source of the data can include the participant, a healthcare provider, or a researcher.

In the Dear et al. (2015) study described earlier, the researchers were examining the construct of GAD. They used the variable self-reported GAD symptoms to represent the construct of GAD. They used the GAD-7 scale as a measurement instrument to assess the GAD symptoms.

Considering the Source of the Data: Who Should Provide the information?

Data on symptoms, distress, and impairment can be provided by many different sources, including the participant himself or herself, a researcher observing or testing a participant, an expert interviewing or observing a participant, a family member or peer reporting on their observations of a participant, and from devices (e.g., an electronic diary) collecting information from a participant.

Each measurement method provides valuable information. But there are also limitations to each method. Identifying the costs and benefits of each method is part of the process of designing the study and recognizing the potential threats to validity.

Researchers testing hypotheses about risk factors which are associated with GAD diagnosis could use the variable self-reported diagnosis of GAD (Table 16.2). The measurement instrument might include a survey or an interview with questions that ask: "Are you currently diagnosed with GAD?" or "Have you ever been diagnosed with GAD?"

TABLE 16.2 Self-reported diagnoses of generalized anxiety disorder (GAD).

Question	Responses	
Did your healthcare provider tell you that you have GAD?	Yes	No
Have you ever received a diagnosis of GAD?	Yes	No

If they use this measurement method, they are assuming the participant's healthcare provider has made the correct diagnosis. Researchers are also assuming the healthcare provider gave the participant information about this diagnosis. And they are assuming the participant remembers the diagnosis and is willing to report it to the researcher.

If these assumptions are not met, the measurement instrument may not be valid—that is, the measurement instrument may not measure what it is intended to measure. Some people might report they do not have GAD despite having the diagnosis. Some people may have a GAD diagnosis but were not informed of this diagnosis by their healthcare provider or they might not have understood the diagnostic information. These difficulties can present a threat to the internal validity of the study.

To use the variable "Self-reported diagnosis of GAD," researchers need to document that participants can reliably provide information on their own diagnoses. They need to demonstrate that using self-reported diagnoses does not exclude many people who were unaware they had GAD.

Alternatively, researchers could use the variable "Healthcare provider diagnosed GAD." If they use this variable, the measurement method could include reviews of medical records. In this case, the diagnostic data come from the healthcare provider based on information provided by the patient (Table 16.3).

TABLE 16.3 Example of diagnostic data obtained from a healthcare provider.

Medical record for patient XX		
Problem list, including all formal diagnoses and complaints		
Date of visit	**Diagnosis**	**ICD-10 diagnosis code**
January 1, 2001	Generalized anxiety disorder	F41.1

Relying on medical record reviews assumes that all the healthcare providers apply the same criteria for diagnosing GAD in the same way. If they do not, the symptoms and impairments associated with GAD may vary across participants. This can present a threat to internal validity as not all participants may have the same types of symptoms.

There are also threats to external validity. If researchers use the variable "Healthcare provider diagnosed GAD," this approach may eliminate many people who do not have access to healthcare providers. These individuals will not have a medical record, so they will not be eligible for a study relying on medical records for the diagnosis.

As another approach, researchers could use a variable such as "Structured interview diagnosis of GAD." The participant is still providing information about GAD, but the information is obtained during a structured interview. A trained interviewer or a healthcare provider asks standardized questions about the symptoms of GAD. A standard algorithm is applied to the data from the participant to enable the interviewer to determine if a diagnosis of GAD applies to the participant. The algorithm indicates how many and what kinds of responses are needed to meet criteria for a diagnosis of GAD (Fig. 16.2).

FIGURE 16.2 "Structured interview".

Using the variable "Structured interview diagnosis" costs more time, effort, and money than using the variable "Self-reported diagnosis." But this approach insures that the procedures for collecting information on symptoms are consistent across participants. All participants receive the same questions. When participants have difficulty remembering or thinking about their symptoms, they receive the same types of prompts from the interviewers. This standardized approach can reduce threats to internal validity which are present if interviewers ask different questions or use different prompts.

As still another approach, you could use "Self-reported symptoms of GAD." Asking the participants to provide information about themselves is often the easiest and least expensive method for collecting data. The measurement instrument could be a survey which asks questions about the different symptoms of GAD. For example, the GAD-7 (Spitzer, Kroenke, Williams, & Löwe, 2006) used in the Dear et al. (2015) study is one example of a measurement instrument which assesses GAD and has been shown to be reliable and valid (Fig. 16.3).

Generalized Anxiety Disorder 7-item (GAD-7) scale

Over the last 2 weeks, how often have you been bothered by the following problems?	Not at all sure	Several days	Over half the days	Nearly every day
1. Feeling nervous, anxious, or on edge	0	1	2	3
2. Not being able to stop or control worrying	0	1	2	3
3. Worrying too much about different things	0	1	2	3
4. Trouble relaxing	0	1	2	3
5. Being so restless that it's hard to sit still	0	1	2	3
6. Becoming easily annoyed or irritable	0	1	2	3
7. Feeling afraid as if something awful might happen	0	1	2	3
Add the score for each column	+	+	+	
Total Score *(add your column scores)* =				

If you checked off any problems, how difficult have these made it for you to do your work, take care of things at home, or get along with other people?

Not difficult at all ________
Somewhat difficult ________
Very difficult ________
Extremely difficult ________

Source: Spitzer RL, Kroenke K, Williams JBW, Lowe B. A brief measure for assessing generalized anxiety disorder. *Arch Inern Med.* 2006;166:1092-1097.

FIGURE 16.3 GAD-7 scale.

If the researcher uses a measurement instrument to assess self-reported symptoms of GAD, he or she can use a standardized approach to determine if the type or intensity of symptoms meets criteria for a probable diagnosis of GAD. For example, scores on the GAD-7 of 5–10 indicate mild symptoms, scores between 10 and 15 indicate moderate symptoms, and scores of 15 or higher indicate severe symptoms. Those with scores above 15 can be considered to have a probable diagnosis of GAD, meaning it would be likely that they would be diagnosed by a mental healthcare provider as having a diagnosis of GAD.

It's worth noting that GAD diagnosis is a categorical variable with only two levels: Yes or No. But there may be consequences for individuals who have some symptoms, even if they do not have enough symptoms to meet the threshold for a diagnosis. A self-report survey or interview of symptoms can permit the researcher to assess the number of symptoms on a continuous scale.

Measurement Methods: How Should the Data Be Collected?

What is the best reliable, valid and efficient method for collecting data? Is a one-time survey adequate or would it be better to obtain data every day using electronic diaries? Are there standardized tests to measure the variable? Can the data be obtained through physiological recordings?

We can look at the costs and benefits of different approaches.

Surveys. Surveys are composed of a series of **items,** with the scores on the survey based on the participants' answers. As you can see in Fig. 16.4, the items could be questions or statements.

Sometimes the response choices have two levels (yes or no, true or false). Sometimes there are more than two response choices. Multiple responses can be presented in a **Likert-type format.** In a Likert-type format the numeric answers correspond to subjective ratings of intensity. For example, "0"" might mean "not at all," "1" might mean "a little," and higher numbers

Sample survey items with different types of response formats:

ITEM/QUESTION: *"Think about your usual week. How often do you worry?"*

Possible response format:

0 = not at all, 1 = a little, 2 = sometimes, 3 = often

Possible response format:

0 = no days, 1 = 1 or 2 days, 2 = 3 to 6 days, 3 = every day

ITEM/QUESTION: *How much do you agree with this statement: "I often worry".*

Possible response format:

-2 = Strongly disagree, -1= Disagree, 0 = neither agree nor disagree, 1= agree, 2 = strongly agree.

****

Researchers can also use **visual analogue scales** in which participants indicate a point along the line which represents the intensity of their response (Lodge, 1981).

ITEM/QUESTION: *How much do you worry ....?*

Possible response format: *(Make a mark on the line indicating your response*

Worry: *not at all* ____ *all the time*

FIGURE 16.4 Sample survey items.

indicate higher levels of intensity or agreement. Participants can complete surveys using a paper-and-pencil format or they can complete them using a computerized format.

Structured interviews. Structured interviews involve **standardized questions.** In some cases, participants can answer with more elaborated responses than they can in survey format. Diagnoses of behavioral health disorders can be made with a structured interview such as the structured clinical interview for DSM-5 (SCID-5; First, Williams, Karg, & Spitzer, 2015).

Diaries. Diaries are brief surveys which can be delivered electronically via smartphone, tablet, or computer, or via paper-and-pencil diaries. Diaries can permit investigators to use **ecological momentary assessment methods**. In these methods, the researchers can give the surveys many times per day or per week. The surveys can be completed in the individuals' natural environment and can capture emotions, behaviors, or experiences as they occur.

Here is an example of a paper-and-pencil diary we used in a study about daily emotions and interpersonal interactions. Participants completed one diary page every 20 min (Broudy et al., 2007) (Fig. 16.5).

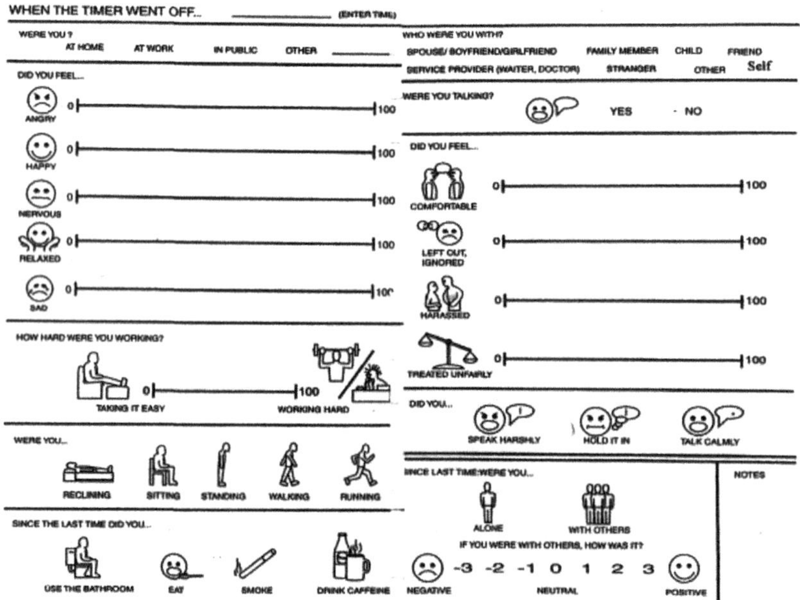

WHEN THE TIMER WENT OFF... ______ (ENTER TIME)

WERE YOU ?
AT HOME AT WORK IN PUBLIC OTHER ______

DID YOU FEEL...
ANGRY 0 —— 100
HAPPY 0 —— 100
NERVOUS 0 —— 100
RELAXED 0 —— 100
SAD 0 —— 100

HOW HARD WERE YOU WORKING?
TAKING IT EASY 0 —— 100 WORKING HARD

WERE YOU...
RECLINING SITTING STANDING WALKING RUNNING

SINCE THE LAST TIME DID YOU...
USE THE BATHROOM EAT SMOKE DRINK CAFFEINE

WHO WERE YOU WITH?
SPOUSE/ BOYFRIEND/GIRLFRIEND FAMILY MEMBER CHILD FRIEND
SERVICE PROVIDER (WAITER, DOCTOR) STRANGER OTHER Self

WERE YOU TALKING?
YES · NO

DID YOU FEEL...
COMFORTABLE 0 —— 100
LEFT OUT, IGNORED 0 —— 100
HARASSED 0 —— 100
TREATED UNFAIRLY 0 —— 100

DID YOU...
SPEAK HARSHLY HOLD IT IN TALK CALMLY

SINCE LAST TIME:WERE YOU...
ALONE WITH OTHERS
IF YOU WERE WITH OTHERS, HOW WAS IT?
NEGATIVE -3 -2 -1 0 1 2 3 POSITIVE
NEUTRAL

NOTES

FIGURE 16.5 Example of a daily diary.

The use of diaries can eliminate problems with **retrospective reporting** and **recall bias**. When participants are asked to remember how they felt or what they did at some point in the past (even the same day), they are using retrospective reporting—reporting on the past. The participant's answers can be affected by recall bias.

Bias can occur for many reasons. Sometimes participants cannot remember how they felt or what they did. Sometimes their current mood can distort their recollection of past events. Using diaries to capture events as they happen can reduce these difficulties.

For more information about the use of diary data collection measures see Stone (2018).

Standardized tests. These are tests in which the questions are administered in the same way across participants, and an individual's scores on the test can be compared to a larger **normative** or **standardization sample**. A normative sample is a large sample containing participants who represent population. Scores from this sample can be used to determine the responses that are typical for participants with similar characteristics (e.g., similar age or gender). Comparing the participants' scores to those of individuals who are part of the normative sample can provide insight into the degree to which the specific participant's scores differ from the average.

For example, intelligence tests like the Wechsler Intelligence Scale for Children or the Stanford-Binet are standardized tests. The researcher can compare the participant's scores to those of the normative sample to determine how much the participant's scores are above or below the scores for people from a comparable population (Tworney, O'Connell, Lillis, Tarpey, & O'Reilly, 2018).

Normative data also can be used to determine if the participant's responses have **clinical significance.** Specifically, researchers can use the normative data to find out if the participant's scores are more like the scores shown by patients with behavioral health disorders versus individuals without these disorders.

Standardized tests can be very useful. Available tests are documented in the **Mental Measurements Yearbook** (https://www.ebsco.com/products/research-databases/mental-measurements-yearbook). However, no tests are available for many behavioral health disorders.

Physiological measurement. Researchers can obtain many different types of physiological data using validated instruments. For example, fMRI machines can be used to obtain data on brain responses, and ambulatory blood pressure or heart rate monitors can be used to obtain data on cardiovascular responses. These data can be very useful, particularly in understanding mechanisms that may contribute to the development of maintenance of symptoms. However, at this point, physiological data are not used to make a diagnosis of a behavioral health disorder.

Achieving Balance

When choosing measurement methods, researchers must balance the burden the assessment approach places on the participant against the need to obtain comprehensive data on the variables. Too little information and the researcher may miss measuring key aspects of the construct. Too many tests and the **participant burden** will be too great.

If the burden is too great, participants may drop out, and it will be difficult to interpret the data. **Dropouts** present threats to validity. For example, if many participants drop out, the final testing sample may only contain highly motivated individuals. It will be difficult to understand if the findings generalize to less motivated participants.

Activity 16.1: Identifying Measurement Strategies

Let's return to the study by Dear et al. (2015). Identify the aim of the study and the hypotheses the researcher wants to test. Examine the measures section. Consider the constructs: generalized anxiety, depression, and social anxiety.

What variables did the researchers use to represent these constructs? What sources of data were used? What methods were used to collect these data? Is the measurement instrument reliable and valid? What are the costs and benefits of this approach? Table 16.4 is filled out for the variable self-reported anxiety. You complete the table for depression and social anxiety.

TABLE 16.4 Identifying measurement methods and instruments.

Author/date			
Construct	Generalized anxiety	Depression	Social anxiety
Variable	Self-reported generalized anxiety disorder symptoms		
Source of data	Participant		
Method of collecting data	Self-report survey		
Measurement tool	GAD-7		
Measurement reliability	Yes, alpha = 0.87		
Measurement validity	Yes, evidence of convergent, divergent validity		
Burden? How many questions/length of time	7 questions, brief survey		
How does this method allow the researcher to test the hypothesis? What are the pros and cons of this choice?	Test is short and easy to understand. Permits rapid evaluation. May have overlap with other self-report measures of other mental health symptoms.		

The Quality of Measurement: Considering Reliability and Validity

Once the researcher has determined the best source of data and determined the best method for obtaining the data, the researcher must choose a measurement instrument. This instrument must be **reliable** and **valid**.

Reliability

Reliability refers to the consistency of measurement (Golafshani, 2003). We count on many measurement instruments to be reliable. A reliable instrument behaves the same way in response to the variable being measured every time it is used.

For example, consider a speedometer and a thermometer. To enable a driver to travel within the speed limit, the speedometer on the driver's car must be reliable. The speed registered on the speedometer must always register the same number when the car is traveling at a given speed.

A thermometer must also be a reliable instrument. If your temperature is 98.6°, you expect the thermometer to register 98.6 every time your temperature is 98.6. The thermometer might also be reliable if it registered 50° every time your temperature was 98.6 and if the thermometer consistently registered 51° when your temperature went to 99.6°. But the absolute value of the temperature readings would not be valid.

Establishing Measurement Reliability

For many instruments, it is straightforward to test reliability. For a thermometer, you can take multiple measurements of temperature and determine if the thermometer gives the same reading each time it is measuring something that has a known temperature.

For psychological measures, establishing reliability is more complicated. Reliability has different meanings depending on the measurement method and the type of study design. For methods involving surveys, researchers need to understand reliability across items in the survey. For observational data, researchers need to understand reliability across observers or raters. For longitudinal studies, researchers need to understand reliability across assessments or test–retest reliability.

Measuring reliability across items in an instrument. To understand if the questions or items in a survey are measuring the same construct, researchers assess **internal consistency reliability**. Internal consistency reliability occurs when the items hypothesized to measure the same construct are related to each other (Henson, 2001).

Here are some items from the SCARED (The Screen for Child Anxiety-Related Emotional Disorders Scale) (Birmaher et al., 1999). This is a scale that can be used to assess anxiety-related disorders in children. The full scale has 38 items which measure different types of anxiety disorder symptoms including those related to social anxiety, school phobia, separation anxiety, generalized anxiety, and panic/somatic anxiety (Fig. 16.6).

1. When I feel frightened, it is hard to breathe
2. I get headaches when I am at school
3. I don't like to be with people I don't know well
4. I get scared if I sleep away from home
5. I worry about other people liking me
6. When I get frightened, I feel like passing out
7. I am nervous
8. I follow my mother or father wherever they go
9. People tell me I look nervous
10. I feel nervous with people I don't know well
11. I get stomachaches at school
12. When I get frightened, I feel like I am going crazy
13. I worry about sleeping alone
14. I worry about being as good as other kids
15. When I get frightened, I feel like things are not real
16. I have nightmares about something bad happening to my parents
17. I worry about going to school
18. When I get frightened, my heart beats fast
19. I get shaky
20. I have nightmares about something bad happening to me

FIGURE 16.6 Some items from the SCARED Scale.

Here are the four items which measure social anxiety:

I don't like to be with people I don't know.
I feel nervous with people I don't know well.
It's hard to talk with people I don't know.
I'm shy with people I don't know well.

Participants were asked to think about how they felt during the last 3 months. They rated these items on a 3-point scale. The response of "0" meant the item was not true for them at all or hardly at all. The response of "1" meant the item was sometimes true, and the response of "2" meant the item was often or always true.

Notice the items are very similar to one another in their meaning. The participant's responses are likely to be consistent across the items. Put another way—a participant who responds with a "2" to the item "*I don't like to be with people I don't know*" is also likely to have a high score on the other items.

Cronbach's alpha is an estimate of the extent of the total relationships among the items on the survey. Researchers can obtain an estimate of the Cronbach's alpha from the correlations among each of the items. Generally, a Cronbach's alpha above 0.80 is considered to reflect good internal consistency. When reliability is high, the researcher can have confidence the items are related to each other (Cortina, 1993).

For the SCARED, the Cronbach's alpha across all 38 items is high—about 0.90. The scores for each of the factors measuring different aspects of anxiety disorders are also moderate to good, ranging from 0.74 to 0.89.

Let's look at an example of a measures section in which the researchers use another social anxiety disorder scale. Notice the researcher reports the Cronbach's alpha for the survey measures of social anxiety (Fig. 16.7).

Social Phobia Scale and Social Interaction Anxiety Scale

The Social Phobia Scale (SPS) and the Social Interaction Anxiety Scale (SIAS; Mattick & Clarke, 1998) are widely used, 20-item measures of performance and interaction anxiety, respectively. The SPS describes situations in which the person is the focus of attention and observed by others, such as eating, drinking, and writing. The SIAS contains items reflecting cognitive, affective, and behavioral reactions to interactional situations, such as nervousness when speaking to authority, mixing with people, and talking to an attractive person of the opposite sex. The 5-point response scale for both scales is *not at all*, *slightly*, *moderately*, *very*, or *extremely* characteristic of me. Internal reliabilities for the SPS ($\alpha = .89$) and SIAS ($\alpha = .93$) are high within clinical samples and these scales have been shown to be sensitive to change (Cox, Ross, Swinson, & Direnfeld, 1998; Mattick, Peters, & Clarke, 1989).

FIGURE 16.7 Excerpt from McEvoy & Mahoney, 2012.

There are also other measures of reliability across items. These approaches are derived from **Item Response Theory**. In these analyses, the measures of reliability examine the degree to which the items are related to the underlying construct (van der Linden, & Hambleton, 2013).

Why is reliability so important? If the measure is not reliable (meaning some items are related to the construct and others are not), the researcher will have difficulty testing hypotheses using this survey to measure a variable. It will be unclear if the researcher did not find the expected outcome because the hypothesis was wrong or because the survey was unreliable.

Measuring reliability across observers. When researchers use **observations** to collect data, they need to insure the observations are reliable across the individual raters who are making the observations. Measures of **inter-rater reliability** are used to determine if the observations are reliable across observers (Hallgren, 2012).

For example, researchers studying childhood social anxiety might observe children in a playground to assess how often a child with social anxiety interacts with another child. The researcher might ask observers to record the child's behavior for 20 min. The observer might break down the 20-minute period into 10 second units and indicate whether the child was interacting at any point in each 10-second period.

The observations of a single observer may not be reliable. The observer could have missed an interaction or made a mistake in coding the interactions. Therefore, researchers often use more than one rater (i.e., observer) and assess the degree to which the observers agree and disagree. The level of inter-rater agreement can be captured in an estimate called the **Kappa coefficient** (Hallgre, 2012).

Here is an example of one type of rating sheet for observations of social behavior. The rater is instructed to give a record a score of 1 if the child interacts with another child during this period and to record a score of 0 if the child does not interact with another child. To assess inter-rater reliability, responses on this rating sheet would be compared with responses on the rating sheet for the second rater (Fig. 16.8).

Rating sheet for children's interactions – Rater # 1						
Minute	**0-10**	**11-20**	**21-30**	**31-40**	**41-50**	**51-60**
1	0	0	1	0	0	0
2	1	0	0	0	0	0
3	0	0	1	0	0	0
4	0	0	0	0	1	0
5	0	0	0	0	0	0
6	0	0	0	0	0	0
Etc.						

FIGURE 16.8 Example of rating sheet in which one rater is coding behavior.

Measuring reliability across assessments. Another type of measurement reliability concerns reliability over time, called **test–retest reliability** (Henrickson, Massey, & Cronan, 1993). This type of reliability is essential if researchers are measuring a characteristic that is a **trait** or stable characteristic of a person. If a scale has good test–retest reliability, participants who had high scores on that scale in comparison to others will continue to show higher scores relative to others the next time the scale is administered.

Sociability and conscientiousness are examples of stable characteristics. People high in sociability will generally be more outgoing than others. They will obtain higher scores than less sociable people on an instrument measuring sociability. They will obtain higher scores than less sociable people, even if they are measured at times when most people are less social (e.g., first thing in the morning).

When researchers develop a measure of trait sociability, they need to find items that assess the stable components of sociability, not the components that might vary from minute to minute. To determine if they have succeeded, they test reliability over time—**test–retest reliability**.

Activity 16.2: Identifying the Reliability of the Measurement Instruments

Read through the measures section for the Dear et al. (2015) article displayed in Fig. 16.1. List two of measures in Table 16.5. Note how the researchers write about the reliability of measures. They often refer to other articles which describe how the measure was developed. For example, when describing the measure of depression, they cite

Kroenke, K., & Spitzer, R. L. (2002). The PHQ-9: a new depression diagnostic and severity measure. *Psychiatric Annals, 32*(9), 509–515.

TABLE 16.5 | Identifying descriptions of reliability and validity.

Author/ date	Construct	Variable	Measurement instrument name	Measurement instrument description	How is reliability described?	Is there a reference for the measure? If so, what type of information is likely to be included in that article?

Measurement Validity

Researchers must also examine the validity of their measurement instruments. Measurement validity refers to the degree to which the instrument measures what it is intended to measure. Put another way—measurement validity indicates the degree to which scores on the measurement instrument are related to the construct the researcher is intending to measure.

Constructs are ideas. But measurement instruments contain specific questions or tasks which are intended to represent the construct. Therefore, researchers must determine if these questions are effective representations of the construct itself.

How is validity determined? Determining the validity of a thermometer is straightforward. Researchers can test the validity of thermometers by examining the readings on the thermometer when it is placed in water at a known temperature. Water is known to boil at 212°F. If the thermometer measures 212° when the water is boiling, and 32° when the water has frozen, the researchers know the thermometer is likely to be a valid measure of temperature.

The situation is not so simple when assessing the validity of psychological measurement instruments. There is no true measure of many psychological constructs such as sociability or shyness, for example. Instead, researchers examine several different dimensions of validity including content validity and construct validity.

Content validity. Content validity refers to the degree to which the items on the measurement instrument capture the full range of concepts incorporated into the construct (Adcock & Collier, 2001). For example, anxiety has many different components: cognitive components including catastrophic thoughts about the future; emotional components such as feelings of nervousness; and somatic components including sweating or blushing. A survey of anxiety may not have content validity if it only includes the somatic or the cognitive symptoms. If a researcher is conducting a treatment outcome study in which the treatment is expected to change many dimensions of anxiety—from catastrophic thoughts to butterflies in the stomach—then the researcher needs an instrument with items representing all different types of symptoms.

Construct validity. Construct validity refers to the degree to which the scores on the measurement instrument are related to the construct it is supposed to represent (Adcock et al., 2001). Since the construct itself often cannot be tested, researchers evaluate construct validity by examining the relations of scores on the measurement instrument to scores on other measures. They are examining whether the relations among these scores are consistent with what would be expected based on theories about the construct.

Researchers differ in their conceptualization of the differences between construct validity and other types of validity, including **criterion validity, convergent validity,** and **divergent validity**. Some psychologists view all these types of validity as components of construct validity (Cronbach & Meehl, 1995). We will use that approach here and explain several types of validity in more detail. We can examine the approaches used by Spitzer and colleagues (2007) Spitzer et al. (2006) to test the measurement validity of the GAD-7, a paper-and-pencil measure of generalized anxiety disorder symptoms discussed earlier in the chapter.

Criterion validity. Researchers can assess the criterion validity of a measurement instrument by comparing scores on that instrument to a "gold standard" measure of the construct (Cichetti, 1994). A gold standard measure is a measure of the construct which relies on data from a different and potentially more objective source. When Spitzer and colleagues were comparing GAD-7 scores to the mental health providers' diagnosis, they were testing criterion validity. The mental health providers' diagnosis was the criterion used to test validity.

When researchers compare the scores on a measure to scores on a criterion measure within the same time frame, they are testing **concurrent criterion validity**. Concurrent means at the same time. For example, if the researcher obtains scores on the GAD-7 and the mental health providers' diagnosis in the same time frame, the researcher is testing concurrent criterion validity.

Researchers can also test **predictive criterion validity** by comparing scores on the measurement instrument to measures of related constructs obtained at a future point in time. For example, if scores on the GAD-7 were found to be related to scores on functional impairment a year later, then the researchers would have evidence of the predictive criterion validity of the GAD-7.

Convergent validity. Convergent validity is obtained when scores on one measurement instrument are related to scores on similar measurement instrument, assessing the same construct. For example, when Spitzer and colleagues were validating the GAD-7, they also examined the relation of the scores on the GAD-7 to other similar self-report measures of anxiety, including the Beck Anxiety Inventory. If the researchers find a significant positive correlation, they can conclude the GAD-7 shows convergent validity (Monga et al., 2000).

Divergent validity. Researchers also establish **discriminant** or **divergent** validity. Tests of divergent validity are done to make sure the measurement instrument is not associated with other constructs that are irrelevant to the hypotheses being tested (Monga et al., 2000). It is important to be able to determine that the independent variable, assessed by the measurement instrument, is the actual variable being assessed. Another variable might be closely related, but not be tied to the underlying theory.

For example, when Spitzer and colleagues are testing the validity of the GAD-7, they need to demonstrate that the scale measures GAD specifically and not simply any type of negative emotion or symptom. They demonstrate that scores on the GAD-7 are not overlapping with scores on a measure of depression. This enables the authors to claim that the scale has divergent validity—the scores on the GAD-7 diverges from scores on a measure of another construct that is related but is not the same as GAD.

Building Human Capital

In this chapter you learned a lot about measurement. You learned about different kinds of measurement methods and instruments and about measurement reliability and validity. This information is important for developing rigorous research methods, but may also important to the way you make judgments in your own life.

Consider the judgments you make about why people act the way they do. Do you use certain behavioral or emotional cues as markers of an underlying personality trait? Do you conclude someone is an angry person because of their facial expressions?

Have you ever been wrong in your judgments? Could it have to do with the way you are measuring your variables? Is it possible that the characteristics you observe are linked to a different construct? For example, sometimes people have a frown on their face because they are angry. But sometimes people wear a frown because they are anxious, but aren't very good about talking about their feelings.

How do you decide whether a hypothesis you have about someone's motivation is right? Do you say "I just know that is the way they are. I know that's the way they think and act." But now that you know more about measurement, can you ask yourself: "What is the evidence I am using for evaluating the reliability and validity of my measurement strategy?"

As you think more about measurement, you can become a better observer and interpreter of people's behavior. You can think more deeply about your own judgments and, you can develop skills to formulate and test hypotheses about other people and yourself. As you learn to think more systematically and rigorously about variables and how to measure them, you can improve your relationships along with improving your coursework.

Terms

Take the time to define each of these terms and consider how to apply them.

Research Terms

Measurement reliability.
Measurement validity.
Coercion.
Likert-style format.
Visual analogue scale.
Open-ended questions.
Structured interviews.
Standardized questions.
Electronic diaries.
Ecological momentary assessment.
Recall bias.
Retrospective reporting.
Reliable reporter.
Normative samples.
Clinical significance.
Mental Measurements Yearbook.
Participant burden.
Internal consistency reliability.
Cronbach's alpha.
Item response theory.

Observational measures.
Inter-rater reliability.
Kappa coefficient.
Trait characteristic.
Test–retest reliability.
Face validity.
Content validity.
Construct validity.
Criterion validity.
Predictive criterion validity.
Concurrent criterion validity.
Discriminant validity/Divergent validity.

References

Adcock, R., & Collier, D. (2001). Measurement validity: A shared standard for qualitative and quantitative research. *American Political Science Review, 95*(3), 529–546.

Birmaher, B., Brent, D. A., Chiappetta, L., Bridge, J., Monga, S., & Baugher, M. (1999). Psychometric properties of the screen for child anxiety related emotional disorders (SCARED): A replication study. *Journal of the American Academy of Child & Adolescent Psychiatry, 38*(10), 1230–1236.

Broudy, R., Brondolo, E., Coakley, V., Brady, N., Cassells, A., Tobin, J. N., & Sweeney, M. (2007). Perceived ethnic discrimination in relation to daily moods and negative social interactions. *Journal of Behavioral Medicine, 30*(1), 31–43.

Cicchetti, D. V. (1994). Guidelines, criteria, and rules of thumb for evaluating normed and standardized assessment instruments in psychology. *Psychological Assessment, 6*(4), 284.

Cortina, J. M. (1993). What is coefficient alpha? An examination of theory and applications. *Journal of Applied Psychology, 78*(1), 98.

Cronbach, L. J., & Meehl, P. E. (1955). Construct validity in psychological tests. *Psychological Bulletin, 52*(4), 281.

Dear, B. F., Staples, L. G., Terides, M. D., Karin, E., Zou, J., Johnston, L., … Titov, N. (2015). Transdiagnostic versus disorder-specific and clinician-guided versus self-guided internet- delivered treatment for generalized anxiety disorder and comorbid disorders: A randomized controlled trial. *Journal of Anxiety Disorders, 36*, 63–77.

First, M. B., Williams, J. B., Karg, R. S., & Spitzer, R. L. (2015). *User's guide to structured clinical interview for DSM-5 disorders (SCID-5-CV) clinical version*. Arlington, VA: American Psychiatric Publishing.

Golafshani, N. (2003). Understanding reliability and validity in qualitative research. *The Qualitative Report, 8*(4), 597–606.

Hallgren, K. A. (2012). Computing inter-rater reliability for observational data: An overview and tutorial. *Tutorials in Quantitative Methods for Psychology, 8*(1), 23.

Hendrickson, A. R., Massey, P. D., & Cronan, T. P. (1993). On the test-retest reliability of perceived usefulness and perceived ease of use scales. *MIS Quarterly*, 227–230.

Henson, R. K. (2001). Understanding internal consistency reliability estimates: A conceptual primer on coefficient alpha. *Measurement and Evaluation in Counseling and Development, 34*(3), 177.

van der Linden, W. J., & Hambleton, R. K. (Eds.). (2013). *Handbook of modern item response theory*. Springer Science & Business Media.

Lodge, M. (1981). *Magnitude scaling: Quantitative measurement of opinions*. London: Sage.

McEvoy, P. M., & Mahoney, A. E. (2006). To be sure, to be sure: Intolerance of uncertainty mediates symptoms of various anxiety disorders and depression. *Behavior Therapy, 43*(3), 533–545.

Monga, S., Birmaher, B., Chiappetta, L., Brent, D., Kaufman, J., Bridge, J., & Cully, M. (2000). Screen for child anxiety-related emotional disorders (SCARED): Convergent and divergent validity. *Depression and Anxiety, 12*(2), 85–91.

Twomey, C., O'Connell, H., Lillis, M., Tarpey, S. L., & O'Reilly, G. (2018). Utility of an abbreviated version of the stanford-binet intelligence scales in estimating 'full scale'IQ for young children with autism spectrum disorder. *Autism Research, 11*(3), 503–508.

Spitzer, R. L., Kroenke, K., Williams, J. B., & Löwe, B. (2006). A brief measure for assessing generalized anxiety disorder: The GAD-7. *Archives of Internal Medicine, 166*(10), 1092–1097.

Stone, A. A. (2018). Ecological Momentary Assessment in Survey Research. In *The Palgrave Handbook of Survey Research* (pp. 221–226). Cham: Palgrave Macmillan.

Chapter 17

Methods: Procedures for study implementation and protection of internal validity

In Chapters 15 and 16, you learned about the methods for selecting a sample and measuring the study variables. In Chapter 17, you will learn about the procedures that are used to implement these methods. Researchers need procedures to implement all aspects of a study, including recruiting participants, delivering the independent variable, assessing all variables, and managing and analyzing the data.

Each of the procedures has implications for the validity of the study. As they design the study, researchers try to anticipate threats to validity and design procedures to limit their effects on the study outcomes. The procedures have implications for internal validity—the degree to which researchers can test the hypotheses they intend to test. The procedures also have implications for the external validity of the study—the degree to which the findings can be generalized beyond the current sample, methods, or circumstances.

Researchers include detailed information about the procedures they use in their articles and proposals. But they don't always include a formal procedures component. Instead, the information about the study procedures may be included in different parts of the article. Researchers might include a description of the procedures in the introduction as they explain the justification for the study. Or they might include a description of procedures as they describe the participants or the measures. You will need to read the full article to insure you understand all the procedures employed.

Psychology Research Methods. https://doi.org/10.1016/B978-0-12-815680-3.00017-7

The procedures from existing articles can help you design the methods for your own proposal or evaluate the methods used in existing research. If you are writing a research proposal to test the effects of a treatment for the disorder you are studying, you will include a component describing the procedures you plan to use in the proposed study. If you are writing a paper evaluating existing research, you will review the procedures of other studies. In your paper you will provide an evaluation of their approaches and the implications for the interpretability of the findings across the articles you have reviewed (Table 17.1).

TABLE 17.1 A Sample of Types of Procedures used in Research Studies.

Procedures	Purpose of including information
Procedures related to sampling participants	
1. Procedures for recruiting participants	To clarify the strategies used to recruit individuals, to indicate potential limitations to external validity.
2. Procedures for testing eligibility	To clarify the processes used to evaluate the characteristics of participants included in the study.
3. Procedures for consenting individuals	To clarify how participants are informed about the study. To understand the participant's expectations, and to explain how to protect the participants' rights.
4. Procedures for evaluating sources of bias in the selection of the sample	To identify sources of bias and to describe how efforts were made to reduce these sources of bias.
Procedures related to measuring variables	
1. Procedures related to the timing of the assessments of each variable	To indicate when assessments will occur. To clarify how the assessment points are appropriate for the design (e.g., cross-sectional, longitudinal).
2. Procedures for assigning and training evaluators	To insure the reliability and validity of measurement. To clarify how the assessment will be free from biases caused by the evaluators' awareness of the participant's status in the experiment (i.e., assignment to experimental or control group).
3. Procedures for training participants to use testing materials, if needed	To explain how the researcher can insure measurement reliability and validity as the participants complete the measurement instruments.
4. Procedures for reducing bias in assessment	To explain how the researcher can insure evaluators conduct unbiased assessments and reduce participant bias.

TABLE 17.1 A Sample of Types of Procedures used in Research Studies.—cont'd

Procedures	Purpose of including information
If conducting an experimental study, procedures for manipulating and delivering the independent variable	
1. Procedures for insuring random, assignment to conditions	To explain how participants are assigned to the levels of the independent variable.
2. Procedures for delivering the independent variable	To explain how the different levels of the independent variable will be delivered to insure the internal validity of the study.
3. Procedures for insuring the comparability of the experimental and control conditions	To explain how the control group(s) will permit the researcher to test hypotheses about the specific aspects of the experimental condition he or she is testing.
Procedures for reducing threats to internal validity by controlling bias and extraneous variables	
1. Procedures for insuring the reliability and validity of the delivery of the independent variable.	To explain how the researcher insures the correct dose of the correct independent variable is delivered. Procedures could include manipulation checks, fidelity checks, experimenter training, among others.
2. Procedures for controlling extraneous variables in experimental studies. Details depend on the specifics of the topic area and instrumentation.	To explain how the researcher will control extraneous variables that may threaten the effects of the independent variable.
Procedures for managing and analyzing data	
1. Procedures for insuring confidentiality and appropriately storing the data	To document how the researchers insured confidentiality. To document the details of efforts to adhere to appropriate rules and regulations.
2. Procedures for handling missing data	To document the strategies used when there is missing data.
3. Procedures for testing if data meet assumptions of analyses	To document how the researcher tested statistical assumptions.
4. Procedures for preliminary data analyses	To document the procedures used to conduct preliminary analyses, including those used to examine potential covariates.
5. Procedures for inferential analyses	To document how the primary, secondary, and other inferential analyses will be performed.

Procedures for Selecting and Recruiting Participants

In Chapter 15, you learned about the steps involved in assembling a sample of participants for a study. You read about establishing appropriate inclusion and exclusion criteria, recruiting the correct number of participants, and protecting the participants' safety and rights. The procedures component includes information about how researchers implement these steps.

Procedures for Recruiting Participants and Screening for Eligibility

Once researchers establish eligibility requirements for participation in their study, they need to screen the participants to see if they meet these criteria. Sometimes researchers ask potential participants to come to the laboratory for screening, other times researchers will conduct brief screening interviews over the phone. They will ask a limited number of questions to determine if the participant meets the eligibility criteria. If a participant seems to meet the criteria, then the researcher can move forward with further testing.

For example, a researcher might be conducting research on individuals who have posttraumatic stress disorder (PTSD), but do not currently have substance use problems. The presence of PTSD is one *inclusion* criterion, and the presence of substance use disorder is one *exclusion* criterion. If participants call to volunteer for the study, the researcher may wish to ask about both PTSD symptoms and substance abuse before the potential participant comes to laboratory for the study.

This brief phone screening can save the researchers much time and money. If they prescreen participants, they reduce the chance of spending too much evaluation time on someone who may not be eligible for the study. Participants will be less likely to waste time traveling to the laboratory, only to find they are not eligible to participate in the study.

But these processes also raise some ethical concerns. Specifically, researchers are obtaining information from participants before they have obtained informed consent from the participant. The Institutional Review Board will help the researcher identify specific approaches that can be used to protect the rights of individuals who are participating in the screening. Depending on how elaborate the eligibility criteria are, it may be necessary to review a consent for screening with the participant.

Researchers also establish possible recruitment sites. They must determine which recruitment procedures are appropriate for the aims of their study and the resources they have. They must also recognize the limitations of the strategies they choose.

Here is an example of procedures used to recruit participants and determine their eligibility from a study by Southam-Gerow et al. (2010). This study examines if cognitive behavioral therapy (CBT) is better than usual care in treating young people with anxiety disorders in community clinics. The authors describe the criteria for eligibility, as well as the procedures used to determine if the participant meets those criteria. They also describe where and how they recruit the participants (Fig. 17.1).

NEW RESEARCH

Does Cognitive Behavioral Therapy for Youth Anxiety Outperform Usual Care in Community Clinics? An Initial Effectiveness Test

Michael A. Southam-Gerow, Ph.D., John R. Weisz, Ph.D., A.B.P.P., Brian C. Chu, Ph.D., Bryce D. McLeod, Ph.D., Elana B. Gordis, Ph.D., Jennifer K. Connor-Smith, Ph.D.

Procedures

Setting/Recruitment. Participants were told about the study during routine intake procedures at six public, urban, community mental health clinics. After institutional review board approval of the assessment sequence, youths were invited to participate in the treatment phase if they (a) met *DSM-IV* criteria for at least one anxiety disorder (i.e., GAD, SAD, SOP, SP) and (b) anxiety was considered the treatment priority by the family. During pretreatment assessment parents and youths reported their top three reasons for seeking services (parent examples: "he worries too much," "has a lot of fears"; youth examples: "afraid to go to school," "too anxious") and rated impairment for each on a 0 (no problem at all) to 10 (huge problem) scale. Diagnosis, symptom, referral problem, and impairment data were discussed by project staff, senior clinic staff, and the family; if it was agreed that one of the four anxiety disorders constituted the family's treatment priority, the youth was invited to enroll in the trial.

FIGURE 17.1 Selected excerpt from Southam-Gerow et al. 2010.

Procedures for Explaining the Study and Obtaining Informed Consent

Researchers often describe the procedures they use to consent participants into the study. They use these procedures to explain how they establish safeguards to ensure participants are fully informed about the study. They may also indicate how their explanations avoid creating expectations or biases that may affect the study.

Here is an example of the procedures used to recruit incarcerated women to participate in a randomized control trial to treat substance use and PTSD. The authors describe the process of recruitment and protecting the participants' rights (Fig. 17.2).

Behavior Therapy 40 (2009) 325–336

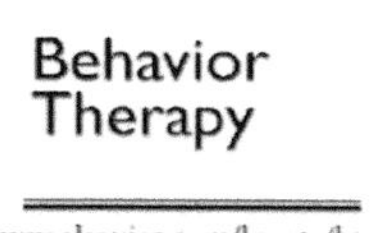

www.elsevier.com/locate/bt

Randomized Controlled Pilot Study of Cognitive-Behavioral Therapy in a Sample of Incarcerated Women With Substance Use Disorder and PTSD

Caron Zlotnick
Butler Hospital/Brown University
Jennifer Johnson
Brown University
Lisa M. Najavits
McLean Hospital/Harvard Medical School

Method

Women were recruited from a residential substance abuse treatment program in a minimum security wing of a women's prison. Admission to the in-prison treatment program is voluntary and those admitted to the program are female inmates who request intensive substance abuse treatment. All participants provided informed consent to participate in the study. The study was approved by the Institutional Review Board (IRB) of Butler Hospital, the IRB of the prison's substance use treatment provider, and the prison's Medical Research Advisory Group. Women who were scheduled to be released from prison within 12 to 16 weeks were approached to be in the study. Of the 103 women approached, 94 women (91%) consented to participate in the study. Of these 94 women, 45 (48%) women were excluded (see Fig. 1). Two women left the substance abuse treatment program prior to randomization. The remaining 43 did not meet inclusion criteria, that is, *DSM-IV* criteria for current PTSD or subthreshold PTSD (i.e., had at least one symptom from all three clusters that were associated with impairment/distress) within the previous month as determined by the Clinician-Administered Posttraumatic Stress Disorder Scale-I (CAPS-I; Blake et al., 1990) or did not meet *DSM-IV* criteria for substance dependence one month prior to entering prison per the Structured Clinical Interview for *DSM-IV*—Patient Version (SCID; First, Spitzer, Gibbon, & Williams, 1996). Women were also excluded if they were actively psychotic (hallucinating or delusional) at the time of recruitment, could not understand English well enough to understand the consent form or measures, or were diagnosed with organic brain impairment. The remaining 49 (52%) of the women were individually randomized to one of the two conditions, after the completion of all study intake measures (see below for details). A simple randomization procedure was used for each cohort of participants (i.e., group of participants who entered the randomized phase of the study at the same time). Each cohort of participants consisted of 5 to 11 women, and there were 7 cohorts of participants.

FIGURE 17.2 Methods from Zlotnick, Johnson, & Najavits, 2009.

Procedures for Detecting Sources of Bias in the Selection of the Sample

There are many sources of possible bias in the selection and retention of participants for a study, including **volunteer bias** and **attrition bias**, among others. Researchers have found that individuals who volunteer for studies differ from those who do not (Nichols & Maner, 2008). Similarly, not all participants complete the study, some participants drop out. Researchers label these participants as lost to attrition. People who drop out of studies may differ from people who remain in the study to completion. If the characteristics of people who volunteer and complete a study are different from those who do not volunteer or who drop out, these characteristics may bias the outcome.

To address this potential source of bias, researchers use several methods. They may report the number of people who volunteer for the study as a proportion of the total number of people approached. This can tell the reader about the representative versus selective nature of the sample. If the data are available, the researcher can provide some information on the differences between those who agreed to be in the study and those who did not (or those who drop out vs. remain).

Here is an example of the way Ali and colleagues addressed this issue in a study examining relapse rates after a low-intensity CBT intervention. The researcher wants to understand if the participants enrolled in the study differ from those in the general population (Fig. 17.3).

Behaviour Research and Therapy 94 (2017) 1–8

Contents lists available at ScienceDirect

Behaviour Research and Therapy

journal homepage: www.elsevier.com/locate/brat

How durable is the effect of low intensity CBT for depression and anxiety? Remission and relapse in a longitudinal cohort study

Shehzad Ali [a], Laura Rhodes [b], Omar Moreea [c], Dean McMillan [d], Simon Gilbody [d], Chris Leach [e], Mike Lucock [e], Wolfgang Lutz [f], Jaime Delgadillo [g, *]

[a] Department of Health Sciences and Centre for Health Economics, University of York, York, UK
[b] Leeds Community Healthcare NHS Trust, Leeds, UK
[c] Centre for Clinical Practice, National Institute for Health and Care Excellence, Manchester, UK
[d] Hull York Medical School and Department of Health Sciences, University of York, York, United Kingdom
[e] South West Yorkshire Partnership NHS Foundation Trust and University of Huddersfield, Huddersfield, UK
[f] Department of Psychology, University of Trier, Trier, Germany
[g] Clinical Psychology Unit, Department of Psychology, University of Sheffield, Sheffield, UK

ARTICLE INFO

Article history:
Received 18 December 2016
Received in revised form
11 April 2017
Accepted 17 April 2017
Available online 18 April 2017

Keywords:
Depression
Anxiety
Relapse
Cognitive behavioural therapy

ABSTRACT

Background: Depression and anxiety disorders are relapse-prone conditions, even after successful treatment with pharmacotherapy or psychotherapy. Cognitive behavioural therapy (CBT) is known to prevent relapse, but there is little evidence of the durability of remission after low intensity forms of CBT (LiCBT).
Method: This study aimed to examine relapse rates 12 months after completing routinely-delivered LiCBT. A cohort of 439 LiCBT completers with remission of symptoms provided monthly depression (PHQ-9) and anxiety (GAD-7) measures during 12 months after treatment. Survival analysis was conducted to model time-to-relapse while controlling for patient characteristics.
Results: Overall, 53% of cases relapsed within 1 year. Of these relapse events, the majority (79%) occurred within the first 6 months post-treatment. Cases reporting residual depression symptoms (PHQ-9 = 5 to 9) at the end of treatment had significantly higher risk of relapse (hazard ratio = 1.90, $p < 0.001$).
Conclusions: The high rate of relapse after LiCBT highlights the need for relapse prevention, particularly for those with residual depression symptoms.

The sample of study participants and the wider pool of potentially eligible participants were comparable in all demographic and clinical characteristics except for four variables. The study participants had a higher mean age ($U[1823] = 345{,}288.00$, $p = 0.001$), a higher mean number of prior treatments ($U[1289] = 159{,}569.00$, $p < 0.02$), a lower mean PHQ-9 score at the final treatment session ($U[1823] = 281{,}739.50$, $p = 0.03$), and a higher mean number of treatment sessions ($U[1823] = 354{,}203.00$, $p < 0.001$).

FIGURE 17.3 Abstract and selected excerpt from Ali et al., 2017.

Cultural biases can also influence the way individuals are recruited and retained in a study. If researchers are unfamiliar with a cultural or racial group or have biases about members of a group, they may fail to recruit participants from this group or may inadvertently increase drop-out among members of this group. Limited participation by some groups may affect the interpretability of the findings, as the study variables may operate in a different manner in different groups. Limited cultural or racial diversity limits the external validity of the study as researchers cannot know if the results will generalize to a sample with members from other cultures or ethnicities. Therefore, researchers may develop procedures for improving their ability to recruit and retain individuals from different cultures or racial and ethnic backgrounds into their studies.

Procedures Related to Measuring Variables

In Chapter 16, you learned about the types of measurement methods and instruments that are used to assess participants' responses. Here you will learn about the procedures used to implement these assessments, and the ways in which these procedures are used to support the reliability and validity of the assessment implementation. These procedures involve standardizing the process, training the assessors, training participants to use measurement instruments, identifying and addressing sources of bias in the assessment process, and establishing the timing of the assessments.

Standardization and Training of the Assessors

Researchers develop procedures to standardize the presentation of the assessment instructions as much as possible across participants. **Standardization** means developing procedures to ensure the measurement instruments are completed in a consistent manner across participants.

To standardize the procedures for each stage of the study, researchers often write a **manual of operations** which carefully describes how the research assistants should conduct the study. A portion of this manual includes instructions for conducting the assessments. Researchers may write a script read by the research assistants to the participants. Researchers also develop procedures to train the assessors (i.e., the research staff who conduct the assessments) to insure they are competent in administering the measurement instruments.

When necessary, researchers implement procedures to evaluate the degree to which standardization was effective and assessors were competent. For example, when researchers are using structured interviews to assess whether the participant meets criteria for a diagnosis, they ensure that the interviewers are reliable in conducting and scoring the interviews. They evaluate inter-rater reliability among the interviewers who are involved in the study and report the reliability in the methods section. With this information, readers can have more confidence the results of the assessment are likely to be reliable and valid.

Here is an example. In a study by Kuyken et al. (2015), researchers were testing the hypothesis that mindfulness-based cognitive therapy is better than continued medication in preventing relapse of depression. To determine if the participants had a relapse (i.e., another episode of depression) over the course of the study, the researchers used careful procedures to determine the reliability of the interviews which used the Depression Module of the Structured Clinical Interview (Levis et al., 2018). More than one research assistant interviewed participants at various points in time, and the researchers checked to determine if there was inter-rater agreement in the identification of a relapse (Fig. 17.4).

Effectiveness and cost-effectiveness of mindfulness-based cognitive therapy compared with maintenance antidepressant treatment in the prevention of depressive relapse or recurrence (PREVENT): a randomised controlled trial

Willem Kuyken, Rachel Hayes, Barbara Barrett, Richard Byng, Tim Dalgleish, David Kessler, Glyn Lewis, Edward Watkins, Claire Brejcha, Jessica Cardy, Aaron Causley, Suzanne Cowderoy, Alison Evans, Felix Gradinger, Surinder Kaur, Paul Lanham, Nicola Morant, Jonathan Richards, Pooja Shah, Harry Sutton, Rachael Vicary, Alice Weaver, Jenny Wilks, Matthew Williams, Rod S Taylor, Sarah Byford

Results

Another assessor rated every first actual or borderline relapse or recurrence and we recorded 90% agreement between the raters (κ=0·62, 95% CI 0·48–0·77, p<0·0001). A subset of 112 SCID interviews were also second rated by an experienced rater who was independent of the trial with 96% agreement being recorded (κ=0·90, 0·82–0·98, p<0·0001).

FIGURE 17.4 Abstract and selected excerpt from Kuyken et al., 2015.

Procedures for Protecting the Assessments from Bias

To protect the internal validity of the study, researchers must reduce potential sources of bias that may affect the outcomes of the assessments. This is a complex task, as there are many sources of bias including both the experimenter's and the participant's expectations about the study. Other sources of bias can be a function of extraneous variables present in the testing situation.

Participant's expectations about the study can be influenced by the **demand characteristics** of the study. Demand characteristics include aspects of the study which generate perceptions of demands for performance. For example, the way the study is advertised or explained to the participant may communicate what is expected of participants. When participants can guess at the intent of the study, they may try to comply (or refuse to comply) with the researcher's expectations.

But the explanation of the study or the advertisements for the study are shaped by the experimenter's conceptualization of the study. Experimenter bias can inadvertently shape these explanations or advertisements (Goodwin & Goodwin, 2016). During the assessment, the researcher's expectations themselves can create the outcome the researcher expected, a phenomenon known as the **Rosenthal effect** or **halo effect** (Rosenthal, 1994).

The participant's own expectations may also bias their responses. For example, if participants are in a treatment study, they may believe a specific treatment will be very helpful to them. Their positive expectations may influence their response to questions about the effects of the treatment.

On the other hand, sometimes participants may believe the treatment will not be helpful or has negative side effects. These expectancies can influence the participants' responses to the procedures and assessments. If the expectations are very negative, they can cause a **nocebo effect**. In a nocebo effect, the participant's negative expectations can make any negative outcome seem worse than it would be without those expectations (Barksy, Saintfort, Rogers, & Borus, 2002).

To avoid biases that arise from the participants' expectations, researchers try to ensure the participants are blind to the experimental condition to which they have been assigned. Researchers use the word "blind" to mean a lack of knowledge about the assignment of the participant to either the control or the experimental condition. When only the participants are blind to their assignment, but the researcher assistants know the assignment, the study is called a **single-blind study** (Heckerling, 2005).

Experimenter bias, sometimes called the **observer-expectancy effect**, can occur because a researcher may have a strong commitment to the theory being tested. To avoid experimenter bias on the part of the research assistants conducting the assessments, researchers will use **double-blind** procedures when this is possible. In a double-blind experiment neither the participants nor the research assistant knows the condition (e.g., experimental or control) to which the participant is assigned. This can prevent expectations from both the research assistant and the participant from affecting the outcome of the assessments (Hughes & Krahn, 1985).

In medical research, researchers can create medication **placebos**. These placebos appear identical to the experimental medication, but do not have the active ingredient(s). Participants are assigned at random to the placebo or the real medication. If the participants are not told which medication they receive, they are blind to the treatment condition. If the research assistants who test the participants do not know whether the participant is taking the real medication or the placebo, the study uses a double-blind procedure (Leuchter, Cook, Witte, Morgan, & Abrams, 2002).

In psychological research it is more difficult to create matched placebo conditions (Moerman, 2002). It can be hard to ensure the participants do not know their treatment condition, as part of the treatment often involves explaining the nature of the treatment and how it affects the disorder. Therefore, as we will discuss later in this chapter, researchers will attempt to develop an appropriate control condition that is equivalent to the experimental condition in as many ways as possible except the key ingredient the researcher is investigating.

In the methods section, the researchers will describe the procedures for creating a single- or double-blind study. They will describe the strategies used to prevent the participants from knowing the treatment condition to which they have been assigned, if this is possible. They will also describe how they are preventing experimenter bias from influencing the assessment process.

Researchers may also institute procedures in which they check whether the participant or research assistant correctly guessed the experimental condition—a procedure known as a **manipulation check.** During this manipulation check, researchers will ask the participants about the treatment they believed they received.

Researchers can also measure expectations about outcomes. They can ask participants what they know about the treatment and what they believe the beneficial and negative effects of treatment may be. This information can be used in additional statistical analyses to determine if these expectations influenced the outcomes.

Cultural factors may also influence the ways in which participants respond to the research assistants. The participants' behavior in the study may differ depending on the research assistants' gender, race, ethnicity, or other characteristics. Sometimes researchers will match the gender or race of the participant to the gender or race of the research assistant when possible.

There are also other issues that must be addressed as the researcher assesses participants. Some are related to the participants' reaction to being assessed, including phenomena such as **response reactivity**, **social desirability effects**, **evaluation apprehension**, **halo or Rosenthal effects**, and **sensitization**. Other issues are related to the burdens of the assessment process itself, including phenomena such as **response bias** or **response set, measurement order effects**, **habituation, fatigue,** among others.

Participants can exhibit **response reactivity** by reacting to being observed and assessed, even if they are not aware of these reactions. **Hawthorne effects** are an example of this type of reactivity. In the famous Hawthorne studies, researchers were studying whether modifying factory conditions improved employees' productivity. The researchers eventually decided that changes in productivity they observed were a function of paying attention to and observing the workers in the factory rather than any specific change they made to the conditions (Sundstrom, McIntyre, Halfhill, & Richards, 2000).

Participants may also adjust their behavior or their descriptions of themselves to present a more favorable or **socially desirable** impression (King & Bruner, 2000). Participants may endorse items on a survey that they believe will make the researcher think about them in a more positive manner. Some participants may experience **evaluation apprehension**, getting anxious or distressed about being measured. This may cause scores on symptom measures or measures of distress to appear more elevated than they would under other circumstances.

To address this bias, researchers may administer additional surveys which measure the tendency to respond in ways that present oneself in a positive light (e.g., the Marlowe–Crowne Social Desirability Scale). The scores on this scale can be used as a control variable in the analyses. For some variables, **implicit association tests** can be used instead of self-reports to measure variables which may elicit concerns about social desirability. For example, implicit association tests are often used to measure nonconscious prejudice or bias against members of different groups. Implicit association tests use reaction time use variations in reaction time instead of self-reports to assess prejudice or bias (see Project Implicit: https://implicit.harvard.edu/implicit/).

In treatment outcome studies and other longitudinal designs, participant's reactions to the test may change as they repeat the tests several times (e.g., at pretest, posttest, follow-up). Some participants may "get used to" the questions and start to **habituate** to questions about a feeling or behavior. Consequently, they may report lower levels of a given behavior or feeling, even when their actual behavior or feeling has not changed.

Alternatively, participants may become **sensitized** to the test, becoming more aware of their behaviors or feelings, and consequently, report higher levels of the behavior over time. Researchers can use different versions of the test to offset some of these effects. For example, they may ask questions in a different order or use different versions of the questions.

Participants may experience **measurement fatigue** if they are given too many tests. Measurement fatigue can lead participants to offer less reliable or valid responses as they become more tired or fatigued. To determine how many tests participants can complete before becoming fatigued, researchers can conduct pilot tests.

Response bias or **response set** can be detected when participants tend to choose the same answer regardless of the question (i.e., they always choose a "3" on a "five-point Likert scale"). The measurement tools themselves can be modified to reduce problems with response bias or response set.

Assessments may also be influenced by **order effects.** Assessments are affected by order effects when the order in which the tests are presented affects the outcome. This can occur when some tests can influence answers to other tests. Researchers may randomize the order of presentation of these tests to permit assessment of order effects and to eliminate their influence.

Information about other sources of bias that can affect assessment can be found in Podsakoff, MacKenzie, & Podsakoff, (2012).

If you are writing a proposal to test the effects of treatment, you will describe the procedures you use to avoid bias in measurement. If you are writing a paper reviewing other studies, you will report on the strategies other researchers used to avoid bias in measurement and indicate if these strategies seemed effective.

Procedures Related to the Timing of the Assessments

Researchers must establish procedures for the timing of assessments. When multiple assessments are needed, researchers must determine how often to assess the participants. They may need to get frequent data to develop reliable estimates, but they must avoid placing too great a burden on the participants.

In a treatment outcome study, assessments to determine eligibility occur before the formal hypothesis-testing begins. Assessments to establish the levels of symptoms occur before the treatment begins. These are often called the **baseline** or **pre-treatment** tests. Assessments to determine if the treatment has produced changes occur after the treatment is complete. These assessments are often called the **posttreatment** tests or **posttests**. Assessments can also be performed to determine if treatment-related changes persist once the treatment has ended. These assessments can be made at one or more points after the treatment has ended. These assessments are often called **follow-up assessments**. Here is one way to visualize the timing of the assessments for a treatment outcome study (Table 17.2).

TABLE 17.2 Potential Timing of Assessments.

Timing/ Group	Eligibility test	Pretreatment test	Posttreatment test	Follow-up test
Experimental	–	–	–	–
Control	–	–	–	–

Fig. 17.5 displays another way to visualize the timing. The experimental and control groups are assessed and then participate in treatment for a specified period of time. In this example, they participate for 5 weeks. Once the treatment is over, participants are tested again, at posttest and at follow-up.

Week 1	Week 2	Week 3	Week 4	Week 5	Week 6	Week 7	Week 8	Week 9	Week 13
Eligibility assessment	Pre-treatment Baseline	Randomization to Experimental or Control Conditions	Intervention					Post-treatment assessment	Follow-up test

FIGURE 17.5 Visualizing the timing of assessments.

Here is an example of a description of the timing of measurements from a longitudinal study by Spinhoven, Elzinga, Van Hemert, de Rooij, and Penninx (2016) (Fig. 17.6).

Research paper

Childhood maltreatment, maladaptive personality types and level and course of psychological distress: A six-year longitudinal study

Philip Spinhoven[a,b,*], Bernet M. Elzinga[a], Albert M. Van Hemert[b], Mark de Rooij[c], Brenda W. Penninx[b,d,e]

2. Methods

2.2. Procedure

A detailed description of the NESDA design and sampling procedures has been given elsewhere (Penninx et al., 2008). The baseline measurement (T0) in 2981 participants included assessment of demographic and personal characteristics, a standardized diagnostic psychiatric interview and a medical assessment including blood samples. The study was approved by the Ethical Committees of participating universities and all respondents provided written informed consent prior to data collection. After two (T2), four (T4), and six years (T6) a face-to-face follow-up assessment was conducted with a response of 87.1% ($n=2596$) at T2, of 80.6% ($n=2402$) at T4 and 75.7% ($n=2256$) at T6. A 1-year follow-up assessment (T1), consisting of a written questionnaire, was completed by 2445 participants (82.0%). Complete measurements for psychological distress at T0 were available for 2947 persons (98.9% of the baseline sample), constituting the present study sample.

FIGURE 17.6 Procedures from Spinhoven et al., 2016.

Procedures Related to Delivering the Independent Variable in Experimental Studies

The aim of experimental research studies is to test the effects of the independent variable, identifying differences in outcomes associated with the experimental and control conditions. Therefore, to protect the internal validity of the study, researchers develop procedures for assigning participants at random, evaluating the reliability and validity of the implementation of the experimental and control conditions, and establishing the comparability of the experimental and control conditions.

Procedures for Random Assignment

One critical approach to reducing bias in experimental studies involves random assignment. As we have discussed earlier (see Chapters 3, 6, and 12), random assignment means that participants are assigned at random to the levels of the independent variable. With random assignment, neither the participant nor the researcher controls assignment to the level of the independent variable (i.e., assignment to the experimental vs. the control conditions). Consequently, unforeseen extraneous variables and other sources of bias are less likely to influence members of one level of the independent variable more than another. When extraneous variables affect level of the independent variable more than the other (i.e., affect the participants in the experimental more than the control), it becomes difficult to determine if the outcome is a function of the extraneous variable or the level of the independent variable.

A Closer Look

Randomization in randomized controlled trials is done differently depending on whether the researcher is using a parallel design or a cross-over design. In parallel design randomized control trials, participants are assigned at random to the experimental and control conditions. In **cross-over RCT** designs, all participants receive both treatments. Consequently, researchers must control potential **carryover effects**. Carryover effects occur when exposure to one treatment influences response to the next. To manage these cross-over effects, the order of presentation of the treatments is **counterbalanced.** Participants are assigned at random to the order of presentation of the conditions (i.e., either receiving the control condition first or the experimental condition first).

There are many strategies for assigning participants at random. There are special computerized programs which generate lists of random numbers to help investigators generate assignments to the experimental and control treatments (https://www.randomizer.org/). The diagram depicting the process of randomization is called a CONSORT diagram. The CONSORT diagram details how participants moved through the study from the initial recruitment to the final phase of testing, clarifying which participants were randomized to the experimental and control conditions.

Procedures for Establishing the Reliability and Validity of the Delivery of the Independent Variable

To protect the internal validity of the study, researchers must ensure that the levels of the independent variable are delivered in a way that is both reliable and valid. Therefore, researchers develop procedures to make sure that the correct "dosage" or type of the levels of the independent variable is consistently administered.

For example, when researchers evaluate the effects of a treatment component such as relaxation training, they clearly describe the relaxation exercises, and they indicate what the therapist and the participant should be doing during these exercises. Then they examine the actual therapy sessions to make sure that the therapists and participants were following the exercise instructions each session.

To understand this further, let's look at two examples of the procedures researchers use to implement the treatment.

In this study by Freeman et al. (2008), the authors describe the experimental treatment for OCD in young children—a family-based treatment. They describe the procedures they use to deliver each component of the treatment.

Researchers evaluate **treatment fidelity,** the quality of adherence to the treatment protocol, a measure of the validity of the treatment implementation. Researchers use several approaches to establish treatment fidelity. They make sure the therapists are well trained and well supervised to ensure their competence in delivering the intervention.

In addition, researchers use **fidelity checks** to determine if the treatment is delivered as intended. They might listen to audio or video tapes to check if the therapists are conducting the sessions in a way that is consistent with the treatment manual and the intent of treatment. In Internet-based therapies, researchers can collect data to determine if the participant completed the treatment module and accompanying exercises.

Fig. 17.7 displays an example of procedures researchers have developed to evaluate treatment fidelity. Treatment fidelity is sometimes called **adherence to the treatment protocol**.

> All therapists were briefly introduced to the treatment program by providing them with the treatment manual, and a 1 h information meeting in separate groups. During the first year of the study, therapists were supervised biweekly by the principal investigator (CvdH) in separate group sessions for MCT and IUT. After the first year, supervision was on average provided once per two months. At these meetings all active cases and therapy notes were reviewed to ensure adherence to protocols and treatment quality. Adherence to the protocol was further evaluated through an assessment of 71 randomly selected recordings of treatment sessions by trained clinical psychology students (at a master level), who rated the therapists' behaviors against session-by-session intervention checklists that closely followed the content of the treatment manuals. This treatment integrity check revealed that the therapists closely followed the treatment manuals (i.e., in only 3% of the sessions they applied interventions that were not described in the manual).

FIGURE 17.7 Selected excerpt from van der Heiden, Muris, & van der Molen, 2012.

Fig. 17.8 displays an example of the procedures that researchers use to ensure the therapists are qualified to deliver the treatment. Freeman et al. (2008) use a series of procedures to ensure the therapy is delivered by highly educated and training therapists who are also well supervised.

> *Therapist Training and Supervision.* All study therapists were clinical psychology interns, postdoctoral fellows, and clinical psychologists with expertise in the application of behavior therapy with anxiety disorders, parent behavior management training, and relaxation and family-based treatment. Doctoral-level clinical psychologists (J.B.F., A.M.G.) provided all of the training and supervision. Training included didactic instruction, familiarization with the treatment manuals, and role-playing of treatment procedures. All of the therapy sessions were videotaped and discussed in weekly group supervision.

FIGURE 17.8 Selected excerpt from Freeman et al., 2008.

Procedures for Insuring the Comparability of the Experimental and Control Conditions

As we discussed in Chapter 11, in both basic and applied experimental studies, a control condition is critical to enable the researcher to understand the effects of the independent variable. Ideally, the control condition contains all aspects of the experimental condition with one exception. This exception is the component hypothesized to cause the effect of the experimental condition. If there are differences in outcomes between the experimental and control conditions, then the researcher can conclude that the differences are caused by the component that is different between the conditions.

The researcher must have procedures for matching the experimental and control conditions on variables that may influence the outcome. Fig. 17.9 provides an example. Dear et al. are comparing two treatments. One treatment is especially designed for the study—the "Worry Course." The other established treatment is called the "Wellbeing Course." In this study, the Worry Course is the experimental condition and the Wellbeing Course is the control condition.

Dear et al. (2016) hypothesize that it is the *content* of the Worry Course that will make it a more effective treatment than the Wellbeing Course. To test the hypothesis that it is the content of the course, and not other aspects of the treatment that determine the outcome, the two treatments must be very similar in every way except the content. As you read the description of the courses, notice the aspects of the treatments, including the length of the course, duration of the sessions, and contact with the therapists that are kept the same across the treatment conditions.

2.3. Interventions

All participants received access to either a DS-CBT course for SAD, the *Social Confidence Course*, or a TD-CBT course, the *Wellbeing Course*. The *Social Confidence Course* was developed specifically for this trial and the Wellbeing Course has been previously demonstrated as clinically efficacious in treating symptoms of anxiety and depression (Titov et al., 2012a,b; Titov et al., 2013a,b; Titov et al., 2014a,b).

← In this section, the authors describe how the content of the courses differs.

Consistent with standard definitions (McEvoy et al., 2009) and the other trials in this series of trials (Dear, Gandy et al., 2015; Dear, Staples et al., 2015; Dear, Zou et al., 2015; Titov, Dear, Staples, Bennett-Levy et al., 2015; Titov, Dear, Staples, Terides et al., 2015; Fogliati, Dear et al., 2016), the TD-CBT intervention was the same for all participants and was not designed to treat any specific psychological disorder. Rather it aimed to present a broad range of therapeutic information and skills relevant to the cognitive, physical and behavioural symptoms of psychological distress generally. Reflecting this, the TD-CBT intervention did not mention specific diagnoses and all vignettes, examples and case stories were presented to cover a broad range of situations and types of psychological distress (e.g., excessive worry, low mood, social anxieties and panic and strong physical sensations). In contrast, the DS-CBT treatment was specifically designed to target symptoms of SAD and presented all therapeutic information and skills in the context of SAD and reducing SAD symptoms. Consequently, all vignettes, examples and case stories focussed on SAD and the management of associated symptoms and no specific mention of other diagnoses or the broader application of therapeutic skills was made. The content and differences between the TD-CBT and DS-CBT interventions are summarised in Table 2.

As with the other trials in this series of studies, participants in the clinician-guided condition (CG-CBT) received weekly contact from a psychologist using telephone or a secure email messaging system. Four accredited and nationally registered psychologists and one provisional psychologist provided treatment. Based on the findings of previous studies (Craske et al., 2009; Johnston, Titov, Spence, Andrews, & Dear, 2011) and to minimise therapist drift (Waller 2009), the nature of the contact was protocolised and key aims included (1) reinforcing the main messages of each lesson, (2) answering questions, (3) reinforcing progress and skills practice, (4) problem solving skills usage, (5) normalising the challenges of recovery, and (6) obtaining feedback about the participant's perception and engagement with the course. Each contact was designed to take ≤ 10 min, but more time was provided when clinically indicated. The psychologists received training in online interventions via the training program at the eCentreClinic and received supervision from BFD and NT during weekly individual and group supervision sessions. Participants in the self-guided condition did not receive weekly contact, but their progress and symptoms were monitored throughout treatment by the clinicians and were able to contact the clinic if technical assistance was required or if they were experiencing a mental health crisis. A research assistant provided technical support for all participants in the trial.

FIGURE 17.9 Selected excerpt from Dear et al., 2016.

Not all experimental and control conditions are matched as carefully as in the Dear et al. (2016) study. In some cases, the experimental and control treatments vary across many dimensions. This makes it difficult to determine what accounts for the outcomes of the study.

If you are writing a proposal for a treatment outcome study, you will choose a control condition which permits a clear test of the active component of the experimental treatment. This involves keeping the experimental and control conditions/treatments as similar as possible, except for the "active ingredient," the component of treatment the researchers hypothesize will improve outcomes. If you are writing a paper reviewing experimental studies, you will review the types of control conditions that have been used and discuss the strengths and limitations of these control conditions. Specifically, you will discuss the hypotheses that can be tested using the experimental and control conditions the researchers have chosen.

Procedures for Reducing Threats to Internal Validity by Controlling Bias and Extraneous Variables

There are many sources of bias which can threaten the internal validity of a treatment outcome study. The internal validity of the study can be threatened if other anticipated or unanticipated extraneous variables affect the ability to deliver or evaluate the treatment or affect the participants' response to treatment. Researchers must develop procedures for handling all these potential sources of bias.

Extraneous Variables

As we discussed in Chapter 13, **extraneous variables** are variables which unintentionally affect the independent or dependent variables, and consequently influence the outcome of the study. When an extraneous variable completely overlaps with an independent variable, then it is called a **confounding variable**. Some extraneous or confounding variables can occur even in the tightly controlled environment of a laboratory. For example, possible extraneous variables could include factors such as unanticipated changes in temperature or noise in the laboratory, technical difficulties, or differences in the way the research assistants interact with the participants.

The introduction of extraneous variables increases dramatically when research is conducted in real-world environments, such as schools, hospitals, or worksites. Researchers cannot always control the circumstances in which treatment is delivered or testing is conducted. Major cultural changes—such as a Presidential election or a natural disaster—can occur as a study is progressing and affect the outcomes. Researchers must attempt to anticipate these variables and try to eliminate or control their effects.

When researchers can anticipate extraneous variables, they can establish procedures for eliminating them or controlling their effects. For example, they can develop procedures to maximize the likelihood the technology functions effectively. In other cases, researchers may develop procedures for recruiting new participants, if some participants drop out of the study because of major life events.

Sometimes there are extraneous variables which may affect the outcome but cannot be directly controlled. Consequently, researchers may measure these variables and adjust for them in statistical analyses. For example, researchers may not wish to eliminate participants taking medications for behavioral health disorders. In these cases, researchers might choose to measure medication use, since they cannot control it. The data on medication use are included in the statistical analyses.

Information about the types of extraneous variables that may serve as a threat to your study can be gathered from meta-analyses and systematic reviews about the disorder you are studying. You can find additional information on extraneous variables by examining the methods section and limitations portion of the discussion section at the end of original research articles. This information can help you understand what types of extraneous variables may affect your study, and help you identify which variables might need to be treated as covariates.

Fig. 17.10 provides an example. In a systematic review of studies of parenting interventions, Flynn and colleagues (2015) report on the quality of the studies in this research area. They identify several difficulties with these studies which limit the interpretability of the data. These difficulties include limitations to the "blinding" of participants or research staff and problems handling missing data. The problems with study quality that are identified by Flynn and colleagues can serve as an important reminder to develop procedures to avoid these limitations.

Published in final edited form as:
Acad Pediatr. 2015 ; 15(5): 480–492. doi:10.1016/j.acap.2015.06.012.

Primary Care Interventions to Prevent or Treat Traumatic Stress in Childhood: A Systematic Review

Anna Flynn, MHS[1], **Kate E. Fothergill, PhD**[2,*], **Holly C. Wilcox, PhD**[1,3], **Elizabeth Coleclough, MPH**[2], **Russell Horwitz, MD**[3], **Anne Ruble, MD**[3], **Matthew D. Burkey, MD**[3], and **Lawrence Wissow, MD**[2,3]

Kate E. Fothergill: kfother1@jhu.edu; Holly C. Wilcox: hwilcox1@jhmi.edu; Elizabeth Coleclough: ecolecl1@jhu.edu; Russell Horwitz: rhorwitz@jhmi.edu; Anne Ruble: aruble@jhmi.edu; Matthew D. Burkey: mburkey1@jhmi.edu; Lawrence Wissow: lwissow@jhmi.edu

[1]Department of Mental Health, Johns Hopkins Bloomberg School of Public Health, 624 N. Broadway, Baltimore, MD, 21205, USA

[2]Department of Health Behavior and Society, Johns Hopkins Bloomberg School of Public Health, 624 N. Broadway, Baltimore, MD, 21205, USA

[3]Department of Psychiatry & Behavioral Sciences, Johns Hopkins University School of Medicine, 600 N. Wolfe Street, Baltimore, 21205, MD, USA

Study Quality

The 10 studies included in this review varied in terms of quality. Over half of the studies were randomized controlled trials. Research staff were blinded to allocation of subjects in only one study[23] though this is understandable given the nature of the interventions; allocation concealment would have been impossible in many instances. Staff assessing outcomes from medical records were blinded in only two studies.[23,29] Those studies for which methods of dealing with missing data were reported dropped subjects with missing outcomes data from the analysis.[30,32] We assessed each of the studies specifically for potential for various forms of bias (see Table 3). Risk of bias was generally low overall though there were some exceptions. In particular, subject/staff blinding, outcome assessment blinding, and incomplete outcome reporting were areas of concern in a number of studies in that our ratings were either high or unclear. The four randomized trials reporting clinical outcomes (e.g. CBCL scores, child maltreatment as measured in the SEEK studies) were of mixed quality, with the two SEEK studies having low or unclear risk of bias and the two studies reporting CBCL scores having relatively high risk of bias (see Table 3).

FIGURE 17.10 Selected excerpt from Flynn et al., 2015

Activity 17.1: Identifying Procedures and Their Implications for the Internal Validity of the Study

Read the excerpts included in Figs. 17.7–17.9 again. Use Table 17.3 to describe the procedures in your own words. Explain how these procedures protect the internal validity of the study.

TABLE 17.3 Identifying and Explaining Procedures.

Authors/Date	Brief descriptions of the key procedures in your own words.	How does each aspect of the procedure protect the internal validity of the study?
Freeman et al. (2008)	–	–
van der Heiden et al. (2012)	–	–

Procedures for Managing and Analyzing Data

As the study is proceeding, the researcher must have procedures to handle the data being collected and prepare the data for analyses. Researchers must ensure the original data are stored to protect confidentiality. The procedures used to store the data must protect the identity of the participant. For example, physical data (e.g., paper-and-pencil surveys) should be stored in locked cabinets, and electronic data should be stored in password protected files. Study identification numbers, rather than names, should be used to identify the participants on the measurement instruments. No personally identifying information, such as addresses, is stored with data that includes confidential health information. The **Health Insurance Portability and Accountability Act (HIPAA)** also has other requirements for ensuring the confidentiality of the data when medical or any type of health records are used. These steps are necessary to protect the rights of the research participants and to protect against threats to internal validity.

Data for analyses must be free from errors and meet the assumptions of the proposed analyses. **Data cleaning** involves the procedures used to insure the data entered into the computer for analysis match the data collected from the participant. For example, sometimes researchers collect paper-and-pencil data, and then they enter it into the computer for analysis. Researchers must have procedures to check that the data entry was done correctly. Some researchers enter data twice and check for differences; others assign one research assistant to enter the data and another to check it. Information about these procedures is included in the Statistical Analysis Plan of the methods section.

Participants do not always complete all measurement instruments, and sometimes the automated data collection strategies fail. To prepare the data for analysis, the researcher must develop procedures for handling **missing data**. For more information on handling missing data, see Buhi, Goodson, & Neilands, 2008.

The researchers must also have procedures for conducting descriptive and inferential analyses. Some of these procedures were discussed in Chapter 9.

Building Human Capital

In this chapter, you learned about many procedures involved in developing and implementing a research study. There is a lot to think about!

Many of those procedures are necessary to prevent bias. Some sources of bias come from the experimenter, some from the participants. Some sources of bias come from the research procedures and some from the research environment.

Learning to identify and address these sources of bias takes conscientiousness and creativity. It helps to be conscientious about reading articles in the area you are studying. These articles can help you identify many sources of bias that have been reported by other researchers. As you learn more, you will get better at recognizing bias. You will be able to think through all the steps and variables involved in the research.

Identifying bias also takes creativity, including the ability to see things from different perspectives. You need to be able to see the research hypothesis and the methods from different points of view. These different points of view include the point of view of the participant, the point of view of someone who really doesn't think your theory is correct, and the point of view of someone who is unfamiliar with this research area. Imagining how the procedures and outcomes look from all these different points of view can help you see sources of bias you did not think of initially. Learning to switch perspectives is a valuable skill.

The hard work you put in to learn about research procedures will help you in any field. You are learning to think through the logistics of working on a project. The logistics involve the step-by-step processes that are involved in researching and implementing any project. Putting these skills to work will help you anticipate problems and guide your efforts to take corrective action. As you master these skills, you can think—"I read about the process, and I thought it through. I can see some possible problems, and I have learned about some possible solutions." People who can think this way are valued members of a team. And they can have fun trying to detect hidden problems.

Terms

Take the time to define each of these terms and consider how to apply them.

Research Terms

Volunteer Bias
Attrition Bias
Standardization
Manual of Operations
Demand Characteristics
Halo Effect
Nocebo Effect

Single-Blind Study
Experimenter Bias
Observer-Expectancy Effect
Double-Blind
Placebo
Manipulation Check
Response Reactivity
Social Desirability Effect
Evaluation Apprehension
Sensitization
Response Bias
Response Set
Measurement Order Effect
Habituation
Implicit Association Test
White Coat Effect
Measurement Fatigue
Baseline (Pretreatment)
Posttreatment (Posttest)
Follow-up Assessment
Cross-Over Randomized Controlled Trial (Cross-Over RCT)
Carryover Effects
Counterbalance
Treatment Fidelity
Fidelity Check
Adherence (to treatment protocol)
Confounding Variable
Health Insurance Portability and Accountability Act (HIPAA)
Data Cleaning
Missing Data
Imputation
Preliminary Analyses

References

Ali, S., Rhodes, L., Moreea, O., McMillan, D., Gilbody, S., Leach, C., ... Delgadillo, J. (2017). How durable is the effect of low intensity CBT for depression and anxiety? Remission and relapse in a longitudinal cohort study. *Behaviour Research and Therapy, 94*, 1–8.

Barsky, A. J., Saintfort, R., Rogers, M. P., & Borus, J. F. (2002). Nonspecific medication side effects and the nocebo phenomenon. *The Journal of the American Medical Association, 287*(5), 622–627.

Brondolo, E., Eichler, B. F., & Taravella, J. (2003). A tailored anger management program for reducing citizen complaints against traffic agents. *Journal of Police and Criminal Psychology, 18*(2), 1.

Buhi, E. R., Goodson, P., & Neilands, T. B. (2008). Out of sight, not out of mind: Strategies for handling missing data. *American Journal of Health Behavior, 32*(1), 83–92.

Dear, B. F., Staples, L. G., Terides, M. D., Fogliati, V. J., Sheehan, J., Johnston, L., … Titov, N. (2016). Transdiagnostic versus disorder-specific and clinician-guided versus self-guided internet-delivered treatment for social anxiety disorder and comorbid disorders: A randomized controlled trial. *Journal of Anxiety Disorders, 42*, 30–44.

Flynn, A. B., Fothergill, K. E., Wilcox, H. C., Coleclough, E., Horwitz, R., Ruble, A., … Wissow, L. S. (2015). Primary care interventions to prevent or treat traumatic stress in childhood: A systematic review. *Academic Pediatrics, 15*(5), 480–492.

Freeman, J. B., Garcia, A. M., Coyne, L., Ale, C., Przeworski, A., Himle, M., … Leonard, H. L. (2008). Early childhood OCD: Preliminary findings from a family-based cognitive- behavioral approach. *Journal of the American Academy of Child & Adolescent Psychiatry, 47*(5), 593–602.

Goodwin, C. J., & Goodwin, K. A. (2016). *Research in psychology methods and design*. John Wiley & Sons.

Heckerling, P. S. (2005). The ethics of single blind trials. *IRB: Ethics & Human Research, 27*(4), 12–16.

Hughes, J. R., & Krahn, D. E. A. N. (1985). Blindness and the validity of the double-blind procedure. *Journal of Clinical Psychopharmacology, 5*(3), 138–142.

van der Heiden, C., Muris, P., & van der Molen, H. T. (2012). Randomized controlled trial on the effectiveness of metacognitive therapy and intolerance-of-uncertainty therapy for generalized anxiety disorder. *Behaviour Research and Therapy, 50*(2), 100–109.

Karlin, W. A., Brondolo, E., & Schwartz, J. (2003). Workplace social support and ambulatory cardiovascular activity in New York City traffic agents. *Psychosomatic Medicine, 65*(2), 167–176.

King, M. F., & Bruner, G. C. (2000). Social desirability bias: A neglected aspect of validity testing. *Psychology and Marketing, 17*(2), 79–103.

Kuyken, W., Hayes, R., Barrett, B., Byng, R., Dalgleish, T., Kessler, D., … Causley, A. (2015). Effectiveness and cost-effectiveness of mindfulness-based cognitive therapy compared with maintenance antidepressant treatment in the prevention of depressive relapse or recurrence (PREVENT): A randomised controlled trial. *The Lancet, 386*(9988), 63–73.

Leuchter, A. F., Cook, I. A., Witte, E. A., Morgan, M., & Abrams, M. (2002). Changes in brain function of depressed subjects during treatment with placebo. *American Journal of Psychiatry, 159*(1), 122–129.

Levis, B., Benedetti, A., Riehm, K. E., Saadat, N., Levis, A. W., Azar, M., … Gilbody, S. (2018). Probability of major depression diagnostic classification using semi-structured versus fully structured diagnostic interviews. *The British Journal of Psychiatry, 212*(6), 377–385.

Moerman, D. E. (2002). *Meaning, medicine, and the" placebo effect"* (Vol. 28). Cambridge: Cambridge University Press.

Nichols, A. L., & Maner, J. K. (2008). The good-subject effect: Investigating participant demand characteristics. *The Journal of General Psychology, 135*(2), 151–166.

Podsakoff, P. M., MacKenzie, S. B., & Podsakoff, N. P. (2012). Sources of method bias in social science research and recommendations on how to control it. *Annual Review of Psychology, 63*, 539–569.

Rosenthal, R. (1994). Interpersonal expectancy effects: A 30-year perspective. *Current Directions in Psychological Science, 3*(6), 176–179.

Southam-Gerow, M. A., Weisz, J. R., Chu, B. C., McLeod, B. D., Gordis, E. B., & Connor- Smith, J. K. (2010). Does cognitive behavioral therapy for youth anxiety outperform usual care in community clinics? An initial effectiveness test. *Journal of the American Academy of Child & Adolescent Psychiatry, 49*(10), 1043–1052.

Spinhoven, P., Elzinga, B. M., Van Hemert, A. M., de Rooij, M., & Penninx, B. W. (2016). Childhood maltreatment, maladaptive personality types and level and course of psychological distress: A six-year longitudinal study. *Journal of Affective Disorders, 191*, 100–108.

Sundstrom, E., McIntyre, M., Halfhill, T., & Richards, H. (2000). Work groups: From the Hawthorne studies to work teams of the 1990s and beyond. *Group Dynamics: Theory, Research, and Practice, 4*(1), 44.

Zlotnick, C., Johnson, J., & Najavits, L. M. (2009). Randomized controlled pilot study of cognitive-behavioral therapy in a sample of incarcerated women with substance use disorder and PTSD. *Behavior Therapy, 40*(4), 325–336.

Chapter 18

Writing about research methods

In Chapters 15–17, you learned about many of the methods used in research studies, including the methods used to choose participants, select and administer measurement instruments, and deliver and monitor the independent variable (IV). In Chapter 18, you will learn about how to write about research methods.

If you are writing a research proposal, the Methods Section will serve as a general instruction manual for the proposed study. In each component of the Methods Section, you include the technical details about the methods you plan to use and a justification for methods you chose. This information enables the reader to evaluate the methodological rigor of the proposed study and to identify potential threats to internal and external validity.

If you are writing a research paper reviewing other studies, you read the methods used in sections of original research articles. As you examine these methods, you provide an evaluation of other researchers' approaches to selecting participants, measuring outcomes, delivering IVs, and controlling bias. You identify consistencies (or inconsistencies) across studies in the methods used.

As you review the studies, you may find their results vary depending on the methods used. In your paper, you describe these variations and your analysis of their causes. You discuss the implications of these methods for the interpretability of the outcomes these studies have obtained. This provides the reader with an understanding of the "state-of-the-science" for the topic area.

In this chapter, the first section describes writing a Methods Section for a research proposal. The second section describes writing about research methods for a paper reviewing other studies.

Psychology Research Methods. https://doi.org/10.1016/B978-0-12-815680-3.00018-9

Writing About the Methods to be Included in a Research Proposal

If you are writing a research proposal, you explain the planned research methods, including the choice of participants, measures, and procedures. You provide a justification for each method, specifically indicating how the methods enable you to test the hypotheses you propose to test. These descriptions help the reader determine if the proposed study will provide a rigorous test of the hypotheses. The Methods Sections can also help the reader recognize potential limitations to the proposed study, including limitations to internal and external validity. This information enables the reader to understand the gaps in knowledge the study will address, and the gaps that may remain.

To develop the methods for a new study, researchers carefully examine the methods used by other researchers. As they incorporate methods from other researchers in their own approach, researchers carefully cite the articles describing the methods they have adopted using APA style. Explaining and citing previous work is part of how the researchers demonstrate that the methods of their study are based on established work and are rigorous.

The general components of a Methods Section for a proposal are described in Table 18.1. More specific components may be necessary depending on the methods used and the degree to which the methods involve equipment or procedures that require technical knowledge. For example, in treatment outcome studies, the IV might be delivered by specialized equipment such as virtual reality or eye movement desensitization technology. The dependent/outcome variables might be assessed using measurement methods which require specialized equipment and procedures to collect the data. The technical details involved in delivering the IV or collecting data on dependent/outcome variables might be described in more detail in separate components in the Methods Section.

In the Methods Section, each component is clearly labeled to allow the reader to quickly find relevant information. Table 18.1 is meant as a guide to help organize your approach to developing a Methods Section for a proposal. But there are no official rules about the order in which this information is presented or how the components are labeled. Not all researchers include all the details described in the table. Share your writing with others to determine if you are as clear and consistent as possible in your description of the methods.

TABLE 18.1 General components of a Methods Section.

Components	Information included
Overview (May be placed at the end of the Introduction or at the beginning of the Methods)	The overall aim of the study. Identifies the predictor/independent variables and the outcome/dependent variables. A brief indication of the research design (e.g., observational, experimental, cross-sectional, longitudinal, mixed), and a brief description of the nature of the sample and study setting (e.g., laboratory, field, workplace).
Participants (and associated procedures)	The number of participants and how that number was determined.
	The inclusion criteria for determining eligibility.
	The exclusion criteria for determining eligibility.
	Descriptions of the procedures for assessing eligibility.
	Reports on proposed or actual sociodemographic characteristics of the sample, information about study setting.
	Description of the procedures for recruitment.
	CONSORT diagram, if needed.
	Identification of steps to insure ethical treatment of participants (e.g., IRB review, use of informed consent, etc.).
	Description of procedures for consenting participants.
Measures (and associated procedures)	Identification of predictor and outcome variables, including primary and secondary outcomes, and other measures. Includes an explanation of the purpose of the measure and a justification of the choice of measurement method.
	Description of measurement instruments. Including details about the measurement method, types of items included, and response formats. Scoring information as appropriate.
	Information about the reliability and validity of the measurement instrument.

Continued

TABLE 18.1 General components of a Methods Section.—cont'd

Components	Information included
	Descriptions of the procedures for timing of assessments, clarifying if this is a cross-sectional study, a longitudinal study, etc.
	Descriptions of procedures for training of assessors (i.e., individuals conducting assessments).
	Descriptions of procedures for protecting against bias (e.g., single or double-blind procedures, etc.)
If an experimental study, description of the independent variable and the experimental manipulation (and associated procedures)	Description of the independent variable, including the different levels of the independent variable (e.g., experimental conditions, control conditions). For treatment outcome studies this includes information about treatment package, treatment components, treatment modality, treatment delivery system, therapist qualifications, and setting.
	Description of comparability across conditions, highlighting differences between experimental and control conditions.
	Descriptions of procedures for random assignment.
	Descriptions of procedures for insuring reliability and validity of treatment delivery.
Statistical analysis plan (and associated procedures)	Descriptions of procedures for entering and storing data, protecting confidentiality.
	Descriptions of procedures for cleaning the data, fixing errors.
	Descriptions of procedures for handling missing data.
	Descriptions of procedures for preliminary analyses to identify covariates.
	Descriptions of procedures for inferential analyses.

In this chapter, we focus on developing a Methods Section for a treatment outcome study. However, Methods Sections of other types of studies also follow these general guidelines. In the following sections, we review strategies for communicating the information included in each component of the Methods Section.

Providing an Overview

To help the reader quickly understand the aim and methods of the study, researchers provide an overview. The goal of the overview is to provide the reader with a clear understanding of the importance of the study and its aims. The overview may start with a short summary of the existing evidence and a brief review of gaps in knowledge. Then, the overview presents a description of the aim of the study and a brief review of the design and methods.

Some authors include this information at the end of the Introduction section, whereas others include this information in the beginning of the Methods Section.

Let's look at two examples.

In the Dear et al. (2015) study, the authors provide a conceptual overview of the aims at the end of the Introduction and include a description of the way the methods will achieve these aims (Fig. 18.1).

The authors provide a statement of the aims of the study in the first paragraph. Later in the paragraph, they identify the specific hypotheses they will test. In the middle of the paragraph, they describe how the methods will permit them to test these hypotheses.

> The present study extends this work by exploring the relative clinical efficacy and acceptability of transdiagnostic and disorder-specific CBT for GAD when provided in both clinician-guided and self-guided formats. Participants ($n = 338$) were randomized to receive either transdiagnostic treatment (TD-CBT) or disorder specific (DS-CBT) treatment for symptoms of GAD, in either a clinician-guided format (CG-CBT) or self-guided format (SG-CBT). Both treatment options consisted of 5 lessons of internet-delivered CBT (iCBT) delivered over 8 weeks. Participants were assessed prior to treatment, immediately post-treatment, and at 3, 12, and 24-months after treatment. It was hypothesized that both TD-CBT and DS-CBT would result in significant reductions in symptoms of GAD, but that TD-CBT would be superior at reducing symptoms of comorbid depression, social anxiety and panic at each time point. It was also hypothesized that CG-CBT would be superior to SG-CBT at every time point for both symptoms of generalized anxiety and comorbid depression, social anxiety, and panic symptoms.

FIGURE 18.1 Excerpt from Dear et al. (2015).

In contrast, Brenes, Divers, Miller, and Danhauer (2018) provide this description at the beginning of the Methods Section (Fig. 18.2).

2. Overview and specific aims

This manuscript describes a two-stage randomized preference trial [26] comparing CBT and yoga for the treatment of worry in a sample of anxious older adults (See Fig. 1). Five hundred participants will be randomized to either the preference trial (participants choose the intervention; N = 250) or to the randomized trial (participants are randomized to one of the two interventions; N = 250) with equal probability. This study design allows for the calculation of traditional intervention effects (differences in outcomes between participants randomized to either CBT or yoga), selection effects [expected difference in outcomes between those who would choose intervention A (if allowed to do so) and those who would choose intervention B (if allowed to do so)], and preference effects (differences in outcomes between participants who received their preferred intervention and those who did not). The primary aim of this study is to compare the effects of two interventions, CBT and yoga, on worry in older ($\geq$60 years) adults. The secondary aims of this study are to compare the effects of these interventions on anxiety and sleep.

FIGURE 18.2 Excerpt from Brenes et al. (2018).

In the overview provided in the Brenes et al. (2018) article, the authors introduce the reader to their complicated study. The careful description of the research design is necessary to understand what the authors are doing. They explain they are asking two questions: (1) Is CBT better than Yoga in improving outcomes, including worry, anxiety, and sleep? (2) Do the effects vary depending on whether the participants prefer the treatment they are provided? The authors explain the sample size and the levels of the two IVs: Type of Treatment and Preferred Treatment. They discuss how they handled random assignment across these two IVs. The overview helps the reader understand the research design and prepares the reader for the additional details to be provided in the remainder of the article.

The authors also use the overview to clarify the outcome measures, explaining that worry is their primary outcome measure, whereas anxiety and sleep are secondary outcomes.

Activity 18.1: Providing an Overview

If you are writing a research proposal, provide an overview summarizing the existing evidence and the gaps in knowledge that need to be addressed. Describe the aims of the study and levels of the independent variables (i.e., experimental and control groups). Provide information about the sample and the outcome variables. Try to keep the overview brief, no more than two paragraphs.

____

____

____

____

____

____

____

____

Describing Participants

In a proposal, the description of the participants is critical to evaluating the scientific rigor of the study. Readers need to understand if the planned sample size is adequate to study the hypothesis. To evaluate both the internal validity and external validity of the study, information on inclusion and exclusion criteria are also included here. Readers need to know the types of characteristics the participants will (or will not) have. A description of the recruitment strategy is also necessary to enable the reader to determine if the recruitment strategy is likely to result in a sample that is appropriate to test the hypothesis.

When writing a proposal, you can model your descriptions of the research participants on the descriptions provided in original research articles. Begin with a description of the proposed sample size, followed by a description of the power analyses, the inclusion and exclusion criteria, and the recruitment strategy. In a proposal, you change the tense used in the description to indicate that that you plan to include a specific number of participants, plan to use certain inclusion and exclusion criteria, and plan to use certain recruitment strategies.

Eligibility and Inclusion and Exclusion Criteria

We can examine the Methods Section of the Brenes et al. article (2018) to see possible strategies for communicating the details of the participants portion of the Methods Section.

In the overview, the authors have indicated they have included 500 people in the study, 250 assigned to each type of IV. They do not explain the power analyses in this section; however, many other authors would include this information when they describe the number of participants they use.

Next, they clearly describe the eligibility criteria, including the inclusion and exclusion criteria. In the participants component of the Brenes et al. (2018) study, the authors clearly explain their inclusion criteria. Notice that they document why they choose the criteria they do and provide citations. The citations take the form of numbers at the end of the sentences. This is a common approach used in medical journals. They do not use APA style (Fig. 18.3).

3.3. Participants

Inclusion criteria include age 60 years and older and a baseline score ≥26 on the Penn State Worry Questionnaire-Abbreviated (PSWQ-A). Older adults may experience anxiety differently than younger adults [27], and traditional diagnostic classifications do not reflect these differences [28,29]. This results in many older adults with symptomatic worry not meeting criteria for DSM diagnoses. Thus, we are targeting people with clinically significant worry for study inclusion rather than relying on a clinical diagnosis. A score of ≥26 on the PSWQ-A represents moderate and severe levels of worry. A score of 26 is 1 standard deviation below the mean in our previous study of late-life GAD [18]; approximately 75% of the sample scored a 26 or higher. Further, participants with a baseline score ≥26 on the PSWQ-A had more than double the reduction in PSWQ-A score (- 10.45 vs. -4.55) than those with a score of 25 or lower. Finally, Stanley and colleagues [30] found that older adults who scored < 26 on the PSWQ-A showed little improvement on measures of worry, anxiety, and depression after intervention with CBT.

Exclusion criteria include currently receiving psychotherapy, currently practicing yoga, current active alcohol/substance abuse, dementia, global cognitive impairment based on the Telephone Interview for Cognitive Status-modified (TICS-m) [31], current psychotic symptoms, active suicidal ideation with plan and intent, change in psychotropic medications within the last month, and hearing loss that would prevent participation in telephone or class sessions.

FIGURE 18.3 Excerpt from Brenes et al. (2018).

Recruitment

The component describing recruitment explains and justifies the location of recruitment and the procedures used. Here is an example of a detailed description of recruitment methods, although the section is labeled "Settings." Brenes et al. (2018) describe both the setting of recruitment (i.e., an academic medical center and the community) and the procedures they will use to implement the recruitment strategies. Notice that they justify their approach. In a proposal, you can use the same type of format, describing your plans for recruitment using future tense (Fig. 18.4).

3.2. Settings

Participants will be recruited through clinics affiliated with an academic medical center and from the community. Clinics participating in the study will include a clinic that provides primary and preventive care to a low-income population; academic and community-based family medicine clinics; a geriatrics clinic; and gynecology clinics. Clinics may use different strategies for referring individuals to the study: administration of an anxiety screening measure by clinic staff with automatic referral of positive screens; mailings to clinic patients; and direct physician referral of patients to the study. Study flyers and brochures will be distributed at local YMCAs, senior centers, senior housing establishments, and restaurants and stores with community boards. Advertisements will be placed in local newspapers, magazines, a newsletter sent to almost 10,000 community-dwelling adults aged ≥60 years who are interested in research studies, and church bulletins.

FIGURE 18.4 Excerpt from Brenes et al. (2018).

Ethical Issues

The component explaining the ethics documents the procedures used to protect the rights of the participants. This component often includes information both about the overall approach to protecting human participants and details about the procedures used to implement these protections. In the Brenes et al. (2018) study, the authors clearly indicate the study has been approved by an Institutional Review Board (Fig. 18.5). In the Ivanova et al. (2016) study, the authors also explicitly state that participants complete a consent prior to participation (Fig. 18.6). In a proposal, you describe the procedures you will use to protect human participants.

3.1. Ethics

This study adheres to the guidelines of the Declaration of Helsinki. It has been approved by Institutional Review Board at Wake Forest School of Medicine.

FIGURE 18.5 Excerpt from Brenes et al. (2018).

2. Method

The current randomized controlled trial was approved by the Regional Ethical Review Board (Regionala Etikprövningsnämnden) in Stockholm, Sweden (Dnr 2013/880-31/5) and preregistered in Clinicaltrials.gov (NCT01963806). See Lindner, Ivanova et al. (2013) for the published study protocol. Participants provided written consent prior to taking part in the study.

FIGURE 18.6 Excerpt from Ivanova et al. (2016).

An Example of a Template for Describing Participants for a Proposal

The level of detail which is included in the participants section depends on the nature of the proposal you are writing and expectations for the course you are taking. The key components are bolded here to draw your attention to the information. They would not be bolded in an actual proposal.

*We plan to **recruit XX** participants using (method of **sampling** such as: convenience, population based, etc.). To arrive at this number, we conducted a **power analysis** (describe). (In the description of the power analysis, include information about the size of the effect you expect based on prior research or your own pilot studies.) The **inclusion criteria** include (list characteristics, measurement methods used to evaluate them, and justify your choices). The **exclusion criteria** include (list characteristics, measurement methods used to evaluate them, and justify the choice of exclusion criteria). The participants will be recruited using (specify the **procedures for recruitment** such as advertisements or other methods) in locations including (specify locations). This recruitment method will permit recruitment of individuals who meet the inclusion criteria, because (justify the choice). The **Institutional Review Board** of (name of institution) approved this study. All participants will provide informed consent (in writing or other method) prior to initiating the study.*

Activity 18.2: Describing the Participants

Describe the participants to be recruited for your proposed study. Make sure you include information on each component of the participants' section. Include the appropriate citations.

____

____

____

____

____

Describing Measures

In a proposal, the measures component explains the way each variable in the study will be measured. The information on the measurement methods helps the reader understand how the researchers conceptualized the variables. Information on the reliability and validity of the measurement instruments helps the reader evaluate the internal validity of the study. Information on the measurement methods helps the reader evaluate any limits to external validity that might occur because of limits to the choice of measurement methods.

Treatment articles will often identify the primary and secondary outcomes. The authors may choose to label the functions of other variables in the analyses, identifying mediators of treatment effects or covariates in the analyses. Researchers may also include information on the timing of assessments.

The measures component may also include a discussion of the ways in which measurement bias can be controlled. The strategies for reducing bias might include procedures for blinding awareness of the experimental and control groups or procedures for minimizing the participants' reactivity to measurement, among others.

In a proposal the researcher writes in future tense, describing measures and procedures to control bias that will be included.

As shown in Fig. 18.7, the measures component of the Freeman et al. (2008) describes the measures used to evaluate a family-based treatment for childhood OCD. In this article, each paragraph includes information about the measurement method, the name and a brief description of the measurement instrument, and information about the reliability and validity of the measurement instrument.

Measures

Children's *DSM-IV* diagnoses were assessed by doctoral-level clinicians using the K-SADS-PL.[15,16] The K-SADS-PL is a semistructured, clinician-rated interview administered to the caregiver(s) and the child that yields *DSM-IV* diagnoses across the major Axis I domains and possesses favorable psychometric properties. The K-SADS is routinely used to assess psychiatric diagnoses in children as young as 5 years old.[17,18]

The CY-BOCS[19] is a well-known 10-item, semistructured, clinician-rated interview merging data from clinical observation and parent and child report. It is adapted from the adult Y-BOCS[20,21] and assesses both OCD symptoms and severity. Adequate reliability and validity have been demonstrated, as well as sensitivity to change after treatment in pharmacological and behavioral therapy studies. Scores range from 0 to 40, with higher scores indicating more severe illness.

The Clinical Global Impressions (CGI)-Improvement scale[22] is used to assess overall clinical improvement based on symptoms observed and impairment reported (7-point scale ranging from 1 [very much improved] to 7 [very much worse]). The clinician-rated scale has been used successfully in patients with OCD.[23,24]

National Institute of Mental Health (NIMH) Global Rating Scales[25] are clinician-rated indices of illness severity. Each scale is a single-item composite rating ranging from 1 (normal) to 15 (very severe) with good interrater reliability. The NIMH Global Impairment, Depression, Anxiety, and OCD Rating Scales have been used in multiple treatment studies.

Conners Parent Rating Scale-Revised (Long Version)[26] is an 80-item parent report of children's behavioral problems that is widely used both clinically and in research efforts and has strong, established psychometric properties. Higher scores on this measure indicate more severe symptoms. For the purpose of this study, we report on only the total score, which corresponds to *DSM-IV* symptoms of combined Inattentive and Hyperactive-Impulsive type ADHD.

Legend

Name of measurement
Measurement method
information about reliability/validity

FIGURE 18.7 Excerpt from Freeman et al. (2008).

An Example of a Possible Template for a Measures Section

The ***primary outcome*** *is (identify variable), and* ***secondary outcomes*** *include (list variables). The primary outcome variable (name) is assessed using (****measurement method****) with data obtained from (identified source of data) using the (measurement instrument or observational procedures, add citation for the measurement instrument or process). The* ***psychometric properties*** *of this measurement instrument have been assessed in prior studies (provide details and citations). In this study, information on the* ***reliability*** *of the instrument indicates (provide data on measurement reliability). (If appropriate, provide information about the* ***validity*** *of the instrument for your sample, if your sample is different from the one originally used to the measurement instrument. For example, if you are including individuals who do not speak English as a native language, and this instrument was developed for people who are native English speakers, you may need to document that the measure is appropriate for use with people who are not native English speakers.)*

Repeat for all outcomes.

Then describe the timing and procedures for measurement.

Participants will be tested by a (research assistant, other type of staff member) who was (blind or not) to the treatment condition. The ***timing of assessments*** *included evaluations conducted (e.g., before, during, after the treatment). Assessments were conducted in (location). The following steps were taken to reduce the influence of extraneous variables or other* ***threats to the validity of measurement*** *(describe).*

Activity 18.3: Describing the Measures

Describe the measures to be used for your proposed study. Make sure you include information on each component of the measures section. Include the appropriate citations in APA style.

____

____

____

____

____

Describing the Independent Variable

In a proposal, this component of the Methods Section provides the reader with essential details about the IV. In a treatment outcome study, this component includes a description of the treatments, including the purpose of the treatment, the components of the treatment, the treatment modality, and the delivery system.

The information on the IV, including the experimental and control conditions, helps the reader understand how the researcher conceptualized the primary aims of the study. Information on the delivery system and treatment modality can further clarify the details of the experimental and control conditions. Information on therapist qualification training and procedures for delivering the IV can help the reader understand how the researcher insures the reliability and validity of the delivery of the IV.

Information about the control condition helps the reader to understand what aspects of the experimental condition are hypothesized to produce the desired outcome. Researchers may include a description of the similarities and differences between the experimental and control treatments. This description permits the reader to understand if the study will effectively test the specific hypothesis under investigation (i.e., how differences between the experimental and control conditions provide an opportunity to test the primary hypothesis). To document the methodological rigor of the study, a reference to a treatment manual with a citation is often included, if available.

Fig. 18.8 displays the descriptions of the interventions used in the Brenes et al. (2018) study which tested the effects of treatments to reduce worry in older adults with GAD. They are contrasting the effects of CBT and Yoga. The authors provide detailed information on the intervention components and the instructions.

3.6. Interventions

3.6.1. Cognitive-behavioral therapy (CBT)

CBT will consist of 10 individual weekly psychotherapy sessions with a study coach and an accompanying workbook. We have used this intervention in two previous randomized controlled trials (RCT) (R01 MH083664 & K23MH065281, Brenes PI). The 10-chapter workbook focuses on techniques that have demonstrated efficacy in treating adults with GAD [32,33] and older adults with GAD [18,[34], [35], [36], [37]]. Chapter 1 describes the intervention and presents a cognitive behavioral model of anxiety. Chapters 2 through 9 each address a specific anxiety management technique or a specific problem that may be comorbid with anxiety, and include relaxation, cognitive restructuring and use of coping statements, problem solving, worry control, behavioral activation, exposure therapy, sleep, and pain. Chapter 10 focuses on relapse prevention. Chapters are approximately 5–10 pages long and written in lay terms. They are presented in a large font, and key points are highlighted and reiterated simply to aid readers in fully understanding the content. Each chapter contains multiple examples of specific situations that an older adult might experience. Chapters are also focused on relevant problems for older adults, such as sleep and pain. Each chapter is followed by a homework exercise to practice the technique described in that chapter. A completed example is provided, followed by blank copies to be completed by the participant. The homework is used to encourage the application of the techniques to daily life.

Weekly telephone sessions with the study coach will last 45–50 min. To ensure privacy, every participant will be asked if he/she needs to reschedule the appointment due to a lack of privacy. All sessions will start with a review of homework and any problems or stressors participants have encountered within the context of the homework. The coach and the participant will discuss whether anxiety coping skills were used and how effective they were. If so, use of the coping techniques will be reinforced. If the worry was not adequately managed, coping skills will be reviewed and ways to incorporate or improve their use will be identified. The study coach will then review the chapter and the exercise with the participant. The participant will be encouraged to ask questions about the reading materials and discuss any difficulties he/she may have experienced when implementing the technique.

FIGURE 18.8 Excerpt from Brenes et al. (2018).

3.6.2. Yoga

Yoga will consist of 20, 75-min group gentle yoga classes held twice weekly using a modified version of an intervention protocol that we have developed and used in 3 previous trials [[38], [39], [40]]. Participants who are randomized to participate in yoga will take classes separately from those who chose to participate in the yoga classes. For both groups, participants will be asked to practice breathing exercises and poses for 15 min at least 5 days per week and record their length of home practice on a tracking form. Participants will enter the yoga classes on a rolling basis rather than waiting until a particular group session begins to mirror “real life.” Class size will be capped at 10 participants so that the instructor can provide adequate attention to each participant. Classes will be offered at different times of day at several locations in the community (e.g., agencies that serve older adults, churches).

In the yoga classes, teachers will emphasize the following yoga practice principles for use with older adults including: do no harm, create a safe environment, meet people where they are, emphasize feeling over form, emphasize fluidity, use skillful language (encourage and invite rather than direct and demand), be a guardian of safety, and teach people rather than poses or conditions [41]. Participants will be told that they should not practice any pose that causes or exacerbates pain. The following additional principles will be followed: (1) It will be made clear to study participants that yoga is not a religious or religious-based program. (2) Classes will not include any designated time for participants to interact verbally or socially, to minimize any “support group” feeling to the classes. We anticipate, though, that unstructured interaction among participants will take place before and after yoga classes, and to some extent, during them. This potential for social interaction is one reason for keeping participants randomized to yoga in the randomized trial separate from those who selected yoga in the preference trial as interaction among these participants could bias the selection and preference estimates.

FIGURE 18.8 Continued.

Researchers also use this component to provide information about procedures to protect the internal validity of the study, including procedures related to random assignment and reducing bias as shown in Fig. 18.9.

3.4. Screening procedures and randomization

Individuals will undergo an initial screening to determine potential eligibility and then provide informed consent either by telephone or in person, depending upon participant preference. Participants will then complete the baseline assessment measures prior to randomization. Once eligibility is determined, randomization will occur. Randomization into the preference and random trials will be stratified by psychotropic medication use to ensure balance and appropriate representation of psychotropic medication users between the intervention groups. Participants who receive CBT will be randomized to one of two study coaches.

FIGURE 18.9 Brenes et al. (2018).

Researchers often include procedures for establishing the reliability and validity of the delivery of the IV. In a treatment outcome study, researchers describe the training and supervision of the therapists, and the procedures for checking their adherence to the treatment protocol, as presented in Chapter 17. Fig. 18.10 displays an example of these procedures as described in Brenes et al. (2018).

3.6.4. Intervention fidelity

CBT Fidelity: To ensure intervention integrity, all weekly participant telephone calls will be recorded; 10% of these sessions will be randomly selected to be coded by a therapist with expertise in CBT. The sessions will be evaluated against the steps outlined in each telephone call protocol using an existing measure of adherence and competence [36,37]. This measure assesses both the competence and adherence of the coach in the delivery of the specific intervention skills (e.g., progressive muscle relaxation, problem solving, etc.) as well as an overall rating of competence and adherence. Data from this measure suggest high internal consistency (alpha = .91-.94) and greater variability in ratings attributed to clinicians (29%) than raters (9%), suggesting good reliability of the instruments (personal communication, Dr. Stanley). The coach may also undergo retraining if mean adherence scores are not good (operationalized as < 6 on adherence rating).

Yoga Fidelity: We have developed a intervention fidelity plan to ensure that the yoga intervention is delivered as intended [42]. Recommended strategies regarding intervention design, training interventionists, delivery of intervention, and receipt of intervention will be implemented as recommended by the Treatment Fidelity Workgroup of the NIH Behavior Change Consortium [48,49] and other investigators [50,51]. Each yoga teacher will receive a two-day training session and demonstrate his/her knowledge of content; complete a checklist for each session; record number of sessions and their length; videotape each yoga class (with the focus on the teacher, not the participants); and report any deviations from the planned protocol. We will also randomly select 10% of the videotaped yoga classes to be reviewed by a yoga instructor/researcher. Yoga teachers will meet bi-monthly with one of the Co-PIs to discuss their experiences and facilitate consistency among sessions.

FIGURE 18.10 Brenes et al. (2018).

An Example of a Template for Describing the Independent Variable

The proposed Experimental Treatment is (label). This treatment is based on (describe theory). (If a treatment manual is available, provide information about this manual. For example: The implementation is conducted according to the manual by (references)). The treatment is intended to address (identify mechanisms and symptoms), by (describe the mechanism of action). The components of the treatment include: (list). The treatment is delivered using a (modality) and (delivery format), by therapists who (list qualifications and training). The treatment is delivered in XX sessions of XX duration.

The proposed Control Treatment or condition is (label). This treatment has been successfully employed in prior studies (provide details). The treatment is intended to address (identify mechanisms and symptoms). The components of the treatment include: (list). The treatment is delivered using a (modality) and (delivery format), by therapists who (list qualifications and training). The treatment is delivered in XX sessions of XX duration.

The differences between the control and experimental treatments include the following: (list). This permits the testing of hypotheses about the effects of (treatment component) on (mechanisms) and/or (symptoms).

Participants are assigned at random to the experimental or control condition using the following randomization procedures (describe).

Therapists are trained and supervised using (describe methods). Treatment fidelity is assessed using the following procedures (describe). Other extraneous variables which might affect treatment include (list) and are addressed by (indicate procedures for reducing effects of possible extraneous variables).

Activity 18.4: Describing the Independent Variable

Describe the experimental and control conditions to be used for your proposed study. Describe the purpose of the control condition and the ways you will insure implementation reliability and validity. Make sure you include information on each component of this section. Include APA style references.

____

____

____

____

____

Analysis Plan

The final section of the methods in a proposal includes information about the analysis plan. You will learn how to write a clear analytic plan as you take more advanced research methods or statistics courses. The details of the analytic plan depend on the specific hypotheses you are studying and the methods you have used.

Writing About the Methods for a Research Review Paper

The goal of a paper reviewing a set of studies on a specific topic is different from the goal of a proposal. In a proposal, you are presenting the hypotheses you want to test and the methods you wish to use to test them. In a paper reviewing studies, you are examining the existing evidence to determine gaps in knowledge and to identify areas in need of future research. But identifying gaps in knowledge based on the methods of research studies can be confusing and difficult. A great deal of information is presented in each article. Therefore, it can help to have a strategy for organizing your approach to reviewing the Methods Sections of the articles you are reading.

The next sections of the chapter provide ideas and suggestions for organizing the information from each component of the Methods Section. A series of tables are provided to help you systematically organize the information provided in the components on participants, measures, and delivery of the IV. As you examine these articles, you may identify aspects of the methods which explain differences in the results or which suggest new ideas for research. Your research paper includes your description of the articles you are reviewing and your analyses of the methods and findings of the research.

A Methods Section for a Research Review

If you are reviewing many articles, you may need to write a Methods Section of your own to describe the methods you used to choose articles to review. You may indicate how you chose articles to review and how many articles you included. This Methods Section might involve identifying the key terms you used to search for articles and the databases you included in the search. Meta-analyses and systematic reviews have very specific criteria for describing the methods of their reviews. For more information, see Moher et al. (2015).

As you prepare your review, you can develop tables for each section of your paper. Specifically, you may develop one table that organizes information about the research participants, another that organizes information about the measurement strategies, and still other tables that organize information about the causes or treatments of the disorder. Creating these tables requires dedication and conscientiousness. However, once you have completed the tables, it is easier to evaluate the research and write about the studies and your analysis of the studies.

Evaluating Research Participants

For a research paper reviewing other studies, you examine the participant selection criteria used in other studies. You can consider the sample sizes, the different inclusion and exclusion criteria, or the different recruitment strategies used in the studies you review. You may wish to examine whether the outcomes of the studies differ depending on the size of the sample, the inclusion or exclusion criteria, or the recruitment strategies. For example, as Brenes et al. (2018) suggest, the outcomes may vary if the participants have mild versus moderate or severe worry.

To help you draw conclusions about the participants included in other studies, you can use adaptations of the tables provided in Chapter 15. We provide one sample table in Activity 18.5.

As you enter the information about the participants in each original research study, you may notice some patterns, and identify some threats to external validity. For example, you may be able to identify groups which have not been studied. Maybe the hypotheses have only been tested in studies of adults (vs. children). Some studies may have included individuals with low levels of symptoms; whereas other studies include individuals with moderate or severe symptoms. Some studies may have excluded individuals with other comorbidities, other may have included them.

In some cases, meta-analyses may have examined the effects of different types of participants on the outcomes of a set of studies. For example, many meta-analyses of treatment outcome studies examine whether the treatment works better for participants with different levels of symptoms or different characteristics (Sanders, Kirby, Tellegen, & Day, 2014).

But if a meta-analysis is not available, you can look at the evidence yourself. You can review the results and compare the findings of studies using different methods. You summarize your observations from the tables you make about the participants in different studies.

Activity 18.5: Completing a Table Reviewing Participants Sections Across Studies

Complete Table 18.2 for several articles you are reading for your review paper. As you review the studies in detail, you will notice limitations to their findings and identify gaps in knowledge, and you will generate ideas for new studies to address these gaps.

TABLE 18.2 Reviewing participants sections across studies.

Authors, Date	n – total sample size	Is method for determining appropriate sample size discussed? (Power analysis described)	Inclusion criteria and method of measuring inclusion criteria	Justification for inclusion criteria	Exclusion criteria and methods of measuring exclusion criteria	Justification for exclusion criteria	Recruitment strategies	Demographic characteristics of the sample.	Implications of eligibility criteria and recruitment strategies for external validity	Study results	Did the study analyses examine differences in outcomes by participants' characteristics (e.g., symptom severity, age, gender, race/ethnicity, comorbidity, etc.?). If so, what were the differences in outcomes?

An Example of a Template to Summarize an Analysis of Participants Included in Studies. *A total of XX studies were reviewed to examine the effects of choices of participants on the outcomes of studies of (topic area under review). Studies used samples of different sizes, ranging from (provide details on the range of sample sizes with references). Samples had different characteristics, with samples varying in age (provide details and references), race and ethnicity (provide details and references), socioeconomic status (provide details and references). Samples also varied in the intensity of the symptoms (provide details and references) and the presence or absence of comorbidity (provide details and references).*

There were (or were not) differences in outcomes depending on sample characteristics. Specifically, (if available) meta-analyses indicated that sample characteristics such as (e.g., age, gender, race/ethnicity, severity of symptoms, presence of comorbidity) were associated with a better (or worse) to treatment. Other characteristics were (or were not) associated with outcomes (describe and provide references).

Or if no meta-analyses are available, conduct your own evaluation and describe the outcomes.

Across studies, sample characteristics such as (e.g., age, gender, race/ethnicity, severity of symptoms, presence of co-morbidity) had a better (worse, equivalent) response (i.e., describe outcomes). Specifically, (describe findings and provide references). Other characteristics were (or were not) associated with outcomes (describe and provided references).

The choices of participants raised concerns about external validity (explain and reference studies used to illustrate the ideas) and/or internal validity (explain and reference studies).

Evaluating the Measures

A research paper reviewing other studies will often evaluate the measures used in the existing research. This review will describe the types of measures used and identify limitations to the interpretation of existing data presented by these measures. For example, if researchers include only self-report measures of symptoms, the conclusions about treatment effects are limited to the participant's perspective. The findings do not permit the researcher to understand changes in behavior or signs of the disorder that participants are not able to observe in themselves. Future research might consider including healthcare provider ratings or family member ratings to capture information that is not reported by the participants.

Meta-analyses can help you understand the differences in outcomes associated with different types of measures. For example, in the Pacella, Hruska, and Delahanty (2013) meta-analysis of the relationship of PTSD to health outcomes discussed in Chapter 3, the authors compare the results across studies and find that the association of PTSD to health is stronger when the measurement method involves self-report of PTSD symptoms versus other measurement methods.

If meta-analyses are not available, you can examine studies yourself to see if the measurement methods or instruments make a difference in the outcome. To help you organize your observation, you can use adaptations of the tables provided in Chapter 16. We provide one sample below in Activity 18.6. This sample table allows you to examine the choices researchers made for primary and secondary outcomes. You can use other tabling approaches for different kinds of variables.

Activity 18.6: Completing a Table to Organize Evaluations of Measures Across Studies

Complete Table 18.3 to review measures of different studies. As you enter the information about the measures in each original research study, you may notice patterns in the choices of measurement methods or instruments. You may consider the strengths and weaknesses of each measurement method and instrument. You may notice that studies vary in primary outcomes, even when they intend to treat the same disorder. Similarly, researchers may choose different secondary outcomes, depending on how they conceptualize the causes for the disorder. As you read the articles carefully and table the measures, you may develop ideas for future studies.

TABLE 18.3 Reviewing measures section across studies.

Author, date	Primary outcome construct	Primary outcome variable	Primary outcome measurement method	Primary outcome measurement instrument	Evidence of reliability and validity?	Secondary outcome construct	Secondary outcome variable	Secondary outcome measurement method	Secondary outcome measurement instrument	Evidence of reliability and validity?	Timing of assessments?	Study results	Did the study analyses examine differences in outcomes across measures different types of measures? If so, what were the differences in outcomes?

An Example of a Template to Summarize an Analysis of Measures Included in Studies

A total of XX studies were reviewed to examine the effects of choices of measures on the outcomes of studies of (topic of the review). Studies testing the theories about the effects of the predictor (describe) on the outcome (describe) used different/similar primary outcome variables (describe and reference). To assess the outcome, studies used similar/different measurement methods (describe and reference). Measurement instruments used to assess the primary outcome included (describe and reference). These instruments had (poor, moderate, good) reliability and (poor, moderate, good) evidence of validity.

There were (or were not) differences in outcomes depending on measurement outcomes. Specifically, (if available) meta-analyses indicated that measurement methods including (describe) were associated with a (better, worse, different) outcome than other measurement methods, such as (describe and reference). Other aspects of measurement, including the timing of assessment, the type of assessors, or way in which the testing was conducted also did/did not affect the outcomes. (Provide details and explain.)

If the measurement methods raised concerns: The measurement methods raised concerns about external validity (explain and reference studies used to illustrate the ideas) and/or internal validity (explain and reference studies).

Evaluating the Independent Variable

A research paper reviewing treatment outcomes research will evaluate the outcomes of the treatment and the procedures used to insure the reliability and validity of treatment delivery. This review will describe the procedures used to insure the reliability and validity of treatment delivery and identify limitations to the interpretation of existing data presented by these procedures. For example, if researchers did not conduct tests of treatment fidelity or did not use highly trained therapists, the conclusions about the effects of the experimental treatment are more limited. Future research might consider including these fidelity checks or more standardized training for the therapists.

Meta-analyses can provide information about these issues. If they are not available, you can examine articles yourself. To help you draw conclusions about the procedures included in other studies, it can be helpful to table the information about the levels of the IV, the procedures used to insure the reliability and validity of the treatment delivery, and the outcomes. One sample table is provided. This sample table included in Activity 18.7 allows you to examine the choices researchers made for experimental and control conditions and for establishing the reliability and validity of treatment delivery. You can use other tabling approaches for different kinds of variables. For example, you may wish to track the types of extraneous variables controlled in these studies.

At the end of the review of methods in research articles, you summarize the methods used, the threats to validity observed, and the gaps in knowledge which are a result of these threats. Then you provide directions for future research.

Activity 18.7: Completing a Table to Organize Evaluations of Independent Variable Implementation Across Studies

Complete Table 18.4 to review the independent variables across studies. As you enter the information about the treatments used in each original research study, you may notice patterns in the procedures used. You may notice that studies vary in the way they offer the same treatments. Some researchers include some components of the treatment, and other include different or fewer components. As you read the articles carefully and table the treatments, you may develop ideas for future studies.

TABLE 18.4 Reviewing experimental manipulation sections across studies.

Author, date	Experimental treatment(s)/ conditions. Provide type of treatment, delivery system, modality, and type of therapist and setting	Control treatment (s)/conditions Provide type of treatment, delivery system, modality, and type of therapist and setting	Components identified as "active component"	Components shared with control treatment	Method for establishing reliability and validity of treatment: Therapist qualifications	Methods for establishing reliability and validity of treatment: Fidelity checks	Methods for establishing validity of treatment: Adherence checks	Methods for establishing validity of evaluation: Assessments of treatment expectations?	Are different control conditions used? If so how do the findings differ across control conditions?	Are different types of therapists or delivery systems used? If so, how do the findings differ across these study methods?

A Possible Template to Summarize an Analysis of Treatments Included in Studies

A total of XX studies were reviewed to examine the effects of treatment for behavioral health disorder (label). Studies examined the following types of treatments (describe and reference). Components of treatments included (describe and reference). The treatment modalities included (describe and reference). The treatment delivery systems included (describe and reference).

There were (or were not) differences in outcomes depending on the treatment. Specifically, (if available) meta-analyses indicated that treatments including (describe) were associated with a (positive, negative, neutral better) outcome. Other aspects of treatment, including the treatment components, delivery format, and modality did/did not affect the outcomes (describe and reference).

Researchers employed a variety of control conditions, including (describe and reference). These conditions permitted researchers to test hypotheses about (describe). Primary outcomes included (describe and reference).

The research indicates that treatment (specify) produces outcomes which are (better/worse/no different) from control conditions such as (e.g., wait list control, active control, etc.) (describe and reference). Other treatments also produced outcomes different from control conditions (describe and reference).

Researchers employed the following methods to insure the reliability and validity of treatment delivery (describe and reference). Outcomes varied (or did not vary) depending on the reliability and validity treatment delivery.

If the methods raise concerns: Overall the study methods raised concerns about external validity (explain and reference studies used to illustrate the ideas). The study methods also raised concerns about internal validity (explain and reference studies).

Building Human Capital: A Final Note on Communication Style

Writing a proposal or paper is very hard work. You build arguments based on the research articles you have read. You integrate your own ideas with the information you learned about the PHS, TOP, TOS, and methods.

You have worked hard to gain the knowledge and skills you need to make these arguments and document your reasoning. When you explain your ideas in a paper or proposal, you want the people who read your work to understand the ideas and information.

To maximize your impact, it is important to communicate your knowledge and ideas clearly and effectively. Short, clear sentences can be the most effective way to tell a scientific story. Each new piece of information should be documented with a citation.

Make sure you have a clear topic sentence for each paragraph. This topic sentence will tell the reader what is coming next. For example, a topic sentence for parts of a PHS section could read: *Disorder XX is common and has serious consequences if left untreated.* The remainder of the sentences in the paragraph can support the initial claim in the topic sentence. The topic sentence for the start of the TOP could read "*One mechanism which triggers (or maintains) symptoms of disorder is (name of mechanism).*" The remainder of this paragraph can provide an operational definition of the mechanism and explain how it is measured and has been tested in other studies.

Make sure your arguments follow in a logical order. If you are writing a proposal, check to make sure that you have systematically justified the study. If you are reviewing research, make sure the issues you raise are clearly explained and justified, and that the chain of ideas is logical.

One great way to check that you are writing clearly is to read your work out loud. Explaining the ideas to yourself is often the best way of insuring you have mastered the material you need to learn. As you read aloud, take the perspective of a future reader. See if you can follow the arguments to make sure you haven't skipped any necessary steps. (Some word processing programs now have the capacity to read your work out loud to you. You can take advantage of this technology to listen to your own work and determine if your writing and thinking are clear.)

Check your writing for ambiguity. Your writing is ambiguous if the meaning can be interpreted in more than one way or if the reader cannot determine what you mean. If your writing seems a little cloudy or confusing, try using several short sentences to explain your ideas in more detail.

Show your ideas to a colleague. Can your colleague follow the arguments? Does your colleague think your meaning is ambiguous or confusing? Take the time to clarify.

When someone listens to your work and evaluates your arguments, they are giving you a great gift. They are sharing their time and thinking with you. It's a good idea to appreciate their effort, even if their criticisms sting a little. Their attention is likely to help you grow and improve your work.

It is also important to take the time to help others. Listen carefully to their ideas. You may improve your understanding of the underlying concepts of writing as you work through someone else's paper or proposal. As you help them understand gaps in their thinking, you are helping yourself understand how to think about gaps.

By the time you finish writing your proposal or paper, you will have gained a great deal of knowledge. And you will have accumulated many different skills. You own these skills and you own the discipline and conscientiousness that you used to learn them.

Just as important, you had the opportunity to develop a clearer sense of your own strengths and interests. As you worked, you observed yourself search for knowledge, analyze and organize information, formulate ideas, and communicate them to others. We hope that as you collaborated with others, you got feedback about areas of competence and areas in need of further growth. This self-knowledge can give you more confidence and focus as you pursue your studies.

You also had the opportunity to see how others solved the problems involved in developed a proposal or papers. We hope you enjoyed working with others and learned more about the kinds of support others need as they grow as learners. The insights you gain about other people will help you develop as a team member and team leader. Learning to be an effective team member and team leader is critical for any work you choose to do.

Thank you for your hard work. Good luck!

References

Brenes, G. A., Divers, J., Miller, M. E., & Danhauer, S. C. (2018). A randomized preference trial of cognitive-behavioral therapy and yoga for the treatment of worry in anxious older adults. *Contemporary Clinical Trials Communications, 10*, 169–176.

Dear, B. F., Staples, L. G., Terides, M. D., Karin, E., Zou, J., Johnston, L., … Titov, N. (2015). Transdiagnostic versus disorder-specific and clinician-guided versus self-guided internet- delivered treatment for generalized anxiety disorder and comorbid disorders: A randomized controlled trial. *Journal of Anxiety Disorders, 36*, 63–77.

Freeman, J. B., Garcia, A. M., Coyne, L., Ale, C., Przeworski, A., Himle, M., … Leonard, H. L. (2008). Early childhood OCD: Preliminary findings from a family-based cognitive- behavioral approach. *Journal of the American Academy of Child and Adolescent Psychiatry, 47*(5), 593–602.

Ivanova, E., Lindner, P., Ly, K. H., Dahlin, M., Vernmark, K., Andersson, G., & Carlbring, P. (2016). Guided and unguided acceptance and commitment therapy for social anxiety disorder and/or panic disorder provided via the internet and a smartphone application: A randomized controlled trial. *Journal of Anxiety Disorders, 44*, 27–35.

Moher, D., Shamseer, L., Clarke, M., Ghersi, D., Liberati, A., Petticrew, M., … Stewart, L. A. (2015). Preferred reporting items for systematic review and meta-analysis protocols (PRISMA-P) 2015 statement. *Systematic Reviews, 4*(1), 1.

Pacella, M. L., Hruska, B., & Delahanty, D. L. (2013). The physical health consequences of PTSD and PTSD symptoms: A meta-analytic review. *Journal of Anxiety Disorders, 27*(1), 33–46.

Sanders, M. R., Kirby, J. N., Tellegen, C. L., & Day, J. J. (2014). The triple P-positive parenting program: A systematic review and meta-analysis of a multi-level system of parenting support. *Clinical Psychology Review, 34*(4), 337–357.

Glossary

Abstract: provides a brief description of the aim of the study, the methods, the results, and the discussion or conclusion.

Adherence (to treatment protocol): compliance with treatment protocols or treatment regimens.

Alpha level: the probability of rejecting the null hypothesis when the null hypothesis is true. The alpha level reflects how much error in the rejection of the null hypothesis researchers are willing to accept. In psychology the alpha level is set at .05, indicating that 5% of the time the null hypothesis may be incorrectly rejected.

American Psychological Association (APA): the APA is a professional organization representing psychologists in the United States. The APA provides information and develops guidelines for research and practice.

American Psychological Association Publication Manual: a guide outlining the APA's established rules governing the ways to cite evidence and to prepare a bibliography.

Analysis of covariance (ANCOVA): a statistical method used to compare differences among levels of the predictor variable as covariates are controlled.

APA style: a writing style and format used for academic research proposals or papers which is consistent with the recommendations of the American Psychological Association.

Applied research: systematic study conducted to solve a "real-world problem"/ practical problem.

Assessment: processes used to evaluate outcomes including behavior, cognitive abilities, and other variables.

Assumptions of the analyses: include the criteria the data must meet to be appropriate for the analyses. For example, some statistical methods require that the data are normally distributed or the relations among variables are linear.

Attrition bias: a form of bias that may affect the outcome of the study, and reflects the possibility that those who drop out (or attrit) from the study may differ in some way from those who remain in the study.

Baseline (Pretreatment): refers to assessments conducted before the independent variable is administered to establish the level of response prior to the delivery of the independent variable.

Basic research: systematic study conducted to understand the characteristics, causes, and effects of a phenomenon.

Belmont report: one of the leading works concerning ethics and healthcare research. Its primary purpose is to educate researchers and the public about the need to protect participants in clinical trials or research studies and to provide guidance for protective actions.

Between-person effects: the comparison across participants.

Bias: in a research context, bias occurs when variables other than the designated predictor variables are unintentionally affecting the outcome.

Carryover effects: a potential source of bias which occurs when exposure to one level of the independent variable (e.g., either the experimental or control condition) influences response to the next.

Case studies: descriptions of studies of evaluations and interventions with individual participants to present an idea or approach.

Categorical outcome: the responses in a study which represent membership in a group or condition. Participants can only be members of one category (e.g., changes in diagnostic status).

Categorical variables: variables in which responses belong to mutually exclusive groups (categories).

Census: process of collecting demographic and economic data on individuals in the population.

Chi-Square analyses: a statistical method to find the differences between groups in a categorical outcome.

Citations: information about the source of evidence, including the authors and year of publication, among other information. The citation is placed after a statement providing evidence.

Clinical significance: the relevance of research findings for health, including the degree to which the outcomes reflect effects on symptoms or functioning that would be meaningful in the context of the participants' experience.

Cluster sampling: members of a population are sorted into clusters. The researcher chooses clusters at random from all possible clusters. In multistage sampling, all possible volunteering individuals within each cluster are selected at random.

Coercion: an implied or direct use of power or influence to affect a participant's response or behavior in a study.

Common method variance: response to different measurement instruments that may overlap because the method of data acquisition or the content of the items are similar.

Compensation for participation: monetary or other forms of payment to participants in return for their voluntary participation in a research study.

Completer analyses: a statistical method used in treatment outcome studies when there are missing data. The researcher only includes those who complete the treatment and have posttest scores.

Concurrent criterion validity: a form of measurement validity. A measurement instrument is regarded as demonstrating concurrent criterion validity if the scores on the measurement instrument are related to scores on a measure of a theoretically related construct.

Confidence interval: provides information about the upper and lower boundaries of the estimate.

Confidentiality: the expectation that information gathered will not be divulged to others without explicit permission.

Confounding variable: a source of bias in which an extraneous variable co-occurs with one level of an independent variable making it difficult to determine if outcomes are a function of the independent variable or the extraneous variable.

Construct validity: the degree to which the scores on the measurement instrument are related to the construct it is intended to represent.

Constructs: the ideas that compose a theory.

Content validity: the degree to which the items on the measurement instrument capture the full range of concepts incorporated into the construct.

Context: the social, environmental, or biological circumstances surrounding and potentially influencing the predictor or outcome variables in a study.

Continuous variables: the scores on a measure of the variable increase in meaningful intervals. The participant's score represents the quantity (or degree or intensity or amount) of the variable the participant has.

Control condition or treatment: in an experimental study, the control is the condition which does not receive the active treatment and enables the investigator to hold constant influential aspects of the experimental condition which are not related to the theory under investigation.

Convenience sampling: sampling in which researchers recruit participants to volunteer for the study. The selection of the participants is not random; it depends on the researchers' recruitment methods and the participants' willingness to volunteer.

Correlated: variables are correlated when the variables have a statistical relationship in which scores on one variable are reliably associated with scores on another.

Correlation/observational design: a type of study design in which researchers examine relations between two or more variables through observation and measurement, but without using the manipulation required to determine causality.

Counterbalance: a potential correction for bias associated with order and carryover effects in which participants are assigned at random to the order of presentation of the conditions.

Criterion validity: the degree to which the measurement instrument is related to a variable representing a theoretically related construct.

Cronbach's alpha: an estimate of internal consistency reliability reflecting the extent of the relationships among the items on the measurement instrument.

Crossover randomized controlled trial (Crossover RCT): a research trial design in which participants received both the control and experimental treatments.

Cross-sectional design: a type of study design in which researchers investigate relationships among variables at one point in time.

Daily diaries: method for collecting individuals' data in their natural environment and real time using paper-and-pencil or electronic data collection devices.

Data: the information collected for a study.

Data cleaning: procedures used to insure the data entered into the computer for analysis match the data collected from the participant.

Degrees of freedom: In an ANOVA analysis, the degrees of freedom adjust the outcomes to reflect the number of comparisons that are being made and the number of observations included, as well as any necessary corrections.

Demand characteristics: aspects of the study which influence the participants' expectations about the study and their own responsibilities in the study. These expectations may influence the participants' performance in unintended ways, potentially creating bias.

Dependent or outcome variable: variable acted upon by the independent or predictor variable.

Descriptive research: research aimed at understanding the characteristics of the construct or phenomenon under investigation.

Difference scores: participant data scores derived from subtracting the posttreatment symptom score from the pretreatment symptom score.

Discussion Section: segment of paper which provides an interpretation of the findings and their implications.

Dose—response relationship: researchers' investigation of whether the amount or dose of the predictor is associated with the magnitude of the response.

Double-blind study: a method for controlling bias in a study in which participants and researchers are unaware of the participants' assignment to the control or experimental condition. This procedure can limit bias due to either the participants' or the researchers' beliefs and expectations about the conditions.

Ecological momentary assessment: a method of data collection in which brief surveys about the participants' experiences are completed in the individuals' natural environment and the assessments are made repeatedly.

Effect size: represents the strength of the relationship between two variables.

Effectiveness: refers to evaluating whether the treatment works under real-world conditions.

Efficacy: refers to evaluating whether a treatment/study produces a good outcome under controlled conditions.

Electronic diaries: a method for collecting brief surveys of participants' activities, thoughts, or feelings or other variables using an electronic device (i.e., smartphone app, tablet, computer, etc.).

Electronic reference manager: electronic platforms that store articles and their bibliographic information (e.g., author, date of publication, journal, etc.).

Eligibility criteria: characteristics that qualify prospective subjects for inclusion in the study; these criteria include characteristics required for inclusion in the study and characteristics which necessitate exclusion from the study.

Empirical article: a research article which presents the findings from a specific research study.

Epidemiology: the study of the prevalence, characteristics, and distribution of a disease or disorder.

Equivalence trial: a type of research design used to determine if two active treatments produce equivalent effects.

Ethical conduct of research: established principles and practices that are required to conduct research involving humans or animals.

Etiology: potential causes of disorders.

Evaluation apprehension: a potential source of bias which may occur when participants have anxiety or distress about being assessed in the study. This distress or apprehension may cause scores on symptom measures to appear more elevated than they would under other circumstances.

Evidence: information or data that can be used to confirm or disconfirm a hypothesis.

Exclusion criteria: characteristics that would render an individual ineligible to participate in the study.

Experimental condition: in an experimental study, the experimental condition is the level of the independent variable which is hypothesized to cause the outcome predicted by the theory.

Experimental confederate: interacts with the research participant, observing or manipulating the participant to achieve the experimenter's goals.

Experimental control: settings and conditions established by the experimenter to reduce the effects of possible extraneous variables.

Experimental design: a type of study design in which researchers can test hypotheses about causal relations among variables.

Experimental treatment: refers to level of the independent variable in a study that contains one or more active ingredients which the researcher believes will produce benefits.

Experimenter: the researcher proposing and formulating the study. The experimenter may also be involved in implementing the study.

Experimenter bias: a source of bias from the experimenter. This bias occurs if a researcher has a strong commitment to the theory being tested. Without controls, these expectations can influence the outcome of the assessment.

Expert ratings: evaluations of a behavior or characteristic or condition made by a relevant expert (e.g., physician, psychiatrist, psychologist).

External validity: the ability to generalize the results of the study across samples, measures, methods, among other dimensions.

Extraneous variables: variables which unintentionally disrupt or influence the relationship among predictor and outcome variables in a research study.

F value: a statistical term generated in an analysis of variance. The F statistic represents the ratio of the variance associated with the model (the predictor variable) to the error.

Face validity: the degree to which the items on the measurement instrument appear to measure the construct it is intended to measure.

Factor analysis: a statistical method used to identify patterns in scores to determine if responses fall along specific dimensions, called factors. This analysis is often used to determine if responses to different items can be grouped together to form a scale.

False negative/type II error: occurs when the researchers accept the null hypothesis, but the null hypothesis is false and a relation between variables exists.

False positive/type I error: occurs when the researchers do not reject the null hypothesis, but the null hypothesis is true and there is no relation between variables.

Fidelity check: monitoring the delivery of the levels of the independent variable to insure the levels are delivered as intended. Specifically, when an experimental treatment is delivered, fidelity checks insure that the treatment components are delivered according to the protocol.

Follow-up assessment: refers to assessments conducted after a predetermined period following the end of exposure to the independent variable (i.e., after the treatment has ended). These assessments can be made at one or more points after the treatment (or other independent variable delivery) terminated. The follow-up assessments permit researchers to determine if effects associated with the independent variable are sustained.

"Gold standard" criterion: is used when researchers are comparing the scores on a new measurement instrument with scores on an established and validated measurement instrument assessing the same construct.

Habituation: a potential source of bias which can occur when repeated exposure to a stimulus decreases responses to that stimulus. Consequently, participants report lower levels of the response over time.

Halo effect: a bias in which positive impressions about one characteristic of a person are generalized to other characteristics.

Hawthorne effect: a source of potential bias in a research study. The Hawthorne effect occurs when participants are aware they are being observed. The effects of observation may influence the outcome and produce effects which are unrelated to the predictor/independent variable.

Health Insurance Portability and Accountability Act (HIPAA): legislation in the United States intended to provide privacy and security of medical information.

Human capital: the skills, knowledge, ethics, values, and other personal characteristics that an individual possesses and develops to enable their personal and professional achievement.

Hypotheses: statement about relations between predictor and outcome variables generated by a theory.

Hypothesis-testing research: research which involves testing predictions or hypotheses about relations among variables.

Implicit association test: a measurement method used to test implicit or nonconscious responses to stimuli. Implicit association tests use reaction time variations instead of self-reports to assess responses to stimuli.

Imputation: a process for calculating values to substitute for missing data.

Incidence: refers to the number of new cases of a disorder which develop in a population over a given time period (e.g., in a 12-month period).

Inclusion criteria: characteristics an individual must have to be included as a participant in the study.

Independent or predictor variable: the variable expected to have an effect on another, called the outcome variable.

Informed consent: a voluntary agreement to participate in research. The subject is informed about the purpose and procedures involved in the research and has an understanding of the research and its risks and benefits.

Institutional review board: an administrative body established to protect the rights and welfare of human research participants in research.

Intent-to-treat Analyses: an approach to analyzing treatment outcome data which includes all participants who were initially included in the study, even if they did not complete the treatment or final post-test assessments.

Inter-rater reliability: the degree of consistency in response across items in a survey. A form of measurement reliability.

Internal consistency reliability: a measurement instrument, such as a survey, has internal consistency reliability if the items hypothesized to measure the same construct are related to each other.

Internal validity: the degree to which the study is able to test the hypothesis it is intended to test.

Intervention: a treatment intended to reduce or prevent the symptoms of a disorder or improve functioning.

Interview: a conversation in which one person asks questions and the other answers.

Introduction section: segment of paper that makes the argument for the study by examining the need for the study and justifying the approach.

Item response theory: a theory about evaluating the psychometric properties of a measurement instrument. The theory proposes specific statistical methods for evaluating the measurement instrument and the ability of the items in the test to represent the construct being measured.

Kappa coefficient: an estimate representing the degree to which multiple researchers agree or disagree on their observations.

Key words: words listed on the title page that indicate the search terms that can be used to find the article. They reflect the key constructs discussed in the paper.

Laboratory tasks: a structured activity given in a laboratory to observe participant responses. These tests are administered in the context of a scientific study.

Likert-type format: a format in which multiple numeric responses are presented in a graded manner. Each response corresponds to a subjective rating of intensity.

Literature review: the written review of the evidence obtained from existing scientific articles. This review provides the background and significance of the issue under investigation and helps establish the scientific premise of a study.

Longitudinal design: a type of study design in which researchers can evaluate changes over time as they test participants at multiple assessment points.

Maintain: to cause or enable (a condition or state) to continue. A maintaining variable is one which permits the symptom to persist or prevents recovery from an initial trigger.

Manipulated: in an experimental study, the researcher manipulates the independent variable by assigning participants at random to different levels of the variable.

Manipulation check: procedures used to evaluate potential sources of bias caused by participants' or researchers' expectations about and responses to the experimental and control conditions. These procedures involve evaluating if the independent variable produced the expected responses and did not produce unintentional responses.

Manual of operations: a guide containing instructions for conducting a study.

Mean squares: in an ANOVA, mean squares are calculated for each of the effects in the model, including the error. The mean square is the sum of squares for the effect adjusted for the degrees of freedom for that effect.

Measurement fatigue: is a source of bias which can occur when participants become tired from completing the assessment protocol. This tiredness can lead participants to give less reliable or valid responses.

Measurement instruments: the specific tools such as survey or interviews used to collect information.

Measurement methods: methods for measuring variables (e.g., surveys, interviews, laboratory tests, diaries, observations, and standardized tests).

Measurement order effect: a source of bias in which responses to measurement instruments are affected by the order in which they are presented.

Measurement reliability: the extent to which the measurement instrument yields a consistent result. Reliability can be assessed over the course of time, across raters, or across items within a measurement instrument.

Measurement validity: the degree to which the measurement instrument assesses the construct it is intended to measure.

Mechanisms: variables which can trigger and/or maintain symptoms and which may explain how people develop and maintain the symptoms.

Mechanisms of action: the processes hypothesized to explain the effects of the treatment.

Mediator: a variable that explains the relationship between predictor and outcome variables.

Medical charts: record of all the treatments and procedures that the patient has received in the context of a medical facility.

Mental measurements yearbook: a handbook which provides a list and description of measurement instruments for assessing psychological phenomena.

Meta-analyses: a type of research study in which researchers combine the quantitative results of many different studies pertaining to a specific research question or theory. They analyze the combined data to understand the strength of the evidence in support of this theory.

Methods section: segment of paper which describes the procedures of the study.

Missing data: data not reported by the participant or not recorded by the researcher.

Mixed models analyses: a statistical method used to test both between-person and within-person effects. For example, mixed models can be used to compare outcomes of two or more treatments (the between-person effect) assessed at multiple points in time (the within-person effect).

Moderator variable: a variable that affects the relations between the predictor and outcome variables.

Mood induction: strategies used to manipulate participants' mood. This approach is used if researchers want to understand the causal effects of variations in mood on any type of functioning.

Multistage sampling: an approach to random selection in which the population is divided into clusters and the individuals within the sampling cluster are selected at random.

National databases: data collected from nationwide sampling and maintained for use of researchers or the public. The American Community Survey is an example of a database of census-related information.

Nationally representative sample: a sample that is representative of the population of the United States (or relevant country).

Nocebo effect: the participant's negative expectations about the outcomes associated with an experimental condition. These expectations can make any negative outcome seem worse than it would be without those expectations.

Noninferiority trial: a type of hypotheses testing which compares treatments to make sure the newer, more efficient or less costly treatment is or non-inferior to effective as the original version.

Normally distributed data: data are distributed more or less evenly around the mean. Normally distributed data look like a bell curve.

Normative samples: samples used to provide information about responses to a measurement instrument in a representative population. These samples can be used to generate estimates of the average response and the variability of response to a measurement instrument. With a normative sample, responses from an individual can be compared to available data for a larger population and permit the evaluation of an individual's performance compared to his or her peers.

Numeric data: data expressed as a number.

Observational measures: an approach used in which researchers directly perceive and record the variables being studied.

Observational study: in an observational study, researchers observe and measure the variables to determine if there is a relationship.

Observations: refer to the data collected on each individual participant.

Observer ratings: observations of behavior or other characteristics of a participant by trained research staff.

Observer-expectancy effect: an effect on the outcome of a study which can occur when a research observer has a strong commitment to the theory being tested. These expectations can influence the outcome of the assessment. Also called the experimenter bias.

Odds ratio: a method used to express the relations between variables. For example, in risk factor studies, the odds ratio expresses the likelihood of having the disorder if the person has versus does not have the risk factor.

Open-ended questions: questions which allow the respondent to answer based on their interpretation of the question and are not confined to any particular response options.

Original research: an empirical investigation using qualitative or quantitative methods.

p value: the significance level of the statistical test. In psychology, if it is less than .05, the test exceeds the standard for statistical significance.

Participant burden: the burden in terms of time, energy, or potential risk that research poses to participants.

Peer nominations: reports from peers, of their reactions to or observations of the research participant.

Peer-reviewed articles: articles that scientists write and other scientists evaluate for quality before they are published.

Physiological measurements: measurement of cardiovascular, endocrine, immune, or brain responses (e.g., blood pressure, heart rate, skin conductance, brain activity). These measures can be made continuously in daily life or in response to structured tasks in the laboratory.

Pilot study: a preliminary study intended to examine the feasibility and validity of an approach that is intended to be used in a larger scale study.

Placebo: a fake or simulated treatment which is comparable to the experimental condition as much as possible, except that the placebo does not contain the "ingredient" or component of the experimental condition which is hypothesized to produce the desired effect. A placebo condition is used as a control condition in an experimental study to permit investigators to test the effects of the experimental condition.

Population: includes all the members of a given group.

Population-based sampling: sampling in which researchers use random selection methods to create a sample that represents the population as a whole.

Post hoc analyses: post hoc analyses are performed if there are multiple levels of the predictor variable. Post hoc analyses permit the investigator to determine which levels of the independent variable produce effects which are significantly different from the effects of the other levels.

Posttest (after treatment): refers to assessments conducted after the independent variable is administered to establish the level of response associated with the delivery of the independent variable.

Power: the likelihood that a study has a sufficient number of participants to detect an effect when there is an effect there to be detected.

Power analysis: helps the researcher determine the sample size required to detect an effect of a given size with a given degree of confidence.

Pretest (before treatment): refers to assessments conducted before the independent variable is administered to establish the level of response prior to the delivery of the independent variable.

Predictive criterion validity: a form of measurement validity. A measurement instrument is regarded as demonstrating predictive criterion validity if the scores on the measurement instrument are related to scores on a measure of a theoretically related construct that are obtained at a future point in time.

Preliminary analyses: the initial steps in data analyses necessary before explicit hypothesis-testing or inferential analyses. For example, preliminary analyses can serve to test assumptions about the data or evaluate potential covariates.

Prevalence: the proportion of a population under study who have ever had the disorder under investigation within a period of time (e.g., lifetime prevalence refers to the proportion with the disorder at any point over their lifespan).

Principles of ethical conduct of research: the underlying principles including respect for persons, beneficence, and justice that support the ethical practice of scientific investigation.

Prospective design: a type of longitudinal design in which a cohort of participants are identified and followed for a given period to determine which members of the cohort experience hypothesized outcomes.

Public health significance: the significance of a study based on its implications for the health of the population. This significance can be established by documenting its prevalence of the disorder and its effects on health and functioning.

Public records (e.g., census data): publicly available information. This includes data which can be accessed by the public and reflects information collected by various agencies of the government, including data on crime rates, health indicators, or sociodemographic data, among other types of information.

Qualitative research: data from exploratory studies in which researchers use interviews or other methods to understand and describe the nature of a phenomena, including individuals' perceptions of the phenomena under investigation. Qualitative research studies can provide detailed information that can be useful for designing interventions, developing quantitative tools, or generating new hypotheses.

Quantify: representing ideas or constructs with measurable variables.

Quantitative research: studies in which researchers collect quantitative or numeric data and use statistical methods to test the researchers' predictions/hypotheses.

Random assignment: the choice of assignment to the level of the independent variable is done at random.

Random digit dialing: method of random selection used to identify possible research participants at random. To reach possible participants, researchers use telephone numbers assembled by selecting digits at random using prespecified methods.

Random selection: each member of the population has an equal chance of being included in the final sample used in the research. The decision about which members of a population are invited to participate is made at random.

Randomized controlled trial (RCT): an experiment in which the causal effects of a treatment can be evaluated. The independent variable is manipulated, with participants assigned at random to the different levels of the independent variable. The independent variable includes both an experimental condition and a control condition. This type of trial is conducted to evaluate differences in the outcomes associated with the experimental versus the control condition(s).

Recall bias: a source of bias related to the participant's recollection of past events or experiences.

Recruitment strategies: plans of action to successfully identify and enroll prospective candidates for the study.

References section: the bibliography of an article or paper. The reference section at the end of the work includes the full list of citations included in the text.

Relative risk ratio: a method used to express the relation between a risk factor and an outcome (disorder). The researcher is expressing the likelihood of having the disorder if the person has versus does not have the risk factor.

Reliable reporter: an individual who provides valid and consistent reports or data on the variables being evaluated.

Representative sample: a sample whose members reflect the characteristics of the general population under study.

Research articles/papers: reports of original research, published in peer-reviewed scholarly journals.

Research design: the strategy used by researchers to test hypotheses about the relations among variables.

Research participants: persons participating in a research study whose responses serve as the data for the study.

Response bias: a source of bias in which the participants' tendency to choose the same answer across questions influences the participants' responses to the questions more than the participants' reaction to any individual question. Also called response set.

Response reactivity: a potential source of bias in which participants react to being observed and assessed, even if they are not aware of these reactions.

Response set: a source of bias in which participants tend to choose the same answer regardless of the question. Also called response bias.

Results section: segment of paper that presents the findings or outcomes from the study.

Retrospective reporting: reporting on past events, emotions, thoughts, behavior, or other phenomena.

Risk factors: characteristics that increase the risk for illness or the problem being studied.

Rosenthal effect: a source of potential bias in a research study. The Rosenthal effect describes a relationship between expectations and performance. The effects of expectations may influence the outcome of the study and produce effects that are unrelated to the predictor/independent variable.

Sampling: the process through which researchers recruit participants into or include observations a research study.

Scientific method: a cycle of proposing ideas; systematically testing and reevaluating the ideas.

Scientific premise: the scientific justification for a proposed study that explains existing knowledge, gaps in the literature, and the ways in which the proposed study addresses those gaps.

Scientific/methodological rigor: quality of the study, particularly its integrity in the face of threats to internal and external validity.

Sensitization: a potential source of bias which can occur when repeated exposure to a stimulus increases responses to that stimulus. Consequently, participants report higher levels of the response over time.

Single-blind study: a method for controlling bias in a study in which participants are unaware of their assignment to the control or experimental condition. This procedure can limit bias due to participants' beliefs and expectations about the conditions.

Skew: data are skewed when the scores are not normally distributed and there are too many scores at the high or low end of the distribution.

Social desirability effect: a potential source of bias reflecting the tendency for participants to respond in a manner they view as presenting them in a positive light.

Standardization: a system or standard process to ensure the methods of a study are implemented in a consistent manner.

Standardized questions: questions which are presented using the same wording across all participants. The validity of these questions as an indicator of the underlying construct has been established.

Standardized testing: a test in which all test-takers respond to all or part of the same set of questions under the same testing conditions.

Statistical analyses: statistical analyses use quantitative data to test hypotheses and to determine the probability of the outcomes.

Statistical analysis plan: the plan for conducting statistical analyses of data collected.

Statistical significance: the likelihood that the outcome of the analysis of a given set of data would be obtained if the null hypothesis were true.

Stratified random sampling: researchers identify groups within the population that they wish to sample (e.g., men and women or children, teens, and adult). Members of these groups are selected at random to permit the final sample to contain the desired proportions of each group.

Structured interviews: a trained interviewer asks questions which are consistent across individuals.

Sum of squares: is a measurement of the variation in scores in a sample.

Superiority trial: a type of hypotheses testing that researchers use to test the hypothesis that the experimental condition is better than the control condition in achieving the desired outcomes.

Surveys: a document which contains questions or items about the construct under study. The research participant answers these questions and the responses are scored.

Systematic reviews: authors examine the results or combine quantitative data across studies to see if there are consistent patterns in the findings.

Test–retest reliability: type of measurement reliability which is obtained when scores on a measurement instrument are consistent over repeated assessments over time.

Theoretical model: a proposal of the hypothesized relationships among constructs included in the theory. These models are often depicted in a figure displaying the relationships. The figure is used to illustrate the direction of the relations among these variables and to indicate if there are causal pathways involved.

Theories: proposals about the relations among ideas or constructs.

Therapist qualifications: can include the training, education, or experience of the therapist.

Trait characteristic: a set of attributes, such as a way of thinking, responding, or behaving, that are stable/consistent within the individual over time.

Transform (data): systematically modifying each score in the same manner to improve the distribution of the data. Two common transformation include taking the square root or the log of the score.

Treatment components: elements of a treatment, such as exercises or educational activities, which are used to achieve changes in symptoms or functioning.

Treatment delivery formats: the medium in which treatment is administered (e.g., face-to-face or on the web).

Treatment fidelity: refers to the quality of adherence to the treatment protocol.

Treatment modalities: the context in which the treatment relationship is established in therapy. For example, treatment can be delivered in the context of individual, group, or family treatment, among other modalities.

Treatment packages: a compilation of multiple treatment components that are delivered together to produce a reduction in symptoms or an improvement in functioning.

Treatment settings: the location in which the therapy takes place (e.g., hospital, patient's home, consulting office, academic medical center, etc.).

Trigger: a variable that initiates a response, feeling, or behavior. A trigger is a variable which may initiate the first episode of symptoms.

Uncontrolled trial: an outcome study in which all participants receive the same treatment. There is no contrasting or control treatment.

Variability: differences among scores which can occur across participants or within a participant over time.

Variables: measurable representations of the underlying constructs.

Visual analogue scale: a line (or other figure) representing the range of possible scores. Participants indicate the point along the line which represents the intensity of their response.

Volunteer bias: a source of potential bias in a research study. Characteristics of those who volunteer in a study may differ from those who do not volunteer, and these characteristics may influence the outcome of the study and produce effects which are unrelated to the predictor variable.

White coat effect: a form of evaluation apprehension in which participants experience anxiety or distress due to being evaluated. The "white coat effect" generally refers to increases in blood pressure associated with evaluation apprehension when blood pressure is measured by a healthcare provider.

Within-person effects: refer to variations in the participants' scores across multiple measurements.

Index

'*Note*: Page numbers followed by "f" indicate figures, "t" indicate tables and "b" indicate boxes.'

Q

R

S

T

9780128156803